PENGUIN CLASSICS

THE PENGUIN BOOK OF RENAISSANCE VERSE

'A stunning job of opening the canon to new possibilities – temporal, geographic, generic, and social – all to the effect of forcing the reader to be more thoughtful about the complex process of canonization. A remarkably daring edition' – Professor Margreta de Grazia, University of Pennsylvania

'An anthology for our time; one which is able to celebrate our own uncertain relationship to the poetic production of the early modern past' – Lisa Jardine in the *Guardian*

'An intelligent and comprehensive anthology, and not the least of its virtues is the social and historical introduction provided by Norbrook ... can be commended for the subtlety and care with which an extraordinary literary period has been restored' – Peter Ackroyd in *The Times*

'[The] admirable historical approach gives us a much fuller and richer portrait of the age ... The result is enlightening' – A. L. Rowse in the *Evening Standard*

'A rich and varied portrait of the Renaissance in England that is both historically convincing and imaginatively impressive ... [Norbrook] succeeds in making his subject accessible to an audience of non-specialists without patronizing their intelligence' – Lucasta Miller in the *New Statesman & Society*

ABOUT THE EDITORS

David Norbrook is Professor of English at the University of Maryland. His publications include *Poetry and Politics in the English Renaissance* (1984), *Writing the English Republic: Poetry, Rhetoric and Politics 1627-1660* (1999) and an edition of Lucy Hutchinson's *Order and Disorder* (2001).

H. R. Woudhuysen was educated at St Paul's School and Pembroke College, Oxford, and was a Junior Research Fellow at Lincoln College, Oxford. Since 1982 he has been a lecturer in the Department of English at University College London. He has edited *Samuel Johnson on Shakespeare* for the New Penguin Shakespeare Library.

THE PENGUIN BOOK OF RENAISSANCE VERSE

SELECTED
AND WITH AN INTRODUCTION
BY DAVID NORBROOK

EDITED BY H. R. WOUDHUYSEN

PENGUIN BOOKS

PENGUIN BOOKS

Published by the Penguin Group
Penguin Books Ltd, 80 Strand, London WC2R 0RL, England
Penguin Putnam Inc., 375 Hudson Street, New York, New York 10014, USA
Penguin Books Australia Ltd, 250 Camberwell Road, Camberwell, Victoria 3124, Australia
Penguin Books Canada Ltd, 10 Alcorn Avenue, Toronto, Ontario, Canada M4V 3B2
Penguin Books India (P) Ltd, 11 Community Centre, Panchsheel Park, New Delhi – 110 017, India
Penguin Books (NZ) Ltd, Cnr Rosedale and Airborne Roads, Albany, Auckland, New Zealand
Penguin Books (South Africa) (Pty) Ltd, 24 Sturdee Avenue, Rosebank 2196, South Africa

Penguin Books Ltd, Registered Offices: 80 Strand, London WC2R 0RL, England

www.penguin.com

First published by Allen Lane The Penguin Press 1992
Publilshed with minor revisions and an additional index in Penguin Books 1993
10

Printed in England by Clays Ltd, St Ives plc

CONTENTS

In this list of contents, titles of poems generally follow those in the edition, with the exception that words in upper case have usually been reduced after the initial letter to lower case. When poems have been given titles from their first lines, the punctuation at the end of the line has been ignored. Titles which have been supplied and titles of works from which extracts have been taken are placed within square brackets.

Abbreviations Used in the Text *xix*
Preface *xxi*
Acknowledgements *xliii*
Introduction *1*
Note on the Text and Annotation *69*

I THE PUBLIC WORLD

1 JOHN SKELTON [*from* A Lawde and Prayse Made for Our Sovereigne Lord the Kyng] *79*
2 SIR THOMAS MORE De Principe Bono Et Malo *80*
3 Quis Optimus Reipublicae Status *80*
4 SIR DAVID LINDSAY [*from* The Dreme] The Complaynt of the Comoun weill of Scotland *82*
5 SIR THOMAS WYATT [Who lyst his welth and eas Retayne] *83*
6 In Spayn *84*
7 [The piller pearisht is whearto I Lent] *85*
8 HENRY HOWARD, EARL OF SURREY [Thassyryans king in peas with fowle desyre] *85*
9 ANONYMOUS John Arm-strongs last good night *86*
10 ROBERT CROWLEY Of unsaciable purchasers *89*
11 JOHN HEYWOOD [*from* A Ballad on the Marriage of Philip and Mary] *90*
12 WILLIAM BIRCH [*from* A songe betwene the Quenes majestie and Englande] *92*

13 QUEEN ELIZABETH I [The dowbt off future foes exiles my present joye] *95*
14 SIR PHILIP SIDNEY [*from* The Countesse of Pembrokes Arcadia] *96*
15 ANONYMOUS Of Sir Frauncis Walsingham Sir Phillipp Sydney, and Sir Christopher Hatton, Lord Chancelor *97*
16 GEORGE PUTTENHAM Her Majestie resembled to the crowned piller *98*
17 ANNE DOWRICHE [*from* The French Historie] *99*
18 SIR WALTER RALEGH [Praisd be Dianas faire and harmles light] *100*
19 [*from* Fortune hath taken the away my love] *100*
20 QUEEN ELIZABETH I [Ah silly pugge wert thou so sore afraid] *101*
21 SIR WALTER RALEGH The 21th: and last booke of the Ocean to Scinthia *102*
22 The Lie *116*
23 ALEXANDER MONTGOMERIE [Remembers thou in Æsope of a taill] *119*
24 SIR JOHN HARINGTON A Tragicall Epigram *119*
25 Of Treason *120*
26 FULKE GREVILLE, LORD BROOKE [*from* Cælica] Sonnet 78 *120*
27 GEORGE PEELE [*from* Anglorum Feriae] *121*
28 JOHN DONNE The Calme *123*
29 [*from* Satire 4] *125*
30 ROBERT DEVEREUX, EARL OF ESSEX [Change thy minde since she doth change] *129*
31 MARY SIDNEY, COUNTESS OF PEMBROKE [To Queen Elizabeth] *131*
32 EDMUND SPENSER [*from* The Faerie Queene Book 5] *134*
33 EOCHAIDH Ó HEÓGHUSA [On Maguire's Winter Campaign] *141*
34 BEN JONSON On the Union *145*
35 SIR ARTHUR GORGES Written upon the death of the most Noble Prince *Henrie* *145*
36 SIR HENRY WOTTON Upon the sudden Restraint of the *Earle* of *Somerset*, then falling from favor *146*
37 WILLIAM BROWNE [*from* Britannia's Pastorals Book 2] *146*
38 ANONYMOUS Feltons Epitaph *148*
39 ANONYMOUS [Epitaph on the Duke of Buckingham] *149*

40 Sir Richard Fanshawe [*from* An Ode Upon occasion of His Majesties Proclamation in the yeare 1630] *149*
41 John Cleveland Epitaph on the Earl of *Strafford* *151*
42 Sir John Denham Coopers Hill *152*
43 Martin Parker Upon defacing of *White-hall* *163*
44 Robert Herrick A King and no King *165*
45 Andrew Marvell An *Horatian* Ode upon *Cromwel's* Return from *Ireland* *166*
46 Sir William Mure [*from* The Cry of Blood, and of a Broken Covenant] *170*
47 Katherine Philips On the 3. of *September*, 1651 *171*
48 John Milton To the Lord Generall Cromwell May 1652 *172*
49 To Sir Henry Vane the younger *173*
50 Andrew Marvell [*from* The First Anniversary of the Government under O.C.] *174*
51 Alexander Brome On Sir *G.B.* his defeat *175*

II IMAGES OF LOVE

52 Anonymous [Westron wynde when wylle thow blow] *181*
53 Sir Thomas Wyatt [They fle from me that sometyme did me seke] *181*
54 [Who so list to hount I knowe where is an hynde] *182*
55 [It may be good like it who list] *183*
56 [My lute awake perfourme the last] *183*
57 Henry Howard, Earl of Surrey [The soote season, that bud and blome furth bringes] *185*
58 Alexander Scott [To luve unluvit it is ane pane] *185*
59 George Turbervile To his Love that sent him a Ring wherein was gravde, *Let Reason rule* *186*
60 Isabella Whitney I. W. To her unconstant Lover *187*
61 George Gascoigne [A Sonet written in prayse of the brown beautie] *192*
62 Anonymous A new Courtly Sonet, of the Lady Greensleeves *193*
63 Sir Philip Sidney [*from* Certain Sonnets: 4] *196*
64 [*from* The Countesse of Pembrokes Arcadia] *197*
65 [*from* Astrophil and Stella] 1 *199*
66 [*from* Astrophil and Stella] 2 *200*
67 [*from* Astrophil and Stella] 9 *201*

68 [*from* Astrophil and Stella] 72 *201*
69 [*from* Astrophil and Stella] 81 *202*
70 [*from* Astrophil and Stella] 83 *203*
71 [*from* Astrophil and Stella] Eight song *203*
72 [*from* Astrophil and Stella] Eleventh song *207*
73 FULKE GREVILLE, LORD BROOKE [*from* Cælica] Sonnet 22 *208*
74 [*from* Cælica] Sonnet 27 *209*
75 [*from* Cælica] Sonnet 39 *210*
76 [*from* Cælica] Sonnet 44 *211*
77 [*from* Cælica] Sonnet 84 *212*
78 MARK ALEXANDER BOYD Sonet *213*
79 ROBERT GREENE *Dorons* description of *Samela* *213*
80 EDMUND SPENSER [*from* The Faerie Queene Book 2] *214*
81 [*from* The Faerie Queene Book 3] *220*
82 [*from* The Faerie Queene Book 3] *224*
83 [*from* Amoretti] *Sonnet 23* *231*
84 [*from* Amoretti] *Sonnet 64* *231*
85 [*from* Amoretti] *Sonnet 67* *232*
86 [*from* Amoretti] *Sonnet 70* *233*
87 [*from* Amoretti] *Sonnet 71* *233*
88 Epithalamion *234*
89 SIR WALTER RALEGH [As you came from the holy land] *247*
90 SAMUEL DANIEL [*from* Delia] Sonnet 13 *249*
91 [*from* Delia] Sonnet 39 *250*
92 [*from* Delia] Sonnet 52 *250*
93 SIR JOHN DAVIES [*from* Gullinge Sonnets] 6 *251*
94 [Faith (wench) I cannot court thy sprightly eyes] *252*
95 THOMAS NASHE The choise of valentines *253*
96 JOHN DONNE To his Mistress going to bed *263*
97 BARNABE BARNES [*from* Parthenophil and Parthenophe] Sonnet 27 *265*
98 CHRISTOPHER MARLOWE The passionate Sheepheard to his love *265*
99 Hero and Leander *266*
100 WILLIAM SHAKESPEARE [*from* Venus and Adonis] *290*
101 [*from* Lucrece] *296*
102 RICHARD BARNFIELD [*from* Cynthia] Sonnet 8 *303*
103 [*from* Cynthia] Sonnet 11 *304*
104 WILLIAM SHAKESPEARE [*from* Sonnets] 19 *304*
105 [*from* Sonnets] 20 *305*

106 [*from* Sonnets] 29 *306*
107 [*from* Sonnets] 35 *306*
108 [*from* Sonnets] 36 *307*
109 [*from* Sonnets] 55 *308*
110 [*from* Sonnets] 56 *308*
111 [*from* Sonnets] 66 *309*
112 [*from* Sonnets] 74 *310*
113 [*from* Sonnets] 94 *310*
114 [*from* Sonnets] 121 *311*
115 [*from* Sonnets] 124 *312*
116 [*from* Sonnets] 129 *312*
117 [*from* Sonnets] 135 *313*
118 [*from* Sonnets] 138 *314*
119 [*from* Sonnets] 144 *314*
120 ROBERT SIDNEY, EARL OF LEICESTER Sonnet 21 *315*
121 Sonnet 25 *316*
122 Sonnet 31 *316*
123 Songe 17 *317*
124 GEORGE CHAPMAN [*from* Hero and Leander Sestiad 3] *317*
125 JOHN MARSTON [*from* The Metamorphosis of Pigmalions Image] *322*
126 THOMAS DELONEY [Long have I lov'd this bonny Lasse] *325*
127 ANONYMOUS [*from* The wanton Wife of Bath] *326*
128 [JOHN DOWLAND] [Fine knacks for ladies, cheape choise brave and new] *328*
129 THOMAS CAMPION [Followe thy faire sunne unhappy shaddowe] *329*
130 [Rose-cheekt *Lawra* come] *330*
131 [There is a Garden in her face] *330*
132 JOHN DONNE His Picture *331*
133 The Sunne Rising *332*
134 The Canonization *333*
135 Loves growth *334*
136 A Valediction of weeping *335*
137 A Valediction forbidding mourning *336*
138 MICHAEL DRAYTON [*from* Idea] 10 *338*
139 [*from* Idea] 61 *338*
140 To His Coy Love, A Canzonet *339*
141 BEN JONSON Why I Write Not Of Love *340*
142 My Picture left in *Scotland* *340*

143 LADY MARY WROTH [*from* Pamphilia to Amphilanthus] 23 *341*
144 [*from* Pamphilia to Amphilanthus] 34 *342*
145 [*from* Pamphilia to Amphilanthus] A crowne of Sonetts dedicated to Love *342*
146 [*from* Pamphilia to Amphilanthus] 2 *349*
147 [*from* The Countesse of Mountgomeries Urania] 7 *350*
148 ROBERT HERRICK Delight in Disorder *351*
149 The Vision *351*
150 The silken Snake *352*
151 Her Bed *352*
152 Upon *Julia's* haire fill'd with Dew *353*
153 Upon *Sibilla* *353*
154 THOMAS CAREW The Spring *353*
155 Ingratefull beauty threatned *354*
156 [*from* A Rapture] *355*
157 MARTIN PARKER [*from* Cupid's Wrongs Vindicated] *356*
158 [*from* Well met Neighbour] *360*
159 EDMUND WALLER The story of *Phœbus* and *Daphne* appli'd *362*
160 Song *363*
161 The Budd *363*
162 SIR JOHN SUCKLING [Out upon it, I have lov'd] *364*
163 JOHN CLEVELAND The Antiplatonick *365*
164 RICHARD LOVELACE Song. To Lucasta, Going to the Warres *367*
165 *Gratiana* dauncing and singing *368*
166 To Althea, From Prison. *Song* *369*
167 Her Muffe *370*
168 [*from* On *Sanazar*'s being honoured with six hundred Duckets by the *Clarissimi* of *Venice*, for composing an *Elegiack Hexastick* of The City. A Satyre] *371*
169 ANDREW MARVELL To his Coy Mistress *372*
170 The Gallery *374*
171 The Definition of Love *376*
172 JAMES HARRINGTON Inconstancy *377*
173 KATHERINE PHILIPS An Answer to another perswading a Lady to Marriage *378*

III TOPOGRAPHIES

174 ALEXANDER BARCLAY [*from* Certayne Egloges 5] *381*

175 George Buchanan Calendæ Maiæ *383*
176 Anonymous [*from* Vox populi vox Dei] *384*
177 Anonymous [*from* Jack of the North] *387*
178 Anonymous The Jolly Pinder of Wakefield *389*
179 Barnabe Googe Goyng towardes Spayne *391*
180 Siôn Phylip [*from* Yr Wylan] *392*
181 Sir Philip Sidney [*from* The Countesse of Pembrokes Arcadia] *394*
182 Edmund Spenser [*from* The Shepheardes Calender] Maye *395*
183 Alexander Hume [*from* Of the day Estivall] *401*
184 Sir John Davies [*from* Epigrammes] In Cosmum 17 *406*
185 Joseph Hall [*from* Virgidemiarum Book 5] *406*
186 Everard Guilpin [*from* Skialetheia Satire 5] *408*
187 Anonymous A Songe bewailinge the tyme of Christmas, So much decayed in Englande *410*
188 John Donne A nocturnall upon S.*Lucies* day, Being the shortest day *412*
189 Æmilia Lanyer The Description of Cooke-ham *414*
190 Ben Jonson To Penshurst *420*
191 Michael Drayton [*from* Pastorals] The Ninth Eglogue *423*
192 [*from* Poly-Olbion Song 6] *428*
193 To The Virginian Voyage *431*
194 Samuel Daniel [*from* Epistle. To Prince Henrie] *433*
195 Anonymous On Francis Drake *437*
196 W. Turner [*from* Turners dish of Lentten stuffe, or a Galymaufery] *437*
197 John Taylor [*from* The Sculler] Epigram 22 *441*
198 William Browne [*from* Britannia's Pastorals Book 2] *442*
199 Edward Herbert, Lord Herbert of Cherbury Sonnet *443*
200 Richard Corbett A Proper New Ballad Intituled The Faeryes Farewell: Or God-A-Mercy Will *444*
201 Sir William Davenant The Countess of Anglesey lead Captive by the Rebels, at the Disforresting of *Pewsam* *446*
202 George Wither [*from* Britain's Remembrancer Canto 4] *447*
203 John Milton Song On *May* morning *449*
204 *L'Allegro* *449*
205 Robert Herrick To *Dean-bourn*, a rude River in *Devon*, by which sometimes he lived *454*
206 *Corinna's* going a Maying *455*
207 To Meddowes *457*

208 The Wassaile *458*
209 RICHARD CRASHAW [*from* Bulla] *459*
210 ABRAHAM COWLEY The Wish *463*
211 ANONYMOUS [The Diggers' Song] *464*
212 HENRY VAUGHAN [*from* To his retired friend, an Invitation to *Brecknock*] *466*
213 RICHARD LOVELACE The Snayl *468*
214 ANDREW MARVELL Bermudas *470*
215 The Mower to the Glo-Worms *471*
216 The Mower against Gardens *472*
217 The Garden *473*
218 [*from* Upon Appleton House, to my Lord *Fairfax*] *476*
219 MARGARET CAVENDISH, DUCHESS OF NEWCASTLE Of many *Worlds* in this *World* *479*
220 A *Dialogue* betwixt *Man*, and *Nature* *480*
221 Similizing the *Sea* to *Meadowes*, and *Pastures*, the *Marriners* to *Shepheards*, the *Mast* to a *May-pole*, *Fishes* to *Beasts* *482*
222 KATHERINE PHILIPS Upon the graving of her Name upon a Tree in *Barnelmes* Walks *483*

IV FRIENDS, PATRONS AND THE GOOD LIFE

223 SIR THOMAS WYATT [Myn owne John poyntz sins ye delight to know] *487*
224 GEORGE GASCOIGNE [Upon the theme: *Magnum vectigal parcimonia*] *490*
225 [Gascoignes wodmanship] *492*
226 EDWARD DE VERE, EARL OF OXFORD [Weare I a Kinge I coulde commande content] *497*
227 THOMAS LODGE [*from* Scillaes Metamorphosis] *497*
228 JOHN DONNE To Sir *Henry Wotton* *498*
229 THOMAS DELONEY The Weavers Song *501*
230 THOMAS DEKKER [Art thou poore yet hast thou golden Slumbers] *503*
231 SAMUEL DANIEL To the Lady Lucie, Countesse of Bedford *504*
232 BEN JONSON To Lucy, Countesse of Bedford, with Mr. Donnes Satyres *507*
233 Inviting A Friend To Supper *507*

234 [Thomas Ravenscroft] [Hey hoe what shall I say] *509*
235 [Sing we now merily] *509*
236 A Belmans Song *510*
237 Thomas Campion [Now winter nights enlarge] *510*
238 Anonymous The Mode of France *511*
239 Michael Drayton These verses weare made By Michaell Drayton Esquier Poett Lawreatt the night before hee dyed *512*
240 Edmund Waller At Pens-hurst *513*
241 Richard Lovelace The Grasse-hopper. To my Noble Friend, Mr. *Charles Cotton*. Ode *514*
242 Alexander Brome [*from* The Prisoners] Written when O.C. attempted to be King *516*
243 John Milton [To Edward Lawrence] *516*
244 Katherine Philips Friendship's Mystery, To My Dearest *Lucasia* *517*
245 Friendship in Embleme, or the Seal. To my dearest *Lucasia* *518*
246 To my Excellent *Lucasia*, on our Friendship *521*

V CHURCH, STATE AND BELIEF

247 John Skelton [*from* Collyn Clout] *525*
248 Anne Askew The Balade whych Anne Askewe made and sange whan she was in Newgate *527*
249 Luke Shepherd [*from* The Upcheringe of the Messe] *529*
250 Anonymous [A Lament for our Lady's Shrine at Walsingham] *531*
251 John Heywood [*from* Epygrams] Of turnyng. 67 *532*
252 George Puttenham [*from* Partheniades] Partheniad 11 Urania *533*
253 Robert Southwell The burning Babe *535*
254 Henry Constable To St Mary Magdalen *536*
255 Sir John Harington A Groome of the Chambers religion in King *Henry* the eights time *536*
256 John Donne Satyre 3 *537*
257 Goodfriday, *1613*. Riding Westward *541*
258 Hymne to God my God, in my sicknesse *542*
259 [*from* Holy Sonnets] 10 *543*
260 [Since she whome I lovd, hath payd her last debt] *544*
261 [Show me deare Christ, thy spouse, so bright and cleare] *545*

262 FULKE GREVILLE, LORD BROOKE [*from* Cælica] Sonnet 89 *546*
263 [*from* Cælica] Sonnet 99 *547*
264 [*from* Cælica] Sonnet 109 *548*
265 GILES FLETCHER [*from* Christs Victorie, and Triumph in Heaven, and Earth, over, and after death] *549*
266 ÆMILIA LANYER [*from* Salve Deus Rex Judæorum] *556*
267 WILLIAM DRUMMOND [For the *Baptiste*] *558*
268 [Content and Resolute] *559*
269 PHINEAS FLETCHER [Vast Ocean of light, whose rayes surround] *559*
270 JOHN MILTON On the morning of Christs Nativity *561*
271 FRANCIS QUARLES [*from* Pentelogia] Fraus Mundi *571*
272 [*from* Divine Fancies] On the contingencie of Actions *572*
273 [*from* Divine Fancies] On the Needle of a Sun-diall *573*
274 [*from* Divine Fancies] On the Booke of Common Prayer *573*
275 [*from* Divine Fancies] On Christ and our selves *573*
276 GEORGE HERBERT Perseverance *574*
277 Redemption *575*
278 Easter wings *576*
279 Prayer *576*
280 Deniall *577*
281 Jordan *578*
282 The Collar *579*
283 The Flower *580*
284 The Forerunners *582*
285 Love *583*
286 [*from* The Church Militant] *584*
287 ANONYMOUS [Yet if his Majestie our Sovareigne lord] *585*
288 SIDNEY GODOLPHIN [Lord when the wise men came from Farr] *586*
289 JOHN TAYLOR [*from* Here followeth the unfashionable fashion, or the too too homely Worshipping of God] *587*
290 EDMUND WALLER Upon His Majesties repairing of Pauls *588*
291 RICHARD CRASHAW A Hymne of the Nativity, sung by the Shepheards *591*
292 To The Noblest and best of Ladyes, the Countesse of Denbigh *594*
293 [*from* The Flaming Heart] *596*
294 ANONYMOUS Upon Arch-bishop Laud, Prisoner in the Tower. 1641 *597*

295 ROBERT WILD [*from* Alas poore Scholler, whither wilt thou goe] *598*
296 JOHN MILTON On the new forcers of Conscience under the Long Parliament *601*
297 MORGAN LLWYD [*from* The Summer] *602*
298 LAURENCE CLARKSON [*from* A Single Eye All Light, no Darkness] *604*
299 HENRY VAUGHAN The Retreate *605*
300 The World *606*
301 Cock-crowing *609*
302 The Water-fall *610*
303 SIR WILLIAM DAVENANT [*from* Gondibert Book 2] *612*
304 ANNA TRAPNEL [*from* The Cry of a Stone] *613*
305 AN COLLINS Another Song exciting to spirituall Mirth *614*
306 ANDREW MARVELL The Coronet *616*

VI ELEGY AND EPITAPH

307 JOHN SKELTON [*from* Phyllyp Sparowe] *621*
308 HENRY HOWARD, EARL OF SURREY [Norfolk sprang thee, Lambeth holds thee dead] *627*
309 [W. resteth here, that quick could never rest] *627*
310 NICHOLAS GRIMALD [*from* A funerall song, upon the deceas of Annes his moother] *629*
311 CHIDIOCK TICHBORNE [My prime of youth is but a froste of cares] *630*
312 WILLIAM SHAKESPEARE [The Phoenix and Turtle] *631*
313 JOHN DONNE [*from* The Second Anniversarie] Of the Progres *of the Soule* *634*
314 BEN JONSON On My First Sonne *637*
315 To the immortall memorie, and friendship of that noble paire, Sir Lucius Cary, and Sir H. Morison *638*
316 SIR WALTER RALEGH [Even suche is tyme that takes in trust] *643*
317 WILLIAM BROWNE On the Countesse *Dowager* of *Pembrooke* *644*
318 HENRY KING An Exequy To his matchlesse never to be forgotten Freind *644*
319 GEORGE HERBERT [*from* Memoriae Matris Sacrum] *648*
320 THOMAS CAREW Epitaph on the Lady *Mary Villers* *648*

321 SIR HENRY WOTTON Upon the death of Sir *Albert Morton's* Wife *649*
322 ROBERT HERRICK To the reverend shade of his religious Father *649*
323 Upon himselfe being buried *650*
324 Upon a child *650*
325 JOHN MILTON *Lycidas* *651*
326 [Methought I saw my late espoused Saint] *658*
327 'ELIZA' To my Husband *659*
328 HENRY VAUGHAN [They are all gone into the world of light] *660*
329 KATHERINE PHILIPS Epitaph. On her Son *H. P.* at St. *Syth's* Church where her body also lies Interred *661*
330 *Orinda* upon little *Hector Philips* *662*
331 JAMES SHIRLEY [The glories of our blood and state] *663*

VII TRANSLATION

332 HENRY HOWARD, EARL OF SURREY [*from* Virgil's Aeneid Book 4] *667*
333 RICHARD STANYHURST [*from* Virgil's Aeneid Book 4] *669*
334 ARTHUR GOLDING [*from* Ovid's Metamorphoses Book 6] *671*
335 EDMUND SPENSER [*from* Ruines of Rome: by Bellay] 5 *676*
336 MARY SIDNEY, COUNTESS OF PEMBROKE Quid gloriaris? Psalm 52 *677*
337 [*from* Psalm 89 Misericordias] *679*
338 Voce mea ad Dominum Psalm 142 *680*
339 CHRISTOPHER MARLOWE [*from* Ovids Elegies Book 1] Elegia. 13. *Ad Auroram ne properet* *681*
340 [*from* Lucan's Pharsalia Book 1] *682*
341 SIR JOHN HARINGTON [*from* Ariosto's Orlando Furioso Book 34] *683*
342 EDWARD FAIRFAX [*from* Tasso's Godfrey of Bulloigne Book 4] *689*
343 JOSUAH SYLVESTER [*from* Saluste du Bartas' Devine Weekes] *693*
344 GEORGE CHAPMAN [*from* Homer's Iliad Book 12] *695*
345 JOHN MILTON The Fifth Ode of *Horace*. Lib. *I* *698*

VIII WRITER, LANGUAGE AND PUBLIC

346 John Skelton [*from* A Replycacion] *701*
347 Thomas Churchyard [*from* A Musicall Consort] *702*
348 Edmund Spenser [*from* The Faerie Queene Book 6] *703*
349 Sir John Harington Of honest Theft. To my good friend Master *Samuel Daniel* *709*
350 John Donne The triple Foole *709*
351 William Shakespeare [*from* Sonnets] 108 *710*
352 John Marston [*from* The Scourge of Villanie] *In Lectores prorsus indignos* *711*
353 Samuel Daniel [*from* Musophilus] *715*
354 Ben Jonson A Fit of Rime against Rime *717*
355 An Ode. To himselfe *719*
356 George Chapman [*from* Homer's Iliad, To the Reader] *721*
357 Sir Walter Ralegh To the Translator *722*
358 William Browne [*from* Britannia's Pastorals Book 2] *722*
359 Rachel Speght [*from* The Dreame] *725*
360 Michael Drayton [*from* Idea] 25 *727*
361 To my most dearely-loved friend Henery Reynolds Esquire, of *Poets and Poesie* *728*
362 [*from* The Muses Elizium] The Description of Elizium *734*
363 John Milton [*from* At a Vacation Exercise] *738*
364 John Taylor [*from* A comparison betwixt a *Whore* and a *Booke*] *740*
365 Thomas Carew An Elegie upon the death of the Deane of Pauls, Dr. John Donne *741*
366 A Fancy *744*
367 Robert Herrick To the Detracter *744*
368 Posting to Printing *745*
369 George Wither [*from* Vox Pacifica] *745*
370 Sir William Davenant [*from* Gondibert Book 2] *749*
371 Margaret Cavendish, Duchess of Newcastle The Claspe *751*
372 [The Common Fate of Books] *751*
373 Abraham Cowley The Muse *752*
374 Henry Vaughan The Book *755*

Notes to the Text *757*

Appendix 1: Index of Genres *853*
Appendix 2: Index of Metrical and Stanzaic Forms *857*
Appendix 3: Glossary of Classical Names *863*
Appendix 4: Biographical Notes on Authors *879*
Appendix 5: Index of Authors *898*

Index of First Lines *901*
Index of Titles *911*

Abbreviations Used in the Text

The following abbreviations have been used:

BL	British Library
c.	circa
ch.	chapter
cp.	compare
ed.	edited by
edn(s)	edition(s)
f(f).	folio(s)
intro.	introduction by, introduced by
MS(S)	manuscript(s)
no(s).	number(s)
p(p).	page(s)
r	recto
rev.	revised
sig(s).	signature(s)
v	verso
vol(s).	volume(s)

Where no place of publication is given for works which are cited, it can be assumed to be London.

PREFACE

Compiling an anthology of a field as rich as British Renaissance verse is an exciting but frustrating task: the more one includes, the more one draws attention to omissions. In the spirit of the Renaissance, this selection is greedily inclusive and as much has been crammed in as possible. An anthology is among other things an incentive towards further reading, however, and it is hoped that readers will be stimulated, and perhaps provoked, rather than satiated. Since a major purpose of the book is to suggest a revaluation of the prevailing canon of Renaissance verse, a brief account will be given in Section 1 of the various fluctuations in the canon over the last hundred years or so, in order to give a context for the present selection. Readers who want an overview of the book's contents and a discussion of its principles of selection should turn straight to Section 2.

1: THE RENAISSANCE AND THE CANON

The word 'anthology' comes from the Greek for 'gathering of flowers', and that is how anthologists often approach their task: pressing the very choicest blossoms, abstracting them from their own season of growth and arranging them decoratively in a timeless album. For F. T. Palgrave, editor of *The Golden Treasury*, the aim was to pass over 'extreme or temporary phases in style' in search of 'something neither modern, nor ancient, but true in all ages'.[1] The present anthology certainly aims to give pleasure, but not to achieve timelessness. Coverage is given to poems concerned with topical religious and political issues of the day as well as with the perennial lyric themes of love, nature and death – which themselves are confronted in different ways in different periods. The point of this historicizing approach is not to reduce the poems' meaning to a single, limited context: poetry works on many different levels, and its meanings are never entirely exhausted by one frame of reference. But to read poems in their social and ideological contexts, as parts of a social process rather than static objects, is often to gain dimensions of meaning that are lost in a homogenizing, timeless approach. Moreover, those contexts are themselves not fixed and static: they are historical processes in which we are still involved in our own time, and our understanding of the contexts will be heavily influenced by our own point of view.[2] The 'rediscoveries' of Donne and Marvell in the later nineteenth century, and of women poets in more recent times, were means of exploring the literary and political possibilities of the present as well as of the past. To read historically is not to reduce texts to a dead past but to heighten our awareness of the complex transactions between past and present that occur whenever we read a text, whether it be a poem or a historical narrative.

The idea of the Renaissance is an example of such a process of active reinterpretation. Succeeding ages have redefined their conception of Renaissance poetry as they have changed their ideas of what the Renaissance might be – or indeed whether there ever was such a thing.[3] For it must be conceded right away that the status of the concept of 'the Renaissance' is questionable.[4] For one thing, it is an evaluative as much as a descriptive term, and gives the highly misleading impression that the thousand years before that period amounted to nothing. Already in 1603 Samuel Daniel was complaining about the humanist habit of describing the previous age as 'barbarous': 'Nor can it be but a touch of arrogant ignorance, to hold this or that nation Barbarous, these or those times grosse, considering how this manifold creature man, wheresoever hee stand in the world, hath alwayes some disposition of worth.'[5] The early modern usage of the word 'renaissance' was at least relatively constricted: people spoke of engaging in a 'renaissance' of letters or of painting. In the nineteenth century, however, there arose the much more ambitious concept of a culture as a unified system in which economic, social and political factors all had their influence on the arts; and the idea of a general 'spirit of an age' tends to flatten a society's differences and contradictions into an artificial uniformity.

And yet, when all these points have been made, there is a case for retaining the 'Renaissance' label. The question of whether or not there 'really was' a Renaissance is in the end unanswerable because what is at issue is a way of interpreting a period, not a set of neutral facts. We cannot read the past without models, and the important thing is to be aware that they are just models, to use them for what they can reveal with a full awareness of alternative ways of seeing. If the idea of the Renaissance has been so consistent in nineteenth- and twentieth-century thought, it is because it seems to offer a way of understanding how modernity changed the world. It was in the nineteenth century that historians who confronted an unprecedented acceleration in the rate of technological and social change first formulated the notion of the Renaissance in a broad historical sense. It was in that age, they found, that traditional feudal social loyalties were undermined, and the authority of the Church was rejected in the name of the individual conscience; sometimes religion was rejected altogether for a defiant this-worldliness. The nineteenth century began increasingly to look for an explanation of these cultural changes in terms not just of an abstract spirit of the age but of deep-rooted economic changes; Marx and Weber located in the Renaissance the origins of capitalism.[6]

According to such interpretations, then, Renaissance culture was a force for modernization; it was also, potentially, a democratizing force, levelling traditional religious and social distinctions. Divisions quickly emerged, however, over the extent of that democratic element. In *The Civilization of the Renaissance in Italy* (1860), Jacob Burckhardt focused his attention not on the republican culture of the city-states but on court society.[7] Burckhardt was sceptical of democratic ideas and drawn to Nietzsche's aristocratic radicalism: he tended to see the freedom of Renaissance man as an inner, individual freedom, the leisurely pursuit of self-fulfilment. Such a pursuit did not necessarily depend on political liberty: in fact it might find its most congenial locale at court, where life itself became a work of art. The Renaissance, then, had already acquired a political double edge: progressives often celebrated the period as ushering in democratic progress, while for conservatives it could be valued as a kind of bastion against the more threatening aspects of a democratic political life.

By the 1890s, Burckhardt's version of the Renaissance was beginning to mould readings of the English sixteenth century, and anthologists like Arthur Symons helped to construct a Burckhardtian image of the age.[8] They placed their emphasis on the courtly lyric, on Elizabethan sonnets and on the previously neglected work of 'cavalier' lyricists like Herrick and Lovelace: writers who seemed to be aspiring to a kind of 'pure' poetry. These priorities were continued even in an anthology as comprehensive as E. K. Chambers's *The Oxford Book of Sixteenth Century Verse* (Oxford 1932), which concentrated overwhelmingly on the love-lyric and neglected many other kinds of poetry. The preference was for what C. S. Lewis termed 'golden' poetry, the courtly and pastoral verse of the high Elizabethan period – verse, as he put it, which celebrates 'all that is naturally delightful'.[9]

That highly courtly notion of the Renaissance, however, gave a one-sided picture of English culture in the sixteenth and seventeenth centuries, and indeed it was formed in conscious opposition to alternative models. Like Burckhardt himself, the devotees of courtly culture were reacting against the ideology of nineteenth-century progressive thought with its cults of inevitable progress and the Protestant work-ethic. The image of the poet as a lyricist devoted to turning his life into a work of art powerfully rejected the demands made on nineteenth-century poets to turn their art to the causes of progress and morality. For one counter-image to the newly-created

'Renaissance', we can turn to the editorial labours of that indefatigable scholar and amateur oarsman F. J. Furnivall (1825–1910). For Furnivall, a somewhat eccentric but steadfast political radical with a commitment to constitutional reform and women's rights, the great English poets had been prophets of political and social reform.[10] Though his own literary judgement was erratic and his methodology somewhat mechanistic, he did make available huge tracts of early English poetry which illustrated public struggles as well as private sensibilities, poetry which Lewis described as 'drab' rather than 'golden'. He drew attention to the traditions of popular religious individualism and protest which prefigured the Reformation (cp. no. 176). For whereas Italian critiques of the Church had tended to be confined to a self-conscious élite, in northern Europe they had more democratic roots. Furnivall was no puritan himself and preferred the downrightness of popular verse on sexual matters to the idealizing of court poetry. He resisted the tendency, visible even in the editorial labours of the great ballad scholar F. J. Child (1825–96), to present an idealized and bowdlerized version of the 'folk' from which the lower orders had subsequently declined.[11] To Child's great consternation, he offered to subscribers of his edition of the Percy ballad manuscript a fourth volume including ballads which were 'loose' in more than one sense, having been censored from the standard printing.[12] Furnivall was only one of many nineteenth-century scholars who were more preoccupied with popular than with courtly poetry.

The formation of a new canon of 'Renaissance' poetry, then, had involved a process of exclusion and sublimation, a shift away from popular and public poetry towards a courtly and apolitical idea of the aesthetic. To some extent, that shift has persisted to the present day. Many of the great printed collections of early modern ballads appeared in the nineteenth century and, despite the editorial labours of figures like H. E. Rollins, criticism has paid relatively little attention to this corpus.[13] There has, however, been a steady rehabilitation of non-courtly verse. Yvor Winters made a strong case for figures whom Lewis would have considered 'drab', such as Googe, Turbervile and Greville.[14] And the outspoken directness of Donne's poetry appealed to those who were dissatisfied with what they saw as the dreamy abstractions of Sidney and Spenser. For William Empson and many poets and critics who began writing in the interwar period, Donne was the pattern for a truly modern poetry. T. S. Eliot had played a leading part in the revaluation of Donne, but he began to express reservations when he found Donne being taken up as a champion of modernity, and he claimed that in Donne thought and feeling were split, rather than unified as he had previously argued.[15] Eliot was heavily influenced by T. E. Hulme's highly critical view of the Renaissance as the beginning of a decadent 'humanism', opening the way to the fuzzy, sentimental thought and art of modern liberalism.[16]

Just like the Renaissance itself, however, the image of Donne could be constructed in many different ways. His reaction against the public world could be seen as affirming an aristocratic, rather than democratic, individualism in harmony with the Nietzschean model. His later movement towards the Anglican Church could be seen as translating this aristocratic spirit into a religious order which was less dogmatic than the Catholic Church but still kept at bay the iconoclastic and democratic tendencies of Puritanism. For Cleanth Brooks and the 'New Critics', Donne's lyrics were of the essence of poetry in so far as they transcended the debased currency of everyday language and took on an almost sacramental status. Donne's religious temper was certainly more important than the simpler appropriations of him as a secular humanist allowed, but there was something odd in the process by which the love-poems he had anxiously suppressed for fear of scandal when he entered the Church came to be seen virtually as embodiments of the divine presence. Meantime, poets who showed strong Puritan and reforming sympathies, most notably Milton, were in F. R. Leavis's phrase 'dislodged' from the canon as being tainted with an emergent modernity.

This conservative reading of English Renaissance culture inevitably generated a reaction. Critics variously labelled 'new historicists' or 'cultural materialists' have insisted that poetry does not transcend its age but is closely bound up with structures of social power; they have argued that the formation of a restricted canon of great poetry functions to defend the status of a social élite, relegating to the margin the voices of those who do not qualify as sufficiently literary.[17] Feminists have been especially sensitive to this process of marginalization, noting how the poetic canon tends to be presented as an august succession of great male minds. Literary theorists have questioned the New Critical notion of the poem as a self-contained, tightly unified artefact, arguing for the inescapable plurality of texts and interpretations. The newer readings of Renaissance culture run parallel to developments in 'post-modern' writing. Where Renaissance writers in the name of modernity defined themselves in relation to the 'Middle Ages', writers are now starting to define themselves as against the whole project of modernity. They tend to see 'Renaissance individualism' not as heroic but as an egotistical, aggressive, narrowing phenomenon. From a different political angle, 'humanism' has again come under attack (see Section 4 of the Introduction). Yet, because the newer model of individuality was still experimental and problematic, the period has continued to fascinate. The present anthology responds to these critical concerns. The poets of the New Critical canon can certainly be found here, but alongside the poised, 'mature', refined texts favoured by the New Critics can be found some rawer kinds of poetry, voices of public engagement and polemic, raw satire, subversive masculine eroticism, and female criticism of those male voices.

2: USING THIS ANTHOLOGY: STRUCTURE, INCLUSIONS, PRESENTATION OF TEXTS

The eight groups of poems in this anthology have been arranged thematically rather than by author, with a view both to variety and to stimulating debate. The categories are by no means hard and fast, and do not necessarily correspond to strict generic divisions. Section I presents poets' engagement with affairs of State, and offers an overview of the major political developments from 1509 to 1660. In Section II the focus shifts from politics to love, but the distinction was not a clear-cut one in this period, when 'courting' was a political as well as an amatory phenomenon, and when the libertine poets' radical experimentation with sexual norms was felt to constitute a major threat to social order. Anthologies of Renaissance love-poetry have often tended to emphasize Neoplatonic idealization at the expense of more earthy material; an attempt has been made here to redress the balance. Women poets intervened in the debates about love to a degree that is only now being fully recognized, and their viewpoints are extensively represented.[18] The third section presents the poets' exploration of landscapes, ranging from idealizations of the countryside as reviving the golden age to denunciations of enclosures and depopulation, and from prophetic glorification of expansion into the New World to prophetic doubts about colonization. Section IV presents poetic debates about the good life and the poet's role in society. Section V presents the most acutely debated questions of all: those concerning the true religion. As will be seen, the debates were not just between Catholics and Protestants, or Anglicans and Puritans, but extended to Puttenham's deism or atheism and the Ranters' belief in a God within (nos. 252, 298). Death of course provokes extremely intense questions, and Section VI illustrates a range of attitudes, from the controlled mourning of public ritual to restless questioning – both being potentially present in the same poem, as most notably in 'Lycidas' (no. 325). Section VII presents English poets' dialogues with their forebears and foreign contemporaries in the art of translation. In the final section the production of poetry itself is the subject of the dialogue, from the scepticism about the whole poetic process expressed in Daniel's *Musophilus* (no. 353) to Wither's almost Romantic confidence in his poetic vision (no. 369). Within each section, the arrangement is generally chronological. Datings cannot always be established with absolute precision, however, and the chronological principle has occasionally been varied to allow suggestive juxtapositions or to enable groups of poems by a single poet to be read together. Ballads are particularly hard to date, and these have sometimes been inserted under the date of the events they commemorate even though surviving versions may be considerably later.

The extensive Introduction consists of four sections which are largely self-contained within the framework of a general line of argument. Its scope is designed to counterbalance the inherent tendency of any anthology to abstract poems from their contexts. In the case of the Renaissance, such a practice tends to exaggerate the period's individualism at the expense of its public concerns; to highlight this point, poets' relations with the public world are discussed, in Section 2, before consideration turns in Section 3 to the traditionally private concerns of love, sexuality and the relations between the sexes. Broadly speaking, Section 2 provides a context for the poems in Sections I, III, IV and V of the anthology, while Section 3 of the Introduction covers the poems in Section II; but the analysis sets out to show how conventional public–private distinctions tend to break down when the texts are viewed in context. The central narrative focus in Section 2 is on 'high' politics, on changes in policy at the centre of power. This is, of course, not the only history that matters, but it provides a useful connection between diverse areas of poetic production. Moreover, public policy mattered greatly to writers, whose careers were often heavily dependent on political patronage. They were not just the creatures of patronage, however; a central aim of the Introduction is to show that, despite their celebrated individualism, Renaissance poets did have an articulate and independent sense of public responsibility. Section 3 of the Introduction asks how far 'Renaissance man' was an unredeemable chauvinist, and how far 'Renaissance woman' was allowed to speak. The question of Renaissance 'humanism' involves attitudes to language: the period's concern with rhetoric is often seen as another manifestation of the will to power, and Section 4 of the Introduction explores the poets' attitudes to language and rhetoric, with particular reference to the poems in Section VIII of the anthology.

The information provided in the Introduction is complemented by the notes at the end and by a series of appendices on genres, verse forms, classical names and authors' lives.

The Introduction sets out to situate the poems historically, but it does not make any claim to limit them to a single, fixed historical meaning. Because they consider 'literary evidence' to be flawed, historians are often sceptical of the use of poems in interpreting the past. In fact, poems can provide much illumination of past societies, but only if they are treated as participating in social processes rather than simply reflecting them. Poems are not transparent windows on history: they are formed by engagement with existing genres and conventions. The 'raw material' they deal with, whether it be political power, landscape or sexual desire, itself comes to poets in a codified, conventionalized form.

Genres have their more general equivalents in speech and writing in what have come to be termed 'discourses': sets of shared assumptions, concepts and words which govern a particular field of knowledge or social interaction and lay down its limits.[19] For example, we can say that many of the poems in this anthology explore man's attitude to the landscape, but, as Sir John Denham observed, landscapes in poetry are not just described but are created – a matter of the boundless 'Fancy' as well as the finite 'eie' (no. 42 ll. 1–12). One of the earliest recorded occurrences of the word 'landscape' occurs in one of the poems in this anthology (no. 343 l. 2); Milton's spelling 'Lantskip' (no. 204 l. 70) is a reminder that the word was a borrowing from a Dutch term to describe paintings. In *The Oxford English Dictionary*, Milton's is the first recorded use of the word in the extended metaphorical sense of a view perceived rather than a view painted. That metaphor has become obscured by time, and the process of active intervention as opposed to passive reflection in organizing one's perceptions has tended to be forgotten, but it can be brought to the fore when contending discourses are juxtaposed. Thus some poems in Section III see the countryman as a prophet of religious reform, others see him as a deferential supporter of the gentry; these poems are of little value in determining the historical reality of country life, but by juxtaposing them we can follow the poets in the process not just of mirroring but of creating their preferred landscapes. Denham's own vision of the landscape was strongly politicized (cp. Section 2 of the Introduction).

Discourses are formed in a process of opposition to other ways of seeing; they are normally linked with specific institutions which may well be in conflict, as with the debates between the monarchy and the common lawyers in the period, so it is highly misleading to try to explicate Renaissance poetry by reference to a single 'Elizabethan World Picture'.[20] Section 2 of the Introduction tries to bring out the complex interactions of political discourses in the period. Poems do not simply reproduce discourses but transform them through their own particular resources of genre and language, and may then have a reciprocal influence on received discourses. As will have become clear from the account of different interpretations of the Renaissance, a further dimension to these complexities is that any account of poems and discourses in the period is itself involved in negotiating between contending discourses in our own time. It will be clear, then, that the Introduction cannot aspire to unlock the final secrets of the poems' historical background; its aim is to provide contexts for critical and historical debate.

The anthology covers the period from the accession of Henry VIII in 1509 to the crisis of the English republic in 1659. This is a massive span of time, but it has a coherence which is missed by the common practice of splitting off sixteenth-century from seventeenth-century verse, and it helps to show the ways in which the political struggles of the 1640s connected with the earlier phases of Renaissance culture. It is of course impossible to give a precise date for the beginning of the English Renaissance, but Henry VIII's accession has been chosen as a starting-point for this anthology. This event aroused the hopes of humanists like More and Erasmus for a rebirth of learning and did indeed begin an advance in humanist educational programmes in universities and schools. The impact of humanist ideas on literary culture was complex and uneven, and older literary conventions persisted until much later, but there is a case for locating a major break around the second decade of the sixteenth century: Douglas Gray has argued that a coherent 'late medieval' tradition can be traced from 1400 down to about 1520.[21] At the other end of the period, the restoration of the monarchy in 1660 marks a phase of political reaction in which conservatives like the philosopher Thomas Hobbes saw the humanist championship of education as leading to political disorder. Hobbes was also in the vanguard of an intellectual reaction against rhetoric, a growing quest for a transcendent rational truth to whose discovery language was a hindrance more than a help. In the early 1650s, Milton could see the foundation of the republic as a triumphant fulfilment of the promise of Renaissance culture. By the end of the decade he was beginning work on *Paradise lost*, the last great Renaissance epic, in a spirit of depression at the collapse of such dreams. The poem presents itself as carrying the spirit of an earlier epoch into new dark days, and its rhetoric of address marks it in this sense as a Restoration poem; it is appropriate that it should be given a prominent place in Harold Love's *The Penguin Book of Restoration Verse*. A number of the selections, however, are designed in part to serve as contexts for *Paradise lost* (for example, nos. 342–3).

The anthology's geographical limits present problems of a different kind. The idea of the 'Renaissance' may have narrowed the canon in some respects, but it did at least draw attention to international influences on English culture. Furnivall belonged to an English populist tradition for which foreign influences were often signs of political decadence and effeminacy, and for which Anglo-Saxon words had intrinsically more value than Continental- or Latin-derived ones. Something of the same English nationalism can be found in F. R. Leavis's criticism. As Daniel Defoe long ago pointed out, however, 'The True-Born Englishman' has always been culturally hybrid, and this anthology tries to put the status of Englishness in question. The period saw the process which one scholar described as the 'Triumph of the English Language', but which may seem from Irish, Welsh or Scottish perspectives to be more a matter of cultural imperialism.[22] In fact, English historians of the Renaissance were well aware that their cultural legacy was radically heterogeneous, with Roman, Celtic, Anglo-Saxon, Danish and Norman elements all having played their part, not to mention later immigrants. Attempts to emphasize any one element as essentially English therefore ran into difficulties. Spenser set his epic *The Faerie Queene* in the world of the ancient Britons, thus complimenting the Tudors, whose ancestry was Welsh, and yet in writing in a language with a Germanic root he undermined the notion of direct cultural continuity that on one level his poem was designed to dramatize. Like it or not – and some poets did not (no. 360) – the English had to recognize that few Continentals would trouble to learn their obscure northern dialect, and that outside England it was only in Scotland, Wales and Ireland that they could find a fully understanding audience.

In trying to avoid a triumphalist notion of Englishness, it is difficult to know exactly what concept to put in its place. Seamus Heaney has protested against being included in an anthology of 'British' verse.[23] The historian J. G. A. Pocock has proposed the label 'the Atlantic archipelago' to describe the islands inhabited by the English, Scots, Irish and Welsh; but it could doubtless be objected that even this label has its problems, being weighted unduly towards American connections.[24] The present anthology does not include English writing in America; instead, taking up Pocock's suggestion, some attempt is made to draw attention to the interaction of different literary cultures and languages within these islands. This is not a matter of counterposing a single Irish, Welsh or Scots identity to an English one, but rather of trying to indicate the complex networks of different ethnic, cultural and religious traditions which have been simplified by later nationalisms into absolute metaphysical identities. Following Ezra Pound's robustly optimistic principle that 'one does not need to learn a whole language in order to understand some one or some dozen poems',[25] samples of Welsh and Irish verse are given in the original (with literal translations). A number of Scottish poets are included: while no attempt has been made to represent the age of the great 'makars' which ended with Dunbar and Douglas, from the reign of James VI onward the fortunes of Scottish and English literary cultures were more and more closely bound together.[26] Within the scope of this anthology it is impossible to give more than a token representation to these different cultural traditions; but, at a time when the notion of Englishness is coming under political pressure, it is hoped that even this limited contribution may help stimulate an interest in other forms of writing within the archipelago.

Critical emphasis on Englishness has led to the neglect not only of the northern and western cultures but also of the continuing significance of Latin as the medium of international literary culture. As the Soviet critic Mikhail Bakhtin pointed out, the humanist exaltation of classical Latin was a sharp ideological challenge to the different form of Latin that had become the language of medieval officialdom, and the return to Latin was part of the move to modernity: 'This world with all that was new threw light upon the face of Cicero's Latin and disclosed a beautiful but dead face.'[27] It was some time before the death was quite apparent: down to the mid seventeenth century, some writers were uncertain about the future of English as a literary language. Latin also offered the attraction of seeming less insular, less bound up with restrictive traditions, than English, and much of the period's scholarly work was conducted in Latin.[28] Writers like More and Buchanan gained a European reputation for their skill as Latin rather than English poets. General anthologies have almost uniformly ignored Latin poems, but it seems time to pay them some attention.[29] More's Latin epigrams (nos. 2–3) present a radical political viewpoint not found in his English verse. George Herbert had to abandon his mother tongue to voice his response to his mother's death (no. 319). In 'Bulla', Crashaw was able to indulge a baroque sensibility of a kind that has always seemed rather alien in England: the conventional moralizing expected of poems about soap-bubbles is overcome by an attentive, and obliquely erotic, celebration of beauty not in order but in transient 'Chaos' (no. 209 l. 38).

Some comment about particular inclusions and omissions is called for. An attempt has been made to offer a more representative picture of early modern British culture than is customary in anthologies, and this has meant including a number of poems whose interest may be regarded as more historical than literary. Those categories, however, need careful scrutiny; all too often judgements of literary value have been used to exclude significant bodies of writing from attention. The sonnets of Lady Mary Wroth almost completely dropped from view for centuries, while the sonnets of some very minor Elizabethans were admitted to the canon. Such fluctuations do not necessarily mean that value judgements are totally arbitrary – to speak of minor sonneteers is to acknowledge that some sonnet sequences are a great deal more tedious than others – but evaluations do need constant weighing against alternative possibilities. There are limits to the degree to which a canon of poetry can be politically representative: poetry can never precisely 'represent' its society in the same way as an elected chamber. The 'voices' it offers us have always been mediated by convention, and the most interesting poetry points us beyond its immediate context. An attempt can be made, however, to draw attention to the limits of inclusion and exclusion, whether they are drawn by explicit censorship or by conventional discourses of the behaviour appropriate to different social groups.[30] The anthology thus responds to the current movements to question the canon and reclaim alternative voices. At the same time, an attempt is made in the Introduction to show that the 'established' canon is by no means politically monolithic or cravenly conformist: it would be short-sighted to dislodge it without being aware of such complexities. 'Alternative' canons may have their own limitations, bringing the concerns of the present so heavily to bear on the past that they suppress differences; the challenge of difference can be as stimulating as the challenge of relevance. Space has been given here for writing that is neither canonical nor 'alternative', for poets who were widely popular for various reasons in their own day and whose writing throws light on the interests and concerns of more central figures. Michael Drayton spent a lifetime spurring on a modest talent with the determination to be a major poet spanning all the genres; the ambition tells us something of the age, and did indeed at times make him excel himself. Francis Quarles and George Wither are unlikely to return to critical favour, but they played a significant part in mediating between 'high' literary culture and a wider popular audience. In juxtaposing Herbert and Quarles, the anthology is not presenting them as poetic equals; but reading them together may give a sharper sense of the ideological inflections of Herbert's verse and the kind of impact he would have made on his contemporaries. In such cases readers may feel that in the end they want to endorse the consensus of posterity; but the question of value is a complex one which constantly needs posing anew so that judgements do not become ossified.

In including some less familiar poems, it has become necessary to omit other familiar and easily available ones. Verse from the drama has been almost entirely excluded, although of course the relations between poetry and drama were especially close in this period. The works of the major dramatists are not hard to come by, and it has been felt more important to make room for less accessible poetic texts. Songs may be thought to be under-represented: on the other hand, they have often been over-represented in Elizabethan anthologies, giving a somewhat disproportionate impression of the age and its poetic production as a whole.[31] At the other end of the generic scale, narrative and historical poetry may be considered under-represented, though Marlowe's *Hero and Leander* has been included in full. Drayton's *Mortimeriados* and Daniel's *The civile warres* spawned many imitations and certainly deserve attention, but brief extracts seemed wholly inadequate to give a sense of these poems; both poets have, however, been represented across a broader range of genres than is normally found in anthologies. *The Faerie Queene* is something of an exception in the degree to which its major episodes, being linked with the poem as a whole by theme as much as by narrative, have a certain self-contained life. As an encyclopaedic poem which confronts so many central issues of the period, *The Faerie Queene* demands extensive representation. Defenders of Spenser have often been detractors of Donne, and vice versa; an attempt has been made to bring out the interest of both Spenserian and 'metaphysical' lines of poetry, but in terms of line-count the Spenserians win. The amount of space given to poets is not necessarily to be taken as a final value judgement. Anyone interested in the period will want to read widely in Donne, whose works are readily available in separate editions and in Helen Gardner's Penguin anthology *The Metaphysical Poets*. Spenser's conventions are somewhat more remote from a modern audience, and it is hoped that his writing will gain in interest when viewed in the context of Renaissance poetic debates. The present anthology is to some degree complementary to *The Metaphysical Poets*, but it also tries to suggest that there are important common factors between 'Spenserian' and 'metaphysical' schools, a point explored more fully in Section 4 of the Introduction. Many other well-known poets are represented by a fairly limited selection, but enough, it is hoped, to convince any new reader that they deserve to be explored far beyond the limits of an anthology. An attempt has been made to introduce some major genres of popular poetry which are not easily available today; but within the confines of a widely ranging anthology it has been impossible to do more than scratch the surface. It is hoped that what is here will provoke readers into further exploration.

The anthology seeks to stimulate discussion about ways of reading as well as about what is read. It presents poems as social acts rather than as isolated objects, and this has implications for the way they are presented on the page. If poems are viewed as static, timeless 'well-wrought urns', then there is a logic in modernizing the texts, removing them from the external dress of their particular epoch so that the reader can gain immediate contact with the original. Modernization does have the advantage of easier initial accessibility, but it also homogenizes the poems and often effectively rewrites them, ironing out their contradictions and ambiguities and the processes of linguistic change. Some of the power of Ralegh's poem to Cynthia (no. 21) is lost when editors chop the manuscripts' verse paragraphs into quatrains, and there is a similar loss in over-punctuating; the poem is presented here in something very close to its original form. Punctuation in the Renaissance was undergoing significant changes, reflecting the shift in status of poetry from a predominantly oral, rhetorical medium, linked with bodily rhythms – punctuation marks would indicate points to draw breath – to an abstract, written discourse governed by strict rules of grammar.[32] Spelling also tended to be a mixture of the phonetic and the conventional and had not yet become standardized. Robert Graves and Laura Riding long ago protested that editors of Shakespeare's Sonnet 129 (no. 116) had been too ready to emend the text because it did not make obvious sense to them; the oblique, enigmatic argumentation of the sonnets often suffers from being packaged into a clear-cut modern structure.[33] In the case of Shakespeare's sonnets and many other texts, the versions printed here are closer to early texts than in most modern editions.

This does not mean, however, as Graves and Riding supposed, that following early texts is necessarily to restore 'the original spelling'. Compositors felt themselves free to modify the spelling and punctuation of the authorial manuscript. Nor is the situation necessarily easier when we try to get behind printed texts to authorial manuscripts. Many leading poets in the period, from Wyatt down to Donne and Carew, circulated their verse almost entirely in manuscript. Print still had to endure a social stigma: in a society strongly marked by an aristocratic disdain for commerce, words that could be circulated everywhere, like common coin, were felt to be devalued (cp. no. 364). Marston was ready to launch spirited abuse at his potential audience for presuming to read him (no. 352). Quite apart from the social stigma of the market-place, it was not clear that publication offered a good chance of profit. There were no copyright laws, and once authors parted with a manuscript to the printer they lost any further financial reward: Spenser's livelihood came from government positions and pensions, not from the somewhat disappointing sales of *The Faerie Queene*. Presenting a manuscript to an influential patron like the Countess of Bedford (nos. 231–2) might offer a better prospect of gain.

Up to a certain point, manuscript circulation allowed the poet more control over the text than passing it to the printer. But when manuscripts circulated widely, this control was lost. Poets did not necessarily regret this loss of control. Renaissance readers did not take such an exclusive interest in authorship as we tend to do: poems circulated as a dialogue between friends rather than as a monologue by an isolated genius. Sir Robert Sidney's poems remained in manuscript until the present century. Those who copied out poems often felt entitled to vary the texts according to their own interests and judgements, and poems might be arranged in manuscript miscellanies by theme rather than by author – rather as in the present anthology. Donne did not take a proprietary attitude over his texts: when in 1614 he came under pressure from a patron to publish a collection of his verse, he had to write to friends to ask them for copies of his own poems. Poems originally written for one occasion would be freely adapted by later copyists for new circumstances (cp. no. 36). The ideal of some older textual critics of restoring an 'original' authorial text purified of later 'corruptions' is the mirror image of the completely modernized text: in each case, the poem is made into a fixed and static object, and the processes of social interaction in which texts were involved are abstracted away. Recent editors have become far more aware of the need to examine the whole range of manuscript circulation, and for many poets the necessary work is still in progress. An anthology like the present one cannot cover such a huge field comprehensively, but the textual notes offer a wide range of variants and provide the information necessary for readers to explore textual circulation more fully.

This edition, then, does not offer fixed or final versions: the texts, it could be said, have been not modernized but lightly post-modernized. Recent work in textual criticism has been influenced by literary theorists who have questioned our culture's obsession with the individual self and emphasized the social dimension in the production of meaning.[34] At the same time, it is possible to exaggerate the fragmentation of authorial identity in the period: the Renaissance did see the growth of distinctively modern attitudes to the poet's role and the transmission of texts. Poets like Drayton and Wither scorned the gentlemen amateurs who confined their verse to manuscript, and they had an exalted sense of their public role: Wither was ready to set his *Britain's remembrancer* (no. 202) in type himself when he could not find a publisher. And we should be wary about exaggerating the differences between manuscript and print circulation: poetry could be published without being printed. Print-runs of poetry would seldom exceed a thousand, while poems circulated in manuscript might reach more readers than a volume printed by a small poetry press today. Women were particularly liable to censure for the alleged immodesty of appearing in print, but a poet like Katherine Philips could achieve a considerable reputation by circulating her poems among friends long before her work appeared in print.

There was often a conflict between a traditional disdain for printing and an interest in the new medium's possibilities: we can be sceptical about the repeated claims by poets of the 1590s that their poems had appeared only because unscrupulous printers or devious friends had spirited the manuscripts away from them. Ben Jonson, like Spenser a model for many later poets, was able to move between the worlds of court patronage and the public press, though there were often tensions in the process. The fact that poets might resist rushing into print did not necessarily mean that they were indifferent to their posthumous reputation: Donne's extreme statements of self-deprecation need to be set against his perhaps equally hyperbolical but equally significant assumption that his poems will form the basis for a future religion (no. 134). He knew that he might become 'Canonicall', even though he was aware of his perhaps precarious status in any conventional canon (no. 29 l. 143). '*Ile not haste*', wrote Herrick, but he intended his life's work to be committed to the press in the end (no. 368). The new possibilities offered by the printing-press in controlling the reader's response were taken up by many poets, not only in the vogue for pattern-poems (cp. nos. 16, 278) but in the structuring of whole volumes of poems.[35] One of the main projects of Renaissance humanists was to establish accurate and widely available texts of classical poets, to restore a hidden textual purity; it was only to be expected that similar procedures would eventually be adopted for their own works.

The transition from an oral culture to a print culture was a very complex and uneven process, and the presentation of texts in this anthology is designed to make the process visible, opening out the very real differences in attitude towards publication, but avoiding a spuriously antiquarian effect. The common practice of modernizing other poets while publishing Spenser in old spelling has the effect of making him look misleadingly quaint: while he did aim at a certain distancing effect, Spenser was closer to modern spelling practice than many of his contemporaries. Moreover, 'modern' British spelling practice is itself not consistently 'modern' in the sense of adhering to consistent rational principles: it is an unstable and inconsistent compound, a blend of deference to custom and intermittent rationalism (rather like the British constitutional settlement). Already in Spenser's day there were many demands for modernization: 'no one in sound mind can defend our writing', wrote one of Spenser's great admirers, the schoolteacher Alexander Gil.[36] The Greeks and Romans, after all, had benefited from reasonably standardized spelling practices. Gil presented extracts from *The Faerie Queene* in a reformed spelling, and Gil's friend Wither, his pupil John Milton and others experimented with reformed spelling, though no single project gained much public support. But, as a glance at the sequences of poems will show, throughout the period of the anthology there was a steady move towards a regularization of spelling practices.

One effect of presenting texts in Renaissance spelling is to draw attention to differences in language: the glosses in this anthology will be found to be unusually full. Readers new to the period need to be alerted to obvious possibilities of misunderstanding, of course: unless we know that Sidney's 'pide weedes' (no. 71 l. 3) are clothes rather than plants, our picture of the landscape will be curiously distorted. Some differences of meaning are relatively straightforward and unambiguous; but other cases are much more complex, and to read historically entails being open to processes of change.[37] For the period covered by this anthology, nearly 27,000 new words are recorded in *The Shorter Oxford English Dictionary* alone, with a particular clustering in the period 1588–1612.[38] Some of the difficulties posed by the language of Renaissance poetry stem not from its hoary antiquity but from its attempts at modernity, from the many words which poets launched on the world without success. Such innovations could also be regarded as restorations, recovering semantic nuances that had been possessed by the ancients but lost in the intervening years. In Horace's much-quoted phrase, 'multa renascentur quae iam cecidere, cadentque/quae nunc sunt in honore vocabula, si volet usus': 'many words which have now fallen from use will be reborn, and those which are now in honour will fall, if usage should so wish'.[39] When confronted with a period of such linguistic fertility, it is more than usually misleading to claim that glosses represent the real, single 'historical' meaning of the word. This edition indicates with asterisks significant usages which constitute, or predate, the first recorded usage in *The Oxford English Dictionary*. As is explained more fully in the Note on the Text and Annotation, this does not by any means prove that the asterisked usage was really the first: not only is the coverage of *The Oxford English Dictionary* sometimes patchy – particularly for 'vulgar' and colloquial words – but written usage may well lag behind speech. The density of the asterisks will, however, serve as a useful reminder that, while for today's readers the language of these poets may have a patina of age, for contemporary readers it was exuberantly inventive. That applies even to Spenser, the poet whose language today seems most remote and archaic. Ben Jonson commented that 'in affecting the ancients' Spenser 'writ no language'; and a word like 'approvance' in the Bower of Blisse episode (no. 80 l. 57) may sound as if it had been borrowed from some medieval poet. In fact, however, this is listed by *The Oxford English Dictionary* as a first occurrence, so it is a decidedly modern archaism. Moreover, the same word had already occurred in a letter by Spenser's patron Lord Grey: far from being fancifully 'poetical' in connotation, the word could appear in the context of hard-headed political analysis. Glosses and asterisks, then, are to be treated as aids to interpretation, not as final truths. To recover the poetry of a past era is never simply a passive process: to recover is also to become actively engaged, and to some extent to recreate. As the Introduction will argue at greater length, that is, after all, what 'Renaissance' means.

NOTES TO THE PREFACE

1. F. T. Palgrave, *The Golden Treasury of the Best Songs and Lyrical Poems in the English Language*, Cambridge and London 1861, p. 308.
2. On the need to acknowledge 'the historicity of texts and the textuality of history', see Louis Adrian Montrose, 'Professing the Renaissance: The Poetics and Politics of Culture', in H. Aram Veeser (ed.), *The New Historicism*, New York and London 1989, pp. 15–36 (20).
3. Wallace K. Ferguson, *The Renaissance in Historical Thought: Five Centuries of Interpretation*, Boston 1948; for a defence of the concept, see Erwin Panofsky, *Renaissance and Renascences in Western Art*, Uppsala 1960.
4. For a sceptical view, see E. M. W. Tillyard, *The English Renaissance: Fact or Fiction?*, 1952.
5. Samuel Daniel, *Poems and A Defence of Ryme*, ed. Arthur Colby Sprague, Chicago and London 1965, pp. 139–40.
6. For a useful survey of these theoretical models, see R. J. Holton, *The Transition from Feudalism to Capitalism*, 1985, and, for a modern application, Perry Anderson, *Lineages of the Absolutist State*, 1974, pp. 421ff.
7. For a recent, fundamentally positive, assessment of Burckhardt's model, see William Kerrigan and Gordon Braden, *The Idea of the Renaissance*, Baltimore and London 1989; see also David Norbrook, 'Life and Death of Renaissance Man', *Raritan*, 8:4 (Spring 1989), 89–110.
8. Arthur Symons, *A Sixteenth-Century Anthology*, 1905, p. iii.
9. C. S. Lewis, *English Literature in the Sixteenth Century Excluding Drama*, Oxford 1954, p. 65.
10. Karl Marx's daughter Eleanor worked as a research assistant for Furnivall, and Marx himself, though somewhat bemused by Furnivall's very English brand of liberalism, took an interest in his scholarly projects: William Benzie, *Dr. F. J. Furnivall: Victorian Scholar Adventurer*, Norman, Oklahoma, 1983, pp. 141, 247.
11. For a highly polemical account of the issues, see Dave Harker, *Fakesong: The Manufacture of British 'Folksong', 1700 to the Present Day*, Milton Keynes and Philadelphia 1985.
12. The poem from vol. iv included in the present anthology (no. 238) is unlikely to shock modern readers.

13. For a recent survey, see Bernard Capp, 'Popular Literature', in *Popular Culture in Seventeenth-Century England*, ed. Barry Reay, 1985, pp. 198–243.
14. Yvor Winters, 'The Sixteenth Century Lyric in England: A Critical and Historical Reinterpretation', *Poetry*, 53–4 (1939), reprinted in Paul J. Alpers (ed.), *Elizabethan Poetry: Modern Essays in Criticism*, London, Oxford and New York 1967, pp. 93–125. Winters's influence can be found in Thom Gunn's selection of Greville's poems, 1968.
15. T. S. Eliot, 'The Metaphysical Poets', in *Selected Essays*, 1951, pp. 281–91, and 'Donne in Our Time', in Theodore Spencer (ed.), *A Garland for John Donne*, Cambridge, Mass., and London 1931, pp. 3–19; see William Empson, 'Donne in the New Edition', *Critical Quarterly*, 8 (1966), 255–80 (255).
16. T. E. Hulme, *Speculations: Essays on Humanism and the Philosophy of Art*, ed. Herbert Read, 1924, pp. 49ff. On Hulme and 'dissociation', see Frank Kermode, *Romantic Image*, 1957.
17. Stephen J. Greenblatt, *Renaissance Self-Fashioning: From More to Shakespeare*, Chicago and London 1980, is the seminal 'new historicist' work; other significant works include Jonathan Goldberg, *James I and the Politics of Literature*, Baltimore and London 1983, and Gary Waller, *English Poetry of the Sixteenth Century*, London and New York 1986. For a manifesto of 'cultural materialism' see Jonathan Dollimore, *Radical Tragedy: Religion, Ideology and Power in the Drama of Shakespeare and his Contemporaries*, 2nd edn, New York and London 1989.
18. Neither of the generally excellent Penguin anthologies covering this period, Helen Gardner's *The Metaphysical Poets*, revised edn, Harmondsworth 1972, and Edward Lucie-Smith's *The Penguin Book of Elizabethan Verse*, Harmondsworth 1965, contains a single poem by a woman. Betty Travitsky (ed.), *The Paradise of Women: Writings by Englishwomen of the Renaissance*, rev. edn, New York 1989, provides brief extracts from a wide range of women writers; Katharina M. Wilson (ed.), *Women Writers of the Renaissance and Reformation*, Athens, Georgia, and London 1987, sets English poets in a European context. Particularly valuable for the seventeenth century is *Kissing the Rod: An Anthology of Seventeenth-Century Women's Verse*, ed. Germaine Greer, Susan Hastings, Jeslyn Medoff and Melinda Sansone, 1988. For a general survey, see Elaine V. Beilin, *Redeeming Eve: Women Writers of the English Renaissance*, Princeton 1987.
19. Differing conceptions of 'discourse' are offered by the French 'anti-humanist' theorists, for example, Michel Foucault, 'The Order of Discourse', in Robert Young (ed.), *Untying the Text: A Post-Structuralist Reader*, 1981, pp. 48–78, and by Anglo-American historians of political thought, see for example James Tully (ed.), *Meaning and Context: Quentin Skinner and his Critics*, Princeton 1988.
20. Cp. E. M. W. Tillyard, *The Elizabethan World Picture*, 1943.
21. Douglas Gray, *The Oxford Book of Late Medieval Verse and Prose*, Oxford 1985, p. iii; for the argument that the full influence of humanism on poetry begins around the 1520s, see Alistair Fox, 'Reinterpreting English Humanism', in Alistair Fox and John Guy (eds.), *Reinterpreting the Henrician Age: Humanism, Politics and Reform, 1500–1550*, Oxford 1986, ch. 1.

22. Richard Foster Jones, *The Triumph of the English Language: A Survey of Opinions Concerning the Vernacular from the Introduction of Printing to the Restoration*, Stanford 1953.
23. Seamus Heaney, 'An Open Letter', in Field Day Theatre Company, *Ireland's Field Day*, 1985, pp. 23–30.
24. J. G. A. Pocock, 'The Limits and Divisions of British History: In Search of the Unknown Subject', *American Historical Review*, 87 (1982), 311–36.
25. *Literary Essays of Ezra Pound*, ed. T. S. Eliot, 1954, p. 37.
26. For fuller coverage, see R. D. S. Jack (ed.), *A Choice of Scottish Verse 1560–1660*, 1978.
27. Mikhail Bakhtin, *Rabelais and his World*, translated by Hélène Iswolsky, Cambridge, Mass., 1968, pp. 466–7.
28. J. W. Binns, *Intellectual Culture in Elizabethan and Jacobean England: The Latin Writings of the Age*, Leeds 1990.
29. Fred J. Nichols's introduction to *An Anthology of Neo-Latin Poetry*, New Haven and London 1979, offers a stimulating and accessible way in to the whole field of Neo-Latin writing; there are also recent anthologies by Alessandro Perosa and John Sparrow, *Renaissance Latin Poetry*, 1979, and I. D. McFarlane, *Renaissance Latin Poetry*, Manchester 1980. See also Leicester Bradner, *Musae Anglicanae: A History of Anglo-Latin Poetry, 1500–1925*, New York 1940.
30. The extent and effect of censorship in the period are controversial matters. Some scholars deny that censorship was a significant factor; Christopher Hill, 'Censorship and English Literature', in *Writing and Revolution in Seventeenth-Century England* (*The Collected Essays of Christopher Hill*, vol. i), Brighton 1985, pp. 32–71, emphasizes its restrictive effect; Annabel Patterson, *Censorship and Interpretation: The Conditions of Writing and Reading in Early Modern England*, Madison and London 1984, argues that writers were to some extent able to come to terms with it through creative ambiguity.
31. For full coverage, see E. H. Fellowes, *English Madrigal Verse 1588–1632*, 3rd edn, revised and enlarged by Frederick W. Sternfeld and David Greer, Oxford 1967.
32. See Mindele Treip, *Milton's Punctuation and Changing English Usage 1582–1676*, 1970.
33. 'A Study in Original Punctuation and Spelling', in Robert Graves, *The Common Asphodel: Collected Essays on Poetry 1922–1949*, 1949, pp. 84–95; Thomas M. Greene, 'Anti-hermeneutics: The Case of Shakespeare's Sonnet 129', in *Poetic Traditions of the English Renaissance*, ed. Maynard Mack and George deForest Lord, New Haven and London 1982, pp. 143–61 (the essay also appears in Greene's *The Vulnerable Text: Essays on Renaissance Literature*, New York 1986, pp. 159–74). See also John Barrell, *Poetry, Language and Politics*, Manchester 1988, pp. 31ff.
34. For an introduction to the new textual criticism, see Jerome J. McGann, *A Critique of Modern Textual Criticism*, Chicago and London 1983.
35. Cp. Graham Parry, *Seventeenth-Century Poetry: The Social Context*, 1985.

36. Alexander Gill, *Logonomia Anglica*, ed. Bror Danielsson and Arvid Gabrielson, 2 vols., Stockholm 1972, ii.94.
37. Cp. Raymond Williams, *Keywords: A Vocabulary of Culture and Society*, 1976.
38. Bryan A. Garner, 'Shakespeare's Latinate Neologisms', *Shakespeare Studies*, 15 (1982), 149–70. It needs to be borne in mind that the documentation in *The Oxford English Dictionary* and *The Shorter Oxford English Dictionary* is much fuller for the later than for the earlier sixteenth century: see Jürgen Schäfer, *Documentation in the O.E.D.: Shakespeare and Nashe as Test Cases*, Oxford 1980. Garner does, however, make a case for the exceptional creativity of Shakespeare and the late Elizabethans.
39. Horace, *Ars poetica*, ll. 70–1.

ACKNOWLEDGEMENTS

While the editors have worked closely in collaboration, David Norbrook is responsible for the selection of the texts and the arrangement of the anthology as well as the Preface and Introduction, and Henry Woudhuysen edited the texts and provided the textual notes and glosses. As well as collaborating in writing the appendices, both editors have read and criticized the drafts of each other's work. The editors are jointly responsible for any errors that remain in this edition. They are grateful to Paul Keegan of Penguin Books for his consistent support and encouragement, and to Bob Davenport for his meticulous copy-editing. They are also greatly indebted to the following individuals and institutions for their permission to include, and help in preparing, poems in their possession: the late Viscount De L'Isle, Penshurst Place, Kent; His Grace The Duke of Norfolk; the Marquess of Salisbury; Dr B. E. Juel-Jensen; the National Library of Wales, Aberystwyth; Cambridge University Library; Corpus Christi College, Cambridge; Trinity College, Cambridge; South Glamorgan Libraries Department; the Trustees of the National Library of Scotland; Edinburgh University Library; Sir John Clerk of Penicuik; the Brotherton Collection, Leeds University Library; the British Library; the Masters of the Bench of the Inner Temple; the Public Record Office, London; Chetham's Library, Manchester; the Bodleian Library, Oxford; the Governing Body of Christ Church, Oxford; the Provost and Fellows of Worcester College, Oxford; Archbishop Marsh's Library, Dublin; the Board of Trinity College, Dublin; the Master and Fellows, Magdalene College, Cambridge; Dr Williams's Library, London; the Society of Antiquaries of London; the School of Celtic Studies of the Dublin Institute for Advanced Studies; the Henry W. and Albert A. Berg Collection, The New York Public Library, Astor, Lenox and Tilden Foundations; the Huntington Library, San Marino, California; the Harry Ransom Humanities Research Center, The University of Texas at Austin; The Folger Shakespeare Library, Washington DC., and Louisiana State University Press.

David Norbrook would like first of all to thank Sandra Sherman for encouraging him to persevere with the anthology at a difficult time. Heather Glen, Margot Heinemann, Lorna Hutson, Patricia Ingham, John Kerrigan, Frank Romany, Erica Sheen and Kate Ward-Perkins commented on various versions of the Introduction, though they bear no responsibility for what became of their painstaking advice. David Norbrook drafted the Latin translations but consulted with Andrew Laird, David Levene and Oliver Taplin, who are thanked for their help. Ceridwen Lloyd Morgan and Bernard O'Donoghue kindly provided the translations from Welsh and Irish respectively. Other valuable advice was given by Tom Cogswell, Ann Coiro, David Cressy, Felicity Heal, Kate Lilley and Nigel Smith.

H. R. Woudhuysen would like to thank Miss Katherine Duncan-Jones, Professor Noel J. Kinnamon, Dr J. B. Loudon, Dr John Pitcher, Professor Josephine A. Roberts, Professor John Scattergood, Dr Keith Walker and Dr P. N. R. Zutshi for help, encouragement and the loan of books. In editing and annotating the poems in this anthology he has drawn heavily on the researches of previous scholars; he would particularly like to acknowledge his great debt to the work of Dr Peter Beal.

Note to the second edition

A few minor corrections and changes, including an index of titles, have been made for this edition.

Introduction

1: Rebirth and Restoration

Renaissance: rebirth. That is an audacious claim to make for any period of literary history; but it can be justified.[1] The period covered by this anthology, from 1509 to 1659, was one of unprecedented poetic productivity. Poets thought through the meaning of their art systematically, from the writer's social responsibility to the minutiae of rhythm and verse form. The contemporary who acclaimed John Donne as a 'Copernicus in Poëtrie' was responding to an originality that discovered new poetic worlds.[2] Edmund Spenser created his own fictive world or 'Faerie Land': his disciple Michael Drayton could hail him as 'our first late great Reformer'.[3] Sir Philip Sidney argued that, far from simply imitating the external world, the poet could emulate God in creating a wholly new world:

Only the poet, disdaining to be tied to any such subjection, lifted up with the vigour of his own invention, doth grow in effect another nature, in making things either better than nature bringeth forth, or, quite anew, forms such as never were in nature ... Nature never set forth the earth in so rich tapestry as divers poets have done; neither with so pleasant rivers, fruitful trees, sweet-smelling flowers, nor whatsoever else may make the too much loved earth more lovely. Her world is brazen, the poets only deliver a golden.[4]

The poet can effectively undo the Fall and put us in touch with a primal golden age.

Sidney sees nature as a 'rich tapestry': his language unembarrassedly celebrates his delight in richly ornate objects. To post-Romantic readers, for whom poets are expected to disguise their art, there may seem something shameless about the Elizabethan poets' conspicuous consumption of artifice. But Renaissance writers could look to their God for a pattern. The French poet du Bartas, who was enormously popular in the period, and was translated by Sidney, imagines God admiring His creation like a 'cunning Painter' who

> Forgets his paines; and inly fill'd with glee,
> Still on his Picture gazeth greedilie.
>
> (no. 343 ll. 1, 7–8)

The artist's aim was not simply to copy the surface of appearances but to re-enact the primal act of creation. Blurred and worn down with mutability, an everyday language could be transfigured into a vision of origins: 'a *New world* leaps forth', writes Cowley of the poet, 'when *Thou* say'st, *Let it Be*' (no. 373 l. 35). Even when Alexander Hume describes meadows whose green spreads 'naturallie but [without] artifice' (no. 183 l. 95), he sees the landscape essentially as a manifestation of God's art: ideal landscapes were sown with flowers of rhetoric. The creation of such 'golden worlds' was not seen as mere escapism: on the contrary, by giving a sharp realization to the utopian ideal, making their readers feel 'more then humane', 'out of themselves remov'd' (no. 353 ll. 75–6), poets could move them to action, to creating new worlds themselves. Armed with these defences, poets could celebrate their golden worlds with an undisguised sensuous relish (nos. 81, 88, 175, 190, 206, 214, 362). Spenser's Calidore is so overcome by the vision of 'An hundred naked maidens lilly white' that he envies his own eyes; the vision has been created by Colin Clout – that is, Spenser himself (no. 348 ll. 16–17). Even a spare description of the 'dead sticks' of a winter landscape will rest on a contrast with the rich dress of summer (no. 122). Sensuousness could easily verge on self-parody, as in Campion's comparison of a woman's face to a garden (no. 131), or the song of Herrick's wassailers who compare cowslips to cream, then abandon their metaphors when they realize they are not going to be given beer (no. 208). And self-parody becomes high camp in Marlowe's luxuriantly inventive portrayal of Hero's costume, in which art outdoes nature so far that a handmaid follows Hero to put water in the artificial sparrows that chirrup as she walks (no. 99).

The word 'Renaissance' often conjures up poetry of this highly self-conscious kind, which may seem to owe more to ancient Arcadia and the courts of Italy than to southern England. But the British Renaissance transformed those southern landscapes as it transformed so many poetic conventions it had borrowed from other cultures. Samuel Daniel, whose discursive, meditative mode is very different from the familiar textbook notions of Renaissance verse, declared that

> . . . all that ever hotter spirits exprest
> Comes bettered by the patience of the North.
>
> (no. 353 ll. 53–4)

That 'patience' often expressed itself in a critical distance from the most flamboyantly artificial modes of poetry. In his unjustly neglected sequence *Cælica*, Daniel's friend Fulke Greville steadily undermined the conventions of courtly praise in mordant self-ironies (nos. 73–7, 262–4); in Sir Walter

Ralegh's 'The 21th: and last booke of the Ocean to Scinthia' (no. 21), the rhetorical polish and patterned artifice of the conventional sequence of love-poems start to collapse into poetry of an almost 'confessional' rawness. Spenser's epic *The Faerie Queene* is a critique as well as an imitation of Italian romance, and one of his most powerful images of evil is a parody of the kind of richly ornate landscape he himself loved to describe (no. 80). The point about Calidore's vision is that it is fragile: it is in the end the product of a visionary way of seeing, not an object that can be kept on the connoisseur's shelf. Poets were well aware that their age's taste for conspicuous ornament might have a deadening effect on the landscape: a formal garden could be seen as enclosing 'A dead and standing pool of Air' (no. 216 l. 6), and a stately home might be a blight on its surroundings,

> The marble pavement hid with desart weede,
> With house-leeke, thistle, docke, and hemlock-seed.
> (no. 185 ll. 29–30)

In Renaissance poetry, especially in the earlier seventeenth century (for example nos. 198, 220), we can find exaltations of nature above art that seem to anticipate poetry of a much later period. Henry Vaughan could see a book not as a triumph of artifice but as the tomb of a once vibrant natural life (no. 374).

Generalization about Renaissance poetry is always liable to be defeated by the period's immense range: if in some respects it seems to anticipate the visionary, prophetic ambitions of the Romantic era, the Renaissance is also rich in a poetry of personal address and discussion more often associated with the eighteenth century. The verse epistle in a 'low' or 'plain' style becomes a favourite medium. Its plainness may be the vehicle for an austere critique of the artifice of the public world (cp. nos. 223, 228). The form is also open, however, to Jonson's self-mocking hedonism in inviting a friend to supper and claiming that he will lie about the goods in store to make sure he comes (no. 233). Such poetry often conjured up an all-male world, but women poets began to celebrate their own networks of friendship (nos. 189, 244–6). The period's wit encompassed the self-deprecating, socially poised irony most prized by the eighteenth century, but ranged more widely across genres, bringing a sardonic cast to religious melancholy and amatory compliment. Alexander Pope acknowledged the wit of Donne's satires, even though he found them unpolished, and despite the constraints of censorship there was an increasingly vigorous body of political satire. Denham's *Coopers Hill* combined satire with the celebration of a classical balance in poetry as well as in politics:

> O could I flow like thee, and make thy stream
> My great example, as it is my theme!
> Though deep, yet clear, though gentle, yet not dull,
> Strong without rage, without ore-flowing full.
>
> (no. 42 ll. 189–92)

The poets of the later seventeenth century looked back to writers like Denham and Edward Fairfax (no. 342) as pioneers of their favoured manner. Yet there was much in Renaissance verse that failed to match later standards of good taste and propriety, from the harsh, populist manner of the poetry of social and religious protest to the erotic extravagance of Crashaw's lyrics (for example no. 293). Against the patterned rhetoric of the sonneteers can be set the vigorously colloquial voice of the balladeer's Wife of Bath confronting St Peter:

> Alas for you, good sir she said,
> now gip you doting Knave.
>
> (no. 127 ll. 15–16)

The Renaissance was more at ease than the succeeding era with the fantastic and supernatural. Sir John Harington was well placed to catch the tone of Ariosto's exuberantly self-mocking fantasy (no. 341). Spenser, who set himself to 'overgo' Ariosto, may have tried to strike a more sober note but matched the Italian poet in an almost surreal inventiveness.

Amid all this variety, one generalization that does have some plausibility is that Renaissance poets were distinguished from their predecessors by a heightened awareness of subjectivity and individuality. Poets had not always made such high claims for their work as Sidney does in *A Defence of Poetry*. In Chaucer's *The House of Fame*, the poet's role is to perpetuate others' fame, not to glorify his own. The new self-assertiveness of poets corresponded to a new insistence in Renaissance culture on the significance of the individual voice. One reason Renaissance poetry often seems so immediate and 'modern' today is that our culture places so much value on the individual. It is easy for modern readers to sympathize with Wyatt's refusal to play the games of court politics – 'I cannot I, no no it will not be' (no. 223 l. 76) – and with Shakespeare's challenge to social convention, 'Noe, I am that I am' (no. 114 l. 9). Sidney's Astrophil urges himself with deceptive simplicity to 'looke in thy heart and write' (no. 65 l. 14). When Spenser declares:

> So I unto my selfe alone will sing,
> The woods shall to me answer and my Eccho ring
>
> (no. 88 ll. 17–18)

he is signalling his departure from convention, contrasting the poem he has written for his own marriage with the ceremonial verse which poets were normally expected to compose for patrons and a court audience; his poetry is moving towards a more modern idea of individual authenticity. The period's religious poets approach God and eternity in an intimate, personal way, as in Vaughan's celebrated opening: 'I saw Eternity the other night' (no. 300 l. 1). Milton rushes to 'prevent' the three Magi by having 'the honour first, thy Lord to greet' and joining his voice directly to 'the Angel Quire' (no. 270 ll. 24–7). On occasion such individualism becomes conscious blasphemy, as in Laurence Clarkson's declaration that God is within, in what he punningly calls 'this *Single Eye*' (no. 298 l. 23). When Marvell claimed that

> Two Paradises 'twere in one
> To live in Paradise alone
> (no. 217 ll. 63–4)

he was jokingly pushing to its extreme a real current of thought in his age.

In its openness to individuality, Renaissance poetry may seem strikingly modern. Whether or not that is a good thing is another matter, and has repeatedly been debated. For T. E. Hulme, T. S. Eliot and Ezra Pound, the individualistic humanism of the Renaissance displaced God and tried to put man in His place, and the result was a disastrous arrogance. Socialists have criticized the Renaissance from a different angle, seeing competitive individualism as an evasion of responsibility to the community.[5] When Daniel's Philocosmus says that he lives in a 'wiser profit-seeking age' (no. 353 l. 8), a degree of irony hovers around the world 'profit', which is becoming increasingly specialized from a general sense of benefit to a narrower sense of personal financial advantage. Another word whose modern sense had not yet become fully established, 'purchase', still retained older connotations, being linked with 'chase' in the sense of 'hunt' (see no. 10).

The period's fascination with creating fictive worlds was in part a rehearsal of the process of conquering new worlds: the period marks a significant stage in the ideology of colonialism. The lover in Donne's 'To his Mistress going to bed' (no. 96) wants to possess his mistress like a colonist plundering a new continent, and in a punning excess of acquisitiveness he calls her 'My Myne'. This parallel between nature and woman as objects to be possessed can be found in much of the period's writing.[6] Enclosure and the clearing of forests aroused protest at the time as expressions of a new, more manipulative attitude to the land as private property by people whose 'self will is theire law' (no. 211 l. 16) at the expense of traditional communal rights (cp. nos. 177, 201). The poets' almost physical pleasure in imaginative possession of their landscapes can be said to offer an encloser's eye view: Sidney did much of his writing in a recently enclosed landscape. In a lyrical description of the light on a forest floor, Lord Herbert observes that its beauty can 'cloath the poorest' (no. 199 l. 7); his brother George imagined his mind as a deer-park (no. 284 l. 3). In Wyatt's 'Who so list to hount' (no. 54), the King has shut up the woman the poet desires like a deer in his own private forest, and Wyatt's frustration is tinged with envy. Renaissance man as free individual often depended on a considerably less free Renaissance woman. 'Mee, brought to light, your tender arms sustaynd', writes Nicholas Grimald in an elegy for his mother (no. 310 l. 3), his syntax indicating how his grief is almost outweighed by concern about how far she acknowledged him.[7] Women in the period often found their own individuality a burden rather than a liberation, a restriction to a domestic space in which they were not able to voice their feelings: 'When others hunt, my thoughts I have in chase', writes Lady Mary Wroth (no. 143 l. 9). Katherine Philips had to rework Donne's language to imagine a less limiting world of female friendship. Whereas for Donne

> She'is all States, and all Princes, I,
> Nothing else is
> (no. 133 ll. 21–2)

for Philips

> We are our selves but by rebound,
> And all our Titles shuffled so,
> Both Princes, and both Subjects too.
> (no. 244 ll. 23–5)

Where Donne's famous compass analogy makes the woman the static centre, the man the active wanderer (no. 137 ll. 25–36), Philips imagines each friend in either position (no. 245 ll. 27–8).

Even the period's most extravagant assertions of selfhood, in fact, often prove to be significantly qualified: 'not alone', writes Donne, 'My lonenesse is' (no. 29 ll. 7–8). The compass had often figured male self-sufficiency, and in insisting on the interdependence of the two legs Donne was shifting it in the direction of mutuality. The final stanzas of 'A Valediction forbidding mourning' (no. 137) gain some of their power from our awareness that when the compass is finally lifted to its greatest height it will be balanced at its most precarious on a tiny point.[8] Shakespeare transmutes the possessiveness of the lovers' 'mine' into a utopian interchange: 'Either was the others mine', and their love appalled 'Propertie' – implying more mundane legal possessions as well as abstract metaphysical laws (no. 312 ll. 36–7). Daniel argues that it is only by setting aside the pursuit of worldly goals that one can avoid becoming 'a possession held for others use' (no. 231 l. 62); Shakespeare, however, finds something disturbing in the stoical self-withdrawal of those who desire to be 'Lords and owners of their faces' (no. 113 l. 7).

Religious poets were both inward-looking and acutely uneasy about what Fulke Greville termed 'selfe-nesse' (*Cælica*, Sonnet 18): 'We seeme more inwardly to know the Sonne', he wrote (no. 262 l. 7), but this might be one more form of idolatry. The later Donne can affirm himself only in total subjugation:

> Take mee to you, imprison mee, for I
> Except you'enthrall mee, never shall be free,
> Nor ever chast, except you ravish mee.
> (no. 259 ll. 12–14)

Donne's 'I' dangles at the end of its line, precarious in its assertive humility. Francis Quarles urges God to

> . . . keepe me from *my Selfe*; 'Tis best for me,
> Never to owne my *Selfe*, if not in *Thee*.
> (no. 275 ll. 19–20)

And even in answering such fears, Herbert makes God turn individualism back on the speaker: 'Who made the eyes but I?' (no. 285 l. 12).

The status of the individual is in fact called in question by the very concept of the Renaissance: it affirms itself as doing something new and individual, but also as repeating something that has been done already – not a birth but a rebirth, not a discovery but a recovery. The art of 'discovery' or 'invention' in logic and rhetoric involved finding ideas and themes in an existing store rather than creating new ones. When Sidney's Astrophil declares that invention is 'Natures child' and flees 'step-dame Studie' (no. 65), we can sense an ironic distance from his creator, for whom study and imitation were essential parts of the poetic process. Such imitation, however, was not so much a denial of selfhood as a way of finding it: 'invention' was in fact beginning to be opposed to mere 'imitation' (cp. no. 365 l. 27), and we can sense something of that tension between innovation and respect for tradition in the by no means entirely stable gap between Sidney and Astrophil. Words like 'reformation', 'restoration' and 'revolution' in the period served to negotiate between tradition and change: going back to a remote past was a way of criticizing the present while accommodating traditional prejudices against innovation. Opposing political factions would vie with each other for the claim to be restoring the past correctly. Edmund Waller saw Charles's repairing of St Paul's Cathedral as a heroic bid to

> . . . higher clime,
> And things half swallow'd from the jaws of time
> Reduce . . .
>
> (no. 290 ll. 33–5)

Charles's adversaries, the architects of the English Revolution of 1649, spoke of themselves as restoring ancient liberties. The word 'revolution' itself was pivoting between old and new senses: it originally meant the return of a wheel to its original position (cp. no. 194 l. 92), but it was coming to be applied to radical innovations, too.[9]

In the same way, Renaissance individualism began as a process of imitation, of recovering lost voices from the past. What was reborn in the Renaissance was in the first instance the culture of classical antiquity. That culture, of course, had never been entirely lost, and there had been many earlier periods of recovery. In the medieval academic curriculum, however, which came to centre on Aristotle, the Greek texts were studied in Latin translations and overlaid by elaborate commentaries which sought to systematize them into an all-embracing canon of knowledge. This 'scholastic' syllabus aroused opposition from a group who became known as 'humanists': it was too abstract and dogmatic, it lost sight of the concrete human complexities in the impossible attempt to find universal rules of behaviour. The humanists revived the ancient quarrel between philosophy and rhetoric which went back to Plato's attacks on the sophists, and often enlisted poetry along with rhetoric in what Sir Philip Sidney termed a 'civil war among the Muses'.[10] Poetry and drama could be valuable sources of political wisdom precisely because they did not aim at a timeless and transcendent truth but examined generalities in the context of specific situations, offering dialogue rather than monologue.[11] The humanists wanted to revive the priorities of the classical educational system, to privilege the *studia humanitatis* – disciplines like grammar, rhetoric, poetics, history and moral philosophy. In the texts of classical antiquity they found voices which seemed to them startlingly fresh and contemporary – the voices of a culture which was in certain respects more secular and individualistic than their own epoch.[12] The fourteenth-century Italian humanist Petrarch felt acute shock and excitement when he discovered copies of Cicero's letters and recognized an individual more problematic and deviously political than the traditional image of a pious dispenser of moral maxims.

Hunting through monasteries for such fragments as might have survived of ancient manuscripts, the humanists experienced the full pathos of what had been lost by time, and often also by conscious censorship exercised by the Christian Church, and they tried to recover as much as possible. Such texts as had survived had been copied and recopied until multiple errors had crept in. Petrarch compared such corrupt texts to the Roman ruins that still dominated many parts of the Italian landscape: if one were skilful enough, perhaps one could reconstruct them, but the danger of error was ever-present.[13] On a larger scale, the Romance languages themselves were ruined Latin, a palimpsest beneath which the original words could be uncovered by the archaeological technique of the etymologist. The humanists' sensitivity to language heightened their historical consciousness: their philological techniques exposed as a forgery the 'Donation of Constantine' by which the papacy had claimed special powers passed on to it from the Roman Emperors (no. 341 ll. 95–6), thus highlighting the gulf between their own traditions and the quite different political structures of classical antiquity: textual criticism became a political critique. Scholars investigating the etymology of the word 'feudum' became aware that it was derived not from Roman but from Germanic laws of landholding, and thus began to formulate a historical model involving a sharp break between classical antiquity and feudalism. It became possible to call for a restoration of classical political forms and agrarian policies – what James Harrington termed 'ancient prudence' – to counter the corruptions of feudal social and political forms.[14] Humanists experimented with what would today be called theories of ideology as they exposed the rhetorical strategies, the mystifying images and representations, with which corrupt institutions had justified their power.

The poets' sense of their belatedness, of the need to repeat what had been said before, could of course become intimidating, with the dispiriting idea that, as Shakespeare put it, love 'makes antiquitie for aye his page', so that the lover's 'thou mine, I thine' is no more than repetition (no. 351). In repudiating many of their own political and cultural traditions as a falling-off from classical purity, Renaissance humanists cast themselves as the heirs to barbarians. Renaissance classicism, however, was a great deal more confident than the more rigidly rule-bound neoclassicism of the succeeding era. Renaissance poets freely mingled traditional genres and invented new ones (cp. Appendix 1). The period was a great age of translation, but there was no clear dividing-line between translation and imitation. Rhetoricians described imitation as a process of struggle, of wrestling with the texts of the great antecedents, and the metaphor implied that the struggle was an even one.[15] The ancient world had been neglected for so long that it was a new continent much like the new worlds being discovered by the navigators. Both forms of discovery, it was sometimes argued, were signs of a providential dispensation, of long-lost truths that were being at last yielded to a favoured age. Discovery could be hard to separate from plunder. Sir John Harington directly compared the processes:

> You'le spoile the Spaniards, by your writ of Mart:
> And I the Romanes rob, by wit, and Art.
>
> (no. 349 ll. 9–10)

In his dedicatory sonnet to *The Faerie Queene*, Ralegh presented Spenser's recovery of the poetic creations of Petrarch and Homer as a kind of grave-robbing. Spenser himself had translated a poem in which the French humanist du Bellay compared the rediscovery of Rome to necromancy, raising the 'Idole' of the dead by 'Magicke skill' (no. 335).[16] Renaissance humanists could thus be figured both as vindicators of the classical world against the barbarians and as barbarians sacking it anew. Predatory though their greedy acquisition of classical poetry might sometimes seem, however, it included a genuine respect for the otherness of the past, a scholarly interest in words and cultural forms whose very distance from the present provided a stimulus to the imagination: a process of dialogue rather than simple appropriation. Marlowe could find equal stimulus in the irreverent eroticism of Ovid (no. 339) and the acerbic anti-courtly rhetoric of Lucan (no. 340), and adopt very different voices in response. Chapman was fuelled in his project of translating Homer (no. 344) by the conviction that he had been possessed by the Greek poet's spirit. Marvell probed his response to the revolutionary events of 1649–50 by going back as scrupulously as possible to the voice of Horace's public odes (no. 45).

The excitement of recovery extended beyond particular literary genres to the timbre and rhythm of the verse line. Renaissance poets considered the accentual metre they had inherited from the Middle Ages to be too crude, too pedestrian, and sought a new metrical basis for English verse (cp. Appendix 2). For a time they experimented with restoring the metrical forms of classical poetry, which were based on syllable length rather than stress (cp. nos. 181, 333, 337). Pedantic as these largely unsuccessful projects may seem today, they had the visionary aim of making English words dance in a lost harmony. It was believed that Greek verse had been based on a principle of musical proportion, and that the ancients had been able to match the meanings of words with their sensuous properties in a particularly exquisite way.[17] The philosopher Pythagoras was known to have believed that numerical proportions were the key to the cosmos: complex harmonies structured everything from the positions of the heavenly bodies to musical notes. The pioneers of Renaissance opera and song were trying to regain a pristine unity of words and music: it was appropriate that Monteverdi should have taken as the plot of one of the first great operas the myth of Orpheus, who tried by the beauty of his song to recover his loved one from the underworld. Spenser and other poets soon abandoned their quantitative experiments, but they tried to create, or recreate, an equivalent harmony in the 'iambic pentameter' line with its complex interplay of stress and syllable-counting. In Spenser's *Epithalamion*, the elaborate vowel-patterns of the carefully structured stanzas culminate with an Orphean appeal for the landscape to answer and echo his song. The whole poem has an elaborate numerical structure, its patterns of long and short lines enacting the precise proportions between light and dark on the day of his wedding in Ireland, so that the text becomes part of the cosmic processes it celebrates.[18]

For the poets of the northern Renaissance, the process of imitation was a doubly complicated one: in one sense they were particularly belated, for Italian humanism had a massive lead over them; on the other hand, northern humanists drawing on new principles of textual criticism had helped to stimulate a process of religious reformation more thoroughgoing than anything undertaken in Italy. Humanist scholarship on the Donation of Constantine had undermined the authority of the Roman Church; and northern humanists were increasingly dissatisfied with the traditional Latin translation of the Bible, the Vulgate. Sidney was excited by the prospect that scholars were at last discovering the secret of the metrical basis of the Hebrew Psalms after centuries of neglect, and he and his sister could find a voice in David's poems (nos. 31, 336–8). It was by checking the Vulgate against the original Hebrew and Greek forms that reformers fuelled their challenge to Catholic tradition and called for a renaissance of the simplicity of the early Church. Erasmus, the pioneer of humanism in the Netherlands and northern Europe in the early sixteenth century, campaigned for widely available vernacular translations of the Bible at a time when this was seen as a dangerous transfer of interpretative authority away from the priest toward the individual.

It was certainly true that new methods of interpretation could become increasingly challenging to the traditional order. A growing body of interpreters argued that the last book of the Bible, the Revelation of St John the Divine, concealed behind its cloudy allegories some very specific prophecies. Its references to the reign of Christ for a thousand years could be taken to refer to the era from Christ's birth to the growing corruption of the medieval Church (cp. no. 261), but it could also be held to point forward to a future reign of Christ and his saints over a renewed earth: the years 1650 and 1666 were looked forward to as marking crucial transformations in mankind's history. Thus advances in textual interpretation, the unveiling of hidden meanings, became for radical Protestants at once a herald to and a sign of the revelation or renaissance of true religion after epochs of corruption. While Protestantism did encourage greater attention to individual religious practice at the expense of the status of the Church, it also provided a strong imperative towards collective action in reforming abuses in Church and State. Milton's first major poem, 'On the morning of Christs Nativity' (no. 270), reveals the growing apocalyptic fervour of many Protestants by the 1630s; its vision goes far beyond the individual's destiny, yet it also displays a virtually unprecedented confidence in the poet's prophetic status. Milton outdoes classical poetry with a poetic evocation of the music of divine creation which pagan myths only dimly recalled. The young Milton was already foreshadowing his epic project of lifting 'Human imagination to such highth/Of Godlike Power' that it could overcome the Fall, and re-enact the creation of Eden itself (*Paradise lost*, VI ll. 300–1).

2: POETS AND THE PUBLIC WORLD

If the Renaissance nurtured individualism, then, it was as part of a process of imitation and recovery. Moreover, the dominance of individualism in the Renaissance has often been exaggerated by later epochs which have read back their own individualism into the period. Poetry anthologies have often heightened this distortion by concentrating narrowly on the lyric. The period is characterized as much by dialogue as by monologue, and its poets displayed a growing concern with their public responsibility. The idea of constructing a 'golden world' might seem escapist, anticipating later theories of the total independence of poetry from society, but for Sidney its aim was didactic, inspiring the translation of its ideal visions into everyday practice. This idea was certainly not without problems, and throughout the period there was a tension between the humanist insistence on the value of the active life and the attractions of the *umbra*, the shade, of contemplative life (cp. no. 31 ll. 1–8, 43, no. 45 l. 3, no. 353 l. 48). For many poets of the period, however, the gap between poetry and the active life was in any case a narrow one. Shelley might speak of poets as 'unacknowledged legislators', but in the Renaissance they were acknowledged: More, Wyatt, Sidney, Greville, Ralegh, Davies, Donne, Herbert, Waller and Marvell were among the leading poets who sat in Parliament. For them, poetry was not necessarily a total escape; but its devices of formal distancing – parody, allusion, irony, genre, metre – helped to form an imaginative distance from the everyday discourses of public life which could facilitate political and intellectual independence. Constructing a golden world could be a means of criticizing the given world.

This emphasis on the practical social function of poetry meant that it was seldom sharply distinguished from rhetoric (cp. no. 265 ll. 63–4): Daniel saw poetry as rhetoric's 'mother' (no. 353 l. 67), and many poetic genres were subsumed under classical oratorical categories (see Appendix 1). The recovery of classical rhetoric had important political implications. In the republican phases of Greek and Roman culture, rhetoric had been a central means of participation in public life: citizens were trained in rhetoric in order to claim their rightful place in the processes of decision-making. When power passed from republic to empire under Augustus's dynasty, however, rhetoric had dwindled in its practical significance as public dialogue was reduced to an imperial monologue and citizens dwindled to subjects. The dominant rhetorical modes shifted from the 'deliberative', the art of political persuasion, to 'demonstrative' or 'epideictic' rhetoric, the ceremonial praise of rulers and patrons. The triumph of Christianity had resulted in a further undermining of classical political ideals. For St Augustine, the earthly city, the secular political order, was inherently inferior to the heavenly city, and the contemplative life took priority over the active life. The 'civic humanists' of the Renaissance challenged this devaluation of the active life and hence of political rhetoric; they tended to favour republican forms of government.[19] Their cult of liberty distanced them from feudal and absolutist political orders, though it would be anachronistic to equate their views with modern liberalism. The values they derived from classical writers emphasized the priority of the common good over the individual, and their concept of liberty was a positive one, implying a duty to participate in public life, rather than a negative defence against State encroachment.[20] The Roman ruling élite had been a small and selective one, and Renaissance republicanism often had an aristocratic rather than a democratic emphasis. None the less, it provided a discourse which challenged many traditional institutions.

For pioneering humanists in northern Europe, such as Sir Thomas More, the discourse of civic humanism was compelling but disturbingly powerless, so alien to their everyday world that it was most easily addressed not in their own language but in Latin, the language of the international humanist republic of letters. It was in Latin that More most directly confronted the tension between civic humanist ideals and his own political context, both in verse (no. 3) and in his sceptical fantasy of a rationally ordered republic, the *Utopia* (1516). Soon after publishing the *Utopia*, More entered the royal service: as so often in the sixteenth century, the humanist rhetorician turned courtier. This was partly a matter of bowing to the inevitable. More's Utopia had been founded by an enlightened prince, reflecting the fact that the monarchy alone had the immediate power to institute humanist educational reforms. It needed articulate administrators, and joined with the humanists in distrusting the traditional aristocratic cult of military honour. The nobility must be civilized: in helping to transform them into polished courtiers, sublimating their pursuit of individual honour into a new cult of honour gained in the service of the State, humanists could feel that they were serving the cause of political rationality. Henry VIII did encourage classical studies in the universities, and there began what has been termed an 'educational revolution' which extended from the aristocracy, who developed a considerably higher level of education than their Continental counterparts, to local grammar schools. The overall literacy rate may have remained as low as 30 per cent by 1642, but in some areas it was very much higher and extended well beyond the ruling élite.[21] This 'revolution' helped to lay the foundations for the cultural Renaissance. It also introduced generations of pupils to a world of republican values, to writers like Cicero for whom monarchy was a barbaric and archaic form of government: though civic humanist discourse remained marginal within the institutions of court, Church and common law, it became a significant element in the period's complex medley of political discourses.[22]

The immediate prospect of an active life for an ambitious young writer lay not in dreaming of Roman antiquity but in serving the Crown. The prospect of an alliance with the Crown was an appealing one for many poets in the period. In adopting the demonstrative rhetoric of the court, writing panegyrics of the ruler and leading courtiers, they could think of themselves as in effect writing the script of the public world, fulfilling the humanist imperative of making their verbal skill serve the State. The resultant compromises with courtly discourse, however, were often uneasy. More himself went to the block in 1535 not only for his loyalty to the Roman Church but also for his resistance to Henry's unconstitutional methods of rule. John Skelton, who had hailed Henry's accession with enthusiasm, also had a turbulent career. Skelton was no radical humanist: he was hostile to the new Greek learning, and the Latin that sounds through 'Phyllyp Sparowe' (no. 307) is the medieval Latin of the liturgy rather than the humanists' academic language. The characteristic Skeltonic metre, with its heaped, accumulated rhymes, strongly resists the humanists' idea that rhyme was a clumsy, 'barbaric' cultural form which the classical age had wisely avoided (cp. no. 354). Yet Skelton did share with the humanists a heightened sense of the poet's dignity and right to mould public events. His bids for advancement from the young Henry VIII on his accession to the throne in 1509 (no. 1) met limited encouragement, his way apparently being blocked by the King's chief minister, Cardinal Wolsey. Skelton eventually fought back by adopting an increasingly oppositional rhetoric. Turning from a courtly to a city audience, in *Collyn Clout* (1522) he adopted the persona of a plain-speaking rustic denouncing abuses in the Church (no. 247). Although he covered himself by attacking the emergent underground groups of Protestants, his poem was probably sponsored by a Londoner with Protestant leanings and designed to gain favour with a wider public.[23] Looking back from the 1570s, Spenser could see Skelton as a pioneer of Protestant humanism and take up his persona as Colin. There was, however, no security in writing satires, even if they did gain public fame, and within a year Skelton had sought Wolsey's pardon and was back in favour. Before long he was calling for the burning of the heretics his satires had helped to inspire; and yet he was doing so in a poem which claimed for the poet precisely the kind of prophetic individuality to which Protestants laid claim (no. 346).

Skelton's involvement with Protestantism and humanism was not deep-rooted; Sir Thomas Wyatt, by contrast, took a keen interest in contemporary Continental humanism on his travels in the royal service, and was a pioneer in translating Petrarch's poetry. He is sometimes seen as quintessentially a court poet, but his poems take a sceptical view of the courtly rhetoric of praise and he did not write public poems for ceremonial occasions. His lyrics take us behind the public scenes, into a world where political and erotic life are both composed of ever-shifting tactical alliances, and even the occasional success is attributed to 'fortune' (no. 53 l. 8). His intrigues became dangerous when his relationship with Anne Boleyn brought him into direct conflict with the King. Desperate to produce a male heir, Henry had determined to divorce Catherine of Aragon and had settled on Anne Boleyn as her successor. Wyatt seems to have voiced his frustration in some of his poems (cp. no. 54), and the King's suspicions of his loyalty led to several periods of imprisonment.

It was probably soon after one imprisonment, in 1536, that Wyatt composed 'Myn owne John poyntz' (no. 223), which draws on contemporary republican discourse. The poem is generically innovative: Skelton's satires followed a vernacular tradition of harsh denunciation, speaking with a collective voice, whereas Wyatt turns to the classical verse satire, whose voice was more personal and ironic, discussing his grievances with a specific individual. Wyatt is drawing not directly on Roman poetry but on a classicizing satire by the Florentine poet Luigi Alamanni. In the early sixteenth century, Florence had see-sawed between monarchical and republican forms of government, an oscillation reflected in the writings of her leading political theorist, Niccolò Machiavelli. Despite his notoriety as an apologist for ruthless authoritarian rule in *The Prince* (written around 1513), he later celebrated the cult of republican liberty in his *Discourses* on the Roman historian Livy. Machiavelli had made Alamanni one of the speakers in his dialogue *The Art of War*. It was as an exile after his involvement in a republican plot that Luigi Alamanni wrote the satire which Wyatt imitated. Wyatt declares, with Alamanni, that he cannot 'alow the state' of Julius Caesar with his monarchical aspirations. Though he removes a reference to Brutus, who had assassinated Julius Caesar in the name of republican liberty, it is only to substitute a glance at More's fate, with an allusion to the innocent victim Cato.[24] Wyatt refers his reader to Livy, who was not in fact an important source for the story of Cato; the reference evokes the world of Machiavelli's *Discourses*. Wyatt uses the term 'comonn wele', whose democratic associations were to cause the more conservative humanist Sir Thomas Elyot to call for its replacement by 'publike weal'.[25] Wyatt's reservations about monarchs who owe their authority not to God but to 'fortune' (l. 8) certainly did not make him a radical democrat, however, and the whole poem may seem somewhat disingenuous: the real 'cause' he fled the court was not so much moral integrity as the fact that he had been banished, and before long he would be back in search of further advancement: despite the repeated cries of 'I cannot', he could. It is possible to be too cynical about such dilemmas, however: even if we see Wyatt as simply trying to rationalize his self-interests at any particular moment, he had to do so by means of discourses which demanded that he universalize his situation.

Like More, Wyatt found it impossible to find a public discourse which would satisfactorily harmonize humanist suspicion of the court's structural inequalities and the strong humanist imperative toward the active life. At this time of crisis, he turns to a more private discourse which none the less has political resonances: like-minded friends could address each other in their letters without the evasions of courtly rhetoric, helping to build up a republic of letters whose boundaries cut across the geographical limits of monarchies. 'Myn owne John poyntz' is not just a transparent expression of personality: in adapting a new kind of literary model, Wyatt was creating a new kind of space for discourse. The work involved in that activity included the arduous process of introducing into English the difficult metre of Alamanni's *terza rima*, which was associated in Italian with popular, non-courtly poetry. Wyatt's retreat from the court is acknowledged as less than perfect or complete – his local liberty is a house arrest, so that even while hunting he has points in common with the captured hind (no. 54), leaving tracks in the snow for his enemies to read. Writing to a friend made a more secure mark.

In his later years Wyatt seems to have turned increasingly toward Protestant ideas, which coloured his versions of the *Penitential Psalms*. The religious situation, however, was insecure and unpredictable. The King's increasingly desperate desire for a male heir overruled his respect for traditional restrictions on divorce and pushed him into breaking with Rome and declaring himself head of the English Church. The new Church of England was thus established from above rather than from below; how far it would lead to a full establishment of Protestant ideas and religious practices remained unclear. The reformers received a sharp setback in 1540 when Thomas Cromwell, who had been sympathetic to their views, suddenly fell from power; Wyatt's sonnet on his fall (no. 7) registers his intense disquiet.

Wyatt's death the following year produced a tribute from Henry Howard, Earl of Surrey, which revealed the common humanist bonds that could cut across differing political alignments (no. 309). Surrey's pride in his Howard ancestry made him hostile to Cromwell and his allies. His poetry evokes the world of chivalry and tournaments more colourfully than Wyatt's. The epitaph on Clere (no. 308) enacts the social bonds of aristocratic tradition by placing the deceased man's name in a subordinate clause, giving pride of place to the Howards' Norfolk estate. Clere was buried in the family vault, and Surrey makes even his death an obliging act of deference towards the family.[26] The still-innovative form of the sonnet, however, establishes Surrey's interest in new humanist ideas. His translation of Virgil (no. 332) pioneered blank verse, which reflected the humanists' disparagement of rhyme and their quest for a metre which would capture in the vernacular something of the flavour of classical unrhymed verse. Stale as that metre may seem today, for the sixteenth century blank verse would have had a quality of risk as each line in turn launched out on its ten-syllable progress without the safety net of rhyme. The 'lordly port' (no. 332 l. 31) of Surrey's Virgil translation is more self-consciously stately than the immediately preceding version by Gavin Douglas or its successor by Stanyhurst (no. 333). Surrey's humanism was courtly in emphasis, and he saw cultural innovativeness as a means of giving a new lustre to traditional social rank.

Surrey's concern with decorous order and proportion has made his poetry less popular in the present century than Wyatt's; closer reading, however, reveals the edge behind the apparent blandness. The artistic discipline he sought was in part a form of self-discipline against the periodic eruption of an unregenerate aristocratic violence and unruliness. Surrey's pride in his birth made him extremely resistant to royal authority, and he was eventually executed for allegedly conspiring to take the throne himself on Henry's death; his poetry can be as sharp as Wyatt's in its critique of tyranny (no. 8).

In 1549 the stately mansion which Surrey had built outside Norwich was occupied by agrarian rebels led by Robert Kett. The political pendulum had swung rapidly: the Protestant faction at court had eventually prevailed, and their influence over the boy-king Edward VI when he came to the throne in 1547 led to a relaxation of censorship controls on Protestant writings and a substantial expansion of the public sphere.[27] The Edwardian period saw the interpenetration of several different discourses of social protest. In a tradition going back to Langland's *Piers Plowman*, which was edited in 1550 by the reforming poet Robert Crowley (cp. no. 10), religious reformers had adopted the persona and the rugged, uncourtly diction of the ploughman or shepherd. Luke Shepherd – the name may be an appropriate pseudonym – pushes the rhetoric of Skelton's *Collyn Clout* in a more radical direction, parodying the authoritarian language of courtly Latin (no. 249). Such populist rhetoric drew on traditions of secular complaint and protest, which were articulating a new wave of resistance to the disruption of the traditional agrarian order by enclosures. Large areas of land which had formerly been in common ownership were being taken over for sheep farming, dispossessing the traditional occupants who were driven to work as hired wage labourers.

Encouraged by some humanist advisers, the government began to take measures against unduly disruptive enclosures. Humanist anti-aristocratic discourse could converge with protests based on an older ethic of rural solidarity: Machiavelli had blamed the decline of the Roman republic on the aristocracy's selfish refusal to accept agrarian reform, and More had attacked enclosures in his *Utopia*, which was translated from its humanist Latin into English in the Edwardian period. For humanist writers, the figure of the protesting ploughman in popular culture could fuse with the shepherd of the classical eclogue. Virgil's first eclogue, a key schoolroom text (no. 361 l. 37), opened with a complaint by Meliboeus that was read as a protest against Augustus's redistribution of land after the Roman civil wars.[28] Some poems of the mid-century were ready to present the rebels' viewpoint (cp. no. 177).

Such sympathy, however, was easily lost: it was one thing for social reforms to be proposed from above, another for the people to take matters into their own hands. Kett's supporters were not the mindless anarchists of hostile propaganda: for example, their occupation of Surrey's house seems to have been carefully targeted, reflecting their resentment at his family's notorious resistance to freeing their feudally subordinated 'bondmen'. The opponents of enclosure had set themselves to 'restore' a traditional order which they saw as threatened by selfish individualism (no. 177 l. 71). Nevertheless, the spectacle of dispossessed labourers occupying a nobleman's home starkly juxtaposed culture and anarchy. After 1549, humanists tended to become more and more assertive in distancing themselves from populist tendencies and, since Roman humanists like Cicero had been élitists with an acute anxiety about popular protest and demagoguery, they could find classical precedents for such an attitude. The masses, they assumed, would never be capable of the level of education necessary for full participation in the civic life.

The humanists' economic programmes in any case tended to offer limited consolation to the rural poor, insisting on the need for a strict social discipline which hit both aristocratic conspicuous consumption and some of the traditional safety-valves of feasting and recreation.[29] Humanists were anxious to encourage the wool trade, whose prosperity depended on further enclosures. In later Elizabethan pastoral, the shepherd often changes from a voice of protest to an emblem of the leisure secured for the gentry by agrarian change.[30] May Day festivities had often been a rallying point for social protest, with Robin Hood and Maid Marion as festive agents of misrule. In many later versions of the legend, however, Robin becomes promoted to an earl and purged of his populist associations. The figure of the Pinder of Wakefield similarly oscillates between subversion and respectability; he often figures as a law-abiding opponent of Robin, yet within a single version of the ballad (no. 178) his status seems to shift from a yeoman who considers himself equal to any baron to a hireling eager to escape wage-slavery by joining the outlaws.[31] In the later sixteenth century, Protestant radicals – who became widely known as 'Puritans' – grew more and more hostile to traditional rural rituals, which they saw as vestiges of superstition and idolatry, while traditionalists idealized these rituals as maintaining a deep-rooted harmony with the rhythms of nature. Representations of rural festivities had become loaded with contradictory meanings, making it possible for Spenser in his 'Maye' eclogue to pit different literal and allegorical representations of rural festivity against each other in a complex dialogue which still leaves critics in doubt as to which view prevails and how 'Puritan' he was (no. 182).[32]

Anxiety about social upheavals contributed to the limited support obtained by a Protestant faction which attempted to stave off a Catholic succession with the rival claim of Lady Jane Grey in 1553. Historians still debate whether Protestantism was so deeply rooted at this time that Mary's attempts to bring the nation back to the Catholic fold were doomed to failure. Certainly, the ruthlessly pragmatic means by which Henry VIII had broken with Rome left a lasting residue of scepticism (nos. 251, 255), and there had been popular risings against religious reform in 1549. But that scepticism could also undermine any attempt to return to a purified Catholicism. Heywood's poem on Mary's marriage to Philip II of Spain (1554) indicates some of the ideological problems her regime encountered (no. 11). As a woman, she was expected to subordinate herself to a husband; but in choosing to marry the king of a powerful Catholic country she aroused nationalistic as well as religious fears. The persecutions and burnings that ensued reconciled many conservative waverers to the accession of Mary's Protestant sister Elizabeth in 1558. A more pragmatic motivation was alarm at Mary's attempts to reclaim the Church's lands. Henry VIII's Reformation had resulted in a massive transfer of lands into the secular domain, and much of this land had been sold off. In the short term these measures gave large sections of the gentry a vested interest in a Protestant monarchy. To the Crown, however, these sales also represented a hostage to fortune, an exchange of long-term power for short-term interest; lacking a standing army and a large professional bureaucracy, the monarchy needed the cooperation of the gentry, both inside and outside Parliament.

Elizabeth learned from the mistakes of her half-sister Mary. She and her supporters made a virtue of her sex, exploiting its complex symbolic resonances. Her refusal to marry became ultimately a symbol of national independence, and she became the centre of an enthusiastic literary cult of monarchy. Although she did not contribute very much directly to literary patronage, her court was a great deal less forbidding in atmosphere than Henry's. While she was not puritanical, she insisted that the cult of royal virginity should be taken seriously, and her court did not attract the lurid denunciations of sexual immorality so often found in Renaissance anti-court satire. Her virgin status also acquired religious meanings. John Foxe, a friend of the prophetic poet Robert Crowley, gave definitive form to an enormously influential apocalyptic monarchism. On this view, the Roman Church, justifying its actions by the notorious Donation of Constantine, had usurped not only true religion but also the State, subordinating royal power to the Pope. The Reformation thus restored if not the primitive Church then at least the status quo of the reign of the Emperor Constantine. Queen Elizabeth, as a female ruler, fitted neatly into this symbolism, becoming likened to the Woman Clothed with the Sun, the antitype of the villainous Whore of Babylon of Revelation.[33] Protestants' belief that an apocalyptic struggle between good and evil was in progress was sharpened after the Council of Trent in 1562 called for militant doctrinal and political opposition to the heretics: in 1570 Elizabeth was excommunicated.

As head of the Church, Elizabeth presided over a complicated compromise. The thrust of reformed Protestantism was to diminish the mediating role of the priesthood and of ritual in the struggle for salvation. The spiritual forces at work in the relations between man and God were too immense to be represented in the ornamental, external forms of images. In one of her Psalm translations, the Countess of Pembroke elaborated on the original to express this Protestant vision of a transcendent cosmic order testifying to God's unbreakable covenant with the elect: 'who is above that may compare with mighty Jehova?' (no. 337 l. 15).[34] If faith alone gave salvation, if God's election took precedence over man's freedom, then the role of the Church's rituals was sharply diminished. The Elizabethan settlement was not a radical one, however: many of the old rituals remained, and there was space in the Church for those who had doubts about Calvinist teaching on predestination.

This compromise reflected the fact that Elizabeth herself was no militant evangelical; but she had been imprisoned under Mary's reign, and for many of her subjects she became a potent symbol of virtuous opposition finally gaining divine recognition (no. 12). A group of prominent aristocrats, led by the Earl of Leicester, urged her to greater activism in abolishing the remains of superstition at home and in rallying Protestant forces throughout Europe. They also sponsored cultural change, a 'reformation' of poetry along Protestant lines. God's word was to be relished not just for its divine content but for its poetic power too: in their translations of the Psalms, Leicester's nephew and niece, Philip and Mary Sidney, set themselves to match David's divine eloquence with their own formal virtuosity. Mary Sidney praised the Queen as a new David, combining the roles of godly prince and champion of the Muses (no. 31). Elizabeth had after all received a humanist education, and she wrote a number of translations and original poems (cp. nos. 13, 20). It was thus appropriate that in Spenser's *The Faerie Queene* she should have served at once as muse and as symbol of political and religious reformation.[35] Sidney, Ralegh and many other poets joined in the chorus of praise.

The cult of Elizabeth was not without political tensions, however. She feared that the Leicester circle's militancy risked kindling subversion at home, and that their keen support of the godly struggle against Catholic oppression on the Continent might threaten the prestige of monarchical rule. The circle's social self-definition was complex: many of them had gained wealth and titles relatively recently, but they often identified themselves with the feudal aristocracy who recalled a time when monarchs had been no more than first among equals. They feared that the monarchy's growing power might threaten their traditional liberties, that '*Honor*' was becoming '*the creature of Authoritie*' (no. 26 l. 16).[36] Their militancy reflected not only godly zeal but also a strong desire for the profits to be gained from imperial expansion. The Dudley–Sidney–Devereux dynasties were to play an important part in cultural and political life down to the Civil War, when they sided with Parliament against the monarchy. In *The Faerie Queene*, Elizabeth may serve as a static image of virtue, but the main agency in the poem is reserved for masculine knights or for Amazonian females like Britomart, who loves the militant Artegall (cp. no. 32). In a manner characteristic of the period, Spenser revises a backward-looking chivalric imagery in the name of a new Protestant–humanist discourse, an aristocratic populism.

Sir Philip Sidney followed a similar programme in his prose epic the *Arcadia*. Though he is today celebrated as a dashing courtier, his relations with the Queen were somewhat strained, and his 'Ister Bank' eclogue (no. 14) shows why. The poem alludes to his conversations with the French Protestant Hubert Languet, who kept Sidney in contact with Continental theorists of resistance to absolutism. The poem adopts the populist modes of the beast-fable, the vernacular pastoral and the golden-age myth, but it gives them an aristocratic twist, insisting that even in early times there was 'order', specific-ally the rule of the 'beasts with courage clad' who made up the 'Senators'. The poem reveals the Sidney circle's political ambivalence, with their call for liberty against royal encroachments being sharply qualified by the fear that the common people might threaten their own privileges. Monarchy and people are here presented as forming an unholy alliance: the multitude institute monarchy out of spite at the nobility's privileges. The biblical story of God's warning the Israelites against kingship is shifted into a sardonic mode, with the call for a king becoming a dissonant medley of animal cries. Although the poem's final political sympathies remain open to debate, it is not surprising that the Queen found Sidney politically un-reliable. When he was killed in a campaign in the Netherlands, intense popular mourning contrasted with the lack of an adequate official monument (no. 15).

Sidney's literary output had been by no means uniformly pious, revealing a tension between Christian and secular discourses, but in his later years he had turned increasingly to religious poetry, including the ambitious translation of the Psalms, which his sister Mary, the Countess of Pembroke, continued. The Sidney Psalms drew heavily on the French versions by Clément Marot and Théodore de Bèze, whose militancy served to marshal resistance to the Catholic monarchy in France. Bèze invoked Psalm 52, in which David denounces a massacre of the godly, as a precedent for Protestant resistance after the massacre of 'heretics' on St Bartholomew's Day 1572 (cp. Anne Dowriche's treatment of this episode, no. 17). The Countess of Pembroke's ringing address to the 'Tyrant' is secure in the confidence that God will 'crush' him (no. 336). Even the stars, in her version, become 'armed squadrons' (no. 337 l. 4). Such vehemence was not altogether reassuring to monarchs, however godly they might consider themselves to be.

It was Sir Walter Ralegh who gave the negative subtext of the cult of Elizabeth its fullest expression. In *The Faerie Queene*, Spenser portrays Ralegh as the squire Timias, concerned exclusively with the Queen's private person, Belphoebe, and indeed Ralegh's relationship with Elizabeth was a fundamentally private one of personal dependence. His unorthodox religious views and political restlessness gave his court career a particular degree of insecurity. He risked Elizabeth's disfavour by challenging the cult of the Virgin Queen: ladies of her bedchamber were meant to be virgins, and he married one without royal permission. For this offence he was consigned to the Tower. It may have been during this imprisonment that he began work on 'The 21th: and last booke of the Ocean to Scinthia' (no. 21), which is at once an ironically incomplete epic, a ruined sonnet sequence, a self-woven funeral shroud, a complaint, a pastoral, a satire, a recantation and, almost despite the author, a love-poem to a remarkable woman. The poem constantly undermines its panegyric by misogynistic outbursts against being governed by a mere woman whose castigations gave his 'longe arections' a 'suddayne fall' (no. 21 l. 230); Ralegh revealingly presents the court poet's art as one of 'hydinge' all 'trespase, and mischance, for her own glorye'. And yet he cannot rest in satire: he is constantly tugged back to a real wonder. The Queen has come to signify not just a particular woman but the lost beauty of the deities of antiquity, 'Th'Idea remayninge of thos golden ages', which Ralegh's poetic skill has been able to recapture. In the humanist tradition, however, Ralegh cannot remain content with contemplating an abstract symbol: he has willed himself to link this ideal with the real person of the Queen, to make abstract beauty and truth engage with the practical political world. And for all his frustration, Ralegh knew that she was in fact an exceptionally able ruler; that awareness had to some degree to trouble the sexual stereotypes. The poem is torn apart by its uncertainties, and its climactic line abandons any attempt to unify the opposing forces: 'Shee is gonn, Shee is lost, shee is found, shee is ever faire' (l. 493).

Ralegh was able to regain favour, and even in its despair his poem draws resonance from the dominant traditions of public poetry. For a younger generation, however, the cult of Elizabeth was becoming less and less meaningful. Donne's early satires powerfully evoke the emergence of London as a centre of political debate – what Nashe termed an 'open Theater of opinions'.[37] Jürgen Habermas has analysed the development of what he termed a 'bourgeois public sphere', a realm of debate in which citizens could participate as equals, independently of pressure from monopolies of power.[38]

Though he dates the full emergence of the public sphere to 1695, its development in England, while uneven, was also remarkably precocious, and precipitated countermeasures by the authorities, who were anxious to limit public discussion of 'mysteries of state'.[39] Young men about town gathered outside and inside St Paul's Cathedral, where all three forces Foxe had singled out as great vehicles of the reforming spirit – preachers, players and printers – were offering their wares.

The literary market-place had reached a point that was making a career as a professional writer just barely viable, permitting greater independence from court patronage. The remarkable institution of the public theatre became a highly significant forum for dialogue on ideas that would be considered unorthodox at court or in the universities, and many of the period's leading poets wrote partly or primarily for the stage.[40] We may owe Shakespeare's narrative poems (nos. 100–1) to a temporary closure of the theatres because of the plague. The theatres might still notionally be under the patronage of the monarch or leading noblemen, but their financial basis was increasingly independent of the Crown. The space of the stage could serve as an imaginary 'world' permitting a significant distance from received ideas. For an audience aware that the actors might be wearing cast-off clothes from the court, the rituals of power became demystified, a commodity like the tourist-guide's endlessly repeated patter (no. 29 ll. 14, 122). Theatres also quickly became familiar enough to serve as an allegory for mental processes (no. 184), and poets would spend an evening reciting to each other their favourite passages from plays (no. 361 l. 9). Critics have often ascribed the increasingly dramatic quality of lyric poetry in the 1590s and 1600s to the theatre's influence – Donne, though not a playwright, was a great playgoer (no. 28 l. 33, no. 29 l. 33). It can also be said that a tendency to drama and dialogue was itself intrinsic to humanism, and that the astonishingly rapid development of the public stage owed something to humanist educational practice. Even poets like Greville who suspected the public stage as breeding immorality could explore sensitive political issues in dialogue form in their closet dramas.

A theatrical career was financially precarious, however. Nor was the market for printed books secure, especially in the absence of authorial copyright. In any case, the major public demand was for the kind of moral didacticism that the young intellectuals of the 1590s were starting to view sceptically. While bad harvests in the 1590s provoked an economic crisis for the rural poor, the very success of humanist policies for limiting domestic consumption was starting to pay off for many members of the gentry, who found themselves with new possibilities as consumers.[41] Protests against enclosures are to be found in writers like the balladeer Deloney and the satirist Joseph Hall (no. 185), but many young wits were ready to turn their satire against the moralizing stance of the satirist. They might attack the luxury of the court, and yet they were themselves indulging in the intoxications of new modes of conspicuous consumption, from plays to tobacco, and mocking puritanical moralists. The naïve celebration of consumer power in 'Greensleeves' (no. 62) would have been too blatant for them, but neither could they go along with the moralizing replies which the ballad had provoked. Furthermore, social criticism was inhibited by the savage crackdown by the authorities on the irreverent 'Martin Marprelate' tracts which had called for systematic reforms in the Church. Donne's satires of the 1590s represent the young poet about town as finding it very difficult to position himself, alike rejecting retirement in his study, the noise and dirt of the streets, and a court which he compares to Dante's Inferno (nos. 28, 29, 256). Donne's verse of this period was circulated only in manuscript, and its sceptical view of all forms of public morality and political authority certainly ventured on dangerous ground: the State is 'rotten' and all branches of Christianity are equally suspect. Donne's Catholic origins made him especially vulnerable to official displeasure, and his involuted poetry communicates the vertiginous sense of being a 'spyed Spie' (no. 29 l. 136). The authorities were indeed keeping an eye on the wits, and in June 1599 further satires were banned and books by several satirists were ordered to be burned.[42]

By the late 1590s the regime was facing a crisis of legitimacy. The second Earl of Essex, Robert Devereux, the political heir of the Leicester circle, became the focus for discontent with what was felt to be the regime's dilatoriness on religious reform and on the international Protestant struggle. The Queen's sex came to count against her as courtiers lamented the realm's lack of manly resolution (cp. no. 30). Sir John Harington dared to hint that it would be better if there were no more female rulers (nos. 24–5). There were fears that corrupt courtiers would monopolize the most likely successor, James VI of Scotland, or even that there might be a Spanish succession. Sir Philip Sidney's brother Robert was denied court advancement, and his discontent at his semi-exile in the Netherlands perhaps coloured his melancholic love-lyrics (nos. 120–3). In the later books of *The Faerie Queene*, the cult of Elizabeth plays a less prominent part: Book 6, the Legend of Courtesy, pointedly does not contain a court (no. 348). In 1601 Essex and his followers risked staging a *coup d'état* to force the Queen's hand. The plot was an ignominious failure, but even figures like Greville and Donne who had had their reservations about the Earl's erratic temperament were shaken by his fall.

For Spenser, one of the central causes for complaint had been the government's Irish policy. In *A view of the present state of Ireland*, completed around 1596, Spenser had drawn on Machiavelli's authority in calling for Essex to be given special powers to achieve a decisive victory in Ireland. Partly because of its championship of Essex, the treatise failed to be printed until 1633. It was a manifesto of humanist modernity, calling for a radical remodelling of the island's social structure, decisively ending the power of the Irish aristocracy and the Catholic Church. Colonists were to be brought in to dispossess the unproductive natives and transform the basis of Irish agriculture. Such a programme was popular with the 'new English' settlers led by men like the first Earl of Essex and Sir Philip's father Sir Henry Sidney, but it overrode the complexities of Irish society, most notably the divisions between the original Irish-speaking inhabitants and the descendants of earlier English settlers, the 'old English'.[43] Many of the 'old English' had begun to adapt to Irish traditions, and sometimes to the Irish language, though others insisted strongly on the English element in the Anglo-Irish compound. Something of the resultant cultural tension can perhaps be seen in Richard Stanyhurst's almost Joycean metrical and linguistic experiments (no. 333). Especially after the establishment in 1541 of Ireland as a separate kingdom, it seemed possible that these processes of cultural coexistence might persist. In Wales, the power-base of the Tudor dynasty, directly comparable cultural forms were allowed to survive and were invested with a patriotic lustre (cp. nos. 180, 192). While Spenser had drawn on Welsh legends for the dynastic framework of *The Faerie Queene*, however, he extended no such tolerance to Irish traditions. Uneasy about the 1541 Act, he insisted that by its medieval right of conquest England had no need to concede to Ireland the political rights enjoyed by the English. Book 5 of *The Faerie Queene*, written at about the same time as *A view*, celebrates his patron Lord Grey's past achievements against the rebels and calls for resolution in future campaigns. Like many committed English Protestants down to Cromwell and Algernon Sidney and well beyond, he saw Ireland as a kind of laboratory for advanced social engineering, with the Gaelic inhabitants as awkward encumbrances.[44]

The inevitable result of such policies was a hardening of religious and political sentiments on the other side: Protestantism imposed from above, with sword and halter, was not calculated to win a people's devotion. The ancestors of today's Ulster Protestants ironically helped to create Catholic nationalism. There is a certain mirroring effect in juxtaposing Spenser's celebration of Grey's role in defeating the Irish rebels with Eochaidh Ó Heóghusa's praise of Hugh Maguire's valour against the English (nos. 32–3).

Maguire was serving with the forces of Hugh O'Neill, whose campaign in Munster in 1598 had led to the destruction of Spenser's estate at Kilcolman. Both poems celebrate violence, though James Mangan's famous translation of Ó Heóghusa, obeying the romanticizing imperatives of a later nationalism, plays down the poem's militancy in favour of its pathos.[45] The poets' discourses, however, remain radically distinct, reflecting different social as well as national positions. Ó Heóghusa is a bard in an oral tradition, celebrating his personal bonds to his patron and lamenting the decline of the old aristocratic order. In a later poem he complained that he now had to compose poems for the common people in rough accentual measures, there being no more audience for the traditional, intricate syllabic metre.[46] Spenser's mode is more impersonal and less aristocratic. It is true that his poem retains a courtly framework, drawing on medieval and Renaissance romance. Artegall/Grey, the focus of personal allegiance, is represented as a chivalric knight obeying the rules of single combat. He is reinforced, however, by the impersonal killing-machine Talus, and the campaign is given an elaborate ideological defence as a manifestation of cosmic justice. Spenser's poem as a whole, notionally addressed to a patron who is herself the representative of an entire State, in fact aims through the printed medium at a wide readership going far beyond the aristocracy.

In the short term Spenser's views did not prevail: his house was burned down by rebels, and Essex, who had paid for his funeral, disastrously failed in his Irish campaign and was then discredited by his failed coup. Before long, however, a more effective military campaign had cleared the way for the colonization of Ulster, and the traditional basis of bardic culture had been destroyed. Some English voices were raised against the harsh treatment of Irish Catholics, notably that of the genial and witty Sir John Harington. But the remarkable episode when he read to the 'barbaric' O'Neill from his translation of Ariosto (no. 341) had few parallels, and men like Wither and Milton were to show no regrets about Cromwell's ruthless campaign of reconquest in 1649–50.[47]

The Ulster plantations were the work of King James VI and I, the first ruler with the opportunity of unifying all the different cultures of England, Scotland and Ireland: he tried to fuse England and Scotland into the entity of 'Great Britain'. Scotland itself was of course no homogeneous cultural entity: the Gaelic culture of the north and west was viewed with suspicion from the Lowlands. In the sixteenth century, however, a Scottish national identity was in the process of formation, with its political balance significantly different from England's.[48] There was an important tradition of court poetry, which continued despite political vicissitudes through to the court's departure to England in 1603. The monarchy was weaker than in England, however, and the discourses of law, politics, education and religion were more open to anti-monarchical currents. Whereas the English reformation was presented as the achievement of a godly monarch handed down to the people, in Scotland religious reform had come more obviously from pressure from below. There was a strong vein of vernacular literature of social protest which was reinforced by the reception of radical currents in humanism and by the Reformers' campaign for widely available public education. Sir David Lindsay's poetry could span idioms from the courtly to the popular (cp. no. 4) and his *Satire of the thrie estaitis* was to be found in many country people's cottages. While writers could thus address a growing popular audience, the reading public was still very small in comparison with that in England, and the very isolation of the Scots in European terms encouraged many of their writers to address an international humanist audience in Latin. The most celebrated neo-Latin poet, George Buchanan, was in some senses less circumscribed by local political traditions than his English counterparts. His lyrics could fuse traditional seasonal celebrations with classical golden-age myths and the prophetic discourse of the apocalypse (no. 175). As an historian and a political theorist, he criticized absolutism and championed the austerity of the Roman republic. With such a man as tutor to the young King James VI, many writers in England looked forward to James's probable accession to the English throne as marking a great opportunity. Was not James a patron of court poets and a poet himself?[49]

The exaggerated expectations which some writers entertained of the new reign were quickly dashed. James was keen to push through a political and cultural union between the two nations (no. 34), but the terms on which this union was to be effected seemed to many both in England and in Scotland to involve an aggrandisement of royal powers: James had reacted strongly and publicly against Buchanan's democratic tendencies. The advent of large numbers of Scottish courtiers put great strains on the patronage system. The most celebrated and notorious court occasion of the reign saw Frances Howard, a member of an old dynasty with absolutist leanings, marrying the Earl of Somerset, the King's Scottish favourite, after divorcing her first husband, the third Earl of Essex. The marriage was a slight to the old Sidney and Essex groups; and when it emerged that Frances Howard had arranged the murder of Sir Thomas Overbury, an opponent of the match, those like Ben Jonson who had written in praise of the wedding were left in an embarrassing position.

Jonson was the only major poet to enjoy large-scale patronage from James, and his court masques were a long way from the austere humanism he had espoused in the 1590s, when he had been as alienated and sceptical politically as his friend John Donne, verging on republican discourse in his Roman play *Sejanus* (1603). Jonson always tried to establish for himself a broader public role than that of court poet, however, being ready to risk ridicule by publishing plays as well as poems in his collected works. His poetry of praise celebrated a network of friendships that cut across political factions and public honours, and he was patronized by men like the Earl of Pembroke and Sir Robert Sidney who maintained a stance of independence from the court (no. 190). Yet one thing that saves his more 'plain' poetic modes from the risk of blandness is the very difficulty Jonson had in maintaining a position of serene detachment. In his last years, increasingly sick, he turned savagely from the public which had failed to appreciate his late plays and vowed to sing of King Charles instead, but the most powerful work of this late period is not his last masque but the Cary–Morison ode (no. 315). In this poem, the cult of friendship and of the good life has to be fought for in the face of the dark opening, which imitates the baffling obliqueness of Pindar and presents a powerful vision of human futility.

Jonson was not merely a court poet; but he did manage to achieve a public eminence which no other contemporary quite matched, and less favoured poets developed a more directly oppositional style of writing. Fulke Greville, ousted from office, presented an alternative programme for English Protestantism in his idealizing life of Sidney. Greville's friend Samuel Daniel, who had been widely viewed as the pre-eminent English poet on Spenser's death, was outflanked by Jonson in the quest for court favour and became critical of the new regime. Like many poets, he found more sympathetic patronage from James's son Prince Henry, though Daniel had his reservations about the militant colonialism popular in Henry's circle (no. 194). Henry's early death in 1612 came as a devastating blow to many, notably to Sir Walter Ralegh, who had hoped that Henry might obtain his release from the Tower where James had had him thrown early in his reign. Ralegh warmly welcomed his friend Sir Arthur Gorges's project of translating the anti-courtly epic of Lucan (no. 357; cp. no. 35).

Henry's death marked a stage in the growing alienation from the monarchy of the Jacobean 'Spenserian' poets – Michael Drayton, William Browne and George Wither – who began to abandon dynastic compliment as a centre for their major poems, and turned from the court and literary coteries to a wider reading public (cp. no. 361 ll. 183–9). They celebrated the countryside rather than the court and the Union. Despite its title, Browne's *Britannia's pastorals* did not venture beyond England and Wales, and Drayton did not take his description of the counties of England in *Poly-Olbion* north of the border. This failure was not necessarily due to chauvinism – Drayton was an admirer of the Scottish poet William Drummond, who had not joined the southward rush of so many Scottish court poets and who was developing a British rather than a Scots literary language which was to win Milton's admiration (nos. 267–8). A celebration of English national identity, however, was gradually becoming a means for writers to distance themselves from the court.[50] Parts of Drayton's ninth eclogue (no. 191) were recast in *Poly-Olbion*, where there is a sense of decline as the muse passes from the Cotswolds to London and the court. The Spenserians' pastorals are generically eclectic, drawing on the discourses of Spenserian political pastoral and on Virgil's *Georgics*, which emphasized the role of labour in the countryside, as well as the *Eclogues*. Browne uses the '*glasse prospective*' of his poetic vision to correct the gaze of a monarch used only to the flattering perspectives of court masque, and to draw attention to the economic pressures on the traditional rural order (no. 37 l. 35).[51]

For all their poetic self-consciousness, Browne and his friends were genuinely seeking a more open and spontaneous poetic, one characterized by generic 'mixtures' and resembling the subtle gradations of the rainbow's colours rather than the strict patternings of courtly ceremonial genres; the weaving and flower-arranging of country women can thus serve as its paradigm (no. 358 ll. 49–70).[52] Browne's description of a rural dawn exemplifies this 'loose' poetic, with the sharp itemization of particulars playing against the structure of the pentameter couplets (no. 198). This 'natural' poetic was to be rediscovered by Keats and his generation of Romantic writers as a political as well as a poetic alternative to neoclassicism.

For poets who continued to seek advancement at court, a humiliatingly high price in flattery had often to be paid. Donne's tortuous poetry of courtly compliment in the Jacobean period contrasts strongly with his bold irreverence in the 1590s. His struggles to win the favour of an arbitrary, capricious God in the 'Holy Sonnets' (for example no. 259) are coloured by the passive aggression of the courtly dependent. It was in the Church rather than the State that Donne eventually found advancement. The Jacobean Church was of course itself a political institution, and as Dean of St Paul's Donne found himself preaching sermons in defence of unpopular royal policies. The Jacobean Church was something more than a puppet of the State, however. The Elizabethan compromise had seemed botched and makeshift to many of its critics, but by James's reign the Church was starting to attract gifted intellectuals like Donne and Herbert. Despite the best efforts of scholars of rival denominations to categorize them, Donne's religious lyrics cut across the conventional modes of Calvinist and Counter-Reformation devotion.[53] He came from a Catholic background and he was sympathetic to rituals that many Puritans attacked as ungodly, but his religious poetry is not ritualistic in any simple way: it often plays on his unwillingness to represent God directly (cp. no. 257). Carew's elegy sees Donne's role at St Paul's as that of an inspiring preacher rather than a ritualist (no. 365).

The same emphasis on the Word, on God's eloquence, characterizes the poetry of Donne's friend George Herbert. Izaak Walton's lives of Donne and Herbert have fixed an image of both men as ritualists associated with a High Church faction under Charles I. It is true that both Donne and Herbert attacked Puritans who called for further assaults on ecclesiastical ritual. Herbert took an interest in the semi-monastic religious community at Little Gidding which T. S. Eliot's poem made famous again in the twentieth century, and which was attacked by Puritans as crypto-Catholic. Herbert's verse, however, is close in spirit to the more open atmosphere of the Jacobean Church, and much of it was probably composed at that time.[54] While his poetry constantly invokes the physical rituals and buildings of the Church, these function more on an allegorical than a literal level. One poem (no. 286), probably composed in the 1620s, reflects Puritan fears that the invisible Church of the elect might have to leave England and move to America, and the passage ran into trouble with the censors in 1633.

In Herbert's verbal temple, words themselves are always in danger of becoming 'too rich' (no. 281 l. 11). Herbert's poetry could speak to readers right across the religious spectrum, from Charles I to Ranters. His 'plainness' gives him something in common with the immensely popular didactic poet Francis Quarles (nos. 271–5), and yet few poets have written so powerfully of the pleasures of composing (no. 283 ll. 36–9). Like Donne, Herbert looked back to the Sidneys' Psalm translations as reminders that there was scriptural authority for the poetic vocation, and his formal virtuosity owes much to their example. In 'The Forerunners' (no. 284), religious asceticism becomes a means of stifling regret at an anticipated loss of poetic power. There is a characteristically tough wit in the idea of his white hair as the chalk-mark anticipating death's occupation; but at the conclusion this white writing gains a vividness that suddenly outdoes the fading colours:

> Let a bleak palenesse chalk the doore,
> So all within be livelier then before.

By the time of Herbert's death, it was becoming increasingly difficult to establish a devotional voice with such a broad appeal. Already in James's last years the always precarious factional balance within the Church had been shattered. There was an explosion of public controversy on political and religious matters, a notable expansion of the public sphere. The debates were intensified by the international situation. In 1619 James's son-in-law, Frederick V of the Palatinate, was elected King of Bohemia, upsetting the balance of power between Protestant and Catholic states and escalating the European conflict that became the Thirty Years War. In England, militant Protestants saw this conflict as an apocalyptic struggle between good and evil and urged the government to support the international Protestant cause. An immense appetite for news of current events was fed by the first regular newspapers and by manuscript newsletters. Parliamentary elections became increasingly contentious, and increases in the size of the electorate meant that more members of the general public were becoming involved in political life. Parliamentarians increasingly spoke out on matters that James considered inviolable mysteries of State. The mystique of monarchy was being undermined by irreverent satires against the King and his favourite the Duke of Buckingham, who was hated for his alleged homosexual relationship with the King and his monopolizing of the patronage system on behalf of his friends and relatives (see no. 39).[55] Large tracts of land were awarded to his relatives, and his sister-in-law was kidnapped by agrarian rebels who were less swayed than Sir William Davenant by her divine voice (no. 201). Buckingham's political influence continued on the accession of Charles I in 1625. A measure of the crisis of confidence in traditional power structures can be found in the chorus of praise directed at John Felton when he assassinated Buckingham in 1628 (no. 38): he was celebrated as belonging to the tradition of classical tyrannicides.

Such exaltation of spiritual freedom over external forms caused widespread alarm, and James and Charles set themselves to limit the damage. Increasingly vigorous attempts by the monarchs to control Parliaments culminated in 1629 when Charles dissolved Parliament; he was to rule without it until 1640. James and Charles also decided that the traditional Church settlement had been too unstable, too open to potentially subversive forces. In cooperation with conservative clergymen led by William Laud, Charles used the Church to help to contain the emergence of a public sphere of criticism and dissension. The Laudians called for greater reverence to be given to the Church visible and its external forms. With the predominance of Calvinists in the Church, preaching from the pulpit had taken precedence over the altar, whose adoration was regarded as superstitious, and there was a gradual dilapidation of church buildings and ornaments (no. 289). This lack of reverence for external forms was felt to parallel a general breakdown in respect for social discipline. The Laudians' opponents dubbed them 'Arminians', after the Dutch theologian Jacobus Arminius who criticized the orthodox

Calvinist position on predestination.[56] The impulse behind the movement, however, involved Church discipline as much as doctrine – the more vigorously the Calvinists challenged free will, the more they undermined the authority of priests and rituals in affecting salvation. The Laudians' triumph was marked in church architecture by returning the altar to its supremacy over the pulpit (cp. no. 294), a measure which had a clear political significance. Outdoor sermons in St Paul's, that symbolic centre of the public sphere, were stopped and the news-gatherers were displaced from the aisles to the shelter of Inigo Jones's massive new portico, where royal statues emphasized the unity of Church and State (no. 290).

The poet whose work most clearly bears the trace of the new religious movement is Richard Crashaw. The Laudians reacted against what was seen as the excessively cerebral nature of Calvinist piety: in the traditional association of the rational with the masculine, a return to the emotive involved a revaluation of female imagery, including the cult of the Virgin Mary. Crashaw aroused much controversy for the devotion he showed to the Virgin in his preaching, and his poetry concentrates again and again on the fertilizing fluidity of the female saints. He is often seen as a distinctively Catholic poet, yet his conversion came only after his ousting from his living in 1644, by which time he had composed many of his best-known poems. In the 1630s it seemed possible that his religious temper could be accommodated within the Church of England.[57] Pastor-poets like Robert Herrick and the celebrated wit Richard Corbett, who were in a very different mould from Donne and Herbert, can also be seen as reinforcing the Laudian programme, celebrating the old ritual calendar which Protestant rationalism had been trying to eradicate (nos. 200, 206). (Since Herrick lived in an area with a strong Puritan presence, however, his view of the country people was somewhat ambivalent: cp. no. 205.) Laud himself was anxious to maintain a certain distance from Rome, but more and more poets became involved in a cult of Queen Henrietta Maria which effectively repudiated the traditional cult of Elizabeth the Virgin Queen and brought back the worship of the Virgin Mary.[58]

For its supporters, the Laudian Church represented a return to the central traditions of the English Church. For its opponents, however, it was effectively a return to Catholicism, with Laud as 'our English *Pope*' (no. 295 l. 32). Many Protestant humanists were uneasy with strict Calvinist predestinarianism; it was challenged by Wither, and Milton was himself to become a staunch believer in free will. But the political context of the Laudian reformers aroused both men's suspicions. Milton denounced the Laudians not only as enemies of reformed religion but also as antagonistic to humanist principles: in satirizing the bishops' 'lean and flashy songs' (no. 325 l. 123) he links their authoritarianism with their insensitivity to language. The Laudians wanted to restrict debate about the interpretation of Scripture, closing dialogue in a dismal monologue, and Milton saw them as the heirs to the humanists' old enemies, the scholastic philosophers, who substituted arid abstractions and empty rituals for a response to the full richness of the Word. Milton does not repudiate verbal beauty, on the contrary he self-consciously relishes it (cp. no. 363) and offers it as a pattern of heavenly harmony; but he also insists that it is only a pattern, and his poems thus have a dual movement of both offering and subverting a sensuous fulfilment. Thus the Nativity ode (no. 270) looks forward to the apocalypse before coming to rest in the very last stanza on the conventional image of the child in the manger, the serenely incarnate Word; and in 'Lycidas' (no. 325) restless questionings, and disruptions of anticipated regularity in the rhyme scheme, clash with the ritual of elegy. The Jacobean Spenserians who most influenced Milton's early poetry, figures like Giles and Phineas Fletcher, placed great emphasis on the extreme difficulty of bringing the infinite within the limitations of human descriptions (nos. 265, 269): the problem with the Laudians was that they seemed too confident of their ability to do so. Music is Milton's favourite symbol of divine discourse precisely because it seems less corporeal, more transcendent, than visual images: other poets contrasted Laud's idolatrous church bells with the deeper harmony of the 'constant Sermon-Bell' (no. 294). For Milton, there was no incompatibility between vehement Puritanism and a commitment to the art of poetry: it was the Laudians who were betraying humanist positions.

The motives behind Charles's support of the Laudians had been partly political, an attempt to contain emergent democratic and individualistic tendencies in the polity. The attempt failed. Whether it could in the long term have succeeded has been much debated: there is evidence of popular support for Laudianism, and also of fierce resistance. One crucial factor was the difficulty of uniting not just one but three kingdoms in a single religious order. The Scots saw his attempt to impose the new English liturgy and prayer-book as a blow to national pride. When a Scots army invaded England in 1639 it received a sympathetic greeting from many citizens, and before long Puritans in England were to form an alliance with the Scots to force the King's hand in religious and political reforms. For a time it seemed as if a compromise could be patched up, with the King accepting far-reaching constitutional and religious reforms; many of his most hated ministers fled (no. 295). Religious radicalism in England, however, provoked panic in Ireland, where there was a Catholic rising in 1641; and the massacres there provoked further reaction in England. A rumoured alliance between the King and the forces of Counter-Reformation Catholicism conjured up deep-rooted anxieties.[59] Such an alliance, it was believed, would help to swing the European balance of power and consolidate absolute monarchy throughout Europe. Gentlemen like Sir Thomas Fairfax feared for lands their ancestors had gained from the Church (cp. no. 218); the Inquisition would undo centuries of struggle for free access to the Gospel. Neither side trusted the other to control the armed forces, and the crisis escalated throughout the spring and summer of 1642.

Sir John Denham's *Coopers Hill* (no. 42), written as the conflict moved towards civil war, registers the ideological crisis in part by what it cannot represent. In the manner of Caroline pastoral, the poet still celebrates a harmonious and peaceful rural landscape, and he salutes Waller's tribute to the rebuilding of St Paul's (no. 290). Below the cathedral, however, there hangs a pall of smoke which for Denham symbolizes the restless activism of a city that has abandoned order for anarchy. And the rural landscape is itself darkened: the stag hunt at the end allegorizes the fall of Strafford, the King's favourite minister, to whose death he had consented in a vain attempt to propitiate the opposition (cp. no. 41). For Denham, the subject's liberties are gifts from above, not rights, and if subjects press monarchs too hard for concessions they will provoke a deluge of tyranny. A few weeks after *Coopers Hill* was published, the King raised his standard against Parliament. He took his court to Oxford, where he was joined in time by Denham and by many other poets, including Cowley, Davenant and Fanshawe, who were alarmed by the breakdown of the traditional political order and by the parliamentarian leaders' appeal beyond the traditional political élite to the London crowds. Thomas Hobbes claimed that humanist studies had been a main factor in provoking the Civil War by intoxicating the literati with the ideal of liberty; his friend Davenant insisted that monarchs should clothe their minds in mystery (no. 370 l. 22).

The royalist poets tended to brand their enemies as base-born philistines, and saw the monarchy as the natural guardian of the arts. It was certainly true that the demise of court patronage was a devastating blow for many poets, artists and musicians. But humanism had always had an ambivalent attitude to the court, and other poets sided enthusiastically with the parliamentarian cause. George Wither, who found himself directly opposed to forces led by Denham when war broke out in 1642, campaigned against the royalists by poetic as well as military means. Where Denham attacked prophetic individualism and exemplified civil order in his disciplined couplets, Wither's poems became ever more rambling and open to prophetic spontaneity (no. 369): his goal was to make both poetry and Parliament more representative of the popular voice. In Wither and in other poets of the mid-century (cp. no. 373), the breakdown of traditional political controls was paralleled by a breakdown of traditional poetic forms.

The public appetite for news and the collapse of traditional restrictions led to the precocious emergence of a lively press. The immensely popular medium of the almanac was also used to prophesy doom to the enemy.[60] In these unprecedented circumstances, even political conservatives engaged with new forms of communication. The balladeers Martin Parker (no. 43) and John Taylor sided with the royalists but showed considerable flair in turning from the ballad to the newspaper. Their long-term aim, however, was to limit the damage, to restore as much as possible of the old political and religious order; and by the mid-1640s the parliamentary group which became known as the 'Presbyterians', alarmed by tendencies to democracy, was seeking a compromise settlement with a strong, though reformed, State Church. The 'Independents' pressed instead for a more vigorous pursuit of the war with the aid of Oliver Cromwell's New Model Army. Wither and Milton both became aligned with this group.

Milton attacked any attempt to produce a new Presbyterian State Church (no. 296), and his *Areopagitica* (1644) celebrated division and dissension in a society as a sign not of weakness but of commitment to the ideals of radical Protestantism and civic humanism. Sidney's 'civil war among the Muses' had become a real conflict. The royalists, in Milton's view, were aligned with authoritarian dogmatism, the domination of social and intellectual life by the private interests of courtiers and churchmen, and the parliamentarians with the spirit of inquiry and the revival of public rhetoric. Milton's pamphlets of the 1640s mingle rhetoric and poetry, fierce invective and visionary prophecies, and offer the poet a new form of engagement in a society no longer offering the traditional lures of courtly advancement.

Andrew Marvell's '*Horatian* Ode' suggests that it took the exceptional force of Oliver Cromwell to translate republicanism into practice, to

> . . . ruine the great Work of Time,
> And cast the Kingdome old
> Into another Mold.
> (no. 45 ll. 34–6)

Certainly the trial and execution of Charles I in January 1649 would not have been possible without the overwhelming military successes of Cromwell's New Model Army, which brought Charles's forces to surrender in 1646 and again after a second civil war in 1648. Cromwell was in fact more vacillating on political matters than Marvell's poem suggests; caught between the fierce hostility of his more radical soldiers and the King's refusal to compromise what he saw as the divine dignity of his office, Cromwell eventually allowed his forces to be used to put pressure on Parliament for the King's trial. Marvell lays so much emphasis on Cromwell's devious role in events that many critics have read his poem as a satire; but the poem's terse, demystifying idiom can also be seen as an attempt to cut through courtly mystification and recover the tougher discourse of classical republicanism. In the process it overgoes its Horatian model and has more in common with Machiavelli, for whom the hero who decisively seizes the occasion for a political transformation is to be applauded despite a lack of moral purity. Unlike Waller's Charles I, who ornaments an old building (no. 290), Marvell's Cromwell lays the foundations for a wholly new structure, recovering and potentially surpassing the strengths of the Roman republic. Revolutions in political and artistic forms are seen as running parallel.

The new republic did for a time succeed where Charles had failed in bringing England, Scotland and Ireland under a uniform system of government. Marvell's poem registers the exultation felt by many English Protestants in the decisive crushing of Catholic resistance, which at last made possible the kind of Protestant cultural revolution long ago urged by Spenser – whose grandson received a pension from Cromwell. And the concluding prophecy of victory against the Scots was to be justified by events. Marvell's darkly violent language, however, registers some of the cost of those victories.[61] The Scots, critical though they might have been of Charles's absolutist pretensions, disliked the English presumption that their king could be disposed of without consulting them (no. 46). In Wales, attempts to graft radical Puritan ideology on to traditional bardic measures (cp. no. 297) met with limited success. The greatest Welsh poet of the period, Henry Vaughan, strongly opposed the new regime, although his poetry perhaps reflects the breakdown of traditional religious forms: in comparison with his chief poetic model, George Herbert, Vaughan's own lyrics are looser in form and more personal and visionary in discourse (nos. 299–302, 328, 374). The republican government strongly repressed internal dissent not only from the right but also from the left; its republicanism was more oligarchic than democratic, and it cracked down on the democratic 'Leveller' movement and the agrarian reformers known as the 'Diggers' (no. 211). The new republic brought freedom on the point of a sword.

Throughout the 1650s, political life was dominated by the implications of Marvell's terse maxim:

> The same *Arts* that did *gain*
> A *Pow'r* must it *maintain*.
> (no. 45 ll. 119–20)

The politicians needed the army but also suspected it; military rule without constitutional forms lacked long-term legitimacy. In April 1653 Cromwell dissolved the Long Parliament by military force; in December he took on semi-regal power as Protector. The pragmatic Marvell praised Cromwell as enhancing England's newly expansionist imperial role (no. 50, cp. no. 214). But was the new order concerned primarily with commercial prosperity or republican virtue? Royalists like Waller and Denham could reconcile themselves to Cromwell's regime in part because it did seem to offer social stability and economic growth: if in the pre-revolutionary version of *Coopers Hill* the River Thames mainly signified royal power, in successive revisions it became increasingly the medium of a less and less 'guilty' (l. 167) process of commercial exchange. James Harrington, the decade's leading republican theorist, could reject the traditional moralizing that denounced women's ornamentation: the claims of commerce had to be heard (no. 172). His admired Machiavelli had celebrated the expansion of the Roman republic as a sign of its constitutional strength. Harrington insisted, however, that commercial prosperity depended on far-reaching agrarian and institutional reforms; he and an emergent republican opposition feared that England under Cromwell was sacrificing liberty for the sake of material wealth. A society's poetry, Harrington believed, might be an index of social change: so Virgil's eclogues registered the decay of agrarian relations under the Empire.[62] Harrington's friend Marvell's portraits of rural landscapes, while containing the expected compliments to his patron and disparagements of rural disorder, register some unease about how 'natural' the established agrarian order might be (nos. 215–18, cp. no. 220): in a post-revolutionary order, the landscape has to be painted anew (no. 218 ll. 40–63), and Marvell's mower has a far more ambiguous relationship to his environment than the traditional shepherd. Milton's sonnet to Vane, Cromwell's most influential opponent, articulates the acute tensions between the demands of military security and the claims of religious liberty (no. 49).

By Cromwell's death, the divisions between Cromwellians and republicans were so deep that no stable consensus could be established, resulting in the giddy political instability captured by one of Brome's ballads (no. 51). When the merry-go-round stopped in 1660, England was left with the restoration not of the golden age but of Charles II. This event, which was celebrated by scores of panegyrists, has often been seen as manifesting a deep-rooted affinity between poetry and the English monarchy. One aim of the foregoing survey has been to suggest that their interrelations were in fact always problematic. Before long, Marvell and other poets were putting pressure on Charles to try to prevent his regime from putting the clock back too far, and in the deposition of James II in 1688 absolutism was to be given a sharp check. Many of the institutional changes of the previous decades had been undone, however, and remain so to this day. Britain was to move into its maturity as a commercial society and a world power in a heavily archaic monarchical costume; some of the constitutional projects of the revolutionary period remain unfinished business.

3: WRITING AND GENDER

Despite their reputation for individualism, Renaissance poets did consistently show a sense of public responsibility. It is in the realm of love, marriage and desire that we might expect to find the poets at their most individualistic. The Renaissance did indeed make a distinction between the 'political' and the 'economical', by the latter category meaning the realm of the household (from the Greek *oikos*, cp. no. 213 l. 38). But in the early modern period that distinction was not yet a sharp one. Under a personal monarchy, there was no clear-cut dividing-line between the administration of the State and the household of the ruler. Conversely, many political theorists saw the household as a little State, with the father as the natural ruler. It was in the early sixteenth century that the English word 'courtship' became extended from political relationships to the rituals preceding marriage; in such central texts as *The Faerie Queene* and Shakespeare's sonnets, the discourses of patronage and of love are inextricably intermingled.[63] To explore the world of sexual relations, then, is by no means to lose sight of political issues altogether.

It is true that the libertine poets of the Renaissance did sometimes turn to sexuality as a force that unsettled the conventional hierarchies of State and household, upholding a hedonistic anarchism. As in the political sphere, however, their rebellion against convention was often expressed by recovering voices from the past. While Donne characteristically insisted on seeking out a wholly new world of love (no. 96), such quests were often encouraged by the recovery of an ancient world with very different views of sexuality from Christian orthodoxy. Lucretius's *De rerum natura* (*On the Nature of the Universe*), which had been effectively lost until 1417, offered a materialist account of knowledge and sexuality. Ovid's *Metamorphoses*, with its sympathetic exploration of the unpredictable extremes of sexuality, had been saved for medieval orthodoxy by allegorical interpretations, but humanist methods of textual interpretation tended to undermine such moralism and concentrate instead on the poem's sceptical rhetoric. From the Renaissance through to the Enlightenment, libertine poetry inspired by the erotic elegies of Ovid, Catullus and other Roman poets became one rallying-point for those who challenged religious and political orthodoxy. Nashe proclaimed himself as restoring a lost classical eloquence in his erotic poem 'The choise of valentines' (no. 95): 'Complaints and praises everie one can write' (a fact which can be verified at length from Section II of this anthology), but modern poets have neglected 'loves pleasure's'. The idealizing poetry of Petrarch, who had sublimated troubadour eroticism into a highly rarefied idiom, had its admirers, but English imitators from Wyatt onward (no. 54) revised his conventions in a more critical – or, some would say, misogynistic – direction.

New currents of love-poetry were more uncompromising in their physicality. In Italy, Pietro Aretino (cp. no. 29 l. 10) acquired a European reputation as the 'scourge of princes' and also as an accomplished pornographer, benefiting from the relatively free press of the Venetian republic. In England, however, such libertine writing faced opposition from the ethos of humanist and Protestant moralism. Many young Elizabethan poets followed what became a familiar path of beginning in defiant eroticism and ending in pious recantation. The love-poems of George Gascoigne's *A hundreth sundrie flowres* (no. 61) hardly strike modern readers as inflammatory, yet they were much criticized and a second edition of them was banned; Gascoigne turned increasingly to didactic and panegyrical verse.[64] He could point to the model of grave divines who had written love-poetry in their youth, and one strategy for poets who ventured on dangerous ground was indeed to establish an ironic distance between the personae of the individual poems and the authoritative position of the moralist. Thus Sir Philip Sidney could detach himself from the 'trewand pen' of Astrophil (no. 65) by various formal distancing devices, notably the pattern of numerical symbolism in which the 108 sonnets of the complete sequence paralleled Astrophil with the ultimately unsuccessful suitors of Penelope in Homer's *Odyssey*.[65] Critics rightly warn against the dangers of naïve autobiographical readings of such texts.[66] All the same, the sonnet was a particularly sensitive instrument for exploring personal experience in a society which still disapproved of too much individualism, and sonnets must have seemed at times as raw and personal as the work of modern 'confessional' poets.[67] It is unlikely that the poets chose this form simply in order to record moralistic disapproval: rather, the moralizing structures of sonnet sequences were to some degree retrospective, an attempt to impose an external moral order. In some cases, as in Chapman's continuation of Marlowe's *Hero and Leander*, fellow poets cooperated in the work of moralization (nos. 99, 124). Much less plausibly, another of Marlowe's friends, Thomas Nashe, claimed that 'The choise of valentines' (no. 95) was merely written to put him in training for singing the praises of his patron, Lord Strange – who doubtless agreed that the poem presented 'strange moralitie' (no. 95 l. 11).

Humanist scholarship often had difficulties with a particularly vexed difference between Christian and pagan mores, the attitude to homosexuality. Current scholarship warns against anachronism in projecting the twentieth-century concept of homosexuality into a period whose assumptions were different and in which friendship between those of the same sex could assume great intensity.[68] The fact remains that sodomy had been made a capital offence in 1533 and the Protestant reformers had campaigned vigorously for closer regulation of sexual conduct. The humanist interest in antiquity, however, drew attention to very different attitudes. Reading the classics from the perspective of compulsory heterosexuality was always an act of bowdlerization. Erasmus advised teachers of Virgil's second eclogue, in which Corydon declares his love for Alexis, to distract students from its subject-matter by directing their attention to the grammar.[69] Clearly such strategies did not always succeed. Plato, the humanists' favourite amongst classical philosophers, had declared love between men to be more noble and elevated than other kinds. The familiar textbook phrases 'Renaissance Platonism' and 'Neoplatonism' often gloss over this fact, which certainly raised complex questions for commentators like the Florentine Marsilio Ficino. The myth recorded by Plato of a primal androgyne from whom both men and women descended caught the imagination of many poets, including Spenser.[70] Marlowe is alleged to have provocatively compared Christ's relationship with John the Baptist to that of Virgil's Corydon with Alexis. In *Hero and Leander* he presents a pagan world in which orthodox sexual boundaries are constantly undermined. Hero is compared to the androgynous nymph Salmacis, while Leander resembles Jove's favourite Ganymede; when Leander professes to misunderstand Neptune's advances, the god simply smiles (no. 99 l. 677). The eroticism of Neptune's wooing quickly found an imitator in Richard Barnfield, author of the first known English sequence of love-poems to employ a homosexual persona or speaker (nos. 102–3).

In this period of erotic experimentation, Shakespeare began his own sequence of sonnets, most of which are addressed to the man he called 'the Master Mistris of my passion', regrettably 'prickt ... out for womens pleasure' (no. 105). The theme of androgyny is highlighted by the sequence of 'feminine' rhymes ending on unstressed syllables, and by a series of bawdy puns. The description of his friend's penis as 'one thing to my purpose nothing' is probably reinforced by a play on 'nothing' as 'female genitals', and there may be similar bawdy undertones in 'acquainted' and 'controwling'. The poem's verbal restlessness belies its attempts to establish a conventional distinction between heterosexual love and masculine friendship, and later poems to the young man have sexual undertones (for example, no. 110). His affair with the poet's mistress provokes an outpouring of sexual puns (no. 117).

Some of these poems embarrassed the editor of the 1640 text so much that he tampered with the language: thus in Sonnet 108 (no. 351 l. 5) 'boy' became 'love', and some words were converted to feminine forms. The response of later critics has sometimes recalled Erasmus's advice to teachers: they steer discussion away from problematic areas of sexuality in order to get on to the safer ground of rhetorical convention. The compulsion to rearrange the sonnets in a more 'natural' order seems to be a defence against the scandal of finding the national bard tainted by sexual irregularity. Some critics deny the existence of any erotic charge in the poems to the young man, though the 1640 edition suggests that some at least among Shakespeare's early readers were disturbed by this feature. Others argue that Shakespeare invented the bisexual persona as a rhetorical exercise, or as a means of ingratiating himself in an aristocratic circle where homosexuality was fashionable.[71] It would indeed be insensitive to reduce the sonnets to autobiographical outpourings, and to deny their philosophical expansiveness. The relationship with the young man is a complex one, blending the discourses of erotic desire, platonic admiration, male bonding and literary patronage. The 'dark lady' is a systematic inversion of the Petrarchans' blonde paragon. But critics are sometimes over-eager to monumentalize the sonnets as transcendental statements on Love, Beauty and Friendship – or, more recently, Language: such readings gloss over their raw edges, the uneasiness of the transition to the universal from a situation painfully perceived as highly particular. The poet's defiance of conventional opinion pushes him into an 'I am that I am' which blasphemously echoes God's words to Moses (no. 114; Exodus 3:14).

Shakespeare was tired of 'arte made tung-tide by authoritie' (no. 111); and the bishops' ban on dangerous texts in June 1599 included erotic works by Marlowe, Davies and Marston. Even a playful ballad like 'The wanton Wife of Bath' (no. 127) came under suspicion. As has been seen, the authorities' main worry may have been about political rather than sexual matters; but there does also seem to have been public concern from moralists about the wave of libertinism. The debate still continues: with the emergence of feminism, these erotic texts have become liable to censure on somewhat different grounds, as reinforcing an acquisitive, domineering male ego. The vogue in the sixteenth century for the blazon, the detailed enumeration of the parts of a woman's body, can be seen as reflecting the new scientific mentality with its mastering gaze, its passion for mapping the world in order to gain power over it: Donne makes the connection in 'To his Mistress going to bed' (no. 96).[72] Women had to be far more careful about where they directed their gaze (no. 144). There is certainly something proprietary about the way in which Spenser displays his wife's body to the admiring gaze of the 'merchants daughters' (no. 88 l. 167); and the blazon often served as a form of soft – sometimes not so soft – pornography. The strategy was indeed so blatant that it quickly lent itself to self-parody (no. 67) or to milder variations, such as Spenser's transmutation of the anticipated visual pleasure to pastoral scents (no. 84); and the genre could assume spiritual resonances from the blazons in the Song of Solomon, which were frequently allegorized in a religious sense (cp. no. 265). There was an intrinsic gender inequality in the genre, in that praise of the gifts of nature, of external beauty, rather than public virtue was assumed to be especially suited to the confined state of women. Marlowe, however, characteristically broke the boundaries in his comically erotic blazon of Leander (no. 99 ll. 61–89). And on the Continent, where women poets could sometimes be more outspoken, some female blazons of men were written; but Lady Mary Wroth was considerably more restrained than Gaspara Stampa or Louise Labé.

The idea of women as subjects as opposed to objects of poetic praise caused male poets many problems. Donne's mistress seems to be holding out against his rhetoric so effectively that he has to remove his clothes himself, resorting to what the rhetoricians termed 'inartificial proof' – displaying physical evidence to supplement verbal arguments. On the other hand, Leander's barrage of rhetorical arguments is comically disproportionate, for Hero is won already; but to acknowledge this openly would be to expose herself as wanton. In the event, 'her toong tript' in saying 'Come thither' (no. 99 l. 357), and we are left in doubt as to how voluntary the 'trip' may be. Eloquence was much admired in men, but too much eloquence in a woman was traditionally suspect: Venus's impassioned wooing of Adonis (no. 100) has its pathos but also a comic edge, and her moist hand is a sign of unruly desire. However much civic humanists might idealize rhetorical debate among equal citizens, they were rarely prepared to admit women to the public sphere.

The crucial question was not just how the image of women was represented in poetry but how much chance women had of representing themselves. As will be shown, they were starting to do so; but male writers took an ambivalent view of the process. Some of them, it is true, were ready to turn aside from their own amatory monologues and try to represent the voice of women's wrongs; the vogue for the amatory sonnet was accompanied by a great interest in the complaint, the lament of the seduced woman. Shakespeare showed his interest in the genre not only in *A lover's complaint*, which was printed at the end of his sonnet sequence, but also in *Lucrece* (no. 101). Here the wronged woman is conscious of the imbalance in the resources available to men and to women for representing their views. Tarquin is presented in civic humanist terms as epitomizing tyrants' hostility to rhetoric, to open debate, and Lucrece is made to defend such debate, but Tarquin turns from rhetoric to violence. After the rape, seeking a means of articulating her grief, Lucrece looks for a woman whose situation mirrors her own in a painting of the fall of Troy. She is so angry that the painter cannot give the widowed Hecuba 'a tong' that she threatens to scratch out the eyes of Hecuba's tormentors, intervening in the canvas to redress the injustice it depicts. The remainder of the poem explores Lucrece's own search for a tongue; in the climax she gains her voice only at a tragically self-destructive cost. She comes close to naming her assailant as the royal Tarquin only in her final sentence, and in a sudden syntactic twist she evades the name to the end and kills herself, leaving the men to draw the inference and execute their revenge.[73]

Lucrece's self-annihilating agency may be presented as tragic, but male writers were frequently unsympathetic to more direct forms of female self-assertion. In one of his sonnets (no. 87), Spenser has his bride-to-be take control of the images of love; she weaves an image of the poet as a spider and herself as a bee about to be entangled in his 'cunning snare'. The poet's reply is not exactly reassuring: no doubt with an intended playful tone, he compares the pleasures of marriage to flowers adorning a prison cell – an analysis not so far removed from that of radical feminism. The woman is wittily inverting conventional images, for the bee was a traditional figure of the poet, while the spider was said to have originated as a female weaver. In Ovid's *Metamorphoses*, Arachne is a weaver who claims to be as skilful at her craft as the goddess Minerva and challenges her to a competition. Minerva's tapestry portrays the gods as wise, controlling deities; Arachne's tapestry presents them as treacherous and sexually rapacious, but it is every bit as good as Minerva's. Exasperated, Minerva is about to strike her when Arachne puts her head in a noose to hang herself; Minerva spares her life and allows her to continue weaving – but only as a spider. Ovid tells the story with some sympathy for Arachne, and indeed his own endlessly fluid poem in some sense resembles her web, a challenge to the will to finality and dynastic triumph embodied in the epic genre; but Renaissance moralists like the Calvinist translator Arthur Golding moralized the story from the gods' point of view (no. 334). The myth provides a link between verbal representation and gender. Conventional moralists insisted that too much learning was not for women, that they should turn from the pen to the spinning-wheel. In the Arachne myth, a woman takes control of a medium of representation and uses it to criticize authority; Minerva, by contrast, had been born directly from her father Jupiter's head, and represented a form of creativity which was directly under masculine control. Spenser was fascinated by the story, narrating it directly in *Muiopotmos* and alluding to it again in the Bower of Blisse episode of *The Faerie Queene*, where the enchantress Acrasia with her 'subtile web' is compared to Arachne (no. 80 l. 70). The tapestries in the wicked enchanter Busirane's house echo Arachne's (no. 82 ll. 19–144, no. 334 ll. 117–51). (In another sonnet (no. 83) it is Spenser whose web of courtship is compared to a spider's.)

Spenser's presentation of the relations between the sexes is complex, however. In libertine poetry, love becomes so much a projection of anarchic individual desires that it turns to idolatry (cp. the claim of Marston's narrator to prefer an image to a real woman, no. 125). *The Faerie Queene* abounds in male figures whose fetishistic relationship with their loved ones, their desire to map the mistress's body precisely, becomes a cruel idolatry. The enchanter Busirane is defeated by the active woman Britomart (no. 82). By giving her many associations with Minerva, however, Spenser emphasizes her fidelity to an ultimately masculine order. His response to the libertines is to champion the 'companionate' marriage. In the Renaissance there was increasing idealization of marriages in which husband and wife were brought together by spiritual affinity rather than merely by dynastic property relations: thus Henry King could make a point of mourning his wife as his 'Freind' (no. 318). The Protestant emphasis on spiritual equality, though certainly not its sole cause, was one motivation behind this change.[74] Spenser's *Amoretti* sequence ends, unconventionally, with an epithalamium, and one written not for a great patron but for the poet himself; similarly, the climax of his legend of Courtesy celebrates his own wife rather than the Queen (no. 348). The poem to some degree questions conventional double standards of sexuality, representing chastity as an ideal which is relevant for both sexes. Generative power is celebrated above chastity, and Spenser places a discreetly veiled celebration of the female genitals at the mid-point of the first part of his epic (no. 81 ll. 127–35). In thus exalting affective relations above the public sphere – and implicitly suggesting that the unmarried state of the Virgin Queen was perhaps not so ideal – he was also insisting on his wife's confinement to a private realm.[75] Katherine Philips wrote of an unmarried friend:

> She is a publick Deity,
> And were't not very odd
> She should depose her self to be
> A petty Houshold God?
> (no. 173 ll. 5–8)

Many historians have debated the question of how far women's lives were enriched or confined by the new marital ideals; inevitably there are many different answers.[76] Spenser's poetry does seem to have been popular with female readers: he gained the patronage of some leading women aristocrats.

Donne's poetry of the 1590s, by contrast, often seems designed to shock ladylike sensibilities. In 'His Picture' (no. 132), the speaker presents a kind of counter-blazon of his own body, imagining himself on his return from the wars as a grotesque 'sack of bones'. This self-image is presented as ultimately truer than the idealizing portrait he will soon outgrow, so that the poem is designed to wean the woman toward a more 'tough' aesthetic (cp. Jonson's portrayal of his grotesque body, no. 142). If that toughness often seems aggressive, reducing the woman's body to a terrain to be colonized, his cartographical conceits can also indicate the delicacy and vulnerability of a mutual relationship, the mapped globe quivering with the surface tension of a tear (no. 136; see further Section 4). The greater complexity of some of the lyrics in comparison with the 'Elegies' is often ascribed to Donne's marriage to Ann More, which lost him his employer's favour, so that the marriage relationship had to bear much of the weight of his earlier aspirations to the public world. Donne's marriage, at least in its early years, may indeed have had a crucial effect; Ann was descended from Sir Thomas More, and repeated puns on 'More' in his lyrics (no. 135) connect his love with utopian exploration. There is no hard and fast evidence, however, to make a complete chronological divide between the poet of 1590s libertinism and the poet of companionate marriage, and the narrative thus constructed by critics may seem too much like Chapman's capping Marlowe's libertine narrative with a ceremonious marriage. What Donne's verse does suggest is that the dialogue between assertive masculine libertinism and a more mutual ideal of love, whether or not tied down to marriage, was taking place within individuals and not just between opposing schools of writers.

The censorship restrictions of 1599 seem to have had an effect in quelling the popularity of libertine verse. Donne himself had none of his love-poetry printed in his lifetime. When his collected poems eventually appeared in

1633, they had an immense impact. Thomas Carew's famous tribute (no. 365) presents all subsequent love-poetry as weak and derivative. It is certainly true that no later love-poet of the period commanded the same range; Carew's own erotic verse is strongly indebted to Donne (cp. nos. 96 and 156). The 'school of Donne', of whom the most significant was Abraham Cowley, were able to reproduce his witty analogies but not his subtlety and range.

In the growing political polarization of the 1620s and 1630s, opponents of royal policies tended to associate sexual libertinism with the court and to affirm a strict morality. The libertine poems of Carew, who had held a minor court post, were listed as a grievance of the realm in a petition to the Long Parliament in 1640. While censured by Puritans, however, courtiers like Carew, Suckling and Davenant, with their erratic private lives and unstable religious views, were not popular with the severe Archbishop Laud. There was always a potential tension between their sceptical tempers and their role as court poets celebrating the marital purity of the King and Queen.[77] Richard Lovelace, best known today for lyrics which associate royalist honour with gallant love, could also allude knowingly to female masturbation (nos. 164, 166, 167). Beneath the idealizing façade of Caroline courtly discourse, the concerns of Restoration verse were emerging.

Such differences of emphasis were of little significance to Puritans like Milton, however. Rejecting courtly poetic fashions, he turned back to Spenser, though he eventually pushed the Spenserian championship of companionate marriage in a more radical direction. The celebration of the element of individual choice and ideological commitment in marriage, as opposed to simply accepting the marital bond out of reverence for custom, carried with it the implication that divorce might be the best solution for a marriage that proved unsuitable. Milton saw the tracts he published in defence of divorce in the 1640s as directly parallel to his defences of freedom of the press and of a republican constitution: all these changes offered a greater dignity to individual choices over prearranged conventions.

But choice for whom? Women were not granted the same degree of autonomy as men in their society. They were endlessly addressed in Renaissance poetry; they were hymned, abused, exhorted, enticed, cajoled; but their chances for answering back in verse were limited. Feminists have asked whether women had a Renaissance, and some have answered in the negative.[78] Though some early humanists championed education for women, the humanist programme was designed above all as a qualification for entry into the public world: since women were denied a public political identity, their education was sharply circumscribed. The growing emphasis on marriage as woman's central role heightened the split between public and private spheres, relegating many characteristic female activities to a private margin. Despite such restrictions, many women did embrace learning as the 'key' to escape 'that prison' of their 'Sex' (no. 231 ll. 37–8); just how many has only become fully apparent with the recent revival of feminist scholarship.[79]

Male prejudices against female intellectuals remained strong, however, as Rachel Speght recorded (no. 359), and those who made their mark normally had the additional support of high social rank or an exceptionally strong religious conviction. Even those of noble birth tended to shy away from writing love-poetry, a kind of assertion of sexual agency, a control of the images, which society still frowned on. If even Sir Philip Sidney was defensive about writing love-sonnets rather than some more serious kind of verse, his sister Mary confined herself mainly to translations. The very uncertainty of how to name her reflects the tensions inherent in her public role. With her marriage, her identity was officially subsumed in her husband's: she became Countess of Pembroke. Some contemporaries, however, continued to describe her as Mary Sidney, but this name itself subsumed her under another identity, authorizing her writings as a continuation of her brother's projects. In her dedication of the Psalm translations to Elizabeth (no. 31), she defers to superior authority: she has merely completed a task begun by her brother, the translation is itself far inferior to the original and, as a woman addressing a monarch, she concedes that her poetic lines break through the lines conventionally constricting female conduct. She authorizes this activity by comparing poetry to the appropriately female activity of weaving, though this move in turn is carefully qualified by making Sidney responsible for the warp while she contributed the woof. But she has a further authorization for her utterance in the Queen's own transcendence of traditional social roles by her personal merit as ruler and as writer – 'Men drawne *by worth* a woman to obay' (no. 31 l. 83; emphasis added).[80] She is able to make her own the denunciatory, prophetic power of David's voice.

Dynastic legitimation certainly helped female poets, especially those who tackled secular themes. The first major sonnet sequence by a woman appeared in a romance by Lady Mary Wroth, the niece of Sir Philip Sidney and the Countess of Pembroke and daughter of Sir Robert Sidney. Wroth signalled her Sidney connections by using the Sidney coat of arms, her father's rank as Earl being considered to overrule her marital status. She closed the circle of her Sidney connections even more defiantly after her husband's death by having two children by the Countess of Pembroke's son, the third Earl of Pembroke. Her boldness in committing her writings to print provoked a bitter attack from Lord Denny, who contrasted her 'lascivious tales and amorous toyes' with her aunt who had 'translated so many godly books and especially the holly psalmes of David'.[81] Wroth's sonnets are hardly 'lascivious'. Her poetic persona was the constant but unrequited lover, and in her reshaping of the stock conventions of love-poetry we can see the pressures of the emergent social roles prescribed for women. Where Sir Philip Sidney often sees love, however mockingly, as a distraction from affairs of State, Wroth's poems centre on the situation of retreating into a shaded, private world and waiting for some sign of affection. Although her Pamphilia adopts the role of the patient, constant platonic lover rejecting male fickleness, Wroth herself seems to have acknowledged that that role could be a trap. The darkening tone of the *Urania* accords with the disillusion reigning among many Jacobean courtiers by the second decade of the reign, and manifested more directly by other members of the Sidney connection such as William Browne. The woman's role of retreat could acquire a further public resonance. The shifts in tone and diction in Wroth's poetry work through these complex intertwinings of the public and the private: her verse was her Ariadne's thread (no. 145).

Wroth belonged to a circle of prominent Jacobean women patrons who maintained the poetic and political interests of the old Leicester–Sidney and Essex circles and helped to maintain a community of female authorship. Though the old Essex faction had been disgraced by the 1601 rebellion, many of them found a favourable reception at the court of Queen Anne, who maintained considerable independence from her husband. The Countess of Bedford, whose husband had been involved in the rebellion, was an important patron for Donne (no. 188 and its note), Daniel (no. 231), Jonson (no. 232) and Gorges, and herself wrote poetry. When Æmilya Lanyer published her collection *Salve deus rex Judæorum* in 1611, she addressed poems to this charmed circle, led by the Countess of Pembroke, whose Psalm translations she praised. Lanyer's bids for patronage seem to have been unsuccessful, however, and the collection betrays her anxieties.

There is an instructive difference between Lanyer's 'The Description of Cooke-ham' (no. 189) and Jonson's 'To Penshurst' (no. 190). Though the credit for inventing the genre of the country-house poem has traditionally gone to Jonson, Lanyer's poem may well precede his. But where Jonson celebrates a confident and easy relationship with his patron Sir Robert Sidney, Lanyer's poem reflects the less stable relations involved in a woman's seeking patronage from a female patron. She appeals for a renewal of former patronage to the Countess of Cumberland, who, despite her elevated rank, herself held a somewhat precarious status. Her estranged husband had cut off her daughter from succession to the earldom's estates, and the Countess was under great pressure to abandon her attempts to gain her daughter what she considered her rights.[82] When Lanyer looks back to the time of their association, it is to recall a shared activity of reading and study. Her invocation of the harmony between patron and nature conventionally assimilates the discourses of love and of patronage, but her gender complicates the relationship. She invokes a utopian solidarity in which the client shared a common cause with her female patrons in the process of studying the Bible. She laments that social distance has now reasserted itself: 'rich' though they may be, the ties of obligation between patron and client are still 'chaines' (l. 210). She makes a bold opposition between 'degree' and 'love', in which 'the lowest alwayes are above', and her immediate apology for her boldness only prepares the way for a further challenge (ll. 106–10, 111–13):

> But whither am I carried in conceit?
> My Wit too weake to conster of the great.
> Why not?

The same questioning note informs Pilate's wife's apology for Eve:

> . . . why should you disdaine
> Our beeing your equals, free from tyranny?
> (no. 266 ll. 67–8)

Such questions were posed more urgently during the upheavals of the 1640s and 1650s. Women engaged in political activity as petitioners and protesters, and increasing numbers demanded a greater role in religious life. The Protestant belief that the divine voice, like Christ's, could emanate from any social station, however lowly, could give authority to the voice of women prophets. John Foxe had celebrated courageous women like Anne Askew (no. 248) in his catalogue of Protestant martyrs. Even here, an elevated social background certainly helped: the most prominent female prophet and poet of the pre-revolutionary period, Lady Eleanor Douglas, invoked her noble birth as well as divine inspiration as a sanction for provocative denunciations of King Charles and his allies. In the 1640s and 1650s, however, many women began taking a more active role in their sects.[83] Anna Trapnel aroused great wonder and admiration for her ability to improvise lengthy verse commentaries on the prophetic books of Scripture; these were transcribed and widely circulated (no. 304).

The fact that the number of publications by women rose sharply during the turbulent decades from 1640 to 1660 does not necessarily mean that the women in question welcomed the revolution. The Caroline court had provided a space for female literary activity and patronage which was now lost; and An Collins, Katherine Philips and Margaret Cavendish, Duchess of

Newcastle, were all in differing degrees critical of the new republic. And yet their boldness of thinking went beyond the pre-war era. Cavendish's verse was the most aristocratic in tone, insisting through her own self-assertion as a woman on her wealthy husband's noble status. Even while rejecting traditional forms and vindicating female self-expression, she appealed to an aristocratic magnanimity:

> ... that seemes *Noble*, which is *Easie*, *Free*,
> Not to be bound with ore-nice *Pedantry*.
> (no. 371 ll. 7–8)

But Cavendish was willing to challenge many orthodoxies. Unable to empathize with the expansive imaginations of many male contemporaries, she turned her quest for new worlds inward (no. 219); her concern about the despoliation of nature by an aggressive modernizing consciousness anticipates the themes of feminist ecology (no. 220).[84] Philips came from a Puritan background and her husband was a parliamentarian, but she moved in royalist literary circles. Her portrayal of the monarchy's apparently terminal crisis, however, was ambivalent rather than purely elegiac (no. 47). She responded to Donne's imagery of finding new social worlds, and her lyrics explore a new kind of female utopia, a space free of patriarchal influences (nos. 173, 244–6). Like Cavendish, she responded to the age's political turbulence with a heightened sensitivity to the natural world; there are similarities between their works and Marvell's, and the traditional assumption that Marvell must have been the originator has been strongly questioned.[85] Philips was to become the first Englishwoman to have a dramatic work publicly performed (1663). Aphra Behn was about to begin her career as a dramatist. Though their gains were by no means secure, women writers had shown that they could make their mark in the public sphere.

4: RHETORIC, POETRY AND PHILOSOPHY

Spenser's Bower of Blisse (no. 80) is a place of female temptation and also of rhetoric. Acrasia's Arachne-like weaving severs the power of representation from its divine function of mirroring eternal truths. She is in league with Archimago, a villainous fabricator of deceitful images. Her veil serves to entice rather than enlighten, and she leaves the 'signes' of identity on the knights' shields 'fowly ra'st' and turns them into debasedly sensuous 'figures', surrendering themselves to the pleasures of the body in a world of 'vile difference'. Guyon and the Palmer destroy the Bower in the name of economy: Verdant is 'wastfull' in spending his days, goods and body in dalliance, abandoning his chances of 'advauncement'. In disfiguring the Bower, Guyon moves from sign to thing signified, from concrete to abstract, and this is also presented as a move from feminine to masculine. The very violence of the move, registered in the hissing sibilants of ll. 118–26, seems to betray a certain unease. Spenser himself proceeds by transforming abstract concepts into concrete 'figures', and his own style could well be regarded as wasteful in its rhetorical profusion: this is in fact the longest canto in the poem. Spenser was an enormously 'uneconomical' poet in linguistic terms: this particular passage contains seven words not previously recorded by *The Oxford English Dictionary*, and, despite his reputation for 'archaisms', the majority of his usages were innovative.[86] It could be argued that Spenser is projecting on to the female figure of Acrasia his own anxiety about his role as a poet, which itself involves a retreat from direct public actions. The anxiety was widespread: poetry, declares Daniel's Philocosmus, 'unmans you quite' (no. 353 l. 22). Acrasia's gaze has a castrating effect, parting Verdant from his 'warlike armes' which become 'idle instruments' hanging on a tree; it takes the combined efforts of Guyon and the Palmer with his 'vertuous staffe' to restore him.[87]

Much Renaissance poetry does indeed betray a certain unease about its own status, and a concomitant will to master the enticing differences of language and flatten them into a clear-cut meaning. Carew praised Donne for a 'masculine expression' which could make 'Our stubborne language' bend to his 'imperious wit' (no. 365 ll. 39–50). Such will to mastery has been seen by feminist critics as characteristic of an increasingly assertive patriarchal attitude, which accompanied the rapacious individualism and the calculating rationalism of the Renaissance. There is some force in this analysis; but, like other generalizations about Renaissance individualism, it needs qualification. It can be argued that the Renaissance was characterized by a heightened sensitivity to the texture of language, by a challenge to the arrogance of those who would struggle to master it too easily. In fact, 'conceited' poetry of the kind represented in England by Donne and his school came in for just such criticism from the poet William Drummond, who complained that they had carried their 'reformation' of poetry too far, and had 'endevured to abstracte her [poetry: note the female personification] to Metaphysicall Ideas, and Scholasticall Quiddityes'.[88]

The terms of Drummond's argument here are very significant. The 'metaphysical' label is now so familiar that we are in danger of missing its original point. It emerged not as a complimentary but as a derogatory label, and it evoked a whole discourse of hostility to metaphysics. Humanism, as has been seen, originated in a defence of rhetoric against scholastic philosophy. Abstract metaphysics was attacked because it was too generalized and detached from the practical concerns of the active life, and one aspect of this abstraction was its insensitivity to language. The scholastics – rather like some twentieth-century linguistic philosophers – had tried to purify everyday language of its imperfections and invent a new set of technical terms which would permit the precise delimitation of concepts without the intervention of irrelevant connotations. The humanists insisted that at least in the areas of practical reasoning, of ethical and political questions, it was futile to try to 'purify' language in this way, because the crucial answers had to be related to particular human contexts, and language was the most subtle and precise instrument for engaging the practical choices.[89] Poetry and rhetoric were not just inferior supplements to philosophy or theology but were media on the very cutting edge of intellectual inquiry, capable of taking on and even surpassing abstract discursive thought. The poet, wrote Sidney, 'yieldeth to the powers of the mind an image of that whereof the philosopher bestoweth but a wordish description'.[90] And he went on the counter-offensive, enlisting the philosopher Plato on behalf of the poets: 'in the body of his work, though the inside and strength were philosophy, the skin, as it were, and beauty depended most of poetry: for all standeth upon dialogues'.[91] (Plato's uneasiness with rhetoric perhaps leaves a trace, however, in the suggestion that poetry's beauty is but skin-deep.) The poet, wrote Sidney, was a 'right popular philosopher'.[92]

Such glorification of dramatic dialogue over philosophical monologue was a powerful intellectual incentive for Elizabethan poets to write for the public stage, and much of the period's non-dramatic poetry works as a dialogue. Milton continued this humanist tradition in proposing an ideal syllabus which would turn from the 'most intellective abstractions of Logick & metaphysicks' to a greater concern with language, which was 'obvious to the sence'. Pride of place must go to rhetoric and to poetry, which was 'more simple, sensuous and passionate' than prose – note the emphasis on the sensuous, bodily character of poetry.[93] When Milton wrote that Spenser was 'a better teacher then *Scotus* or *Aquinas*',[94] he was making the same kind of opposition between poetry and metaphysics as Drummond.

In response to this philosophical turn to language, Renaissance rhetoricians scrutinized the details of verbal texture and figuration with a minuteness that makes even twentieth-century techniques of 'close reading' look vague and impressionistic.[95] In modern criticism, metaphor has become the dominant figure to the extent of eclipsing virtually all others with the possible exception of metonymy; Renaissance criticism listed hundreds of figures.[96] Editors of poetic and dramatic texts were not content simply to gloss unfamiliar words: they would also note significant figures and rhetorical strategies. Absurdly elaborate as the received rhetorical terminology may seem today, Renaissance readers would perhaps react to the dominant modern critical vocabulary rather as some inhabitants of the Arctic Circle might do on discovering that English has only one word for 'snow'. These terms may seem abstract rather than 'sensuous' to us; but in the translations offered by George Puttenham – significantly, to a female audience, for whom too much erudition was considered unbecoming – we can see the exuberant physicality that underlay these apparently very abstract terms in their original languages. He rendered metaphor as the 'figure of transport', and other figures included the 'changeling', the 'middlemarcher', the 'fleering frumpe', the 'privie nippe', the 'dismembrer', the 'rebound', the 'crossecoople', the 'underlay'.[97] The word 'figure' evoked a physical form or shape; a 'trope' was a 'turning'. The word 'scheme' was said by one rhetorician to be derived from the movement made by a victorious dancer,[98] and schemes were the figures that made language dance; metre was included among the schemes.

In this insistence on the bodily characteristics of language, in fact, Renaissance humanists can be said to have something in common with post-modern and feminist writers who have tried to reaffirm rhetorical play against philosophical asceticism. Rather like the humanists, they have attacked the aridities of metaphysics and have tried to break down the clear-cut distinctions between philosophy, rhetoric and poetry.[99] And some Renaissance poets seem to verge on the post-modern outlook. Marlowe's *Hero and Leander* (no. 99) presents a world where there is no absolute truth, only a series of different rhetorics. The hero is like 'a bold sharpe Sophister'; the barrage of arguments he uses against virginity parodies the certainties of scholastic logic. Like Arachne's web, the pictures in the temple represent the gods in an extremely unfavourable light. And the inset fable presents Mercury, the god of rhetoric, as a figure of political and moral subversion, overthrowing the king of the gods. Mercury was the god of the market-place, the place where ideas are exchanged by the medium of words and goods by the medium of money, and where in each case the values involved seem totally arbitrary. We know that Marlowe was arrested for coining – usurping the authority of the monarch to stamp coins with the signs of legitimacy – and there is a similar impulse in his poem's sceptical scrutiny of traditional signs and representations. The fragmentary status of Marlowe's poem may well be deliberate: he refuses to carry the story to a tragic conclusion that would permit a traditional moral. The poem dissolves the normal categories of linear narrative, social order and personal identity.

It is not surprising that Marlowe scandalized his contemporaries. In general, rhetoric played a more conservative social role, with the emphasis on maintaining rather than subverting social order. This could be done by emphasizing the principle of decorum: language could be integrated with the rules of social honour and dishonour in a hierarchical society.[100] In his completion of Marlowe's poem, Chapman brought in '*Comelinesse*', decorum, along with Morality, as attendants on Ceremony, the goddess who 'all estates of men distinguisheth' (no. 124 ll.134–5): these figures turn arbitrary currency into 'civill forms' in tune with the order of nature. The rules of decorum in Renaissance England prescribed that princes were to be described in a 'high' style, country people in a 'low' or plain style. Poems were to observe principles of precedence in their structure: thus a description of a ruler might often be positioned at the middle line of a poem, and the moral disorder of Busirane's house is revealed by the way aristocrats are 'heap'd together with the vulgar sort' on its tapestries (no. 82 l. 164). In practice, however, such neat distinctions were hard to maintain: arguments about just what counted as decorum were ultimately circular, implying a previous ideological agreement. Classical writers of the republican era might insist on a sharp dividing-line between the élite and the plebeians, but they would have regarded the more extravagant encomia which Renaissance poets showered on their princes as somewhat indecorous. Christian ideology cut across classical divisions between high and low: Christ provided a pattern for authentic popular speech which could be imitated by the poetry of pastoral complaint and by prophets like Anna Trapnel (no. 304). Women poets challenged some standards of decorum by their very existence. It is hard to know exactly how to interpret the decorum of Marvell's placing Charles I at the centre of a poem praising a regicide (no. 45). Like so many concepts in the period, the principle of decorum was open to debate.

Reason was at least as important in constraining rhetorical invention as social custom. In recent literary theory, the opposition between rhetoric and philosophy has been pushed so far that rhetoric comes to be seen as the subversion of any process of rational communication.[101] Few Renaissance poets were prepared to go so far; they were concerned with the pragmatic, communicative aspects of language and, while they wanted logic to be more relevant to practical argumentation, they certainly did not advocate its overthrow.[102] Renaissance rhetoricians brought together the logical and verbal sides of their art. In the Middle Ages, 'elocution', the art of verbal ornamentation, had tended to develop in separation from logical argument; 'rhetoric' in popular parlance today often refers simply to figures of speech. It had a much wider meaning for the Renaissance, which restored the classical integrity of the art, with 'invention' – finding arguments – and 'disposition' – structuring arguments – preceding 'elocution' and the other two parts of rhetoric, 'memory' and 'action' or gesture.[103] Renaissance editions of literary texts would regularly provide breakdowns of their arguments as well as analyses of their elocution or figures of speech. Some logicians in the sixteenth century began to argue that invention and disposition actually belonged with logic rather than rhetoric, that there was no such thing as a separate rhetorical mode of argumentation; Abraham Fraunce used Spenser's eclogues as central examples of logical debate.[104] Whatever the demarcation disputes between the different arts, an interest in strategies of reasoning was central to the period. The more writers learned about the power of rhetoric to deceive and dazzle, the more of an interest they would find in being able to disentangle an opponent's fallacious arguments and deceitful images: in modern terms, to criticize ideology.

That tension between rhetoric and logic helps to explain the dualism, the split between the intellectual and the sensuous, which has been noted in the Bower of Blisse episode. Spenser's reader is expected to be able to demystify, to be alert to deceptive images and arguments. Yet the poem's movement is dialectical rather than merely schematic. Guyon is not necessarily the ideal reader, for his responses are somewhat rigid, and the force of his resistance to Acrasia's bodily allurements may reflect his limitations: alone of the protagonists, he is not in love. Reading the poem becomes a long-term process rather than a communion with static types of beauty; readers are both invited to lose themselves in this 'golden world', to respond to the sensuous properties of the language, and jerked back into contact with their own world, encouraged to paraphrase what they have been reading. The value of the experience lies in the process rather than in the paraphrasable content. Spenser would not have subscribed to the claim of some twentieth-century writers and critics that 'A poem should not mean/But be';[105] it must both mean and be, and must resist too simple a movement from the one to the other.

The apparent dualism of such an attitude to poetry, the split between form and content, led critics like F. R. Leavis to disparage Spenser and Milton at the expense of Donne and the metaphysicals; but it was precisely on the grounds of dualism that poets in the Spenserian tradition criticized the metaphysicals. Drummond complained that they made poetry a mere vehicle for 'Scholasticall Quiddityes'; Milton attacked the 'late fantasticks' who failed to give their ideas the 'gay'st attire' of language (no. 363 ll. 20–1). This was in turn a misunderstanding, of Donne if not of some of his lesser followers: Donne was too recent and too powerful a precursor for Milton to be able to engage with him properly. But it is true that Donne repeatedly dismisses conventional poetic taste as effeminate, as too much bound up with the body, and presents himself as the poet of pure mind. In 'To his Mistress going to bed' (no. 96), the stripping away of the woman's clothes matches the poet's quest for a less ornate style of love-poetry – though it is noteworthy that he sees men rather than women as liable to be deceived by mere externality. Donne is fond of figures drawn from the prelinguistic, deductive science of geometry. But he is more an 'anti-metaphysical' than a 'metaphysical' poet. His poems constantly explore the difficulties of relationship by means of the difficulties of representation. The cartographer's geometry has a totally different logic in two and in three dimensions (no. 136 ll. 10–16), the lovers' convex tears try to mirror each other but must acknowledge failure.[106]

Donne may draw attention to the argumentative structures of his poems, as in 'Loves growth' (no. 135): 'I scarce beleeve', 'But if', 'And yet', 'If'. The case the poem makes is not a rigorously logical one, however: the speaker is working with enthymemes, the merely approximate arguments of rhetorical proof, rather than the logician's syllogisms. He begins, after all, by blithely assuring us that he has 'lyed all winter', so we are hardly prepared to take his words at face value. The poem works by assertion and counter-assertion: he insists that his love has changed but is also keen to deny that change may entail decay and death, so that by line 15 he is protesting that it only seems subjectively to have changed, and his final declaration that the winter will not change his love takes us back to the previous winter's lies. The argument is clinched by a series of analogies, which were considered by Renaissance logicians to represent a low level of proof. Critics have made much of Renaissance beliefs in natural analogies between the human body and the world at large, which meant that metaphor and simile might have a literal truth; but it should also be remembered that rhetorical training encouraged a profound scepticism about the literal truth of any analogy. In any case, literal truth, for the rhetorician, is not the point: analogies are significant because they involve the emotional nuances which are more significant for exploring concrete human relations than metaphysical categories. It is in the way he uses his far-fetched analogies or 'conceits', rather than the conceits themselves, that Donne stands out so sharply from his lesser imitators.

The poem firmly challenges scholastic aspirations to other-worldly transcendence. The speaker's love is not a 'quintessence', a fifth element that could transcend the material mutability of the other four: rather than 'pure, and abstract', it is material, 'mixt of all stuffes, paining soule, or sense'. Donne deploys the language of the humanist exaltation of the active life: 'Love sometimes would contemplate, sometimes do.' In a bawdy pun, 'doing' or making love becomes an exemplum of the active life in the world. But the element of phallic boasting so often found in Donne's poetry is tempered by the ensuing 'And yet': what is at issue is not the physical 'growth' of, among other things, the poet's erection, but the revelation of ever-new facets of the original relationship, and these are now figured by the stars around the sun, the budding blossoms, and the ever-increasing circles spreading from the loved one. A buried sexual pun in 'concentrique' counters Donne's phallicism by placing the woman's body at the centre. In the traditional cosmology the spheres are fixed and perfect, the earth mutable and imperfect; Donne makes the expanding ripples of love part of a process rather than a static perfection. Yet such an acknowledgement readmits the possibility of decay, and in a final bid to dispel such doubts Donne resorts to one of his dazzling switches of discourse:

> As princes doe in times of action get
> New taxes, and remit them not in peace,
> No winter shall abate the springs encrease.

Not being timeless, Donne's love cannot be shut up in the closed economy of the household, the *oikos*, for the 'economy' is increasingly being perceived as an impersonal mechanism that mediates between individual and State. And we realize that on one level this is a poem about inflation: the inflation of language in the lover's hyperboles as well as the inflation caused by the internecine competition of nation-states. In such a world there is no stable currency, words cannot become the reliable counters for timeless concepts towards which the scholastics aspired. Yet the poem's rueful wit at the end does not imply disillusion: the lovers can still make their own commitment, can dedicate their love to embracing and outdoing the world's changes rather than flying from them. Donne's love is made more by spring, it 'cures all sorrow/With more': it may be that his poem's language finds its own precarious moment of stability in addressing his wife, Ann More.

The humanist commitment to rhetoric, then, cuts across conventional oppositions between literary schools. It remains true that the later part of the period sees an increasingly sharp reaction against the deceitful properties of language, a movement towards ideals of plainness in style. This movement reflects in part a loss of confidence in the public ceremonious language of the court and, more generally, the emergence of rationalist currents of thought. In *Leviathan* (1651), Thomas Hobbes took geometry rather than rhetoric as his model for political science, and scathingly anatomized the errors caused by the misuse of language. In the best poetry of the period, however, there is always a tension between the desire to subordinate language to an unambiguous meaning and an awareness of the medium's productive resistances.

In Fulke Greville and his friend Samuel Daniel we can trace a persistent wrestling with the question of poetic truth and poetic artifice. Daniel wrote an interesting defence of rhymed verse, and yet his own poetic practice reveals a certain scepticism about the validity of imposing external rhyme structures on rational argument (cp. nos. 194, 353). Ben Jonson, who railed only half-ironically against over-ornate verse forms (no. 354), tended to compose his poems in prose before casting them into verse. Verse was no mere external ornament for him, however. In the Cary–Morison ode (no. 315) the 'lines of life' become the cosmic dance and the workings of his own adaptation of the Pindaric form, and at the poem's most audacious moment (ll. 84–5) the enjambment from stanza to stanza, pivoting on an ambiguously placed period, suspends his massive bulk between heaven and earth.[107]

Jonson's 'plainness' is very different from that of the Puritan George Wither with his sharply antagonistic attitudes to religious and poetic forms. Wither aimed at plainness of a rather different kind, presenting his poetry as the spontaneous overflowing of a spiritual essence, a 'VOICE', which transcended the material 'Forme' of language (no. 369 ll. 19–21). Wither's 'loose', spontaneous style, repudiating conventional formal structures, has led to his being compared to modern confessional writers, even to William Burroughs.[108] Yet Wither was careful to insist that his inspiration was not 'immediate' and that care was needed to articulate his visions in poetic language (in fact the poem's stanzas are formally structured as sonnets). The poet's particular gift, he said, was to move the emotions through language, by catching

> At all advantages of *Place* and *Time*,
> Of *Actions*, or *Expressions*; . . .
> (no. 369 ll. 62–3)

These are the skills of the orator, mediating between universal truths and particular human contexts.

Wither may not have been quite as spontaneously disorderly as he sometimes liked to claim, but his poetry did represent an extreme face of individualism. It enacted on a formal level that process of breaking free from traditional rituals which the Puritan revolutionaries were putting into practice. Conservatives responded by insisting on more decorous modes of poetic and religious formality. Waller praised the remodelling of St Paul's Cathedral under King Charles in revealing terms: the building

... Spouse-like may with comly grace command
More then by force of argument or hand.
For doubtfull reason few can apprehend,
And war brings ruine, where it should amend.
But beauty with a bloodlesse conquest findes
A welcome sovereignty in rudest mindes.
(no. 290 ll. 37–42)

In such self-consciously temperate verse, the unsettling conflicts between rhetoric and logic, beauty and deceit, that motivated so much Renaissance poetry are subsiding. It would not become a gentleman to be too logical in matters of religion, and the beauty of rhetoric has lost its associations with visionary harmony or with energetic argumentation and has become the domestic composure of a good wife, reassuringly subordinated to her husband's authority. The closed couplets and the antithetical patterning admit a degree of obtrusive artifice but keep it under firm control. To the later seventeenth century, such poetry seemed to look forward from the immediate turmoil of the Civil War to a new era of refinement and social concord. In surveying the huge, and often disorderly, variety of Renaissance verse, it may also be thought that much was lost in that process of refinement.

NOTES TO THE INTRODUCTION

1. Many points in the Introduction are argued more fully in David Norbrook, *Poetry and Politics in the English Renaissance*, 1984. In a general survey of this kind it is impossible to make full acknowledgement of the many critical works that have been drawn on, but the notes refer readers to books which will provide fuller guidance, and further reading is also recommended in the editions referred to in the textual notes.
2. Thomas Pestell, quoted in A. J. Smith (ed.), *John Donne: The Critical Heritage*, 1975, p. 108.
3. Drayton, 'To the Reader', in *The barons warres, Poems*, 1619, sig. [2A2r]. On the creation of fictive worlds, see Harry Berger, Jr., 'The Renaissance Imagination: Second World and Green World', in *Second World and Green World: Studies in Renaissance Fiction-Making*, selected and arranged, with an introduction, by John Patrick Lynch, Berkeley, Los Angeles and London 1988, pp. 3–40.
4. Sir Philip Sidney, *A Defence of Poetry*, in *Miscellaneous Prose of Sir Philip Sidney*, ed. Katherine Duncan-Jones and Jan van Dorsten, Oxford 1973, p. 78.
5. See, for example, the critiques of 'humanism' in Francis Barker, *The Tremulous Private Body: Essays on Subjection*, 1984, and Catherine Belsey, *The Subject of Tragedy: Identity and Difference in Renaissance Drama*, 1985.

6. Cp. Peter Stallybrass, 'Patriarchal Territories: The Body Enclosed', in Margaret W. Ferguson, Maureen Quilligan and Nancy J. Vickers (eds.), *Rewriting the Renaissance: The Discourses of Sexual Difference in Early Modern Europe*, Chicago and London 1986, pp. 123–42.
7. Cp. G. W. Pigman III, *Grief and English Renaissance Elegy*, Cambridge 1985, pp. 47–52; Pigman offers a valuable survey of elegiac conventions.
8. Karl Josef Höltgen, *Aspects of the Emblem: Studies in the English Emblem Tradition and the European Context*, Kassel 1986, pp. 82–90, notes that Donne's patron Lord Hay used the compass figure with the King at the centre and the courtier on the circumference.
9. Christopher Hill, 'The Word "Revolution"', in *A Nation of Change and Novelty: Radical Politics, Religion and Literature in Seventeenth-Century England*, London and New York 1990, pp. 82–101.
10. Sidney, *A Defence of Poetry*, p. 74.
11. See Joel Altman, *The Tudor Play of Mind: Rhetorical Inquiry and the Development of Elizabethan Drama*, Berkeley, Los Angeles and London 1978.
12. See R. R. Bolgar, *The Classical Heritage and its Beneficiaries*, Cambridge 1954.
13. Thomas M. Greene, 'Petrarch and the Humanist Hermeneutic', in *The Light in Troy: Imitation and Discovery in Renaissance Poetry*, New Haven and London 1982, pp. 81–103.
14. J. G. A. Pocock, *The Ancient Constitution and the Feudal Law: A Study of English Historical Thought in the Seventeenth Century*, reissue, Cambridge 1987; James Harrington, *The Commonwealth of Oceana*, in J. G. A. Pocock (ed.), *The Political Works of James Harrington*, Cambridge 1977, pp. 161ff. and *passim*. On criticism and critique, see Paul Connerton, *The Tragedy of Enlightenment: An Essay on the Frankfurt School*, Cambridge 1980, pp. 16ff.
15. G. W. Pigman III, 'Versions of Imitation in the Renaissance', *Renaissance Quarterly*, 33 (1980), 1–32.
16. On this sense of possession by the past, see D. J. Gordon, 'Giannotti, Michelangelo and the Cult of Brutus', in *The Renaissance Imagination: Essays and Lectures by D. J. Gordon*, ed. Stephen Orgel, Berkeley, Los Angeles and London 1975, pp. 233–45.
17. S. K. Heninger, Jr., *Touches of Sweet Harmony: Pythagorean Cosmology and Renaissance Poetics*, San Marino 1974.
18. A. Kent Hieatt, *Short Time's Endless Monument*, New York 1960.
19. In practice, humanist education often bred political conformity rather than opposition: see Anthony Grafton and Lisa Jardine, *From Humanism to the Humanities: Education and the Liberal Arts in Sixteenth- and Seventeenth-Century Europe*, 1986.
20. On civic humanism, see J. G. A. Pocock, *The Machiavellian Moment: Florentine Political Thought and the Atlantic Republican Tradition*, Princeton 1975.
21. See Joan Simon, *Education and Society in Tudor England*, Cambridge 1966, and, for a useful anthology of humanist educational writings, Joanna Martindale, *English Humanism: Wyatt to Cowley*, 1985. On literacy, see Keith Wrightson, *English Society 1580–1680*, 1982, pp. 184–91.

22. See Pocock's extremely rich and suggestive account in *The Machiavellian Moment*, ch. 10, and, on the full range of political discourses, J. P. Sommerville, *Politics and Ideology in England, 1603–1640*, 1986.
23. On Skelton's politics, see Greg Walker, *John Skelton and the Politics of the 1520s*, Cambridge 1988, and Alistair Fox, *Politics and Literature in the Reigns of Henry VII and Henry VIII*, Oxford 1989, chs. 8–10.
24. Fox, *Politics and Literature in the Reigns of Henry VII and Henry VIII*, p. 271.
25. Sir Thomas Elyot, *The Boke Named The Governour*, ed. H. S. Croft, 2 vols., 1880, i.1–3.
26. S. P. Zitner, 'Truth and Mourning in a Sonnet by Surrey', *Journal of English Literary History*, 50 (1983), 509–29.
27. For a full discussion, see John N. King, *English Reformation Literature: The Tudor Origins of the Protestant Tradition*, Princeton 1982.
28. On critical elements in the pastoral tradition, see Annabel Patterson, *Pastoral and Ideology: Virgil to Valéry*, Oxford 1988.
29. On humanist social policy in relation to literature, see Lorna Hutson, *Thomas Nashe in Context*, Oxford 1989, ch. 1.
30. Louis Adrian Montrose, '"Eliza, Queene of shepheardes," and the Pastoral of Power', *English Literary Renaissance*, 10 (1980), 153–82.
31. See Peter Stallybrass, '"Drunk with the Cup of Liberty": Robin Hood, the Carnivalesque, and the Rhetoric of Violence in Early Modern England', in Nancy Armstrong and Leonard Tennenhouse (eds.), *The Violence of Representation: Literature and the History of Violence*, London and New York 1989, pp. 45–76.
32. For discussion of differing interpretations, see John N. King, 'Was Spenser a Puritan?', in *Spenser's Poetry and the Reformation Tradition*, Princeton 1990, pp. 233–8.
33. See Frances A. Yates, *Astraea: The Imperial Theme in the Sixteenth Century*, 1975.
34. For Calvin's reading of this Psalm as warning against idolatry, see Arthur Golding's translation, *The psalmes of David*, 1571, commentary on Psalm 89; on the politics of the Psalm translations generally, see Margaret P. Hannay, *Philip's Phoenix: Mary Sidney, Countess of Pembroke*, New York and Oxford 1990, ch. 4.
35. See Robin Headlam Wells, *Spenser's 'Faerie Queene' and the Cult of Elizabeth*, 1983.
36. For differing views, see Richard C. McCoy, *The Rites of Knighthood: The Literature and Politics of Elizabethan Chivalry*, Berkeley, Los Angeles and London 1989, and Martin N. Raitiere, *Faire Bitts: Sir Philip Sidney and Renaissance Political Theory*, Pittsburgh 1984.
37. Thomas Nashe, *Pierce Penilesse his supplication to the divell*, in *Works*, ed. R. B. McKerrow, revised edn, ed. F. P. Wilson, 5 vols., Oxford 1958, i.193.
38. Jürgen Habermas, *The Structural Transformation of the Public Sphere: An Inquiry into a Category of Bourgeois Society*, translated by Thomas Burger with the assistance of Frederick Lawrence, Cambridge, Mass., 1989.
39. David Norbrook, 'The Monarchy of Wit and the Republic of Letters: Donne's

Politics', in Katharine Maus and Elizabeth Harvey (eds.), *Soliciting Interpretation: Literary Theory and Seventeenth-Century English Poetry*, Chicago and London 1990, pp. 3–36.

40. On political debate in the theatre, see Margot Heinemann, *Puritanism and Theatre: Thomas Middleton and Opposition Drama under the Early Stuarts*, Cambridge 1980.

41. Hutson, *Thomas Nashe in Context*, pp. 82ff.

42. Richard A. McCabe, 'Elizabethan Satire and the Bishops' Ban of 1599', *Yearbook of English Studies*, 11 (1981), 188–93.

43. For an excellent introduction, see Roy Foster, *Modern Ireland 1600–1972*, 1988, chs. 1–3.

44. See Ciarán Brady, 'Spenser's Irish Crisis: Humanism and Experience in the 1590s', *Past and Present*, 111 (1986), 17–49, and Patricia Coughlan (ed.), *Spenser and Ireland: An Interdisciplinary Perspective*, Cork 1989.

45. Mangan's translation can be found in Thomas Kinsella's *The New Oxford Book of Irish Verse*, Oxford 1986, pp. 277–8, and can be instructively compared with Kinsella's own translation, pp. 159–61.

46. 'On a Change in Literary Fashions', in Osborn Bergin, *Irish Bardic Poetry*, Dublin 1970, p. 127.

47. Thomas Park (ed.), *Nugae Antiquae*, 2 vols., 1804, i.249.

48. See Arthur H. Williamson, *Scottish National Consciousness in the Age of James VI: The Apocalypse, the Union, and the Shaping of Scotland's Public Culture*, Edinburgh 1979.

49. Helena Mennie Shire, *Song, Dance and Poetry of the Court of Scotland under King James VI*, Cambridge 1969.

50. Richard Helgerson, 'The Land Speaks: Cartography, Chorography, and Subversion in Renaissance England', *Representations*, 16 (1986), 51–85.

51. On the mingling of pastoral and georgic in Browne and other Jacobean poets, see Patterson, *Pastoral and Ideology*, pp. 142ff. Patterson argues that Browne's denunciation of abuses (no. 37) inverts the georgic praise of the 'happy man'.

52. The weaving thus has elements both of Minerva's and of Arachne's tapestries in the *Metamorphoses*: cp. no. 334 and the discussion in Section 3.

53. It has been possible to claim Donne and Herbert both for Anglo-Catholicism and for orthodox Calvinism. For influential analyses, see Louis L. Martz, *The Poetry of Meditation*, New Haven 1954, and Barbara K. Lewalski, *Protestant Poetics and the Seventeenth-Century Religious Lyric*, Princeton 1979.

54. Amy M. Charles, *A Life of George Herbert*, Ithaca and London 1977, pp. 80ff., 138, emphasizes early dates for many of the poems, though the evidence is inconclusive.

55. Thomas Cogswell, 'England and the Spanish Match', in Richard Cust and Ann Hughes (eds.), *Conflict in Early Stuart England: Studies in Religion and Politics 1603–1642*, 1989, pp. 107–33. The ensuing analysis of this very controversial period draws heavily on this volume; for alternative 'revisionist' perspectives, questioning the degree of long-term political and social polarization, see Conrad Russell (ed.), *The*

Origins of the English Civil War, 1973, and Conrad Russell, *The Causes of the English Civil War*, Oxford 1990.

56. See Nicholas Tyacke, *Anti-Calvinists: The Rise of English Arminianism c. 1590–1640*, Oxford 1987.

57. Cp. Thomas F. Healy, *Richard Crashaw*, Leiden 1986, p. 3 and *passim*.

58. Erica Veevers, *Images of Love and Religion: Queen Henrietta Maria and Court Entertainments*, Cambridge 1989.

59. See Peter Lake, 'Anti-Popery: The Structure of a Prejudice', in Cust and Hughes (eds.), *Conflict in Early Stuart England*, pp. 72–106.

60. See Bernard Capp, *Astrology and the Popular Press: English Almanacs 1500–1800*, London and Boston 1979, pp. 71ff.

61. For this reading, see David Norbrook, 'Marvell's "Horatian Ode" and the Politics of Genre', in Thomas Healy and Jonathan Sawday (eds.), *Literature and the English Civil War*, Cambridge 1990, pp. 147–69, and cp. John M. Wallace, *Destiny His Choice: The Loyalism of Andrew Marvell*, Cambridge 1968; on apocalyptic themes, see Margarita Stocker, *Apocalyptic Marvell: The Second Coming in Seventeenth Century Poetry*, Brighton 1986.

62. James Harrington, *An essay upon two of Virgil's Eclogues*, 1658, sig. A8r–v. I am indebted to David Armitage for discussion of Harrington.

63. Catherine Bates, *The Rhetoric of Courtship in Elizabethan Language and Literature*, Cambridge 1992.

64. Richard C. McCoy, 'Gascoigne's "*Poëmata Castrata*": The Wages of Courtly Success', *Criticism*, 27 (1985–6), 29–55. It was probably the prose work *The adventures of Master F. J.* that gave most offence.

65. Alastair Fowler, *Triumphal Forms: Structural Patterns in Elizabethan Poetry*, Cambridge 1970, pp. 175–6.

66. See, for example, Thomas P. Roche, Jr., *Petrarch and the English Sonnet Sequences*, New York 1989.

67. One of the leading 'confessionals', John Berryman, had a scholarly interest in Elizabethan poetry, and his first venture into confessional poetry was a sonnet sequence. Berryman's protestations that the escapades of his fictional 'Henry' had nothing to do with him can be compared with the attempt to make a radical separation between Sidney and Astrophil: in each case there is room for argument.

68. See Alan Bray, *Homosexuality in Renaissance England*, 1982.

69. Erasmus, *De ratione studii*, in *Literary and Educational Writings 2*, ed. Craig R. Thompson (*Collected Works of Erasmus*, vol. 24), Toronto, Buffalo and London 1978, pp. 683ff.

70. Stevie Davies, *The Idea of Woman in Renaissance Literature: The Feminine Reclaimed*, Brighton 1986.

71. On the sonnets as a revision of the conventions of epideictic complimentary poetry, see Joel Fineman, *Shakespeare's Perjured Eye: The Invention of Poetic Subjectivity in the Sonnets*, Berkeley, Los Angeles and London 1986; on the sonnets' triangle as figuring general 'homosocial' bonds between males, see Eve Kosofsky Sedgwick,

Between Men: English Literature and Male Homosocial Desire, New York and London 1985; for a homosexual reading, see Joseph Pequigney, *Such Is My Love: A Study of Shakespeare's Sonnets*, Chicago and London 1985.

72. On the gender politics of the blazon, see Patricia Parker, *Literary Fat Ladies: Rhetoric, Gender, Property*, London and New York 1987, pp. 126–54.

73. On rhetoric and representation in the poem, see Nancy Vickers, '"The blazon of sweet beauty's best": Shakespeare's *Lucrece*', in Patricia Parker and Geoffrey Hartman (eds.), *Shakespeare and the Question of Theory*, London and New York 1985, pp. 95–115.

74. William and Malleville Haller, 'The Puritan Art of Love', *Huntington Library Quarterly*, 5 (1941–2), 235–72; more recent authorities have played down the 'Puritan' element and emphasized the degree of traditional consensus on marriage, for example Wrightson, *English Society 1580–1680*, ch. 4.

75. For differing views of Spenser on marriage, cp. Davies, *The Idea of Woman in Renaissance Literature*, and Philippa Berry, *Of Chastity and Power: Elizabethan Literature and the Unmarried Queen*, London and New York 1989, pp. 153–65.

76. On the ways in which the universalizing language of citizenship could marginalize women, see Hilda L. Smith, *Reason's Disciples: Seventeenth-Century English Feminists*, Urbana, Ill., Chicago and London 1982, pp. 58–9.

77. Kevin Sharpe, *Criticism and Compliment: The Politics of Literature in the England of Charles I*, Cambridge 1987, and cp. John Kerrigan, 'Thomas Carew', *Proceedings of the British Academy*, 74 (1988), 311–50.

78. See Joan Kelly-Gadol, 'Did Women Have a Renaissance?', in Renate Bridenthal and Claudia Koonz (eds.), *Becoming Visible: Women in European History*, Boston 1977, pp. 137–64; on the limitations of Renaissance education of women, see Grafton and Jardine, *From Humanism to the Humanities*, ch. 2, and Lisa Jardine, *Still Harping on Daughters: Women and Drama in the Age of Shakespeare*, Brighton 1983, pp. 38ff.

79. 'Revival' because there was a substantial wave of interest in women's history in the late nineteenth and early twentieth centuries, a movement that subsequently became eclipsed for a long time.

80. See Hannay, *Philip's Phoenix: Mary Sidney, Countess of Pembroke*, pp. 84–105.

81. *The Poems of Lady Mary Wroth*, ed. Josephine A. Roberts, Baton Rouge and London 1983, p. 239. On her romance *The Countesse of Mountgomeries Urania*, [1621], see Carolyn Ruth Swift, 'Feminine Identity in Lady Mary Wroth's Romance *Urania*', *English Literary Renaissance*, 14 (1984), 328–46.

82. On the context of the Cookham poem, see Barbara K. Lewalski, 'Of God and Good Women: The Poems of Aemilia Lanyer', in Margaret Patterson Hannay (ed.), *Silent But for the Word: Tudor Women as Patrons, Translators, and Writers of Religious Works*, Kent, Ohio, 1985, pp. 203–24.

83. See Elaine Hobby, *Virtue of Necessity: English Women's Writing 1649–1688*, 1988, chs. 2–3.

84. Sara Heller Mendelson, *The Mental World of Stuart Women: Three Studies*, Brighton 1987, pp. 38–9.

85. Allan Pritchard, 'Marvell's "The Garden": A Restoration Poem?', *Studies in English Literature*, 23 (1983), 371–88. This anthology's chronological limits may have been broken to illustrate this interaction (cp. nos. 217, 222).
86. I am indebted to Patricia Ingham for discussion of this point.
87. Cp. Patricia Parker, *Literary Fat Ladies*, pp. 126ff.
88. William Drummond of Hawthornden, 'A Letter on the True Nature of Poetry, addressed to Dr. Arthur Johnston', in *Poems and Prose*, ed. Robert H. MacDonald, Edinburgh and London 1976, p. 191.
89. There is thus a confusing disparity between the phenomenon labelled by Heidegger as 'humanism', an exaltation of metaphysics at the expense of sensitivity to language, and the Renaissance conception of humanism: cp. Martin Heidegger, *Basic Writings*, ed. David Farrell Krell, New York, Hagerstown, San Francisco and London 1977, pp. 189–242.
90. Sidney, *A Defence of Poetry*, p. 85.
91. Ibid., p. 75.
92. Ibid., p. 87.
93. *Of Education*, in *Complete Prose Works of John Milton*, ed. Don M. Wolfe et al., 8 vols., New Haven 1953–82, ii.374, 403.
94. Ibid., ii.516.
95. For an excellent introduction, see Richard A. Lanham, *A Handlist of Rhetorical Terms*, Berkeley, Los Angeles and London 1968.
96. On the gradual reduction of rhetorical figures to the master-trope of metaphor, or the structuralist binary opposition between metaphor and metonymy, see Gérard Genette, 'Rhetoric Restrained', in *Figures of Literary Discourse*, trans. Alan Sheridan, introduction by Marie-Rose Logan, Oxford 1982, pp. 103–24.
97. George Puttenham, *The Arte of English Poesie*, ed. Gladys Doidge Willcock and Alice Walker, Cambridge 1936, pp. 311–13. Puttenham lists 'figurative' itself as a recent term which the language cannot do without (p. 147).
98. Richard Sherry, *A treatise of schemes and tropes*, [1550], sig. b5v.
99. For parallels between humanist rhetorical theory and contemporary 'deconstruction', see Terence Cave, *The Cornucopian Text: Problems of Writing in the French Renaissance*, Oxford 1979. Jacques Derrida's 'deconstruction' derives from and moves beyond Martin Heidegger's critique of metaphysics; a somewhat parallel response to Heidegger can be found in the return to medieval and Renaissance rhetoric by North American scholars like Walter J. Ong, SJ (*Ramus, Method and the Decay of Dialogue: From the Art of Discourse to the Art of Reason*, Cambridge, Mass., 1958) and Marshall McLuhan (cp. *The Gutenberg Galaxy: The Making of Typographical Man*, London and Toronto 1962, p. 248). McLuhan's doctoral thesis discussed rhetoric in Nashe.
100. On decorum, see Rosemond Tuve, *Elizabethan and Metaphysical Imagery: Renaissance Poetic and Twentieth-Century Critics*, Chicago 1947, ch. 9, and Daniel Javitch, *Poetry and Courtliness in Renaissance England*, Princeton 1978. For particularly

precise analyses of structural decorum, see Alastair Fowler, *Conceitful Thought: The Interpretation of English Renaissance Poems*, Edinburgh 1975.

101. Cp. Paul de Man, *The Resistance to Theory*, Manchester 1986, p. 17: 'Rhetoric, by its actively negative relationship to grammar and to logic, certainly undoes the claims of the *trivium* (and, by extension, of language) to be an epistemologically stable construct.'

102. Cp. Victoria Kahn, 'Humanism and the Resistance to Theory', in Patricia Parker and David Quint (eds.), *Literary Theory/Renaissance Texts*, Baltimore and London 1986, pp. 373–96.

103. Brian Vickers, *In Defence of Rhetoric*, Oxford 1988, ch. 5.

104. Lisa Jardine, 'Humanistic Logic', in Charles B. Schmitt and Quentin Skinner (eds.), *The Cambridge History of Renaissance Philosophy*, Cambridge 1988, pp. 173–98. On the possible influence on poetry of Petrus Ramus's transferral of 'invention' and 'disposition' from rhetoric to logic, see Tuve, *Elizabethan and Metaphysical Imagery*, pp. 331ff., and cp. Abraham Fraunce, *The lawiers logike*, 1588.

105. Archibald MacLeish, '*Ars poetica*', *Poems*, 1935, p. 123.

106. Cp. Jean-Marie Benoist, 'La géométrie des poètes métaphysiques', *Critique*, 27 (1971), 730–69.

107. For a subtle and illuminating analysis of this poem, see Richard S. Peterson, *Imitation and Praise in the Poems of Ben Jonson*, New Haven and London 1981, ch. 5.

108. Thomas O. Calhoun, 'George Wither: Origins and Consequences of a Loose Poetics', *Texas Studies in Literature and Language*, 16 (1974), 263–79.

Note on the Text and Annotation

Poetry in the Renaissance circulated in both manuscript and print. Some authors, like Sir Philip Sidney and John Donne, generally preferred to allow their poems to be copied by hand; others, like Spenser and Drayton, published their works mainly in printed form. Each medium had distinct advantages and disadvantages. The copying of manuscripts could, up to a point, be controlled and the audience limited; printed texts allowed authors to see their works in forms which they approved. Scribes and copyists, however, sometimes liked to 'improve' poems and in a sense make them their own, and printers were subject to all sorts of external pressures – social, economic and technical. By modern standards the copying of manuscripts often therefore appears to be highly inaccurate, and many printed texts contain what we would regard as corruptions – among them simplifications, revisions, adaptations and the rewriting of religious, political and sexual matters – which, in effect, produced 'edited' versions of the poems.

The concept of an accurate, correct text representing what an author had finally decided upon was therefore an unfamiliar one in the Renaissance. Once it was in circulation, a poem could easily change its form, being adapted for different purposes at different times by different people. The whole notion of authors' control over, or ownership of, their texts was a relative one.

These circumstances have led to the decision that the editing of texts for this edition proceed on pragmatic principles. Many of the authors represented here have had their works edited by modern scholars to a very high standard. Others, among them most notably Edmund Waller, have yet to receive full scholarly attention. As well as recording the copy-text from which the text in this edition is taken, the Notes on the Text refer to the best or most accessible (usually Penguin) modern edition of a poet's works, from which further information about textual matters can be gathered; references to standard editions not cited in the textual notes can be found in Appendix 4. The texts of the poems in those editions and those printed here will often be found to differ quite considerably.

In addition to the scholarly editions which have been used in the editing of this book, the chief sources for the listing of early printed texts are *A Short-Title Catalogue of Books Printed in England, Scotland, & Ireland and of English Books Printed Abroad 1475–1640*, first compiled by A. W. Pollard and G. R. Redgrave, 2nd edn, revised and enlarged by W. A. Jackson and F. S.

Ferguson, completed by Katherine F. Pantzer, 3 vols., 1976–91, and Donald G. Wing, *Short-Title Catalogue of Books Printed in England and America 1641–1700*, 2nd edn, 3 vols., New York 1972–88. Further information about publishing and printing is contained in the Registers of the Stationers' Company in which many works, both extant and lost, were entered; these were published by Edward Arber in *A Transcript of the Registers of the Company of Stationers of London: 1554–1640*, 5 vols., London and Birmingham 1875–94. References to the Stationers' Registers in the Notes on the Text are by date.

The cataloguing of the manuscripts of major poets (and other writers) has been undertaken by Peter Beal in the important *Index of English Literary Manuscripts* project. Volume 1, covering the years 1450 to 1625, appeared in two parts in 1980; of volume 2, covering the years 1625–1700, the first part describing the manuscripts of a range of authors (alphabetically) from Aphra Behn to Henry King was published in 1987. This edition is much indebted to Dr Beal's invaluable work. A further published source cataloguing poetry in manuscript is provided by Margaret Crum's *First-Line Index of English Poetry 1500–1800 in Manuscripts of the Bodleian Library Oxford*, 2 vols., Oxford 1969. The listing of printed texts of early English verse was begun by William A. Ringler, Jr., in *Bibliography and Index of English Verse Printed 1476–1558*, London and New York 1988.

This edition is based on a fresh examination of almost all the original texts reprinted here. For some authors, notably Donne, whose poems survive in at least seventy early manuscripts, the researches and collations of earlier editors have had to be heavily relied upon. With other authors, the texts of previous editions have been compared against their originals and some corruptions have been corrected and original readings restored. Many variants are printed here for the first time. The recording of variant readings in the Notes on the Text is necessarily selective. It is designed to give the user an idea of some of the main variants between editions and among manuscripts, as well as a sense of their range. All departures from the copy-texts, with the exception of evident printers' and scribes' errors, have been recorded. Where no source is given in the Notes on the Text for a reading, it can be assumed to be an editorial emendation. The punctuation at the end of variant readings has generally been omitted.

In the Notes on the Text references are given to the pages on which a poem or an extracted part of a poem are to be found. These are supplied by giving page numbers; or, in the case of early printed books, the signatures (usually in the form of a letter and number printed at the foot of the page to show the sequence of folded sheets or gatherings); or, in the case of manuscripts, the folio numbers. In the last two cases it is noted whether the poem is to be found on the recto (right-hand) leaf or the verso (left-hand) leaf.

The choice of copy-texts for poems has generally been based on the earliest and most complete available. Sometimes, as in the case of the extract from Harington's Ariosto (no. 341), later revisions, where they appear to be authorial, have been incorporated into the text. Revisions which appear to have been made after or just before the Restoration, as is the case with the poems of Margaret Cavendish, Duchess of Newcastle, have been recorded selectively in the Notes on the Text. Some poems, particularly ballads, have had to be taken from texts which were printed after the Restoration, because earlier versions do not survive. Composite texts have in general been avoided, with the exception of Wyatt's satire no. 223 and the text in Welsh of Siôn Phylip's poem no. 180.

The rationale for this edition is to provide readers with texts in as close a form as possible to that in which they circulated in the Renaissance. The versions of the poems printed here may not represent their authors' earliest or final intentions (if such things exist), but they do consist of versions which, more or less, existed at about the time when they were written.

While old spelling and original punctuation may, inevitably, cause some local difficulties, the translation of Renaissance poetry into modernized forms results in wholesale alterations. Modernization entails an imposition of sense and structure which may distort poetry's meaning and effect. An editorial decision to rely on the practice of previous editors would be unsatisfactory. Nineteenth- and twentieth-century editions produced in Great Britain and North America modernize and punctuate according to different principles and at different times. Furthermore, consistency in modernizing a wide variety of texts, each of which poses particular problems, is impossible to achieve: the problem is especially acute with authors writing in a consciously archaic style, such as Spenser.

On the other hand, while modernized texts may smooth difficulties away and be subject to their editors' idiosyncratic habits, they follow in a long tradition. It has to be remembered that scribes and compositors imposed their own personal and printing-house styles on the texts for which they were responsible. Orthography and punctuation were usually felt to be the responsibility of the scribe or compositor. The choice of which words were begun with a capital letter (to which modern readers often attach an unwarranted importance) and which words were italicized was not the author's alone. Some authors would have expected these editorial services to be performed on their behalf when they sent their manuscripts to the press.

Even then, typographic and scribal habits varied widely and also varied in consistency within the same text.

Despite this, there is no effective substitute for studying texts in their original forms. For this reason, references to facsimiles of books (especially those issued by the Scolar Press) and of manuscripts have been included in the Notes on the Text. Not all facsimiles of printed books are entirely accurate, however, and facsimiles can generally reproduce only one particular copy of a book with all its distinctive features. Many copies of the same edition of early printed books differ from each other in minor and major ways. Changes could be made to the type while books passed through the press (see no. 370 l. 1), so that some poems survive in corrected and uncorrected forms, sometimes with whole sheets in different settings (see, for example, the textual note to no. 366). Lists of errata might be added to some copies of books but not to all. In a few cases, the author or a scribe corrected the printed text by hand (see, for example, the textual notes to nos. 303 and 325).

In this edition the original spelling and punctuation of the early texts have been retained, with a few exceptions. Following Latin usage, writers in the sixteenth and seventeenth centuries did not discriminate between i and j and u and v in both upper- and lower-case letters. These have been regularized following modern practice, although in a few cases the correct form is uncertain: see, for example, the famous crux 'proud' or 'provd' in Shakespeare's Sonnet 129 (no. 116 l. 11), or Stanyhurst's 'Troians' (no. 333 l. 14) who may be 'Troyans' or 'Trojans'. The long s, which resembles an f without the cross-stroke, has been modernized throughout, and the initial double ff used in Renaissance handwriting has been changed to a capital F, as in 'ffoo' printed here as 'Foo' in no. 223 l. 65. The numerous contractions and abbreviations used in both printed books and manuscripts of this period, including the ampersand ('&') and the tilde above a letter indicating an omitted m or more usually n, have been silently expanded; the various forms of *et cetera* have been regularized to 'etc.'. Raised letters – as in M$^{r.}$ – have been lowered.

Some other typographical features have also been regularized. Many poems printed in the sixteenth and seventeenth centuries have their first word or their first few words (or their beginnings) set in capitals; also the first letter in the poem may be set in a larger size of capital than the subsequent capitals, and it may rise above the line or drop below it. All of this capitalization of the opening words of poems (other than the first letter of the first word) has generally been changed to lower-case. This has sometimes led to some difficult decisions. For example, the general practice in the 1609 quarto of Shakespeare's sonnets was to set the first letter of the poem as a large drop capital and the second in upper-case. Sonnet 20 (no. 105) begins in 1609 'A Womans face', but given the typographical practice of the volume this has been reprinted in this anthology as 'A womans face'. The same convention of drop capital followed by a standard-size capital is found in Robert Herrick's *Hesperides*, 1648, and this has led to printing the opening of 'Delight in Disorder' (no. 148) as 'A sweet disorder' rather than as 'A Sweet disorder'.

The titles of poems have always been printed in roman with some words in italics, even where the reverse obtains in the originals. Full stops at the end of the titles of poems have been eliminated. With the important exception of no. 228, authors' names at the end of poems and, with the exception of no. 298, words or phrases like 'Finis' or 'The End' have been omitted. The reversed question mark, occasionally used during this period, has been changed around, but the use of the question mark for an exclamation mark and vice versa has been retained. Marks introducing new paragraphs have been omitted, but the inverted commas used to mark 'sententiae' (sentences or maxims felt to be of particular importance or usefulness to the reader) have been retained, as in nos. 21 and 26.

Punctuation has been changed only where it seemed essential to do so: the virgule, a slanting line like the modern slash, /, used in some of the earlier texts as a mark of punctuation, has generally been rendered as a comma. With some manuscript texts it is probable that a comma was sometimes intended where the author used a full stop: this is the case with the autograph manuscript of Ralegh's 'The 21th: and last booke of the Ocean to Scinthia', no. 21. In one case, that of Daniel's verse epistle to Prince Henry (no. 194), because of the difficulty of the poem, the punctuation has been lightly modernized and on account of the large number of necessary changes these have not been recorded in this edition. In another, no. 33, the editor's punctuation of the Gaelic text has been retained.

The layout of the poems on the page follows that of the originals as closely as possible. Modern editors often rearrange texts to bring out their rhyme structure by supplying functional indentation, that is by indenting from the left-hand margin lines whose endings rhyme with each other so that they are aligned: this edition does not do so. For typographic reasons, editors also sometimes prefer to avoid having poems in long lines, and divide them up into stanzas. Robert Southwell's 'The burning Babe' (no. 253), for example, was first printed as a poem of sixteen lines, but has been rearranged by his modern editors into eight four-line stanzas. On the other hand, the layout of no. 20 differs from its original manuscript, where, for reasons of saving space, a poem of twenty-one lines was copied in ten and a half long lines. In side-notes, however, line divisions and word breaks are not necessarily as in the originals, and all side-notes have been rendered in roman type except for emphases in the original.

In poems without titles, headings have been supplied within square brackets, some consisting of the familiar titles by which they are generally known and others merely reprinting their first line. Poems which are represented by extracts have titles supplied, also within square brackets: sometimes these have been supplied by the editor (for example, no. 11), on other occasions (as the unmodernized spelling indicates) these titles are original ones (for example, no. 12). Extracted poems all have their titles preceded by the designation '*from*'. The omission of material before or after the extracted poem is not indicated by an ellipsis (three points, thus: '. . .'). This is the case except where a line (as at the beginning of no. 29) or a verse (as in no. 218 l. 17) is left incomplete. However, an ellipsis is supplied to indicate where lines are omitted within a poem (for example, in no. 12 l. 72, or in no. 40 l. 4). The one exception to the editorial use of the ellipsis in this edition occurs in Ralegh's autograph poem 'The 21th: and last booke of the Ocean to Scinthia', no. 21 (printed here in full), where he himself used ellipses of three points and of four points (including after a comma in l. 473).

In this edition, Roman numerals have been changed to Arabic ones in the titles of poems from sequences, for example in Fulke Greville's *Cælica* and Daniel's *Delia*, but Roman numerals for stanza numbers have been retained.

The annotation to this edition is largely concerned with glossing unfamiliar and obsolete words and words which have significantly changed their meanings. Elaborate exploration of all the possible meanings, especially punning ones, of words in their contexts has not been attempted. Different senses in which words may be understood are separated by a semicolon. A certain amount of historical material about the poems and their approximate dates is contained in the Notes on the Text.

In the glossing, much use has been made of *The Oxford English Dictionary* and asterisks have been supplied to designate usages of particular interest. A single asterisk indicates that the passage (or work) in question contains the earliest citation for the word in the *OED*. Two asterisks indicate that the particular usage, including figurative usages, antedates the *OED*'s earliest citation. This material needs to be used with caution, since the *OED*'s use of illustrative quotations varies in fullness between the earlier and later letters of the alphabet, and since the dating of many works is only approximate. Furthermore, these early citations have not been checked against the *Middle English Dictionary* (Ann Arbor 1952–; in progress), nor against the second edition of the *OED*, nor its electronic version. The asterisks do not, therefore, necessarily mean that a word is being used in a particular sense for the first time, but are meant to draw attention to the expanding and developing nature of the English language during this period.

In the annotation, the word or phrase being glossed exactly follows its form in the poem, except that italics have been ignored; the same applies to the Notes on the Text at the end of the volume. References to classical names will be found in Appendix 3. Words and names are usually glossed only on their first appearance in a poem.

Quotations from the Bible are taken from a modern-spelling text of the 1611 Authorized Version; quotations from classical authors are generally taken from the Penguin editions.

In the Notes on the Text, titles of books printed before 1700 are transcribed in the manner of the short-title catalogues, generally ignoring upper-case initial letters and not noting omitted words by ellipses. Square brackets have been used to signal material which is not present in the original.

PART ONE

THE PUBLIC WORLD

John Skelton

1 [*from* A Lawde and Prayse Made for Our Sovereigne Lord the Kyng]

The Rose both white and Rede
In one Rose now dothe grow:
Thus thorow every stede
There of the fame dothe blow:
Grace the sede did sow: Candida punica etc
England Now gaddir flowris
Exclude now all dolowrs.

Noble Henry the eight
Thy loving sovereine lorde
Of kingis line moost streight
His titille dothe Recorde: Nobilis henricus etc
In whome dothe wele Acorde
Alexis yonge of Age
Adrastus wise and sage:

Astrea Justice hight
That from the starry sky
Shall now com and do Right: Sedibus etheriis etc
This hunderd yere scantly
A man kowd not Aspy
That Right dwelt us Among
And that was the more wrong:

1 3 *stede* place 5 side-note *Candida punica* white and red 11 side-note *Nobilis henricus* noble Henry 12 *Acorde* exist harmoniously with 13 *Alexis* perhaps the character in Virgil, *Eclogues* 2, mentioned here as a representative of youth 15 *hight* called 17 side-note *Sedibus etheriis* in heavenly thrones

Right shall the foxis chare
The wolvis the beris also
That wrowght have moche care
And browght Englond in wo Arcebit vulpes etc
They shall wirry no mo
Nor wrote the Rosary
By extort Trechery.

SIR THOMAS MORE

2 DE PRINCIPE BONO ET MALO

Quid bonus est princeps? Canis est custos gregis inde
  Qui fugat ore lupos. Quid malus? ipse lupus.

2 The Good Prince and the Bad Prince

What is a good prince? He is the sheepdog who puts the wolves to flight by his barking. What is a bad one? The wolf itself.

3 QUIS OPTIMUS REIPUBLICAE STATUS

Quæris uter melius, Rex ne imperet an ne Senatus.
  Neuter (quod sæpe est) si sit uterque malus.
Sin sit uterque bonus, numero præstare Senatum,
  Inque bonis multis plus reor esse boni.
Difficile est numerum forsan reperire bonorum,
  Sic facile est unum sæpius esse malum,
Et fuerit medius sæpe inter utrunque Senatus,
  Sed tibi vix unquam Rex mediocris erit.
Consilioque malus regitur meliore Senator,
  Rex consultores sed regit ipse suos.

1 22 *chare* turn aside 24 side-note *Arcebit vulpes* he will keep off the foxes 27 *wrote* uproot

Alter ut eligitur populo, sic nascitur alter.
Sors hic cæca regit, certum ibi consilium.
Illeque se factum populo, populum sibi factum,
Scilicet hic ut sint quos regat ipse putat.
Rex est in primo semper blandissimus anno,
Omni anno consul rex erit ergo novus.
Rex cupidus longo populum corroserit ævo.
Si consul malus est, spes melioris adest.
Nec me nota movet quæ pastam fabula muscam
Ferre iubet, subeat ne male pransa locum.
Fallitur, expleri regem qui credit avarum,
Nunquam hæc non vacuam mittet hirudo cutem.
At patrum consulta gravis dissensio turbat,
Regi dissentit nemo, malum hoc gravius.
Nam quum de magnis varia est sententia rebus,
Quæstio sed tamen hæc nascitur unde tibi?
Est ne usquam populus, cui regem sive Senatum
Præficere arbitrio tu potes ipse tuo?
Si potes hoc, regnas: nec iam cui, consule, tradas
Imperium: prior est quæstio, an expediat.

3 What is the Best Form of Government

You ask which is better, whether a king or a senate rules. Neither, if, as often happens, each of them is bad. But if both are good, I think that a senate is superior from its greater number, and that more good comes from many good people. Perhaps it is difficult to find a number of good people, but it is more often easy for a single person to be bad, and there will often be a middle way between the opposing sides of the senate, but you will hardly ever have a king who will be moderate. A bad senator is ruled by better counsel, but the king himself rules his counsellors. As the senator is elected by the people, so the king – is born. Under the latter system blind chance rules, under the former, firm counsel. The one thinks he has been made by the people, the other thinks they have been made for him so that he may have people to rule. A king is always very pleasant in his first year, a consul will be a new king every year. An avaricious king will gnaw away the people over a long period. If one consul is bad, there is hope of a better one on the way. Nor does the famous fable move me which orders us to bear with the well-fed fly lest a badly fed one take its place. He is mistaken who thinks that a greedy king can be satiated, this

3 19 *fabula* told by Aesop, but deriving from Aristotle's *Rhetoric* 2.20

leech will never leave behind a skin which is not completely empty. 'But a serious disagreement throws a senate's decrees into disorder' – no one disagrees with a king, and that is a more serious ill. For when there is a difference of opinion about great matters – but where did this question of yours come from? Is there really anywhere a people over whom you can place in authority a king or a senate by your own decision? If you can do this, you are reigning: do not now think to whom you may hand over power: the prior question is, whether it would do any good.

Sir David Lindsay

4 [*from* The Dreme]

THE COMPLAYNT OF THE Comoun weill of Scotland

And thus as we wer talking to and fro,
We saw a boustius berne cum ovir the bent
But hors on fute, als fast as he mycht go
Quhose rayment wes all raggit rewin and rent
With wisage leyne, as he had fastit lent
And fordwart fast, his wayis he did advance
With ane rycht malancolious countynance

With scrip on hip, and pyikstaff in his hand
As he had purposit, to passe fra hame
Quod I gude man, I wald faine understand
Geve that ye plesit, to wyt quhat wer your name.
Quod he my Sonne, of that I think gret schame
Bot sen thow wald of my name have ane feill
Forsuith thay call me Jhone the comoun weill.

4 2 *boustius* large, strong, rough *berne* man *bent* grass 3 *But* without 4 *Quhose* whose *rewin* torn 8 *scrip* bag 11 *wyt* know 13 *sen* since *feill* knowledge

Schir Commoun weill, quho hes yow so disgysit
Quod I, or quhat makis yow so miserabyll
I have marvell, to se yow so supprysit
The quhilk that I have sene so honorabyll
To all the warld, ye have bene proffitabyll
And weill honorit, in everilk Natioun
How happinnis now your tribulatioun.

Allace quod he, thow seis how it dois stand
With me, and quhow I am disherisit
Off all my grace, and mon pas of Scotland
And go afore, quhare I was cherisit
Remane I heir, I am bot perysit
For thare is few to me, that takis tent
That garris me go, so raggit rewin, and rent

Sir Thomas Wyatt

5 [Who lyst his welth and eas Retayne]

V. Innocentia
Veritas viat Fides
circumdederunt me inimici mei

Who lyst his welth and eas Retayne
  hym selffe let hym unknowne contayne
  presse not to Fast in at that gatte
  wher the Retorne standes by desdayne
  for sure, circa Regna tonat.

4 15 *disgysit* changed for the worse 23 *disherisit* disinherited 24 *mon pas of* must go from 26 *perysit* perished 27 *tent* heed, care 28 *garris* makes

5 Title *V ... mei* the Latin motto (cp. Psalm 17:9) presents Wyatt's name ('V.') as surrounded with Innocence, Truth and Faith while 'my deadly enemies have compassed me about' 1 *lyst* wants, wishes *welth* well-being, prosperity; riches 4 *standes by* is in the hands of 5, 10, 15, 20, 25 *circa ... tonat* the motto (where it refers to Jove who 'thunders around thrones') and the first two verses of the poem are derived from Seneca's *Phaedra*

the hye montayns ar blastyd oft
when the lowe vaylye ys myld and soft
Fortune with helthe stondis at debate
the Fall ys grevous Frome Aloffte
and sure, circa Regna tonat

these blodye Dayes have brokyn my hart
my lust my youth dyd thenc departe
and blynd desyre of astate
who hastis to clyme sekes to reverte
of truthe circa Regna tonat

the bell towre showed me suche syght
that in my hed stekys day and nyght
ther dyd I lerne out of a grate
For all vavore glory or myght
that yet circa regna tonat

by proffe I say ther dyd I lerne
wyt helpythe not deffence to yerne
of innocence to pled or prate
ber low therffor geve god the sterne
For sure circa Regna tonat

6 In Spayn

Tagus fare well that westward with thy strems
torns up the grayns off gold alredy tryd
with spurr and sayle for I go seke the tems
gaynward the sonne that shewth her welthi pryd
and to the town wych brutus sowght by drems
like bendyd mone doth lend her lusty syd.
My kyng my Contry alone for whome I lyve
of myghty love the winges for this me gyve

5 8 *helthe* well-being, safety *at debate* at variance 12 *lust* youthfulness, joy 13 *astate* office, rank, status 14 *reverte* fall back 16 *bell towre*** 18 *grate* grating; prison; cage 19 *vavore* favour 22 *yerne* earn 24 *ber low* remain humble *geve . . . sterne* allow God to steer the ship (?)

6 3 *tems* Thames 4 *gaynward** towards 5 *drems* dreams 6 *lusty* vigorous, strong

7 [The piller pearisht is whearto I Lent]

The piller pearisht is whearto I Lent
the strongest staye of myne unquyet mynde
The lyke of it no man agayne can fynde
From East to west still seking thoughe he went
To myne unhappe for happe away hath rent
Of all my joye the vearye bark and rynde
And I (alas) by chaunce am thus assynde
Dearlye to moorne till death do it relent
but syns that thus it is by destenye
What can I more but have a wofull hart
My penne in playnt, my voyce in wofull crye
My mynde in woe, my bodye full of smart
And I my self, my self alwayes to hate
Till dreadfull death, do ease my dolefull state

Henry Howard, Earl of Surrey

8 [Thassyryans king in peas with fowle desyre]

Thassyryans king in peas with fowle desyre
And filthye lustes that staynd his regall harte
In warr that should sett pryncelye hertes afyre
vaynquyshd dyd yelde for want of marcyall arte
The dent of swordes from kysses semed straunge
and harder then hys ladyes syde his targe
from glotton feastes to sowldyers fare a chaunge
his helmet far above a garlandes charge

7 5 *unhappe* misfortune *happe* fortune 8 *Dearlye* from the heart, earnestly *it* my misfortune

8 1 *king* Sardanapalus *peas* peace 6 *targe* shield

who scace the name of manhode dyd retayne
Drenched in slouthe and womanishe delight
Feble of sprete unpacyent of payne
when he hadd lost his honor and hys right
Prowde tyme of welthe, in stormes appawld with drede
murdred hym self to shew some manfull dede

ANONYMOUS

9 John Arm-strongs last good night.

DECLARING How John Arm-strong and his eightscore men, fought a bloody Bout with a Scottish King at Edenborough. To a pretty Northern Tune, called, Fare you well guilt Knock-hall

Is there never a man in all *Scotland*
from the highest state to the lowest degree,
That can shew himself now before the King,
Scotland is so full of their Traitery?

Yes, there is a man in *Westmerland*,
and *John Arm-strong* some do him call,
He has no Lands nor Rents coming in,
yet he keeps eightscore men within his hall.

He has horse and harness for them all,
and goodly steeds that be milk white,
With their goodly belts about their necks,
with hats and feathers all alike.

The King he writ a lovely letter,
with his own hand so tenderly,
And has sent it unto *John Arm-strong*
to come and speak with him speedily.

8 9 *scace* scarcely 11 *sprete* spirit 13 *appawld . . . drede* made pale with fear

9 3 *King* James V of Scotland 4 *Traitery* treachery, treason

When *John* he looked the letter upon,
then Lord he was as blithe as a bird in a tree,
I was never before no King in my life,
my Father, my Grandfather, nor none of us three

But seeing we must before the King,
Lord we will go most valiantly,
You shall every one have a velvet coat,
laid down with golden laces three;

And you shall every one have a scarlet cloak,
laid down with silver laces five,
With your golden belts about your necks,
with hats, brave feathers all alike.

But when *John* he went from guilt Knock-hall,
the wind it blew hard, and full sore it did rain
Now fare you well brave guilt Knock-hall,
I fear I shall never see thee again.

Now *John* he is to *Edenborough* gone,
and his eightscore men so gallantly,
And every one of them on a milk-white steed,
with their bucklers and swords hanging down to the knee

But when *John* he came the King before,
with his eightscore men so gallant to see,
The King he moved his bonnet to him,
he thought he had been a King as well as he.

O pardon, pardon, my Soveraign Leige.
pardon for my eightscore men and me,
For my name it is *John Arm-strong*,
and a subject of yours my Leige said he.

Away with thee thou false Traitor,
no pardon I will grant to thee,
But to morrow before eight of the clock,
I will hang thy eightscore men and thee.

9 18 cp. the proverbial 'As merry as bird on briar' 24 *laid down* inlaid 29 *guilt Knock-hall* Giltnock Hall in Westmorland

O how *John* looked over his left shoulder,
and to his merry men thus said he,
I have asked grace of a graceless face,
no pardon here is for you nor me.

Then *John* pull'd out a nut-brown sword,
and it was made of mettle so free,
Had not the King moved his foot as he did,
John had taken his head from his body.

Come follow me my merry men all,
we will scorn one foot away to fly.
It never shall be said we were hung like doggs
no wee'l fight it out most manfully.

Then they fought on like Champions bold,
for their hearts was sturdy, stout, and free,
Till they had killed all the Kings good Guard.
there was none left alive but onely three.

But then rise up all *Edenborough*,
they rise up by thousands three,
Then a cowardly Scot came *John* behind.
and run him thorow the fair body.

Said *John*, fight on my merry men all,
I am a little hurt, but I am not slain
I will lay me down for to bleed a while,
then Ile rise, and fight with you again.

Then they fought on like mad men all,
till many a man lay dead on the plain,
For they were resolved before they would yield
that every man would there be slain.

So there they fought couragiously,
till most of them lay dead there, and slain,
But little *Musgrave* that was his foot-page,
with his bonny grissel got away untain.

9 80 *grissel** grey horse

But when he came up to guilt Knock-hall,
  the Lady spyed him presently.
What news what news thou little Foot-page,
  what news from thy Master and his company?

My news is bad, Lady he said,
  which I do bring as you may see,
My Master *John Arm-strong* he is slain
  and all his gallant company.

Yet thou art welcom home my bonny Grisel,
  full oft thou hast fed at the corn and hay,
But now thou shalt be fed with bread and wine
  and thy sides shall be spurred no more I say

O then bespoke his little Son,
  as he was set on his Nurses knee,
If ever I live for to be a man,
  my Fathers blood revenged shall be.

ROBERT CROWLEY

10 Of unsaciable purchasers

An unreasonable ryche manne
dyd ryde by the way,
Who for lacke of menne
hadde wyth hym a boye.
And as he paste by a pasture
most pleasaunte to se,
Of late I have purchased
thys grounde Jacke, quod he.
Marye maister (quod the boye)
men saye over all,

10 Title *purchasers* people intent on acquiring possessions in a selfish, luxurious way

That your purchase is greate
but your housholde is smal.
Why Jacke (quod this riche man)
what have they to do?
Woulde they have me to purchase
and kepe greate house to? Luk. xiiii
I can not tell (quod the boye)
what maketh them to brawle.
But they saye that ye purchase
the Devill, his dame and all.

JOHN HEYWOOD

11 [*from* A Ballad on the Marriage of Philip and Mary]

The egles byrde hath spred his wings
And from far of, hathe taken flyght
In whiche meane way by no leurings
On bough or braunch this birde wold light
Till on the rose, both red and whight
He lighteth now, moste lovinglie
And therto moste behovinglie.

The monthe ensuing next to June
This birde, this floure for perche doth take
Rejoysinglie him selfe to prune
He rousith, rypelie to awake
Upon this perche to chose his make
Concluding strayght for rype right rest
In the lions boure, to bilde his nest

10 16 side-note cp. Luke 14:16–24 18 *brawle* quarrel noisily and indecently

11 3 *leurings* allurements 7 *behovinglie*** appropriately 10 *Rejoysinglie***
12 *make* mate

A birde, a beast to make to choose
Namelie the beaste most furious
It may seeme straunge, and so it doose
And to this birde injurious
It semthe a case right curious
To make construction in suche sens
As may stande for this birds defens

But marke, this lion so by name
Is properlie a lambe tassyne
No lion wilde, a lion tame
No rampant lion masculyne
The lamblike lion feminyne
Whose milde meeke propertie aleurth
This birde to light, and him asseurth

The egles birde, the egles eyre
All other birds far surmounting
The crounid lion, matcheth feyre
Croune unto croune, this birde dothe bring
A queenelie queene, a kinglie king
Thus, lyke to lyke here matched is
What matche may match more mete then this

11 15 *to make* as a mate 23 *tassyne* to specify, to designate 26 *lamblike***
35 *mete* meet, fit, appropriate

William Birch

12 [*from* A songe betwene the Quenes majestie and Englande]

E Come over the born bessy,
come over the born bessy
  Swete bessy come over to me
And I shall the take,
and my dere lady make
  Before all other that ever I see.

B My thinke I hear a voice,
at whom I do rejoyce
  and aunswer the now I shall
Tel me I say,
what art thou that biddes me com away
  and so earnestly doost me call.

E I am thy lover faire,
hath chose the to mine heir
  and my name is mery Englande
Therefore come away,
and make no more delaye
  Swete bessie give me thy hande.

B Here is my hand,
my dere lover Englande
  I am thine both with mind and hart
For ever to endure,
thou maiest be sure
  Untill death us two depart.

12 Title: the speakers are England and Bessy, or Queen Elizabeth 1 *born* small stream, brook

E Lady this long space,
have I loved thy grace
more then I durste well saye
Hoping at the last,
when all stormes were past
For to see this joyfull daye.

B yet my lover England,
ye shall understand
How Fortune on me did lowre
I was tombled and tost,
from piller to post
and prisoner in the Towre.

E Dere Lady we do know,
how that tiraunte*s* not a fewe
went about for to seke thy bloude
And contrarie to right,
they did what they might
That now bare two faces in one hood.

B Then was I caried to wodstock,
and kept close under lock
That no man mighte with me speake
And against all reason,
they accused me of treason
And tirably thei did me threate.

E Oh my lover faire,
my dearlinge and mine heire
Full sore for the I did lament
But no man durst speak,
but thei wuld him threat
and quickly make him repent.

12 42 to bear, carry, have two faces in one hood, proverbial for to act hypocritically 43 *wodstock* Woodstock in Oxfordshire, where Elizabeth was held in 1554 48 *tirably* terribly

B Then was I deliverd their hands,
but was faine to put in bands
  and good suerties for my forth comminge
Not from my house to departe,
nor no where els to sterte
  as though I had ben away runninge.

E why dere Lady I trow,
those mad men did not knowe
  That ye were doughter unto Kinge Hary
And a princesse of birth,
one of the noblest on earth
  and sister unto Quene Mary.

B yes, yet I must forgeve,
al such as do live
  if they wil hereafter amend
And for those that are gone,
God forgeve them every one
  and his mercy on them extend. . . .

E Oh swete virgin pure,
longe may ye endure
  To reigne over us in this lande
For your workes do accord,
ye are the handmaid of the lord
  For he hath blessed you with his hand.

B My swete realme be obedient,
To gods holy commaundement
  and my procedinges embrace
And for that that is abused,
shalbe better used
  and that within shorte space.

QUEEN ELIZABETH I

13 [The dowbt off future foes exiles my present joye]

The dowbt off future foes exiles my present joye
 and wytte me warnes to shunne suche snares as threaten mine anoye
For falshode nowe dothe flowe and subjects faithe dothe ebbe
 which shuld not be yf reason rulde or wisdome weaved the webbe
but clowdes of joyes untryed do cloke aspirynge mynds
 which turnes to raigne of late repent bi chaunged course of windes
the toppe of hope supprest the roote upreard shalbe
 and fruictles all there grafted guile, as shortlye you shall see
the dayseled eyes with pride, which greate ambition blyndes
 shalbe unseelde bi worthie wyghts, whose foresight falshode finds
the dawghter off debatte, that discord aye doth sowe
 shall reape no gayne, where former rule styll peace hathe tawght to know
no Forrene banished wight shall ancore in this port
 our realme brokes not seditious sects, lett them els where resort
my rustye sword throwghe rest shall first his eydge imploye
to poule there toppes that sekes suche chaunge or gape for future joye.

13 6 *raigne* rain 7 *upreard* raised in dignity, exalted 10 *unseelde* unsewn (of the eyes of a hawk), opened *wyghts* people 16 *poule . . . toppes* cut off their heads *gape for* long for

SIR PHILIP SIDNEY

14 [*from* The Countesse of Pembrokes Arcadia]

Such maner time there was (what time I n'ot)
When all this Earth, this damme or mould of ours
Was onely won'd with such as beastes begot:
Unknowne as then were they that builden towers:
The cattell wild, or tame, in natures bowers
  Might freely rome, or rest, as seemed them:
  Man was not man their dwellings in to hem.

The beastes had sure some beastly pollicie:
For nothing can endure where order n'is.
For once the Lion by the Lambe did lie;
The fearefull Hinde the Leopard did kisse:
Hurtles was Tygers pawe and Serpents hisse.
  This thinke I well, the beasts with courage clad
  Like Senators a harmeles empire had.

At which whether the others did repine,
(For envie harbreth most in feeblest hartes)
Or that they all to chaunging did encline,
(As even in beasts their dammes leave chaunging parts)
The multitude to *Jove* a suite empartes,
  With neighing, blaying, braying, and barking,
  Roring, and howling for to have a King.

14 1 *I n'ot* I know not 2 *damme or mould* mother or shaper 3 *won'd* inhabited 5 *cattell* animals 8 *pollicie* system or form of government; expedient course of action; political cunning 9 *n'is* is not 20 *blaying* bleating of lambs

A King, in language theirs they said they would:
(For then their language was a perfect speech)
The birdes likewise with chirpes, and puing could
Cackling, and chattring, that of *Jove* beseech.
Onely the owle still warnde them not to seech
So hastily that which they would repent:
But sawe they would, and he to deserts went.

Jove wisely said (for wisedome wisely sayes)
O beasts, take heed what you of me desire.
Rulers will thinke all things made them to please
And soone forget the swincke due to their hire.
But since you will, part of my heav'nly fire
I will you lende; the rest your selves must give,
That it both seene and felte may with you live.

ANONYMOUS

15 Of Sir Frauncis Walsingham Sir Phillipp Sydney, and Sir Christopher Hatton, Lord Chancelor

Sir *Frauncis* and *Sir Phillip* have noe Tombe
Sir *Christofer* hath Tombe enoughe for three
And yet they lye not soe for want of roome
or want of Love in there posteritye
who wold from livinge hartes entombe such ones
to bury under a fewe marble stones,
Vertue dyes not, her Tombe you neede not rayse
let them trust tombes that have owtelived theire praise

14 24 *puing* plaintive crying 26 *seech* seek 32 *swincke* labour, toil

15 3 *they* Walsingham and Sidney 4 *posteritye* descendants

George Puttenham

16 Her Majestie resembled to the crowned piller. Ye must read upward.

Is blisse with immortalitie.
Her trymest top of all ye see,
Garnish the crowne
Her just renowne
Chapter and head,
Parts that maintain
And womanhead
Her mayden raigne
In te gri tie:
In ho nour and
With ve ri tie:
Her roundnes stand
Strengthen the state.
By their increase
With out de bate
Concord and peace
Of her sup port,
They be the base
With stedfastnesse
Vertue and grace
Stay and comfort
Of Al bi ons rest,
The sounde Pillar
And seene a farre
Is plainely exprest
Tall stately and strayt
By this no ble pour trayt

ANNE DOWRICHE

17 [*from* The French Historie]

So him at first *De Nance* commanded was to kill;
But he most stoutlie did [a]refuse this guiltlesse blood to spill.
"[b]Shall I, said he, consent to doo this fearfull thing
"To shed this blood, because I am commanded by the King?
"No, God forbid, I know I have a soule to save;
"So bloodie spot, to save my life my name shall never have.
"I know there is a day, a day that [c]Saints desire;
"When of our deeds the king above a reckoning will require.
"*Obaie the* [d]*King*; that's true, in things that honest be:
"When I obey in wicked hests, wo worth the time to me. . . .
"A murder to be done the King doth now request,
"My God commands the contrary: now which to chuse wer best?
"The King doth threaten death, and God doth threaten hell,
"If for the King I should forsake my God, should I doo well?

a Mounsier De Nance Captaine of the gard, refuseth to kill the Countie Rouchfoucault.
b His speeches used both privatelie to his frends, and also to the King upon the refusall.
c Rev. 6. 10.
d Rom. 13.1 1 Pet. 2.13 Tit. 3.1.

17 10 *hests* commands 7 *c* Revelation 6:10 'How long, O Lord, holy and true, dost thou not judge and avenge our blood on them that dwell on the earth?' 9 *d* Romans 13:1 'Let every soul be subject unto the higher powers. For there is no power but of God: the powers that be are ordained of God.' 1 Peter 2:13 'Submit yourselves to every ordinance of man for the Lord's sake: whether it be to the king, as supreme' Titus 3:1 'Put them in mind to be subject to principalities and powers, to obey magistrates, to be ready to every good work'

Sir Walter Ralegh

18 [Praisd be Dianas faire and harmles light]

Praisd be Dianas faire and harmles light,
Praisd be the dewes, wherwith she moists the ground;
Praisd be hir beames, the glorie of the night,
Praisd be hir powre, by which all powres abound.

Praisd be hir Nimphs, with whom she decks the woods,
Praisd be hir knights, in whom true honor lives,
Praisd be that force, by which she moves the floods,
Let that Diana shine, which all these gives.

In heaven Queene she is among the spheares,
In ay she Mistres like makes all things pure,
Eternitie in hir oft chaunge she beares,
She beautie is, by hir the faire endure.

Time weares hir not, she doth his chariot guide,
Mortalitie belowe hir orbe is plaste,
By hir the vertue of the starrs downe slide,
In hir is vertues perfect image cast.

A knowledge pure it is hir worth to kno,
With Circes let them dwell that thinke not so.

19 [*from* Fortune hath taken the away my love]

Thus now I leave my love in fortunes { handes / bandes }

and onlie love the sorowes due to me
sorowe henceforth it shal my princes be

18 5 *decks* decorates, ornaments, arrays 10 *In ay* for ever

I joy in this that fortune conquers kinges
fortune that rules on earth and earthly thinges
hath taken my love in spight of Cupids might
so blinde a dame did never cupid right.

With wisdomes eyes had but blind Cupid seene
then had my love my love for ever bene
but love farewell though fortune conquer the
no fortune base shal ever alter me.

Queen Elizabeth I

20 [Ah silly pugge wert thou so sore afraid]

Ah silly pugge wert thou so sore afraid,
mourne not (my Wat) nor be thou so dismaid,
it passeth fickle fortunes powere and skill,
to force my harte to thinke thee any ill.
No fortune base thou saiest shall alter thee,
and may so blinde a Witche so conquere me?
No no my pugg, thoughe fortune were not blinde,
assure thy self she could not rule my mynde.
fortune I knowe somtimes doth conquere kinges,
and rules and raignes on earth and earthly thinges
But never thinke fortune can beare the sway,
if vertue watche and will her not obay
Ne chose I thee by fickle fortunes rede,
ne she shall force me alter with suche spede
But if to try this mistres jest with thee, . . .
Pull up thy harte suppresse thy brakishe teares,
Torment thee not, but put away thy feares;
Dead to all joyes and livinge unto woe,
slaine quite by her that nere gave wiseman blowe
Revive againe and live without all drede,
the lesse afraid the better thou shalt spede.

20 1 *pugge* a term of personal endearment 2 *Wat* diminutive of Walter 13 *rede* counsel, advice

SIR WALTER RALEGH

21 The 21th: and last booke of the Ocean to Scinthia

Sufficeth it to yow my joyes interred,
in simpell wordes that I my woes cumplayne,
Yow that then died when first my fancy erred,
joyes under dust that never live agayne:
if to the livinge weare my muse adressed,
or did my minde her own spirrit still inhold,
weare not my livinge passion so repressed,
as to the dead, the dead did thes unfold,
sume sweeter wordes, sume more becumming vers,
should wittness my myshapp in hygher kynd,
but my loves wounds, my fancy in the hearse,
the Idea but restinge, of a wasted minde,
the blossumes fallen, the sapp gon from the tree,
the broken monuments of my great desires,
from thes so lost what may th'affections bee,
what heat in Cynders of extinguisht fiers?
Lost in the mudd of thos hygh flowinge streames
which through more fayrer feilds ther courses bend,
slayne with sealf thoughts, amasde in fearfull dreams,
woes without date, discumforts without end,
from frutfull trees I gather withred leves
and glean the broken eares with misers hands,
who sumetyme did injoy the waighty sheves
I seeke faire floures amidd the brinish sand,
all in the shade yeven in the faire soon dayes
Under thos healthless trees I sytt a lone
wher joyfull byrdds singe neather lovely layes
nor phillomen recounts her direfull mone,
No feedinge flockes, no sheapherds cumpunye

21 Title *21th* one and twentieth *Scinthia* Cynthia 6 *inhold*** contain, enclose
25 *yeven* even *soon dayes* sunny days

that might renew my dollorus consayte
while happy then, while love and fantasye
confinde my thoughts onn that faire flock to waite
no pleasinge streames fast to the ocean wendinge
the messengers sumetymes of my great woe
but all onn yearth as from the colde stormes bendinge
shrinck from my thoughts in hygh heavens and below.
"Oh, hopefull love my object, and invention,
"Oh, trew desire the spurr of my consayte
"Oh, worthiest spirrit, my minds impulsion
"Oh, eyes transpersant my affections bayte
"Oh, princely forme, my fancies adamande
"Devine consayte, my paynes acceptance,
"Oh all in onn, oh heaven on yearth transparant,
"the seat of joyes, and loves abundance
"Out of that mass of mirakells, my Muse,
gathered thos floures, to her pure sences pleasinge
"Out of her eyes (the store of joyes) did chuse
equall delights, my sorrowes counterpoysinge
Her regall lookes, my rigarus sythes suppressed
Small dropes of joyes, sweetned great worlds of woes,
one gladsume day a thowsand cares redressed.
Whom love defends, what fortune overthrowes?
When shee did well, what did ther elce a miss.
when shee did ill what empires could have pleased
no other poure effectinge wo, or bliss,
Shee gave, shee tooke, shee wounded, shee apeased.

The honor of her love, love still devisinge
woundinge my mind with contrary consayte
transferde it sealf sumetyme to her aspiringe
sumetyme the trumpett of her thoughts retrayt
To seeke new worlds, for golde, for prayse, for glory,
to try desire, to try love severed farr
when I was gonn shee sent her memory
more stronge then weare tenthowsand shipps of warr

21 30 *consayte* thought, conception, imagination 35 *yearth* earth 40 *transpersant* (not in *OED*) piercing through 41 *adamande*** adamant, magnet, centre of attraction 49 *sythes* sighs 55 *poure* power

to call mee back, to leve great honors thought
to leve my frinds, my fortune, my attempte
to leve the purpose I so longe had sought
and holde both cares, and cumforts in contempt.
Such heat in Ize, such fier in frost remaynde
such trust in doubt, such cumfort in dispaire
mich like the gentell lamm, though lately waynde
playes with the dug though finds no cumfort ther,
But as a boddy violently slayne
retayneath warmth although the spirrit be gonn,
and by a poure in nature moves agayne
till it be layd below the fatall stone
Or as the yearth yeven in cold winter dayes
left for a tyme by her life gevinge soonn,
douth by the poure remayninge of his rayes
produce sume green, though not as it hath dunn,
Or as a wheele forst by the fallinge streame
although the course be turnde sume other way
douth for a tyme go rounde uppon the beame
till wantinge strenght to move, it stands att stay,
So my forsaken hart, my withered minde
widdow of all the joyes it once possest
my hopes cleane out of sight with forced wind
to kyngdomes strange, to lands farr of addrest
Alone, forsaken, frindless onn the shore
with many wounds, with deaths cold pangs imbrased
writes in the dust as onn that could no more
whom love, and tyme, and fortune had defaced,
of things so great, so longe, so manefolde
with meanes so weake, the sowle yeven then departing
the weale, the wo, the passages of olde
and worlds of thoughts discribde by onn last sythinge,
as if when after phebus is dessended
and leves a light mich like the past dayes dawninge,
and every toyle and labor wholy ended
each livinge creature draweth to his restinge
wee should beginn by such a partinge light
to write the story of all ages past

21 71 *mich* much 96 *sythinge* sighing

and end the same before th'aprochinge night.
Such is agayne the labor of my minde
whose shroude by sorrow woven now to end
hath seene that ever shininge soonn declynde
so many yeares that so could not dissende
but that the eyes of my minde helde her beames
in every part transferd by loves swift thought
farr of or nire, in wakinge or in dreames
Imagination stronge their luster brought
"such force her angellike aparance had
"to master distance, tyme, or crueltye
"such art to greve, and after to make gladd
"such feare in love, such love in majestye.
"My weery lymes, her memory imbalmed,
"my darkest wayes her eyes make cleare as day
"what stormes so great but Cinthias beames apeased.
"what rage so feirce that love could not allay.
Twelve yeares intire I wasted in this warr
twelve yeares of my most happy younger dayes,
butt I in them, and they now wasted ar
of all which past the sorrow only stayes,
So wrate I once and my mishapp fortolde
my minde still feelinge sorrowfull success
yeven as before a storme the marbell colde
douth by moyste teares tempestious tymes express,
so fealt my hevy minde my harmes att hande
which my vayne thought in vayne sought to recure
att middell day my soonn seemde under land
when any littell cloude did it obscure
"and as the Isakells in a winters day
when as the soonn shines with unwounted warme
so did my joyes mealt into secreat teares
so did my hart desolve in wastinge dropps
and as the season of the year outweares
and heapes of snow from of the mountayn topps
with suddayne streames the valles overflow
so did the tyme draw on my more dispaire

21 123 the same line occurs in Ralegh's 'Farewell to the Court' 125 *sorrowfull success* the sorrow that was to follow

then fludds of sorrow and whole seas of wo
the bancks of all my hope did overbeare
and dround my minde in deapts of missery
sumetyme I died sumetyme I was distract
my sowle the stage of fancies tragedye
then furious madness wher trew reason lackt
wrate what it would, and scurgde myne own consayte.
Oh, hevy hart who cann thee wittnes beare
what tounge, what penn could thy tormentinge treat
but thyne owne mourning thoughts which present weare
what stranger minde beleve the meanest part
what altered sence conceve the weakest wo
that tare, that rent, that peirsed thy sadd hart.
"And as a man distract, with trebell might
bound in stronge chaynes douth strive, and rage in vayne
till tyrde and breathless, he is forst to rest
fyndes by contention but increas of payne
and fiery heat inflamde in swollen breast,
So did my minde in change of passion
from wo to wrath, from wrath returne to wo,
struglinge in vayne from loves subjection
"Therfore all liveless, and all healpless bounde
"my fayntinge spirritts sunck, and hart apalde
"my joyes and hopes lay bleedinge on the ground
"that not longe since the highest heaven scalde,
I hated life and cursed destiney
the thoughts of passed tymes like flames of hell,
kyndled a fresh within my memorye
the many deere achivements that befell
in thos pryme yeares and infancy of love
which to discribe weare butt to dy in writinge
ah thos I sought, but vaynly, to remove
and vaynly shall, by which I perrish livinge
And though strong reason holde before myne eyes
the Images, and formes of worlds past
teachinge the cause why all thos flames that rize
from formes externall, cann no longer last,
then that thos seeminge bewties hold in pryme,
loves ground, his essence, and his emperye,
all slaves to age, and vassalls unto tyme

of which repentance writes the tragedye,
But this, my harts desire could not conceve
"whose Love outflew the fastest fliinge tyme
"A bewty that cann easely deseave
"Th'arrest of yeares, and creepinge age outclyme,
"a springe of bewties which tyme ripeth not
"tyme that butt workes onn frayle mortallety
"a sweetness which woes wronges outwipeth not
"whom love hath chose for his devinnitye
"A vestall fier that burnes, but never wasteth
"that looseth nought by gevinge light to all
"that endless shines eachwher and endless lasteth
"blossumes of pride that cann nor vade nor fall,
"Thes weare thos marvelous perfections,
"the parents of my sorrow and my envy
"most deathfull and most violent infections
"Thes be the Tirants that in fetters tye
"their wounded vassalls, yet nor kill nor cure,
but glory in their lastinge missery
that as her bewties would our woes should dure
thes be th'effects of pourfull emperye . . .

"Yet have thes wounders want which want cumpassion,
"yet hath her minde some markes of humayne race
"yet will shee bee a wooman for a fashion
"so douth shee pleas her vertues to deface
"and like as that immortall pour douth seat
"an element of waters to allay
"the fiery soonn beames that on yearth do beate
"and temper by cold night the heat of day
"so hath perfection which begatt her minde
"added therto a change of fantasye
"and left her the affections of her kynde
"yet free from evry yevill but crueltye

But leve her prayse, speak thow of nought but wo
write onn the tale that Sorrow bydds the tell
strive to forgett, and care no more to know
thy cares ar known, by knowinge thos to well,

21 192 *vade* fade; disappear 216 *to* too

discribe her now as shee apeeres to thee
not as shee did apeere in dayes fordunn
in love thos things that weare no more may bee
for fancy seildume ends where it begunn.
And as a streame by stronge hand bounded in
from natures course wher it did sumetyme runn
by sume small rent or loose part douth beginn
to finde escape, till it a way hath woone
douth then all unawares in sunder teare
the forsed bounds and raginge, runn att large
in th'auncient channells as the wounted weare
such is of weemens love the carefull charge
helde, and mayntaynde with multetude of woes
of longe arections such the suddayne fall
onn houre deverts, onn instant overthrowes
for which our lives, for which our fortunes thrale
so many yeares thos joyes have deerely bought
of which when our fonde hopes do most assure
all is desolvde, our labors cume to nought
nor any marke therof ther douth indure
no more then when small dropps of rayne do fall
uppon the parched grounde by heat up dried
no coolinge moysture is percevde att all
nor any shew or signe of weet douth byde
But as the feildes clothed with leves and floures
the bancks of roses smellinge pretious sweet
have but ther bewties date, and tymely houres
and then defast by winters cold, and sleet,
so farr as neather frute nor forme of floure
stayes for a wittnes what such branches bare
butt as tyme gave, tyme did agayne devoure
and chandge our risinge joy to fallinge care,
So of affection which our youth presented
when shee that from the soonn reves poure and light
did but decline her beames as discontented
convertinge sweetest dayes to saddest night

21 218 *fordunn* exhausted, wearied 227 *the* they 228 *carefull* full of care, uneasy, sorrowful 232 *thrale* thrall 240 *weet* wet 250 *reves* steals, deprives

all droopes, all dyes, all troden under dust
the person, place, and passages forgotten
the hardest steele eaten with softest ruste
the firme and sollide tree both rent and rotten,
thos thoughts so full of pleasure and content
that in our absence weare affections foode
ar rased out and from the fancy rent
in highest grace and harts deere care that stood
ar cast for pray to hatred, and to scorne
our deerest treasors and our harts trew joyes
the tokens hunge onn brest, and kyndly worne
ar now elcewhere disposde, or helde for toyes
and thos which then our Jelosye removed
and others for our sakes then valued deere
the on forgot the rest ar deere beloved
when all of ours douth strange or vilde apeere,
Thos streames seeme standinge puddells which before,
Wee saw our bewties in, so weare the cleere
Bellphebes course is now observde no more
that faire resemblance weareth out of date
our Ocean seas ar but tempestius waves
and all things bass that blessed wear of late ...
And as a feilde wherin the stubbell stands
of harvest past, the plowmans eye offends
hee tills agayne or teares them up with hands
and throwes to fire as foylde and frutless ends
and takes delight another seed to sow ....
So douth the minde root up all wounted thought
and scornes the care of our remayninge woes
the sorrowes, which themsealvs for us have wrought
ar burnt to Cinders by new kyndled fiers
the ashes ar dispeirst into the ayre
the sythes, the grones of all our past desires
ar cleane outworne, as things that never weare ...

21 270 *the* they 271 *Bellphebes* the name means, literally, 'handsome' and 'pure'. Spenser used the same name in *The Faerie Queene* for a character whom he described in his letter to Ralegh prefixed to the first edition of Books 1–3 as 'a most vertuous and beautifull Lady'; in both cases, she is undoubtedly meant to reflect the character of Queen Elizabeth 278 *foylde* trampled down

With youth, is deade the hope of loves returne
who lookes not back to heare our after cryes
wher hee is not, hee laughts att thos that murne
whence hee is gonn, hee scornes the minde that dyes,
when hee is absent hee beleves no words
when reason speakes hee careless stopps his ears
whom hee hath left hee never grace affords
but bathes his wings in our lamentinge teares.

Unlastinge passion, soune outworne consayte
wheron I built, and onn so dureless trust,
my minde had wounds, I dare not say desaite
weare I resolvde her promis was not Just?
Sorrow was my revendge, and wo my hate
I pourless was to alter my desire
my love is not of tyme, or bound to date
my harts internall heat, and livinge fier
would not, or could be quencht, with suddayn shoures
my bound respect was not confinde to dayes
my vowed fayth not sett to ended houres
I love the bearinge and not bearinge sprayes
Which now to others do ther sweetnes send
th'incarnat, snow driven white, and purest asure,
who from high heaven douth onn their feilds dissend
fillinge their barns with grayne, and towres with treasure,
erringe or never erringe, such is Love
as while it lasteth scornes th'accompt of thos
seekinge but sealf contentment to improve
and hydes if any bee, his inward woes,
and will not know while hee knowes his own passion
the often and unjust perseverance
in deeds of love, and state, and every action
from that first day and yeare of their joyes entrance,

But I unblessed, and ill borne creature
that did inebrace the dust her boddy bearinge
that loved her both, by fancy, and by nature
that drew yeven with the milke in my first suckinge

21 296 *dureless** not lasting, unenduring 308 *incarnat* flesh-coloured, crimson 320 *inebrace* embrace

affection from the parents brest that bare mee
have found her as a stranger so severe
improvinge my mishapp in each degree
But love was gonn. So would I, my life weare.
a Queen shee was to mee, no more Belphebe
a Lion then, no more a milke white Dove,
a prissoner in her brest I could not bee
shee did untye the gentell chaynes of love
Love was no more the love of hydinge
all trespase, and mischance, for her own glorye
It had bynn such, it was still for th'elect
but I must bee th'exampell in loves storye
this was of all forpast the sadd effect ...

But thow my weery sowle and hevy thought
made by her love a burden to my beinge
dust know my error never was forthought
or ever could proceed from sence of Lovinge
of other cause if then it had proceedinge
I leve th'excuse syth Judgment hath bynn geven
the lymes devided, sundred and a bleedinge
cannot cumplayne the sentence was unyevunn.

"This did that natures wonnder, Vertues choyse
"the only parragonn of tymes begettinge
"Devin in wordes angellicall in voyse
"that springe of joyes, that floure of loves own settinge
"Th'Idea remayninge of thos golden ages
"that bewtye bravinge heavens, and yearth imbaulminge
"which after worthless worlds but play onn stages,
"such diddst thow her longe since discribe, yet sythinge,
"that thy unabell spirrit could not fynde ought
"in heavens bewties, or in yearths delighte
"for likeness, fitt to satisfy thy thought
Butt what hath it avaylde thee so to write
shee cares not for thy prayse, who knowes not thers

21 333 *th'elect* those in favour at court, compared to those chosen by God (in Calvinist doctrine) 341 *syth* since 342 *lymes* limbs 343 *unyevunn* unjust 351 *sythinge* sighing

Its now ann Idell labor and a tale
tolde out of tyme that dulls the heerers eares
a marchandize wherof ther is no sale
leve them, or lay them up with thy dispaires
shee hath resolvde, and Judged thee longe ago
thy lines ar now a murmeringe to her eares
like to a fallinge streame which passinge sloe
is wount to nurrishe sleap, and quietnes
So shall thy paynfull labors bee perusde
and draw onn rest, which sumetyme had regard
but thos her cares, thy errors have excusde
thy dayes foredun have had ther dayes reward,
so her harde hart, so her estranged minde
in which above the heavens, I once reposed
so to thy error have her eares inclined,
and have forgotten all thy past deservinge,
holdinge in minde butt only thyne offence
and only now affecteth thy depravinge
and thincks all vayne that pleadeth thy defence.
Yet greater fancye bewtye never bredd
a more desire the hart bludd never nowrished
her sweetness an affection never fedd
which more in any age hath ever floryshedd
The minde and vertue never have begotten
a firmer love, since love onn yearth had poure
a love obscurde, but cannot be forgotten
to great and stronge for tymes Jawes to devoure,
contayninge such a fayth as ages wound not
Care, wackfull ever of her good estate
feare, dreadinge loss, which sythes, and joyes not
a memory, of the joyes her grace begate
a lastinge gratfullness, for thos cumforts past
of which the cordiall sweetness cannot dye
thes thoughts knitt up by fayth shall ever last
thes, tyme assayes, butt never cann untye.
Whose life once lived in her perrellike brest
whose joyes weare drawne but from her happines

21 365 *paynfull* strenuous 385 *wackfull* watchfull 392 *perrellike* like pearls or jewellery

whose harts hygh pleasure, and whose minds trew rest
proceeded from her fortunes blessedness,
who was intentive, wakefull, and dismayde
in feares, in dreames, in feeverus Jelosye
who longe in sylence served, and obayed
with secret hart, and hydden loyaltye,
which never change to sadd adversetye
which never age, or natures overthrow
which never sickness, or deformetye
which never wastinge care, or weeringe wo,
If subject unto thes she could have bynn . . . .
which never words, or witts mallicious
which never honors bayte, or worlds fame
atchyved by attemptes adventerus,
or ought beneath the soonn, or heavens frame
can so desolve, dissever, or distroye
the essentiall love, of no frayle parts cumpounded
though of the same now buried bee the joy
the hope, the cumfort, and the sweetness ended,
but that the thoughts, and memores of thees
worke a relapps of passion, and remayne
of my sadd harte the sorrow suckinge bees
the wrongs recevde, the scornes perswade in vayne, . . .
And though thes medcines worke desire to end
and ar in others the trew cure of likinge
the salves that heale loves wounds and do amend
consuminge woe, and slake our harty sythinge
the worke not so, in thy minds long deseas
externall fancy tyme alone recurethe
all whose effects do weare away with ease
love of delight while such delight indureth
stayes by the pleasure, but no longer stayes. . . .
But in my minde so is her love inclosde
and is therof not only the best parte
but into it the essence is disposde . . .
"Oh love (the more my wo) to it thow art
"yeven as the moysture in each plant that growes
"yeven as the soonn unto the frosen ground

21 396 *intentive* attentive 421 *the* they 422 *recurethe* brings to recovery

"yeven as the sweetness, to th'incarnate rose
"yeven as the Center in each perfait rounde,
"as water to the fyshe, to men as ayre
"as heat to fier, as light unto the soonn
"Oh love it is but vayne, to say thow weare,
"ages, and tymes, cannot thy poure outrun. . . .

"Thow art the sowle of that unhappy minde
"which beinge by nature made an Idell thought
"begann yeven then to take immortall kynde
"when first her vertues in thy spirrights wrought, ...
"from thee therfore that mover cannot move
"because it is becume thy cause of beinge
what ever error may obscure that love
what ever frayle effect in mortall livinge,
what ever passion from distempered hart
what absence, tyme, or injures effect,
what faythless frinds, or deipe dissembled art
present, to feede her most unkynde suspect.
Yet as the eayre in deip caves under ground
is strongly drawne when violent heat hath rent
great clefts therin, till moysture do abound
and then the same imprisoned, and uppent,
breakes out in yearthquakes teringe all asunder,
So in the Center of my cloven hart,
my hart, to whom her bewties wear such wounder
lyes the sharpe poysoned heade of that loves dart
which till all breake and all desolve to dust
thence drawne it cannot bee, or therin knowne
ther, mixt with my hart bludd, the fretting rust
the better part hath eaten, and outgrown. . . .
Butt what of thos, or thes, or what of ought
of that which was, or that which is, to treat
what I possess is butt the same I sought
my love was falce, my labors weare desayte
nor less then such the ar esteemde to bee,
a fraude bought att the prize of many woes
a guile, wherof the profitts unto mee
coulde it be thought premeditate for thos?

21 447 *injures* injury's

wittnes thos withered leves ieft on the tree
the sorrow worren face, the pensive minde,
the xternall shews what may th'internall bee
cold care hath bitten both the roote, and rinde, ...

Butt stay my thoughts, make end, geve fortune way
harshe is the voice of woe and sorrows sounde
cumplaynts cure not, and teares do butt allay
greifs for a tyme, which after more abounde
to seeke for moysture in th'arabien sande
is butt a losse of labor, and of rest
the lincks which tyme did break of harty bands
words cannot knytt, or waylings make a new,
seeke not the soonn in cloudes, when it is sett . . . .
On highest mountaynes wher thos Sedars grew
agaynst whose bancks, the trobled ocean bett
and weare the markes to finde thy hoped port
into a soyle farr of them sealves remove
on Sestus shore, Leanders late resorte
Hero hath left no lampe to Guyde her love
Thow lookest for light in vayne, and stormes arize
Shee sleaps thy death, that erst thy danger syth-ed
strive then no more bow down thy weery eyes
eyes, which to all thes woes thy hart have guided

Shee is gonn, Shee is lost, shee is found, shee is ever faire,
Sorrow drawes weakly, wher love drawes not too
Woes cries, sound nothinge, butt only in loves eare
Do then by Diinge, what life cannot doo . . . .
Unfolde thy flockes, and leve them to the feilds
to feed on hylls, or dales, wher likes them best
of what the summer, or the springetyme yeildes
for love, and tyme, hath geven thee leve to rest
Thy hart which was their folde now in decay
by often stormes, and winters many blasts
all torne and rent becumes misfortunes pray,
falce hope, my shepherds staff now age hath brast

21 471 *worren* worn 484 *bett* beat 486 *of* off 490 *erst* before *syth-ed* sighed for 504 *brast* burst, broken

My pipe, which loves own hand, gave my desire
to singe her prayses, and my wo uppon
Dispaire hath often threatned to the fier
as vayne to keipe now all the rest ar gonn.
Thus home I draw, as deaths longe night drawes onn
yet every foot, olde thoughts turne back myne eyes
constraynt mee guides as old age drawes a stonn
agaynst the hill, which over wayghty lyes
for feebell armes, or wasted strenght to move
my steapps ar backwarde, gasinge onn my loss,
my minds affection, and my sowles sole love,
not mixte with fances chafe, or fortunes dross,
to god I leve it, who first gave it me,
and I her gave, and she returnd agayne,
as it was herrs, so lett his mercies bee,
of my last cumforts, the essentiall meane.

But be it so, or not, th'effects, ar past,
her love hath end, my woe must ever last.

22 The Lie

Goe soule the bodies guest
upon a thankelesse arrant,
Feare not to touch the best
the truth shall be thy warrant.
Goe since I needs must die
and give the world the lie.

Say to the Court it glowes
and shines like rotten wood,
Say to the Church it showes
what's good, and doth noe good.
If Church and Court reply
then give them both the lie.

21 511 *stonn* stone 516 *fances* fancies

Tell potentates they live
  acting by others action,
Not loved unlesse they give,
  not strong but by affection:
If potentates reply
  give potentates the lie.

Tell men of high condition,
  that manage the Estate,
Their purpose is ambition,
  their practise only hate,
And if they once reply
  then give them all the lie.

Tell them that brave it most,
  they beg for more by spending
Who in their greatest cost
  seek nothing, but commending.
And if they make reply,
  then give them all the lie.

Tell zeale it wants devotion
  tell love it is but lust,
Tell time it meets but motion
  tell flesh it is but dust.
And wish them not reply
  For thou must give the lie.

Tell age it daily wasteth,
  tell honor how it alters.
Tel beauty how she blasteth
  tell favour how it falters
And as they shall reply,
  give every one the lie.

Tell wit how much it wrangles
  In tickle points of nycenesse,
Tell wisedome she entangles
  her selfe in over wisenesse.
And when they do reply
  straight give them both the lie.

22 33 *meets* measures 44 *tickle* uncertain, unreliable

Tell Phisick of her boldnes,
  tel skill it is prevention
Tel charity of coldnes,
  tell Law it is contention,
And as they doe reply
  so give them still the lie.

Tell Fortune of her blindnesse,
  tel nature of decay,
Tel friendship of unkindnesse,
  tel Justice of delay.
And if they wil reply,
  then give them all the lie.

Tell Arts they have no soundnes,
  but vary by esteeming,
Tel schooles they want profoundnes
  and stand to much on seeming.
If Arts and Schooles reply,
  give arts and schooles the lie.

Tell faith it's fled the Citie,
  tell how the country erreth
Tel manhood shakes of pitty
  tel vertue least preferreth,
And if they doe reply,
  spare not to give the lie.

So when thou hast as I,
  commanded thee, done blabbing,
Because to give the lie,
  deserves no lesse then stabbing,
Stab at thee, he that will,
  no stab thy soule can kill.

22 49 *Phisick* medicine 50 *prevention* forestalling, getting in first 69 *of* off

Alexander Montgomerie

23 [Remembers thou in Æsope of a taill]

Remembers thou in Æsope of a taill
A loving Dog wes of his Maister fane
To faun on him wes all his Pastym haill
His courteous Maister clappit him agane.
By stood ane Asse a beist of blunter brane
Perceiving this bot looking to no freet
To pleis hir Maister with the counterpane
Sho clambe on him with hir foull clubbit feet
To play the Messan thoght sho wes not meit
Sho meinit weill I grant hir mynd wes guid
Bot vhair sho troude hir Maister suld hir treit
They battound hir vhill that they sau hir bluid
So stands with me vho loves with all my hairt
My Maister best, some taks it in ill pairt

Sir John Harington

24 A Tragicall Epigram

When doome of Peeres and Judges fore-appointed,
By racking lawes beyond all reach of reason,
Had unto death condemn'd a Queene anointed,
And found, (oh strange!) without allegeance, treason;
The Axe that should have done that execution,
Shunn'd to cut off a head that had beene crowned,

23 2 *fane* fond 3 *haill* whole 4 *clappit* patted, fondled 6 *freet* omen, superstition 7 *counterpane* like, or similar, act 9 *Messan* little dog *meit* meet, fit 11 *vhair* where *troude* trusted 12 *battound* beat *vhill* until

Our hangman lost his wonted resolution,
To quell a Queene of noblenesse so renowned.
Ah, is remorse in hangmen and in steele,
When Peeres and Judges no remorse can feele?
  Grant Lord, that in this noble Ile, a Queene
  Without a head, may never more be seene.

25 Of Treason

Treason doth never prosper, what's the reason?
For if it prosper, none dare call it Treason.

FULKE GREVILLE, LORD BROOKE

26 [*from* Cælica]

SONNET 78.

The little Hearts, where light-wing'd Passion raignes,
Move easily upward, as all frailties doe;
Like *Strawes to Jeat*, these follow Princes veines,
And so, by pleasing, doe corrupt them too.
  Whence as their raising proves Kings can create;
  So *States prove sicke, where toyes beare Staple-rate*.

"Like *Atomi* they neither rest, nor stand,
"Nor can erect; because they nothing be
"But baby-thoughts, fed with time-presents hand,
"Slaves, and yet darlings of Authority;
  "*Eccho's* of wrong; shadowes of Princes might;
  "Which glow-worme-like, by shining, show 'tis night.

26 1 *light-wing'd*** 3 *veines* humours, moods 6 *toyes* knick-knacks, trinkets *beare* are bought at the high cost of *Staple-rate** price fixed by commercial monopolies 8 *erect* raise or set themselves upright

"Curious of fame, as foule is to be faire;
"Caring to seeme that which they would not be;
"Wherein Chance helpes, since *Praise is powers heyre*,
"*Honor the creature of Authoritie:*
  "So as borne high, in giddie *Orbes* of grace,
  "These pictures are, which are indeed but Place.

"And as the Bird in hand, with freedome lost,
"Serves for a stale, his fellowes to betray:
"So doe these Darlings rays'd at Princes cost
"Tempt man to throw his libertie away;
  "And sacrifice Law, Church, all reall things
  "To soare, not in his owne, but Eagles wings.

Whereby, like *Æsops* dogge, men lose their meat,
To bite at glorious shadowes, which they see;
And let fall those strengths which make all States great
By free Truths chang'd to servile flatterie.
  Whence, *while men gaze upon this blazing starre,*
  Made slaves, not subjects, they to Tyrants are.

George Peele

27 [*from* Anglorum Feriae]

Write write yow Croniclers of Tyme and Fame,
Elizabeth by miracles preserved
From perrills imminent and infinite;
Clio proclayme with golden trumpe and pen
hir happier daies Englandes highe hollydaies;
Ore Europes boundes take winge and make thy flight,
throughe meltinge aire from where the risinge sune,
gallops the Zodiack in his fierie wayne,
even to the brincke where Thetis in hir bowre,
of pummey and tralucent peble stones,

26 20 *stale* decoy-bird 25 *Æsops dogge* snapped at his own reflection in water

27 10 *pummey* pummice stone *tralucent* translucent

receaves the wearie Bridegrome of the sea,
beyonde Graunde Chaire, by Nilus slimie banck
over the wilde and sandie Africk plaines
Alonge the frozen shoare of Tanais
Whose ycie crust Apollo cannot thawe
Even there and rownde aboute this earthly ball
Proclayme the day of Englandes happines;
The daies of Peace the daies of quietnes,
And let hir gladsome birth:day be the first
Hir day of birthe beginninge of our bliss.
Sett downe the day in caracters of golde
And marke it with a stone as white as milke,
that cheirfull sunnie day: weare Eglantine
And wreathes of Roses red and white put on,
in honor of that day yow Lovelie Nymphes,
And pæans singe and sweete melodious songes:
Alonge the chaulkie clyffes of Albion
Leade Englandes Lovely Shepherdes in a daunce
Ore hill and dale and downes and daysie plotts
And bee that Day Englandes highe Hollyday
And hollydayes and highe daies be they all
highe hollydaies, daies minutes monethes and howres
that multyplie the number of hir yeares
Yeares that for us begett this golden age
Wherein we live in safety under hir
Wherein she raignes in honor over us.
So may she longe and ever may she so,
untoucht of traitrous hande or trecherous foe.

27 12 *Chaire* Cairo 14 *Tanais* the river Don 23 *Eglantine* sweet-brier

John Donne

28 THE CALME

Our storme is past, and that storms tyrannous rage,
A stupid calme, but nothing it, doth swage.
The fable is inverted, and farre more
A blocke afflicts, now, then a storke before.
Stormes chafe, and soone weare out themselves, or us;
In calmes, Heaven laughs to see us languish thus.
As steady'as I can wish, that my thoughts were,
Smooth as thy mistresse glasse, or what shines there,
The sea is now. And, as those Iles which wee
Seeke, when wee can move, our ships rooted bee.
As water did in stormes, now pitch runs out
As lead, when a fir'd Church becomes one spout.
And all our beauty, and our trimme, decayes,
Like courts removing, or like ended playes.
The fighting place now seamens ragges supply;
And all the tackling is a frippery.
No use of lanthornes; and in one place lay
Feathers and dust, to day and yesterday.
Earths hollownesses, which the worlds lungs are,
Have no more winde then the upper valt of aire.
We can nor lost friends, nor sought foes recover,
But meteorlike, save that wee move not, hover.
Onely the Calenture together drawes
Deare friends, which meet dead in great fishes jawes:
And on the hatches as on Altars lyes
Each one, his owne Priest, and owne Sacrifice.

28 2 *stupid*** lacking consciousness or feeling 3 *fable* in Aesop's fable, asked by the frogs for a king, Zeus gave them a log; when they asked for another he sent a stork which ate them all 15 probably a reference to the seamen's washing 16 *frippery* a secondhand-clothes shop 23 *Calenture* a tropical madness in which sailors, imagining the sea to be green meadows, threw themselves overboard

Who live, that miracle do multiply
Where walkers in hot Ovens, doe not dye.
If in despite of these, wee swimme, that hath
No more refreshing, then our brimstone Bath,
But from the sea, into the ship we turne,
Like parboyl'd wretches, on the coales to burne.
Like *Bajazet* encag'd, the sheepheards scoffe,
Or like slacke sinew'd *Sampson*, his haire off,
Languish our ships. Now, as a Miriade
Of Ants, durst th'Emperours lov'd snake invade,
The crawling Gallies, Sea-goales, finny chips,
Might brave our venices, now bed-ridde ships.
Whether a rotten state, and hope of gaine,
Or, to disuse mee from the queasie paine
Of being belov'd, and loving, or the thirst
Of honour, or faire death, out pusht mee first,
I lose my end: for here as well as I
A desperate may live, and a coward die.
Stagge, dogge, and all which from, or towards flies,
Is paid with life, or pray, or doing dyes.
Fate grudges us all, and doth subtly lay
A scourge, 'gainst which wee all forget to pray,
He that at sea prayes for more winde, as well
Under the poles may begge cold, heat in hell.
What are wee then? How little more alas
Is man now, then before he was? he was
Nothing; for us, wee are for nothing fit;
Chance, or our selves still disproportion it.
Wee have no power, no will, no sense; I lye,
I should not then thus feele this miserie.

28 28 the victims of Nebuchadnezzar's fiery furnace (see no. 256 l. 24) 29 *these* the fish 30 *brimstone Bath* sulphur baths were used to treat syphilis 33 *Bajazet* Emperor of the Turks; in Christopher Marlowe's *1 Tamburlaine* the play's eponymous hero captures him and puts him in a cage to be mocked 34 Samson lost his extraordinary strength when his hair was shaved off, see Judges 16:17–20 35–6 the Emperor Tiberius' pet snake was eaten by ants 37 *Sea-goales* jails at sea *finny chips* chips of wood with fins 38 *venices* each ship is imagined as a city rising above the waters 44 *desperate*** desperado

29 [*from* Satire 4]

. . . Then, as if he would have sold
His tongue, he praised it, and such wonders told
That I was faine to say, If you'had liv'd, Sir,
Time enough to have beene Interpreter
To Babells bricklayers, sure the Tower had stood.
He adds, If of court life you knew the good,
You would leave lonenesse; I said, not alone
My lonenesse is, but Spartanes fashion,
To teach by painting drunkards, doth not last
Now; Aretines pictures have made few chast;
No more can Princes courts, though there be few
Better pictures of vice, teach me vertue;
He, like to a high stretcht lute string squeakt, O Sir,
'Tis sweet to talke of Kings. At Westminster,
Said I, The man that keepes the Abbey tombes,
And for his price doth with who ever comes,
Of all our Harries, and our Edwards talke,
From King to King and all their kin can walke:
Your eares shall heare nought, but Kings; your eyes meet
Kings only; The way to it, is Kingstreet.
He smack'd, and cry'd, He's base, Mechanique, coarse,
So are all your Englishmen in their discourse.
Are not your Frenchmen neate? Mine? as you see,
I have but one frenchman, looke, hee followes mee.
Certes they are neatly cloth'd. I, of this minde am,
Your only wearing is your Grogaram;

29 5 *Babells bricklayers* the story of the building of the Tower of Babel, whose builders could not understand each other, is told in Genesis 11:1–9 10 *Aretines pictures* a set of erotic engravings by the sixteenth-century Italian artist Giulio Romano, popularly known in England as 'Aretines pictures' from the verses which accompanied them by the satirist Pietro Aretino 15 *Abbey tombes* the tombs in Westminster Abbey were one of the favourite sights for visitors to London 20 *Kingstreet* led from Charing Cross to the royal palace at Westminster 21 *smack'd* his lips *Mechanique* working-class, artisan 26 *Grogaram* a fabric made of silk and coarser material

Not so Sir, I have more. Under this pitch
He would not flie; I chaff'd him; But as Itch
Scratch'd into smart, and as blunt iron grown'd
Into an edge, hurts worse: So, I foole found,
Crossing hurt mee; To fit my sullennesse,
He to another key, his stile doth addresse.
And askes, what newes? I tell him of new playes.
He takes my hand, and as a Still, which staies
A Sembriefe, 'twixt each drop, he nigardly,
As loth to enrich mee, so tells many a lie,
More then ten Hollensheads, or Halls, or Stowes,
Of triviall houshold trash he knowes; He knowes
When the Queene frown'd, or smil'd, and he knowes what
A subtle States-man may gather of that;
He knowes who loves; whom; and who by poyson
Hasts to an Offices reversion;
He knowes who'hath sold his land, and now doth beg
A licence, old iron, bootes, shooes, and egge-
shels to transport; Shortly boyes shall not play
At span-counter, or blow-point, but shall pay
Toll to some Courtier; And wiser then all us,
He knowes what Ladie is not painted; Thus
He with home-meats tries me; I belch, spue, spit,
Looke pale, and sickly, like a Patient; Yet
He thrusts on more; And as if he'undertooke
To say Gallo-Belgicus without booke
Speakes of all States, and deeds, that hath been since
The Spaniards came, to the losse of Amyens.
Like a bigge wife, at sight of loathed meat,
Readie to travaile: So I sigh, and sweat
To heare this Makeron talke: In vaine: For yet,
Either my humour, or his owne to fit,

29 27 *pitch* high-flown style of speaking; the height to which a trained hawk flies 35 *Sembriefe* semibreve 37 Raphael Holinshed (?–1580?) compiler of the *Chronicles* which Shakespeare used; Edward Hall (?–1547) and John Stow (1525–1605) old-fashioned chroniclers 42 *reversion*** right to succeed 46 *span-counter* a game like marbles *blow-point* a game played with the points used to fasten the hose to the doublet 49 *home-meats* domestic gossip 52 *Gallo-Belgicus* the Latin journal of current events 54 from the Armada of 1588 to the fall of Amiens in March 1597 55 *bigge* pregnant 56 *travaile* give birth 57 *Makeron** macaroon; buffoon, blockhead, dolt; fop, dandy

He like a priviledg'd spie, whom nothing can
Discredit, Libells now 'gainst each great man.
He names a price for every office paid;
He saith, our warres thrive ill, because delai'd;
That offices are entail'd, and that there are
Perpetuities of them, lasting as farre
As the last day; And that great officers,
Doe with the Pirates share, and Dunkirkers.
Who wasts in meat, in clothes, in horse, he notes;
Who loves Whores, who boyes, and who goats.
I more amas'd then Circes prisoners, when
They felt themselves turne beasts, felt my selfe then
Becomming Traytor, and mee thought I saw
One of our Giant Statutes ope his jaw
To sucke me in; for hearing him, I found
That as burnt venom'd Leachers doe grow sound
By giving others their soares, I might grow
Guilty, and he free: Therefore I did shew
All signes of loathing; But since I am in,
I must pay mine, and my forefathers sinne
To the last farthing; Therefore to my power
Toughly and stubbornly I beare this crosse; But the'houre
Of mercy now was come; He tries to bring
Me to pay a fine to scape his torturing,
And saies, Sir, can you spare me; I said, willingly;
Nay, Sir, can you spare me a crowne? Thankfully I
Gave it, as Ransome; But as fidlers, still,
Though they be paid to be gone, yet needs will
Thrust one more jigge upon you: so did hee
With his long complementall thankes vexe me.
But he is gone, thankes to his needy want,
And the prerogative of my Crowne: Scant
His thankes were ended, when I, (which did see
All the court fill'd with more strange things then hee)
Ran from thence with such or more hast, then one
Who feares more actions, doth make from prison;

29 63 *entail'd* settled in succession 64 *Perpetuities* perpetual possessions 66 *Dunkirkers*** privateering vessels and their crews 72 *Statutes* relating to treason 88 *complementall*** formal, ceremonial; complimentary 94 *actions* lawsuits against him

At home in wholesome solitarinesse
My precious soule began, the wretchednesse
Of suiters at court to mourne, and a trance
Like his, who dreamt he saw hell, did advance
It selfe on mee, Such men as he saw there,
I saw at court, and worse, and more; Low feare
Becomes the guiltie, not the accuser; Then,
Shall I, nones slave, of high borne, or rais'd men
Feare frownes? And, my Mistresse Truth, betray thee
To th'huffing, braggart, puft Nobility.
No, no, Thou which since yesterday hast beene
Almost about the whole world, hast thou seene,
O Sunne, in all thy journey, Vanitie,
Such as swells the bladder of our court? I
Thinke he which made your waxen garden, and
Transported it from Italy to stand
With us, at London, flouts our Presence, for
Just such gay painted things, which no sappe, nor
Tast have in them, ours are, And naturall
Some of the stocks are, their fruits, bastard all.
'Tis ten a clock and past; All whom the Mues,
Baloune, Tennis, Dyet, or the stewes,
Had all the morning held, now the second
Time made ready, that day, in flocks, are found
In the Presence, and I, (God pardon mee.)
As fresh, and sweet their Apparrells be, as bee
The fields they sold to buy them; For a King
Those hose are, cry the flatterers; And bring
Them next weeke to the Theatre to sell;
Wants reach all states; Me seemes they doe as well
At stage, as court; All are players; who e'r lookes
(For themselves dare not goe) o'r Cheapside books,
Shall finde their wardrops Inventory; . . .

29 96 *precious* particular, fastidious 98 *his* Dante's 102 *rais'd* not born to noble rank 109 *waxen garden* nothing certain is known of this phenomenon 111 *flouts* mocks, ridicules 115 *Mues** stabling in a mews for carriages and their horses 116 *Baloune* a ball game 118 *made ready* got dressed 124 *Wants . . . states* everyone is in need, hard up 126 *Cheapside books* the accounts of the tailors in Cheapside

Tyr'd, now I leave this place, and but pleas'd so
As men which from gaoles to'execution goe,
Goe through the great chamber (why is it hung
With the seaven deadly sinnes?); Being among
Those Askaparts, men big enough to throw
Charing Crosse for a barre, men that doe know
No token of worth, but Queenes man, and fine
Living, barrells of beefe, flaggons of wine;
I shooke like a spyed Spie. Preachers which are
Seas of Wit and Arts, you can, then dare,
Drowne the sinnes of this place, for, for mee
Which am but a scarce brooke, it enough shall bee
To wash the staines away; though I yet
With *Macchabees* modestie, the knowne merit
Of my worke lessen: yet some wise man shall,
I hope, esteeme my writs Canonicall.

Robert Devereux, Earl of Essex

30 [Change thy minde since she doth change]

1 Change thy minde since she doth change,
Let not Fancy still abuse thee:
Thy untruth cannot seeme strange,
When her falshood doth excuse thee.
Love is dead and thou art free,
She doth live but dead to thee.

29 128 *this place* the Court 132 *Askaparts* Ascapart was a giant, thirty feet tall, whom Sir Bevis of Hampton defeated in the old romance; here the giants are the halberdiers guarding the monarch 133 *barre* their weapon; a wooden or iron bar used in exercise 134 *Queenes man* in the service of the Queen 141 *Macchabees modestie* cp. 2 Maccabees 15:38 'And if I have done well, and as is fitting the story, it is that which I desired: but if slenderly and meanly, it is that which I could attain unto'; for Protestants the two books of Maccabees belong to the uncanonical Apocrypha

2 Whilst she lov'd thee best a while,
See how she hath still delaid thee:
Using shewes for to beguile,
Those vaine hopes that have deceiv'd thee.
  Now thou seest although too late,
  Love loves truth which women hate.

3 Love no more since she is gone,
Shee is gone and loves another:
Being once deceiv'd by one,
Leave her love but love none other.
  She was false bid her adew,
  She was best but yet untrue.

4 Love farewell more deere to mee
Then my life which thou preservest;
Life all joyes are gone from thee,
Others have what thou deservest.
  Oh my death doth spring from hence
  I must dye for her offence.

5 Dye, but yet before thou dye
Make her know what she hath gotten:
She in whom my hopes did lye,
Now is chang'd, I quite forgotten.
  She is chang'd, but changed base,
  Baser in so vilde a place.

30 30 *vilde* vile, lowly

Mary Sidney, Countess of Pembroke

31 [To Queen Elizabeth]

Even now that Care which on thy Crowne attends
and with thy happy greatnes dayly growes
Tells mee thrise sacred Queene my Muse offends,
and of respect to thee the line out goes,
One instant will, or willing can shee lose
I say not reading, but receiving Rimes,
On whom in chiefe dependeth to dispose
what Europe acts in theise most active times?

Yet dare I so, as humblenes may dare
cherish some hope they shall acceptance finde;
not waighing less thy state, lighter thy Care,
but knowing more thy grace, abler thy minde.
What heav'nly powrs thee highest throne assign'de,
assign'd thee goodnes suting that Degree:
and by thy strength thy burthen so defin'de,
To others toile, is Exercise to thee.

Cares though still great, cannot bee greatest still,
Busines most ebb, though Leasure never flowe:
Then these the Postes of Dutie and Goodwill
shall presse to offer what their Senders owe;

31 Title: the first of two poems written to accompany a presentation MS of a translation of the Psalms intended to be given to Queen Elizabeth 4 *line out goes* breaks, exceeds the metre 18 *most* must 19 *these* two poems accompanying the translation of the Psalms *Postes* postmen, letter-carriers 20 *presse* ride hard

Which once in two, now in one Subject goe,
the poorer left, the richer reft awaye:
Who better might (O might ah word of woe.)
have giv'n for mee what I for him defraye.

How can I name whom sighing signes extend,
and not unstopp my teares eternall spring?
but hee did warpe, I weav'd this webb to end;
the stuffe not ours, our worke no curious thing,
Wherein yet well wee thought the Psalmist King
Now English denizend, though Hebrue borne,
woold to thy musicke undispleased sing,
Oft having worse, without repining worne;

And I the Cloth in both our names present,
A liverie robe to bee bestowed by thee:
small parcell of that undischarged rent,
from which nor paines, nor paiments can us free.
And yet enough to cause our neighbours see
wee will our best, though scanted in our will:
and those nighe feelds where sow'n thy favors bee
unwalthy doo, not elce unworthie till.

For in our worke what bring wee but thine owne?
what English is, by many names is thine.
There humble Lawrells in thy shadowes growne
To garland others, woold themselves repine.
Thy brest the Cabinet, thy seat the shrine,
where Muses hang their vowed memories:
where Wit, where Art, where all that is divine
conceived best, and best defended lies.

31 21 *two* the Countess of Pembroke and her dead brother Sir Philip Sidney 22 *reft* snatched 23 *O . . . woe* cp. Sidney, *Astrophil and Stella* 33 ll. 1–2 'I might, unhappie word, ô me, I might,/And then would not, or could not see my blisse' 27 *this webb* the translation of the Psalms 28 *stuffe* raw material *curious* elaborate 29 *King* David 30 *denizend* naturalized 32 *repining* complaining 35 *parcell* portion *undischarged* unpaid 38 *scanted* diminished, restricted 40 *unwalthy* unwealthy 43–4 laurels (poems) grown in the Queen's shadow would themselves complain at being used to garland others

Which if men did not (as they doe) confesse,
and wronging worlds woold otherwise consent:
Yet here who mynds so meet a Patrones
for Authors state or writings argument?
A King should onely to a Queene bee sent.
Gods loved choise unto his chosen love:
Devotion to Devotions President:
what all applaud, to her whom none reprove.

And who sees ought, but sees how justly square
his haughtie Ditties to thy glorious daies?
How well beseeming thee his Triumphs are?
his hope, his zeale, his praier, plaint, and praise,
Needles thy person to their height to raise:
lesse need to bend them downe to thy degree:
Theise holy garments each good soule assaies,
some sorting all, all sort to none but thee.

For ev'n thy Rule is painted in his Raigne:
both cleere in right: both nigh by wrong opprest:
And each at length (man crossing God in vaine)
Possest of place, and each in peace possest.
proud Philistines did interrupt his rest,
The foes of heav'n no lesse have beene thy foes;
Hee with great conquest, thou with greater blest;
Thou sure to winn, and hee secure to lose.

Thus hand in hand with him thy glories walke:
but who can trace them where alone they goe?
Of thee two hemispheres on honor talke,
and Lands and seas thy Trophees jointly showe.
The very windes did on thy partie blowe,
and rocks in armes thy foe men eft defie:
But soft my muse, Thy pitch is earthly lowe;
forbeare this heav'n, where onely Eagles flie.

31 51 *mynds* brings to mind *meet* fitting 57 *square* correspond 58 *his* David's *haughtie* exalted, elevated, high-minded 64 *sort* consort, are fitting 69 *Philistines* the ancient enemy of the Israelites in Palestine 77–8 these lines probably refer to the destruction of the Armada in 1588 78 *eft* afterwards 80 eagles are traditionally supposed to be able to fly up to the sun

Kings on a Queene enforst their states to lay;
Main-lands for Empire waiting on an Ile;
Men drawne by worth a woman to obay;
one moving all, herselfe unmov'd the while:
Truthes restitution, vanitie exile,
wealth sprung of want, warr held without annoye,
Let subject bee of some inspired stile,
Till then the object of her subjects joye.

Thy utmost can but offer to hir sight
Her handmaids taske, which most her will endeeres;
and pray unto thy paines life from that light
which lively lightsome, Court, and Kingdome cheeres,
what wish shee may (farre past hir living Peeres
and Rivall still to Judas Faithfull King)
In more then hee and more triumphant yeares,
Sing what God doth, and doo What men may sing.

Edmund Spenser

32 [*from* The Faerie Queene Book 5]

Tho when they came to the sea coast, they found
  A ship all readie (as good fortune fell)
  To put to sea, with whom they did compound,
  To passe them over, where them list to tell:
  The winde and weather served them so well,
  That in one day they with the coast did fall;
  Whereas they readie found them to repell,
  Great hostes of men in order martiall,
Which them forbad to land, and footing did forstall.

31 85 *restitution* restoration 94 *Judas* David was King of Judaea

32 3 *compound* make terms, contract 6 *they* ... *fall* they came to the coast, landed

But nathemore would they from land refraine,
But when as nigh unto the shore they drew,
That foot of man might sound the bottome plaine,
Talus into the sea did forth issew,
Though darts from shore and stones they at him threw;
And wading through the waves with stedfast sway,
Maugre the might of all those troupes in vew,
Did win the shore, whence he them chast away,
And made to fly, like doves, whom the Eagle doth affray.

The whyles Sir *Artegall*, with that old knight
Did forth descend, there being none them neare,
And forward marched to a towne in sight.
By this came tydings to the Tyrants eare,
By those, which earst did fly away for feare
Of their arrivall: wherewith troubled sore,
He all his forces streight to him did reare,
And forth issuing with his scouts afore,
Meant them to have incountred, ere they left the shore.

But ere he marched farre, he with them met,
And fiercely charged them with all his force;
But *Talus* sternely did upon them set,
And brusht, and battred them without remorse,
That on the ground he left full many a corse;
Ne any able was him to withstand,
But he them overthrew both man and horse,
That they lay scattred over all the land,
As thicke as doth the seede after the sowers hand.

Till *Artegall* him seeing so to rage,
Willd him to stay, and signe of truce did make:
To which all harkning, did a while asswage
Their forces furie, and their terror slake;
Till he an Herauld cald, and to him spake,

32 10 *nathemore* never the more 15 *sway* force 16 *Maugre* in spite of 18 *affray* frighten 19 *knight* Sir Sergis 25 *reare* raise, levy, gather 30 *sternely* fiercely, cruelly 31 *brusht* rushed at

Willing him wend unto the Tyrant streight,
And tell him that not for such slaughters sake
He thether came, but for to trie the right
Of fayre *Irenaes* cause with him in single fight.

And willed him for to reclayme with speed
His scattred people, ere they all were slaine,
And time and place convenient to areed,
In which they two the combat might darraine.
Which message when *Grantorto* heard, full fayne
And glad he was the slaughter so to stay,
And pointed for the combat twixt them twayne
The morrow next, ne gave him longer day.
So sounded the retraite, and drew his folke away.

That night Sir *Artegall* did cause his tent
There to be pitched on the open plaine;
For he had given streight commaundement,
That none should dare him once to entertaine:
Which none durst breake, though many would right faine
For fayre *Irena*, whom they loved deare.
But yet old *Sergis* did so well him paine,
That from close friends, that dar'd not to appeare,
He all things did purvay, which for them needfull weare.

The morrow next, that was the dismall day,
Appointed for *Irenas* death before,
So soone as it did to the world display
His chearefull face, and light to men restore,
The heavy Mayd, to whom none tydings bore
Of *Artegals* arryvall, her to free,
Lookt up with eyes full sad and hart full sore;
Weening her lifes last howre then neare to bee,.
Sith no redemption nigh she did nor heare nor see.

32 46 *reclayme** call back, recall 48 *convenient* suitable, appropriate *areed* declare 49 *darraine* engage 57 *he* Grantorto *streight* strict 61 *him paine* took pains, or trouble, on his behalf 64 *dismall* unlucky, fatal 68 *Mayd* Irena

Then up she rose, and on her selfe did dight
Most squalid garments, fit for such a day,
And with dull countenance, and with doleful spright,
She forth was brought in sorrowfull dismay,
For to receive the doome of her decay.
But comming to the place, and finding there
Sir *Artegall*, in battailous array
Wayting his foe, it did her dead hart cheare,
And new life to her lent, in midst of deadly feare.

Like as a tender Rose in open plaine,
That with untimely drought nigh withered was,
And hung the head, soone as few drops of raine
Thereon distill, and deaw her daintie face,
Gins to looke up, and with fresh wonted grace
Dispreds the glorie of her leaves gay;
Such was *Irenas* countenance, such her case,
When *Artegall* she saw in that array,
There wayting for the Tyrant, till it was farre day.

Who came at length, with proud presumpteous gate,
Into the field, as if he fearelesse were,
All armed in a cote of yron plate,
Of great defence to ward the deadly feare,
And on his head a steele cap he did weare
Of colour rustie browne, but sure and strong;
And in his hand an huge Polaxe did beare,
Whose steale was yron studded, but not long,
With which he wont to fight, to justifie his wrong.

Of stature huge and hideous he was,
Like to a Giant for his monstrous hight,
And did in strength most sorts of men surpas,
Ne ever any found his match in might;
Thereto he had great skill in single fight:

32 73 *dight* clothe, dress 74 *squalid* foul, dirty 77 *doome ... decay* punishment of death 79 *battailous* warlike 83 *untimely* unseasonable 85 *distill* gently fall 87 *Dispreds* opens out 88 *case* condition, plight 90 *farre day* late in the day 91–9 Spenser's description of Grantorto suggests he is armed like a galloglas or Irish foot soldier 94 *ward ... feare* guard, repel the fear of death 97 *Polaxe* battleaxe 98 *steale* handle 100 *hideous* monstrously large

His face was ugly, and his countenance sterne,
That could have frayd one with the very sight,
And gaped like a gulfe, when he did gerne,
That whether man or monster one could scarse discerne.

Soone as he did within the listes appeare,
With dreadfull looke he *Artegall* beheld,
As if he would have daunted him with feare,
And grinning griesly, did against him weld
His deadly weapon, which in hand he held.
But th'Elfin swayne, that oft had seene like sight,
Was with his ghastly count'nance nothing queld,
But gan him streight to buckle to the fight,
And cast his shield about, to be in readie plight.

The trompets sound, and they together goe,
With dreadfull terror, and with fell intent;
And their huge strokes full daungerously bestow,
To doe most dammage, where as most they ment.
But with such force and furie violent,
The tyrant thundred his thicke blowes so fast,
That through the yron walles their way they rent,
And even to the vitall parts they past,
Ne ought could them endure, but all they cleft or brast.

Which cruell outrage when as *Artegall*
Did well avize, thenceforth with warie heed
He shund his strokes, where ever they did fall,
And way did give unto their gracelesse speed:
As when a skilfull Marriner doth reed
A storme approching, that doth perill threat,
He will not bide the daunger of such dread,
But strikes his sayles, and vereth his mainsheat,
And lends unto it leave the emptie ayre to beat.

32 106 *frayd* frightened 107 *gerne* show his teeth, snarl 109 *listes* area of battle 114 *Elfin swayne* knightly man 119 *fell* fierce, savage, deadly 126 *brast* burst 128 *avize* notice 130 *gracelesse* merciless, cruel 131 *reed* see, perceive 134 but shortens his sails and raises the rope which secures the mainsail to reduce the amount of wind behind the ship

So did the Faerie knight himselfe abeare,
And stouped oft his head from shame to shield;
No shame to stoupe, ones head more high to reare,
And much to gaine, a litle for to yield;
So stoutest knights doen oftentimes in field.
But still the tyrant sternely at him layd,
And did his yron axe so nimbly wield,
That many wounds into his flesh it made,
And with his burdenous blowes him sore did overlade.

Yet when as fit advantage he did spy,
The whiles the cursed felon high did reare
His cruell hand, to smite him mortally,
Under his stroke he to him stepping neare,
Right in the flanke him strooke with deadly dreare,
That the gore bloud thence gushing grievously,
Did underneath him like a pond appeare,
And all his armour did with purple dye;
Thereat he brayed loud, and yelled dreadfully.

Yet the huge stroke, which he before intended,
Kept on his course, as he did it direct,
And with such monstrous poise adowne descended,
That seemed nought could him from death protect:
But he it well did ward with wise respect,
And twixt him and the blow his shield did cast,
Which thereon seizing, tooke no great effect,
But byting deepe therein did sticke so fast,
That by no meanes it backe againe he forth could wrast.

Long while he tug'd and strove, to get it out,
And all his powre applyed thereunto,
That he therewith the knight drew all about:
Nathlesse, for all that ever he could doe,
His axe he could not from his shield undoe.

32 136 *abeare** comport 144 *overlade* overburden, overload 146 *felon* villain, monster 149 *deadly dreare* the sadness and gloom of death 150 *gore bloud* clotted blood 156 *poise* forcible impact 158 *respect* care, attention 162 *wrast* wrest, pull away

Which *Artegall* perceiving, strooke no more,
But loosing soone his shield, did it forgoe,
And whiles he combred was therewith so sore,
He gan at him let drive more fiercely then afore.

So well he him pursew'd, that at the last,
He stroke him with *Chrysaor* on the hed,
That with the souse thereof full sore aghast,
He staggered to and fro in doubtfull sted.
Againe whiles he him saw so ill bested,
He did him smite with all his might and maine,
That falling on his mother earth he fed:
Whom when he saw prostrated on the plaine,
He lightly reft his head, to ease him of his paine.

Which when the people round about him saw,
They shouted all for joy of his successe,
Glad to be quit from that proud Tyrants awe,
Which with strong powre did them long time oppresse;
And running all with greedie joyfulnesse
To faire *Irena*, at her feet did fall,
And her adored with due humblenesse,
As their true Liege and Princesse naturall;
And eke her champions glorie sounded over all.

Who streight her leading with meete majestie
Unto the pallace, where their kings did rayne,
Did her therein establish peaceablie,
And to her kingdomes seat restore agayne;
And all such persons, as did late maintayne
That Tyrants part, with close or open ayde,
He sorely punished with heavie payne;
That in short space, whiles there with her he stayd,
Not one was left, that durst her once have disobayd.

32 169 *forgoe* let go 172 *pursew'd* harassed, attacked 173 *Chrysaor* Artegall's sword, called 'Golden' 174 *souse* heavy blow, thump 175 *sted* state 178 *fed* bit the dust 180 *reft* robbed him of, took away 183 *awe* terror 185 *greedie* keen, eager 188 *naturall* legitimate 190 *meete* suitable, fit

During which time, that he did there remaine,
His studie was true Justice how to deale,
And day and night employ'd his busie paine
How to reforme that ragged common-weale:
And that same yron man which could reveale
All hidden crimes, through all that realme he sent,
To search out those, that usd to rob and steale,
Or did rebell gainst lawfull government;
On whom he did inflict most grievous punishment.

But ere he could reforme it thoroughly,
He through occasion called was away,
To Faerie Court, that of necessity
His course of Justice he was forst to stay,
And *Talus* to revoke from the right way,
In which he was that Realme for to redresse.
But envies cloud still dimmeth vertues ray.
So having freed *Irena* from distresse,
He tooke his leave of her, there left in heavinesse.

Eochaidh Ó Heóghusa

33 [On Maguire's Winter Campaign]

Fúar liom an adhaighsi dh'Aodh,
cúis tuirse truime a ciothbhraon;
mo thrúaighe sein dár seise,
neimh fhúaire na hoidhcheise.

Anocht, is neimh rem chridhe,
fearthar frasa teintidhe
a gcomhdháil na gclá seacdha
mar tá is orghráin aigeanta.

32 211 *stay* halt, interrupt 212 *revoke* recall

Do hosgladh ós ochtaibh néll
doirse uisgidhe an aiér:
tug sé minlinnte 'na muir,
do sgé an fhirminnte a hurbhuidh.

Gémadh fiaidhmhíol a bhfiodhbhaidh,
gémadh éigne ar inbhiormhuir,
gémadh ealta, is doiligh dhi
soighidh ar eachtra an úairsi.

Sáoth leamsa Aodh Mhág Uidhir
anocht a gcrích chomhoidhigh,
fá ghrís ndeirg gcáorshoighnén gceath
fá fheirg bhfáobhoirnél bhfuileach.

A gcóigeadh Chloinne Dáire
dursan linn dár leannáinne
idir dhorchladh bhfúairfhliuch bhfeóir
is confadh úaibhreach aieóir.

Fúar liom dá leacain shubhaigh
fráoch na n-iodhlann n-earrchamhail,
ag séideadh síongháoth na reann
fá ríoghláoch ngéigeal nGaileang.

Sáoth linn, do loit ar meanmain,
learg thais a thaoibh míndealbhaigh
'gá meilt a ngrúamoidhche ghairbh,
a mbeirt fhúarfhoirfe íairn.

Bos tláith na dtachar n-édtláth,
síon oighridh dá fhúaighealtáth
re crann rionnfhúar gcáol gceise
ionnfhúar dh'Aodh san oidhcheise.

Nárab aithreach leis ná leam
a thurus timcheall Éireann;
go ndeach tharainn—ná ti m'olc—
an ní fá ngabhaim gúasacht.

33 21 *Dáire* West Munster 28 *nGaileang* a tribe living around Meath, Sligo, Cavan

Dá dtí ris an toisg do thríall,
do chur chúarta Chráoi Mhaicniadh—
ní tháirtheamar séd mar soin—
créd acht snáithghearradh sáoghail?

Líonaid re hucht na n-ánrath
brúaigh ísle na n-úaránshroth;
clúana sgor fá sgingbheirt reóidh
dá gcor tar ingheilt d'aimhdheóin.

Folchar a gciomhsa cheana,
nach léir do lucht foirgneamha
brúaigh easgadh na ngríanshroth nglan,
seasgadh fíanbhoth ní fédtar.

Eagail dó, díochra an anbhúain,
coill eachraidh is aradhshlúaigh,
sul dighthir tar síothLáoi síar,
a slighthibh míonchráoi Mhaicniadh.

Ní hé budh uireasbhaidh linn,
a thurus an tráth smúainim;
lór do chor chúarta ar gcridhe
gomh fhúachta na haimsire.

Gidh eadh, is adhbhar téighthe
dhá ghnúis shúaithnidh shoiléirthe
slios gach múir ghormsháothraigh gil
'na dhlúimh thonngháothmhair theintigh.

Téighidh teannál an adhnaidh
sging reóidh an ruisg shocarghlain,
geimhle chuisne a chorrghlac ndonn,
donnbhrat luisne nos leaghonn.

Seachnóin Mhumhan na múr ngeal
iomdha ó airgtheóir fhuinn Gháoidheal
cúirte brúachnochta a mbeirt smóil,
ag ceilt fhúardhochta an aieóir.

33 42 *Chráoi Mhaicniadh* Munster

Iomdha ó chuairt Aoidh Mhéig Uidhir
feadh íarthair fhóid fhionnfhuinidh
cúirt 'na doighir, ní díoth núa,
críoch gan oighir gan íarmhúa.

33 [On Maguire's Winter Campaign]

I think this night is cold for Hugh; the heaviness of its downpour is a cause of misery. I grieve that this befalls our comrade, the poison of this night's cold. Tonight it is poison to my heart that the fiery showers prevail; his encountering the weapons of frost, as he is, is inner anguish for me. The upper air's water-doors were opened above the clouds' breasts. It changed small pools into seas, as the firmament vented its destruction. Whether for the wild hare in the woods or the salmon in the estuary, or the flocking birds, it is deadly to travel at this time. It is my grief that Hugh Maguire is in foreign territory tonight, beneath the red burning of streaming thunder and the raging of bloody clouds of violence. It is heartbreak to us that our loved one is in the province of the people of Dáire, between the dark of the cold-wet ground and the arrogant frenzy of the sky. I think too cold for his gentle cheeks is the ferocity of the stormy attacks, blowing the tempest-winds of the constellations on to the radiant warrior-king of the Gaileanga. It is our grief, and it has destroyed our heart, that the soft smoothness of his sleek sides should be pounded by the savage boor-night while in the steel grip of age-cold. A gentle grasp in ungentle conflict, icy ill-weather binding it to the piercing shaft of a sharp spear: bitter it is for Hugh this night! May his journey around Ireland not prove a cause of regret for him and for me! May the thing that would be my ruin pass by me; may my ill not come! If the journey he is travelling on should prove ill for him, his visiting all the Fold of Maicnia, what would it be but the severing of our life's thread, since we have found no jewel like this one? The low banks of the spring-streams have swollen against the heroes; the champions' plains are under a blanket of ice, irresistibly making them pastureless. Their bounds are already flooded, so that house-builders cannot see the banks of the clear sunlit rivers, now they are deluged, and the tents cannot be dried. There is a danger (and it is a terrible threat) of losing horses and trappings before they can cross west over the Lee, tranquil again, on the level roads of Maicnia. But that is not such a loss to us, when I think by comparison of how he fares now. It's enough to put our hearts astray, so cold is the weather. And yet a theme to warm his noble, shining face is the side of every blue-worked castle bright with the blazing of wind-driven fire. The heat of that beacon-fire warms the veil of frost from the clear-firm eye. A red-brown cloak of flame will melt the fetters of ice off his brown wrists. Throughout Munster of the bright castle-walls, in response to the plunderers of the territory of the Gaels, courts stand stark naked, disguising the coldness of the air. Because of Hugh Maguire's journey, all through the west of this bright-lit land, courts are in flames, far and wide, a land without heir or descendant.

BEN JONSON

34 ON THE UNION

When was there contract better driven by *Fate?*
  Or celebrated with more truth of state?
The world the temple was, the priest a king,
  The spoused paire two realmes, the sea the ring.

SIR ARTHUR GORGES

35 Written upon the death of the most Noble Prince *Henrie*

Whilst my heart bleeding writes that deadlie wound
  Receaved of late in honnors overthrow
With our brave Prince, whose worth noe words can sound
  Sorrow must dictate, what my zeale would shew
Sorrow for that deare Treasure wee have loste,
  Zeale to the memorie of what wee had,
And that is all they cann, that cann saye moste.
  Soe sings my Muse, in zeale and sorrow clad.
Soe sung *Achilles* to his Silver Harpe,
  When fowle affroont had reft his faire delight,
Soe sings sweet *Philomel* against the sharpe
  Soe sings the *Swan*, when lyfe is taking flight.

Soe sings my Zeale the notes that sorrow weepes
Which antheme sung my Muse for ever sleepes.

35 11 *sharpe* sharp edge, thorn

SIR HENRY WOTTON

36 Upon the sudden Restraint of the *Earle* of *Somerset*, then falling from favor

Dazel'd thus, with height of place,
Whilst our hopes our wits beguile,
No man markes the narrow space
'Twixt a prison, and a smile.

Then, since fortunes favours fade,
You, that in her armes doe sleep,
Learne to swim, and not to wade;
For, the Hearts of Kings are deepe.

But, if Greatness be so blind,
As to trust in towers of Aire,
Let it be with Goodness lin'd,
That at'least, the Fall be faire.

Then though darkned, you shall say,
When Friends faile, and Princes frowne,
Vertue is the roughest way,
But proves at night a *Bed of Downe*.

WILLIAM BROWNE

37 [*from* Britannia's Pastorals Book 2]

O! should all Potentates whose higher birth
Enroles their titles, other *Gods on earth*,

36 16 *Bed of Downe* soft feather bed

Should they make private search, in vaile of night,
For cruell wrongs done by each Favorite;
Here should they finde a great one paling in
A meane mans land, which many yeeres had bin
His charges life, and by the others heast,
The poore must starve to feede a scurvy beast.
If any recompence drop from his fist,
His time's his owne, the mony, what he list.
There should they see another that commands
His Farmers Teame from furrowing his lands,
To bring him stones to raise his building vast,
The while his Tenants sowing time is past.
Another (spending) doth his rents inhance,
Or gets by trickes the poores inheritance.
But as a man whose age hath dim'd his eyes
Useth his Spectacles, and as he pryes
Through them all Characters seeme wondrous faire,
Yet when his glasses quite removed are
(Though with all carefull heed he neerly looke)
Cannot perceive one tittle in the Booke
So if a King behold such favourites
(Whose being great, was being *Parasites*,)
With th'eyes of favour; all their actions are
To him appearing plaine and regular:
But let him lay his sight of grace aside,
And see what men hee hath so dignifide,
They all would vanish, and not dare appeare,
Who *Atom-like*, when their *Sun* shined cleare,
Danc'd in his beame; but now his rayes are gone,
Of many hundred we perceive not one.
Or as a man who standing to descry
How great floods farre off run, and vallies lye,
Taketh a *glasse prospective* good and true,
By which things most remote are full in view:
If Monarchs, so, would take an Instrument
Of truth compos'd to spie their Subjects drent

37 3 *in vaile* under cover 5 *paling* fencing 7 *heast* behest, command 12 *furrowing* ploughing 15 *inhance* raise, increase 21 *neerly* closely, minutely 27 *sight of grace* aid to better vision; spectacles 35 *glasse prospective*** telescope 38 *drent* drowned

In foule oppression by those high in seate,
(Who care not to be good but to be great)
In full aspect the wrongs of each degree
Would lye before them; and they then would see.
The divelish *Polititian* all convinces,
In murdring Statesmen and in poisning Princes;
The *Prelate* in *pluralities* asleepe
Whilst that the *Wolfe* lyes preying on his sheepe;
The drowsie *Lawyer*, and the false *Atturnies*
Tire poore mens purses with their life-long-journyes;
The *Country Gentleman*, from's neighbours hand
Forceth th'inheritance, joynes land to land,
And (most insatiate) seekes under his rent
To bring the worlds most spacious continent;
The fawning *Citizen* (whose love's bought deerest)
Deceives his brother when the Sun shines clearest,
Gets, borrowes, breakes, lets in, and stops out light,
And lives a Knave to leave his sonne a Knight;
The griping *Farmer* hoords the seede of bread,
Whilst in the streets the poore lye famished:
And free there's none from all this worldly strife,
Except the Shepheards heaven-blest happy life.

ANONYMOUS

38 Feltons Epitaph

Heere uninterr'd suspendes (though not to save
Surviving Frendes th'expences of a grave)
Feltons dead Earth; which to the world must bee
Its owne sadd Monument. His Elegie

37 43 *convinces* overcomes, conquers, vanquishes 45 *pluralities* two or more benefices held by one person 48 *life-long*** livelong, long as life, enduring 57 *griping* grasping, avaricious

38 1 *uninterr'd*** after his execution, the body of Buckingham's assassin, John Felton, was hung in chains

As large as Fame; but whether badd or good
I say not: by himself 'twas writt in blood:
For which his bodie is entomb'd in Ayre,
Archt o're with heaven, sett with a thousand faire
And glorious Diamond Starrs. A Sepulchre
That time can never ruinate, and where
Th'impartiall Worme (which is not brib'd to spare
Princes corrupt in Marble) cannot share
His Flesh; which yf the charitable skies
Embalme with teares; doeing those Obsequies
Belong to men shall last; till pittying Fowle
Contend to beare his bodie to his soule.

Anonymous

39 [Epitaph on the Duke of Buckingham]

This little Grave embraces
One Duke and twentie places.

Sir Richard Fanshawe

40 [*from* An Ode Upon occasion of His Majesties Proclamation in the yeare 1630. Commanding the Gentry to reside upon their Estates in the Country]

Now warre is all the world about,
And every where *Erynnis* raignes,
Or else the Torch so late put out
The stench remaines. . . .

39 2 *places* offices, official posts

40 1 *warre* the Thirty Years War (1618–48)

Onely the Island which wee sowe,
(A world without the world) so farre
From present wounds, it cannot showe
An ancient skarre.
White Peace (the beautiful'st of things)
Seemes here her everlasting rest
To fix, and spreads her downy wings
Over the nest.
As when great *Jove* usurping Reigne
From the plagu'd world did her exile
And ty'd her with a golden chaine
To one blest Isle:
Which in a sea of plenty swamme
And Turtles sang on ev'ry bowgh,
A safe retreat to all that came
As ours is now:
Yet wee, as if some foe were here,
Leave the despised Fields to clownes,
And come to save our selves as twere
In walled Townes.
Hither we bring Wives, Babes, rich clothes
And Gemms; Till now my Soveraigne
The growing evill doth oppose:
Counting in vaine
His care preserves us from annoy
Of enemyes his Realmes to'invade,
Unlesse hee force us to enjoy
The peace hee made.
To rowle themselves in envy'd leasure
He therefore sends the Landed Heyres,
Whilst hee proclaimes not his owne pleasure
So much as theirs.
The sapp and bloud o'th land, which fled
Into the roote, and choackt the heart,
Are bid their quickning pow'r to spread
Through ev'ry part.

40 6 *A ... world* cp. Virgil, *Eclogues* 1.66, in which the Britons are described as 'cut off from the whole width of the world' 16 *blest Isle* the tradition that Britain was especially fortunate was an ancient one 18 *Turtles* turtle-doves 22 *clownes* rustics, peasants 39 *quickning* animating, vivifying

O, 'twas an act, not for my muse
To celebrate, nor the dull Age
Untill the country aire infuse
A purer rage!
And if the Fields as thankfull prove
For benefits receiv'd, as seed,
They will, to quite so great a love,
A *Virgill* breed.
A *Tytirus*, that shall not cease
Th' *Augustus* of our world to praise
In equall verse, author of peace
And *Halcyon* dayes.

JOHN CLEVELAND

41 Epitaph on the Earl of *Strafford*

Here lies Wise and Valiant Dust,
Huddled up 'twixt Fit and Just:
STRAFFORD, who was hurried hence
'Twixt Treason and Convenience.
He spent his Time here in a Mist;
A *Papist*, yet a *Calvinist*.
His Prince's nearest Joy, and Grief.
He had, yet wanted all Reliefe.

40 47 *quite* requite, pay back 49 *Tytirus* the name of a goatherd or shepherd, especially used by Virgil in the *Eclogues* 52 *Halcyon* kingfishers, whose nesting for a week or two at midwinter supposedly calms the seas, bringing a time of peace

41 Title *Strafford* Sir Thomas Wentworth (1593–1641), first Earl of Strafford, courtier and statesman, adviser to Charles I who assented to his execution after Parliament had passed a bill of attainder for high treason against him. Strafford was executed on 12 May 1641 6 Strafford was popularly thought to be a Roman Catholic, although privately he was a Calvinist

The Prop and Ruine of the State;
The People's violent Love, and Hate:
One in extreames lov'd and abhor'd.
Riddles lie here; or in a word,
Here lies Blood; and let it lie
Speechlesse still, and never crie.

SIR JOHN DENHAM

42 Coopers Hill

Sure there are Poets which did never dream
Upon *Parnassus*, nor did tast the stream
Of *Helicon*, we therefore may suppose
Those made not Poets, but the Poets those.
And as Courts make not Kings, but Kings the
Court,
So where the Muses and their train resort,
Parnassus stands; if I can be to thee
A Poet, thou *Parnassus* art to me.
Nor wonder, if (advantag'd in my flight,
By taking wing from thy auspicious height)
Through untrac't ways, and aery paths I fly,
More boundless in my Fancy than my eie:
My eye, which swift as thought contracts the space
That lies between, and first salutes the place
Crown'd with that sacred pile, so vast, so high,
That whether 'tis a part of Earth, or sky,
Uncertain seems, and may be thought a proud
Aspiring mountain, or descending cloud,

42 Title *Coopers Hill* near Egham, Surrey, close to Windsor and Runnymede; at least four counties can be seen from the top of the Hill 1–4 cp. Persius, *Satires* 1, Prologue 1–3 translated by Dryden as 'I never did on cleft Parnassus dream,/Nor taste the sacred Heliconian stream;/Nor can remember when my brain, inspir'd,/Was by the Muses into madness fir'd' 10 *auspicious* lucky, favourable; promising success 15 *pile* St Paul's Cathedral

Pauls, the late theme of such a Muse whose flight *M. W.*
Has bravely reach't and soar'd above thy height:
Now shalt thou stand though sword, or time, or
fire,
Or zeal more fierce than they, thy fall conspire,
Secure, whilst thee the best of Poets sings,
Preserv'd from ruine by the best of Kings.
Under his proud survey the City lies,
And like a mist beneath a hill doth rise;
Whose state and wealth the business and the crowd,
Seems at this distance but a darker cloud:
And is to him who rightly things esteems,
No other in effect than what it seems:
Where, with like hast, though several ways, they
run
Some to undo, and some to be undone;
While luxury, and wealth, like war and peace,
Are each the others ruine, and increase;
As Rivers lost in Seas some secret vein
Thence reconveighs, there to be lost again.
Oh happiness of sweet retir'd content!
To be at once secure, and innocent.
Windsor the next (where *Mars* with *Venus*
dwells, *Windsor.*
Beauty with strength) above the Valley swells
Into my eye, and doth it self present
With such an easie and unforc't ascent,
That no stupendious precipice denies
Access, no horror turns away our eyes:
But such a Rise, as doth at once invite
A pleasure, and a reverence from the sight.
Thy mighty Masters Embleme, in whose face
Sate meekness, heightned with Majestick Grace
Such seems thy gentle height, made only proud
To be the basis of that pompous load,

42 19 side-note *M. W.* Master (Edmund) Waller, see his poem 'Upon his *Majesties* repairing of *Pauls*' (no. 290) 22 *zeal* Puritan extremism 33–4 proverbial 35–6 a traditional theory explaining the source of rivers 47 *Masters Embleme* Windsor Hill and Castle are Charles I's natural emblems 50 *pompous* dignified

Than which, a nobler weight no Mountain bears,
But *Atlas* only that supports the Sphears.
When Natures hand this ground did thus advance,
'Twas guided by a wiser power than Chance;
Mark't out for such a use, as if 'twere meant
T' invite the builder, and his choice prevent.
Nor can we call it choice, when what we chuse,
Folly, or blindness only could refuse.
A Crown of such Majestick towrs doth Grace
The Gods great Mother, when her heavenly race
Do homage to her, yet she cannot boast
Amongst that numerous, and Celestial host,
More *Hero's* than can *Windsor*, nor doth Fames
Immortal book record more noble names.
Not to look back so far, to whom this Isle
Owes the first Glory of so brave a pile,
Whether to *Cæsar*, *Albanact*, or *Brute*,
The Brittish *Arthur*, or the Danish *Knute*,
(Though this of old no less contest did move,
Then when for *Homers* birth seven Cities strove)
(Like him in birth, thou should'st be like in fame,
As thine his fate, if mine had been his Flame)
But whosoere it was, Nature design'd
First a brave place, and then as brave a mind.
Not to recount those several Kings, to whom
It gave a Cradle, or to whom a Tombe,
But thee (great *Edward*) and thy greater son,
(The lillies which his Father wore, he won)
And thy *Bellona*, who the Consort came
Not only to thy Bed, but to thy Fame,
She to thy Triumph led one Captive King,
And brought that son, which did the second bring.

Edward the third, and the *Black Prince*.

Queen *Philip*.

The Kings of *France* and *Scotland*.

42 60 *Mother* Cybele 65–6 cp. Waller's poem on St Paul's (no. 290 ll. 5–6) 68 *Arthur* legendary King of Britain *Knute* Canute, King of the English, Danes and Norwegians (994?–1035) 78 *lillies* fleurs-de-lis, the emblem of France 79 side-note *Queen Philip* Edward III's wife, Philippa of Hainault 81 *Captive King* David II of Scotland was captured in 1346 82 *the second* King John of France was captured in 1356

Then didst thou found that Order (whither love
Or victory thy Royal thoughts did move)
Each was a noble cause, and nothing less,
Than the design, has been the great success:
Which forraign Kings, and Emperors esteem
The second honour to their Diadem.
Had thy great Destiny but given thee skill,
To know as well, as power to act her will,
That from those Kings, who then thy captives were,
In after-times should spring a Royal pair
Who should possess all that thy mighty power,
Or thy desires more mighty, did devour;
To whom their better Fate reserves what ere
The Victor hopes for, or the Vanquisht fear;
That bloud, which thou and thy great Grandsire
shed,
And all that since these sister Nations bled,
Had been unspilt, had happy *Edward* known
That all the bloud he spilt, had been his own.
When he that Patron chose, in whom are joyn'd
Souldier and Martyr, and his arms confin'd
Within the Azure Circle, he did seem
But to foretell, and prophesie of him,
Who to his Realms that Azure round hath joyn'd,
Which Nature for their bound at first design'd.
That bound, which to the Worlds extreamest ends,
Endless it self, its liquid arms extends;

42 83 *that Order* the Order of the Knights of the Garter, probably founded in about 1349 either to celebrate the victory of the battle of Calais, or to strengthen bonds of love and loyalty between knights, or as a result of Edward III's picking up the Countess of Salisbury's garter and placing it on his own knee, proclaiming the Order's motto 'Honi soit qui mal y pense' 92 *Royal pair* Charles I was descended from the royal house of Scotland and his wife Henrietta Maria from the French house of Bourbon 97 *great Grandsire* Edward III's grandfather, Edward I, fought both the Scots and the French 101 *that Patron* St George of Cappadocia 102 *his arms* a red cross on a white shield 103 *Azure Circle* the blue garter of the Order 104 *him* Charles I 105–6 the reference to the seas around Britain may allude to Charles I's shipbuilding programme

Nor doth he need those Emblemes which we paint,
But is himself the Souldier and the Saint.
Here should my wonder dwell, and here my praise,
But my fixt thoughts my wandring eye betrays,
Viewing a neighbouring hill, whose top of late
A Chappel crown'd, till in the Common Fate,
The adjoyning Abby fell: (may no such storm
Fall on our times, where ruine must reform.)
Tell me (my Muse) what monstrous dire offence,
What crime could any Christian King incense
To such a rage? was't Luxury, or Lust?
Was he so temperate, so chast, so just?
Were these their crimes? they were his own much
more:
But wealth is Crime enough to him that's poor,
Who having spent the Treasures of his Crown,
Condemns their Luxury to feed his own.
And yet this Act, to varnish o're the shame
Of sacriledge, must bear devotions name.
No Crime so bold, but would be understood
A real, or at least a seeming good.
Who fears not to do ill, yet fears the Name,
And free from Conscience, is a slave to Fame.
Thus he the Church at once protects, and spoils:
But Princes swords are sharper than their stiles.
And thus to th' ages past he makes amends,
Their Charity destroys, their Faith defends.
Then did Religion in a lazy Cell,
In empty, airy contemplations dwell;
And like the block, unmoved lay: but ours,
As much too active, like the stork devours.
Is there no temperate Region can be known,
Betwixt their Frigid, and our Torrid Zone?

42 109 in 1629 Rubens painted Charles I as St George rescuing Henrietta Maria from the dragon in a pastoral setting 113 *neighbouring hill* St Anne's Hill, near Chertsey 115 *Abby* Chertsey Abbey 118 *King* Henry VIII 119 *Luxury* lasciviousness; self-indulgence 132 *stiles* styluses, pens; styles, titles 134 *Faith defends* cp. Henry VIII's title conferred on him by the Pope of 'Fidei defensor', 'Defender of the faith' 137–8 in Aesop's fable, the frogs appealed to Zeus for a king; when they were dissatisfied with his gift of a log, the stork sent to replace it devoured them

Could we not wake from that Lethargick dream,
But to be restless in a worse extream?
And for that Lethargy was there no cure,
But to be cast into a Calenture?
Can knowledge have no bound, but must advance
So far, to make us wish for ignorance?
And rather in the dark to grope our way,
Than led by a false guide to erre by day?
Who sees these dismal heaps, but would demand
What barbarous Invader sackt the land?
But when he hears, no Goth, no Turk did bring
This desolation, but a Christian King;
When nothing, but the Name of Zeal, appears
'Twixt our best actions and the worst of theirs,
What does he think our Sacriledge would spare,
When such th' effects of our devotions are?
Parting from thence 'twixt anger, shame, and fear,
Those for whats past, and this for whats too near:
My eye descending from the Hill, surveys
Where *Thames* amongst the wanton vallies strays. *Thames.*
Thames, the most lov'd of all the Oceans sons,
By his old Sire to his embraces runs,
Hasting to pay his tribute to the Sea,
Like mortal life to meet Eternity.
Though with those streams he no resemblance hold,
Whose foam is Amber, and their Gravel Gold;
His genuine, and less guilty wealth t' explore,
Search not his bottom, but survey his shore;
Ore which he kindly spreads his spacious wing,
And hatches plenty for th' ensuing Spring.
Nor then destroys it with too fond a stay,
Like Mothers which their Infants overlay.
Nor with a sudden and impetuous wave,
Like profuse Kings, resumes the wealth he gave.

42 144 *Calenture* tropical disease in which sailors imagine the sea to be green fields 148 *erre* be mistaken; wander 149 *dismal heaps* the ruins of Chertsey Abbey 158 *Those* anger and shame *this* fear 160 *wanton* luxurious, lush 165 *those streams* Tagus and Pactolus 172 *overlay* suffocate in sleep 174 *resumes* takes back again

No unexpected inundations spoyl
The mowers hopes, nor mock the plowmans toyl:
But God-like his unwearied Bounty flows;
First loves to do, then loves the Good he does.
Nor are his Blessings to his banks confin'd,
But free, and common, as the Sea or Wind;
When he to boast, or to disperse his stores
Full of the tributes of his grateful shores,
Visits the world, and in his flying towers
Brings home to us, and makes both *Indies* ours;
Finds wealth where 'tis, bestows it where it wants
Cities in deserts, woods in Cities plants.
So that to us no thing, no place is strange,
While his fair bosom is the worlds exchange.
O could I flow like thee, and make thy stream
My great example, as it is my theme!
Though deep, yet clear, though gentle, yet not dull,
Strong without rage, without ore-flowing full.
Heaven her *Eridanus* no more shall boast,
Whose Fame in thine, like lesser Currents lost,
Thy Nobler streams shall visit *Jove's* aboads,
To shine amongst the Stars, and bath the Gods.
Here Nature, whether more intent to please — The Forrest.
Us or her self, with strange varieties,
(For things of wonder give no less delight
To the wise Maker's, than beholders sight.
Though these delights from several causes move
For so our children, thus our friends we love)
Wisely she knew, the harmony of things,
As well as that of sounds, from discords springs.
Such was the discord, which did first disperse
Form, order, beauty through the Universe;
While driness moysture, coldness heat resists,
All that we have, and that we are, subsists.
While the steep horrid roughness of the Wood
Strives with the gentle calmness of the flood.

42 175–6 cp. Denham's translation of Virgil's *Aeneid* 2.305–6 '. . . Torrents raging course/Bears down th'opposing Oaks, the fields destroys/And mocks the Ploughmans toil . . .' 184 *both Indies* the East and West Indies 209 *horrid* bristling, shaggy

Such huge extreams when Nature doth unite,
Wonder from thence results, from thence delight
The stream is so transparent, pure, and clear,
That had the self-enamour'd youth gaz'd here, *Narcissus.*
So fatally deceiv'd he had not been,
While he the bottom, not his face had seen.
But his proud head the aery Mountain hides
Among the Clouds; his shoulders, and his sides
A shady mantle cloaths; his curled brows
Frown on the gentle stream, which calmly flows,
While winds and storms his lofty forehead beat:
The common fate of all that's high or great.
Low at his foot a spacious plain is plac't,
Between the mountain and the stream embrac't:
Which shade and shelter from the Hill derives,
While the kind river wealth and beauty gives;
And in the mixture of all these appears
Variety, which all the rest indears.
This scene had some bold Greek, or Brittish Bard
Beheld of old, what stories had we heard,
Of Fairies, Satyrs, and the Nymphs their Dames,
Their feasts, their revels, and their amorous flames
'Tis still the same, although their aery shape
All but a quick Poetick sight escape.
There *Faunus* and *Sylvanus* keep their Courts,
And thither all the horned hoast resorts,
To graze the ranker mead, that noble heard
On whose sublime and shady fronts is rear'd
Natures great Master-piece; to shew how soon
Great things are made, but sooner are undone.
Here have I seen the King, when great affairs
Give leave to slacken, and unbend his cares,
Attended to the Chase by all the flower
Of youth, whose hopes a Nobler prey devour:

42 214 *self-enamour'd*** 223 *spacious plain* Egham Mead, which includes Runnymede and Long Mead 237 *ranker* more luxuriant, richer 241–322 these lines describing the stag hunt probably originally referred to the trial and execution of Strafford (see no. 41), but by 1655 could be read as alluding to the trial and execution of Charles I

Pleasure with Praise, and danger, they would buy,
And wish a foe that would not only fly.
The stagg now conscious of his fatal Growth,
At once indulgent to his fear and sloth,
To some dark covert his retreat had made,
Where nor mans eye, nor heavens should invade
His soft repose; when th' unexpected sound
Of dogs, and men, his wakeful ear doth wound.
Rouz'd with the noise, he scarce believes his ear,
Willing to think th' illusions of his fear
Had given this false Alarm, but straight his view
Confirms, that more than all he fears is true.
Betray'd in all his strengths, the wood beset,
All instruments, all Arts of ruine met;
He calls to mind his strength, and then his speed,
His winged heels, and then his armed head;
With these t'avoid, with that his Fate to meet:
But fear prevails, and bids him trust his feet.
So fast he flyes, that his reviewing eye
Has lost the chasers, and his ear the cry;
Exulting, till he finds, their Nobler sense
Their disproportion'd speed does recompense.
Then curses his conspiring feet, whose scent
Betrays that safety which their swiftness lent.
Then tries his friends, among the baser herd,
Where he so lately was obey'd, and fear'd,
His safety seeks: the herd, unkindly wise,
Or chases him from thence, or from him flies.
Like a declining States-man, left forlorn
To his friends pity, and pursuers scorn,
With shame remembers, while himself was one
Of the same herd, himself the same had done.
Thence to the coverts, and the conscious Groves,
The scenes of his past triumphs, and his loves;
Sadly surveying where he rang'd alone
Prince of the soyl, and all the herd his own;

42 263 *reviewing* surveying 271 *unkindly* unnaturally, not according to their kind 277 *conscious* sharing in, witnesses to, human affairs

And like a bold Knight Errant did proclaim
Combat to all, and bore away the Dame;
And taught the woods to eccho to the stream
His dreadful challenge, and his clashing beam.
Yet faintly now declines the fatal strife;
So much his love was dearer than his life.
Now every leaf, and every moving breath
Presents a foe, and every foe a death.
Wearied, forsaken, and pursu'd, at last
All safety in despair of safety plac'd,
Courage he thence resumes, resolv'd to bear
All their assaults, since 'tis in vain to fear.
And now too late he wishes for the fight
That strength he wasted in Ignoble flight:
But when he sees the eager chase renew'd,
Himself by dogs, the dogs by men pursu'd:
He straight revokes his bold resolve, and more
Repents his courage, than his fear before;
Finds that uncertain waies unsafest are,
And Doubt a greater mischief than Despair.
Then to the stream, when neither friends, nor force,
Nor speed, nor Art avail, he shapes his course;
Thinks not their rage so desperate t' assay
An Element more merciless than they.
But fearless they pursue, nor can the floud
Quench their dire thirst; alas, they thirst for bloud.
So towards a Ship the oarefin'd Gallies ply,
Which wanting Sea to ride, or wind to fly,
Stands but to fall reveng'd on those that dare
Tempt the last fury of extream despair.
So fares the Stagg among th' enraged Hounds,
Repels their force, and wounds returns for wounds.
And as a Hero, whom his baser foes
In troops surround, now these assails, now those,
Though prodigal of life, disdains to die
By common hands; but if he can descry

42 281–2 cp. the note to l. 109 above 303 *assay* try 307 *oarefin'd* with oars like fins

Some nobler foes approach, to him he calls,
And begs his Fate, and then contented falls.
So when the King a mortal shaft lets fly
From his unerring hand, then glad to dy,
Proud of the wound, to it resigns his bloud,
And stains the Crystal with a Purple floud.
This a more Innocent, and happy chase,
Than when of old, but in the self-same place,

Runny Mead where that great Charter was first sealed.

Fair liberty pursu'd, and meant a Prey
To lawless power, here turn'd, and stood at bay.
When in that remedy all hope was plac't
Which was, or should have been at least, the last.
Here was that Charter seal'd, wherein the Crown

Magna Charta.

All marks of Arbitrary power lays down:
Tyrant and slave, those names of hate and fear,
The happier stile of King and Subject bear:
Happy, when both to the same Center move,
When Kings give liberty, and Subjects love.
Therefore not long in force this Charter stood;
Waiting that seal, it must be seal'd in bloud.
The Subjects arm'd, the more their Princes gave,
Th' advantage only took the more to crave:
Till Kings by giving, give themselves away,
And even that power, that should deny, betray.
"Who gives constrain'd, but his own fear reviles
"Not thank't, but scorn'd; nor are they gifts, but spoils.
Thus Kings, by grasping more than they could hold,
First made their Subjects by oppression bold:
And popular sway, by forcing Kings to give
More than was fit for Subjects to receive,
Ran to the same extreams; and one excess
Made both, by striving to be greater, less.
When a calm River rais'd with sudden rains,
Or Snows dissolv'd, oreflows th' adjoyning Plains,

42 324 side-note *Charter* King John signed Magna Carta at Runnymede in 1215; in the seventeenth century it was often cited as a charter of 'English liberty' 336 *that seal* love 341–2 these lines are marked to show that they are sententiae

The Husbandmen with high-rais'd banks secure
Their greedy hopes, and this he can endure.
But if with Bays and Dams they strive to force
His channel to a new, or narrow course;
No longer then within his banks he dwells,
First to a Torrent, then a Deluge swells:
Stronger, and fiercer by restraint he roars,
And knows no bound, but makes his power his
shores.

MARTIN PARKER

43 Upon defacing of *White-hall*

1\. What *Booker* doth prognosticate
Concerning Kings or Kingdoms state,
I think my self to be as wise,
As some that gazeth on the skyes:
My skill goes beyond, the depth of a *Pond*,
Or *Rivers* in the greatest rain,
Whereby I *can tell, all things will be well,*
When the King enjoys his own again.

2\. There's neither *Swallow, Dove,* nor *Dade,*
Can soar more high, or deeper wade;
Nor shew a reason from the stars,
What causeth Peace or Civil Wars:

42 353 *Bays* embankments, dams

43 1 *What* whatever *Booker* John Booker (1603–67) astrologer and almanac-maker 5 *Pond* Edward Pond, almanac-maker, who died in 1629 6 *Rivers* Peregrine and William Rivers both published almanacs under their names from 1625 9 *Swallow* almanacs appeared under Thomas Swallow's name from 1628 *Dove* Jonathan Dove's almanacs appeared from 1627 *Dade** wading-bird; William Dade's almanacs appeared from 1615

The man in the Moon, may wear out his shoo'n
By runing after *Charls* his Wain,
But all's to no end, for the times will not mend
Till the King, etc.

3. Full forty years this Royal Crown
Hath been his fathers and his own:
And is there anyone but He,
That in the same should sharers be?
For who better may, the Scepter sway,
Than he that hath such right to reign?
Then let's hope for a peace, for the Wars will not
cease
Till the King enjoys, etc.

4. Though for a time we see *White-hall*
With Cobweb-hangings on the wall,
In stead of gold and silver brave,
Which formerly 'twas wont to have,
With rich perfume in every room,
Delightful to that Princely Train,
Which again shall be, when the time you see,
That the King enjoys, etc.

5. Did *Walker* no predictions lack
In *Hammonds* bloody Almanack?
Foretelling things that would ensue,
That all proves right, if lies be true:

43 13 *The ... Moon* may refer to the scurrilous newspaper edited by John Crouch, April 1649 to June 1650; Crouch had edited a competing version of the newspaper *Mercurius melancholicus* in which Parker was involved 14 *Charls ... Wain* the constellation so named, a frequent motif in Caroline court poetry 27 *brave* fine, splendid 33 *Walker* the parliamentarian journalist Henry Walker, who was repeatedly satirized by Parker 34 *Hammonds ... Almanack* on the outbreak of the Civil War almanacs became increasingly politicized; the Presbyterian ballad-maker John Hammond issued *The new bloody almanack for this insuing yeare* in 1644

But why should not he, the pillory foresee,
Wherein poor *Toby* once was ta'ne?
And also foreknow, to'th Gallows he must go,
When the King enjoys, etc.

6. Till then upon Ararats-hill,
My hope shall cast his Anchor still,
Untill I see some peaceful *Dove *Gen. *Monck*
Bring home the Branch I dearly love:
Then will I wait till the waters abate,
Which most disturbs my troubled brain,
Else never rejoyce till I hear the voice,
That the King enjoys his own again.

ROBERT HERRICK

44 A King and no King

That Prince, who may doe nothing but what's just,
Rules but by leave, and takes his Crowne on trust.

43 38 *poor Toby* Henry Walker was pilloried in July 1642 for inciting the people to take up arms against the King. In the celebrated satire *A seasonable lecture*, 1642, 'Thorny Ailo', alias John Taylor who shared Parker's political views, put in Walker's mouth an absurd sermon on Tobias's dog (see Tobit 5:16) 41 *Ararats-hill* where the Ark came to rest, see Genesis 8:4 43–6 cp. Genesis 8:11 'And the dove came in to him in the evening; and, lo, in her mouth was an olive leaf pluckt off: so Noah knew that the waters were abated from off the earth' 43 side-note *Monck* George Monck (1608–70), a military commander who served Charles I in Ireland and Cromwell in Scotland; with some hesitation and equivocation he supported the Restoration

ANDREW MARVELL

45 An *Horatian* Ode upon *Cromwel's* Return from *Ireland*

The forward Youth that would appear
Must now forsake his *Muses* dear,
Nor in the Shadows sing
His Numbers languishing.
'Tis time to leave the Books in dust,
And oyl th' unused Armours rust:
Removing from the Wall
The Corslet of the Hall.
So restless *Cromwel* could not cease
In the inglorious Arts of Peace,
But through adventrous War
Urged his active Star.
And, like the three-fork'd Lightning, first
Breaking the Clouds where it was nurst,
Did thorough his own Side
His fiery way divide.
For 'tis all one to Courage high
The Emulous or Enemy;
And with such to inclose
Is more then to oppose.
Then burning through the Air he went,
And Pallaces and Temples rent:
And *Cæsars* head at last
Did through his Laurels blast.
'Tis Madness to resist or blame
The force of angry Heavens flame:

45 Title *Horatian*★★ 1 *forward* ready, prompt, eager, spirited; presumptuous, bold, immodest; precocious *appear* come before the public as if on stage 4 *Numbers* poems, verses *languishing* pining with love 8 *Corslet* piece of body armour 9 *cease* rest 15 *his own Side* his own party, the parliamentary leaders; the cloud's side through which the lightning flashes 19–20 to enclose, shut in, such a man is more trying than to oppose him

And, if we would speak true,
Much to the Man is due.
Who, from his private Gardens, where
He liv'd reserved and austere,
As if his highest plot
To plant the Bergamot,
Could by industrious Valour climbe
To ruine the great Work of Time,
And cast the Kingdome old
Into another Mold.
Though Justice against Fate complain,
And plead the antient Rights in vain:
But those do hold or break
As Men are strong or weak.
Nature that hateth emptiness,
Allows of penetration less:
And therefore must make room
Where greater Spirits come.
What Field of all the Civil Wars,
Where his were not the deepest Scars?
And *Hampton* shows what part
He had of wiser Art.
Where, twining subtile fears with hope,
He wove a Net of such a scope,
That *Charles* himself might chase
To *Caresbrooks* narrow case.
That thence the *Royal Actor* born
The *Tragick Scaffold* might adorn
While round the armed Bands
Did clap their bloody hands.
He nothing common did or mean
Upon that memorable Scene:
But with his keener Eye
The Axes edge did try:

45 32 *Bergamot* fine kind of pear, also known as 'prince's pear' or 'pear of kings' 42 *penetration*** the occupation of the same space by two bodies at the same time 47 *Hampton* Hampton Court, which Charles fled in November 1647 49 *twining* weaving *subtile* fine, delicate 50–1 *such* ... *That* such ... as 52 *Caresbrooks* Carisbrooke Castle on the Isle of Wight, whose Governor betrayed him *case* cage 53 *born* borne, carried 54 *Scaffold* stage 60 *try* test

Nor call'd the *Gods* with vulgar spight
To vindicate his helpless Right,
But bow'd his comely Head,
Down as upon a Bed.
This was that memorable Hour
Which first assur'd the forced Pow'r.
So when they did design
The *Capitols* first Line,
A bleeding Head where they begun,
Did fright the Architects to run;
And yet in that the *State*
Foresaw it's happy Fate.
And now the *Irish* are asham'd
To see themselves in one Year tam'd:
So much one Man can do,
That does both act and know.
They can affirm his Praises best,
And have, though overcome, confest
How good he is, how just,
And fit for highest Trust:
Nor yet grown stiffer with Command,
But still in the *Republick's* hand:
How fit he is to sway
That can so well obey.
He to the *Commons Feet* presents
A *Kingdome*, for his first years rents:
And, what he may, forbears
His Fame to make it theirs:
And has his Sword and Spoyls ungirt,
To lay them at the *Publick's* skirt.
So when the Falcon high
Falls heavy from the Sky,
She, having kill'd, no more does search,
But on the next green Bow to pearch;
Where, when he first does lure,
The Falckner has her sure.

45 66 *assur'd* ensured *forced* imposed, enforced 74 Cromwell landed at Dublin in August 1649 82 *still* yet, always 90 *Publick's* state's, nation's

What may not then our *Isle* presume
While Victory his Crest does plume!
   What may not others fear
   If thus he crown each Year!
A *Cæsar* he ere long to *Gaul*,
To *Italy* an *Hannibal*,
   And to all States not free
   Shall *Clymacterick* be.
The *Pict* no shelter now shall find
Within his party-colour'd Mind;
   But from this Valour sad
   Shrink underneath the Plad:
Happy if in the tufted brake
The *English Hunter* him mistake;
   Nor lay his Hounds in near
   The *Caledonian* Deer.
But thou the Wars and Fortunes Son
March indefatigably on;
   And for the last effect
   Still keep thy Sword erect:
Besides the force it has to fright
The Spirits of the shady Night,
   The same *Arts* that did *gain*
   A *Pow'r* must it *maintain*.

45 104 *Clymacterick* critical, marking an epoch 105 *Pict* Scot, from 'picti' in Latin, meaning 'painted', 'tattooed' 106 *party-colour'd* a punning reference to Scottish factionalism 107 *sad* steadfast, grave 108 *Plad* plaid, Scottish outer garment 109 *tufted brake* thicket formed out of tufts of bushes, trees 110 *mistake* fail to see because of his clothes 111 *lay* put 116 in Homer's *Odyssey* and Virgil's *Aeneid* the heroes wield swords to ward off the spirits of the dead in the underworld

Sir William Mure

46 [*from* The Cry of Blood, and of a Broken Covenant]

O Heavens! O Earth! heer I must pause a space.
Griefs tide flows higher, then, in this sad case,
Can calm'd be by expression: But, to speak,
Allegiance pleads. Men soberest, minds most meek,
Most free of passion, cannot but resent
This high Injustice; yea, in freedome vent
Their Thoughts, and what a dialect to use,
This bloody prelude speaks. Then free-born Muse
Tell Britaine, tell the World, that hence, in vain
Words shall be heard of any milder straine
Then Martiall eloquence. In trumpets sound
Be Scotlands Musick henceforth deeply
drown'd
From Heav'ns th'alarme, attended Orders bee,
All doubts discust, all judgments clear and free.
Let Colours fly, Drums beat. Gird on your
swords.
Arme Gallants, Arme. The Battell is the
Lords.

Treaties and parleyes to be suspected, the parties being in an unequall posture.

Arms therefore necessary to be ordered and made use of, as the God of Arms shall call for, and imploy.
1 Sam. 25.28.
2 Chr. 20.15

46 side-notes 1 Samuel 25:28 'I pray thee, forgive the trespass of thine handmaid [Abigail]: for the Lord will certainly make my lord a sure house; because my lord fighteth the battles of the Lord, and evil hath not been found in thee all thy days' 2 Chronicles 20:15 '... Thus saith the Lord unto you, Be not afraid nor dismayed by reason of this great multitude; for the battle is not yours but God's'

KATHERINE PHILIPS

47 On the 3. of *September*, 1651

As when the glorious Magazine of Light
Approches to his Canopy of Night,
He with new splendour clothes his dying Rays,
And double brightness to his Beams conveys;
And (as to brave and check his ending fate)
Puts on his highest looks in's lowest state,
Drest in such terrour as to make us all
Be *Anti-Persians*, and adore his Fall;
Then quits the world depriving it of Day,
While every Herb and Plant does droop away:
So when our gasping *English* Royalty
Perceiv'd her Period was now drawing nigh,
She summons her whole strength to give one blow,
To raise her self, or pull down others too.
Big with revenge and hope she now spake more
Of terror than in many months before;
And musters her Attendants, or to save
Her from, or else attend her to, the Grave:
Yet but enjoy'd the miserable fate
Of setting Majesty, to die in State.
Unhappy Kings, who cannot keep a Throne,
Nor be so fortunate to fall alone!
Their weight sinks others: *Pompey* could not fly,
But half the World must bear him company;
And captiv'd *Sampson* could not life conclude,
Unless attended with a multitude.

47 Title Cromwell defeated the future Charles II at the battle of Worcester on 3 September 1651 1 *Magazine* storehouse, warehouse *Light* the sun 8 *Persians* traditionally thought to worship the sun 12 *Period* termination, end 25 *Sampson* the Israelite Samson destroyed the Philistine house where three thousand men and women were revelling; see Judges 16:27

Who'd trust to Greatness now, whose food is air,
Whose ruine sudden, and whose end despair?
Who would presume upon his Glorious Birth,
Or quarrel for a spacious share of Earth,
That sees such Diadems become so cheap,
And Heros tumble in a common heap?
Oh give me Vertue then, which sums up all,
And firmly stands when Crowns and Scepters fall.

JOHN MILTON

48 To the Lord Generall Cromwell May 1652

On the proposalls of certaine ministers at the Commitee for Propagation of the Gospell

Cromwell, our cheif of men, who through a cloud
Not of warr onely, but detractions rude,
Guided by faith and matchless Fortitude
To peace and truth thy glorious way hast plough'd,
And on the neck of crowned Fortune proud
Hast reard Gods Trophies and his work pursu'd,
While Darwen stream with blood of Scotts imbru'd,
And Dunbarr feild resounds thy praises loud,

47 27 *whose … air* who live on nothing, false hopes

48 1–2 *cloud … of warr* cp. Virgil, *Aeneid* 10.809–10 '… so Aeneas, with the weapons showering upon him from every side, held off this thunder-cloud of war till its last discharge was spent' 5 *crowned Fortune* Charles I and his son 7 *Darwen* the river Darwen, near Preston, where Cromwell defeated the Scots in August 1648 *imbru'd* stained, dyed 8 *Dunbarr feild* Cromwell defeated the Scots at Dunbar in September 1650

And Worsters laureat wreath; yet much remaines
To conquer still; peace hath her victories
No less renownd then warr, new foes aries
Threatning to bind our soules with secular chaines:
Helpe us to save free Conscience from the paw
Of hireling wolves whose Gospell is their maw.

49 To Sir Henry Vane the younger

Vane, young in yeares, but in sage counsell old,
Then whome a better Senatour nere held
The helme of Rome, when gownes not armes repelld
The feirce Epeirot and the African bold,
Whether to settle peace or to unfold
The drift of hollow states hard to be spelld,
Then to advise how warr may best, upheld,
Move by her two maine nerves, Iron and Gold
In all her equipage; besides to know
Both spirituall powre and civill, what each meanes
What severs each thou'hast learnt, which few have don.
The bounds of either sword to thee wee ow.
Therfore on thy firme hand religion leanes
In peace, and reck'ns thee her eldest son.

48 9 *Worsters* in September 1651 Cromwell defeated the Scots under Charles II at Worcester 11 *aries* arise 14 cp. John 10:12 'But he that is an hireling, and not the shepherd, whose own the sheep are not, seeth the wolf coming, and leaveth the sheep, and fleeth: and the wolf catcheth them, and scattereth the sheep' *maw* stomach

49 3 *gownes not armes* cp. Cicero, *De officiis* 1.22.77 'cedant arma togae' ('arms yield to the toga') 4 *Epeirot* Pyrrhus, King of Epirus *African* Hannibal 6 *hollow states* the Low Countries; insincere, false countries. In June Vane served on a committee appointed to deal with the Dutch ambassadors following a naval incident in May of the year *spelld* deciphered, understood 12 *either sword* spiritual or civil

Andrew Marvell

50 [*from* The First Anniversary of the Government under O. C.]

'Is this, saith one, the Nation that we read
'Spent with both Wars, under a Captain dead?
'Yet rig a Navy while we dress us late;
'And ere we Dine, rase and rebuild their State.
'What Oaken Forrests, and what golden Mines!
'What Mints of Men, what Union of Designes!
'Unless their Ships, do, as their Fowle proceed
'Of shedding Leaves, that with their Ocean breed.
'Theirs are not Ships, but rather Arks of War,
'And beaked Promontories sail'd from far;
'Of floting Islands a new Hatched Nest;
'A Fleet of Worlds, of other Worlds in quest;
'An hideous shole of wood-Leviathans,
'Arm'd with three Tire of brazen Hurricans;
'That through the Center shoot their thundring side
'And sink the Earth that does at Anchor ride.
'What refuge to escape them can be found,
'Whose watry Leaguers all the world surround?

50 2 *both Wars* the Civil War and the war against the Dutch of 1652–4 7–8 solan geese were traditionally thought to come from the leaves of a certain tree falling into water 10 cp. Milton's 'Lycidas' (see no. 325), l. 94 13 *Leviathans*** huge ships 14 *brazen Hurricans* bronze cannons 18 *watry Leaguers* besiegers by sea

ALEXANDER BROME

51 On Sir *G. B.* his defeat

1.

Pray why should any man complain,
Or why *disturb* his brest or brain,
At this new *alteration*?
Since that which has been done's no more,
Then what has oft been done before,
And that which will be done agen,
As long's there are ambitious men,
That strive for domination.

2.

In this mad age there's nothing firm,
All things have periods and their *terme*,
Their *Rise* and *Declinations*,
Those gaudy *Nothings* we admire,
Which get above, and shine like fire,
Are empty *vapours*, rais'd from dust
Whose mock-shine past, they quickly must
Fall down like *Exhalations*.

3.

But still we *Commons* must be made
A gald, a lame, thin, hackney jade,
And all by turnes will ride us,
This side and that, no matter which,
For *both* do ride with *spur* and *switch*,
Till we are tyr'd, and then at last,
We stumble, and our riders cast
Cause *they'ld* nor *feed nor guide us*.

51 Title *Sir G. B.* Sir George Booth (1622–84); after some initial success, his uprising against the Rump and in support of the future Charles II was quashed in battle by John Lambert at Nantwich, near Chester, on 16 August 1659 3 *new alteration* the restoration of the Rump Parliament on 6 May 1659

4.

The insulting Clergy quite mistook,
In thinking Kingdoms past by book,
  Or Crowns were got by prating;
'Tis not the blackcoat, but the red
Has power to make, or be the head,
Nor is it words, or oaths, or tears,
But *Muskets* or full *Bandoleers*
  Have power of *Legislating*.

5.

The Lawyers must lay by their book,
And study *Lambert* more then *Cook*,
  The sword's the *learnedst pleader*,
Reports and *judgments* will not do't,
But 'tis *Dragoons*, and *Horse* and *foot*,
Words are but wind, but *blowes* come home,
A stout tongu'd *Lawyer*'s but a Mome,
  Compar'd to a stout *File-leader*.

6.

Luck, wit or valour, rule all things,
They pull *down* and they set *up* Kings,
  All lawes are in their bosome;
That side is always *right* that's *strong*,
And that that's beaten must be *wrong*,
An he that thinks it is not so,
Unlesse he's sure to *beat* 'um too,
  Is but a fool t'oppose 'um.

7.

Let them impose taxes or rates,
'Tis but on those that have estates,
  Not such as I and thou are,
But it concerns those worldlings, which

51 25 *Clergy* Puritan ministers 28 *blackcoat* clergyman *red* soldier 32 *Legislating*** making laws 34 *Lambert* John Lambert (1619–83), parliamentarian soldier *Cook* Sir Edward Coke (1552–1634), judge and champion of the common law 36 *Reports* law reports of cases 39 *Mome* blockhead, dolt, fool 40 *File-leader* leader of a file, body of soldiers 46 *An* and

Are left, or made, or else grow rich,
Such as have studied all their dayes,
The saving and the thriving wayes,
  To be the mules of power.

8.

If they reform the Church or State,
We'l ne're be troubled much thereat,
  Let each man takes opinion,
If we don't like the *Church* you know,
Taverns are free and there we go,
And if every one would be
As cleerly unconcern'd as we,
  They'd ne're fight for *Dominion*.

51 59 *takes* take his

PART TWO

IMAGES OF LOVE

Anonymous

52 [Westron wynde when wylle thow blow]

Westron wynde when wylle thow blow
the smalle rayne downe can Rayne
Cryst yf my love were in my Armys
And I yn my bed A gayne

Sir Thomas Wyatt

53 [They fle from me that sometyme did me seke]

They fle from me that sometyme did me seke
  with naked fote stalking in my chambre
  I have sene theim gentill tame and meke
  that nowe are wyld and do not remembre
  that sometyme they put theimself in daunger
  to take bred at my hand and nowe they raunge
  besely seking with a continuell chaunge
Thancked be fortune it hath ben othrewise
  twenty tymes better but ons in speciall
  in thyn arraye after a pleasaunt gyse
  When her lose gowne from her shoulders did fall
  and she me caught in her armes long and small
  therewithall swetely did me kysse
  and softely said dere hert howe like you this

53 5 *daunger* subjection, the object of another's power 7 *besely* busily 10 *gyse* style or fashion of attire

It was no dreme I lay brode waking
but all is torned thorough my gentilnes
into a straunge fasshion of forsaking
and I have leve to goo of her goodenes
and she also to use new fangilnes
but syns that I so kyndely ame served
I would fain knowe what she hath deserved

54 [Who so list to hount I knowe where is an hynde]

Who so list to hount I knowe where is an hynde
but as for me helas I may no more
the vayne travaill hath weried me so sore
I ame of theim that farthest cometh behinde
yet may I by no meanes my weried mynde
drawe from the Deere but as she fleeth afore
faynting I folowe I leve of therefor
sethens in a nett I seke to hold the wynde
Who list her hount I put him owte of dowbte
as well as I may spend his tyme in vain
and graven with Diamondes in letters plain
There is written her faier neck rounde abowte
noli me tangere for Cesars I ame
and wylde for to hold though I seme tame

53 20 *kyndely* according to the law of nature, naturally; kindly, pleasantly

54 1 *list* likes, pleases 2 *may* can 3 *travaill* effort, labour 8 *sethens* since; the phrase is proverbial 13 *noli . . . tangere* 'Touch me not', Christ's words to Mary Magdalene after the Resurrection (John 20:17) and said to be the motto inscribed on the collars of Caesar's hinds *Cesars I ame* cp. Matthew 22:21 'Render therefore unto Caesar the things which are Caesar's'

55 [It may be good like it who list]

It may be good like it who list
but I do dowbt who can me blame
for oft assured yet have I myst
and now again I fere the same
The wyndy wordes the Ies quaynt game
of soden chaunge makth me agast
for dred to fall I stond not fast
Alas I tred an endles maze
that seketh to accorde two contraries
and hope still and nothing hase
imprisoned in libertes
as oon unhard and still that cries
alwaies thursty and yet nothing I tast
for dred to fall I stond not fast
Assured I dowbt I be not sure
and should I trust to suche suretie
that oft hath put the prouff in ure
and never hath founde it trusty
nay sir In faith it were great foly
and yet my liff thus I do wast
for dred to fall I stond not fast

56 [My lute awake perfourme the last]

My lute awake perfourme the last
labor that thou and I shall wast
and end that I have now begon
for when this song is song and past
my lute be still for I have done

55 1 *list* pleases 5 *wyndy* changeable *Ies* eyes' *quaynt* cunning, clever, knowing 10 *hase* perhaps, 'hazard' 17 *ure* operation, action, practice

56 4 *is song* is sung

As to be herd where ere is none
as lede to grave in marbill stone
my song may perse her hert as sone
should we then sigh or syng or mone
no no my lute for I have done
The Rokkes do not so cruelly
repulse the waves continuelly
as she my suyte and affection
so that I ame past remedy
whereby my lute and I have done
Prowd of the spoyll that thou hast gott
of simple hertes thorough loves shot
by whome unkynd thou hast theim wone,
thinck not he haith his bow forgot
all tho my lute and I have done
Vengeaunce shall fall on thy disdain
that makest but game on ernest pain
thinck not alone under the sonne
unquyt to cause they lovers plain
all tho my lute and I have done
Perchaunce the lye wethered and old
the wynter nyghts that are so cold
playnyng in vain unto the mone
thy wisshes then dare not be told
care then who lyst for I have done
And then may chaunce the to repent
the tyme that thou hast lost and spent
to cause thy lovers sigh and swoune
then shalt though knowe beaultie but lent
and wisshe and want as I have done
Now cesse my lute this is the last
labor that thou and I shall wast
and ended is that we begon
now is this song boeth song and past
my lute be still for I have done

56 6–8 it is as difficult to be heard, for my song to reach her heart, as for soft lead to engrave hard marble 24 *unquyt* unrequited; without penalty

Henry Howard, Earl of Surrey

57 [The soote season, that bud and blome furth bringes]

The soote season, that bud and blome furth bringes,
With grene hath clad the hill and eke the vale:
The nightingale with fethers new she singes:
The turtle to her make hath tolde her tale:
Somer is come, for every spray nowe springes,
The hart hath hong his olde hed on the pale:
The buck in brake his winter cote he flinges:
The fishes flote with newe repaired scale:
The adder all her sloughe awaye she slinges:
The swift swalow pursueth the flyes smale:
The busy bee her honye now she minges:
Winter is worne that was the flowers bale:
And thus I see among these pleasant thinges
Eche care decayes, and yet my sorow springes.

Alexander Scott

58 [To luve unluvit it is ane pane]

To luve unluvit it is ane pane
For scho that is my soverane
Sum wantoun man so he hes set hir
That I can get no lufe agane
Bot brekis my hairt and nocht the bettir

57 1 *soote* sweet 11 *minges* remembers; mixes 12 *bale* evil, harm

58 2 *scho* she 3 *he* high, haughty

Quhen that I went with that sweit may
To dance to sing To sport and pley
And oft tymes in my armis plet hir
I do now murne both nycht and day
And brekis my hart and nocht the bettir

Quhair I wes wont to se hir go
Rycht trymly passand to and fro
With cumly smylis quhen that I met hir
And now I leif in pane and wo
And brekis etc.

Quhattane ane glaikit fule am I
To slay my self with malancoly
Sen weill I ken I may nocht get hir
Or quhat suld be the caus and quhy
To brek etc.

My hairt sen thou may nocht hir pleis
Adew as gud lufe cumis as gais
Go chus ane udir and foryet hir
God gif him dolour and diseis
That brekis thair hairt and nocht the bettir

George Turbervile

59 To his Love that sent him a Ring wherein was gravde, *Let Reason rule*

Shall *Reason* rule where *Reason* hath no right?
Nor never had? shall *Cupid* loose his landes?
His claim? his crown? his kingdome? name of might
And yeeld himselfe to be in *Reasons* bandes?

58 6 *Quhen* when *may* maiden 8 *plet* entwined, clasped 11 *Quhair* where 12 *Rycht trymly* right smartly 14 *leif* live 16 *Quhattane* how like, what *glaikit* foolish, silly 18 *Sen* since 22 *gais* goes 24 *dolour and diseis* grief and trouble

59 4 *bandes* a company or troop of men; a ring

No, (Friend) thy Ring doth wil me thus in vaine,
Reason and *Love* have ever yet beene twaine.
They are by kinde of such contrarie mould
As one mislikes the others lewde devise,
What *Reason* willes *Cupido* never would,
Love never yet thought *Reason* to be wise.
To *Cupid* I my homage earst have donne,
Let *Reason* rule the harts that she hath wonne.

ISABELLA WHITNEY

60 I.W. To her unconstant Lover

As close as you your weding kept
yet now the trueth I here:
Which you (yer now) might me have told
what nede you nay to swere?

You know I alwayes wisht you wel
so wyll I during lyfe:
But sith you shal a Husband be
God send you a good wyfe.

And this (where so you shal become)
full boldly may you boast:
That once you had as true a Love,
as dwelt in any Coast.

Whose constantnesse had never quaild
if you had not begonne:
And yet it is not so far past,
but might agayne be wonne.

If you so would: yea and not change
so long as lyfe should last:
But yf that needes you marry must?
then farewell hope is past,

60 3 *yer* ere, before

And if you cannot be content
   to lead a single lyfe?
(Although the same right quiet be)
   then take me to your wife.

So shall the promises be kept,
   that you so firmly made:
Now chuse whether ye wyll be true,
   or be of SINONS trade.

Whose trade if that you long shal use,
   it shal your kindred stayne:
Example take by many a one
   whose falshood now is playne.

As by ENEAS first of all,
   who dyd poore DIDO leave,
Causing the Quene by his untrueth
   with Sword her hart to cleave,

Also I finde that THESEUS did,
   his faithfull love forsake:
Stealyng away within the night,
   before she dyd awake.

JASON that came of noble race,
   two Ladies did begile:
I muse how he durst shew his face,
   to them that knew his wile.

For when he by MEDEAS arte,
   had got the Fleece of Gold
And also had of her that time,
   al kynd of things he wolde.

He toke his Ship and fled away
   regarding not the vowes:
That he dyd make so faithfully,
   unto his loving Spowes,

60 52 *Spowes* spouse

How durst he trust the surging Seas
  knowing himselfe forsworne?
Why dyd he scape safe to the land,
  before the ship was torne?

I think king Aeolus stayd the winds
  and Neptune rulde the Sea:
Then might he boldly passe the waves
  no perils could him slea.

But if his falsehed had to them,
  bin manifest befor:
They wold have rent the ship as soone
  as he had gon from shore.

Now may you heare how falsenes is
  made manyfest in time:
Although they that commit the same,
  think it a veniall crime.

For they, for their unfaithfulnes,
  did get perpetuall Fame:
Fame? wherfore dyd I terme it so?
  I should have cald it shame.

Let Theseus be, let Jason passe,
  let Paris also scape:
That brought destruction unto Troy
  all through the Grecian Rape,

And unto me a Troylus be,
  if not you may compare:
With any of these parsons that
  above expressed are.

But if I can not please your minde,
  for wants that rest in me:
Wed whom you list, I am content,
  your refuse for to be.

 60 *slea* slay 79 *parsons* persons 84 *refuse* that which has been refused

It shall suffise me simple soule,
of thee to be forsaken:
And it may chance although not yet
you wish you had me taken.

But rather then you shold have cause
to wish this through your wyfe:
I wysh to her, ere you her have,
no more but losse of lyfe.

For she that shal so happy be,
of thee to be elect:
I wish her vertues to be such,
she nede not be suspect.

I rather wish her HELENS face,
then one of HELENS trade:
With chastnes of PENELOPE
the which did never fade.

A LUCRES for her constancy,
and Thisbie for her trueth:
If such thou have, then PETO be
not PARIS, that were rueth.

Perchance, ye will think this thing rare
in on woman to fynd:
Save Helens beauty, al the rest
the Gods have me assignd.

These words I do not spek thinking
from thy new Love to turne thee:
Thou knowst by prof what I deserve
I nede not to informe thee.

But let that passe: would God I had
Cassandraes gift me lent:
Then either thy yll chaunce or mine
my foresight might prevent.

60 94 *elect* chosen 103 *Peto* possibly William Peto (d. 1558), a strong supporter of Catherine of Aragon and confessor to her daughter, Mary Tudor 104 *rueth* pity 106 *on* one

But all in vayne for this I seeke,
  wishes may not attaine it
Therfore may hap to me what shall,
  and I cannot refraine it.

Wherfore I pray God be my guide
  and also thee defend:
No worser then I wish my selfe,
  untill thy lyfe shal end.

Which life I pray God, may agayne,
  King Nestors lyfe renew:
And after that your soule may rest
  amongst the heavenly crew.

Therto I wish King Xerxis wealth,
  or els King Cressus Gould:
With as much rest and quietnesse
  as man may have on Mould.

And when you shall this letter have
  let it be kept in store?
For she that sent the same, hath sworn
  as yet to send no more.

And now farewel, for why at large
  my mind is here exprest?
The which you may perceive, if that
  you do peruse the rest?

60 120 *refraine* restrain, hold back 132 *Mould* earth

George Gascoigne

61 [A Sonet written in prayse of the brown beautie]

The thriftles thred which pampred beauty spinnes,
In thraldom binds the foolish gazing eyes:
As cruell Spyders with their crafty ginnes,
In worthlesse webbes doe snare the simple Flies.
The garments gay, the glittring golden gite,
The tysing talk which floweth from *Pallas* pooles:
The painted pale, the (too much) red made white,
Are smyling baytes to fishe for loving fooles.
But lo, when eld in toothlesse mouth appeares,
And whoary heares in steed of beauties blaze:
Than Had I wist, doth teach repenting yeares,
The tickle track of craftie *Cupides* maze.
Twixt faire and foule therfore, twixt great and small,
A lovely nutbrowne face is best of all.

Si fortunatus infœlix.

61 1 *thriftles* unprofitable, worthless; wasteful, spendthrift 3 *ginnes* traps 5 *gite* dress or gown 6 *tysing* enticing *Pallas pooles* the eyes 7 *pale* paleness 9 *eld* old age 11 *Had I wist* if only I had known 12 *tickle* unreliable, fickle [15] *Si . . . infœlix* if lucky, unhappy

ANONYMOUS

62 A new Courtly Sonet, of the Lady Greensleeves.

To the new tune of Greensleeves

Alas my love, ye do me wrong,
  to cast me off discurteously:
And I have loved you so long,
  Delighting in your companie.
    Greensleeves was all my joy,
      Greensleeves was my delight:
    Greensleeves was my heart of gold,
      And who but Ladie Greensleeves,
I have been readie at your hand,
  to grant what ever you would crave.
I have both waged life and land,
  your love and good will for to have.
    Greensleeves was all my joy, etc.,
I bought thee kerchers to thy head,
  that were wrought fine and gallantly:
I kept thee both at boord and bed,
  Which cost my purse wel favouredly,
    Greensleeves was all my joie, etc.
I bought thee peticotes of the best,
  the cloth so fine as fine might be:
I gave thee jewels for thy chest,
  and all this cost I spent on thee.
    Greensleeves was all my joie, etc.
Thy smock of silk, both faire and white,
  with gold embrodered gorgeously:
Thy peticote of Sendall right:
  and thus I bought thee gladly.
    Greensleeves was all my joie, etc.

62 2 *discurteously*★ 14 *kerchers* cloths used to cover the head 26 *Sendall* thin, rich silken material

Thy girdle of gold so red,
with pearles bedecked sumptuously:
The like no other lasses had,
and yet thou wouldst not love me,
Greensleeves was all my joy, etc.
Thy purse and eke thy gay guilt knives,
thy pincase gallant to the eie:
No better wore the Burgesse wives,
and yet thou wouldst not love me.
Greensleeves was all my joy, etc.
Thy crimson stockings all of silk,
with golde all wrought above the knee,
Thy pumps as white as was the milk,
and yet thou wouldst not love me.
Greensleeves was all my joy, etc.
Thy gown was of the grassie green,
thy sleeves of Satten hanging by:
Which made thee be our harvest Queen,
and yet thou wouldst not love me.
Greensleeves was all my joy, etc.
Thy garters fringed with the golde,
And silver aglets hanging by,
Which made thee blithe for to beholde,
And yet thou wouldst not love me.
Greensleeves was all my joy, etc.
My gayest gelding I thee gave,
To ride where ever liked thee,
No Ladie ever was so brave,
And yet thou wouldst not love me.
Greensleeves was all my joy, etc.
My men were clothed all in green,
And they did ever wait on thee:
Al this was gallant to be seen,
and yet thou wouldst not love me.
Greensleeves was all my joy, etc.

62 41 *pumps* light shoes 50 *aglets* metal ends or tags of a lace 51 *blithe* glad, happy

They set thee up, they took thee downe,
 they served thee with humilitie,
Thy foote might not once touch the ground
 and yet thou wouldst not love me.
  Greensleeves was all my joy, etc.
For everie morning when thou rose,
 I sent thee dainties orderly:
To cheare thy stomack from all woes,
 and yet thou wouldst not love me.
  Greensleeves was all my joy, etc.
Thou couldst desire no earthly thing,
 But stil thou hadst it readily:
Thy musicke still to play and sing,
 And yet thou wouldst not love me.
  Greensleeves was all my joy, etc.
And who did pay for all this geare,
 that thou didst spend when pleased thee
Even I that am rejected here,
 and thou disdainst to love me.
  Greensleeves was all my joy, etc.
Wel, I wil pray to God on hie,
 that thou my constancie maist see:
And that yet once before I die,
 thou wilt vouchsafe to love me.
  Greensleeves was all my joy, etc.
Greensleeves now farewel adue,
 God I pray to prosper thee:
For I am stil thy lover true,
 come once againe and love me.
  Greensleeves was all my joy, etc.

62 79 *geare* dress, apparel

SIR PHILIP SIDNEY

63 [*from* Certain Sonnets]

[4]

The Nightingale as soone as Aprill bringeth
Unto her rested sense a perfect waking,
While late bare earth, proud of new clothing springeth,
Sings out her woes, a thorne her song-booke making:
   And mournfully bewailing,
   Her throate in tunes expresseth
   What griefe her breast oppresseth,
   For *Thereus* force on her chaste will prevailing.
      O *Philomela* faire, ô take some gladnesse,
      That here is juster cause of plaintfull sadnesse:
      Thine earth now springs, mine fadeth,
      Thy thorne without, my thorne my heart invadeth.

Alas she hath no other cause of anguish
But *Thereus* love, on her by strong hand wrokne,
Wherein she suffring all her spirits languish,
Full womanlike complaines her will was brokne.
   But I who dayly craving,
   Cannot have to content me,
   Have more cause to lament me,
   Since wanting is more woe then too much having.
      O *Philomela* faire, ô take some gladnesse,
      That here is juster cause of plaintfull sadnesse:
      Thine earth now springs, mine fadeth:
      Thy thorne without, my thorne my heart invadeth.

63 4 *thorne* used to make prick-song (an accompanying melody to a simple theme, which was noted down), but also traditionally by the nightingale to keep herself awake   14 *wrokne* wreaked

64 [*from* The Countesse of Pembrokes Arcadia]

Strephon. Yee Gote-heard Gods, that love the grassie mountaines,
Yee Nimphes that haunt the springs in pleasant vallies,
Ye Satyrs joyde with free and quiet forrests,
Vouchsafe your silent eares to playning musique,
Which to my woes gives still an early morning:
And drawes the dolor on till wery evening.

Klaius. O *Mercurie*, foregoer to the evening,
O heavenlie huntresse of the savage mountaines,
O lovelie starre, entitled of the morning,
While that my voice doth fill these wofull vallies,
Vouchsafe your silent eares to plaining musique,
Which oft hath *Echo* tir'd in secrete forrests.

Strephon. I that was once free-burges of the forrests,
Where shade from Sunne, and sporte I sought in evening,
I that was once esteem'd for pleasant musique,
Am banisht now among the monstrous mountaines
Of huge despaire, and foule afflictions vallies,
Am growne a shrich-owle to my selfe each morning.

Klaius. I that was once delighted every morning,
Hunting the wilde inhabiters of forrests,
I that was once the musique of these vallies,
So darkened am, that all my day is evening,
Hart-broken so, that molehilles seeme high mountaines,
And fill the vales with cries in steed of musique.

Strephon. Long since alas, my deadly Swannish musique
Hath made it selfe a crier of the morning,
And hath with wailing strength clim'd highest mountaines:
Long since my thoughts more desert be then forrests:
Long since I see my joyes come to their evening,
And state throwen downe to over-troden vallies.

64 8 *huntresse* Diana 9 *starre* Lucifer 13 *free-burges* citizen 25 *Swannish* musique* swans are supposed to sing only when they are dying

Klaius. Long since the happie dwellers of these vallies,
Have praide me leave my strange exclaiming musique,
Which troubles their dayes worke, and joyes of evening:
Long since I hate the night, more hate the morning:
Long since my thoughts chase me like beasts in forrests,
And make me wish my selfe layd under mountaines.

Strephon. Me seemes I see the high and stately mountaines,
Transforme themselves to lowe dejected vallies:
Me seemes I heare in these ill changed forrests,
The Nightingales doo learne of Owles their musique:
Me seemes I feele the comfort of the morning
Turnde to the mortall serene of an evening.

Klaius. Me seemes I see a filthie clowdie evening,
As soon as Sunne begins to clime the mountaines:
Me seemes I feele a noysome sent, the morning
When I doo smell the flowers of these vallies:
Me seemes I heare, when I doo heare sweete musique,
The dreadfull cries of murdred men in forrests.

Strephon. I wish to fire the trees of all these forrests;
I give the Sunne a last farewell each evening;
I curse the fidling finders out of Musicke:
With envie I doo hate the loftie mountaines;
And with despite despise the humble vallies:
I doo detest night, evening, day, and morning.

Klaius. Curse to my selfe my prayer is, the morning:
My fire is more, then can be made with forrests;
My state more base, then are the basest vallies:
I wish no evenings more to see, each evening;
Shamed I hate my selfe in sight of mountaines,
And stoppe mine eares, lest I growe mad with Musicke.

64 42 *mortall serene*** a fine rain after sunset in hot countries, thought to be deadly poisonous 45 *noysome* ill-smelling, offensive

Strephon. For she, whose parts maintainde a perfect musique,
Whose beawties shin'de more then the blushing morning,
Who much did passe in state the stately mountaines,
In straightnes past the Cedars of the forrests,
Hath cast me wretch into eternall evening,
By taking her two Sunnes from these darke vallies.

Klaius. For she, with whom compar'd, the Alpes are vallies,
She, whose lest word brings from the spheares their musique,
At whose approach the Sunne rase in the evening,
Who, where she went, bare in her forhead morning,
Is gone, is gone from these our spoyled forrests,
Turning to desarts our best pastur'de mountaines.

Strephon. These mountaines witnesse shall, so shall these vallies,
Klaius. These forrests eke, made wretched by our musique,
Our morning hymne this is, and song at evening.

65 [*from* Astrophil and Stella]

1

Loving in truth, and faine in verse my love to show,
That she (deare she) might take some pleasure of my paine:
Pleasure might cause her reade, reading might make her know,
Knowledge might pitie winne, and pitie grace obtaine,

I sought fit words to paint the blackest face of woe,
Studying inventions fine, her wits to entertaine:
Oft turning others leaves, to see if thence would flow
Some fresh and fruitfull showers upon my sunne-burn'd braine.

64 68 *lest* least

65 6 *inventions* in rhetoric the finding out or selection of topics or arguments to be used (cp. no. 281 l. 3) 8 *sunne-burn'd*** scorched or dried up by the heat of the sun

But words came halting forth, wanting Inventions stay,
Invention Natures child, fled step-dame Studies blowes,
And others feete still seem'd but strangers in my way.
Thus great with child to speake, and helplesse in my throwes,
Biting my trewand pen, beating my selfe for spite,
Foole, said my Muse to me, looke in thy heart and write.

66 [*from* Astrophil and Stella]

2

Not at first sight, nor with a dribbed shot
Love gave the wound, which while I breathe will bleed:
But knowne worth did in mine of time proceed,
Till by degrees it had full conquest got.

I saw and liked, I liked but loved not,
I loved, but straight did not what *Love* decreed:
At length to *Loves* decrees, I forc'd, agreed,
Yet with repining at so partiall lot.

Now even that footstep of lost libertie
Is gone, and now like slave-borne *Muscovite*,
I call it praise to suffer Tyrannie;

And now employ the remnant of my wit,
To make my selfe beleeve, that all is well,
While with a feeling skill I paint my hell.

65 11 *feete* footsteps to be followed; metrical units 12 *throwes* throes 13 *trewand* truant, lazy, loitering

66 1 *dribbed* ineffectual, random 3 *mine* underground tunnelling 8 *repining* grumbling, discontent 9 *footstep*** vestige, trace 10 *Muscovite* alludes to the contemporary belief that the Russians enjoyed being ruled by tyrants 14 *paint* give a false colour to

67 [*from* Astrophil and Stella]

9

Queene *Vertues* court, which some call *Stellas* face,
  Prepar'd by Natures chiefest furniture,
  Hath his front built of Alablaster pure;
  Gold is the covering of that stately place.

The doore by which sometimes comes forth her Grace,
  Red Porphir is, which locke of pearle makes sure:
  Whose porches rich (which name of cheekes endure)
  Marble mixt red and white do enterlace.

The windowes now through which this heav'nly guest
  Looks over the world, and can find nothing such,
  Which dare claime from those lights the name of best.

Of touch they are that without touch doth touch,
  Which *Cupids* selfe from Beauties myne did draw:
  Of touch they are, and poore I am their straw.

68 [*from* Astrophil and Stella]

72

Desire, though thou my old companion art,
  And oft so clings to my pure Love, that I
  One from the other scarcely can descrie,
  While each doth blow the fier of my hart;

67 3 *front* forehead 6 *Porphir* a beautiful, hard stone 12 they are made of touchstone or black marble which moves those who see them without touching them 14 they are a touchstone which when rubbed, can pick up straw; or, they are touchwood burning straw to get a light

Now from thy fellowship I needs must part,
Venus is taught with *Dians* wings to flie:
I must no more in thy sweet passions lie;
Vertues gold now must head my *Cupids* dart.

Service and Honor, wonder with delight,
Feare to offend, will worthie to appeare,
Care shining in mine eyes, faith in my sprite.

These things are left me by my only Deare;
But thou Desire, because thou wouldst have all,
Now banisht art, but yet alas how shall?

69 [*from* Astrophil and Stella]

81

O kisse, which doest those ruddie gemmes impart,
Or gemmes, or frutes of new-found *Paradise*,
Breathing all blisse and sweetning to the heart,
Teaching dumbe lips a nobler exercise.

O kisse, which soules, even soules together ties
By linkes of *Love*, and only Natures art:
How faine would I paint thee to all mens eyes,
Or of thy gifts at least shade out some part.

But she forbids, with blushing words, she sayes,
She builds her fame on higher seated praise:
But my heart burnes, I cannot silent be.

Then since (deare life) you faine would have me peace,
And I, mad with delight, want wit to cease,
Stop you my mouth with still still kissing me.

68 8 Cupid's golden arrow traditionally inflames love; his lead one makes the wounded victim reject it

69 12 *faine* gladly, willingly *peace* keep silence

70 [*from* Astrophil and Stella]

83

Good brother *Philip*, I have borne you long,
I was content you should in favour creepe,
While craftily you seem'd your cut to keepe,
As though that faire soft hand did you great wrong.

I bare (with Envie) yet I bare your song,
When in her necke you did *Love* ditties peepe;
Nay, more foole I, oft suffered you to sleepe
In Lillies neast, where *Loves* selfe lies along.

What, doth high place ambitious thoughts augment?
Is sawcinesse reward of curtesie?
Cannot such grace your silly selfe content,

But you must needs with those lips billing be?
And through those lips drinke Nectar from that toong;
Leave that sir *Phip*, least off your necke be wroong.

71 [*from* Astrophil and Stella]

Eight song

In a grove most rich of shade,
Where birds wanton musicke made,
May then yong his pide weedes showing,
New perfumed with flowers fresh growing,

70 1 *Philip* Catullus' poem (*Carmina* 2) to Lesbia's sparrow and John Skelton's poem *Phyllyp Sparowe* (see no. 307) have contributed to the bird's traditional association with lechery 3 *your ... keepe* act with modesty, propriety 11 *silly* simple 14 *sir* used contemptuously

71 2 *wanton* gay, lively 3 *pide* many-coloured *weedes* clothes, garments

Astrophil with *Stella* sweete,
Did for mutuall comfort meete,
Both within themselves oppressed,
But each in the other blessed.

Him great harmes had taught much care,
Her faire necke a foule yoke bare,
But her sight his cares did banish,
In his sight her yoke did vanish.

Wept they had, alas the while,
But now teares themselves did smile,
While their eyes by love directed,
Enterchangeably reflected.

Sigh they did, but now betwixt
Sighs of woes were glad sighs mixt,
With armes crost, yet testifying
Restlesse rest, and living dying.

Their eares hungry of each word,
Which the deere tongue would afford,
But their tongues restraind from walking,
Till their harts had ended talking.

But when their tongues could not speake,
Love it selfe did silence breake;
Love did set his lips asunder,
Thus to speake in love and wonder:

Stella soveraigne of my joy,
Faire triumpher of annoy,
Stella starre of heavenly fier,
Stella loadstar of desier.

Stella, in whose shining eyes,
Are the lights of *Cupids* skies,
Whose beames where they once are darted,
Love therewith is streight imparted.

71 19 *armes crost* a sign of melancholy

Stella, whose voice when it speakes,
Senses all asunder breakes;
Stella, whose voice when it singeth,
Angels to acquaintance bringeth.

Stella, in whose body is
Writ each character of blisse,
Whose face all, all beauty passeth,
Save thy mind which yet surpasseth.

Graunt, ô graunt, but speech alas,
Failes me, fearing on to passe,
Graunt, ô me, what am I saying?
But no fault there is in praying.

Graunt, ô deere, on knees I pray,
(Knees on ground he then did stay)
That not I, but since I love you,
Time and place for me may move you.

Never season was more fit,
Never roome more apt for it;
Smiling ayre allowes my reason,
These birds sing; now use the season.

This small wind which so sweete is,
See how it the leaves doth kisse,
Ech tree in his best attiring,
Sense of love to love inspiring.

Love makes earth the water drinke,
Love to earth makes water sinke;
And if dumbe things be so witty,
Shall a heavenly grace want pitty?

There his hands in their speech, faine
Would have made tongues language plaine;
But her hands his hands repelling,
Gave repulse all grace excelling.

Then she spake; her speech was such,
As not eares but hart did tuch:
While such wise she love denied,
As yet love she signified.

Astrophil sayd she, my love
Cease in these effects to prove:
Now be still, yet still beleeve me,
Thy griefe more then death would grieve me.

If that any thought in me,
Can tast comfort but of thee,
Let me fed with hellish anguish,
Joylesse, hopelesse, endlesse languish.

If those eyes you praised, be
Half so deere as you to me,
Let me home returne, starke blinded
Of those eyes, and blinder minded.

If to secret of my hart,
I do any wish impart,
Where thou art not formost placed,
Be both wish and I defaced.

If more may be sayd, I say,
All my blisse in thee I lay;
If thou love, my love content thee,
For all love, all faith is meant thee.

Trust me while I thee deny,
In my selfe the smart I try,
Tyran honour doth thus use thee,
Stellas selfe might not refuse thee.

Therefore, Deere, this no more move,
Least though I leave not thy love,
Which too deep in me is framed,
I should blush when thou art named.

Therewithall away she went,
Leaving him so passion rent,
With what she had done and spoken,
That therewith my song is broken.

71 73–4 stop testing my love by these declarations

72 [*from* Astrophil and Stella]

Eleventh song

Who is it that this darke night,
Underneath my window playneth?
It is one who from thy sight,
Being (ah) exild, disdayneth
Every other vulgar light.

Why alas, and are you he?
Be not yet those fancies changed?
Deere when you find change in me,
Though from me you be estranged,
Let my chaunge to ruine be.

Well in absence this will dy,
Leave to see, and leave to wonder:
Absence sure will helpe, if I
Can learne, how my selfe to sunder
From what in my hart doth ly.

But time will these thoughts remove:
Time doth worke what no man knoweth,
Time doth as the subject prove,
With time still the affection groweth
In the faithfull Turtle dove.

What if you new beauties see,
Will not they stir new affection?
I will thinke theye pictures be,
(Image like of Saints perfection)
Poorely counterfeting thee.

But your reasons purest light,
Bids you leave such minds to nourish?
Deere, do reason no such spite,
Never doth thy beauty florish
More, then in my reasons sight.

72 27 *minds* states of mind

But the wrongs love beares, will make
Love at length leave undertaking;
No the more fooles it do shake,
In a ground of so firme making,
Deeper still they drive the stake.

Peace, I thinke that some give eare:
Come no more, least I get anger.
Blisse, I will my blisse forbeare,
Fearing (sweete) you to endanger,
But my soule shall harbour there.

Well, be gone, be gone I say,
Lest that *Argus* eyes perceive you,
O unjustest fortunes sway,
Which can make me thus to leave you,
And from lowts to run away.

FULKE GREVILLE, LORD BROOKE

73 [*from* Cælica]

SONNET 22.

I with whose colors *Myra* drest her head,
I, that ware posies of her owne hand making,
I, that mine owne name in the chimnies read
By *Myra* finely wrought ere I was waking:
  Must I looke on? in hope time comming may
  With change bring backe my turne againe to play.

73 3 *in the chimnies* in the soot

I, that on Sunday at the Church-stile found,
A Garland sweet, with true-love knots in flowers,
Which I to weare about mine arme was bound,
That each of us might know that all was ours:
  Must I now lead an idle life in wishes?
  And follow *Cupid* for his loaves, and fishes?

I, that did weare the ring her Mother left,
I, for whose love she gloried to be blamed,
I, with whose eyes her eyes committed theft,
I, who did make her blush when I was named;
  Must I lose ring, flowers, blush, theft and go naked,
  Watching with sighs, till dead love be awaked?

I, that when drowsie *Argus* fell asleep,
Like Jealousie o'rewatched with desire,
Was even warned modestie to keepe,
While her breath speaking kindled Natures fire:
  Must I looke on a-cold, while others warme them?
  Doe *Vulcans* brothers in such fine nets arme them?

Was it for this that I might *Myra* see?
Washing the water with her beauties, white,
Yet would she never write her love to me;
Thinks wit of change while thoughts are in delight?
  Mad Girles must safely love, as they may leave,
  No man can print a kisse, lines may deceive.

74 [*from* Cælica]

SONNET 27.

Cupid, in *Myra's* faire bewitching eyes,
(Where Beauty shewes the miracles of pleasure)
When thou laist bound for honours sacrifice,
Sworne to thy hate, equalitie and measure.

73 12 hope to be one of the five thousand fed miraculously (see Matthew 15:32) 15 *theft* as in stealing glances

74 4 bound by oath to your foes, proportion and moderation

With open hand thou offeredst me her heart,
Thy bow and arrowes, if I would conspire,
To ruine honour, with whose frozen Art
She tyranniz'd thy Kingdome of desire.

I glad to dwell, and raigne in such perfections,
Gave thee my reason, memory, and sense,
In them to worke thy mysticall reflexions,
Against which Nature can have no defence;
And wilt thou now to nourish my despaire,
Both head and feather all thy shafts with feare?

75 [*from* Cælica]

SONNET 39.

The *nurse-life* Wheat within his greene huske growing,
Flatters our hope, and tickles our desire,
Natures true riches in sweet beauties shewing,
Which set all hearts, with labours love, on fire.

No lesse faire is the Wheat when golden eare,
Shewes unto hope the joyes of neare enjoying:
Faire and sweet is the bud, more sweet and faire
The Rose, which proves that time is not destroying.

Cælica, your youth, the morning of delight,
Enamel'd o're with beauties white and red,
All sense and thoughts did to beleefe invite,
That Love and Glorie there are brought to bed;
And your ripe yeeres love none; he goes no higher,
Turnes all the spirits of Man into desire.

74 11 *reflexions* during the siege of Syracuse, Archimedes burned the Roman fleet by means of reflecting mirrors

75 1 *nurse-life* life-fostering 13 *love none* love's noon, when the morning sun can go no higher

76 [*from* Cælica]

SONNET 44.

Absence, the noble truce
Of *Cupids* warre:
Where though desires want use,
They honoured are.
Thou art the just protection,
Of prodigall affection,
Have thou the praise;
When bankrupt *Cupid* braveth,
Thy mines his credit saveth,
With sweet delayes.

Of wounds which presence makes
With Beauties shot,
Absence the anguish slakes,
But healeth not:
Absence records the Stories,
Wherein Desire glories,
Although she burne,
She cherisheth the spirits
Where Constancy inherits
And Passions mourne.

Absence, like dainty Clouds,
On glorious-bright,
Natures weake senses shrowds,
From harming light.
Absence maintaines the treasure
Of pleasure unto pleasure,
Sparing with praise;
Absence doth nurse the fire,
Which starves and feeds desire
With sweet delayes.

Presence to every part
Of Beauty tyes,
Where Wonder rules the heart
There Pleasure dyes:

Presence plagues minde and senses
With modesties defences,
Absence is free:
Thoughts doe in absence venter
On *Cupids* shadowed center,
They winke and see.

But Thoughts be not so brave,
With absent joy;
For you with that you have
Your selfe destroy:
The absence which you glory,
Is that which makes you sory,
And burne in vaine:
For Thought is not the weapon,
Wherewith *thoughts-ease* men cheapon,
Absence is paine.

77 [*from* Cælica]

SONNET 84.

Farewell sweet Boy, complaine not of my truth;
Thy Mother lov'd thee not with more devotion;
For to thy Boyes play I gave all my youth,
Yong Master, I did hope for your promotion.

While some sought Honours, Princes thoughts observing,
Many woo'd *Fame, the child of paine and anguish*,
Others judg'd inward good a chiefe deserving,
I in thy wanton Visions joy'd to languish.

I bow'd not to thy image for succession,
Nor bound thy bow to shoot reformed kindnesse,
Thy playes of hope and feare were my confession,
The spectacles to my life was thy blindnesse:
  But *Cupid* now farewell, I will goe play me,
  With thoughts that please me lesse, and lesse betray me.

77 9 *succession* inheriting his position; heirs, descendants

Mark Alexander Boyd

78 SONET

Fra banc to banc fra wod to wod I rin
Ourhailit with my feble fantasie
Lyc til a leif that fallis from a trie
Or til a reid ourblawin with the wind.
Twa gods gyds me the ane of tham is blind,
Ye and a bairn brocht up in vanitie.
The nixt a wyf ingenrit of the se,
And lichter nor a dauphin with hir fin.
Unhappie is the man for evirmaire
That teils the sand and sawis in the aire,
Bot twyse unhappier is he I lairn
That feidis in his hairt a mad desyre,
And follows on a woman throw the fyre
Led be a blind and teichit be a bairn

Robert Greene

79 *Dorons* description of *Samela*

Like to *Diana* in her Summer weede
Girt with a crimson roabe of brightest die,
goes faire *Samela*.
Whiter than be the flockes that straggling feede,
When washt by *Arethusa* faint they lie:
is faire *Samela*.

78 2 *Ourhailit* harassed, oppressed 5 *gods* Cupid and Venus 7 *ingenrit* engendered 8 *nor* than 10 *teils* tills, ploughs *sawis* sows 14 *teichit* taught

79 Title *Samela* is the name taken by the shipwrecked princess Sephestia while she is in Arcadia; *Doron* is a rustic character

As faire *Aurora* in her morning gray
Deckt with the ruddie glister of her love,
is faire *Samela.*
Like lovelie *Thetis* on a calmed day,
When as her brightnesse *Neptunes* fancie move,
shines faire *Samela.*
Her tresses gold, her eyes like glassie streames,
Her teeth are pearle, the breasts are yvorie
of faire *Samela.*
Her cheekes like rose and lilly yeeld foorth gleames,
Her browes bright arches framde of ebonie:
Thus faire *Samela.*
Passeth faire *Venus* in her bravest hiew,
And *Juno* in the shew of majestie,
for she'is *Samela.*
Pallas in wit, all three if you well view,
For beautie, wit, and matchlesse dignitie
yeeld to *Samela.*

Edmund Spenser

80 [*from* The Faerie Queene Book 2]

Eftsoones they heard a most melodious sound,
Of all that mote delight a daintie eare,
Such as attonce might not on living ground,
Save in this Paradise, be heard elswhere:
Right hard it was, for wight, which did it heare,
To read, what manner musicke that mote bee:
For all that pleasing is to living eare,
Was there consorted in one harmonee,
Birdes, voyces, instruments, windes, waters, all agree.

79 8 *glister* brilliance, lustre

80 1 *they* Guyon and his companion the Palmer 3 *attonce* at one time, together 6 *read* discover, perceive 8 *consorted** combined in music

The joyous birdes shrouded in chearefull shade,
Their notes unto the voyce attempred sweet;
Th'Angelicall soft trembling voyces made
To th'instruments divine respondence meet:
The silver sounding instruments did meet
With the base murmure of the waters fall:
The waters fall with difference discreet,
Now soft, now loud, unto the wind did call:
The gentle warbling wind low answered to all.

There, whence that Musick seemed heard to bee,
Was the faire Witch her selfe now solacing,
With a new Lover, whom through sorceree
And witchcraft, she from farre did thither bring:
There she had him now layd a slombering,
In secret shade, after long wanton joyes:
Whilst round about them pleasauntly did sing
Many faire Ladies, and lascivious boyes,
That ever mixt their song with light licentious toyes.

And all that while, right over him she hong,
With her false eyes fast fixed in his sight,
As seeking medicine, whence she was stong,
Or greedily depasturing delight:
And oft inclining downe with kisses light,
For feare of waking him, his lips bedewd,
And through his humid eyes did sucke his spright,
Quite molten into lust and pleasure lewd;
Wherewith she sighed soft, as if his case she rewd.

The whiles some one did chaunt this lovely lay;
Ah see, who so faire thing doest faine to see,
In springing flowre the image of thy day;
Ah see the Virgin Rose, how sweetly shee
Doth first peepe forth with bashfull modestee,

80 11 *attempred* attuned, brought into harmony 13 *respondence* meet* fitting response, answer 14 *meet* agree, accord 16 *difference discreet* distinct variation 20 *Witch* Acrasia, 'weakness of will', 'bad mixture' 27 *toyes* flirtings, amorous behaviour 31 *depasturing* grazing on 36 *rewd* rued 38–54 the song imitates one in Tasso's *Gerusalemme liberata* 16.14–15 38 *faine* rejoice in, delight

That fairer seemes, the lesse ye see her may;
Lo see soone after, how more bold and free
Her bared bosome she doth broad display;
Loe see soone after, how she fades, and falles away.

So passeth, in the passing of a day,
Of mortall life the leafe, the bud, the flowre,
Ne more doth flourish after first decay,
That earst was sought to decke both bed and bowre,
Of many a Ladie, and many a Paramowre:
Gather therefore the Rose, whilest yet is prime,
For soone comes age, that will her pride deflowre:
Gather the Rose of love, whilest yet is time,
Whilest loving thou mayst loved be with equall crime.

He ceast, and then gan all the quire of birdes
Their diverse notes t'attune unto his lay,
As in approvance of his pleasing words.
The constant paire heard all, that he did say,
Yet swarved not, but kept their forward way,
Through many covert groves, and thickets close,
In which they creeping did at last display
That wanton Ladie, with her lover lose,
Whose sleepie head she in her lap did soft dispose.

Upon a bed of Roses she was layd,
As faint through heat, or dight to pleasant sin,
And was arayd, or rather disarayd,
All in a vele of silke and silver thin,
That hid no whit her alablaster skin,
But rather shewd more white, if more might bee:
More subtile web *Arachne* can not spin,
Nor the fine nets, which oft we woven see
Of scorched deaw, do not in th'aire more lightly flee.

80 51 *prime* its best, most flourishing, state 52 *pride* magnificence, splendour 54 *crime* wrong-doing, sin 56 *attune** bring into musical accord 57 *approvance*** approof, proof, approbation 61 *display** discover, get sight of 65 *dight to* made ready, arranged, for 72 *scorched** dried up; gossamer was thought to be formed from dried-up dew

Her snowy brest was bare to readie spoyle
Of hungry eies, which n'ote therewith be fild,
And yet through languour of her late sweet toyle,
Few drops, more cleare then Nectar, forth distild,
That like pure Orient perles adowne it trild,
And her faire eyes sweet smyling in delight,
Moystened their fierie beames, with which she thrild
Fraile harts, yet quenched not; like starry light
Which sparckling on the silent waves, does seeme more bright.

The young man sleeping by her, seemd to bee
Some goodly swayne of honorable place,
That certes it great pittie was to see
Him his nobilitie so foule deface;
A sweet regard, and amiable grace,
Mixed with manly sternnesse did appeare
Yet sleeping, in his well proportiond face,
And on his tender lips the downy heare
Did now but freshly spring, and silken blossomes beare.

His warlike armes, the idle instruments
Of sleeping praise, were hong upon a tree,
And his brave shield, full of old moniments,
Was fowly ra'st, that none the signes might see;
Ne for them, ne for honour cared hee,
Ne ought, that did to his advauncement tend,
But in lewd loves, and wastfull luxuree,
His dayes, his goods, his bodie he did spend:
O horrible enchantment, that him so did blend.

The noble Elfe, and carefull Palmer drew
So nigh them, minding nought, but lustfull game,
That suddein forth they on them rusht, and threw
A subtile net, which onely for the same

80 74 *n'ote* could not 77 *trild* flowed 79 *thrild* pierced 80 *quenched* destroyed, killed 83 *place* rank 88 *Yet sleeping* while he slept 93 *moniments* marks 94 *ra'st* erased 99 *blend* blind 103 *subtile* finely woven *the same* that purpose

The skilfull Palmer formally did frame.
So held them under fast, the whiles the rest
Fled all away for feare of fowler shame.
The faire Enchauntresse, so unwares opprest,
Tryde all her arts, and all her sleights, thence out to wrest.

And eke her lover strove: but all in vaine;
For that same net so cunningly was wound,
That neither guile, nor force might it distraine.
They tooke them both, and both them strongly bound
In captive bandes, which there they readie found:
But her in chaines of adamant he tyde;
For nothing else might keepe her safe and sound;
But *Verdant* (so he hight) he soone untyde,
And counsell sage in steed thereof to him applyde.

But all those pleasant bowres and Pallace brave,
Guyon broke downe, with rigour pittilesse;
Ne ought their goodly workmanship might save
Them from the tempest of his wrathfulnesse,
But that their blisse he turn'd to balefulnesse:
Their groves he feld, their gardins did deface,
Their arbers spoyle, their Cabinets suppresse,
Their banket houses burne, their buildings race,
And of the fairest late, now made the fowlest place.

Then led they her away, and eke that knight
They with them led, both sorrowfull and sad:
The way they came, the same retourn'd they right,
Till they arrived, where they lately had
Charm'd those wild-beasts, that rag'd with furie mad.
Which now awaking, fierce at them gan fly,
As in their mistresse reskew, whom they lad;
But them the Palmer soone did pacify.
Then *Guyon* askt, what meant those beastes, which there did ly.

80 104 *formally* expressly; skilfully 108 *wrest* twist, escape 110 *wound* twined, woven 111 *distraine* tear apart 114 *adamant* a hard rock or mineral resembling diamond 116 *Verdant* literally 'green-giving', abundant, flourishing; the name is associated with spring 118 *brave* beautiful, fair 122 *balefulnesse** distress, sadness 124 *Cabinets* bowers 125 *banket* banquet *race* raze 131 *wild-beasts* protecting the Bower of Blisse, see Book 2, Canto 12, verses 39–40

Said he, these seeming beasts are men indeed,
Whom this Enchauntresse hath transformed thus,
Whylome her lovers, which her lusts did feed,
Now turned into figures hideous,
According to their mindes like monstruous.
Sad end (quoth he) of life intemperate,
And mournefull meed of joyes delicious:
But Palmer, if it mote thee so aggrate,
Let them returned be unto their former state.

Streight way he with his vertuous staffe them strooke,
And streight of beasts they comely men became;
Yet being men they did unmanly looke,
And stared ghastly, some for inward shame,
And some for wrath, to see their captive Dame:
But one above the rest in speciall,
That had an hog beene late, hight *Grille* by name,
Repined greatly, and did him miscall,
That had from hoggish forme him brought to naturall.

Said *Guyon*, See the mind of beastly man,
That hath so soone forgot the excellence
Of his creation, when he life began,
That now he chooseth, with vile difference,
To be a beast, and lacke intelligence.
To whom the Palmer thus, The donghill kind
Delights in filth and foule incontinence:
Let *Grill* be *Grill*, and have his hoggish mind,
But let us hence depart, whilest wether serves and wind.

80 140 monstrous according to the corruption of their minds; Spenser modifies the myth of Homer's Circe 142 *meed* reward 143 *aggrate* please, gratify 145 *vertuous* possessing virtues, powers 151 *Grille* according to Plutarch, Ulysses' companion who was changed by Circe into a hog and refused to be changed back into human shape 152 *Repined* complained *miscall* revile, abuse 157 *difference* discrimination, preference

81 [*from* The Faerie Queene Book 3]

She brought her to her joyous Paradize,
Where most she wonnes, when she on earth does dwel.
So faire a place, as Nature can devize:
Whether in *Paphos*, or *Cytheron* hill,
Or it in *Gnidus* be, I wote not well;
But well I wote by tryall, that this same
All other pleasant places doth excell,
And called is by her lost lovers name,
The *Gardin* of *Adonis*, farre renowmd by fame.

In that same Gardin all the goodly flowres,
Wherewith dame Nature doth her beautifie,
And decks the girlonds of her paramoures,
Are fetcht: there is the first seminarie
Of all things, that are borne to live and die,
According to their kindes. Long worke it were,
Here to account the endlesse progenie
Of all the weedes, that bud and blossome there;
But so much as doth need, must needs be counted here.

It sited was in fruitfull soyle of old,
And girt in with two walles on either side;
The one of yron, the other of bright gold,
That none might thorough breake, nor over-stride:
And double gates it had, which opened wide,
By which both in and out men moten pas;
Th'one faire and fresh, the other old and dride:
Old *Genius* the porter of them was,
Old *Genius*, the which a double nature has.

He letteth in, he letteth out to wend,
All that to come into the world desire;
A thousand thousand naked babes attend
About him day and night, which doe require,

81 1 *She brought her* Venus brought Amoret 2 *wonnes* dwells, lives 13 *seminarie** seed-plot 15 *kindes* natures 16 *account* recount, relate 20 *girt* surrounded, encircled 26 *Genius* god of generation 31 *require* request

That he with fleshly weedes would them attire:
Such as him list, such as eternall fate
Ordained hath, he clothes with sinfull mire,
And sendeth forth to live in mortall state,
Till they againe returne backe by the hinder gate.

After that they againe returned beene,
They in that Gardin planted be againe;
And grow afresh, as they had never seene
Fleshly corruption, nor mortall paine.
Some thousand yeares so doen they there remaine;
And then of him are clad with other hew,
Or sent into the chaungefull world againe,
Till thither they returne, where first they grew:
So like a wheele around they runne from old to new.

Ne needs there Gardiner to set, or sow,
To plant or prune: for of their owne accord
All things, as they created were, doe grow,
And yet remember well the mightie word,
Which first was spoken by th'Almightie lord,
That bad them to increase and multiply:
Ne doe they need with water of the ford,
Or of the clouds to moysten their roots dry;
For in themselves eternall moisture they imply.

Infinite shapes of creatures there are bred,
And uncouth formes, which none yet ever knew,
And every sort is in a sundry bed
Set by it selfe, and ranckt in comely rew:
Some fit for reasonable soules t'indew,
Some made for beasts, some made for birds to weare,
And all the fruitfull spawne of fishes hew
In endlesse rancks along enraunged were,
That seem'd the *Ocean* could not containe them there.

81 32 *fleshly weedes* bodies, flesh 42 *hew* form, shape 43 *chaungefull*** changing, inconstant 49 *word* see Genesis 1:22 'And God blessed them, saying, Be fruitful, and multiply, and fill the waters in the seas, and let fowl multiply in the earth' 54 *eternall* essential, inherent *imply* enfold, involve 59 *reasonable . . . indew* human beings to assume, put on

Daily they grow, and daily forth are sent
Into the world, it to replenish more;
Yet is the stocke not lessened, nor spent,
But still remaines in everlasting store,
As it at first created was of yore.
For in the wide wombe of the world there lyes,
In hatefull darkenesse and in deepe horrore,
An huge eternall *Chaos*, which supplyes
The substances of natures fruitfull progenyes.

All things from thence doe their first being fetch,
And borrow matter, whereof they are made,
Which when as forme and feature it does ketch,
Becomes a bodie, and doth then invade
The state of life, out of the griesly shade.
That substance is eterne, and bideth so,
Ne when the life decayes, and forme does fade,
Doth it consume, and into nothing go,
But chaunged is, and often altred to and fro.

The substance is not chaunged, nor altered,
But th'only forme and outward fashion;
For every substance is conditioned
To change her hew, and sundry formes to don,
Meet for her temper and complexion:
For formes are variable and decay,
By course of kind, and by occasion;
And that faire flowre of beautie fades away,
As doth the lilly fresh before the sunny ray.

Great enimy to it, and to all the rest,
That in the *Gardin* of *Adonis* springs,
Is wicked *Time*, who with his scyth addrest,
Does mow the flowring herbes and goodly things,

81 75 *feature* aspect *ketch* take, seize 80 *Doth* ... *consume* is it consumed
83 *But th'only* except only the 88 *kind* nature, species 93 *addrest* armed

And all their glory to the ground downe flings,
Where they doe wither, and are fowly mard:
He flyes about, and with his flaggy wings
Beates downe both leaves and buds without regard,
Ne ever pittie may relent his malice hard.

Yet pittie often did the gods relent,
To see so faire things mard, and spoyled quight:
And their great mother *Venus* did lament
The losse of her deare brood, her deare delight;
Her hart was pierst with pittie at the sight,
When walking through the Gardin, them she spyde,
Yet no'te she find redresse for such despight.
For all that lives, is subject to that law:
All things decay in time, and to their end do draw.

But were it not, that *Time* their troubler is,
All that in this delightfull Gardin growes,
Should happie be, and have immortall blis:
For here all plentie, and all pleasure flowes,
And sweet love gentle fits emongst them throwes,
Without fell rancor, or fond gealosie;
Franckly each paramour his leman knowes,
Each bird his mate, ne any does envie
Their goodly meriment, and gay felicitie.

There is continuall spring, and harvest there
Continuall, both meeting at one time:
For both the boughes doe laughing blossomes beare,
And with fresh colours decke the wanton Prime,
And eke attonce the heavy trees they clime,
Which seeme to labour under their fruits lode:
The whiles the joyous birdes make their pastime
Emongst the shadie leaves, their sweet abode,
And their true loves without suspition tell abrode.

81 97 *flaggy* drooping, pendulous 106 *no'te* could not 113 *fits* paroxysms, exciting experiences (?) 114 *fond* foolish 115 *Franckly* openly *leman* lover, mistress 121 *Prime* springtime

Right in the middest of that Paradise,
There stood a stately Mount, on whose round top
A gloomy grove of mirtle trees did rise,
Whose shadie boughes sharpe steele did never lop,
Nor wicked beasts their tender buds did crop,
But like a girlond compassed the hight,
And from their fruitfull sides sweet gum did drop,
That all the ground with precious deaw bedight,
Threw forth most dainty odours, and most sweet delight.

82 [*from* The Faerie Queene Book 3]

For round about, the wals yclothed were
With goodly arras of great majesty,
Woven with gold and silke so close and nere,
That the rich metall lurked privily,
As faining to be hid from envious eye;
Yet here, and there, and every where unwares
It shewd it selfe, and shone unwillingly;
Like a discolourd Snake, whose hidden snares
Through the greene gras his long bright burnisht backe declares.

And in those Tapets weren fashioned
Many faire pourtraicts, and many a faire feate,
And all of love, and all of lusty-hed,
As seemed by their semblaunt did entreat;
And eke all *Cupids* warres they did repeate,
And cruell battels, which he whilome fought
Gainst all the Gods, to make his empire great;
Besides the huge massacres, which he wrought
On mighty kings and kesars, into thraldome brought.

81 128 *Mount* the 'mons Veneris', pudenda 134 *bedight* bedecked

82 2 *arras* richly woven tapestry 6 *unwares* unexpectedly 8 *discolourd* multi-coloured 10 *Tapets* tapestries, hangings 11 *pourtraicts* designs, figures 12 *lusty-hed* lustfulness, libidinousness 13 *semblaunt* demeanour, look *entreat* treat 14 *repeate* recount, relate 18 *kesars* emperors

Therein was writ, how often thundring *Jove*
Had felt the point of his hart-percing dart,
And leaving heavens kingdome, here did rove
In straunge disguize, to slake his scalding smart;
Now like a Ram, faire *Helle* to pervart,
Now like a Bull, *Europa* to withdraw:
Ah, how the fearefull Ladies tender hart
Did lively seeme to tremble, when she saw
The huge seas under her t'obay her servaunts law.

Soone after that into a golden showre
Him selfe he chaung'd faire *Danaë* to vew,
And through the roofe of her strong brasen towre
Did raine into her lap an hony dew,
The whiles her foolish garde, that little knew
Of such deceipt, kept th'yron dore fast bard,
And watcht, that none should enter nor issew;
Vaine was the watch, and bootlesse all the ward,
Whenas the God to golden hew him selfe transfard.

Then was he turnd into a snowy Swan,
To win faire *Leda* to his lovely trade:
O wondrous skill, and sweet wit of the man,
That her in daffadillies sleeping made,
From scorching heat her daintie limbes to shade:
Whiles the proud Bird ruffing his fethers wyde,
And brushing his faire brest, did her invade;
She slept, yet twixt her eyelids closely spyde,
How towards her he rusht, and smiled at his pryde.

Then shewd it, how the *Thebane Semelee*
Deceiv'd of gealous *Juno*, did require
To see him in his soveraigne majestee,
Armd with his thunderbolts and lightning fire,

82 20 *hart-percing** 23 *pervart* turn away from, corrupt 26 *lively* in a lifelike way 27 *servaunts* lover's 31 *hony dew* ideally sweet, luscious, substance 36 *transfard* transported 42 *ruffing** ruffling

Whence dearely she with death bought her desire.
But faire *Alcmena* better match did make,
Joying his love in likenesse more entire;
Three nights in one, they say, that for her sake
He then did put, her pleasures lenger to partake.

Twise was he seene in soaring Eagles shape,
And with wide wings to beat the buxome ayre,
Once, when he with *Asterie* did scape,
Againe, when as the *Trojane* boy so faire
He snatcht from *Ida* hill, and with him bare:
Wondrous delight it was, there to behould,
How the rude Shepheards after him did stare,
Trembling through feare, least down he fallen should
And often to him calling, to take surer hould.

In *Satyres* shape *Antiopa* he snatcht:
And like a fire, when he *Aegin'* assayd:
A shepheard, when *Mnemosyne* he catcht:
And like a Serpent to the *Thracian* mayd.
Whiles thus on earth great *Jove* these pageaunts playd,
The winged boy did thrust into his throne,
And scoffing, thus unto his mother sayd,
Lo now the heavens obey to me alone,
And take me for their *Jove*, whiles *Jove* to earth is gone.

And thou, faire *Phœbus*, in thy colours bright
Wast there enwoven, and the sad distresse,
In which that boy thee plonged, for despight,
That thou bewray'dst his mothers wantonnesse,
When she with *Mars* was meynt in joyfulnesse:
For thy he thrild thee with a leaden dart,
To love faire *Daphne*, which thee loved lesse:
Lesse she thee lov'd, then was thy just desart,
Yet was thy love her death, and her death was thy smart.

82 52 *entire* perfect 56 *buxome* yielding, unresisting 57 *scape* escape 58 *boy* Ganymede 61 *rude* simple, unlearned 67 *mayd* Proserpina 68 *pageaunts* tricks 69 *boy* Cupid 70 *mother* Venus 77 *meynt* mingled, joined sexually 78 *For thy* therefore *thrild* pierced *leaden dart* of unhappy love

So lovedst thou the lusty *Hyacinct*,
So lovedst thou the faire *Coronis* deare:
Yet both are of thy haplesse hand extinct,
Yet both in flowres do live, and love thee beare,
The one a Paunce, the other a sweet breare:
For griefe whereof, ye mote have lively seene
The God himselfe rending his golden heare,
And breaking quite his gyrlond ever greene,
With other signes of sorrow and impatient teene.

Both for those two, and for his owne deare sonne,
The sonne of *Climene* he did repent,
Who bold to guide the charet of the Sunne,
Himselfe in thousand peeces fondly rent,
And all the world with flashing fier brent,
So like, that all the walles did seeme to flame.
Yet cruell *Cupid*, not herewith content,
Forst him eftsoones to follow other game,
And love a Shepheards daughter for his dearest Dame.

He loved *Isse* for his dearest Dame,
And for her sake her cattell fed a while,
And for her sake a cowheard vile became,
The servant of *Admetus* cowheard vile,
Whiles that from heaven he suffered exile.
Long were to tell each other lovely fit,
Now like a Lyon, hunting after spoile,
Now like a Hag, now like a faulcon flit:
All which in that faire arras was most lively writ.

Next unto him was *Neptune* pictured,
In his divine resemblance wondrous lyke:
His face was rugged, and his hoarie hed
Dropped with brackish deaw; his three-forkt Pyke

82 82 *lusty* youthful, strong, vigorous 86 *Paunce* pansy 87 *lively* living, lifelike 90 *teene* grief, affliction 91 *sonne* Phaethon 94 *fondly* foolishly 95 *brent* burned 107 *Hag* haggard, untamed hawk (?) *flit** swift, nimble 112 *Pyke* pikestaff

He stearnly shooke, and therewith fierce did stryke
The raging billowes, that on every syde
They trembling stood, and made a long broad dyke,
That his swift charet might have passage wyde,
Which foure great *Hippodames* did draw in temewise tyde.

His sea-horses did seeme to snort amayne,
And from their nosethrilles blow the brynie streame,
That made the sparckling waves to smoke agayne,
And flame with gold, but the white fomy creame,
Did shine with silver, and shoot forth his beame.
The God himselfe did pensive seeme and sad,
And hong adowne his head, as he did dreame:
For privy love his brest empierced had,
Ne ought but deare *Bisaltis* ay could make him glad.

He loved eke *Iphimedia* deare,
And *Aeolus* faire daughter *Arne* hight,
For whom he turnd him selfe into a Steare,
And fed on fodder, to beguile her sight.
Also to win *Deucalions* daughter bright,
He turnd him selfe into a Dolphin fayre;
And like a winged horse he tooke his flight,
To snaky-locke *Medusa* to repayre,
On whom he got faire *Pegasus*, that flitteth in the ayre.

Next *Saturne* was, (but who would ever weene,
That sullein *Saturne* ever weend to love?
Yet love is sullein, and *Saturnlike* seene,
As he did for *Erigone* it prove)
That to a *Centaure* did him selfe transmove.
So proov'd it eke that gracious God of wine,
When for to compasse *Philliras* hard love,
He turnd himselfe into a fruitfull vine,
And into her faire bosome made his grapes decline.

82 117 *Hippodames* hippocamps, sea-horses *in temewise* as a team 118 *amayne* with all their might 131 *daughter* Melantho 136 *weene* think 140 *transmove** transform, transmute 141 *God of wine* Bacchus

Long were to tell the amorous assayes,
And gentle pangues, with which he maked meeke
The mighty *Mars*, to learne his wanton playes:
How oft for *Venus*, and how often eek
For many other Nymphes he sore did shreek,
With womanish teares, and with unwarlike smarts,
Privily moystening his horrid cheek.
There was he painted full of burning darts,
And many wide woundes launched through his inner parts.

Ne did he spare (so cruell was the Elfe)
His owne deare mother, (ah why should he so?)
Ne did he spare sometime to pricke himselfe,
That he might tast the sweet consuming woe,
Which he had wrought to many others moe.
But to declare the mournfull Tragedyes,
And spoiles, wherewith he all the ground did strow,
More eath to number, with how many eyes
High heaven beholds sad lovers nightly theeveryes.

Kings Queenes, Lords Ladies, Knights and Damzels gent
Were heap'd together with the vulgar sort,
And mingled with the raskall rablement,
Without respect of person or of port,
To shew Dan *Cupids* powre and great effort:
And round about a border was entrayld,
Of broken bowes and arrowes shivered short,
And a long bloudy river through them rayld,
So lively and so like, that living sence it fayld.

And at the upper end of that faire rowme,
There was an Altar built of pretious stone,
Of passing valew, and of great renowme,
On which there stood an Image all alone,

82 145 *assayes* assaults, attempts 146 *pangues* pangs 150 *unwarlike** 151 *horrid* bristly 154 *Elfe* malicious, supernatural being 155 *mother* Venus 161 *eath* easy 163 *gent* gentle, noble 166 *port* social status 167 *Dan* Master 168 *entrayld* entwined, interlaced 169 *shivered* broken, splintered 170 *rayld* flowed, gushed 171 *fayld* deceived

Of massy gold, which with his owne light shone;
And wings it had with sundry colours dight,
More sundry colours, then the proud *Pavone*
Beares in his boasted fan, or *Iris* bright,
When her discolourd bow she spreds through heaven bright.

Blindfold he was, and in his cruell fist
A mortall bow and arrowes keene did hold,
With which he shot at randon, when him list,
Some headed with sad lead, some with pure gold;
(Ah man beware, how thou those darts behold)
A wounded Dragon under him did ly,
Whose hideous tayle his left foot did enfold,
And with a shaft was shot through either eye,
That no man forth might draw, ne no man remedye.

And underneath his feet was written thus,
Unto the Victor of the Gods this bee:
And all the people in that ample hous
Did to that image bow their humble knee,
And oft committed fowle Idolatree.
That wondrous sight faire *Britomart* amazed,
Ne seeing could her wonder satisfie,
But ever more and more upon it gazed,
The whiles the passing brightnes her fraile sences dazed.

82 176 *massy* heavy, solid 177 *dight* adorned 178 *Pavone** peacock (Italian) 180 *discolourd* of differing colours 187 *enfold** clasp, embrace

83 [*from* Amoretti]

SONNET. 23.

Penelope for her *Ulisses* sake,
Deviz'd a Web her wooers to deceave:
in which the worke that she all day did make
the same at night she did againe unreave,
Such subtile craft my Damzell doth conceave,
th'importune suit of my desire to shonne:
for all that I in many dayes doo weave,
in one short houre I find by her undonne.
So when I thinke to end that I begonne,
I must begin and never bring to end:
for with one looke she spils that long I sponne,
and with one word my whole years work doth rend.
Such labour like the Spyders web I fynd,
whose fruitlesse worke is broken with least wynd.

84 [*from* Amoretti]

SONNET. 64.

Comming to kisse her lyps, (such grace I found)
Me seemd I smelt a gardin of sweet flowres:
that dainty odours from them threw around
for damzels fit to decke their lovers bowres.
Her lips did smell lyke unto Gillyflowers,
her ruddy cheekes lyke unto Roses red:
her snowy browes lyke budded Bellamoures,
her lovely eyes lyke Pincks but newly spred,

83 4 *unreave* unravel 6 *importune* pressing, urgent

84 5 *Gillyflowers* a variety of pinks 7 *Bellamoures** an unidentified, white flower, literally 'fair loves' 8 *spred* unfurled, opened

Her goodly bosome lyke a Strawberry bed,
her neck lyke to a bounch of Cullambynes:
her brest lyke lillyes, ere theyr leaves be shed,
her nipples lyke yong blossomd Jessemynes.
Such fragrant flowres doe give most odorous smell,
but her sweet odour did them all excell.

85 [*from* Amoretti]

SONNET. 67.

Lyke as a huntsman after weary chace,
Seeing the game from him escapt away:
sits downe to rest him in some shady place,
with panting hounds beguiled of their pray:
So after long pursuit and vaine assay,
when I all weary had the chace forsooke,
the gentle deare returnd the selfe-same way,
thinking to quench her thirst at the next brooke.
There she beholding me with mylder looke,
sought not to fly, but fearelesse still did bide:
till I in hand her yet halfe trembling tooke,
and with her owne goodwill hir fyrmely tyde.
Strange thing me seemd to see a beast so wyld,
so goodly wonne with her owne will beguyld.

84 10 *Cullambynes* columbines, small plants with inverted flowers, which are often pale pink 12 *Jessemynes* jasmines, which have white or yellow flowers

85 4 *beguiled* cheated, deprived 5 *assay* attempt, endeavour 14 *beguyld* charmed, diverted

86 [*from* Amoretti]

SONNET. 70.

Fresh spring the herald of loves mighty king,
In whose cote armour richly are displayd
all sorts of flowers the which on earth do spring
in goodly colours gloriously arrayd.
Goe to my love, where she is carelesse layd,
yet in her winters bowre not well awake:
tell her the joyous time wil not be staid
unlesse she doe him by the forelock take.
Bid her therefore her selfe soone ready make,
to wayt on love amongst his lovely crew:
where every one that misseth then her make,
shall be by him amearst with penance dew.
Make hast therefore sweet love, whilest it is prime,
for none can call againe the passed time.

87 [*from* Amoretti]

SONNET. 71.

I joy to see how in your drawen work,
Your selfe unto the Bee ye doe compare;
and me unto the Spyder that doth lurke,
in close awayt to catch her unaware.
Right so your selfe were caught in cunning snare
of a deare foe, and thralled to his love:
in whose streight bands ye now captived are
so firmely, that ye never may remove.

86 2 *cote armour* coat armour, coat of arms, vest or tabard worn over armour and embroidered with heraldic devices 8 *forelock* Occasion, or Opportunity, was emblematically pictured as having a long forelock over the forehead which had to be grasped 11 *make* mate 12 *amearst* amerced, punished, usually by a fine 13 *prime* the best, most perfect moment

87 1 *drawen work* patterned ornamental work in fabric 4 *close awayt* hidden, secret, ambush 7 *streight* tight, close

But as your worke is woven all above,
with woodbynd flowers and fragrant Eglantine:
so sweet your prison you in time shall prove,
with many deare delights bedecked fyne.
And all thensforth eternall peace shall see,
betweene the Spyder and the gentle Bee.

88 Epithalamion

Ye learned sisters which have oftentimes
Beene to me ayding, others to adorne:
Whom ye thought worthy of your gracefull rymes,
That even the greatest did not greatly scorne
To heare theyr names sung in your simple layes,
But joyed in theyr prayse.
And when ye list your owne mishaps to mourne,
Which death, or love, or fortunes wreck did rayse,
Your string could soone to sadder tenor turne,
And teach the woods and waters to lament
Your dolefull dreriment.
Now lay those sorrowfull complaints aside,
And having all your heads with girland crownd,
Helpe me mine owne loves prayses to resound,
Ne let the same of any be envide,
So Orpheus did for his owne bride,
So I unto my selfe alone will sing,
The woods shall to me answer and my Eccho ring.

Early before the worlds light giving lampe,
His golden beame upon the hils doth spred,
Having disperst the nights unchearefull dampe,
Doe ye awake and with fresh lusty hed,

87 10 *woodbynd* woodbine, honeysuckle *Eglantine* sweet-brier rose

88 1 *sisters* Muses 3 *gracefull** conferring grace, honour 4 *greatest* Spenser dedicated *The Faerie Queene* to Queen Elizabeth I 5 *layes* songs 11 *dreriment* dismal state: the opposite, perhaps, of 'merriment' 13 *girland* a garland, wreath of flowers 16 *bride* Eurydice 22 *lusty hed* lustihead, pleasure, delight

Go to the bowre of my beloved love,
My truest turtle dove,
Bid her awake; for Hymen is awake,
And long since ready forth his maske to move,
With his bright Tead that flames with many a flake,
And many a bachelor to waite on him,
In theyr fresh garments trim.
Bid her awake therefore and soone her dight,
For lo the wished day is come at last,
That shall for al the paynes and sorrowes past,
Pay to her usury of long delight,
And whylest she doth her dight,
Doe ye to her of joy and solace sing,
That all the woods may answer and your eccho ring.

Bring with you all the Nymphes that you can heare
Both of the rivers and the forrests greene:
And of the sea that neighbours to her neare,
Al with gay girlands goodly wel beseene.
And let them also with them bring in hand,
Another gay girland
For my fayre love of lillyes and of roses,
Bound truelove wize with a blew silke riband.
And let them make great store of bridale poses,
And let them eeke bring store of other flowers
To deck the bridale bowers.
And let the ground whereas her foot shall tread,
For feare the stones her tender foot should wrong
Be strewed with fragrant flowers all along,
And diapred lyke the discolored mead.
Which done, doe at her chamber dore awayt,
For she will waken strayt,
The whiles doe ye this song unto her sing,
The woods shall to you answer and your Eccho ring.

88 26 *maske* pageant, procession 27 *Tead* tede, wood-torch *flake* flash, spark 30 *dight* dress 40 *wel beseene* well provided for, furnished; seen to look well 45 *poses* posies, bunches of flowers 51 *diapred** strewn in a diaper pattern *discolored* differently coloured

Ye Nymphes of Mulla which with carefull heed,
The silver scaly trouts doe tend full well,
And greedy pikes which use therein to feed,
(Those trouts and pikes all others doo excell)
And ye likewise which keepe the rushy lake,
Where none doo fishes take,
Bynd up the locks the which hang scatterd light,
And in his waters which your mirror make,
Behold your faces as the christall bright,
That when you come whereas my love doth lie,
No blemish she may spie.
And eke ye lightfoot mayds which keepe the dere,
That on the hoary mountayne use to towre,
And the wylde wolves which seeke them to devoure,
With your steele darts doo chace from comming neer
Be also present heere,
To helpe to decke her and to help to sing,
That all the woods may answer and your eccho ring.

Wake now my love, awake; for it is time,
The Rosy Morne long since left Tithones bed,
All ready to her silver coche to clyme,
And Phœbus gins to shew his glorious hed.
Hark how the cheerefull birds do chaunt theyr laies
And carroll of loves praise.
The merry Larke hir mattins sings aloft,
The thrush replyes, the Mavis descant playes,
The Ouzell shrills, the Ruddock warbles soft,
So goodly all agree with sweet consent,
To this dayes merriment.
Ah my deere love why doe ye sleepe thus long,
When meeter were that ye should now awake,
T'awayt the comming of your joyous make,

88 56 *Mulla* Spenser's name for the river Awbeg which flowed through his estate at Kilcolman in Ireland 60 *rushy* full of, covered by, rushes 68 *hoary* covered in trees, scrub *towre* tower, rise up high 81 *Mavis* song thrush 82 *Ouzell* blackbird *Ruddock* robin 86 *meeter* more fitting, appropriate 87 *make* mate

And hearken to the birds lovelearned song,
The deawy leaves among.
For they of joy and pleasance to you sing,
That all the woods them answer and theyr eccho ring.

My love is now awake out of her dreame,
And her fayre eyes like stars that dimmed were
With darksome cloud, now shew theyr goodly beams
More bright then Hesperus his head doth rere.
Come now ye damzels, daughters of delight,
Helpe quickly her to dight,
But first come ye fayre houres which were begot
In Joves sweet paradice, of Day and Night,
Which doe the seasons of the yeare allot,
And al that ever in this world is fayre
Doe make and still repayre.
And ye three handmayds of the Cyprian Queene,
The which doe still adorne her beauties pride,
Helpe to addorne my beautifullest bride
And as ye her array, still throw betweene
Some graces to be seene,
And as ye use to Venus, to her sing,
The whiles the woods shal answer and your eccho ring.

Now is my love all ready forth to come,
Let all the virgins therefore well awayt,
And ye fresh boyes that tend upon her groome
Prepare your selves; for he is comming strayt.
Set all your things in seemely good aray
Fit for so joyfull day,
The joyfulst day that ever sunne did see.
Faire Sun, shew forth thy favourable ray,
And let thy lifull heat not fervent be
For feare of burning her sunshyny face,
Her beauty to disgrace.

88 88 *lovelearned** 103 *handmayds* the Graces *Queene* Aphrodite 118 *lifull* lifeful, life-giving *fervent* hot, burning 119 *sunshyny* bright as with sunshine

O fayrest Phœbus, father of the Muse,
If ever I did honour thee aright,
Or sing the thing, that mote thy mind delight,
Doe not thy servants simple boone refuse,
But let this day let this one day be myne,
Let all the rest be thine.
Then I thy soverayne prayses loud wil sing,
That all the woods shal answer and theyr eccho ring.

Harke how the Minstrels gin to shrill aloud
Their merry Musick that resounds from far,
The pipe, the tabor, and the trembling Croud,
That well agree withouten breach or jar.
But most of all the Damzels doe delite,
When they their tymbrels smyte,
And thereunto doe daunce and carrol sweet,
That all the sences they doe ravish quite,
The whyles the boyes run up and downe the street,
Crying aloud with strong confused noyce,
As if it were one voyce.
Hymen io Hymen, Hymen they do shout,
That even to the heavens theyr shouting shrill
Doth reach, and all the firmament doth fill,
To which the people standing all about,
As in approvance doe thereto applaud
And loud advaunce her laud,
And evermore they Hymen Hymen sing,
That al the woods them answer and theyr eccho ring.

Loe where she comes along with portly pace,
Lyke Phœbe from her chamber of the East,
Arysing forth to run her mighty race,
Clad all in white, that seemes a virgin best.
So well it her beseemes that ye would weene
Some angell she had beene.

88 124 *boone* favour, request 129 *shrill** utter in shrill tones 131 *Croud* fiddle 132 *agree* keep harmony 134 *tymbrels* tambourines 138 *confused* mixed, blended 140 *io* (Greek) hurra! ho! 144 *approvance* approval 145 *laud* praise 148 *portly* stately, dignified 151 *seemes* becomes, befits

Her long loose yellow locks lyke golden wyre,
Sprinckled with perle, and perling flowres a tweene,
Doe lyke a golden mantle her attyre,
And being crowned with a girland greene,
Seeme lyke some mayden Queene.
Her modest eyes abashed to behold
So many gazers, as on her do stare,
Upon the lowly ground affixed are.
Ne dare lift up her countenance too bold,
But blush to heare her prayses sung so loud,
So farre from being proud.
Nathlesse doe ye still loud her prayses sing,
That all the woods may answer and your eccho ring.

Tell me ye merchants daughters did ye see
So fayre a creature in your towne before,
So sweet, so lovely, and so mild as she,
Adornd with beautyes grace and vertues store,
Her goodly eyes lyke Saphyres shining bright,
Her forehead yvory white,
Her cheekes lyke apples which the sun hath rudded,
Her lips lyke cherryes charming men to byte,
Her brest like to a bowle of creame uncrudded,
Her paps lyke lyllies budded,
Her snowie necke lyke to a marble towre,
And all her body like a pallace fayre,
Ascending uppe with many a stately stayre,
To honors seat and chastities sweet bowre.
Why stand ye still ye virgins in amaze,
Upon her so to gaze,
Whiles ye forget your former lay to sing,
To which the woods did answer and your eccho ring.

But if ye saw that which no eyes can see,
The inward beauty of her lively spright,
Garnisht with heavenly guifts of high degree,
Much more then would ye wonder at that sight,

88 155 *perling**...*tweene* forming flowers between, made out of pearls 165 *ye* the 'gazers' of l.160 173 *rudded* made ruddy 175 *uncrudded** uncurdled, fresh

And stand astonisht lyke to those which red
Medusaes mazeful hed.
There dwels sweet love and constant chastity,
Unspotted fayth and comely womanhood,
Regard of honour and mild modesty,
There vertue raynes as Queene in royal throne,
And giveth lawes alone.
The which the base affections doe obay,
And yeeld theyr services unto her will,
Ne thought of thing uncomely ever may
Thereto approch to tempt her mind to ill.
Had ye once seene these her celestial threasures,
And unrevealed pleasures,
Then would ye wonder and her prayses sing,
That al the woods should answer and your echo ring.

Open the temple gates unto my love,
Open them wide that she may enter in,
And all the postes adorne as doth behove,
And all the pillours deck with girlands trim,
For to recyve this Saynt with honour dew,
That commeth in to you.
With trembling steps and humble reverence,
She commeth in, before th'almighties vew,
Of her ye virgins learne obedience,
When so ye come into those holy places,
To humble your proud faces.
Bring her up to th'high altar that she may
The sacred ceremonies there partake,
The which do endlesse matrimony make,
And let the roring Organs loudly play
The praises of the Lord in lively notes,
The whiles with hollow throates
The Choristers the joyous Antheme sing,
That al the woods may answere and their eccho ring.

88 189 *red* saw 190 *mazeful** bewildering, confounding

Behold whiles she before the altar stands
Hearing the holy priest that to her speakes
And blesseth her with his two happy hands,
How the red roses flush up in her cheekes,
And the pure snow with goodly vermill stayne,
Like crimsin dyde in grayne,
That even th'Angels which continually,
About the sacred Altare doe remaine,
Forget their service and about her fly,
Ofte peeping in her face that seemes more fayre,
The more they on it stare.
But her sad eyes still fastened on the ground,
Are governed with goodly modesty,
That suffers not one looke to glaunce awry,
Which may let in a little thought unsownd.
Why blush ye love to give to me your hand,
The pledge of all our band?
Sing ye sweet Angels Alleluya sing,
That all the woods may answere and your eccho ring.

Now al is done; bring home the bride againe,
Bring home the triumph of our victory,
Bring home with you the glory of her gaine,
With joyance bring her and with jollity.
Never had man more joyfull day then this,
Whom heaven would heape with blis.
Make feast therefore now all this live long day,
This day for ever to me holy is,
Poure out the wine without restraint or stay,
Poure not by cups, but by the belly full,
Poure out to all that wull,
And sprinkle all the postes and wals with wine,
That they may sweat, and drunken be withall.
Crowne ye God Bacchus with a coronall,
And Hymen also crowne with wreathes of vine,

88 227 *vermill* vermeil, red 228 *dyde in grayne* fast dyed, dyed thoroughly 234 *sad* solemn, serious 237 *unsownd** not soundly based in reasoning or fact (?); immodest 239 *band* bond 245 *joyance* merrymaking, festivities

And let the Graces daunce unto the rest;
For they can doo it best:
The whiles the maydens doe theyr carroll sing,
To which the woods shal answer and theyr eccho ring.

Ring ye the bels, ye yong men of the towne,
And leave your wonted labors for this day:
This day is holy; doe ye write it downe,
That ye for ever it remember may.
This day the sunne is in his chiefest hight,
With Barnaby the bright,
From whence declining daily by degrees,
He somewhat loseth of his heat and light,
When once the Crab behind his back he sees.
But for this time it ill ordained was,
To chose the longest day in all the yeare,
And shortest night, when longest fitter weare:
Yet never day so long, but late would passe.
Ring ye the bels, to make it weare away,
And bonefiers make all day,
And daunce about them, and about them sing:
That all the woods may answer, and your eccho ring.

Ah when will this long weary day have end,
And lende me leave to come unto my love?
How slowly do the houres theyr numbers spend?
How slowly does sad Time his feathers move?
Hast thee O fayrest Planet to thy home
Within the Westerne fome:
Thy tyred steedes long since have need of rest.
Long though it be, at last I see it gloome,
And the bright evening star with golden creast
Appeare out of the East.
Fayre childe of beauty, glorious lampe of love
That all the host of heaven in rankes doost lead,
And guydest lovers through the nights dread,
How chearefully thou lookest from above,

88 266 see the textual note 269 the sun moves out of Cancer into Leo in mid-June 282 *Planet* the sun 285 *gloome** grow dark 286 *star* Venus

And seemst to laugh atweene thy twinkling light
As joying in the sight
Of these glad many which for joy doe sing,
That all the woods them answer and their echo ring.

Now ceasse ye damsels your delights forepast,
Enough is it, that all the day was youres:
Now day is doen, and night is nighing fast:
Now bring the Bryde into the brydall boures.
Now night is come, now soone her disaray,
And in her bed her lay;
Lay her in lillies and in violets,
And silken courteins over her display,
And odourd sheetes, and Arras coverlets.
Behold how goodly my faire love does ly
In proud humility;
Like unto Maia, when as Jove her tooke,
In Tempe, lying on the flowry gras,
Twixt sleepe and wake, after she weary was,
With bathing in the Acidalian brooke.
Now it is night, ye damsels may be gon,
And leave my love alone,
And leave likewise your former lay to sing:
The woods no more shal answere, nor your echo ring.

Now welcome night, thou night so long expected,
That long daies labour doest at last defray,
And all my cares, which cruell love collected,
Hast sumd in one, and cancelled for aye:
Spread thy broad wing over my love and me,
That no man may us see,
And in thy sable mantle us enwrap,
From feare of perrill and foule horror free.
Let no false treason seeke us to entrap,
Nor any dread disquiet once annoy
The safety of our joy:

88 294 *many* crowd, company 296 *forepast* previously passed 299 *boures* bowers, chambers, bedrooms 303 *display* unfold, spread out 304 *odourd* scented *Arras* tapestry from the French town of Arras 313 *leave* cease, stop 316 *defray* pay for

But let the night be calme and quietsome,
Without tempestuous storms or sad afray:
Lyke as when Jove with fayre Alcmena lay,
When he begot the great Tirynthian groome:
Or lyke as when he with thy selfe did lie,
And begot Majesty.
And let the mayds and yongmen cease to sing:
Ne let the woods them answer, nor theyr eccho ring.

Let no lamenting cryes, nor dolefull teares,
Be heard all night within nor yet without:
Ne let false whispers breeding hidden feares,
Breake gentle sleepe with misconceived dout.
Let no deluding dreames, nor dreadful sights
Make sudden sad affrights;
Ne let housefyres, nor lightnings helpelesse harmes,
Ne let the Pouke, nor other evill sprights,
Ne let mischivous witches with theyr charmes,
Ne let hob Goblins, names whose sence we see not,
Fray us with things that be not.
Let not the shriech Oule, nor the Storke be heard:
Nor the night Raven that still deadly yels,
Nor damned ghosts cald up with mighty spels,
Nor griesly vultures make us once affeard:
Ne let th'unpleasant Quyre of Frogs still croking
Make us to wish theyr choking.
Let none of these theyr drery accents sing;
Ne let the woods them answer, nor theyr eccho ring.

But let stil Silence trew night watches keepe,
That sacred peace may in assurance rayne,
And tymely sleep, when it is tyme to sleepe,
May poure his limbs forth on your pleasant playne,
The whiles an hundred little winged loves,
Like divers fethered doves,

88 326 *quietsome** quiet 329 *Tirynthian groome* Hercules 330 *thy selfe* Night 331 *Majesty* the product of the union of Jove and Night seems to derive from Spenser's own imagination 341 *Pouke* Puck, Robin Goodfellow, a hobgoblin 344 *Fray* frighten 356 *poure* spread

Shall fly and flutter round about your bed,
And in the secret darke, that none reproves,
Their prety stealthes shal worke, and snares shal spread
To filch away sweet snatches of delight,
Conceald through covert night.
Ye sonnes of Venus, play your sports at will,
For greedy pleasure, carelesse of your toyes,
Thinks more upon her paradise of joyes,
Then what ye do, albe it good or ill.
All night therefore attend your merry play,
For it will soone be day:
Now none doth hinder you, that say or sing,
Ne will the woods now answer, nor your Eccho ring.

Who is the same, which at my window peepes?
Or whose is that faire face, that shines so bright,
Is it not Cinthia, she that never sleepes,
But walkes about high heaven al the night?
O fayrest goddesse, do thou not envy
My love with me to spy:
For thou likewise didst love, though now unthought,
And for a fleece of woll, which privily,
The Latmian shephard once unto thee brought,
His pleasures with thee wrought.
Therefore to us be favorable now;
And sith of wemens labours thou hast charge,
And generation goodly dost enlarge,
Encline thy will t'effect our wishfull vow,
And the chast wombe informe with timely seed,
That may our comfort breed:
Till which we cease our hopefull hap to sing,
Ne let the woods us answere, nor our Eccho ring.

88 361 *stealthes* thefts 364 *sonnes of Venus* Cupids 378 *unthought** not regarded, unremembered 380 *Latmian shephard* Endymion 384 *generation* begetting of children *enlarge* increase 385 *wishfull* longed-for, desired 388 *hopefull hap* wished-for event

And thou great Juno, which with awful might
The lawes of wedlock still dost patronize,
And the religion of the faith first plight
With sacred rites hast taught to solemnize:
And eeke for comfort often called art
Of women in their smart,
Eternally bind thou this lovely band,
And all thy blessings unto us impart.
And thou glad Genius, in whose gentle hand,
The bridale bowre and geniall bed remaine,
Without blemish or staine,
And the sweet pleasures of theyr loves delight
With secret ayde doest succour and supply,
Till they bring forth the fruitfull progeny,
Send us the timely fruit of this same night.
And thou fayre Hebe, and thou Hymen free,
Grant that it may so be.
Til which we cease your further prayse to sing,
Ne any woods shal answer, nor your Eccho ring.

And ye high heavens, the temple of the gods,
In which a thousand torches flaming bright
Doe burne, that to us wretched earthly clods
In dreadful darknesse lend desired light;
And all ye powers which in the same remayne,
More then we men can fayne,
Poure out your blessing on us plentiously,
And happy influence upon us raine,
That we may raise a large posterity,
Which from the earth, which they may long possesse,
With lasting happinesse,
Up to your haughty pallaces may mount,
And for the guerdon of theyr glorious merit
May heavenly tabernacles there inherit,

88 391 *patronize** act as a patron saint, tutelary deity 392 *plight* plighted, pledged 395 *smart* pain 398 *Genius* the god of generation 399 *geniall* nuptial, generative 411 *clods** bodies 414 *fayne* imagine 421 *guerdon* reward

Of blessed Saints for to increase the count.
So let us rest, sweet love, in hope of this,
And cease till then our tymely joyes to sing,
The woods no more us answer, nor our eccho ring.

Song made in lieu of many ornaments,
With which my love should duly have bene dect,
Which cutting off through hasty accidents,
Ye would not stay your dew time to expect,
But promist both to recompens,
Be unto her a goodly ornament,
And for short time an endlesse moniment.

Sir Walter Ralegh

89 [As you came from the holy land]

As you came from the holy land
of Walsinghame
Mett you not with my true love
by the way as you came
How shall I know your trew love
That have mett many one
As I went to the holy lande
That have come that have gone
She is neyther whyte nor browne
Butt as the heavens fayre
There is none hathe a form so divine
In the earth or the ayre

88 428 *duly* rightly, properly 429 *cutting off* preventing, cutting short *accidents* events; misfortunes 430 *Ye* the poem *stay* remain; delay 431 *both* his bride and the poem, or time

89 2 *Walsinghame* the important and popular shrine of the Holy House of Nazareth at Walsingham in Norfolk had been destroyed in 1538 (see no. 250) 5 cp. Ophelia's 'How should I your true-love know' in *Hamlet* IV.5.23

Such an one did I meet good Sir
Suche an Angelyke face
Who lyke a queene lyke a nymph did appere
by her gate by her grace:
She hath lefte me here all alone
All allone as unknowne
Who somtymes did me lead with her selfe
And me lovde as her owne:
Whats the cause that she leaves you alone
And a new waye doth take:
Who loved you once as her owne
And her joye did you make:
I have lovde her all my youth
butt now ould as you see
Love lykes not the fallyng frute
From the wythered tree:
Know that love is a careless chylld
And forgets promysse paste:
He is blynd, he is deaff when he lyste
And in faythe never faste:
His desyre is a dureless contente
And a trustless joye
He is wonn with a world of despayre
And is lost with a toye:
Of women kynde suche indeed is the love
Or the word Love abused
Under which many chyldysh desyres
And conceytes are excusde:
Butt trwe Love is a durable fyre
In the mynde ever burnynge:
Never sycke never ould never dead
from itt selfe never turnynge:

SAMUEL DANIEL

90 [*from* Delia]

SONNET. 13.

Behold what hap *Pigmalion* had to frame
  And carve his proper griefe upon a stone;
  My heavie fortune is much like the same,
  I worke on flint, and thats the cause I mone.
For haplesse loe even with mine owne desires,
  I figurde on the table of mine hart,
  The fairest forme, that all the world admires,
  And so did perish by my proper art.
And still I toyle, to change the Marble brest
  Of her, whose sweetest grace I do adore,
  Yet cannot finde her breathe unto my rest,
  Hard is her hart, and woe is me therefore.
But happie he that joy'd his stone and art,
Unhappie I, to love a stonie hart.

90 1 *hap* luck, fortune 8 *proper* own

91 [*from* Delia]

SONNET. 39.

When winter snowes upon thy sable haires,
And frost of age hath nipt thy beauties neere,
When darke shall seeme thy day that never cleares,
And all lies withred that was held so deere.
Then take this picture which I here present thee,
Limned with a Pensill not all unworthy:
Here see the gifts that God and nature lent thee.
Here read thy selfe, and what I suffred for thee.
This may remaine thy lasting monument,
Which happily posteritie may cherrish,
These colours with thy fading are not spent,
These may remain when thou and I shal perrish.
If they remaine, then thou shalt live thereby,
They will remaine, and so thou canst not die.

92 [*from* Delia]

SONNET. 52.

Let others sing of Knights and Palladines;
In aged accents, and untimely words:
Paint shadowes in imaginarie lines,
Which wel the reach of their high wits records;
But I must sing of thee, and those faire eies,
Autentique shall my verse in time to come,
When yet th'unborn shall say, Lo where she lies,
Whose beautie made him speak that else was dombe.

91 6 *Limned* painted *Pensill* brush 10 *happily* by chance, perhaps

92 1 *others* probably Spenser in the first three books of *The Faerie Queene*, 1590 *Palladines** paladins, heroic knights 2 *untimely* old-fashioned (?) 6 *Autentique** authenticate 8 *dombe* dumb

These are the Arkes, the Trophies I erect,
That fortifie thy name against old age:
And these thy sacred vertues must protect,
Against the darke and Tymes consuming rage.
Though th'error of my youth in them appeare,
Suffise, they shew I liv'd and lov'd thee deare.

Sir John Davies

93 [*from* Gullinge Sonnets]

6

The sacred Muse that firste made love devine
hath made him naked and without attyre
but I will cloth him with this penn of myne
that all the world his fashion shall admyre
his hatt of hope, his bande of beautye fine
his cloake of crafte, his doblett of desyre
greife for a girdell, shall aboute him twyne
his pointes of pride, his Iletholes of yre
his hose of hate, his Codpeece of conceite
his stockings of sterne strife, his shirte of shame
his garters of vaine glorie gaye and slyte
his pantofels of passions I will frame,
Pumpes of presumption shall adorne his feete
and Socks of sullennes excedinge sweete.

92 9 *Arkes* sacred chests

93 5 *bande* collar 8 *pointes* ties with metal ends joining doublet to hose *Iletholes* eyelet holes 11 *slyte* slashed 12 *pantofels* overshoes

94 [Faith (wench) I cannot court thy sprightly eyes]

Faith (wench) I cannot court thy sprightly eyes,
With the base Viall placed betweene my Thighes
I cannot lispe, nor to some Fiddle sing,
Nor run uppon a high strecht Minikin.

I cannot whine in puling Elegies,
Intombing Cupid with sad obsequies.
I am not fashioned for these amorous times,
To court thy beutie with lascivious rimes.

I cannot dally, caper, daunce and sing,
Oyling my saint with supple sonneting.
I cannot crosse my armes, or sigh ay me,
Ay me Forlorne: egregious Fopperie.

I cannot busse thy fist, play with thy hayre,
Swearing by Jove, Thou art most debonaire.
  Not I by Cock, but shall I tel thee roundly,
  Harke in thine eare, zounds I can ( ) thee soundly.

94 2 *base Viall* bass vial; bass vile; bass viol 4 *Minikin* treble string of a viol; girl, sweetheart 10 *Oyling*** flattering 11 *crosse my armes* a pose of the melancholy lover 13 *busse* kiss 15 *by Cock* variant oath of 'by God' (see textual note) *roundly* readily, without hesitation 16 ( ) the omitted word is presumably 'fuck'

THOMAS NASHE

95 The choise of valentines

To the right Honorable the lord S.

Pardon sweete flower of matchless Poetrie,
And fairest bud the red rose ever bare;
Although my Muse devor'st from deeper care
Presents thee with a wanton Elegie.
Ne blame my verse of loose unchastitie
For painting forth the things that hidden are,
Since all men acte what I in speache declare,
Onelie induced by varietie.
Complaints and praises everie one can write,
And passion-out their pangu's in statelie rimes,
But of loves pleasure's none did ever write
That hath succeeded in theis latter times.
Accept of it Deare Lord in gentle gree,
And better lynes ere long shall honor thee.

The choosing of valentines.

It was the merie moneth of Februarie
When yong-men in their jollie roguerie
Rose earelie in the morne fore breake of daie
To seeke them valentines so trimme and gaie.
With whom they maie consorte in summer sheene,
And dance the heidegeies on our toune-greene.
At Ale's at Easter or at Pentecost
Perambulate the fields that flourish most,
And goe to som village abbordring neere
To taste the creame, and cakes and such good cheere,

95 Title *valentines* sweethearts Sonnet title *the lord S.* Ferdinàndo Stanley, Lord Strange 10 *pangu's* pangs 13 *gree* favour, goodwill 4 *trimme* smartly dressed 6 *heidegeies* hay-de-guys, hays, dances 7 *Ale's* ale-drinking festivals

Or see a playe of strange moralitie
Shewen by Bachelrie of Maningtree;
Whereto the Contrie franklins flock-meale swarme,
And Jhon and Jone com marching arme in arme,
Even on the hallowes of that blessed Saint,
That doeth true lovers with those joyes acquaint,
I went poore pilgrim to my ladies shrine
To see if she would be my valentine.
But woe-alass, she was not to be found,
For she was shifted to an upper-ground.
Good Justice Dudgein-haft, and crab-tree face
With bills and staves had scar'd hir from the place;
And now she was compell'd for Sanctuarie
To flye unto an house of venerie.
Thither went I, and bouldlie made enquire
If they had hackneis to lett-out to hire,
And what they crav'd by order of their trade
To lett one ride a journie on a jade.
Therwith out stept a foggie three-chinnd dame,
That us'd to take yong wenches for to tame,
And ask't me, if I ment as I profest,
Or onelie ask't a question but in jest.
In jest? quoth I; that terme it as you will,
I com for game, therfore give me my Jill,
Why Sir, quoth shee, if that be your demande,
Com, laye me a Gods-pennie in my hand;
For, in our Oratorie siccarlie,
None enters heere to doe his nicerie.
But he must paye his offertorie first,
And then perhaps wee'le ease him of his thirst.
I hearing hir so ernest for the box
Gave hir hir due, and shee the dore unlocks.

95 11–12 the famous old plays performed by unmarried men at Manningtree in Essex 13 *franklins* freeholders *flock-meale* in companies 15 *hallowes* saints' days 20 *upper-ground* the name of a street in Southwark near the brothels of London 21 *Dudgein-haft* the hilt of a dagger made of dudgeon wood 24 *venerie* sexual pleasure 26 *hackneis* horses; prostitutes 28 *jade* horse of low quality; whore 29 *foggie* bloated, gross 36 *a Gods-pennie* an earnest, deposit 37 *siccarlie* sickerly, undoubtedly, certainly 38 *nicerie*** lust, depravity

In am I entered: venus be my speede;
  But where's this female, that must doe this deede?
By blinde meanders, and by crankled wayes
  Shee leades me onward (as my Aucthor saies)
Untill we came within a shadie loft
  Where venus bounzing vestalls skirmish oft.
And there shee sett me in a leather chaire,
  And brought me forth of prettie Trulls a paire,
To chuse of them which might content myne eye;
  But hir I sought I could nowhere espie.
I spake them faire, and wisht them well to fare,
  Yett so it is, I must have fresher ware.
Wherfore, dame Bawde, as daintie as yow bee,
  Fetch gentle mistris Francis forth to me.
By Halliedame, quoth she, and Gods oune mother,
  I well perceave yow are a wylie brother.
For, if there be a morsell of more price,
  Yow'l smell it out, though I be ner'e so nice.
As yow desire, so shall yow swive with hir,
  But think your purse-strings shall abye-it deare;
For, he that will eate quaile's must lavish croune's;
  And mistris Francis in hir velvet goune's,
And ruffs, and periwigs as fresh as Maye
  Can not be kept with half a croune a daye.
Of price good hostess, we will not debate,
  Though yow assize me at the highest rate;
Onelie conduct me to this bonnie bell,
  And tenne good gobbs I will unto thee tell
Of golde or silver, which shall lyke thee best,
  So much doe I hir companie request.
Awaie she went: So sweete a thing is golde,
  That (mauger) will invade the strongest holde.
Hey-ho, she coms, that hath my heart in keepe,
  Sing lullabie my cares, and falle a-sleepe.

95 43 *speede* helper, patroness 45 *meanders*** labyrinthine paths *crankled*** twisting 48 *bounzing* big, strapping 50 *Trulls* prostitutes 57 *Halliedame* halidom, something holy 61 *swive* fuck 62 *abye-it* pay for it 68 *assize* value, assess 70 *gobbs* large sums of money 74 *mauger* notwithstanding

Sweeping she coms, as she would brush the ground,
   Hir ratling silke's my sences doe confound.
Oh, I am ravish't; voide the chamber streight;
   For, I must neede's upon hir with my weight.
My Tomalin, quoth shee, and then she smilde,
   I, I, quoth I; so more men are beguilde
With smiles, with flatt'ring worde's, and fained cheere,
   When in their deede's their falsehood doeth appeere.
As how my lambkin? (blushing, she replide)
   Because I in this dancing-schoole abide?
If that be it, that breede's this discontent,
   We will remove the camp incontinent.
For shelter onelie, sweete heart came I hither,
   And to avoide the troblous stormie weather.
But now the coaste is cleare, we wilbe gonne,
   Since but thy self, true lover I have none.
With that she sprung full lightlie to my lips,
   And fast about the neck me colle's and clips.
She wanton faint's, and falle's upon hir bed,
   And often tosseth too and fro hir head.
She shutts hir eyes, and waggles with hir tongue:
   Oh, who is able to abstaine so long?
I com, I com; sweete lyning be thy leave,
   Softlie my fingers, up theis curtaine, heave
And make me happie stealing by degreese.
   First bare hir leggs, then creepe up to hir kneese.
From thence ascend unto hir mannely thigh.
   (A pox on lingring when I am so nighe)
Smock climbe a-pace, that I maie see my joyes.
   Oh heaven, and paradize are all but toyes,
Compar'd with this sight, I now behould,
   Which well might keepe a man from being olde.
A prettie rysing wombe without a weame,
   That shone as bright as anie silver streame;
And bare out lyke the bending of an hill,
   At whose decline a fountaine dwelleth still,

95 81 *Tomalin* little Thomas 88 *incontinent* immediately 94 *colle's and clips* embraces and kisses 97 *waggles*** 99 *lyning be* linen by 106 *toyes* knick-knacks, worthless things, trash 109 *weame* bodily blemish, scar 111 *bare out* stuck out

That hath his mouth besett with uglie bryers
  Resembling much a duskie nett of wyres.
A loftie buttock barred with azure veine's,
  Whose comelie swelling, when my hand distreine's,
Or wanton checketh with a harmeless stype,
  It makes the fruites of love eftsoone be rype;
And pleasure pluckt too tymelie from the stemme
  To dye ere it hath seene Jerusalem.
Oh Gods, that ever anie thing so sweete
  So suddenlie should fade awaie and fleete.
Hir arme's are spread, and I am all unarm'd
  Lyke one with Ovids cursed hemlock charm'd,
So are my limm's unwealdie for the fight,
  That spend their strength in thought of hir delight.
What shall I doe to shewe my self a man?
  It will not be for ought that beawtie can.
I kisse, I clap, I feele, I view at will,
  Yett dead he lyes not thinking good or ill.
Unhappie me, quoth shee, and wilt' not stand?
  Com, lett me rubb and chafe it with my hand.
Perhaps the sillie worme is labour'd sore,
  And wearied that it can doe no more.
If it be so (as I am greate a-dread)
  I wish tenne thousand times, that I were dead.
How ere it is; no meanes shall want in me,
  That maie availe to his recoverie.
Which saide, she tooke and rould it on hir thigh,
  And when she lookt' on't, she would weepe and sighe,
And dandled it, and dance't it up and doune,
  Not ceasing, till she rais'd it from his swoune.
And then he flue on hir as he were wood,
  And on hir breeche did thack, and foyne a-good;
He rubd', and prickt, and pierst hir to the bones,
  Digging as farre as eath he might for stones.

95 115 *loftie* proud 116 *distreine's* clasps 117 *stype* steep, slope (?) 124 *Ovids Amores* 3.7.13: 'My member hung slack, as though frozen by hemlock' 130 *he* the narrator's penis 143 *wood* mad, crazy 144 *thack* slap, clap, strike *foyne* thrust, prick 146 *eath* easily

Now high, now lowe, now stryking short and thick;
  Now dyving deepe he toucht hir to the quick.
Now with a gird, he would his course rebate;
  Streite would he take him to a statelie gate,
Plaie while him list; and thrust he neare so hard,
  Poore pacient Grisill lyeth at hir warde,
And give's, and take's as blythe and free as Maye,
  And ere-more meete's him in the midle waye.
On him hir eyes continualy were fixt,
  With hir eye-beames his melting looke's were mixt,
Which lyke the Sunne, that twixt tuo glasses plaies
  From one to th' other cast's rebounding rayes.
He lyke a starre, that to reguild his beames
  Sucks-in the influence of Phebus streames,
Imbathe's the lynes of his descending light
  In the bright fountaines of hir clearest sight.
She faire as fairest Planet in the Skye
  Hir puritie to no man doeth denye.
The verie chamber, that enclowds hir shine,
  Looke's lyke the pallace of that God devine,
Who leade's the daie about the zodiake,
  And everie even discends to th' Oceane lake:
So fierce and fervent is hir radiance,
  Such fyrie stake's she darts at everie glance,
As might enflame the icie limmes of age,
  And make pale death his surquedrie aswage
To stand and gaze upon hir Orient lamps
  Where Cupid all his chiefest joyes encamps,
And sitts, and playes with everie atomie
  That in hir Sunne-beames swarme aboundantlie.
Thus gazing, and thus striving we persever,
  But what so firme, that maie continue ever?
Oh not so fast, my ravisht Mistriss cryes,
  Leaste my content, that on thy life relyes

95 149 *with a gird* suddenly 152 *pacient Grisill* the heroine of Chaucer's 'Clerk's Tale': the representative of (female) enduring fortitude *warde* gatehouse, guarded entrance 161 *Imbathe's* immerses, dips 166 *God* Apollo 172 *surquedrie* presumption, pride

Be brought too-soone from his delightfull seate,
  And me unwares of hoped bliss defeate.
Togeather lett our equall motions stirr
  Togeather let us live and dye my deere
Together lett us marche unto content,
  And be consumed with one blandishment.
As she prescrib'd, so kept we crotchet-time,
  And everie stroake in ordre lyke a chyme.
Whilst she, that had preserv'd me by hir pittie,
  Unto our musike fram'd a groaning dittie.
Alass, alass, that love should be a sinne,
  Even now my blisse and sorrow doeth beginne.
Hould wyde thy lap, my lovelie Danae,
  And entretaine the golden shoure so free,
That trilling falles into thy treasurie,
  As Aprill-drops not half so pleasant be,
Nor Nilus overflowe, to Ægipt-plaines,
  As this sweete-streames, that all hir joints imbaynes;
With Oh, and Oh, she itching moves hir hipps,
  And to and fro, full lightlie starts and skips.
She jerks hir leggs, and sprauleth with hir heeles,
  No tongue maie tell the solace that she feeles.
I faint, I yeald; Oh death rock me a-sleepe;
  Sleepe – sleepe desire, entombed in the deepe.
Not so my deare; my dearest Saint replyde;
  For, from us yett thy spirit maie not glide
Untill the sinnowie channels of our blood
  Withould their source from this imprisoned flood;
And then will we (that then will com to soone)
  Dissolved lye as-though our dayes were donne.
The whilst I speake, my soule is fleeting hence,
  And life forsakes his fleshie residence.
Staie, staie sweete joye, and leave me not forlorne,
  Why shouldst thow fade, that art but newelie borne?
Staie but an houre; an houre is not so much,
  But half an houre; if that thy haste be such:

95 184 *dye* come to orgasm 186 *blandishment* pleasing experience 195 *trilling* rolling, flowing 197 *Nilus* the Nile 198 *imbaynes* embathes, drenches, suffuses

Naie but a quarter; I will aske no more,
That thy departure (which torments me sore)
Maie be alightned with a little pause,
And take awaie this passions sudden cause.
He heare's me not, hard-hearted as he is:
He is the sonne of Time, and hate's my blisse.
Time ner'e looke's back, the rivers ner'e returne;
A second spring must help me or I burne.
No, no, the well is drye that should refresh me,
The glasse is runne of all my destinie.
Nature of winter learneth nigardize,
Who, as he over-beare's the streame with ice,
That man nor beaste maie of their pleasance taste,
So shutts she up hir conduit all in haste,
And will not let hir Nectar over-flowe,
Least mortall men immortall joyes should knowe.
Adiew unconstant love, to thy disporte,
Adiew false mirth, and melodie too-short.
Adiew faint-hearted instrument of lust,
That falselie hast betrayde our equale trust.
Hence-forth no more will I implore thine ayde,
Or thee, or men of cowardize upbrayde.
My little dilldo shall suplye their kinde:
A knave, that moves as light as leaves by winde;
That bendeth not, nor fouldeth anie deale,
But stands as stiff, as he were made of steele,
And playes at peacock twixt my leggs right blythe,
And doeth my tickling swage with manie a sighe;
For, by Saint Runnion he'le refresh me well,
And never make my tender bellie swell.
Poore Priapus, whose triumph now must falle,
Except thow thrust this weakeling to the walle.
Behould how he usurps in bed and bowre,
And undermine's thy kingdom everie howre.
How slye he creepe's betwixt the barke and tree,
And sucks the sap, whilst sleepe detaineth thee.

95 219 *alightned* lightened, relieved 227 *nigardize* parsimony, meanness 228 *over-beare's* thrusts, drives, down 239 *dilldo*** artificial penis 243 *playes at peacock* behaves very proudly *blythe* joyfully 245 *Runnion* a mangy or fat woman

He is my Mistris page at everie stound,
And soone will tent a deepe intrenched wound.
He wayte's on Courtlie Nimphs, that be so coye,
And bids them skorne the blynd-alluring boye.
He give's yong guirls their gamesom sustenance,
And everie gaping mouth his full sufficeance.
He fortifies disdaine with forraine artes,
And wanton-chaste deludes all loving hearts.
If anie wight a cruell mistris serve's,
Or in dispaire (unhappie) pine's and sterv's
Curse Eunuke dilldo, senceless, counterfet,
Who sooth maie fill, but never can begett:
But if revenge enraged with dispaire,
That such a dwarf his wellfare should empaire,
Would faine this womans secretarie knowe,
Lett him attend the marks' that I shall showe.
He is a youth almost tuo handfulls highe,
Streight, round, and plumb, yett having but one eye,
Wherin the rhewme so ferventlie doeth raigne,
That Stigian gulph maie scarce his teares containe;
Attired in white velvet or in silk,
And nourisht with whott water or with milk;
Arm'd otherwhile in thick congealed glasse,
When he more glib to hell be lowe would passe,
Upon a charriot of five wheeles he rydes,
The which an arme strong driver stedfast guide's,
And often alters pace, as wayes growe deepe;
(For, who in pathe's unknowen, one gate can keepe?)
Sometimes he smoothlie slideth downe the hill;
Another while the stones his feete doe kill:
In clammie waies he treaddeth by and by,
And plasheth and sprayeth all that be him nye.
So fares this jollie rider in his race,
Plunging, and soursing forward in lyke case,

95 253 *stound* moment; pleasurable thrill 254 *tent* apply a linen bandage to 256 *boye* Cupid 262 *sterv's* starves, dies 267 *secretarie* one entrusted with secrets 270 *plumb* vertical, erect 276 *glib* smoothly, easily 286 *soursing* rising, surging

Bedasht, bespurted, and beplodded foule,
God give thee shame, thow blinde mischapen owle.
Fy—fy for grief; a ladies chamberlaine,
And canst not thow thy tatling tongue refraine?
I reade thee beardles blab, beware of stripes,
And be advised what thow vainelie pipes.
Thow wilt be whipt with nettles for this geare
If Cicelie shewe but of thy knaverie heere.
Saint Denis shield me from such female sprites.
Regarde not Dames, what Cupids Poete writes.
I pennd this storie onelie for my self,
Who giving suck unto a childish Elfe,
And quitte discourag'd in my nurserie,
Since all my store seemes to hir, penurie.
I am not as was Hercules the stout,
That to the seaventh journie could hould out.
I want those hearbe's and rootes of Indian soile,
That strengthen wearie members in their toile;
Druggs and Electuaries of new devise
Doe shunne my purse; that trembles at the price.
Sufficeth, all I have, I yeald hir hole,
Which for a poore man is a princelie dole.
I paie our hostess scott and lott at moste,
And looke as leane and lank as anie ghoste.
What can be added more to my renowne?
She lyeth breathlesse, I am taken doune,
The waves doe swell, the tydes climbe or'e the banks,
Judge gentlemen if I deserve not thanks,
And so good night unto yow eve'rie one,
For loe, our threed is spunne, our plaie is donne.

Claudito iam rivos Priape, sat prata biberunt.

95 287 *bespurted* befouled 291 *reade* advise, warn *blab* blabber 293 *geare* business, affair 294 *Cicelie* not identified 295 *Saint Denis* patron saint of France 305 *Electuaries* medical pastes 309 *scott and lott* local taxes; thoroughly, in full 317 'Priapus, drop the sluice-gates now: the meadows have had enough to drink'; cp. Virgil, *Eclogues* 3.111, which reads 'pueri' ('boys') instead of 'Priape'

Thus hath my penne presum'd to please my friend;
Oh mightst thow lykewise please Apollo's eye.
No: Honor brooke's no such impietie;
Yett Ovids wanton Muse did not offend.
He is the fountaine whence my streames doe flowe.
Forgive me if I speake as I was taught,
A lyke to women, utter all I knowe,
As longing to unlade so bad a fraught.
My mynde once purg'd of such lascivious witt,
With purifide word's, and hallowed verse
Thy praises in large volumes shall rehearce,
That better maie thy graver view befitt.
Meanewhile yett rests, yow smile at what I write,
Or for attempting, banish me your sight.

JOHN DONNE

96 To his Mistress going to bed

Come, Madam, come, all rest my powers defie,
Until I labour, I in labour lie.
The foe oft-times having the foe in sight,
Is tir'd with standing though he never fight.
Off with that girdle, like heavens Zone glittering,
But a far fairer world incompassing.
Unpin that spangled breastplate which you wear,
That th' eyes of busie fooles may be stopt there.
Unlace your self, for that harmonious chyme,
Tells me from you, that now it is bed time.
Off with that happy busk, which I envie,
That still can be, and still can stand so nigh.
Your gown going off, such beautious state reveals,
As when from flowry meads th' hills shadow steales.

95 Sonnet 8 *fraught* burden, load

96 2 *in labour* in the painful exertion of childbirth 5 *Zone* the girdle of Orion 9 *chyme* chiming watch 11 *busk* corset

Off with that wyerie Coronet and shew
The haiery Diadem which on you doth grow:
Now off with those shooes, and then safely tread
In this loves hallow'd temple, this soft bed.
In such white robes, heaven's Angels us'd to be
Receavd by men; thou Angel bringst with thee
A heaven like Mahomets Paradice, and though
Ill spirits walk in white; we easly know,
By this these Angels from an evil sprite,
Those set our hairs, but these our flesh upright.
  Licence my roaving hands, and let them go,
Before, behind, between, above, below,
O my America! my new-found-land,
My kingdome, safeliest when with one man man'd.
My Myne of precious stones: My Emperie,
How blest am I in this discovering thee?
To enter in these bonds, is to be free;
Then where my hand is set, my seal shall be.
  Full nakedness! All joyes are due to thee,
As souls unbodied, bodies uncloth'd must be,
To taste whole joyes. Jems which you women use
Are like Atlanta's balls: cast in mens views,
That when a fools eye lighteth on a Jem,
His earthly soul may covet theirs, not them:
Like pictures or like books gay coverings made,
For lay-men are all women thus arrayed.
Themselves are mystick books, which only wee
(Whom their imputed grace will dignifie)
Must see revealed. Then since that I may know;
As liberally, as to a Midwife shew
Thy self: cast all, yea, this white lynnen hence
Here is no pennance much lesse innocence.
  To teach thee I am naked first, why than
What needst thou have more covering then a man.

96 29 *Emperie* emperor's land 34 *unbodied* removed from the body 42 *imputed* attributed, ascribed (cf. no. 256 l. 13) 45–6 Church courts made sexual transgressors wear white in penitence

Barnabe Barnes

97 [*from* Parthenophil and Parthenophe]

SONNET 27.

Why do I draw this coole releeving ayer
  And breathe it out in scaulding sighes as fast?
  Since all my hopes dye buried in dispayer
  In which hard soyle mine endlesse knottes be cast:
Where when I come to walke be soundry mazes
  With bewties skilfull finger lyned out,
  And knottes whose borders set with double dazes,
  Doubles my dazed muse with endlesse doubt
How to finde easie passage through the time
  With which my mazes are so long beset,
  That I can never passe but fall and clyme
  According to my passions which forget
The place where they with loves guide should have met:
  But when faint-wearied all me thinkes is past
The maze returning makes me turne as fast.

Christopher Marlowe

98 The passionate Sheepheard to his love

Come live with mee, and be my love,
And we will all the pleasures prove,
That Vallies, groves, hills and fieldes,
Woods, or steepie mountaine yeeldes.

97 4 *knottes* main point of difficulty; flower-bed laid out in a fanciful design or pattern 7 *dazes* daisies 10 *mazes* puzzles, bewilderment

And wee will sit upon the Rocks,
Seeing the Sheepheards feede theyr flocks,
By shallow Rivers, to whose falls,
Melodious byrds sing Madrigalls.

And I will make thee beds of Roses,
And a thousand fragrant poesies,
A cap of flowers, and a kirtle,
Imbroydred all with leaves of Mirtle.

A gowne made of the finest wooll,
Which from our pretty Lambes we pull,
Fayre lined slippers for the cold:
With buckles of the purest gold.

A belt of straw, and Ivie buds,
With Corall clasps and Amber studs,
And if these pleasures may thee move,
Come live with mee, and be my love.

The Sheepheards Swaines shall daunce and sing,
For thy delight each May-morning,
If these delights thy minde may move;
Then live with mee, and be my love.

99 Hero and Leander

On *Hellespont* guiltie of True-loves blood,
In view and opposit two citties stood,
Seaborderers, disjoin'd by *Neptunes* might:
The one *Abydos*, the other *Sestos* hight.
At *Sestos*, *Hero* dwelt; *Hero* the faire,
Whom young *Apollo* courted for her haire,
And offred as a dower his burning throne,
Where she should sit for men to gaze upon.
The outside of her garments were of lawne,
The lining, purple silke, with guilt starres drawne,

98 11 *kirtle* skirt, smock

99 3 *Seaborderers** by the sea 4 *hight* named, called 9 *lawne* fine linen

Her wide sleeves greene, and bordered with a grove,
Where *Venus* in her naked glory strove,
To please the carelesse and disdainfull eies,
Of proud *Adonis* that before her lies.
Her kirtle blew, whereon was many a staine,
Made with the blood of wretched Lovers slaine.
Upon her head she ware a myrtle wreath,
From whence her vaile reacht to the ground beneath.
Her vaile was artificiall flowers and leaves,
Whose workmanship both man and beast deceaves.
Many would praise the sweet smell as she past,
When t'was the odour which her breath foorth cast.
And there for honie, bees have sought in vaine,
And beat from thence, have lighted there againe.
About her necke hung chaines of peble stone,
Which lightned by her necke, like Diamonds shone.
She ware no gloves, for neither sunne nor wind
Would burne or parch her hands, but to her mind,
Or warme or coole them, for they tooke delite
To play upon those hands, they were so white.
Buskins of shels all silvered, used she,
And brancht with blushing corall to the knee;
Where sparrowes pearcht, of hollow pearle and gold,
Such as the world would woonder to behold:
Those with sweet water oft her handmaid fils,
Which as shee went would cherupe through the bils.
Some say, for her the fairest *Cupid* pyn'd,
And looking in her face, was strooken blind.
But this is true, so like was one the other,
As he imagyn'd *Hero* was his mother.
And oftentimes into her bosome flew,
About her naked necke his bare armes threw.
And laid his childish head upon her brest,
And with still panting rockt, there tooke his rest.
So lovely faire was *Hero*, *Venus* Nun,

99 11 *bordered* embroidered 15 *kirtle* gown, skirt 17 *myrtle* sacred to Venus 31 *Buskins* short boots 32 *brancht*** embroidered with patterns of flowers or foliage 35 *sweet* fresh 36 *cherupe*** chirrup 40 *mother* Venus 44 *still* constant, continual

As nature wept, thinking she was undone;
Because she tooke more from her than she left,
And of such wondrous beautie her bereft:
Therefore in signe her treasure suffred wracke,
Since *Heroes* time, hath halfe the world beene blacke.
Amorous *Leander*, beautifull and yoong,
(Whose tragedie divine *Musæus* soong)
Dwelt at *Abidus*, since him, dwelt there none,
For whom succeeding times make greater mone.
His dangling tresses that were never shorne,
Had they beene cut, and unto *Colchos* borne,
Would have allur'd the ventr'ous youth of *Greece*,
To hazard more, than for the golden Fleece.
Faire *Cinthia* wisht, his armes might be her spheare,
Greefe makes her pale, because she mooves not there.
His bodie was as straight as *Circes* wand,
Jove might have sipt out *Nectar* from his hand.
Even as delicious meat is to the tast,
So was his necke in touching, and surpast
The white of *Pelops* shoulder, I could tell ye,
How smooth his brest was, and how white his bellie,
And whose immortall fingars did imprint,
That heavenly path, with many a curious dint,
That runs along his backe, but my rude pen,
Can hardly blazon foorth the loves of men,
Much lesse of powerfull gods, let it suffise,
That my slacke muse, sings of *Leanders* eies,
Those orient cheekes and lippes, exceeding his
That leapt into the water for a kis
Of his owne shadow, and despising many,
Died ere he could enjoy the love of any.
Had wilde *Hippolitus*, *Leander* seene,
Enamoured of his beautie had he beene,
His presence made the rudest paisant melt,

99 52 *divine* divinely inspired; absolutely excellent 57 *vent'rous* adventurous 59 *her spheare* in her orbit; Leander is compared to Endymion 62 Leander is compared to Ganymede 68 *curious* elaborate, skilfully made *dint* indentation 70 *blazon foorth* describe fitly 72 *slacke* idle, remiss; weak, slow 73 *orient* shining, glowing, radiant *his* Narcissus'

That in the vast uplandish countrie dwelt,
The barbarous *Thratian* soldier moov'd with nought,
Was moov'd with him, and for his favour sought.
Some swore he was a maid in mans attire,
For in his lookes were all that men desire,
A pleasant smiling cheeke, a speaking eye,
A brow for love to banquet roiallye,
And such as knew he was a man would say,
Leander, thou art made for amorous play:
Why art thou not in love, and lov'd of all?
Though thou be faire, yet be not thine owne thrall.
The men of wealthie *Sestos*, everie yeare,
(For his sake whom their goddesse held so deare,
Rose-cheekt *Adonis*) kept a solemne feast,
Thither resorted many a wandring guest,
To meet their loves; such as had none at all,
Came lovers home, from this great festivall.
For everie street like to a Firmament
Glistered with breathing stars, who where they went,
Frighted the melancholie earth, which deem'd,
Eternall heaven to burne, for so it seem'd,
As if another *Phaeton* had got
The guidance of the sunnes rich chariot.
But far above, the loveliest *Hero* shin'd,
And stole away th'inchaunted gazers mind,
For like Sea-nimphs inveigling harmony,
So was her beautie to the standers by.
Nor that night-wandring pale and watrie starre,
(When yawning dragons draw her thirling carre,
From *Latmus* mount up to the glomie skie,
Where crown'd with blazing light and majestie,
She proudly sits) more over-rules the flood,
Than she the hearts of those that neere her stood.
Even as, when gawdie Nymphs pursue the chace,
Wretched *Ixions* shaggie footed race,

99 80 *uplandish* inland, remote 85 *speaking* very expressive 90 *thrall* slave 99 *melancholie* according to the theory of the humours, the earth was melancholy, that is cold and dry 107 *starre* the moon 108 *thirling* darting, whirling 111 *over-rules* rules over 114 *shaggie footed** hairy-footed

Incenst with savage heat, gallop amaine,
From steepe Pine-bearing mountains to the plaine:
So ran the people foorth to gaze upon her,
And all that view'd her, were enamour'd on her.
And as in furie of a dreadfull fight,
Their fellowes being slaine or put to flight,
Poore soldiers stand with fear of death dead strooken,
So at her presence all surpris'd and tooken,
Await the sentence of her scornefull eies:
He whom she favours lives, the other dies.
There might you see one sigh, another rage,
And some (their violent passions to asswage)
Compile sharpe satyrs, but alas too late,
For faithfull love will never turne to hate.
And many seeing great princes were denied,
Pyn'd as they went, and thinking on her died.
On this feast day, O cursed day and hower,
Went *Hero* thorow *Sestos*, from her tower
To *Venus* temple, were unhappilye,
As after chaunc'd, they did each other spye.
So faire a church as this, had *Venus* none,
The wals were of discoloured *Jasper* stone,
Wherein was *Proteus* carved, and o'rehead,
A livelie vine of greene sea agget spread;
Where by one hand, light headed *Bacchus* hoong,
And with the other, wine from grapes out wroong.
Of Christall shining faire, the pavement was,
The towne of *Sestos*, cal'd it *Venus* glasse,
There might you see the gods in sundrie shapes,
Committing headdie ryots, incest, rapes:
For know, that underneath this radiant floure,
Was *Danaes* statue in a brazen tower,
Jove, slylie stealing from his sisters bed,
To dallie with *Idalian Ganimed:*

99 115 *Incenst* inflamed, enraged *amaine* with all speed 116 *Pine-bearing*** 121 *dead strooken** struck dead 127 *satyrs* satires 133 *were* where 136 *discoloured* multicoloured 138 *livelie* lifelike *greene sea agget** agate with green, wavelike markings (?); agate of sea-green colour (?) 144 *headdie* violent, passionate 145 *underneath* below, on the surface of *floure* floor

And for his love *Europa*, bellowing loud,
And tumbling with the Rainbow in a cloud,
Blood-quaffing *Mars*, heaving the yron net,
Which limping *Vulcan* and his *Cyclops* set:
Love kindling fire, to burne such townes as *Troy*,
Sylvanus weeping for the lovely boy
That now is turn'd into a *Cypres* tree,
Under whose shade the Wood-gods love to bee.
And in the midst a silver altar stood,
There *Hero* sacrificing turtles blood,
Vaild to the ground, vailing her eie-lids close,
And modestly they opened as she rose:
Thence flew Loves arrow with the golden head,
And thus *Leander* was enamoured.
Stone still he stood, and evermore he gazed,
Till with the fire that from his count'nance blazed,
Relenting *Heroes* gentle heart was strooke,
Such force and vertue hath an amorous looke.
  It lies not in our power to love, or hate,
For will in us is over-rul'd by fate.
When two are stript long ere the course begin,
We wish that one should loose, the other win.
And one especiallie doe we affect,
Of two gold Ingots like in each respect,
The reason no man knowes, let it suffise,
What we behold is censur'd by our eies.
Where both deliberat, the love is slight,
Who ever lov'd, that lov'd not at first sight?
  He kneel'd, but unto her devoutly praid;
Chast *Hero* to her selfe thus softly said:
Were I the saint hee worships, I would heare him,
And as shee spake those words, came somewhat nere
    him.
He started up, she blusht as one asham'd;
Wherewith *Leander* much more was inflam'd.

99 158 *turtles* turtle-doves' 159 *Vaild** bowing down to the ground 166 *vertue* power 169 *course* race 171 *affect* prefer 174 *censur'd* judged, criticized 176 cp. Shakespeare, *As You Like It* III.5.81–2 'Dead shepherd, now I find thy saw of might:/Who ever lov'd that lov'd not at first sight?'

He toucht her hand, in touching it she trembled,
Love deepely grounded, hardly is dissembled.
These lovers parled by the touch of hands,
True love is mute, and oft amazed stands.
Thus while dum signs their yeelding harts entangled,
The aire with sparkes of living fire was spangled,
And night deepe drencht in mystie *Acheron*,
Heav'd up her head, and halfe the world upon, A periphrasis of night.
Breath'd darkenesse forth (darke night is *Cupids* day.)
And now begins *Leander* to display
Loves holy fire, with words, with sighs and teares,
Which like sweet musicke entred *Heroes* eares,
And yet at everie word shee turn'd aside,
And alwaies cut him off as he replide,
At last, like to a bold sharpe Sophister,
With chearefull hope thus he accosted her.
Faire creature, let me speake without offence,
I would my rude words had the influence,
To lead thy thoughts, as thy faire lookes doe mine,
Then shouldst thou bee his prisoner who is thine.
Be not unkind and faire, mishapen stuffe
Are of behaviour boisterous and ruffe.
O shun me not, but heare me ere you goe,
God knowes I cannot force love, as you doe.
My words shall be as spotlesse as my youth,
Full of simplicitie and naked truth.
This sacrifice (whose sweet perfume descending,
From *Venus* altar to your footsteps bending)
Doth testifie that you exceed her farre,
To whom you offer, and whose Nunne you are,
Why should you worship her, her you surpasse,
As much as sparkling Diamonds flaring glasse.
A Diamond set in lead his worth retaines,
A heavenly Nimph, belov'd of humane swaines,

99 184 *hardly* with difficulty 185 *parled* spoke 197 *Sophister* at Cambridge an undergraduate in his second or third year; a specious reasoner 203 *mishapen stuffe* ugly-looking people 210 *bending* turning 214 *flaring*** showy, gaudy

Receives no blemish, but oft-times more grace,
Which makes me hope, although I am but base,
Base in respect of thee, divine and pure,
Dutifull service may thy love procure,
And I in dutie will excell all other,
As thou in beautie doest exceed loves mother.
Nor heaven, nor thou, were made to gaze upon,
As heaven preserves all things, so save thou one.
A stately builded ship, well rig'd and tall,
The Ocean maketh more majesticall:
Why vowest thou then to live in *Sestos* here,
Who on Loves seas more glorious wouldst appeare?
Like untun'd golden strings all women are,
Which long time lie untoucht, will harshly jarre.
Vessels of Brasse oft handled, brightly shine,
What difference betwixt the richest mine
And basest mold, but use? for both not us'de,
Are of like worth. Then treasure is abus'de,
When misers keepe it; being put to lone,
In time it will returne us two for one.
Rich robes, themselves and others do adorne,
Neither themselves nor others, if not worne.
Who builds a pallace and rams up the gate,
Shall see it ruinous and desolate.
Ah simple *Hero*, learne thy selfe to cherish,
Lone women like to emptie houses perish.
Lesse sinnes the poore rich man that starves himselfe,
In heaping up a masse of drossie pelfe,
Than such as you: his golden earth remains,
Which after his disceasse, some other gains.
But this faire jem, sweet in the losse alone,
When you fleet hence, can be bequeath'd to none.
Or if it could, downe from th'enameld skie,
All heaven would come to claime this legacie,

99 222 *loves mother* Venus 231–40 cp. Marlowe's translation of Ovid's *Elegies* 1.8.51–2 'Brasse shines with use; good garments would be worne,/Houses not dwelt in, are with filth forlorne' 233 *mold* earth 244 *drossie pelfe* worthless wealth 248 *fleet* slip away, fly; die

And with intestine broiles the world destroy,
And quite confound natures sweet harmony.
Well therefore by the gods decreed it is,
We humane creatures should enjoy that blisse.
One is no number, mayds are nothing then,
Without the sweet societie of men.
Wilt thou live single still? one shalt thou bee,
Though never-singling *Hymen* couple thee.
Wild savages, that drinke of running springs,
Thinke water farre excels all earthly things:
But they that dayly tast neat wine, despise it.
Virginitie, albeit some highly prise it,
Compar'd with marriage, had you tried them both,
Differs as much, as wine and water doth.
Base boullion for the stampes sake we allow,
Even so for mens impression do we you.
By which alone, our reverend fathers say,
Women receave perfection everie way.
This idoll which you terme *Virginitie*,
Is neither essence subject to the eie,
No, nor to any one exterior sence,
Nor hath it any place of residence,
Nor is't of earth or mold celestiall,
Or capable of any forme at all.
Of that which hath no being, doe not boast,
Things that are not at all, are never lost.
Men foolishly doe call it vertuous,
What vertue is it, that is borne with us?
Much lesse can honour bee ascrib'd thereto,
Honour is purchac'd by the deedes wee do.
Beleeve me *Hero*, honour is not wone,
Untill some honourable deed be done.
Seeke you for chastitie, immortall fame,
And know that some have wrong'd *Dianas* name?

99 251 *intestine* internal, domestic, civil 255 cp. Shakespeare, *Sonnets* 136 l. 8 'Among a number one is reckon'd none' 258 *singling* that renders single, separates 261 *neat* pure, undiluted 265 *boullion* bullion *allow* praise, commend, sanction 270 *essence* something that exists 273 *mold* mould, form

Whose name is it, if she be false or not,
So she be faire, but some vile toongs will blot?
But you are faire (aye me) so wondrous faire,
So yoong, so gentle, and so debonaire,
As *Greece* will thinke, if thus you live alone,
Some one or other keepes you as his owne.
Then *Hero* hate me not, nor from me flie,
To follow swiftly blasting infamie.
Perhaps, thy sacred Priesthood makes thee loath,
Tell me, to whom mad'st thou that heedlesse oath?
   To *Venus*, answered shee, and as shee spake,
Foorth from those two tralucent cesternes brake,
A streame of liquid pearle, which downe her face
Made milk-white paths, wheron the gods might trace
To *Joves* high court. Hee thus replide: The rites
In which Loves beauteous Empresse most delites,
Are banquets, Dorick musicke, midnight-revell,
Plaies, maskes, and all that stern age counteth evill.
Thee as a holy Idiot doth she scorne,
For thou in vowing chastitie, hast sworne
To rob her name and honour, and thereby
Commit'st a sinne far worse than perjurie.
Even sacrilege against her Dietie,
Through regular and formall puritie.
To expiat which sinne, kisse and shake hands,
Such sacrifice as this, *Venus* demands.
   Thereat she smild, and did denie him so,
As put thereby, yet might he hope for mo.
Which makes him quickly re-enforce his speech,
And her in humble manner thus beseech.
   Though neither gods nor men may thee deserve,
Yet for her sake whom you have vow'd to serve,
Abandon fruitlesse cold Virginitie,
The gentle queene of Loves sole enemie.

99 286 *blot* slander 296 *tralucent* translucent *cesternes* cisterns, her eyes 298 *trace* walk, go 301 *Dorick* rustic; cp. Milton, 'Lycidas' (no. 325) l. 189 303 *Idiot* ignorant, simple person; layman 307 *Dietie* deity 308 *formall* satisfying the forms, conventional 312 *put* put off, repelled *mo* more 313 *re-enforce* give fresh strength to

Then shall you most resemble *Venus* Nun,
When *Venus* sweet rites are perform'd and done.
Flint-brested *Pallas* joies in single life,
But *Pallas* and your mistresse are at strife.
Love *Hero* then, and be not tirannous,
But heale the heart, that thou hast wounded thus,
Nor staine thy youthfull years with avarice,
Faire fooles delight, to be accounted nice.
The richest corne dies, if it be not reapt,
Beautie alone is lost, too warily kept.
These arguments he us'de, and many more,
Wherewith she yeelded, that was woon before.
Heroes lookes yeelded, but her words made warre,
Women are woon when they begin to jarre.
Thus having swallow'd *Cupids* golden hooke,
The more she striv'd, the deeper was she strooke.
Yet evilly faining anger, strove she still,
And would be thought to graunt against her will.
So having paus'd a while, at last shee said:
Who taught thee Rhethoricke to deceive a maid?
Aye me, such words as these should I abhor,
And yet I like them for the Orator.
With that *Leander* stoopt, to have imbrac'd her,
But from his spreading armes away she cast her,
And thus bespake him. Gentle youth forbeare
To touch the sacred garments which I weare.
Upon a rocke, and underneath a hill,
Far from the towne (where all is whist and still,
Save that the sea playing on yellow sand,
Sends foorth a ratling murmure to the land,
Whose sound allures the golden *Morpheus*,
In silence of the night to visite us.)
My turret stands, and there God knowes I play
With *Venus* swannes and sparrowes all the day,
A dwarfish beldame beares me companie,
That hops about the chamber where I lie,

99 326 *nice* shy, coy; fastidious, dainty 328 *alone* on its own 332 *jarre* quarrel 346 *whist* silent

And spends the night (that might be better spent)
In vaine discourse, and apish merriment.
Come thither; As she spake this, her toong tript,
For unawares (*Come thither*) from her slipt,
And sodainly her former colour chang'd,
And here and there her eies through anger rang'd.
And like a planet, mooving severall waies,
At one selfe instant, she poore soule assaies,
Loving, not to love at all, and everie part,
Strove to resist the motions of her hart.
And hands so pure, so innocent, nay such,
As might have made heaven stoope to have a touch,
Did she uphold to *Venus*, and againe,
Vow'd spotlesse chastitie, but all in vaine,
Cupid beats downe her praiers with his wings,
Her vowes above the emptie aire he flings:
All deepe enrag'd, his sinowie bow he bent,
And shot a shaft that burning from him went,
Wherewith she strooken, look'd so dolefully,
As made Love sigh, to see his tirannie.
And as she wept, her teares to pearle he turn'd,
And wound them on his arme, and for her mourn'd.
Then towards the pallace of the destinies,
Laden with languishment and griefe he flies.
And to those sterne nymphs humblie made request,
Both might enjoy ech other, and be blest.
But with a ghastly dreadfull countenaunce,
Threatning a thousand deaths at everie glaunce,
They answered Love, nor would vouchsafe so much
As one poore word, their hate to him was such.
Harken a while, and I will tell you why:
Heavens winged herrald, *Jove-borne Mercury*,
The selfe-same day that he asleepe had layd
Inchaunted *Argus*, spied a countrie mayd,

99 356 *apish* silly, trifling 361 in the Ptolemaic system, planets moved in their own orbit, but could also be moved by other planetary influences 370 *emptie aire* the sphere of air which, traditionally, lay between the spheres of earth and fire (cp. no. 313 l. 50) 371 *sinowie* sinewy 377 *destinies* fates 382 the line is identical with one in Marlowe's *Dido, Queen of Carthage* II.1.231 388 *mayd* Io

Whose carelesse haire, in stead of pearle t'adorne it,
Glist'red with deaw, as one that seem'd to skorne it:
Her breath as fragrant as the morning rose,
Her mind pure, and her toong untaught to glose,
Yet prowd she was, (for loftie pride that dwels
In tow'red courts, is oft in sheapheards cels.)
And too too well the faire vermilion knew,
And silver tincture of her cheekes, that drew
The love of everie swaine: On her, this god
Enamoured was, and with his snakie rod,
Did charme her nimble feet, and made her stay,
The while upon a hillocke downe he lay,
And sweetly on his pipe began to play,
And with smooth speech, her fancie to assay,
Till in his twining armes he lockt her fast,
And then he woo'd with kisses, and at last,
As sheap-heards do, her on the ground hee layd,
And tumbling in the grasse, he often strayd
Beyond the bounds of shame, in being bold
To eie those parts, which no eie should behold.
And like an insolent commaunding lover,
Boasting his parentage, would needs discover
The way to new *Elisium:* but she,
Whose only dower was her chastitie,
Having striv'ne in vaine, was now about to crie,
And crave the helpe of sheap-heards that were nie.
Herewith he stayd his furie, and began
To give her leave to rise, away she ran,
After went *Mercurie*, who us'd such cunning,
As she to heare his tale, left off her running.
Maids are not woon by brutish force and might,
But speeches full of pleasure and delight.
And knowing *Hermes* courted her, was glad
That she such lovelinesse and beautie had
As could provoke his liking, yet was mute,
And neither would denie, nor graunt his sute.

99 390 *it* pearl 392 *glose* flatter 398 *snakie rod* Mercury's caduceus 402 *her ... assay* try, assail her amorous inclination, love 410 *Boasting his parentage* see Ovid, *Metamorphoses* 2.744

Still vowd he love, she wanting no excuse
To feed him with delaies, as women use:
Or thirsting after immortalitie,
All women are ambitious naturallie,
Impos'd upon her lover such a taske,
As he ought not performe, nor yet she aske.
A draught of flowing *Nectar*, she requested,
Wherewith the king of Gods and men is feasted.
He readie to accomplish what she wil'd,
Stole some from *Hebe* (*Hebe*, *Joves* cup fil'd,)
And gave it to his simple rustike love,
Which being knowne (as what is hid from *Jove*)
He inly storm'd, and waxt more furious,
Than for the fire filcht by *Prometheus*;
And thrusts him down from heaven, he wandring here,
In mournfull tearmes, with sad and heavie cheare
Complaind to *Cupid*, *Cupid* for his sake,
To be reveng'd on *Jove*, did undertake,
And those on whom heaven, earth, and hell relies,
I mean the Adamantine Destinies,
He wounds with love, and forst them equallie,
To dote upon deceitfull *Mercurie*.
They offred him the deadly fatall knife,
That sheares the slender threads of humane life,
At his faire feathered feet, the engins layd,
Which th'earth from ougly *Chaos* den up-wayd:
These he regarded not, but did intreat,
That *Jove*, usurper of his fathers seat,
Might presently be banisht into hell,
And aged *Saturne* in *Olympus* dwell.
They granted what he crav'd, and once againe,
Saturne and *Ops*, began their golden raigne.
Murder, rape, warre, lust and trecherie,
Were with *Jove* clos'd in *Stigian* Emprie.

99 426 *use* are accustomed to 432 *king* Jove 440 *tearmes* condition, state *cheare* demeanour, appearance 444 *Adamantine* made of unbreakable, immovable adamant 449 *engins* implements, tools 450 *up-wayd* raised, bore up 452 *fathers* Saturn's

But long this blessed time continued not,
As soone as he his wished purpose got;
He recklesse of his promise, did despise
The love of th'everlasting Destinies.
They seeing it, both Love and him abhor'd,
And *Jupiter* unto his place restor'd.
And but that Learning, in despight of Fate,
Will mount aloft, and enter heaven gate,
And to the seat of *Jove* it selfe advaunce,
Hermes had slept in hell with ignoraunce.
Yet as a punishment they added this,
That he and *Povertie* should alwaies kis.
And to this day is everie scholler poore,
Grosse gold, from them runs headlong to the boore.
Likewise the angrie sisters thus deluded,
To venge themselves on *Hermes*, have concluded
That *Midas* brood shall sit in Honors chaire,
To which the *Muses* sonnes are only heire:
And fruitfull wits that inaspiring are,
Shall discontent, run into regions farre;
And few great lords in vertuous deeds shall joy,
But be surpris'd with every garish toy.
And still inrich the loftie servile clowne,
Who with incroching guile, keepes learning downe.
Then muse not, *Cupids* sute no better sped,
Seeing in their loves, the Fates were injured.
  By this, sad *Hero*, with love unacquainted,
Viewing *Leanders* face, fell downe and fainted.
He kist her, and breath'd life into her lips,
Wherewith as one displeas'd, away she trips.
Yet as she went, full often look'd behind,
And many poore excuses did she find,
To linger by the way, and once she stayd,
And would have turn'd againe, but was afrayd,

99 460 *he* Mercury 461 *recklesse* heedless 475 *Midas brood* rich fools 477 *inaspiring* do not aspire (after gold and so on) 480 *surpris'd* delighted, captivated, astonished *toy* trifle, worthless thing 481 *still* continually *clowne* rustic peasant 482 *incroching* wrongfully seizing, intrusive 483 *sped* fared, succeeded 485 *By* at *sad* grave, serious

In offring parlie, to be counted light.
So on she goes, and in her idle flight,
Her painted fanne of curled plumes let fall,
Thinking to traine *Leander* therewithall.
He being a novice, knew not what she meant,
But stayd, and after her a letter sent.
Which joyfull *Hero* answerd in such sort,
As he had hope to scale the beauteous fort,
Wherein the liberall graces lock'd their wealth,
And therefore to her tower he got by stealth.
Wide open stood the doore, hee need not clime,
And she her selfe before the pointed time,
Had spread the boord, with roses strowed the roome,
And oft look't out, and mus'd he did not come.
At last he came, O who can tell the greeting,
These greedie lovers had, at their first meeting.
He askt, she gave, and nothing was denied,
Both to each other quickly were affied.
Looke how their hands, so were their hearts united,
And what he did, she willingly requited.
(Sweet are the kisses, the imbracements sweet,
When like desires and affections meet,
For from the earth to heaven, is *Cupid* rais'd,
Where fancie is in equall ballance pais'd.)
Yet she this rashnesse sodainly repented,
And turn'd aside, and to her selfe lamented.
As if her name and honour had beene wrong'd,
By being possest of him for whom she long'd;
I, and shee wisht, albeit not from her hart,
That he would leave her turret and depart.
The mirthfull God of amorous pleasure smil'd,
To see how he this captive Nymph beguil'd.
For hitherto hee did but fan the fire,
And kept it downe that it might mount the hier.
Now waxt she jealous, least his love abated,
Fearing, her owne thoughts made her to be hated.

99 493 *light* wanton, immodest 496 *traine* allure, entice 504 *pointed* appointed 510 *affied* affianced, betrothed 516 *pais'd* peised, weighed 527 *waxt* grew

Therefore unto him hastily she goes,
And like light *Salmacis*, her body throes
Upon his bosome, where with yeelding eyes,
She offers up her selfe a sacrifice,
To slake his anger, if he were displeas'd,
O what god would not therewith be appeas'd?
Like *Æsops* cocke, this jewell he enjoyed,
And as a brother with his sister toyed,
Supposing nothing else was to be done,
Now he her favour and good will had wone.
But know you not that creatures wanting sence,
By nature have a mutuall appetence,
And wanting organs to advaunce a step,
Mov'd by Loves force, unto ech other lep?
Much more in subjects having intellect,
Some hidden influence breeds like effect.
Albeit *Leander* rude in love, and raw,
Long dallying with *Hero*, nothing saw
That might delight him more, yet he suspected
Some amorous rites or other were neglected.
Therefore unto his bodie, hirs he clung,
She, fearing on the rushes to be flung,
Striv'd with redoubled strength, the more she strived,
The more a gentle pleasing heat revived,
Which taught him all that elder lovers know,
And now the same gan so to scorch and glow,
As in plaine termes (yet cunningly) he crav'd it,
Love alwaies makes those eloquent that have it.
Shee, with a kind of graunting, put him by it,
And ever as he thought himselfe most nigh it,
Like to the tree of *Tantalus* she fled,
And seeming lavish, sav'de her maydenhead.
Ne're king more sought to keepe his diademe,
Than *Hero* this inestimable gemme.

99 533 *slake* moderate, decrease 535 *Æsops cocke* preferred a barleycorn to a precious stone 539 *creatures ... sence* inanimate objects 540 *appetence*** appetite, desire; affinity 541 *organs* means, instruments 542 *lep* leap 545 *rude* unlearned, ignorant 555 *cunningly* skilfully, cleverly 557 *put ... it* put him off, deflected him, thrust him aside 560 *lavish* unrestrained, licentious

Above our life we love a stedfast friend,
Yet when a token of great worth we send,
We often kisse it, often looke thereon,
And stay the messenger that would be gon:
No marvell then, though *Hero* would not yeeld
So soone to part from that she deerely held.
Jewels being lost are found againe, this never,
T'is lost but once, and once lost, lost for ever.
   Now had the morne espy'de her lovers steeds,
Whereat she starts, puts on her purple weeds,
And red for anger that he stayd so long,
All headlong throwes her selfe the clouds among,
And now *Leander* fearing to be mist,
Imbrast her sodainly, tooke leave, and kist,
Long was he taking leave, and loath to go,
And kist againe, as lovers use to do,
Sad *Hero* wroong him by the hand, and wept,
Saying, let your vowes and promises be kept.
Then standing at the doore, she turnd about,
As loath to see *Leander* going out.
And now the sunne that through th'orizon peepes,
As pittying these lovers, downeward creepes.
So that in silence of the cloudie night,
Though it was morning, did he take his flight.
But what the secret trustie night conceal'd,
Leanders amorous habit soone reveal'd,
With *Cupids* myrtle was his bonet crownd,
About his armes the purple riband wound,
Wherewith she wreath'd her largely spreading heare,
Nor could the youth abstaine, but he must weare
The sacred ring wherewith she was endow'd,
When first religious chastitie she vow'd:
Which made his love through *Sestos* to bee knowne,
And thence unto *Abydus* sooner blowne,

99 571 *morne* Aurora *her lovers* Apollo's 572 *weeds* clothes 579 *wroong* wrung 588 *habit* dress, clothing 589 *Cupids myrtle* cp. Marlowe's translation of Ovid's *Elegies* 1.1.33–4 '*Elegian Muse*, that warblest amorous laies,/Girt my shine browe with Sea-banke Mirtle praise' 591 *heare* hair

Than he could saile, for incorporeal Fame,
Whose waight consists in nothing but her name,
Is swifter than the wind, whose tardie plumes,
Are reeking water, and dull earthlie fumes.
Home when he came, he seem'd not to be there,
But like exiled aire thrust from his sphere,
Set in a forren place, and straight from thence,
Alcides like, by mightie violence,
He would have chac'd away the swelling maine,
That him from her unjustly did detaine.
Like as the sunne in a Dyameter,
Fires and inflames objects remooved farre,
And heateth kindly, shining lat'rally;
So beautie, sweetly quickens when t'is ny,
But being separated and remooved,
Burnes where it cherisht, murders where it loved.
Therefore even as an Index to a booke,
So to his mind was yoong *Leanders* looke.
O none but gods have power their love to hide,
Affection by the count'nance is descride.
The light of hidden fire it selfe discovers,
And love that is conceal'd, betraies poore lovers.
His secret flame apparantly was seene,
Leanders Father knew where hee had beene,
And for the same mildly rebuk't his sonne,
Thinking to quench the sparckles new begonne.
But love resisted once, growes passionate,
And nothing more than counsaile, lovers hate.
For as a hote prowd horse highly disdaines,
To have his head control'd, but breakes the raines,
Spits foorth the ringled bit, and with his hoves,
Checkes the submissive ground: so hee that loves,
The more he is restrain'd, the woorse he fares,
What is it now, but mad *Leander* dares?

99 597 *Fame* common talk, rumour 599 *tardie* slow 600 *reeking* vaporous, steamy 602 cp. l. 370 above 605 *maine* ocean 607 *in a Dyameter* directly (above, overhead) 609 *kindly* easily, spontaneously *lat'rally* from the side 610 *quickens* is enlivened, is stimulated 619 *apparantly* openly 627 *ringled** ringed 628 *Checkes* strikes, hits 630 there is nothing but mad Leander would dare to do it

O *Hero*, *Hero*, thus he cry'de full oft,
And then he got him to a rocke aloft.
Where having spy'de her tower, long star'd he on't,
And pray'd the narrow toyling *Hellespont*,
To part in twaine, that hee might come and go,
But still the rising billowes answered no.
With that hee stript him to the yv'rie skin,
And crying, Love I come, leapt lively in.
Whereat the saphir visag'd god grew prowd,
And made his capring *Triton* sound alowd,
Imagining, that *Ganimed* displeas'd,
Had left the heavens, therefore on him hee seaz'd.
Leander striv'd, the waves about him wound,
And puld him to the bottome, where the ground
Was strewd with pearle, and in low corrall groves,
Sweet singing Meremaids, sported with their loves
On heapes of heavie gold, and tooke great pleasure,
To spurne in carelesse sort, the shipwracke treasure.
For here the stately azure pallace stood,
Where kingly *Neptune* and his traine abode.
The lustie god imbrast him, cald him love,
And swore he never should returne to *Jove*.
But when he knew it was not *Ganimed*,
For under water he was almost dead,
He heav'd him up, and looking on his face,
Beat downe the bold waves with his triple mace,
Which mounted up, intending to have kist him,
And fell in drops like teares, because they mist him.
Leander being up, began to swim,
And looking backe, saw *Neptune* follow him.
Whereat agast, the poore soule gan to crie,
O let mee visite *Hero* ere I die.
The god put *Helles* bracelet on his arme,
And swore the sea should never doe him harme.

99 634 *toyling* struggling, raging 638 *lively* nimbly, vigorously 639 *saphir visag'd* god* Neptune *prowd* lustful 640 *capring*** frolicsome dancing 646 *Sweet singing** *sported with* amused, diverted themselves in the company of 648 *sort* manner *shipwracke* shipwrecked

He clapt his plumpe cheekes, with his tresses playd,
And smiling wantonly, his love bewrayd.
He watcht his armes, and as they opend wide,
At every stroke, betwixt them would he slide,
And steale a kisse, and then run out and daunce,
And as he turnd, cast many a lustfull glaunce,
And threw him gawdie toies to please his eie,
And dive into the water, and there prie
Upon his brest, his thighs, and everie lim,
And up againe, and close beside him swim,
And talke of love: *Leander* made replie,
You are deceav'd, I am no woman I.
Thereat smilde *Neptune*, and then told a tale,
How that a sheapheard sitting in a vale,
Playd with a boy so faire and kind,
As for his love, both earth and heaven pyn'd,
That of the cooling river durst not drinke,
Least water-nymphs should pull him from the brinke.
And when hee sported in the fragrant lawnes,
Gote-footed Satyrs, and up-staring Fawnes,
Would steale him thence. Ere halfe this tale was done,
Aye me, *Leander* cryde, th'enamoured sunne,
That now should shine on *Thetis* glassie bower,
Descends upon my radiant *Heroes* tower.
O that these tardie armes of mine were wings,
And as he spake, upon the waves he springs.
Neptune was angrie that he gave no eare,
And in his heart revenging malice bare:
He flung at him his mace, but as it went,
He cald it in, for love made him repent.
The mace returning backe, his owne hand hit,
As meaning to be veng'd for darting it.
When this fresh bleeding wound *Leander* viewd,
His colour went and came, as if he rewd
The greefe which *Neptune* felt. In gentle brests,
Relenting thoughts, remorse and pittie rests.

99 672 *prie* pry 683 *lawnes* woodland clearings 684 *Gote-footed*** *up-staring* with hair standing on end (?) 687 *Thetis . . . bower* the sea 696 *darting* throwing, casting

And who have hard hearts, and obdurat minds,
But vicious, harebraind, and illit'rat hinds?
The god seeing him with pittie to be moved,
Thereon concluded that he was beloved.
(Love is too full of faith, too credulous,
With follie and false hope deluding us.)
Wherefore *Leanders* fancie to surprize,
To the rich *Ocean* for gifts he flies.
'Tis wisedome to give much, a gift prevailes,
When deepe perswading Oratorie failes.
By this *Leander* being nere the land,
Cast downe his wearie feet, and felt the sand.
Breathlesse albeit he were, he rested not,
Till to the solitarie tower he got.
And knockt and cald, at which celestiall noise,
The longing heart of *Hero* much more joies
Then nymphs and sheapheards, when the timbrell rings,
Or crooked Dolphin when the sailer sings;
She stayd not for her robes, but straight arose,
And drunke with gladnesse, to the dore she goes.
Where seeing a naked man, she sriecht for feare,
Such sights as this, to tender maids are rare.
And ran into the darke her selfe to hide,
Rich jewels in the darke are soonest spide.
Unto her was he led, or rather drawne,
By those white limmes, which sparckled through the lawne.
The neerer that he came, the more she fled,
And seeking refuge, slipt into her bed.
Whereon *Leander* sitting, thus began,
Through numming cold, all feeble, faint and wan:
  If not for love, yet love for pittie sake,
Me in thy bed and maiden bosome take,
At least vouchsafe these armes some little roome,
Who hoping to imbrace thee, cherely swome.
This head was beat with manie a churlish billow,
And therefore let it rest upon thy pillow.

99 702 *hinds* boors 717 *timbrell* tambourine 718 *crooked Dolphin* curved dolphin; cp. Ovid, *Heroides* 18.131 'curvi delphines'; the phrase recalls the myth of Arion 734 *cherely* cheerily

Herewith afrighted *Hero* shrunke away,
And in her luke-warme place *Leander* lay.
Whose lively heat like fire from heaven fet,
Would animate grosse clay, and higher set
The drooping thoughts of base declining soules,
Then drerie *Mars*, carowsing *Nectar* boules.
His hands he cast upon her like a snare,
She overcome with shame and sallow feare,
Like chast *Diana*, when *Acteon* spyde her,
Being sodainly betraide, dyv'd downe to hide her.
And as her silver body downeward went,
With both her hands she made the bed a tent,
And in her owne mind thought her selfe secure,
O'recast with dim and darksome coverture.
And now she lets him whisper in her eare,
Flatter, intreat, promise, protest and sweare,
Yet ever as he greedily assayd
To touch those dainties, she the *Harpey* playd,
And every lim did as a soldier stout,
Defend the fort, and keep the foe-man out.
For though the rising yv'rie mount he scal'd,
Which is with azure circling lines empal'd,
Much like a globe, (a globe may I tearme this,
By which love sailes to regions full of blis,)
Yet there with *Sysiphus* he toyld in vaine,
Till gentle parlie did the truce obtaine.
Wherein *Leander* on her quivering brest,
Breathlesse spoke some thing, and sigh'd out the rest;
Which so prevail'd, as he with small ado,
Inclos'd her in his armes and kist her to.
And everie kisse to her was as a charme,
And to *Leander* as a fresh alarme.
So that the truce was broke, and she alas,
(Poore sillie maiden) at his mercie was.

99 739–40 these lines may allude to the story of Prometheus 739 *fet* fetched 742 *drerie* gory, bloody; cruel 744 *sallow* yellow 750 *coverture* bed-cover, quilt 758 *empal'd* surrounded, hedged about; encircled, bordered 768 *alarme* call to arms

Love is not full of pittie (as men say)
But deaffe and cruell, where he meanes to pray.
Even as a bird, which in our hands we wring,
Foorth plungeth, and oft flutters with her wing,
She trembling strove, this strife of hers (like that
Which made the world) another world begat,
Of unknowne joy. Treason was in her thought,
And cunningly to yeeld her selfe she sought.
Seeming not woon, yet woon she was at length,
In such warres women use but halfe their strength.
Leander now like Theban *Hercules*,
Entred the orchard of Th'*esperides*,
Whose fruit none rightly can describe, but hee
That puls or shakes it from the golden tree:
And now she wisht this night were never done,
And sigh'd to thinke upon th'approching sunne,
For much it greev'd her that the bright day light,
Should know the pleasure of this blessed night,
And them like *Mars* and *Ericine* displayd,
Both in each others armes chaind as they layd.
Againe she knew not how to frame her looke,
Or speake to him who in a moment tooke,
That which so long so charily she kept,
And faine by stealth away she would have crept,
And to some corner secretly have gone,
Leaving *Leander* in the bed alone.
But as her naked feet were whipping out,
He on the suddaine cling'd her so about,
That Meremaid-like unto the floore she slid,
One halfe appear'd the other halfe was hid.
Thus neere the bed she blushing stood upright,
And from her countenance behold ye might,
A kind of twilight breake, which through the heare,
As from an orient cloud, glymse here and there.
And round about the chamber this false morne,
Brought foorth the day before the day was borne.

99 773 *wring* hold tightly 779 *woon* won 793 *charily* carefully 804 *glymse* glimpse, shine faintly, glimmer

So *Heroes* ruddie cheeke, *Hero* betrayd,
And her all naked to his sight displayd.
Whence his admiring eyes more pleasure tooke,
Than *Dis*, on heapes of gold fixing his looke.
By this *Apollos* golden harpe began,
To sound foorth musicke to the *Ocean*,
Which watchfull *Hesperus* no sooner heard,
But he the days bright-bearing Car prepar'd.
And ran before, as Harbenger of light,
And with his flaring beames mockt ougly night,
Till she o'recome with anguish, shame, and rage,
Dang'd downe to hell her loathsome carriage.

Desunt nonnulla.

WILLIAM SHAKESPEARE

100 [*from* Venus and Adonis]

Even as the sunne with purple-colourd face,
Had tane his last leave of the weeping morne,
Rose-cheekt Adonis hied him to the chace,
Hunting he lov'd, but love he laught to scorne:
Sick-thoughted Venus makes amaine unto him,
And like a bold fac'd suter ginnes to woo him.

Thrise fairer then my selfe, (thus she began)
The fields chiefe flower, sweet above compare,
Staine to all Nimphs, more lovely then a man,
More white, and red, then doves, or roses are:
Nature that made thee with her selfe at strife,
Saith that the world hath ending with thy life.

99 810 *Dis* Plutus 816 *flaring*** shining brightly and fitfully 818 *Dang'd* dinged, knocked, dashed, drove violently [819] *Desunt nonnulla* 'something is missing'

100 2 *weeping* rainy 3 *hied* hastened 5 *Sick-thoughted** lovesick *amaine* with all speed 6 *suter* suitor 9 *Staine to* eclipsing, casting into the shade 11 *at strife* striving, surpassing

Vouchsafe thou wonder to alight thy steed,
And raine his proud head to the saddle bow,
If thou wilt daine this favor, for thy meed
A thousand honie secrets shalt thou know:
  Here come and sit, where never serpent hisses,
  And being set, Ile smother thee with kisses.

And yet not cloy thy lips with loth'd sacietie,
But rather famish them amid their plentie,
Making them red, and pale, with fresh varietie:
Ten kisses short as one, one long as twentie:
  A sommers day will seeme an houre but short,
  Being wasted in such time-beguiling sport.

With this she ceazeth on his sweating palme,
The president of pith, and livelyhood,
And trembling in her passion, calls it balme,
Earths soveraigne salve, to do a goddesse good,
  Being so enrag'd, desire doth lend her force,
  Couragiously to plucke him from his horse.

Over one arme the lustie coursers raine,
Under her other was the tender boy,
Who blusht, and powted in a dull disdaine,
With leaden appetite, unapt to toy,
  She red, and hot, as coles of glowing fier,
  He red for shame, but frostie in desier.

The studded bridle on a ragged bough,
Nimbly she fastens, (ô how quicke is love!)
The steed is stalled up, and even now,
To tie the rider she begins to prove:
  Backward she pusht him, as she would be thrust,
  And governd him in strength though not in lust.

100 14 *saddle bow* arched front of a saddle 15 *meed* reward, merit 18 *set* set down, seated 24 *wasted* spent 25 *ceazeth* seizes 26 *president* precedent, sign, token *pith* strength, vigour *livelyhood* animation, energy 29 *enrag'd* maddened with desire, aroused 30 *Couragiously* longingly, lustfully 31 *lustie* young, vigorous *coursers* horse's, charger's 34 *unapt* unwilling, uninclined *toy* flirt, make love 39 *stalled up* kept as in a stall 40 *prove* try

So soone was she along, as he was downe,
Each leaning on their elbowes and their hips:
Now doth she stroke his cheek, now doth he frown,
And gins to chide, but soone she stops his lips,
And kissing speaks, with lustful language broken,
If thou wilt chide, thy lips shall never open.

He burnes with bashfull shame, she with her teares
Doth quench the maiden burning of his cheekes,
Then with her windie sighes, and golden heares,
To fan, and blow them drie againe she seekes.
He saith, she is immodest, blames her misse,
What followes more, she murthers with a kisse.

Even as an emptie Eagle sharpe by fast,
Tires with her beake on feathers, flesh, and bone,
Shaking her wings, devouring all in hast,
Till either gorge be stuft, or pray be gone:
Even so she kist his brow, his cheeke, his chin,
And where she ends, she doth anew begin.

Forst to content, but never to obey,
Panting he lies, and breatheth in her face.
She feedeth on the steame, as on a pray,
And calls it heavenly moisture, aire of grace,
Wishing her cheeks were gardens ful of flowers,
So they were dew'd with such distilling showers.

Looke how a bird lyes tangled in a net,
So fastned in her armes Adonis lyes,
Pure shame and aw'd resistance made him fret,
Which bred more beautie in his angrie eyes:
Raine added to a river that is ranke,
Perforce will force it overflow the banke.

100 43 *along* stretched out 53 *misse* misdeed, offence 55 *sharpe* hungry, famished 56 *Tires* preys, feeds ravenously 61 *content* acquiesce, endure 71 *ranke* full

Still she intreats, and prettily intreats,
For to a prettie eare she tunes her tale.
Still is he sullein, still he lowres and frets,
Twixt crimson shame, and anger ashie pale,
Being red she loves him best, and being white,
Her best is betterd with a more delight.

Looke how he can, she cannot chuse but love,
And by her faire immortall hand she sweares,
From his soft bosome never to remove,
Till he take truce with her contending teares,
Which long have raind, making her cheeks al wet,
And one sweet kisse shal pay this comptlesse debt.

Upon this promise did he raise his chin,
Like a divedapper peering through a wave,
Who being lookt on, ducks as quickly in:
So offers he to give what she did crave,
But when her lips were readie for his pay,
He winks, and turnes his lips another way.

Never did passenger in sommers heat,
More thirst for drinke, then she for this good turne,
Her helpe she sees, but helpe she cannot get,
She bathes in water, yet her fire must burne:
Oh pitie gan she crie, flint-hearted boy,
Tis but a kisse I begge, why art thou coy?

I have bene wooed as I intreat thee now,
Even by the sterne, and direfull god of warre,
Whose sinowie necke in battell nere did bow,
Who conquers where he comes in everie jarre,
Yet hath he bene my captive, and my slave,
And begd for that which thou unaskt shalt have.

100 73 *prettily* ingeniously, cleverly 78 *more* greater 79 *how* however, in whatsoever way 82 *take truce* make peace *contending* striving, making war 84 *comptlesse* countless, infinite 86 *divedapper* dabchick 90 *winks* closes his eyes 91 *passenger* traveller 92 *turne* change; sexual encounter 98 *god* Mars 99 *sinowie* sinewy 100 *jarre* quarrel, fight

Over my Altars hath he hong his launce,
His battred shield, his uncontrolled crest,
And for my sake hath learnd to sport, and daunce,
To toy, to wanton, dallie, smile, and jest,
Scorning his churlish drumme, and ensigne red,
Making my armes his field, his tent my bed.

Thus he that over-ruld, I over-swayed,
Leading him prisoner in a red rose chaine,
Strong-temperd steele his stronger strength obayed,
Yet was he servile to my coy disdaine,
Oh be not proud, nor brag not of thy might,
For maistring her that foyld the god of fight.

Touch but my lips with those faire lips of thine,
Though mine be not so faire, yet are they red,
The kisse shalbe thine owne as well as mine,
What seest thou in the ground? hold up thy head,
Looke in mine ey-bals, there thy beautie lyes,
Then why not lips on lips, since eyes in eyes?

Art thou asham'd to kisse? then winke againe,
And I will winke, so shall the day seeme night.
Love keepes his revels where there are but twaine:
Be bold to play, our sport is not in sight,
These blew-veind violets whereon we leane,
Never can blab, nor know not what we meane.

The tender spring upon thy tempting lip,
Shewes thee unripe; yet maist thou well be tasted,
Make use of time, let not advantage slip,
Beautie within it selfe should not be wasted,
Faire flowers that are not gathred in their prime,
Rot, and consume them selves in litle time.

100 104 *uncontrolled* unrestrained, ungoverned 108 *field* field of battle 112 *coy* distant 126 *blab* tell tales 127 *spring* young shoot, downy hair

Were I hard-favourd, foule, or wrinckled old,
Il-nurtur'd, crooked, churlish, harsh in voice,
Ore-worne, despised, reumatique, and cold,
Thick-sighted, barren, leane, and lacking juyce;
  Then mightst thou pause, for then I were not for thee,
  But having no defects, why doest abhor me?

Thou canst not see one wrinckle in my brow,
Mine eyes are grey, and bright, and quicke in turning:
My beautie as the spring doth yearelie grow,
My flesh is soft, and plumpe, my marrow burning,
  My smooth moist hand, were it with thy hand felt,
  Would in thy palme dissolve, or seeme to melt.

Bid me discourse, I will inchaunt thine eare,
Or like a Fairie, trip upon the greene,
Or like a Nimph, with long disheveled heare,
Daunce on the sands, and yet no footing seene.
  Love is a spirit all compact of fire,
  Not grosse to sinke, but light, and will aspire.

Witnesse this Primrose banke whereon I lie,
These forcelesse flowers like sturdy trees support me:
Two strengthles doves will draw me through the skie,
From morne till night, even where I list to sport me.
  Is love so light sweet boy, and may it be,
  That thou should thinke it heavie unto thee?

Is thine owne heart to thine owne face affected?
Can thy right hand ceaze love upon thy left?
Then woo thy selfe, be of thy selfe rejected:
Steale thine own freedome, and complaine on theft.
  Narcissus so him selfe him selfe forsooke,
  And died to kisse his shadow in the brooke.

100 133 *hard-favourd* ugly 134 *churlish* rude, rough 135 *Ore-worne* overworn, worn out *despised* despicable, hateful 136 *Thick-sighted** dull-, dim-sighted 148 *footing* footprint 149 *compact* made up, composed 150 *grosse* heavy, corpulent 152 *forcelesse* powerless 154 *list* please 157 *affected* in love

Torches are made to light, jewels to weare,
Dainties to tast, fresh beautie for the use,
Herbes for their smell, and sappie plants to beare.
Things growing to them selves, are growths abuse,
  Seeds spring from seeds, and beauty breedeth beauty,
  Thou wast begot, to get it is thy duty.

Upon the earths increase why shouldst thou feed,
Unlesse the earth with thy increase be fed?
By law of nature thou art bound to breed,
That thine may live, when thou thy selfe art dead:
  And so in spite of death thou doest survive,
  In that thy likenesse still is left alive.

By this the love-sicke Queene began to sweate,
For where they lay the shadow had forsooke them,
And Titan tired in the midday heate,
With burning eye did hotly over-looke them,
  Wishing Adonis had his teame to guide,
  So he were like him, and by Venus side.

101 [*from* Lucrece]

At last shee cals to mind where hangs a peece
Of skilfull painting, made for PRIAMS Troy,
Before the which is drawn the power of Greece,
For HELENS rape, the Cittie to destroy,
Threatning cloud-kissing ILLION with annoy,
  Which the conceipted Painter drew so prowd,
  As Heaven (it seem'd) to kisse the turrets bow'd.

100 165 *sappie* full of sap, vitality 166 *to* for 168 *get* beget children 177 *tired* attired, dressed; weary 179 *teame* of horses to guide Titan's chariot 180 *he ... him* Titan ... Adonis

101 1 *shee* Lucrece 1–2 *peece ... painting* probably a painted cloth 2 *for* of 3 *drawn* drawn up *power* body of armed men 6 *conceipted* ingenious, clever

A thousand lamentable objects there,
In scorne of Nature, Art gave livelesse life,
Many a dry drop seem'd a weeping teare,
Shed for the slaughtred husband by the wife.
The red bloud reek'd to shew the Painters strife,
  And dying eyes gleem'd forth their ashie lights,
  Like dying coales burnt out in tedious nights.

There might you see the labouring Pyoner
Begrim'd with sweat, and smeared all with dust,
And from the towres of Troy, there would appeare
The verie eyes of men through loop-holes thrust,
Gazing uppon the Greekes with little lust,
  Such sweet observance in this worke was had,
  That one might see those farre of eyes looke sad.

In great commaunders, Grace, and Majestie,
You might behold triumphing in their faces,
In youth quick-bearing and dexteritie,
And here and there the Painter interlaces
Pale cowards marching on with trembling paces.
  Which hartlesse peasaunts did so wel resemble,
  That one would swear he saw them quake and tremble.

In Ajax and Ulysses, ô what Art
Of Phisiognomy might one behold!
The face of eyther cypher'd eythers heart,
Their face, their manners most expreslie told,
In Ajax eyes blunt rage and rigour rold,
  But the mild glance that slie Ulysses lent,
  Shewed deepe regard and smiling government.

101 12 *reek'd** steamed 15 *Pyoner* pioneer, sapper 19 *lust* pleasure, delight 20 *observance* observation of, attention to, detail 24 *quick-bearing* lively behaviour 27 *hartlesse* disheartened 30 *Phisiognomy* the science or art of judging character from the face 31 *cypher'd* wrote out, expressed 35 *regard* attentive thoughtfulness, deliberation

There pleading might you see grave NESTOR stand,
As'twere incouraging the Greekes to fight,
Making such sober action with his hand,
That it beguild attention, charm'd the sight,
In speech it seemd his beard, all silver white,
   Wag'd up and downe, and from his lips did flie,
   Thin winding breath which purl'd up to the skie.

About him were a presse of gaping faces,
Which seem'd to swallow up his sound advice,
All joyntlie listning, but with severall graces,
As if some Marmaide did their eares intice,
Some high, some low, the Painter was so nice.
   The scalpes of manie almost hid behind,
   To jump up higher seem'd to mocke the mind.

Here one mans hand leand on anothers head,
His nose being shadowed by his neighbours eare,
Here one being throng'd, bears back all boln, and red,
Another smotherd, seemes to pelt and sweare,
And in their rage such signes of rage they beare,
   As but for losse of NESTORS golden words,
   It seem'd they would debate with angrie swords.

For much imaginarie worke was there,
Conceipt deceitfull, so compact so kinde,
That for ACHILLES image stood his speare
Grip't in an Armed hand, himselfe behind
Was left unseene, save to the eye of mind,
   A hand, a foote, a face, a leg, a head
   Stood for the whole to be imagined.

101 38 *sober* grave, dignified *action* rhetorical gesture 42 *purl'd** flowed with a whirling motion 47 *high* ... *low* tall ... short *nice* exact, precise 52 *throng'd* pressed by the crowd *boln* swollen, puffed up 53 *pelt** shout out angry words 55 *As* ... *of* if it had not meant missing 58 *compact* solid, fully composed *kinde* natural

And from the wals of strong besieged TROY,
When their brave hope, bold HECTOR march'd to field,
Stood manie Trojan mothers sharing joy,
To see their youthfull sons bright weapons wield,
And to their hope they such odde action yeeld,
That through their light joy seemed to appeare,
(Like bright things staind) a kind of heavie feare.

And from the strond of DARDAN where they fought,
To SIMOIS reedie bankes the red bloud ran,
Whose waves to imitate the battaile sought
With swelling ridges, and their rankes began
To breake uppon the galled shore, and than
Retire againe, till meeting greater ranckes
They joine, and shoot their fome at SIMOIS banck*s*.

To this well painted peece is LUCRECE come,
To find a face where all distresse is steld,
Manie shee sees, where cares have carved some,
But none where all distresse and dolor dweld,
Till shee dispayring HECUBA beheld,
Staring on PRIAMS wounds with her old eyes,
Which bleeding under PIRRHUS proud foot lies.

In her the Painter had anathomiz'd
Times ruine, beauties wracke, and grim cares raign,
Her cheeks with chops and wrincles were disguiz'd,
Of what shee was, no semblance did remaine:
Her blew bloud chang'd to blacke in everie vaine,
Wanting the spring, that those shrunke pipes had fed,
Shew'd life imprison'd in a bodie dead.

101 64 *strong* strongly 68 *odde* extraordinary, unparalleled 69 *light* bright; superficial 70 *staind* disfigured 71 *strond* strand, shore 75 *galled* fretted, sore from being rubbed 79 *steld* stelled, fixed, placed; steeled, portrayed 80 *carved* incised, engraved 85 *anathomiz'd* analysed, laid bare 86 *wracke* wreck, ruin 87 *chops* chaps, cracks

On this sad shadow LUCRECE spends her eyes,
And shapes her sorrow to the Beldames woes,
Who nothing wants to answer her but cries,
And bitter words to ban her cruell Foes.
The Painter was no God to lend her those,
And therefore LUCRECE swears he did her wrong,
To give her so much griefe, and not a tong.

Poore instrument (quoth shee) without a sound,
Ile tune thy woes with my lamenting tongue,
And drop sweet Balme in PRIAMS painted wound,
And raile on PIRRHUS that hath done him wrong;
And with my tears quench Troy that burns so long;
And with my knife scratch out the angrie eyes,
Of all the Greekes that are thine enemies.

Shew me the strumpet that began this stur,
That with my nailes her beautie I may teare:
Thy heat of lust fond PARIS did incur
This lode of wrath, that burning Troy doth beare;
Thy eye kindled the fire that burneth here,
And here in Troy for trespasse of thine eye,
The Sire, the sonne, the Dame and daughter die.

Why should the private pleasure of some one
Become the publicke plague of manie moe?
Let sinne alone committed, light alone
Uppon his head that hath transgressed so.
Let guiltlesse soules be freed from guilty woe,
For ones offence why should so many fall?
To plague a private sinne in generall.

101 92 *shadow* picture; shade of her former self 93 *Beldames* old woman's 95 *ban* curse 100 *tune* give voice to 106 *strumpet* Helen *stur* disturbance, tumult 108 *fond* infatuated, foolish 109 *lode of* load, weight of; loadstone of, magnet which attracts (?) 111 *trespasse of* offence, crime, committed by 114 *moe* more 119 *plague* punish

Lo here weeps HECUBA, here PRIAM dies,
Here manly HECTOR faints, here TROYLUS sounds,
Here friend by friend in bloudie channel lies:
And friend to friend gives unadvised wounds,
And one mans lust these manie lives confounds.
Had doting PRIAM checkt his sons desire,
TROY had bin bright with Fame, and not with fire.

Here feelingly she weeps TROYES painted woes,
For sorrow, like a heavie hanging Bell,
Once set on ringing, with his own waight goes,
Then little strength rings out the dolefull knell,
So LUCRECE set a worke, sad tales doth tell
To pencel'd pensivenes, and colour'd sorrow,
She lends them words, and she their looks doth borrow.

Shee throwes her eyes about the painting round,
And who shee finds forlorne, shee doth lament:
At last shee sees a wretched image bound,
That piteous lookes, to Phrygian sheapheards lent,
His face though full of cares, yet shew'd content,
Onward to TROY with the blunt swains he goes,
So mild that patience seem'd to scorne his woes.

In him the Painter labour'd with his skill
To hide deceipt, and give the harmlesse show
An humble gate, calme looks, eyes wayling still,
A brow unbent that seem'd to welcome wo,
Cheeks neither red, nor pale, but mingled so,
That blushing red, no guiltie instance gave,
Nor ashie pale, the feare that false hearts have.

101 121 *sounds* swounds, swoons 122 *channel* street gutter 123 *unadvised* inadvertent, unintentional 125 *doting* excessively fond, foolish 127 *feelingly* with feeling; understandingly, sympathetically 129 *on* to 131 *set a worke* started off, got going 132 *pencel'd* painted *pensivenes* sadness 136 *image* Sinon 137 *to . . . lent* drew from 139 *blunt* rude, stupid 146 *instance* sign, token

But like a constant and confirmed Devill,
He entertain'd a show, so seeming just,
And therein so ensconc't his secret evill,
That Jealousie it selfe could not mistrust,
False creeping Craft, and Perjurie should thrust
Into so bright a daie, such blackfac'd storms,
Or blot with Hell-born sin such Saint-like forms.

The well-skil'd workman this milde Image drew
For perjur'd SINON, whose inchaunting storie
The credulous old PRIAM after slew.
Whose words like wild fire burnt the shining glorie
Of rich-built ILLION, that the skies were sorie,
And little stars shot from their fixed places,
When their glas fel, wherin they view'd their faces.

This picture shee advisedly perus'd,
And chid the Painter for his wondrous skill:
Saying, some shape in SINONS was abus'd,
So faire a forme lodg'd not a mind so ill,
And still on him shee gaz'd, and gazing still,
Such signes of truth in his plaine face shee spied,
That shee concludes, the Picture was belied.

It cannot be (quoth she) that so much guile,
(Shee would have said) can lurke in such a looke:
But TARQUINS shape, came in her mind the while,
And from her tongue, can lurk, from cannot, tooke.
It cannot be, shee in that sence forsooke,
And turn'd it thus, it cannot be I find,
But such a face should beare a wicked mind.

101 149 *entertain'd a show* kept up an appearance 150 *ensconc't* concealed, buried 151 *Jealousie* suspicion, mistrust *mistrust* suspect that 158 *wild fire* a gun-powder mixture used in siege warfare 160 *stars* cp. Virgil, *Aeneid* 2.693–6 'Scarcely had the aged prince [Anchises] so spoken, when with a sudden crash came thunder on the left, and a shooting star trailing a firebrand slid from the sky through the dark and darted downwards in brilliant light' 161 *their glas* Troy's polished roofs and towers *they* the stars 162 *advisedly* deliberately, carefully 165 *lodg'd* housed 167 *plaine* honest, open 168 *belied* filled with lies

For even as subtill SINON here is painted,
So sober sad, so wearie, and so milde,
(As if with griefe or travaile he had fainted)
To me came TARQUIN armed, to beguild
With outward honestie, but yet defild
  With inward vice: as PRIAM him did cherish,
  So did I TARQUIN, so my Troy did perish.

RICHARD BARNFIELD

102 [*from* Cynthia]

SONNET. 8.

Sometimes I wish that I his pillow were,
  So might I steale a kisse, and yet not seene,
  So might I gaze upon his sleeping eine,
Although I did it with a panting feare:
But when I well consider how vaine my wish is,
  Ah foolish Bees (thinke I) that doe not sucke
  His lips for hony; but poore flowers doe plucke
Which have no sweet in them: when his sole kisses,
Are able to revive a dying soule.
  Kisse him, but sting him not, for if you doe,
  His angry voice your flying will pursue:
But when they heare his tongue, what can controule,
  Their back-returne? for then they plaine may see,
  How hony-combs from his lips dropping bee.

101 176 *subtill* treacherous, cunning 177 *sober sad* grave, serious 178 *travaile* labour, work; travelling 179 *to beguild* too concealed, disguised, with guile; to deceive

102 3 *eine* eyes 8 *sole* single; mere

103 [*from* Cynthia]

SONNET. 11.

Sighing, and sadly sitting by my Love,
He ask't the cause of my hearts sorrowing,
Conjuring me by heavens eternall King
To tell the cause which me so much did move.
Compell'd: (quoth I) to thee I will confesse,
Love is the cause; and onely love it is
That doth deprive me of my heavenly blisse.
Love is the paine that doth my heart oppresse.
And what is she (quoth he) whom thou do'st love?
Looke in this glasse (quoth I) there shalt thou see
The perfect forme of my fælicitie.
When, thinking that it would strange Magique prove,
He open'd it: and taking off the cover,
He straight perceav'd himselfe to be my Lover.

WILLIAM SHAKESPEARE

104 [*from* Sonnets]

19

Devouring time blunt thou the Lyons pawes,
And make the earth devoure her owne sweet brood,
Plucke the keene teeth from the fierce Tygers yawes,
And burne the long liv'd Phænix in her blood,
Make glad and sorry seasons as thou fleet'st,
And do what ere thou wilt swift-footed time
To the wide world and all her fading sweets:
But I forbid thee one most hainous crime,

103 12 *prove* show

104 3 *yawes* jaws 7 *sweets* fine, lovely things

O carve not with thy howers my loves faire brow,
Nor draw noe lines there with thine antique pen,
Him in thy course untainted doe allow,
For beauties patterne to succeding men.
Yet doe thy worst ould Time; dispight thy wrong,
My love shall in my verse ever live young.

105 [*from* Sonnets]

20

A womans face with natures owne hand painted,
Haste thou the Master Mistris of my passion,
A womans gentle hart but not acquainted
With shifting change as is false womens fashion,
An eye more bright then theirs, lesse false in rowling:
Gilding the object where-upon it gazeth,
A man in hew all *Hews* in his controwling,
Which steales mens eyes and womens soules amaseth.
And for a woman wert thou first created,
Till nature as she wrought thee fell a dotinge,
And by addition me of thee defeated,
By adding one thing to my purpose nothing.
But since she prickt thee out for womens pleasure,
Mine be thy love and thy loves use their treasure.

104 10 *antique* antic, fantastic; ancient

105 1 *natures ... painted* coloured by Nature herself; coloured naturally 2 *Haste* hast 5 *rowling* rolling, roving 7 *hew* hue, form, appearance, colouring 10 *a dotinge* became besotted; went mildly mad 11 *addition* honouring you; adding something (a penis) *defeated* deprived 13 *prickt* chose; gave you a penis

106 [*from* Sonnets]

29

When in disgrace with Fortune and mens eyes,
I all alone beweepe my out-cast state,
And trouble deafe heaven with my bootlesse cries,
And looke upon my selfe and curse my fate.
Wishing me like to one more rich in hope,
Featur'd like him, like him with friends possest,
Desiring this mans art, and that mans skope,
With what I most injoy contented least,
Yet in these thoughts my selfe almost despising,
Haplye I thinke on thee, and then my state,
(Like to the Larke at breake of daye arising)
From sullen earth sings himns at Heavens gate,
  For thy sweet love remembred such welth brings,
  That then I skorne to change my state with Kings.

107 [*from* Sonnets]

35

No more bee greev'd at that which thou hast done,
Roses have thornes, and silver fountaines mud,
Cloudes and eclipses staine both Moone and Sunne,
And loathsome canker lives in sweetest bud.
All men make faults, and even I in this,
Authorizing thy trespas with compare,
My selfe corrupting salving thy amisse,
Excusing thy sins more then thy sins are:

106 3 *bootlesse* unavailing, useless 6 *Featur'd* formed, shaped, handsome *possest* endowed 7 *skope** extent of view, outlook; liberties, circumstances 8 *injoy* possess; enjoy 10 *Haplye* by chance; happily 12 *sullen* dark, dull

107 3 *staine* make dim 4 *canker* worm 6 *compare* comparison 7 *salving* softening, palliating as with an ointment *amisse* error, fault, misdeed

For to thy sensuall fault I bring in sence,
Thy adverse party is thy Advocate,
And gainst my selfe a lawfull plea commence,
Such civill war is in my love and hate,
That I an accessary needs must be,
To that sweet theefe which sourely robs from me.

108 [*from* Sonnets]

36

Let me confesse that we two must be twaine,
Although our undevided loves are one:
So shall those blots that do with me remaine,
Without thy helpe, by me be borne alone.
In our two loves there is but one respect,
Though in our lives a seperable spight,
Which though it alter not loves sole effect,
Yet doth it steale sweet houres from loves delight,
I may not ever-more acknowledge thee,
Least my bewailed guilt should do thee shame,
Nor thou with publike kindnesse honour me,
Unlesse thou take that honour from thy name:
But doe not so, I love thee in such sort,
As thou being mine, mine is thy good report.

107 9 *sence* mind, reasoning power 14 *sourely* cruelly, hurtfully

108 3 *blots* stains 5 *respect* regard, consideration, care 6 *seperable** causing separation 7 *effect* accomplishment; property 14 *report* repute, reputation

109 [*from* Sonnets]

55

Not marble, nor the guilded monuments
Of Princes shall out-live this powrefull rime,
But you shall shine more bright in these contents
Then unswept stone, besmeer'd with sluttish time.
When wastefull warre shall *Statues* over-turne,
And broiles roote out the worke of masonry,
Nor *Mars* his sword, nor warres quick fire shall burne
The living record of your memory.
Gainst death, and all oblivious enmity
Shall you pace forth, your praise shall stil finde roome,
Even in the eyes of all posterity
That weare this world out to the ending doome.
So til the judgement that your selfe arise,
You live in this, and dwell in lovers eies.

110 [*from* Sonnets]

56

Sweet love renew thy force, be it not said
Thy edge should blunter be then apetite,
Which but too daie by feeding is alaied,
To morrow sharpned in his former might.
So love be thou, although too daie thou fill
Thy hungrie eies, even till they winck with fulnesse,
Too morrow see againe, and doe not kill
The spirit of Love, with a perpetual dulnesse:

109 2 *out-live** outlast 4 *sluttish* dirty, unchaste, immoral 6 *broiles* tumults, battles 7 *quick* living 13 *that* when

110 6 *winck* close 8 *dulnesse* inactivity; bluntness

Let this sad *Intrim* like the Ocean be
Which parts the shore, where two contracted new,
Come daily to the banckes, that when they see
Returne of love, more blest may be the view.
As cal it Winter, which being ful of care,
Makes Sommers welcome, thrice more wish'd, more rare.

111 [*from* Sonnets]

66

Tyr'd with all these for restfull death I cry,
As to behold desert a begger borne,
And needie Nothing trimd in jollitie,
And purest faith unhappily forsworne,
And gilded honor shamefully misplast,
And maiden vertue rudely strumpeted,
And right perfection wrongfully disgrac'd,
And strength by limping sway disabled,
And arte made tung-tide by authoritie,
And Folly (Doctor-like) controuling skill,
And simple-Truth miscalde Simplicitie,
And captive-good attending Captaine ill.
Tyr'd with all these, from these would I be gone,
Save that to dye, I leave my love alone.

110 9 *Intrim* interim, interlude

111 2 *As* as for example *desert* worth, merit 3 *trimd* dressed, got up *jollitie* finery, fancy clothes 6 *strumpeted* prostituted 7 *disgrac'd* robbed of its grace 8 *sway* rule 9 *authoritie* tradition, precedent; the ruling powers 10 *Doctor-like* like a pompous scholar *controuling* directing, overpowering, refuting 11 *miscalde* wrongly called, slandered as 12 *attending* waiting on; listening to

112 [*from* Sonnets]

74

But be contented when that fell arest,
With out all bayle shall carry me away,
My life hath in this line some interest,
Which for memoriall still with thee shall stay.
When thou revewest this, thou doest revew,
The very part was consecrate to thee,
The earth can have but earth, which is his due,
My spirit is thine the better part of me,
So then thou hast but lost the dregs of life,
The pray of wormes, my body being dead,
The coward conquest of a wretches knife,
To base of thee to be remembred,
  The worth of that, is that which it containes,
  And that is this, and this with thee remaines.

113 [*from* Sonnets]

94

They that have powre to hurt, and will doe none,
That doe not do the thing, they most do showe,
Who moving others, are themselves as stone,
Unmooved, could, and to temptation slow:
They rightly do inherrit heavens graces,
And husband natures ritches from expence,
They are the Lords and owners of their faces,
Others, but stewards of their excellence:

112 1 *fell* fierce, cruel, deadly *arest* seizure by legal warrant; halt, stop 3 *line* of poetry 5 *revewest . . . revew* survey, see again 10 *pray* prey 12 *To* too

113 2 *showe* appear they will do 3 *moving* exciting the feelings of 4 *could* cold 6 *husband* manage, protect *expence* spending, extravagant expenditure

The sommers flowre is to the sommer sweet,
Though to it selfe, it onely live and die,
But if that flowre with base infection meete,
The basest weed out-braves his dignity:
  For sweetest things turne sowrest by their deedes,
  Lillies that fester, smell far worse then weeds.

114 [*from* Sonnets]

121

Tis better to be vile then vile esteemed,
When not to be, receives reproach of being,
And the just pleasure lost, which is so deemed,
Not by our feeling, but by others seeing.
For why should others false adulterat eyes
Give salutation to my sportive blood?
Or on my frailties why are frailer spies;
Which in their wils count bad what I think good?
Noe, I am that I am, and they that levell
At my abuses, reckon up their owne,
I may be straight though they them-selves be bevel.
By their rancke thoughtes, my deedes must not be shown
  Unlesse this generall evill they maintaine,
  All men are bad and in their badnesse raigne.

113 11 *base* foul, vile 12 *basest* lowest, humblest *out-braves* defies; surpasses in fine array

114 5 *adulterat* adulterous; corrupt, impure 6 *sportive* amorous, wanton 9 *I . . . am* cp. Exodus 3:14 'And God said unto Moses, I AM THAT I AM' *levell* guess; aim 10 *abuses* offences *reckon up* count 11 *straight* honest, not bent *bevel* slanting, crooked 12 *rancke* corrupt, lustful, foul-smelling, luxuriating 14 *raigne* rule; prosper

115 [*from* Sonnets]

124

Yf my deare love were but the childe of state,
It might for fortunes basterd be unfathered,
As subject to times love, or to times hate,
Weeds among weeds, or flowers with flowers gatherd.
No it was buylded far from accident,
It suffers not in smilinge pomp, nor falls
Under the blow of thralled discontent,
Whereto th'inviting time our fashion calls:
It feares not policy that *Heriticke*,
Which workes on leases of short numbred howers,
But all alone stands hugely pollitick,
That it nor growes with heat, nor drownes with showres.
  To this I witnes call the foles of time,
  Which die for goodnes, who have liv'd for crime.

116 [*from* Sonnets]

129

Th'expence of Spirit in a waste of shame
Is lust in action, and till action, lust
Is perjurd, murdrous, blouddy full of blame,
Savage, extreame, rude, cruell, not to trust,
Injoyd no sooner but dispised straight,
Past reason hunted, and no sooner had
Past reason hated as a swollowed bayt,
On purpose layd to make the taker mad.

115 1 *but . . . state* only the offspring of circumstances 2 *unfathered* made fatherless, illegitimate 5 *accident* chance 8 *inviting* attractive, seductive 9 *policy* contrivance, crafty scheming 11 *pollitick* provident, prudent 13 *foles of time* followers of time, time-servers

116 1 *expence* extravagant expenditure, loss *Spirit* vital energy; semen *waste* squandering; waist 4 *rude* harsh, brutal 5 *Injoyd* enjoyed; used

Made In pursut and in possession so,
Had, having, and in quest to have, extreame,
A blisse in proofe and proud a very wo,
Before a joy proposd behind a dreame,
  All this the world well knowes yet none knowes well,
  To shun the heaven that leads men to this hell.

117 [*from* Sonnets]

135

Who ever hath her wish, thou hast thy *Will*,
And *Will* too boote, and *Will* in over-plus,
More then enough am I that vexe thee still,
To thy sweet will making addition thus.
Wilt thou whose will is large and spatious,
Not once vouchsafe to hide my will in thine,
Shall will in others seeme right gracious,
And in my will no faire acceptance shine:
The sea all water, yet receives raine still,
And in aboundance addeth to his store,
So thou beeing rich in *Will* adde to thy *Will*,
One will of mine to make thy large *Will* more.
  Let no unkinde, no faire beseechers kill,
  Thinke all but one, and me in that one *Will*.

116 9 *Made* usually modernized to 'mad' 11 *in proofe* when experienced *proud* (usually modernized to 'proved', cp. no. 129 l. 20); erect

117 1 *Will* this and the following sonnet in the sequence (136) play on various senses of the word 'will'. These include: what is willed, desired; lust, desire; the penis; the vagina; and the poet's own name 2 *too boote* in addition, into the bargain 3 *vexe* irritate 5 *large* big, generous, lavish, unrestrained 8 *acceptance* reception, admittance 13 *no* . . . *no* none; the word of denial, 'no'

118 [*from* Sonnets]

138

When my love sweares that she is made of truth,
I do beleeve her though I know she lyes,
That she might thinke me some untuterd youth,
Unlearned in the worlds false subtilties.
Thus vainely thinking that she thinkes me young,
Although she knowes my dayes are past the best,
Simply I credit her false speaking tongue,
On both sides thus is simple truth supprest:
But wherefore sayes she not she is unjust?
And wherefore say not I that I am old?
O loves best habit is in seeming trust,
And age in love, loves not to have yeares told.
Therefore I lye with her, and she with me,
And in our faults by lyes we flattered be.

119 [*from* Sonnets]

144

Two loves I have of comfort and dispaire,
Which like two spirits do sugiest me still,
The better angell is a man right faire:
The worser spirit a woman collour'd il.
To win me soone to hell my femall evill,
Tempteth my better angel from my side,
And would corrupt my saint to be a divel:
Wooing his purity with her fowle pride.

118 2 *lyes* tells untruths; fornicates 9 *unjust* unfaithful; dishonest 11 *habit* clothes; way of behaving *seeming* apparent; handsome; appearing to 12 *told* counted; revealed 14 *flattered* falsely praised; caressed, pampered

119 2 *sugiest* suggest, incite, tempt, lead astray 4 *collour'd il* of dark colouring; unpleasantly painted

And whether that my angel be turn'd finde,
Suspect I may, yet not directly tell,
But being both from me both to each friend,
I gesse one angel in an others hel.
   Yet this shal I nere know but live in doubt,
   Till my bad angel fire my good one out.

Robert Sidney, Earl of Leicester

120 Sonnet 21

Alas why say yow I ame ritch? when I
doe begg, and begging scant a lyfe sustaine:
why doe yow say that I ame well? when paine
lowder then on the rack, in mee doth cry.

O let mee know myself! my poverty
with whitening rotten walls, no stay doth gaine.
and these small hopes yow tell, keep but in vaine
lyfe with hott drincks, in one layd down to dy.

If in my face, my wants and sores, so greate
doe not appeer: A canker (thinck) unseen
the apples hart thogh sownd without doth eate.

Or if on mee from my fayre heaven are seen,
some scattred beames: Know sutch heate gives theyr light
as frosty mornings Sun: as Moonshyne night.

119 9 *finde* usually modernized to 'fiend' 12 *hel* misery; pudenda 14 *fire* drive with fire, smoke; sexually infect

121 Sonnet 25

Yow that take pleasure in yowr cruelty,
and place yowr health in my infections:
yow that add sorrowes to afflictions
and thinck yowr wealth shines in my poverty

Since that there is all inequality
between my wants and yowr perfections
between yowr scorns and my affections
between my bands and yowr soveranity

O love your self: bee yow yowrself yowr care:
Joy in those acts, in which yowr making stood:
Fayre, lovely, good: of these made, these yow are:
pity is fayre, grace lovely, mercy good.

And when Sunn like, yow in yowrself yow show
Let mee the point bee, about which yow goe.

122 Sonnet 31

Forsaken woods, trees with sharpe storms opprest
whose leaves once hidd, the sun, now strew the grownd
once bred delight, now scorn, late usde to sownd
of sweetest birds, now of hoars crowes the nest

Gardens which once in thowsand coulers drest
shewed natures pryde: now in dead sticks abownd
in whome prowd summers treasure late was fownd
now but the rags, of winters torn coate rest

Medows whose sydes, late fayre brookes kist now slyme
embraced holds: feelds whose youth green and brave
promist long lyfe, now frosts lay in the grave

Say all and I with them: what doth not tyme!
But they whoe knew tyme, tyme will finde again
I that fayre tymes lost, on tyme call in vaine

122 4 *hoars* hoarse

123 Songe 17

The Sunn is set, and masked night
vailes heavens fayer eyes.
Ah what trust is there to a light
that so swift flyes.

A new world doth his flames enjoy
New hartes rejoice.
In other eyes is now his joye
in other choice.

GEORGE CHAPMAN

124 [*from* Hero and Leander Sestiad 3]

New light gives new directions, Fortunes new
To fashion our indevours that ensue,
More harsh (at lest more hard) more grave and hie
Our subject runs, and our sterne *Muse* must flie,
Loves edge is taken off, and that light flame,
Those thoughts, joyes, longings, that before became
High unexperienst blood, and maids sharpe plights,
Must now grow staid, and censure the delights,
That being enjoyd aske judgement; now we praise,
As having parted: Evenings crowne the daies.
  And now ye wanton loves, and yong desires,
Pied vanitie, the mint of strange Attires;
Ye lisping Flatteries, and obsequious Glances,
Relentfull Musicks, and attractive Dances,
And you detested Charmes constraining love,
Shun loves stolne sports by that these Lovers prove.
  By this the Soveraigne of Heavens golden fires,
And yong *Leander*, Lord of his desires,

124 1 *New light* the light of the second day of the story 9 *praise* value, appraise
14 *Relentfull*** softening, melting 16 *prove* experience

Together from their lovers armes arose:
Leander into *Hellespontus* throwes
His *Hero*-handled bodie, whose delight
Made him disdaine each other Epethite.
And as amidst the enamourd waves he swims,
The God of gold of purpose guilt his lims,
That this word guilt, including double sence,
The double guilt of his *Incontinence*,
Might be exprest, that had no stay t'employ
The treasure which the Love-god let him joy
In his deare *Hero*, with such sacred thrift,
As had beseemd so sanctified a gift:
But like a greedie vulgar Prodigall
Would on the stock dispend, and rudely fall
Before his time, to that unblessed blessing,
Which for lusts plague doth perish with possessing.
Joy graven in sence, like snow in water wasts;
Without preserve of vertue, nothing lasts.
What man is he that with a welthie eie,
Enjoyes a beautie richer than the skie,
Through whose white skin, softer then soundest sleep,
With damaske eyes, the rubie blood doth peep,
And runs in branches through her azure vaines,
Whose mixture and first fire, his love attaines;
Whose both hands limit, both Loves deities,
And sweeten humane thoughts like Paradise;
Whose disposition silken is and kinde,
Directed with an earth-exempted minde;
Who thinks not heaven with such a love is given?
And who like earth would spend that dower of heaven,
With ranke desire to joy it all at first?
What simply kils our hunger, quencheth thirst,
Clothes but our nakednes, and makes us live?
Praise doth not any of her favours give:
But what doth plentifully minister
Beautious apparell and delicious cheere,

He cals Phœbus the God of Gold, since the vertue of his beams creates it.

124 24 side-note *vertue* power 43 *limit* hold within limits

So orderd that it still excites desire,
And still gives pleasure freenes to aspire
The palme of *Bountie*, ever moyst preserving:
To loves sweet life this is the courtly carving.
Thus *Time*, and all-states-ordering *Ceremonie*
Had banisht all offence: *Times* golden *Thie*
Upholds the flowrie bodie of the earth,
In sacred harmonie, and every birth
Of men, and actions makes legitimate,
Being usde aright; *The use of time is Fate.*
Yet did the gentle flood transfer once more,
This prize of Love home to his fathers shore;
Where he unlades himselfe of that false welth
That makes few rich; treasures composde by stelth;
And to his sister kinde *Hermione*,
(Who on the shore kneeld, praying to the sea
For his returne) he all Loves goods did show
In *Hero* seasde for him, in him for *Hero*.
His most kinde sister all his secrets knew,
And to her singing like a shower he flew,
Sprinkling the earth, that to their tombs tooke in
Streames dead for love, to leave his ivorie skin,
Which yet a snowie fome did leave above,
As soule to the dead water that did love;
And from thence did the first white Roses spring,
(For love is sweet and faire in every thing)
And all the sweetned shore as he did goe,
Was crownd with odrous roses white as snow.
Love-blest *Leander* was with love so filled,
That love to all that toucht him he instilled.
And as the colours of all things we see,
To our sights powers communicated bee:
So to all objects that in compasse came
Of any sence he had; his sences flame

124 57 *moyst* fruitful 58 *carving* covering, adornment 60 *Times . . . Thie* Pythagoras's golden thigh is made to represent the harmony of musical composition, hence the order or harmony of creation 69 Hermione is Chapman's invention 72 *seasde* seized, settled

Flowd from his parts, with force so virtuall,
It fir'd with sence things meere insensuall.
   Now (with warme baths and odours comforted)
When he lay downe he kindly kist his bed,
As consecrating it to *Heros* right,
And vowd thereafter that what ever sight
Put him in minde of *Hero*, or her blisse,
Should be her Altar to prefer a kisse.
   Then laid he forth his late inriched armes,
In whose white circle Love writ all his charmes,
And made his characters sweet *Heros* lims,
When on his breasts warme sea she sideling swims.
And as those armes (held up in circle) met,
He said: see sister *Heros* Carquenet,
Which she had rather weare about her neck,
Then all the jewels that doth *Juno* deck.
   But as he shooke with passionate desire,
To put in flame his other secret fire,
A musick so divine did pierce his eare,
As never yet his ravisht sence did heare:
When suddenly a light of twentie hews
Brake through the roofe, and like the Rainbow views
Amazd *Leander*; in whose beames came downe
The Goddesse *Ceremonie*, with a Crowne
Of all the stars, and heaven with her descended,
Her flaming haire to her bright feete extended,
By which hung all the bench of Deities;
And in a chaine, compact of eares and eies,
She led Religion; all her bodie was
Cleere and transparent as the purest glasse:
For she was all presented to the sence;
Devotion, Order, State, and Reverence,
Her shadowes were; Societie, Memorie;
All which her sight made live; her absence die.

124 89 *virtuall* powerful 90 *insensuall* not in *OED* 96 *prefer* proffer, offer 99 *characters* letters 102 *Carquenet* carcanet, necklace 112 *Goddesse Ceremonie* Chapman's invention

A rich disparent Pentackle she weares,
Drawne full of circles and strange characters:
Her face was changeable to everie eie;
One way lookt ill, another graciouslie;
Which while men viewd, they cheerfull were and holy:
But looking off, vicious, and melancholy:
The snakie paths to each observed law,
Did *Policie* in her broad bosome draw:
One hand a Mathematique Christall swayes,
Which gathering in one line a thousand rayes
From her bright eyes, *Confusion* burnes to death,
And all estates of men distinguisheth.
By it *Morallitie* and *Comelinesse*,
Themselves in all their sightly figures dresse.
Her other hand a lawrell rod applies,
To beate back *Barbarisme*, and *Avarice*,
That followd eating earth, and excrement
And humane lims; and would make proud ascent
To seates of Gods, were *Ceremonie* slaine;
The *Howrs* and *Graces* bore her glorious traine,
And all the sweetes of our societie
Were Spherde, and treasurde in her bountious eie.
Thus she appeard, and sharply did reprove
Leanders bluntnes in his violent love;
Tolde him how poore was substance without rites,
Like bils unsignd, desires without delites;
Like meates unseasond; like ranke corne that growes
On Cottages, that none or reapes or sowes:
Not being with civill forms confirm'd and bounded,
For humane dignities and comforts founded:
But loose and secret all their glories hide,
Feare fils the chamber, darknes decks the Bride.
She vanisht, leaving pierst *Leanders* hart
With sence of his unceremonious part,

124 123 *disparent*** diverse, of various appearance *Pentackle* pentangle 131 *Mathematique* prismatic 144 *Spherde*** enclosed as if in a sphere 156 *unceremonious**

In which with plaine neglect of Nuptiall rites,
He close and flatly fell to his delites:
And instantly he vowd to celebrate
All rites pertaining to his maried state.

John Marston

125 [*from* The Metamorphosis of Pigmalions Image]

1.

Pigmalion, whose hie love-hating minde
Disdain'd to yeeld servile affection,
Or amorous sute to any woman-kinde,
Knowing their wants, and mens perfection.
Yet Love at length forc'd him to know his fate,
And love the shade, whose substance he did hate.

2.

For having wrought in purest Ivorie,
So faire an Image of a Womans feature,
That never yet proudest mortalitie
Could show so rare and beautious a creature.
(Unlesse my Mistres all-excelling face,
Which gives to beautie, beauties onely grace.)

3.

Hee was amazed at the wondrous rarenesse
Of his owne workmanships perfection.
He thought that Nature nere produc'd such fairenes
In which all beauties have their mantion.
And thus admiring, was enamored
On that fayre Image himselfe portraied.

124 158 *close* secretly *flatly* without ceremony

125 8 *feature* build, shape of body 16 *mantion* mansion, dwelling-place

4.

And naked as it stood before his eyes,
Imperious Love declares his Deitie.
O what alluring beauties he descries
In each part of his faire imagery!
Her nakednes, each beauteous shape containes.
All beautie in her nakednes remaines.

5.

He thought he saw the blood run through the vaine
And leape, and swell with all alluring meanes:
Then feares he is deceiv'd, and then againe,
He thinks he see'th the brightnes of the beames
Which shoote from out the fairenes of her eye:
At which he stands as in an extasie.

6.

Her Amber-coloured, her shining haire,
Makes him protest, the Sunne hath spread her head
With golden beames, to make her farre more faire.
But when her cheeks his amorous thoughts have fed,
Then he exclaimes, such redde and so pure white,
Did never blesse the eye of mortall sight.

7.

Then view's her lips, no lips did seeme so faire
In his conceit, through which he thinks doth flie
So sweet a breath, that doth perfume the ayre.
Then next her dimpled chin he doth discry,
And views, and wonders, and yet view's her still.
"Loves eyes in viewing never have their fill.

8.

Her breasts, like polisht Ivory appeare,
Whose modest mount, doe blesse admiring eye,
And makes him wish for such a Pillowbeare.
Thus fond *Pigmalion* striveth to discry
Each beauteous part, not letting over-slip
One parcell of his curious workmanship.

125 22 *imagery* workmanship, image, form 42 the line is intended to be taken as a sententia 44 *mount* mounting, elevation 45 *Pillowbeare* pillowcase

9.

Untill his eye discended so farre downe
That it discried Loves pavillion:
Where *Cupid* doth enjoy his onely crowne,
And *Venus* hath her chiefest mantion:
 There would he winke, and winking looke againe,
 Both eies and thoughts would gladly there remaine.

10.

Who ever saw the subtile Citty-dame
In sacred church, when her pure thoughts shold pray,
Peire through her fingers, so to hide her shame,
When that her eye, her mind would faine bewray.
 So would he view, and winke, and view againe,
 A chaster thought could not his eyes retaine.

11.

He wondred that she blusht not when his eye
Saluted those same parts of secrecie:
Conceiting not it was imagerie
That kindly yeelded that large libertie.
 O that my Mistres were an Image too,
 That I might blameles her perfections view.

12.

But when the faire proportion of her thigh
Began appeare. O *Ovid* would he cry,
Did ere *Corinna* show such Ivorie
When she appear'd in *Venus* livorie?
 And thus enamour'd, dotes on his owne Art
 Which he did work, to work his pleasing smart.

125 53 *winke* close his eyes 55 *Citty-dame*★ 63 *Conceiting* conceiving, thinking 64 *kindly* willingly, generously

THOMAS DELONEY

126 [Long have I lov'd this bonny Lasse]

Man. Long have I lov'd this bonny Lasse,
 yet durst not shew the same.
Wom. Therein you prov'd your selfe an Asse,
Man. I was the more too blame.
 Yet still will I remaine to thee,
 Trang dilly do, trang dilly,
 Thy friend and lover secretly.
Wom. Thou art my owne sweet bully.

Man. But when shall I enjoy thee,
 delight of thy faire love?
Wom. Even when thou seest that fortune doth
 all maner lets remove.
Man. O, I will fold thee in my armes,
 Trang dilly do, trang dilly,
 And keepe thee so from sodaine harmes.
Wom. Thou art my owne sweet bully.

Wom. My husband he is gone from home,
 you know it very well.
Man. But when will he returne againe?
Wom. In troth I cannot tell:
 If long he keepe him out of sight,
 Trang dilly do, trang dilly,
 Be sure thou shalt have thy delight.
Man. Thou art my bonny lassy.

126 8 *bully* sweetheart, darling 12 *lets* obstacles, hindrances

ANONYMOUS

127 [*from* The wanton Wife of Bath]

In *Bath* a wanton wife did dwell
  as *Chaucer* he doth write,
Who did in pleasure spend her days
  in many a fond delight.

Upon a time sore sick she was,
  and at the length did dye:
Her soul at last at Heavens gate,
  did knock most mightily.

Then *Adam* came unto the gate,
  who knocketh there, quoth he,
I am the wife of *Bath* she said,
  and fain would come to thee.

Thou art a sinner *Adam* said,
  and here no place shall have:
Alas for you, good sir she said,
  now gip you doting Knave.

I will come in, in spight, she said,
  of all such churles as thee:
Thou wast the causer of our woe,
  our pain and misery.

And first broke Gods Commandements,
  in pleasure of thy wife:
When *Adam* heard her tell this tale,
  he ran away for life....

With thy two Daughters thou didst lye,
  on them two Bastards got:
And thus most tauntingly she chaft
  against poor silly *Lot*.

127 16 *gip* get out, get along with you 25 *thy* Lot, see Genesis 19

Who knocketh here, quoth *Judith* then,
with such shrill sounding notes?
Alas fine Minks, you cannot hear,
quoth she, for cutting throats.

Good Lord how *Judith* blusht for shame,
when she heard her say so:
King *David* hearing of the same,
he to the gate did go....

Then up starts *Peter* at the last,
and to the gate he hies:
Fond fool, quoth he, knock not so fast,
thou weariest Christ with cries.

Peter, said she, content thy self
for mercy may be won,
I never did deny my Christ
as thou thy self hath done.

When as our Saviour Christ heard this,
with Heavenly Angels bright,
He comes unto this sinful soul,
who trembled at his sight.

Of him for mercy she did crave,
quoth he, thou hast refused
My profer, grace, and mercy both,
and much my name abused.

Sore have I sinned, Oh Lord, said she,
and spent my time in vain,
But bring me like a wandring sheep,
unto thy flock again.

O Lord my God, I will amend
my former wicked vice;
The thief at the poor silly words
past into Paradise.

127 29 *Judith* wife of Holofernes, whose head she cut off, according to the apocryphal Book of Judith 38 *hies* goes 43 the Apostle Peter denied Christ three times; see Matthew 26: 69–75

My Laws and my Commandements
  saith Christ, were known to thee;
But of the same in any wise
  not yet one word did ye.

I grant the same O Lord quoth she
  most lewdly did I live,
But yet the loving Father did
  his Prodigal Son forgive.

And I forgive thy soul, he said,
  through thy repenting cry;
Come therefore enter into my joys,
  I will thee not deny.

[JOHN DOWLAND]

128 [Fine knacks for ladies, cheape choise brave and new]

Fine knacks for ladies, cheape choise brave and new,
Good penniworths but mony cannot move,
I keepe a faier but for the faier to view
A begger may bee liberall of love,
Though all my wares bee trash the hart is true,
            The hart is true,
            The hart is true.

Great gifts are guiles and looke for gifts againe,
My trifles come, as treasures from my minde,
It is a precious Jewell to bee plaine,
Sometimes in shell th'orienst pearles we finde,
Of others take a sheafe, of mee a graine,
            Of mee a graine,
            Of mee a graine.

127 68 *Prodigal Son* see Luke 15: 11–32

128 1 *knacks* trinkets, toys 5 *trash* worthless stuff, dross 11 *orienst* most precious, brilliant

Within this packe pinnes points laces and gloves,
And divers toies fitting a country faier,
But in my hart where duety serves and loves,
Turtels and twins, courts brood, a heavenly paier,
Happy the hart that thincks of no removes,
Of no removes,
Of no removes.

THOMAS CAMPION

129 [Followe thy faire sunne unhappy shaddowe]

Followe thy faire sunne unhappy shaddowe,
Though thou be blacke as night
And she made all of light,
Yet follow thy faire sunne unhappie shaddowe.

Follow her whose light thy light depriveth,
Though here thou liv'st disgrac't,
And she in heaven is plac't,
Yet follow her whose light the world reviveth.

Follow those pure beames whose beautie burneth,
That so have scorched thee,
As thou still blacke must bee,
Til her kind beames thy black to brightnes turneth.

Follow her while yet her glorie shineth,
There comes a luckles night,
That will dim all her light,
And this the black unhappie shade devineth.

128 18 *paier* Gemini, the heavenly twins, Castor and Pollux 19 *removes* changes, shiftings

Follow still since so thy fates ordained,
The Sunne must have his shade,
Till both at once doe fade,
The Sun still prov'd the shadow still disdained.

130 [Rose-cheekt *Lawra* come]

Rose-cheekt *Lawra* come
Sing thou smoothly with thy beawties
Silent musick, either other
Sweetely gracing.
Lovely formes do flowe
From concent devinely framed,
Heav'n is musick, and thy beawties
Birth is heavenly.
These dull notes we sing
Discords neede for helps to grace them,
Only beawty purely loving
Knowes no discord:
But still mooves delight
Like cleare springs renu'd by flowing,
Ever perfet, ever in them-
selves eternall.

131 [There is a Garden in her face]

1 There is a Garden in her face,
Where Roses and white Lillies grow;
A heav'nly paradice is that place,
Wherein all pleasant fruits doe flow.
There Cherries grow which none may buy,
Till Cherry ripe themselves doe cry.

129 20 *prov'd* approved, perhaps with a pun on 'proud', cp. no. 116 l. 11

130 6 *concent* harmony, concord of voices

131 6 *Cherry ripe* a street-seller's cry

2 Those Cherries fayrely doe enclose
Of Orient Pearle a double row,
Which when her lovely laughter showes,
They looke like Rose-buds fill'd with snow.
Yet them nor Peere, nor Prince can buy,
Till Cherry ripe themselves doe cry.

3 Her Eyes like Angels watch them still;
Her Browes like bended bowes doe stand,
Threatning with piercing frownes to kill
All that attempt with eye or hand
Those sacred Cherries to come nigh,
Till Cherry ripe themselves doe cry.

JOHN DONNE

132 His Picture

Here take my Picture, though I bid farewell;
Thine, in my heart, where my soule dwels, shall dwell.
'Tis like me now, but I dead, 'twill be more
When wee are shadowes both, then 'twas before.
When weather-beaten I come backe; my hand,
Perhaps with rude oares torne, or Sun beams tann'd,
My face and brest of haireclоth, and my head
With cares rash sodaine hoarinesse o'rspread,
My body'a sack of bones, broken within,
And powders blew staines scatter'd on my skinne;
If rivall fooles taxe thee to'have lov'd a man,
So foule, and course, as, Oh, I may seeme than,
This shall say what I was: and thou shalt say,
Doe his hurts reach mee? doth my worth decay?
Or doe they reach his judging minde, that hee
Should now love lesse, what hee did love to see?

132 4 *shadowes* ghosts; portraits 7 *haireclоth* coarse fabric 14 *reach* affect

That which in him was faire and delicate,
Was but the milke, which in loves childish state
Did nurse it: who now is growne strong enough
To feed on that, which to disus'd tasts seemes tough.

133 The Sunne Rising

Busie old foole, unruly Sunne,
Why dost thou thus,
Through windowes, and through curtaines call on us?
Must to thy motions lovers seasons run?
Sawcy pedantique wretch, goe chide
Late schoole boyes, and sowre prentices,
Goe tell Court-huntsmen, that the King will ride,
Call countrey ants to harvest offices;
Love, all alike, no season knowes, nor clyme,
Nor houres, dayes, moneths, which are the rags of time.

Thy beames, so reverend, and strong
Why shouldst thou thinke?
I could eclipse and cloud them with a winke,
But that I would not lose her sight so long:
If her eyes have not blinded thine,
Looke, and to morrow late, tell mee,
Whether both the'India's of spice and Myne
Be where thou leftst them, or lie here with mee.
Aske for those Kings whom thou saw'st yesterday,
And thou shalt heare, All here in one bed lay.

She'is all States, and all Princes, I,
Nothing else is.
Princes doe but play us; compar'd to this,
All honor's mimique; All wealth alchimie;

132 20 *disus'd* unaccustomed

133 8 *countrey . . . offices* labouring farmers to their tasks of harvesting 10 *rags* worthless remnants 17 *Myne* the West Indies were a source of gold 24 *mimique* imitative, not real *alchimie* glittering dross

Thou sunne art halfe as happy'as wee,
In that the world's contracted thus.
Thine age askes ease, and since thy duties bee
To warme the world, that's done in warming us.
Shine here to us, and thou art every where;
This bed thy center is, these walls, thy spheare.

134 The Canonization

For Godsake hold your tongue, and let me love,
Or chide my palsie, or my gout,
My five gray haires, or ruin'd fortune flout,
With wealth your state, your minde with Arts improve,
Take you a course, get you a place,
Observe his honour, or his grace,
Or the Kings reall, or his stamped face
Contemplate, what you will, approve,
So you will let me love.

Alas, alas, who's injur'd by my love?
What merchants ships have my sighs drown'd?
Who saies my teares have overflow'd his ground?
When did my colds a forward spring remove?
When did the heats which my veines fill
Adde one more, to the plaguie Bill?
Soldiers finde warres, and Lawyers finde out still
Litigious men, which quarrels move,
Though she and I do love.

Call us what you will, wee are made such by love;
Call her one, mee another flye,
We'are Tapers too, and at our owne cost die,
And wee in us finde the'Eagle and the dove;

133 25 there is only one sun so it is half as happy as two lovers 30 *center* earth *spheare* orbit

134 5 *course* career *place* position at court 6 *honour* ... *grace* aristocratic and religious titles 7 *stamped* on a coin 8 *approve* try out; commend 15 *plaguie Bill* list of those dead from the plague 20 *flye* moth 22 *Eagle* ... *dove* emblems of strength and gentleness, the masculine and the feminine

The Phœnix ridle hath more wit
By us, we two being one, are it.
So, to one neutrall thing both sexes fit,
Wee dye and rise the same, and prove
Mysterious by this love.

Wee can dye by it, if not live by love,
And if unfit for tombes and hearse
Our legend bee, it will be fit for verse;
And if no peece of Chronicle wee prove,
We'll build in sonnets pretty roomes;
As well a well wrought urne becomes
The greatest ashes, as halfe-acre tombes,
And by these hymnes, all shall approve
Us *Canoniz'd* for Love.

And thus invoke us; You whom reverend love
Made one anothers hermitage;
You, to whom love was peace, that now is rage;
Who did the whole worlds soule contract, and drove
Into the glasses of your eyes
So made such mirrors, and such spies,
That they did all to you epitomize,
Countries, Townes, Courts: Beg from above
A patterne of your love.

135 Loves growth

I scarce beleeve my love to be so pure
As I had thought it was,
Because it doth endure
Vicissitude, and season, as the grasse;
Me thinkes I lyed all winter, when I swore,
My love was infinite, if spring make'it more.

134 23 *hath more wit* is cleverer; makes more sense 26–7 *prove/Mysterious* pass beyond human understanding 31 if as timeless lovers we are no part of history 32 *sonnets* love-poems *roomes* stanzas (cp. Italian 'stanza' = 'room') 33 *well wrought* well-made 43 *epitomize*** contain the sum of

135 1 *pure* simple, unchangeable

But if this medicine, love, which cures all sorrow
With more, not onely bee no quintessence,
But mixt of all stuffes, paining soule, or sense,
And of the Sunne his working vigour borrow,
Love's not so pure, and abstract, as they use
To say, which have no Mistresse but their Muse,
But as all else, being elemented too,
Love sometimes would contemplate, sometimes do.

And yet no greater, but more eminent,
Love by the spring is growne;
As, in the firmament,
Starres by the Sunne are not inlarg'd, but showne,
Gentle love deeds, as blossomes on a bough,
From loves awakened root do bud out now.
If, as in water stir'd more circles bee
Produc'd by one, love such additions take,
Those like so many spheares, but one heaven make,
For, they are all concentrique unto thee,
And though each spring doe adde to love new heate,
As princes doe in times of action get
New taxes, and remit them not in peace,
No winter shall abate the springs encrease.

136 A Valediction of weeping

Let me powre forth
My teares before thy face, whil'st I stay here,
For thy face coines them, and thy stampe they beare,
And by this Mintage they are something worth,

135 8 *quintessence* pure essence, purified virtue 13 *elemented* composed of elements, mixed 15 *eminent* high, exalted 24 *concentrique unto* having a common centre about

136 4 *Mintage** making something compared to a coin; coining a word

For thus they bee
Pregnant of thee;
Fruits of much griefe they are, emblemes of more,
When a teare falls, that thou falls which it bore,
So thou and I are nothing then, when on a divers shore.
On a round ball
A workeman that hath copies by, can lay
An Europe, Afrique, and an Asia,
And quickly make that, which was nothing, *All*,
So doth each teare,
Which thee doth weare,
A globe, yea world by that impression grow,
Till thy teares mixt with mine doe overflow
This world, by waters sent from thee, my heaven dissolved so.

O more then Moone,
Draw not up seas to drowne me in thy spheare,
Weepe me not dead, in thine armes, but forbeare
To teach the sea, what it may doe too soone;
Let not the winde
Example finde,
To doe me more harme, then it purposeth;
Since thou and I sigh one anothers breath,
Who e'r sighes most, is cruellest, and hasts the others death.

137 A Valediction forbidding mourning

As virtuous men passe mildly away,
And whisper to their soules, to goe,
Whilst some of their sad friends doe say,
The breath goes now, and some say, no:

So let us melt, and make no noise,
No teare-floods, nor sigh-tempests move,
T'were prophanation of our joyes
To tell the layetie our love.

136 9 *divers* separate

137 6 *teare-floods** floods of tears

Moving of th'earth brings harmes and feares,
Men reckon what it did and meant,
But trepidation of the spheares,
Though greater farre, is innocent.

Dull sublunary lovers love
(Whose soule is sense) cannot admit
Absence, because it doth remove
Those things which elemented it.

But we by a love, so much refin'd,
That our selves know not what it is,
Inter-assured of the mind,
Care lesse, eyes, lips, and hands to misse.

Our two soules therefore, which are one,
Though I must goe, endure not yet
A breach, but an expansion,
Like gold to ayery thinnesse beate.

If they be two, they are two so
As stiffe twin compasses are two,
Thy soule the fixt foot, makes no show
To move, but doth, if the'other doe.

And though it in the center sit,
Yet when the other far doth rome,
It leanes, and hearkens after it,
And growes erect, as that comes home.

Such wilt thou be to mee, who must
Like th'other foot, obliquely runne;
Thy firmnes makes my circle just,
And makes me end, where I begunne.

137 9 *Moving . . . earth* earthquakes 11 *trepidation** the oscillating motion of the eighth or the ninth, the crystalline, sphere 13 *sublunary* beneath, and subject to, the moon 14 *sense* sensuality 19 *Inter-assured** mutually assured 26 *stiffe* firm, constant *compasses* dividers 31 *hearkens* inquires, asks 34 *obliquely* not directly 35 *just* complete, perfect

MICHAEL DRAYTON

138 [*from* Idea]

10.

To nothing fitter can I Thee compare,
Then to the Sonne of some rich Penny-father,
Who having now brought on his end with Care,
Leaves to his Sonne all he had heap'd together;
This new rich Novice, lavish of his chest,
To one Man gives, doth on another spend,
Then heere he riots, yet amongst the rest,
Haps to lend some to one true honest Friend.
Thy Gifts thou in Obscuritie doest waste,
False Friends thy kindnesse, borne but to deceive Thee;
Thy Love, that is on the unworthy plac'd,
Time hath thy Beautie, which with Age will leave thee;
  Onely that little which to Me was lent,
  I give Thee backe, when all the rest is spent.

139 [*from* Idea]

61.

Since ther's no helpe, Come let us kisse and part,
Nay, I have done: You get no more of Me,
And I am glad, yea glad with all my heart,
That thus so cleanly, I my Selfe can free,
Shake hands for ever, Cancell all our Vowes,
And when We meet at any time againe,
Be it not seene in either of our Browes,
That We one jot of former Love reteyne;

138 2 *Penny-father* miser, skinflint

Now at the last gaspe, of Loves latest Breath,
When his Pulse fayling, Passion speechlesse lies,
When Faith is kneeling by his bed of Death,
And Innocence is closing up his Eyes,
Now if thou would'st, when all have given him over,
From Death to Life, thou might'st him yet recover.

140 To His Coy Love, A Canzonet

I pray thee leave, love me no more,
Call home the Heart you gave me,
I but in vaine that Saint adore,
That can, but will not save me:
These poore halfe Kisses kill me quite;
Was ever Man thus served?
Amidst an Ocean of Delight,
For Pleasure to be sterved.

Shew me no more those Snowie Brests,
With Azure Riverets branched,
Where whilst mine Eye with Plentie feasts,
Yet is my Thirst not stanched.
O Tantalus, thy Paines ne'r tell,
By me thou art prevented;
'Tis nothing to be plagu'd in Hell,
But thus in Heaven tormented.

Clip me no more in those deare Armes,
Nor thy Life's Comfort call me;
O, these are but too pow'rfull Charmes,
And doe but more inthrall me.
But see how patient I am growne,
In all this coyle about thee;
Come nice Thing, let thy Heart alone,
I cannot live without thee.

140 Title *Canzonet* little, short song 10 *Riverets*** surface veins like small rivers 12 *stanched* staunched, assuaged 17 *Clip* embrace, hold 22 *coyle* noise, confusion

Ben Jonson

141 Why I write not of Love

Some act of *Love's* bound to reherse,
I thought to binde him, in my verse:
Which when he felt, Away (quoth hee)
Can Poets hope to fetter mee?
It is enough, they once did get
MARS, and my *Mother*, in their net:
I weare not these my wings in vaine.
With which he fled me: and againe,
Into my ri'mes could ne're be got
By any arte. Then wonder not,
That since, my numbers are so cold,
When *Love* is fled, and I grow old.

142 My Picture left in *Scotland*

I now thinke, Love is rather deafe, then blind,
For else it could not be,
That she,
Whom I adore so much, should so slight me,
And cast my love behind:
I'm sure my language to her, was as sweet,
And every close did meet
In sentence, of as subtile feet,
As hath the youngest Hee,
That sits in shadow of *Apollo's* tree.
Oh, but my conscious feares,
That flie my thoughts betweene,
Tell me that she hath seene

141 6 *Mother* Venus 11 *numbers* verses, poems

142 7 *close* cadence, conclusion of a musical phrase or movement 8 *sentence* thought

My hundreds of gray haires,
Told seven and fortie yeares,
Read so much wast, as she cannot imbrace
My mountaine belly, and my rockie face,
And all these through her eyes, have stopt her eares.

LADY MARY WROTH

143 [*from* Pamphilia to Amphilanthus]

23

When every one to pleasing pastime hies
some hunt, some hauke, some play, while some delight
in sweet discourse, and musique showes joys might
yett I my thoughts doe farr above thes prise.

The joy which I take, is that free from eyes
I sitt, and wunder att this daylike night
soe to dispose them-selves, as voyd of right;
and leave true pleasure for poore vanities;

When others hunt, my thoughts I have in chase;
if hauke, my minde att wished end doth fly,
discourse, I with my spiritt tauke, and cry
while others, musique is theyr greatest grace.

O God, say I, can thes fond pleasures move?
Or musique bee butt in deere thoughts of love?

142 16 *wast* waste; waist

143 1 *hies* goes

144 [*from* Pamphilia to Amphilanthus]

34

Take heed mine eyes, how you your lookes doe cast
least they beetray my harts most secrett thought;
bee true unto your selves for nothings bought
more deere then doubt which brings a lovers fast.

Catch you all waching eyes, ere they bee past,
or take yours fixt wher your best love hath sought
the pride of your desires; lett them bee taught
theyr faults with shame, they could noe truer last;

Then looke, and looke with joye for conquest wunn
of those that search'd your hurt in double kinde;
soe you kept safe, lett them themselves looke blinde
watch, gaze, and marke till they to madnes runn,

While you, my eyes injoye full sight of love
contented that such hapinesses move.

145 [*from* Pamphilia to Amphilanthus]

A crowne of Sonetts dedicated to Love

In this strang labourinth how shall I turne?
wayes are on all sids while the way I miss:
if to the right hand, ther, in love I burne;
lett mee goe forward, therin danger is;

If to the left, suspition hinders bliss,
lett mee turne back, shame cries I ought returne
nor fainte though crosses with my fortunes kiss;
stand still is harder, allthough sure to mourne;

145 1 *labourinth* labyrinth of love, out of which Ariadne led Theseus from the Minotaur with her 'thread' (l. 14) 7 *crosses* adversities

Thus lett mee take the right, or left hand way;
goe forward, or stand still, or back retire;
I must thes doubts indure with out allay
or help, butt traveile find for my best hire;

yett that which most my troubled sence doth move
is to leave all, and take the thread of love,

2.

Is to leave all, and take the thread of love
which line straite leads unto the soules content
wher choyce delights with pleasures wings doe move,
and idle phant'sie never roome had lent,

When chaste thoughts guide us then owr minds ar bent
to take that good which ills from us remove,
light of true love, brings fruite which none repent
butt constant lovers seeke, and wish to prove;

Love is the shining starr of blessings light;
the fervent fire of zeale, the roote of peace,
that lasting lampe fed with the oyle of right;
Image of fayth, and wombe for joyes increase.

Love is true vertu, and his ends delight,
his flames ar joyes, his bands true lovers might.

3.

His flames ar joyes, his bands true lovers might,
noe staine is ther butt pure, as purest white,
wher noe clowde can apeere to dimm his light,
nor spott defile, butt shame will soone requite,

Heere are affections, tri'de by loves just might
as gold by fire, and black desernd by white,
Error by truthe, and darknes knowne by light,
wher faith is vallwed for love to requite,

145 22 *prove* experience, try 34 *desernd* discerned 36 *vallwed* valued

Please him, and serve him, glory in his might,
and firme hee'll bee, as innosencye white,
cleere as th'ayre, warme as sunn beames, as day light,
just as truthe, constant as fate, joy'd to requite,

Then love obay, strive to observe his might,
and bee in his brave court a glorious light;

4.

And bee in his brave court a gloriouse light,
shine in the eyes of faith, and constancie,
maintaine the fires of love still burning bright
nott slightly sparkling butt light flaming bee

Never to slack till earth noe stars can see,
till sunn, and Moone doe leave to us dark night,
and secound Chaose once againe doe free
us, and the world from all devisions spite,

Till then, affections which his followers are
governe our harts, and prove his powers gaine
to taste this pleasing sting seek with all care
for hapy smarting is itt with smale paine,

such as although, itt pierce your tender hart
and burne, yett burning you will love the smart;

5.

And burne, yett burning you will love the smart,
when you shall feele the weight of true desire,
soe pleasing, as you would nott wish your part
of burden showld bee missing from that fire;

Butt faithfull and unfained heate aspire
which sinne abolisheth, and doth impart
saulves to all feares, with vertues which inspire
soules with devine love, which showes his chaste art,

145 63 *saulves* salves, healing ointments *vertues* powers

And guide hee is to joyings; open eyes
hee hath to hapines, and best can learne
us means how to deserve, this hee descries,
who blind yett doth our hidenest thought deserne.

Thus may wee gaine since living in blest love
hee may our profitt, and owr Tuter prove,

6.

Hee may owr profitt, and our Tuter prove
in whom alone wee doe this power finde,
to joine tow harts as in one frame to move;
tow bodies, butt one soule to rule the minde;

Eyes with much care to one deere object bind
eares to each others speech as if above
all els they sweet, and learned were; this kind
content of lovers wittniseth true love,

Itt doth inrich the witts, and makes you see
that in your self, which you knew nott before,
forcing you to admire such guifts showld bee
hid from your knowledg, yett in you the store;

Millions of thes adorne the throne of Love
how blest bee they then, who his favours prove

7.

How blest bee they then, who his favors prove
a lyfe wherof the birth is just desire,
breeding sweet flames which hearts invite to move
in those lov'd eyes which kindles Cupids fire,

And nurse his longings with his thoughts intire,
fixt on the heat of wishes formd by love,
yett as wher fire distroys this doth respire,
increase, and foster all delights above;

145 65 *hee* Cupid 70 *profitt* profit; prophet 73 *tow* two 81 *admire* marvel 91 *respire* breathe again; recover hope, courage, strength

Love will a painter make you, such, as you
  shall able bee to drawe your only deere
  more lively, parfett, lasting, and more true
  then rarest woorkmen, and to you more neere,

Thes be the least, then needs must all confess
Hee that shunns love doth love him self the less

8.

Hee that shunns love doth love him self the less
  and cursed hee whos spiritt nott admires
  the worth of love, wher endles blessednes
  raines, and commands, maintaind by heavnly fires

made of Vertu, join'de by truth, blowne by desires
  strengthned by worth, renued by carefullnes
  flaming in never changing thoughts, briers
  of jelousie shall heere miss wellcomnes;

nor coldly pass in the pursuites of love
  like one longe frozen in a sea of ise,
  and yett butt chastly lett your passions move
  noe thought from vertuouse love your minds intise.

Never to other ends your phant'sies place
butt wher they may returne with honors grace,

9.

Butt wher they may returne with honors grace
  wher Venus follyes can noe harbour winn
  butt chased ar as worthles of the face
  or stile of love who hath lasiviouse binn.

Oure harts ar subjects to her sunn; wher sinn
  never did dwell, nor rest one minutes space;
  what faults hee hath, in her, did still begin,
  and from her brest hee suckd his fleeting pace,

145 96 *rarest* most expert, skilled 106 *wellcomnes*** the state of being welcome
117 *sunn* son; the divine Cupid, here opposed to the sensual Venus

If lust bee counted love t'is faulcely nam'd
by wikednes a fayrer gloss to sett
upon that Vice, which els makes men asham'd
in the owne frase to warrant butt begett

This childe for love, who ought like monster borne
bee from the court of Love, and reason torne.

10.

Bee from the court of Love, and reason torne
for Love in reason now doth putt his trust,
desert, and liking are together borne
children of love, and reason parents just,

Reason adviser is, love ruler must
bee of the state which crowne hee long hath worne
yett soe as neither will in least mistrust
the government wher noe feare is of scorne,

Then reverence both theyr mights thus made butt one,
butt wantones, and all those errors shun,
which wrongers bee, impostures, and alone
maintainers of all follyes ill begunn;

Fruit of a sowre, and unwholsome ground
unprofitably pleasing, and unsound

11.

Unprofitably pleasing, and unsound
when heaven gave liberty to frayle dull earth
to bringe forth plenty that in ills abound
which ripest yett doe bring a sertaine dearth.

A timeles, and unseasonable birth
planted in ill, in wurse time springing found,
which hemlock like might feed a sick-witts mirthe
wher unruld vapors swimm in endles rounde,

145 124 *the* its *frase* phrase *warrant* guarantee as true 129 *desert* deserving 137 *impostures* cheats, frauds 139 *sowre* sour, cold and wet

Then joy wee nott in what wee ought to shun
wher shady pleasures showe, butt true borne fires
ar quite quench'd out, or by poore ashes wunn
awhile to keepe those coole, and wann desires.

O noe lett love his glory have and might
bee given to him who triumphs in his right

12.

Bee given to him who triumphs in his right
nor vading bee, butt like those blossooms fayre
which fall for good, and lose theyr coulers bright
yett dy nott, butt with fruite theyr loss repaire

soe may love make you pale with loving care
when sweet injoying shall restore that light
more cleare in beauty then wee can compare
if nott to Venus in her chosen night.

And who soe give them selves in this deere kind
thes hapinesses shall attend them still
to bee suplyd with joys, inrichd in mind
with treasures of contents, and pleasures fill,

Thus love to bee devine doth heere apeere
free from all fogs butt shining faire, and cleere;

13.

Free from all fogs butt shining faire, and cleere
wise in all good, and innosent in ill
wher holly friendship is esteemed deere
with truth in love, and justice in our will,

In love thes titles only have theyr fill
of hapy lyfe maintainer, and the meere
defence of right, the punnisher of skill,
and fraude; from whence directnes doth apeere,

145 156 *vading* fading 174 *meere* pure, unmixed

To thee then lord commander of all harts,
ruller of owr affections kinde, and just
great king of Love, my soule from fained smarts
or thought of change I offer to your trust

This crowne, my self, and all that I have more
except my hart which you beestow'd beefore;

14.

Except my hart which you beestow'd before,
and for a signe of conquest gave away
as worthles to bee kept in your choyse store
yett one more spotles with you doth nott stay.

The tribute which my hart doth truly pay
faith untouch'd is, pure thoughts discharge the score
of debts for mee, wher constancy bears sway,
and rules as Lord, unharm'd by envyes sore,

Yett other mischiefs faile nott to attend,
as enimies to you, my foes must bee;
curst jealousie doth all her forces bend
to my undoing; thus my harmes I see.

Soe though in Love I fervently doe burne,
In this strange labourinth how shall I turne?

146 [*from* Pamphilia to Amphilanthus]

2

Late in the Forest I did Cupid see
colde, wett, and crying hee had lost his way,
and beeing blind was farder like to stray:
which sight a kind compassion bred in mee,

145 185 *store* treasure

146 3 *farder* further

I kindly tooke, and dride him, while that hee
poore child complain'd hee sterved was with stay,
and pin'de for want of his accustom'd pray,
for non in that wilde place his hoste would bee,

I glad was of his finding, thinking sure
this service should my freedome still procure,
and in my armes I tooke him then unharmde,

Carrying him safe unto a Mirtle bowre
butt in the way hee made mee feele his powre,
burning my hart who had him kindly warmd.

147 [*from* The Countesse of Mountgomeries Urania]

7

Some doe, perhaps, both wrong my love, and care,
Taxing me with mistrust, and Jelousie,
From both which sinnes in love like freedome, free
I live, these slanders but new raised are.

What though from griefe, my soule I doe not spare,
When I perceive neglect's slight face on me?
While unto some the loving smiles I see,
I am not Jealous, they so well doe fare.

But doubt my selfe lest I lesse worthy am,
Or that it was but flashes, no true flame,
Dazl'd my eyes, and so my humour fed.

If this be jealousie, then doe I yeeld,
And doe confesse I thus goe arm'd to field,
For by such Jealousie my love is led.

146 6 *stay* delay, halt, waiting

ROBERT HERRICK

148 Delight in Disorder

A sweet disorder in the dresse
Kindles in cloathes a wantonnesse:
A Lawne about the shoulders thrown
Into a fine distraction:
An erring Lace, which here and there
Enthralls the Crimson Stomacher:
A Cuffe neglectfull, and thereby
Ribbands to flow confusedly:
A winning wave (deserving Note)
In the tempestuous petticote:
A carelesse shooe-string, in whose tye
I see a wilde civility:
Doe more bewitch me, then when Art
Is too precise in every part.

149 The Vision

Sitting alone (as one forsook)
Close by a Silver-shedding Brook;
With hands held up to Love, I wept;
And after sorrowes spent, I slept:
Then in a Vision I did see
A glorious forme appeare to me:
A Virgins face she had; her dresse
Was like a sprightly *Spartanesse.*

148 3 *Lawne* a piece of fine linen 6 *Stomacher* an ornamental piece of clothing worn by women under the lacing of the bodice

149 6 *forme* Venus 7–16 cp. Virgil, *Aeneid* 1.315–20, where Aeneas meets his mother, 'She had a maiden's countenance and a maiden's guise, and carried a maiden's

A silver bow with green silk strung,
Down from her comely shoulders hung:
And as she stood, the wanton Aire
Dandled the ringlets of her haire.
Her legs were such *Diana* shows,
When tuckt up she a hunting goes;
With Buskins shortned to descrie
The happy dawning of her thigh:
Which when I saw, I made accesse
To kisse that tempting nakednesse:
But she forbad me, with a wand
Of Mirtle she had in her hand:
And chiding me, said, Hence, Remove,
Herrick, thou art too coorse to love.

150 The silken Snake

For sport my *Julia* threw a Lace
Of silke and silver at my face:
Watchet the silke was; and did make
A shew, as if't'ad been a snake:
The suddenness did me affright;
But though it scar'd, it did not bite.

151 Her Bed

See'st thou that Cloud as silver cleare,
Plump, soft, and swelling every where?
Tis *Julia's* Bed, and she sleeps there.

149 (7–16 cont.) weapons, like some Spartan girl . . . Slung ready on her shoulder she carried a bow as a huntress would, and she had let her hair stream in the wind; her tunic's flowing folds were caught up and tied, and her knees were bare'

150 3 *Watchet* light blue, greenish

152 Upon *Julia's* haire fill'd with Dew

Dew sate on *Julia's* haire,
    And spangled too,
Like Leaves that laden are
    With trembling Dew:
Or glitter'd to my sight,
    As when the Beames
Have their reflected light,
    Daunc't by the Streames.

153 Upon *Sibilla*

With paste of Almonds, *Syb* her hands doth scoure;
Then gives it to the children to devoure.
In Cream she bathes her thighs (more soft then silk)
Then to the poore she freely gives the milke.

Thomas Carew

154 The Spring

Now that the winter's gone, the earth hath lost
Her snow-white robes, and now no more the frost
Candies the grasse, or castes an ycie creame
Upon the silver Lake, or Chrystall streame:
But the warme Sunne thawes the benummed Earth,
And makes it tender, gives a sacred birth

152 2 *spangled* glistened

154 3 *Candies* covers with frost 6 *sacred* swallows were sacred to the household gods of the Romans; nesting all winter, as harbingers of the spring they could be taken as emblematic of the Resurrection

To the dead Swallow; wakes in hollow tree
The drowzie Cuckow, and the Humble-Bee.
Now doe a quire of chirping Minstrels bring
In tryumph to the world, the youthfull Spring.
The Vallies, hills, and woods, in rich araye,
Welcome the comming of the long'd for May.
Now all things smile; onely my *Love* doth lowre:
Nor hath the scalding Noon-day-Sunne the power,
To melt that marble yce, which still doth hold
Her heart congeald, and makes her pittie cold.
The Oxe which lately did for shelter flie
Into the stall, doth now securely lie
In open fields; and love no more is made
By the fire side; but in the cooler shade
Amyntas now doth with his *Cloris* sleepe
Under a Sycamoure, and all things keepe
Time with the season, only shee doth carry
June in her eyes, in her heart *January*.

155 Ingratefull beauty threatned

Know *Celia*, (since thou art so proud,)
'Twas I that gave thee thy renowne:
Thou hadst, in the forgotten crowd
Of common beauties, liv'd unknowne,
Had not my verse exhal'd thy name,
And with it, ympt the wings of fame.

That killing power is none of thine,
I gave it to thy voyce, and eyes:
Thy sweets, thy graces, all are mine;
Thou art my starre, shin'st in my skies;
Then dart not from thy borrowed sphere
Lightning on him, that fixt thee there.

154 13 *Now … smile* cp. Virgil, *Eclogues* 7.55 'Omnia nunc rident', 'The whole world smiles'

155 6 *ympt* imped, grafted a falcon's wing with feathers

Tempt me with such affrights no more,
  Lest what I made, I uncreate;
Let fooles thy mystique formes adore,
  I'le know thee in thy mortall state:
Wise Poets that wrap't Truth in tales,
Knew her themselves, through all her vailes.

156 [*from* A Rapture]

I will enjoy thee now my *Celia*, come
And flye with me to Loves Elizium:
The Gyant, Honour, that keepes cowards out,
Is but a Masquer, and the servile rout
Of baser subjects onely, bend in vaine
To the vast Idoll, whilst the nobler traine
Of valiant Lovers, daily sayle betweene
The huge Collosses legs, and passe unseene
Unto the blissfull shore; be bold, and wise,
And we shall enter, the grim Swisse denies
Only tame fooles a passage, that not know
He is but forme, and onely frights in show
The duller eyes that looke from farre; draw neere,
And thou shalt scorne, what we were wont to feare.
We shall see how the stalking Pageant goes
With borrowed legs, a heavie load to those
That made, and beare him; not as we once thought
The seed of Gods, but a weake modell wrought
By greedy men, that seeke to enclose the common,
And within private armes empale free woman.
  Come then, and mounted on the wings of love
Wee'le cut the flitting ayre, and sore above
The Monsters head, and in the noblest seates
Of those blest shades, quench, and renew our heates.
There, shall the Queens of Love, and Innocence,
Beautie and Nature, banish all offence

156 5 *bend* bow, stoop 10 *Swisse* Switzerland was famous for supplying mercenaries and guards 15 *Pageant* empty show 20 *empale* fence in 22 *flitting* inconstant, unstable; fleeting, insubstantial

From our close Ivy twines, there I'le behold
Thy bared snow, and thy unbraded gold.
There, my enfranchiz'd hand, on every side
Shall o're thy naked polish'd Ivory slide.
No curtaine there, though of transparant lawne,
Shall be before thy virgin-treasure drawne;
But the rich Mine, to the enquiring eye
Expos'd, shall ready still for mintage lye,
And we will coyne young *Cupids*. There, a bed
Of Roses, and fresh Myrtles, shall be spread
Under the cooler shade of Cypresse groves:
Our pillowes, of the downe of *Venus* Doves,
Whereon our panting lims wee'le gently lay
In the faint respites of our active play;
That so our slumbers, may in dreames have leisure,
To tell the nimble fancie our past pleasure;
And so our soules that cannot be embrac'd,
Shall the embraces of our bodyes taste.

MARTIN PARKER

157 [*from* Cupid's Wrongs Vindicated]

To the tune of *Cupid's cruell torments*

Thou knowst I lov'd thee well,
  and purposd thee to have,
Thy conscience this can tell,
  thou false dissembling knave,

156 31 *lawne* fine linen 34 *mintage* minting money, coining 40 *faint* languid, tired

But when I did perceive
  thy fickle wavering mind,
Twas time to take my leave,
  and serve thee in thy kind.
    Then raile no more on love,
    Nor Cupids cruell wrong,
    For thou didst never prove
    What doth to love belong.

Let any one that will
  be judge twixt thee and mee,
Why should I love thee still,
  when thou lov'st two or three.
Dost thinke Ile stand at stake,
  to helpe at the last cast?
When all doe thee forsake,
  then I must serve at last.
    O raile no more on love,
    Nor Cupids cruell wrong,
    For thou didst never prove
    What doth to love belong.

Thou com'st to me ith morne,
  and goest to *Madge* at night,
Thy mind will quickly turne
  to which comes next in sight.
Thou'lt promise and protest
  thou wilt have none but me,
But when thou seest the rest
  those vowes forgotten bee.
    Then raile no more on love,
    Nor Cupids, etc.

Dost thinke I cannot heare
  how thou playst fast and loose,
Long *Mall* gave thee good cheere,
  both Cony Hen and Goose:

157 18 *at . . . cast* in extremity, in death, ruin 37 *Mall* Mary 38 *Cony* rabbit

Alas man I have friends
that note thy actions well,
Thou lov'st for thine owne ends,
but I thy knavery smell.
Then raile no more on love,
Nor Cupids cruell wrong,
For thou didst never prove
What doth to love belong.

I saw last Thurseday night,
when thou wentst to the Swan,
With *Kate* and *Winifrite*,
and after you came *Nan*,
I know what wine you had,
and also what was payd,
Alas poore harmelesse lad,
wilt thou dye for a Mayd!
Fye raile no more on love,
Nor Cupids cruell wrong,
For thou didst never prove
What does to love belong.

I cannot choose but smile
to thinke how cunningly
Thou wouldst the world beguile
with foule hypocrisy:
For I the wrong sustaine,
and thou from griefe art free,
Yet still thou dost complaine
that I am false to thee.
Fye never raile on love,
Nor Cupids cruell wrong,
For thou didst never prove
What doth to love belong.

To either man or Mayd
For censure Ile appeale,
Which of us may be sayd
disloyally to deale;

Did ever I seeme nice
  till I was told for truth,
More oft then once or twice,
  thou was't a faithlesse youth.
    Fye doe not raile, etc.

Thou mak'st the world beleeve,
  thou for my love dost pine,
Indeed thou sore dost grieve
  with wenches, Cakes, and wine,
For my part tis my lot
  to pray for patience still,
Untill I have forgot
  thy over-reaching skill.
    Then doe not raile, etc.

Yet though I suffer wrong
  I needs must prayse thy art,
Sure thou hast study'd long
  to act the Mad-mans part,
Thou canst not sleep nor wake
  for fancies in thy head,
Now I doe thee forsake
  I muse thou art not dead.
    Fye doe not raile, etc.

That Lasse which shall have thee
  Who ere has that ill hap,
Let her learne this of me,
  shee's caught in follies trap.
He that dissemble can
  with one in such a way,
Hee'l nere prove honest man,
  beleeve me what I say.
    Then doe not raile on love,
    Nor Cupids cruell wrong,
    For thou didst never prove
    What doth to love belong.

157 87 *over-reaching* cheating

158 [*from* Well met Neighbour]

To the Tune of Ragged and Torne

Whither away good neighbour,
what makes you to trudge so fast?
I'm going to Margeryes Labour,
I'm sent for in very great hast:
Yet for all this your speed,
I pray you goe softly a while,
For I have a thing in my head
that will hold us talking a mile:
Heard you not lately of Hugh,
how soundly his wife he bangd,
He beat her black and blew
O such a Rogue would be hangd.

Ist possible neighbour Sisse,
that they doe no better agree?
Nay I have more newes then this
of others as bad as he:
And seeing wee both goe one way,
wee'l give to our hast some scope,
Though you from the labour doe stay
sheel doe well enough I hope:
Know you not Laurence the Miller,
O he is as good as ere twangd,
His wife sayes he threatens to kill her,
O such a Rogue would be hangd.

O fye on these dastardly Knaves,
for those that will beate their wives
They dare not with swords or staves
meet men in the field for their lives:
But if that my husband should
not use mee so well as he ought,

158 13 *Sisse* Cicely 22 he has all the good qualities you can name

My hands I should hardly hold
for ide give him as good as he brought:
But know you not Kett the Baker
o he is as good as ere twangd,
Hee threatens his wife to forsake her
O such a Rogue would be hangd.

Why what is his reason for that?
in troth neighbour I doe not know,
But when hees as drunke as a Rat,
then sheel act the part of a shrow:
Tush, thats such a catching disease
few women their silence can keepe,
Let every one say what they please
but a shrew's better then a sheepe:
But know you not Ralph the plummer,
I hee is as good as ere twangd:
He walkes with a wench every summer
O such a Rogue would be hangd. . . .

In sadnesse neighbour Sisse
you have made me my time oreslip,
If Margery should doe amisse
'twould make mee to bite my lip:
And therefore in hast farewell.
o Margery now I come,
Adiew sweet neighbour Nell,
hush, say no more but mum.
For staying from Madge tis true,
I confesse I deserve to be bangd:
And this is all long of Hugh,
O such a Rogue would be hangd.

158 33 *Kett* Kit, Christopher 39 *drunke as a Rat* proverbial 40 *shrow* shrew 50 *oreslip* overslip, slip, pass by 59 *all long* because

EDMUND WALLER

159 The story of *Phœbus* and *Daphne* appli'd

Thirsis a youth of the inspired train,
Fair *Sacharissa* lov'd, but lov'd in vain:
Like *Phœbus* sung the no lesse amorous boy,
Like *Daphne* she as lovely and as coy:
With numbers he the flying Nimph pursues,
With numbers such as *Phœbus* self might use:
Such is the chase when love and fancy leads
Ore craggy mountains, and through flowry meads;
Invoked to testifie the lovers care,
Or form some image of his cruell fair:
Urg'd with his fury like a wounded Deer,
Ore these he fled, and now approaching near:
Had reacht the Nimph with his harmonious lay,
Whom all his charms could not incline to stay.
Yet what he sung in his immortall strain,
Though unsuccessfull, was not sung in vain:
All but the Nimph that should redress his wrong,
Attend his passion, and approve his song.
  Like *Phœbus* thus acquiring unsought praise,
  He catcht at love, and fill'd his arm with bayes.

159 Title *appli'd* given a specific reference 1 *inspired* infused with divine power 2 *Sacharissa* Waller's name ('most sweet') for his patron Dorothy Sidney (1617–84). As Robert Sidney's eldest child she was brought up at Penshurst; in 1639 she married Henry Lord Spencer, who just before his death in 1643 was created Earl of Sunderland; see Waller's entry in Appendix 4 5 *numbers* verses, poetry 20 *bayes* laurels

160 Song

Go lovely Rose,
Tell her that wastes her time and me,
That now she knows
When I resemble her to thee
How sweet and fair she seems to be.

Tell her that's young,
And shuns to have her graces spy'd
That hadst thou sprung
In desarts where no men abide,
Thou must have uncommended dy'd.

Small is the worth
Of beauty from the light retir'd;
Bid her come forth,
Suffer her self to be desir'd,
And not blush so to be admir'd.

Then die that she,
The common fate of all things rare
May read in thee
How small a part of time they share,
That are so wondrous sweet and fair.

161 The Budd

Lately on yonder swelling bush,
Big with many a comming Rose,
This early Bud began to blush,
And did but half it self disclose;
I pluck't it, though no better grown,
Yet now you see how full 'tis blown.

160 4 *resemble* compare, liken

161 6 *blown* in bloom, blossoming

Still as I did the leaves inspire,
With such a purple light they shon
As if they had been made of fire,
And spreading so, would flame anon:
  All that was meant by Air or Sun
  To the young flower my breath has done.

If our loose breath so much can do,
What may the same inform's of love,
Of purest love and musick too
When *Flavia* it aspires to move:
  When that which life-less buds perswades
  To wax more soft her youth invades.

SIR JOHN SUCKLING

162 [Out upon it, I have lov'd]

1.

Out upon it, I have lov'd
  Three whole days together;
And am like to love three more,
  If it prove fair weather.

2.

Time shall moult away his wings
  Ere he shall discover
In the whole wide world agen
  Such a constant Lover.

3.

But the spite on't is, no praise
  Is due at all to me:
Love with me had made no staies,
  Had it any been but she.

161 7 *inspire* breathe in, inhale 8 *purple* crimson, red 13 *loose* free, lax, unchaste, wanton 18 *wax* grow, become *invades* intrudes upon, attacks

4.

Had it any been but she
  And that very Face,
There had been at least ere this
  A dozen dozen in her place.

JOHN CLEVELAND

163 The Antiplatonick

For shame, thou everlasting Woer,
Still saying Grace, and never fall to her!
Love that's in Contemplation plac't,
Is *Venus* drawn but to the Wast.
Unlesse your Flame confesse its Gender,
And your Parley cause surrender;
Y'are Salamanders of a cold desire,
That live untouch't amid the hottest fire.

What though she be a Dame of stone,
The Widow of *Pigmalion*;
As hard and un-relenting She,
As the new-crusted *Niobe*;
Or what doth more of Statue carry
A Nunne of the Platonick Quarrey?
Love melts the rigor which the rocks have bred,
A Flint will break upon a Feather-bed.

163 Title *Antiplatonick* one opposed to the spiritualized, 'Neo-Platonic' love in vogue at the Caroline court 7 *Salamanders* mythical kinds of lizard which because of the coldness of their bodies were supposedly able to live in fire

For shame you pretty Female Elves,
Cease for to Candy up your selves:
No more, you Sectaries of the Game,
No more of your calcining flame.
Women Commence by *Cupids* Dart;
As a Kings Hunting dubs a Hart.
Loves Votaries inthrall each others soul,
Till both of them live but upon Paroll.

Vertue's no more in Women-kind
But the green-sicknesse of the mind.
Philosophy, their new delight,
A kind of Charcoal Appetite.
There's no Sophistry prevails,
Where all-convincing Love assails:
But the disputing Petticoat will Warp,
As skilfull Gamesters are to seek at Sharp.

The souldier, that man of Iron,
Whom Ribs of *Horror* all inviron;
That's strung with Wire, in stead of Veins,
In whose imbraces you're in chains,
Let a Magnetick Girle appear,
Straight he turns *Cupids* Cuiraseer.
Love storms his lips, and takes the Fortresse in,
For all the Brisled Turn-pikes of his chin.

Since Loves Artillery then checks
The Breast-works of the firmest Sex,
Come let's in Affections Riot,
Th'are sickly pleasures keep a Diet.

163 18 *Candy up* preserve by boiling in sugar; congeal in crystals 19 *Sectaries* followers; Puritans 20 *calcining* burning to ashes; purifying 21 *Commence* begin; take their academic degrees 22 *dubs* stabs 26 *green-sicknesse* an anaemic condition in which the resulting paleness made the skin look green 28 *Charcoal Appetite** morbid hunger 31 *Warp* lead astray 32 *to seek at* lacking, wanting *Sharp* a rapier used in duelling 38 *Cuiraseer* cuirassier, a horse-soldier wearing a metal breastplate and backplate 40 *Turn-pikes* defensive spiked barriers across a road 41 *checks* strikes, hits

Give me a Lover bold and free,
Not Eunuch't with Formality;
Like an Embassador that beds a Queen,
With the Nice Caution of a sword between.

RICHARD LOVELACE

164 *Song.* To Lucasta, Going to the Warres

Set by Mr. *John Laniere*

I.

Tell me not (Sweet) I am unkinde,
That from the Nunnerie
Of thy chaste breast, and quiet minde,
To Warre and Armes I flie.

II.

True; a new Mistresse now I chase,
The first Foe in the Field;
And with a stronger Faith imbrace
A Sword, a Horse, a Shield.

III.

Yet this Inconstancy is such,
As you too shall adore;
I could not love thee (Deare) so much,
Lov'd I not Honour more.

163 46 *Eunuch't** castrated

165 *Gratiana* dauncing and singing

I.

See! with what constant Motion
Even, and glorious, as the Sunne,
Gratiana steeres that Noble Frame,
Soft as her breast, sweet as her voyce
That gave each winding Law and poyze,
And swifter then the wings of Fame.

II.

She beat the happy Pavement
By such a Starre made Firmament,
Which now no more the Roofe envies;
But swells up high with *Atlas* ev'n
Bearing the brighter, nobler Heav'n,
And in her, all the Dieties.

III.

Each step trod out a Lovers thought
And the Ambitious hopes he brought,
Chain'd to her brave feet with such arts;
Such sweet command, and gentle awe,
As when she ceas'd, we sighing saw
The floore lay pav'd with broken hearts.

IV.

So did she move; so did she sing
Like the Harmonious spheres that bring
Unto their Rounds their musick's ayd;
Which she performed such a way,
As all th'inamour'd world will say
The *Graces* daunced, and *Apollo* play'd.

165 5 *poyze** poise, balance, equilibrium 8 *Firmament* sky, heavens 21 *Rounds* circular movements, orbits

166 TO ALTHEA, From Prison. *Song.*

Set by Dr. *John Wilson*

I.

When Love with unconfined wings
  Hovers within my Gates;
And my divine *Althea* brings
  To whisper at the Grates:
When I lye tangled in her haire,
  And fetterd to her eye;
The *Gods* that wanton in the Aire,
  Know no such Liberty.

II.

When flowing Cups run swiftly round
  With no allaying *Thames*,
Our carelesse heads with Roses bound,
  Our hearts with Loyall Flames;
When thirsty griefe in Wine we steepe,
  When Healths and draughts go free,
Fishes that tipple in the Deepe,
  Know no such Libertie.

III.

When (like committed Linnets) I
  With shriller throat shall sing
The sweetnes, Mercy, Majesty,
  And glories of my KING;
When I shall voyce aloud, how Good
  He is, how Great should be;
Inlarged Winds that curle the Flood,
  Know no such Liberty.

166 10 *allaying Thames* diluting water 17 *committed* imprisoned 23 *Inlarged* liberated, set free *curle* ripple

IV.

Stone Walls doe not a Prison make,
Nor I'ron bars a Cage;
Mindes innocent and quiet take
That for an Hermitage;
If I have freedome in my Love,
And in my soule am free;
Angels alone that sore above,
Injoy such Liberty.

167 Her Muffe

1.

'Twas not for some calm blessing to receive,
Thou didst thy polish'd hands in shagg'd furs weave;
It were no blessing thus obtain'd,
Thou rather would'st a curse have gain'd,
Then let thy warm driven snow be ever stain'd.

2.

Not that you feared the discolo'ring cold,
Might alchymize their Silver into Gold;
Nor could your ten white Nuns so sin,
That you should thus pennance them in
Each in her course hair smock of Discipline.

3.

Nor *Hero*-like, who on their crest still wore
A Lyon, Panther, Leopard or a Bore,
To look their Enemies in their Herse;
Thou would'st thy hand should deeper pierce,
And, in its softness rough, appear more fierce.

167 1-5 Jacob covered himself with goatskins to deceive his blind father Isaac into blessing him instead of his hairy brother Esau, see Genesis 27 2 *shagg'd* shaggy 7 *alchymize* change by alchemy, transmute 8 *ten . . . Nuns* fingers 9 *pennance* impose a penance on, discipline 13 *Herse* coffin, tomb

4.

No, no, *Lucasta*, destiny Decreed
That Beasts to thee a sacrifice should bleed,
And strip themselves to make you gay;
For ne'r yet Herald did display,
A Coat, where *Sables* upon *Ermin* lay.

5.

This for Lay-Lovers, that must stand at dore,
Salute the threshold, and admire no more:
But I, in my Invention tough,
Rate not this outward bliss enough,
But still contemplate must the hidden Muffe.

168 [*from* On *Sanazar*'s being honoured with six hundred Duckets by the *Clarissimi* of *Venice*, for composing an *Elegiack Hexastick* of The City. A Satyre]

Yet there belongs a Sweetnesse, softnesse too,
Which you must pay, but first pray know to who.
There is a Creature, (if I may so call
That unto which they do all prostrate fall)
Term'd Mistress, when they'r angry, but pleas'd high,
It is a Princesse, Saint, Divinity.
To this they sacrifice the whole days light,
Then lye with their Devotion all night;
For this you are to dive to the Abysse,
And rob for Pearl the Closet of some Fish.
Arabia and *Sabæa* you must strip
Of all their Sweets, for to supply her Lip;

167 20 *Sables* the skins of sables; the heraldic colour black *Ermin* the skins of stoats; in heraldry, white marked with black spots 21 *Lay-Lovers* not professional, not clerical, lovers

168 Title *Sanazar* Jacopo Sannazaro (1455–1530), a Neapolitan poet whose Italian and Latin works were very popular during the Renaissance 2 *you* poets and writers 8 *Devotion* object of their devotion

And steal new fire from Heav'n for to repair
Her unfledg'd Scalp with *Berenice*'s hair;
Then seat her in *Cassiopeia*'s Chair,
As now you're in your Coach. Save you bright Sir
(O spare your thanks) is not this finer far
Then walk un-hided, when that every Stone
Has knock'd acquaintance with your Anckle bone?
When your wing'd papers, like the last dove, nere
Return'd to quit you of your hope or fear,
But left you to the mercy of your Host,
And your days fare, a fortified Toast.

ANDREW MARVELL

169 To his Coy Mistress

Had we but World enough, and Time,
This coyness Lady were no crime.
We would sit down, and think which way
To walk, and pass our long Loves Day.
Thou by the *Indian Ganges* side
Should'st Rubies find: I by the Tide
Of *Humber* would complain. I would
Love you ten years before the Flood:
And you should if you please refuse
Till the Conversion of the *Jews*.
My vegetable Love should grow
Vaster then Empires, and more slow.

168 14 *unfledg'd* imperfect, not fully covered, immature 18 *un-hided** without a hide, skinned 20 *last dove* the bird from Noah's ark which, finding land, did not return; see Genesis 8:12 21 *quit* release, deliver, free

169 7 *Humber* the river in Marvell's hometown, Hull 8–11 there was much discussion in the 1640s and 1650s of the theory that the Great Flood took place 1,656 years from the creation of the world and that the conversion of the Jews, an equally momentous event, heralding the second coming would take place in AD 1656 11 *vegetable* having the primal principle of life and growth (cp. no. 199 l. 14)

An hundred years should go to praise
Thine Eyes, and on thy Forehead Gaze.
Two hundred to adore each Breast:
But thirty thousand to the rest.
An Age at least to every part,
And the last Age should show your Heart.
For Lady you deserve this State;
Nor would I love at lower rate.
  But at my back I alwaies hear
Times winged Charriot hurrying near:
And yonder all before us lye
Desarts of vast Eternity.
Thy Beauty shall no more be found;
Nor, in thy marble Vault, shall sound
My ecchoing Song: then Worms shall try
That long preserv'd Virginity:
And your quaint Honour turn to dust;
And into ashes all my Lust.
The Grave's a fine and private place,
But none I think do there embrace.
  Now therefore, while the youthful glew
Sits on thy skin like morning dew,
And while thy willing Soul transpires
At every pore with instant Fires,
Now let us sport us while we may;
And now, like am'rous birds of prey,
Rather at once our Time devour,
Than languish in his slow-chapt pow'r.
Let us roll all our Strength, and all
Our sweetness, up into one Ball:
And tear our Pleasures with rough strife,
Thorough the Iron gates of Life.
Thus, though we cannot make our Sun
Stand still, yet we will make him run.

169 19 *State* high rank, position; condition 27 *ecchoing*** that causes echoes 29 *quaint* fastidious, prim *Honour* chastity, purity; in *quaint Honour* some editors see a double allusion to the woman's sexual parts 33 *glew* glue; glow (?) 37 *sport* amuse, entertain, recreate 40 *chapt** chapped, having a jaw, hence devouring 45–6 cp. Joshua 10:12 'and he said in the sight of Israel, Sun, stand thou still upon Gibeon'

170 The Gallery

I.

Clora come view my Soul, and tell
Whether I have contriv'd it well.
Now all its several lodgings lye
Compos'd into one Gallery;
And the great *Arras*-hangings, made
Of various Faces, by are laid;
That, for all furniture, you'l find
Only your Picture in my Mind.

II.

Here Thou art painted in the Dress
Of an Inhumane Murtheress;
Examining upon our Hearts
Thy fertile Shop of cruel Arts:
Engines more keen than ever yet
Adorned Tyrants Cabinet;
Of which the most tormenting are
Black Eyes, red Lips, and curled Hair.

III.

But, on the other side, th' art drawn
Like to *Aurora* in the Dawn;
When in the East she slumb'ring lyes,
And stretches out her milky Thighs;
While all the morning Quire does sing,
And *Manna* falls, and Roses spring;
And, at thy Feet, the wooing Doves
Sit perfecting their harmless Loves.

IV.

Like an Enchantress here thou show'st,
Vexing thy restless Lover's Ghost;
And, by a Light obscure, dost rave
Over his Entrails, in the Cave;

170 2 *contriv'd* designed, devised 11 *Examining* testing, trying 24 *harmless* innocent, innocuous

Divining thence, with horrid Care,
How long thou shalt continue fair;
And (when inform'd) them throw'st away,
To be the greedy Vultur's prey.

V.

But, against that, thou sit'st a float
Like *Venus* in her pearly Boat.
The *Halcyons*, calming all that's nigh,
Betwixt the Air and Water fly.
Or, if some rowling Wave appears,
A Mass of Ambergris it bears.
Nor blows more Wind than what may well
Convoy the Perfume to the Smell.

VI.

These Pictures and a thousand more,
Of Thee, my Gallery do store;
In all the Forms thou can'st invent
Either to please me, or torment:
For thou alone to people me,
Art grown a num'rous Colony;
And a Collection choicer far
Then or *White-hall's*, or *Mantua's* were.

VII.

But, of these Pictures and the rest,
That at the Entrance likes me best:
Where the same Posture, and the Look
Remains, with which I first was took.
A tender Shepherdess, whose Hair
Hangs loosely playing in the Air,
Transplanting Flow'rs from the green Hill,
To crown her Head, and Bosome fill.

170 35 *Halcyons* kingfishers were believed to breed at the winter solstice, when they calmed the sea 38 *Ambergris* the odoriferous secretion of the sperm whale, see Marvell's 'Bermudas' (no. 214), l. 28 40 *Convoy* accompany, escort; convey, carry 42 *store* supply, stock 48 Charles I added to his collection of pictures at Whitehall, by buying the paintings belonging to Vincenzo Gonzaga, Duke of Mantua. The collection was sold off after the abolition of the monarchy

171 The Definition of Love

I.

My Love is of a birth as rare
As 'tis for object strange and high:
It was begotten by despair
Upon Impossibility.

II.

Magnanimous Despair alone
Could show me so divine a thing,
Where feeble Hope could ne'r have flown
But vainly flapt its Tinsel Wing.

III.

And yet I quickly might arrive
Where my extended Soul is fixt,
But Fate does Iron wedges drive,
And alwaies crouds it self betwixt.

IV.

For Fate with jealous Eye does see
Two perfect Loves; nor lets them close:
Their union would her ruine be,
And her Tyrannick pow'r depose.

V.

And therefore her Decrees of Steel
Us as the distant Poles have plac'd,
(Though Loves whole World on us doth wheel)
Not by themselves to be embrac'd.

171 5 *Magnanimous* great in courage 10 *extended* stretched out *fixt* intent, fastened 11 cp. Horace, *Odes* 1.35.17–18 'Before you your servant Necessity stalks with spikes and wedges in her brazen hand' 12 *crouds* pushes, shoves 14 *close* join, unite, combine 19 the celestial or terrestrial world revolves around the axis which goes through the two poles 20 *by themselves* by each other; on their own

VI.

Unless the giddy Heaven fall,
And Earth some new Convulsion tear;
And, us to joyn, the World should all
Be cramp'd into a *Planisphere*.

VII.

As Lines so Loves *oblique* may well
Themselves in every Angle greet:
But ours so truly *Paralel*,
Though infinite can never meet.

VIII.

Therefore the Love which us doth bind,
But Fate so enviously debarrs,
Is the Conjunction of the Mind,
And Opposition of the Stars.

James Harrington

172 Inconstancy

He who at first a womans mind
Compar'd to the inconstant wind,
Did it in gratitude, not spleen,
For, had this ever constant been,
We that in wealth to pomp abound
Had scarce for needful uses found.
It is his vary'd dance that leads
Us to the eastern spicy meads,

171 24 be compressed, squeezed into a chart formed by the projection of a sphere on to a plane 25 *oblique* inclined at any angle other than a right angle 26 *greet* meet, intersect 31 *Conjunction* the presence of two heavenly bodies in the same sign of the zodiac; union 32 *Opposition* the position of two heavenly bodies exactly opposite each other when seen from the earth; antagonism, resistance

And back again our course declines
To dig in the rich western mines,
Where should it stand still to one coast
The trafick of the world were lost.

KATHERINE PHILIPS

173 An Answer to another perswading a Lady to Marriage

1.

Forbear bold Youth, all's Heaven here,
 And what you do aver,
To others Courtship may appear,
 'Tis Sacriledge to her.

2.

She is a publick Deity,
 And were't not very odd
She should depose her self to be
 A petty Houshold God?

3.

First make the Sun in private shine,
 And bid the World adieu,
That so he may his beams confine
 In complement to you.

4.

But if of that you do despair,
 Think how you did amiss,
To strive to fix her beams which are
 More bright and large than his.

173 Title *another* another poem

PART THREE

TOPOGRAPHIES

ALEXANDER BARCLAY

174 [*from* Certayne Egloges 5]

Amintas first speaketh.

The winter snowes, all covered is the grounde,
The north wind blowes sharpe and with ferefull sound,
The longe ise sicles at the ewes hang,
The streame is frosen, the night is cold and long,
Where botes rowed nowe cartes have passage,
From yoke the oxen be losed and bondage,
The ploweman resteth avoyde of businesse,
Save when he tendeth his harnes for to dresse,
Mably his wife sitteth before the fyre
All blacke and smoky clothed in rude attire,
Sething some grewell, and sturring the pulment
Of pease or frument, a noble meat for lent,
The summer season men counted nowe laudable
Whose fervour before they thought intollerable,
The frosty winter and wether temperate
Which men then praysed they nowe disprayse and hate,
Colde they desired, but nowe it is present
They braule and grutche their mindes not content.
Thus mutable men them pleased can not holde,
At great heat grutching, and grutching when it is cold.

Faustus

All pleasour present of men is counted small,
Desire obtayned some counteth nought at all,
What men hope after that semeth great and deare,
As light by distaunce appeareth great and cleare,

174 3 *ewes* eaves 7 *avoyde* free 11 *Sething* boiling, stewing *pulment* a kind of pottage 12 *frument* frumenty, wheat boiled in milk 18 *braule* quarrel noisily *grutche* complain

Amintas

Eche time and season hath his delite and joyes,
Loke in the stretes beholde the little boyes,
Howe in fruite season for joy they sing and hop,
In lent is eche one full busy with his top,
And nowe in winter for all the greevous colde
All rent and ragged a man may them beholde,
They have great pleasour supposing well to dine,
When men be busied in killing of fat swine,
They get the bladder and blowe it great and thin,
With many beanes or peason put within,
It ratleth, soundeth, and shineth clere and fayre,
While it is throwen and caste up in the ayre,
Eche one contendeth and hath a great delite
With foote and with hande the bladder for to smite,
If it fall to grounde they lifte it up agayne,
This wise to labour they count it for no payne,
Renning and leaping they drive away the colde.
The sturdie plowmen lustie, strong and bolde
Overcommeth the winter with driving the foote ball,
Forgetting labour and many a grevous fall.

Faustus

Men labour sorer in fruiteles vanitie
Then in fayre workes of great utilitie,
In suche trifles we labour for domage,
Worke we despise which bringeth advauntage.

Amintas

Touching their labour it can not me displease,
While we be in rest and better here at ease
In the warme litter, small payne hath little hire,
Here may we walow while milke is on the fire,
If it be crudded of bread we nede no crome,
If thou bide Faustus thereof thou shalt have some.

174 34 *peason* peas 42 *lustie* lively, vigorous, strong 47 *domage* injury, harm 51 *hire* payment, reward 53 *crudded* curdled *crome* crumb

George Buchanan

175 Calendæ Maiæ

Salvete sacris deliciis sacræ
Maiæ Calendæ, laetitiæ, et mero,
Ludisque dicatæ, iocisque,
Et teneris Charitum choreis.
Salve voluptas, et nitidum decus
Anni recurrens perpetua vice,
Et flos renascentis iuventæ
In senium properantis ævi.
Cum blanda veris temperies novo
Illuxit orbi, primaque secula
Fulsere flaventi metallo
Sponte sua sine lege iusta:
Talis per omnes continuus tenor
Annos tepenti rura Favonio
Mulcebat, et nullis feraces
Seminibus recreabat agros.
Talis beatis incubat insulis
Felicis auræ perpetuus tepor,
Et nesciis campis senectæ
Difficilis, querulique morbi.
Talis silentum per tacitum nemus
Levi susurrat murmure spiritus,
Lethenque juxta obliviosam
Funereas agitat cupressos.
Forsan supremis cum Deus ignibus
Piabit orbem, lætaque secula
Mundo reducet, talis aura
Ætherios animos fovebit.
Salve fugacis gloria seculi,
Salve secunda digna dies nota,
Salve vetustæ vitæ imago,
Et specimen venientis aevi.

175 May Morning

Hail, May Day, dedicated to holy delights, to joy as full as unadulterated wine, devoted to games and mirth and the delicate dances of the Graces. Hail, pleasure, and shining splendour returning with the perpetual succession of the year, and the flower of youth being reborn, hurrying on towards the feebleness of old age. When the friendly temperance of spring dawned on a new world, and the first ages shone with golden metal, just of their own accord without any law; just such a steady course down all the years charmed the countryside with a mild west wind, and renewed the fertile fields without any seeds. Just such a perpetual warmth of happy air hangs over the blessed islands and the fields that know nothing of troublesome old age and querulous illness; such a spirit whispers with a light murmur through the silent grove of the dead, and shakes the funereal cypresses on the far side of Lethe the river of forgetfulness. Perhaps when God purifies the world with the last fires, and brings back the joyful ages to the world, such a breeze will nourish the heavenly souls. Hail, glory of the fleeting age, hail, day worthy of a propitious mark, hail, image of the ancient life and pattern of an age yet to come.

Anonymous

176 [*from* Vox populi vox Dei]

And yett not lowng agoo
was prechares one or tooe
that spake it plene enowgh
To yow, to yow, and to yowe
that it was reght tyme to repente
this develysche intente
of covitis the convente
frome skottland into kente
this precheng was be sprent
and frome the est frunt

176 Title *Vox ... dei* proverbial: 'the voice of the people, the voice of God' 7 *covitis* the covetous (?) *convente* assembly, gathering 9 *be sprent* bespread, scattered 10 *frunt* side, hence coast

unto saynt mychelles montte
this sayeng Did surmownte
a brode to all menes heres
and to youre grasys peres
that frome pyllyr to post
the powr man he was toste
I mene the laboreng man
I mene the husbande man
I mene the plowghe man
I mene the handy craft man
I mene the vytalyng man
and also the gud yoman
that some tyme in this realme
hade plente of key and creme
butter egges and chesse
hony vax and besse
but now a lacke a lacke
all thes men gowe to wrake
that are the bodye and staye
of youre grasis realme alwaye
alwaye and at lenght
they most be youre strenght
youre strenght and your teme
for to defende youre realme
Then yf thes men appall
and lack when ye doe call
Wiche waye maye you, or shall
Resyst youre enymes all
thet over ragynge stremes
wyll wadde frome foren realmes
for me to make Judiciall
This matter ys to mysticall
Juge yowe my lordes for me ye shall
youres ys the charge that governes all

176 11 St Michael's Mount off the Cornish coast (see no. 325 l.161) 14 *youre grasys peres* the King's peers 15 proverbial: from the pillory to the whipping-post 20 *handy craft man*** manual worker 24 *key* cows 25 *chesse* cheese 26 *vax* wax *besse* bees 33 *teme** team 35 *appall** lose heart or resolution 40 *wadde* go 41 *Judiciall* a judgement, decision

for vox populi, me thay call
that maketh but reersall
de parvum but not De totall
de locis but not locall
Therfore ye most not blame
the wyght that wrott the same
for the comenes of this Lande
hath sone this in there sande
plowghyng it with ther hande
I fonde it where I stonnde
And I ame but the hayne
that wrythe new agayne
The copy for to see
that also lerneth me
to take there by good hede
my shepe howe for to fede
for I a sheparde ame
A sory powre man
Yett wolde I wysche my lordes
this myght be youre recordies
and make of it nowe Dreme
for it ys a worthey realme
a reme that in tymes paste
hath made the prowdes a gaste

176 46 *reersall* rehearsal 47 *de parvum* about small thing(s) 48 *de locis* about places 50 *wyght* man 51 *comenes* commons, common people in general 52 *sone* sown; proverbial: producing nothing, wasting labour 55 *hayne* mean wretch 56 *wrythe* writes 68 *prowdes* proud people

ANONYMOUS

177 [*from* Jack of the North]

Now for that slawnders sake
Companye be nyght I take
And with all that I maye make
Cast hedge and dyche in the lake
fyxed with many a stake—
though it war never so faste
yet asondre it is wraste—
Thus I Jake do recompense
ther naughty slawnderous offense,
Wher as they make me a murderor
and of dethe a furderer
I take god to wytnes
I am of it gyltles
for as I am true speaker
I am but a hedge breaker
I reporte me now oute
to thes that be of my rowte
so bragge so bolde and stowte
how sayst thou robyn clowte
Is this nyght wele wroughte—

Robbyn clowte ye syr wythout doughte
be god that me boughte
It is as ye do saye
but Syr without delaye
me thought it but a playe
to see the stakes fast straye

177 Title: the first and last speaker is Jack of the North, who denies that he has committed murder, resolves to return to Stamford in Lincolnshire again and in the final verse subscribes an oath 1 *that slawnders* that he has committed a murder 7 *wraste* wrested, torn 9 *naughty* wicked 15 *hedge breaker*** 17 *rowte* number, company 18 *bragge* spirited, valiant

down into the raye
swymmyng evermore awaye
saylyng towarde the castyll
lyke as they wolde wrastyll
for superyoryte
or elles for the meyraltye . . .

Jake How sayst thou harry clowte
thy bryches botom is torn oute.

harry clowt Syr yf that I speake myght
I wold speake but the ryghte
Gud conscyence shold them move
ther neybors quietly to love
And thus not for to wrynche
the comons styl for to pynche
To take into ther handes
that be other mennes landes
for it gettyth them gret blame
and I wys yet wylt not frame
but ever encrese ther shame
and loseth ther gud name
Thus they to take such payne
Wheras it is no gayne
they may thynke yt playne
to be to them a gret mayne
so many nobles bestowyd
And in the erthe so throwyde
Of it so wastfully spente
they maye chance now repente.

Jake Repent man? so lett it be
Who wyll them pytte?
that thus dothe all encroche
to ther gret shame and reproche
Ever beyng to ther pore
Heavy grevous and sore

177 27 *raye* the river Rea or Lindis, now the Witham in Lincolnshire 29 *castyll* Horncastle in Lincolnshire 30 *wrastyll* wrestle 32 *meyraltye* mayoralty, office of mayor 33 *clowte* rag, patch 39 *wrynche* turn from the right path 44 *wylt not frame* it would not have any effect 50 *mayne* moan, complaint

to them that dyd withstande
thos thynges they had in hande
for somme dyd never consente
to this monye thus spente
the comons thus to defrawde
to them it is gret lawede
seyng they had a conscyence
of that covetous pretence . . .

This I do and wyll do with all my myght
for sclawnderyng me yet do I but ryght
for comon to the comons agayne I restore
Wherever it hathe ben yet comon before
If agayne they enclose it never so faste
agayne a sondre it shall be wraste
they maye be ware by that is paste
to make it agayne is but waste.

ANONYMOUS

178 The Jolly Pinder of WAKEFIELD

In *wakefield* there lives a jolly Pinder,
  in Wakefield all on a green,
  in Wakefield all on a green,
There is neither knight nor Squire said the Pinder
  nor Barron that is so bold,
  nor Barron that is so bold,
Dare make a trespasse to the town of Wakefield
  but his pledge goes to the Pinfold,
  but his pledge goes to the Pinfold.

177 66 *lawede* praise

178 Title *Pinder* impounder of stray beasts 8 *Pinfold* pound

All this beheard three witty youngmen
twas *Robin Hood Scarlet and John*, etc.
With that they spyed the jolly Pinder
as he sate under a Thorn. etc.
Now turn again turn again said the Pinder
for a wrong way have you gone. etc.

For you have forsaken the King his high way
and made a path over the Corn, etc.
O that were great shame said jolly *Robin*
we being three and thou but one, etc.
The Pinder leapt back then thirty good foot,
twas thirty good foot and one. etc.

He leaned his back fast unto a Thorn,
and his foot unto a stone, etc.
And there he fought a long Summers day,
a Summers day so long, etc.
Till that their Swords on their broad Bucklers
were broken fast unto their hands. etc.

Hold thy hand hold thy hand said *Robin Hood*
and my merry men every one, etc.
For this is one of the best Pinders,
that ever I try'd with Sword. etc.
And wilt thou forsake thy Pinder his craft,
and live in green wood with me, etc.

At *Michaelmas* next my Cov'nant comes out,
when every man gathers his Fee, etc.
Ile take my blew Blade all in my hand,
and plod to the Green wood with thee, etc.
Hast thou either meat or drink said *Robin Hood*
for my merry men and me, etc.

178 10 *witty* clever, expert; strong (?) 11, 13 the second, fourth and sixth line of each verse should be repeated; Justice Silence sings l. 11 in Shakespeare's *2 Henry IV* V.3.103 18 *jolly* gallant, brave

I have both bread and beef said the Pinder,
And good Ale of the best etc.
And that is meat good enough said *Robin Hood*
for such unbidden guest etc.
O wilt thou forsake thy Pinder his craft
And go to the green wood with me, etc.

Thou shalt have a Livery twice in the year,
the one green the other brown.
the one green the other brown,
If *Michaelmas* day were once come and gone,
And my Master had paid me my fee
And my Master had paid me my fee,
Then would I set as little by him
As my Master doth set by me
As my master doth set by me.

Barnabe Googe

179 Goyng towardes Spayne

Farewell thou fertyll soyle,
that *Brutus* fyrst out founde,
When he poore soule, was driven clean
from out his Countrey ground.
That Northward layst thy lusty sides
amyd the ragyng Seas.
Whose welthy Land doth foster upp,
thy people all in ease,

178 47 'shall be' has perhaps been omitted at the end of the line

179 5 *lusty* healthy, strong, vigorous

While others scrape and carke abroad,
theyr symple foode to gett,
And selye Soules take all for good,
that commeth to the Net.
Which they with painfull paynes do pynch,
in barrain burning Realmes:
While we have all with out restreint
among thy welthy streames.
O blest of God thou Pleasaunt Ile,
where welth her self doth dwell:
Wherin my tender yeares I past,
I byd thee now farewell.
For Fancy dryves me forth abrode,
and byds me take delyght,
In levyng thee and raungyng far,
to se some straunger syght.
And sayth I was not framed heare,
to lyve at home with eas:
But passynge foorth for knowledge sake
to cut the fomyng seas.

Siôn Phylip

180 [*from* Yr Wylan]

Yr wylan deg ar lan dŵr,
Loywblu gofl, abl o gyflwr,
Ni'th ddeil hebog, ni'th ddilyn,
Ni'th fawdd y dŵr, ni'th fedd dyn.
Crefyddwraig fwydsaig o fôr,
Creigleisferch cyrrau glasfor,
Taro ar lled trwy war y llyn,
Ysgwyd yna sgadenyn.
Amlygwen heulwen heli,
Amlygyn tywyn wyt ti.

179 9 *scrape* scrape a living *carke* labour anxiously 11 *selye* silly, simple 11–12 cp. the proverb, 'All is fish that comes to the net'

Merch fedydd ddedwydd ydwyd,
Is y lan, Neptunus lwyd.
Chwith gennyd o'r symud sydd
Ar dy fyd, oer dy fedydd.
Edn gwrddwyn dan y garwddwr,
A merch gynt ym mreichiau gŵr.

Halsio, fun liwus feinael,
Y'th elwid di i'th wlad hael,
Ac ar ôl d'ŵr, gweryl da,
I'r tonnau yr ait yna,
Ac yn wylan ganolwyllt
Yno y'th droed, edn gwandroed gwyllt.
Byw, esgudferch bysgodfwyd,
Tan yr allt a'r tonnau'r wyd,
A'r un gri am dy briawd
Wyt o waedd braff hyd dydd brawd.

A fu erioed ar fôr iach
Nofyddes wen ufuddach?
Clyw gri bardd clogwyn byrddoeth,
Cywen murn awen môr noeth.
Curiais drwy'r ais o draserch,
Curio i'm hoes yn caru merch.

180 The Seagull

Fair seagull on the water's edge, bright-feathered breast, rich your state, hawk will not catch you or pursue you, the water will not drown you nor man own you. Nun with food-feast from the sea, stony-voiced daughter of the edges of the blue sea, striking out wide through the water's nape, then shaking a herring. Conspicuous white sunshine of the briny water, you are a banner on the seashore. Blessed god-daughter art thou, below the shore, of pale Neptune. You regret the alteration in your life, cold your baptism. Strong white bird below the rough water, once a girl in a man's arms. Fair narrow-browed girl, you were called halcyon in your fruitful land, and after your husband, a good dispute, you then went to the waves, and into a gull, wild to the core, you were changed there,

180 31–2 the bird is to take a message to his loved one across the water

wild, weak-footed bird. You live, swift, fishfed girl, below the slope and the waves, with the same cry for your spouse strong-shouting will you be until the day of judgement. Was there ever on the fresh sea a more obedient swimmer? Hear the cry of a white-cloaked bard, short in wisdom, bright torment of inspiration of the bare sea.

SIR PHILIP SIDNEY

181 [*from* The Countesse of Pembrokes Arcadia]

Then do I thinke in deed, that better it is to be private
In sorrows torments, then, tyed to the pompes of a pallace,
Nurse inwarde maladyes, which have not scope to be breath'd out.
But perforce disgest, all bitter juices of horror
In silence, from a mans owne selfe with company robbed.
Better yet do I live, that though by my thoughts I be plunged
Into my lives bondage, yet may disburden a passion
(Opprest with ruinouse conceites) by the helpe of an outcrye:
Not limited to a whispringe note, the Lament of a Courtier.
But sometimes to the woods somtimes to the heavens do decyphire
With bolde clamor unheard, unmarckt, what I seeke what I suffer:
And when I meete these trees, in the earths faire livory clothed,
Ease I do feele (such ease as falls to one wholly diseased)
For that I finde in them parte of my estate represented.

181 4 *disgest* digest 10 *decyphire* represent, make known 12 *livory* livery 13 *diseased* distressed, troubled

EDMUND SPENSER

182 [*from* The Shepheardes Calender]

Maye

PALINODE. PIERS.

Is not thilke the mery moneth of May,
When love lads masken in fresh aray?
How falles it then, we no merrier bene,
Ylike as others, girt in gawdy greene?
Our bloncket liveryes bene all to sadde,
For thilke same season, when all is ycladd
With pleasaunce: the grownd with grasse, the Wods
With greene leaves, the bushes with bloosming Buds.
Yougthes folke now flocken in every where,
To gather may bus-kets and smelling brere:
And home they hasten the postes to dight,
And all the Kirke pillours eare day light,
With Hawthorne buds, and swete Eglantine,
And girlonds of roses and Sopps in wine.
Such merimake holy Saints doth queme,
But we here sytten as drownd in a dreme.

182 *Palinode* literally, a poem or song in which the author takes back what was said in a previous work *Piers* the name evokes the title of William Langland's poem *Piers Plowman* and suggests a plain-spoken countryman 1 *thilke* 'this same moneth. It is applyed to the season of the moneth, when all menne delight them selves with pleasaunce of fieldes, and gardens, and garments' E. K. (for E. K. and his glosses, see the textual note) 4 *girt* dressed *gawdy greene* yellowish green 5 *bloncket liveryes* 'gray coates' E. K. 6 *ycladd* 'arrayed' E. K. 10 *bus-kets* 'little bushes of hauthorne' E. K. *smelling brere* sweet-smelling briers, rose-bushes 12 *Kirke* 'church' E. K. 13 *Eglantine* sweet-brier 14 *Sopps in wine* gillyflowers 15 *merimake** merrymaking *queme* 'please' E. K.

PIERS.

For Younkers *Palinode* such follies fitte,
But we tway bene men of elder witt.

PALINODE.

Sicker this morrowe, ne lenger agoe,
I sawe a shole of shepeheardes outgoe,
With singing, and shouting, and jolly chere:
Before them yode a lusty Tabrere,
That to the many a Horne pype playd,
Whereto they dauncen eche one with his mayd.
To see those folkes make such jouysaunce,
Made my heart after the pype to daunce.
Tho to the greene Wood they speeden hem all,
To fetchen home May with their musicall:
And home they bringen in a royall throne,
Crowned as king: and his Queene attone
Was Lady Flora, on whom did attend
A fayre flocke of Faeries, and a fresh bend
Of lovely Nymphs. (O that I were there,
To helpen the Ladyes their Maybush beare)
Ah *Piers,* bene not thy teeth on edge, to thinke,
How great sport they gaynen with little swinck?

PIERS.

Perdie so farre am I from envie,
That their fondnesse inly I pitie.
Those faytours little regarden their charge,
While they letting their sheepe runne at large,

182 17 *Younkers* youths, young men 18 *tway* two 19 *Sicker* certainly, surely 20 *shole* 'a multitude; taken of fishe ...' E. K. *shepheardes* pastors 22 *yode* 'went' E. K. *Tabrere* taborer, drummer 23 *many* company, crowd 25 *jouysaunce** pleasure, merriment, mirth; 'joye' E. K. 27 *Tho* then *greene Wood* wood in leaf 28 *May* the lord of the May *musicall* musical instruments, music 30 *attone* together 32 *bend* band 34 *Maybush** branch of hawthorn 36 *swinck* 'labour' E. K. 37 *Perdie* indeed, truly 38 *inly* 'entirely' E. K. 39 *faytours* impostors, cheats, fraudulent vagrants; 'vagabonds' E. K.

Passen their time, that should be sparely spent,
In lustihede and wanton meryment.
Thilke same bene shepeheards for the Devils stedde,
That playen, while their flockes be unfedde.
Well is it seene, theyr sheepe bene not their owne,
That letten them runne at randon alone.
But they bene hyred for little pay
Of other, that caren as little as they,
What fallen the flocke, so they han the fleece,
And get all the gayne, paying but a peece.
I muse, what account both these will make,
The one for the hire, which he doth take,
And thother for leaving his Lords tas-ke,
When great *Pan* account of shepeherdes shall as-ke.

PALINODE.

Sicker now I see thou speakest of spight,
All for thou lackest somedele their delight.
I (as I am) had rather be envied,
All were it of my foe, then fonly pitied:
And yet if neede were, pitied would be,
Rather, then other should scorne at me:
For pittied is mishappe, that nas remedie,
But scorned bene dedes of fond foolerie.
What shoulden shepheards other things tend,
Then sith their God his good does them send,
Reapen the fruite thereof, that is pleasure,
The while they here liven, at ease and leasure?
For when they bene dead, their good is ygoe,
They sleepen in rest, well as other moe.
Tho with them wends, what they spent in cost,
But what they left behind them, is lost.

182 41 *sparely* sparingly 43 *stedde* place 54 *great Pan* 'Christ, the very God of all shepheards, which calleth himselfe the greate and good shepherd. The name is most rightly (me thinkes) applyed to him, for Pan signifieth all or omnipotent, which is onely the Lord Jesus' E. K. 55 *of spight* out of spite 56 *All for* just because *somedele* somewhat 58 *fonly** fondly, foolishly 61 *nas* 'has not' E. K. 67 *ygoe* gone 68 *other moe* many others 69 *cost* time, labour

Good is no good, but if it be spend:
God giveth good for none other end.

PIERS.

Ah *Palinodie*, thou art a worldes childe:
Who touches Pitch mought needes be defilde.
But shepheards (as Algrind used to say,)
Mought not live ylike, as men of the laye:
With them it sits to care for their heire,
Enaunter their heritage doe impaire:
They must provide for meanes of maintenaunce,
And to continue their wont countenaunce.
But shepheard must walke another way,
Sike worldly sovenance he must foresay.
The sonne of his loines why should he regard
To leave enriched with that he hath spard?
Should not thilke God, that gave him that good,
Eke cherish his child, if in his wayes he stood?
For if he mislive in leudnes and lust,
Little bootes all the welth and the trust,
That his father left by inheritaunce:
All will be soone wasted with misgovernaunce.
But through this, and other their miscreaunce,
They maken many a wrong chevisaunce,
Heaping up waves of welth and woe,
The floddes whereof shall them overflowe.
Sike mens follie I cannot compare
Better, then to the Apes folish care,
That is so enamoured of her young one,
(And yet God wote, such cause hath she none)

182 73 *worldes* worldly 74 *mought* must 75 *Algrind* 'the name of a shepheard' E. K.; generally taken to be Edmund Grindal (1519?–83), Archbishop of Canterbury, at the time suspended by order of the Queen from his jurisdictional duties 76 *men . . . laye* 'Lay men' E. K. 77 *sits* is fitting *heire* heirs, inheritors 78 *Enaunter* 'least that' E. K. 80 *wont* wonted, accustomed *countenaunce* position, standing 82 *Sike* such *sovenance* care, 'remembraunce' E. K. *foresay* renounce 84 *spard* spared, put aside 87 *mislive* live a bad life 88 *bootes* avails, profits 90 *misgovernaunce* mismanagement, misuse 91 *miscreaunce* 'despeire or misbeliefe' E. K. 92 *chevisaunce* 'spoyle, or bootie, or enterprise' E. K.

That with her hard hold, and straight embracing,
She stoppeth the breath of her youngling.
So often times, when as good is meant,
Evil ensueth of wrong entent.
   The time was once, and may againe retorne,
(For ought may happen, that hath bene beforne)
When shepeheards had none inheritaunce,
Ne of land, nor fee in sufferaunce:
But what might arise of the bare sheepe,
(Were it more or lesse) which they did keepe.
Well ywis was it with shepheards thoe:
Nought having, nought feared they to forgoe.
For *Pan* himselfe was their inheritaunce,
And little them served for their mayntenaunce.
The shepheards God so wel them guided,
That of nought they were unprovided,
Butter enough, honye, milke, and whay,
And their flockes fleeces, them to araye.
But tract of time, and long prosperitie:
That nource of vice, this of insolencie,
Lulled the shepheards in such securitie,
That not content with loyall obeysaunce,
Some gan to gape for greedie governaunce,
And match them selfe with mighty potentates,
Lovers of Lordship and troublers of states:
Tho gan shepheards swaines to looke a loft,
And leave to live hard, and learne to ligge soft:
Tho under colour of shepeheards, somewhile
There crept in Wolves, ful of fraude and guile,
That often devoured their owne sheepe,
And often the shepheards, that did hem keepe.

182 99 *straight* tight, close 106 *fee in sufferaunce* property kept after the right to it has lapsed 109 *ywis* certainly *thoe* then 110 *forgoe* give up, do without 111 cp. Deuteronomy 10:9 'Wherefore [the tribe of] Levi hath no part nor inheritance with his brethren; the Lord is his inheritance, according as the Lord thy God promised him'; the reference is noted by E. K. 117 *tract* course 121 *Some gan* 'meant of the Pope, and his Antichristian prelates, which usurpe a tyrannical dominion in the Churche . . .' E. K. *gape* long 125 *leave* stop *ligge* lie 126 *colour* pretence

This was the first sourse of shepheards sorowe,
That now nill be quitt with baile, nor borrowe.

PALINODE.

Three thinges to beare, bene very burdenous,
But the fourth to forbeare, is outragious.
Wemen that of Loves longing once lust,
Hardly forbearen, but have it they must:
So when choler is inflamed with rage,
Wanting revenge, is hard to asswage:
And who can counsell a thristie soule,
With patience to forbeare the offred bowle?
But of all burdens, that a man can beare,
Moste is, a fooles talke to beare and to heare.
I wene the Geaunt has not such a weight,
That beares on his shoulders the heavens height.
Thou findest faulte, where nys to be found,
And buildest strong warke upon a weake ground:
Thou raylest on right withouten reason,
And blamest hem much, for small encheason.
How shoulden shepheardes live, if not so?
What? should they pynen in payne and woe?
Nay sayd I thereto, by my deare borrowe,
If I may rest, I nill live in sorrowe.
  Sorrowe ne neede be hastened on:
For he will come without calling anone.
While times enduren of tranquillitie,
Usen we freely our felicitie.
For when approchen the stormie stowres,
We mought with our shoulders beare of the sharpe showres.
And sooth to sayne, nought seemeth sike strife,
That shepheardes so witen ech others life,

182 130 *sourse* 'welspring and originall' E. K. 131 *nill* will not *quitt* freed, released *borrowe* 'pledge or suertie' E. K. 135 *Hardly forbearen* refrain with difficulty 137 *Wanting* lacking 142 *Geaunt* 'the greate Atlas' E. K. 144 *nys* none is 145 *warke* 'worke' E. K. 147 *encheason* 'cause, occasion' E. K. 150 *deare borrowe* 'our saviour, the commen pledge of all mens debts to death' E. K. 151 *nill* will not 156 *stowres* disturbances, bad times 157 *beare* keep 158 *nought seemeth* 'is unseemely' E. K. 159 *witen* 'blame' E. K.

And layen her faults the world beforne,
The while their foes done eache of hem scorne.
Let none mislike of that may not be mended:
So conteck soone by concord mought be ended.

PIERS.

Shepheard, I list none accordaunce make
With shepheard, that does the right way forsake.
And of the twaine, if choice were to me,
Had lever my foe, then my freend he be.
For what concord han light and darke sam?
Or what peace has the Lion with the Lambe?

ALEXANDER HUME

183 [*from* Of the day Estivall]

O Perfite light, quhilk schaid away,
The darkenes from the light, Gen.1.4.16
And set a ruler ou'r the day,
Ane uther ou'r the night.

Thy glorie when the day foorth flies,
Mair vively dois appeare,
Nor at midday unto our eyes,
The shining Sun is cleare.

182 163 *conteck* 'strife, contention' E. K. 164 *accordaunce* agreement 167 *lever* rather 168 *han* 'have' E. K. *sam* 'together' E. K. 169 Piers goes on to tell the tale of the fox which, according to the poem's Argument, 'by such a counterpoynt of craftines deceived and devoured the credulous kidde'

183 Title *Estivall* of the summer solstice 1 *schaid away* separated, divided 2 cp. Genesis 1:4 and 1.16 'And God saw the light, that it was good: and God divided the light from the darkness . . . And God made two great lights; the greater light to rule the day, and the lesser light to rule the night: he made the stars also' 6 *vively* vividly, distinctly 7 *Nor* than

The shaddow of the earth anon,
Remooves and drawes by,
Sine in the East, when it is gon,
Appeares a clearer sky.

The crepuscule matutine

Quhilk Sunne perceaves the little larks,
The lapwing and the snyp,
And tunes their sangs like natures clarks,
Ou'r midow, mure, and stryp.

Bot everie bais'd nocturnall beast,
Na langer may abide,
They hy away baith maist and least,
Them selves in house to hide.

They dread the day fra thay it see,
And from the sight of men.
To saits, and covars fast they flee,
As Lyons to their den.

Oure *Hemisphere* is poleist clein,
And lightened more and more,
While everie thing be clearely sein,
Quhilk seemed dim before.

Except the glistering astres bright,
Which all the night were cleere,
Offusked with a greater light,
Na langer dois appeare.

The golden globe incontinent,
Sets up his shining head,
And ou'r the earth and firmament,
Displayes his beims abread.

A description of the morning.

183 10 side-note *crepuscule matutine* morning twilight 11 *Sine* then 15 *clarks* choristers 16 *mure* moor *stryp* small stream 17 *bais'd* fearful 19 *hy* hie, hurry *maist and least* the largest and the smallest 21 *fra* when 23 *saits* sets, lairs *covars* covers, hiding-places 25 *poleist clein* polished bright 27 *While* until 29 *astres* stars 31 *Offusked* obfuscated, obscured 33 *incontinent* at once 36 *abread* abroad

For joy the birds with boulden throts,
Agains his visage shein,
Takes up their kindelie musicke nots,
In woods and gardens grein.

Up braids the carefull husbandman,
His cornes, and vines to see,
And everie tymous artisan,
In buith worke busilie.

The pastor quits the slouthfull sleepe,
And passis forth with speede,
His little camow-nosed sheepe,
And rowtting kie to feede.

The passenger from perrels sure,
Gangs gladly foorth the way:
Breife, everie living creature,
Takes comfort of the day,

The subtile mottie rayons light,
At rifts thay are in wonne,
The glansing thains, and vitre bright,
Resplends against the sunne.

The dew upon the tender crops,
Lyke pearles white and round,
Or like to melted silver drops,
Refreshes all the ground.

The mystie rocke, the clouds of raine,
From tops of mountaines skails,
Cleare are the highest hils and plaine,
The vapors takes the vails,

183 37 *boulden* swollen 38 *shein* bright 39 *kindelie* according to kind, natural 41 *braids* rises *carefull* painstaking, watchful 43 *tymous* early 44 *buith* booth 47 *camow* snub 48 *rowtting kie* lowing cows 53 *mottie rayons* dusty beams, rays full of motes 54 *rifts* chinks, cracks *wonne* entered 55 *glansing thains* shimmering vanes *vitre* window-glass 56 *Resplends* shines brightly 57 *crops* heads, tops 61 *rocke* steam, vapour 62 *skails* disperses

Begaried is the saphire pend,
With sprainges of skarlet hew,
And preciously from end till end,
Damasked white and blew,

The ample heaven of fabrik sure,
In cleannes dois surpas,
The chrystall and the silver pure,
Or clearest poleist glas.

The time sa tranquill is and still,
That na where sall ye find,
Saife on ane high, and barren hill,
Ane aire of peeping wind.

All trees and simples great and small,
That balmie leife do beir,
Nor thay were painted on a wall,
Na mair they move or steir.

Calme is the deepe, and purpour se,
Yee smuther nor the sand,
The wals that woltring wont to be,
Are stable like the land.

Sa silent is the cessile air,
That every cry and call,
The hils, and dails, and forrest fair,
Againe repeates them all.

The rivers fresh, the callor streames,
Ou'r rockes can softlie rin,
The water cleare like chrystall seames,
And makes a pleasant din.

183 65 *Begaried* begeared, ornamentally dressed *pend* vault 66 *sprainges* streaks 69 *fabrik* fabrication, workmanship 75 *Saife* save, except 76 *peeping* piping 77 *simples* herbs 79 *Nor* than if 81 *purpour se* purple sea 82 *nor* than 83 *wals* waves *woltring* weltering, rolling 85 *cessile* yielding, gentle 89 *callor* cool 90 *rin* run

The fields, and earthly superfice,
With verdure greene is spread,
And naturallie but artifice,
In partie coulors cled.

The flurishes and fragrant flowres,
Throw *Phœbus* fostring heit,
Refresht with dew and silver showres,
Casts up ane odor sweit.

The clogged busie bumming beis,
That never thinks to drowne,
On flowers and flourishes of treis,
Collects their liquor browne.

A description of the midday.

The Sunne maist like a speedie post,
With ardent course ascends,
The beautie of the heavenly host,
Up to our Zenith tends.

Nocht guided be na *Phaeton*,
Nor trained in a chyre,
Bot be the high and haly on,
Quhilk dois all where impire.

183 93 *superfice* surface 95 *but* without 97 *flurishes* blossoms 101 *clogged* loaded, burdened *bumming* humming 102 *drowne* drone, buzz 105 *post* postman, courier 106 *ardent* burning 110 *trained* drawn *chyre* chariot 111 *on* God 112 *impire* rule absolutely. The noon sun is placed centrally in the poem

Sir John Davies

184 [*from* Epigrammes]

In Cosmum 17

Cosmus hath more discoursing in his head,
Then Jove, when Pallas issued from his braine,
And still he strives to be delivered,
Of all his thoughtes at once, but al in vaine.
For as we see at all the play house dores,
When ended is the play, the daunce, and song:
A thousand townsemen, gentlemen, and whores,
Porters and serving-men togither throng,
So thoughts of drinking, thriving, wenching, war,
And borrowing money, raging in his minde,
To issue all at once so forwarde are,
As none at all can perfect passage finde.

Joseph Hall

185 [*from* Virgidemiarum Book 5]

Hous-keping's dead, *Saturio*: wot'st thou where?
For-sooth they say far hence in *Brek-neck* shire.
And ever since they say, that feele and tast,
That men may breake their neck, soone as their fast. . . .

184 1 *discoursing* conversation, talk 9 *thriving* making money

185 1 *Saturio* the name of a parasite in Plautus' *The Persian* 2 *Brek-neck shire* Breconshire in Wales, but an allusion to Cambridge may be intended for Hall's contemporary university audience

There findest thou some stately *Dorick* frame
Or neate *Ionicke* worke;
Like the vaine bubble of *Iberian* pride,
That over-croweth all the world beside.
Which rear'd to raise the crazy Monarches fame,
Strives for a Court and for a Colledge name;
Yet nought within, but louzy coul's doth hold,
Like a scab'd Cuckow in a cage of gold;
So pride above doth shade the shame below:
A golden Periwig on a Black-mores brow.
When *Mævios* first page of his poesie,
Nayl'd to an hundreth postes for noveltie,
With his big title, an *Italian* mot,
Layes siege unto the backward buyers grote.
Which all within is draftie sluttish geere,
Fit for the Oven or the Kitching fire:
So this gay gate adds fuell to thy thought,
That such proud piles were never rays'd for nought.
Beat the broad gates, a goodly hollow sound
With doubled Ecchoes doth againe rebound,
But not a Dog doth barke to welcome thee,
Nor churlish Porter canst thou chafing see:
All dumbe and silent, like the dead of night,
Or dwelling of some sleepy *Sybarite*.
The marble pavement hid with desart weede,
With house-leeke, thistle, docke, and hemlock-seed.
But if thou chance cast up thy wondring eyes,
Thou shalt discerne upon the Frontispice,

185 5 *There* an ostentatious, great house (cp. no. 190 ll. 1–5) 7 *bubble* Philip II of Spain's palace, the Escorial, near Madrid; its buildings included a monastery, a mausoleum and a library 11 *coul's* cowls, monks' hoods, monks 15 *Mævios* the type of the learned scholar who indulges in writing poetry 16 title-pages were often fixed to posts to advertise new works 17 *big* long *mot* motto 18 *grote* groat, coin worth four (old) pence 19 *draftie* rubbishy, worthless *geere* matter, stuff, things 29 *desart* barren, waste 32 *Frontispice** decorated entrance to a building

ΟΥΔΕΙΣ ΕΙΣΙΤΩ graven up on hie,
A fragment of olde *Platoes* Poesie:
The meaning is, Sir foole ye may be gone,
Go backe by leave, for way here lieth none.
Looke to the towred chymneis which should bee
The wind-pipes of good hospitalitie,
Through which it breatheth to the open ayre,
Betokening life and liberall welfaire,
Lo, there th'unthankfull swallow takes her rest,
And fils the Tonnell with her circled nest,
Nor halfe that smoke from all his chymneies goes
Which one Tabacco-pipe drives through his nose;
So rawbone hunger scorns the mudded wals,
And gin's to revell it in Lordly halls.

EVERARD GUILPIN

186 [*from* Skialetheia Satire 5]

What more variety of pleasures can
An idle Citty-walke affoord a man?
More troublesome and tedious well I know
T'will be, into the peopled streets to goe,
Witnes that hotch-potch of so many noyses,
Black-saunts of so many severall voyces,
That Chaous of rude sounds, that harmony,
And *Dyapason* of harsh *Barbary*,
Compos'd of severall mouthes, and severall cries,
Which to mens eares turne both their tongs and eies.

185 33–4 'Let no one enter'; Plato's Academy was supposed by later writers to have had the poesy or motto 'Let no one who is not a geometrician enter' on a notice 42 *Tonnell* tunnel 45 *rawbone* with bones sticking out from hunger

186 6 *Black-saunts* black sanctus, a discord of harsh sounds, expressing contempt 8 *Dyapason* full harmony, concord; deep outburst of sound *Barbary* barbarousness, barbarity; uncultivated, rude speech

There squeaks a cart-wheele, here a tumbrel rumbles
Heere scolds an old Bawd, there a Porter grumbles.
Heere two tough Car-men combat for the way,
There two for looks begin a coward fray,
Two swaggering knaves heere brable for a whore,
There brauls an Ale-knight for his fat-grown score.
  But oh purgation! yon rotten-throated slaves
Engarlanded with coney-catching knaves,
Whores, Bedles, bawdes and Sergeants filthily
Chaunt *Kemps* Jigge, or the *Burgonians* tragedy:
But in good time, there's one hath nipt a bong,
Farewell my harts, for he hath marrd the song.
  Yet might all this, this too bad be excusd,
Were not an Ethicke soule much more abusd,
And her still patience choakt by vanitie,
With unsufferable inhumanitie:
For whose gall is't that would not overflow,
To meete in every streete where he shall goe,
With folly maskt in divers semblances?
The Cittie is the mappe of vanities,
The marte of fooles, the *Magazin* of gulles,
The painters shop of Antickes: walke in Poules,
And but observe the sundry kindes of shapes,
Th'wilt sweare that London is as rich in apes
As *Affricke Tabraca.*

186 13 *Car-men* carters, carriers 15 *brable* quarrel, squabble 16 *Ale-knight* devotee of the ale-house *score* reckoning, bill 18 *Engarlanded** surrounded as with a garland *coney-catching* gulling, swindling 20 *Kemps Jigge* none of the actor William Kemp's jigs, which were short 'revue' pieces with songs and dancing, has survived, although they were popular in the early 1590s *the Burgonians tragedy* in July 1598 John Barrose, a Burgundian, was hanged for murdering a City official who had arrested him for debt 21 *nipt a bong* picked a pocket; cut a purse 31 *Magazin* storehouse, repository 32 *Antickes* clowns, mountebanks; grotesques *Poules* St Paul's Cathedral 35 *Affricke Tabraca* Tabarka in North Africa

ANONYMOUS

187 A Songe bewailinge the tyme of Christmas, So much decayed in Englande

Christmas is my name, Farr have I gone, have I gone, have I gone,
have I gone without regarde,
Whereas great men, by flockes they be flowen, they be flowen
they be flowen, they be flowen to London warde,
Where they in pompe, and pleasure do waste,
that which Christmas had wont to feast
Wellay daie.
Houses where musicke was wonted to ringe,
Nothinge but Batts, and Ouls now do singe
Wellay daie, wallay daie, wallay daie, where should I stay.

Christmas bread and Beefe, is turnd into stons, into stons, into stons,
Into Stones and Silken ragges.
And ladie monie it doth slepe, It doth slepe, It doth sleepe,
It doth sleepe in Mysers bagges.
Where manie gallantes once abounde,
Nought but A dogg and A Sheperd is founde,
Wellay day.
Places where Christmas revells did keepe,
Are now becom habitations for Sheepe.
Wallay day, wallay day, wellay day, where should I stay.

Pan the Shepherdes God, doth deface, doth deface, doth deface,
doth deface, Ladie Ceres crowne,
And Tilliges doth decay, doth decay, doth decay,
doth decay in everie towne.
Landlordes their rentes so highly Inhaunce,
That Peares the plowman, barefoote doth daunce,
Wellay day.

187 23 *Tilliges* tilled, ploughed lands 26 *Peares the plowman* the traditional name for the ploughman; cp. William Langland's poem and no. 182

Farmers that Christmas woulde Intertaine,
hath scarselie withall them selves to mantaine,
Wellay day, wellay day, wellay day, where should I stay.

Go to the Protestant, hele protest, hele protest, hele protest,
he will protest and bouldlie boaste,
And to the Puritine, he is so hote, he is so hote, he is so hote,
he is so hote he will burne the Roast,
The Catholike good deedes will not scorne,
nor will not see pore Christmas forlorne,
Wellay Day.
Since Holines no good deedes will do,
Protestantes had best turn Papistes too,
Wellay day, Wellay day, wellay day, where should I stay.

Pride and Luxurie, doth devoure, doth devoure, doth devoure,
doth devoure house kepinge quite,
And Beggarie, doth beget, doth begett, doth begett,
doth begett in manie A knight.
Madam for sooth in Cooch she must reele
Although she weare her hoose out at heele,
Wellay day.
And on her backe were that for her weede,
that woulde both me, and manie other feede,
Wellay day, Wallay day, wellay day, where should I stay.

Breefelye for to ende, here I fynde, here I fynde,
here I fynde such great vacation
That some great houses, do seeme to have, Seme to have, seeme to have,
for to have some great Purgation,
With Purginge Pills, such effectes they have Shewed,
that out of dores, theyr owners they have spewed.
Wellay day.
And when Christmas goes by and calles,
Nothinge but solitude, and naked walls,
Wellay day, Wellay day, wellay day, where should I staie.

187 52 *vacation* emptying out

Philemels Cottages are turnd into gould, into gould,
Into gould for harboringe Jove.
And great mens houses up for to hould, up for to houlde,
up for to hould, make great men mone,
But in the Cittie they saie they do live,
Where gould by handfulls away they do give
Wellay day.
And therefore thither I purpose to passe,
hopinge at london to fynde the goulden Asse,
Ile away, Ile away, Ile away, Ile no longer staie.

JOHN DONNE

188 A nocturnall upon S.*Lucies* day, Being the shortest day

Tis the yeares midnight, and it is the dayes,
Lucies, who scarce seaven houres herself unmaskes,
The Sunne is spent, and now his flasks
Send forth light squibs, no constant rayes;
The worlds whole sap is sunke:
The generall balme th'hydroptique earth hath drunk,
Whither, as to the beds-feet, life is shrunke,
Dead and enterr'd; yet all these seeme to laugh,
Compar'd with mee, who am their Epitaph.

Study me then, you who shall lovers bee
At the next world, that is, at the next Spring:
For I am every dead thing,
In whom love wrought new Alchimie.
For his art did expresse

187 61 *Philemels* Philemon's 69 *goulden Asse* proverbial for sterile wealth

188 Title *nocturnall** night-piece 3 *flasks* stars, which store the sun's energy as flasks store gunpowder 4 *squibs* fireworks 6 *generall balme* essential oil for preserving everything *hydroptique*** insatiably thirsty 14 *expresse* squeeze out by crushing

A quintessence even from nothingnesse,
From dull privations, and leane emptinesse
He ruin'd mee, and I am re-begot
Of absence, darknesse, death; things which are not.

All others, from all things, draw all that's good,
Life, soule, forme, spirit, whence they beeing have;
I, by loves limbecke, am the grave
Of all, that's nothing. Oft a flood
Have wee two wept, and so
Drownd the whole world, us two; oft did we grow
To be two Chaosses, when we did show
Care to ought else; and often absences
Withdrew our soules, and made us carcasses.

But I am by her death, (which word wrongs her)
Of the first nothing, the Elixer grown;
Were I a man, that I were one,
I needs must know; I should preferre,
If I were any beast,
Some ends, some means; Yea plants, yea stones detest,
And love; all, all some properties invest;
If I an ordinary nothing were,
As shadow, a light, and body must be here.

But I am None; nor will my Sunne renew.
You lovers, for whose sake, the lesser Sunne
At this time to the Goat is runne
To fetch new lust, and give it you,
Enjoy your summer all;
Since shee enjoyes her long nights festivall,
Let mee prepare towards her, and let mee call
This houre her Vigill, and her eve, since this
Both the yeares, and the dayes deep midnight is.

188 17 *re-begot* born again 21 *limbecke* alembic, used for chemical distillation 37 *None* no ordinary nothing 39 *Goat* the star-sign of Capricorn

ÆMILIA LANYER

189 The Description of Cooke-ham

Farewell (sweet *Cooke-ham*) where I first obtain'd
Grace from that Grace where perfit Grace remain'd;
And where the Muses gave their full consent,
I should have powre the virtuous to content:
Where princely Palace will'd me to indite,
The sacred Storie of the Soules delight.
Farewell (sweet Place) where Virtue then did rest,
And all delights did harbour in her breast:
Never shall my sad eies againe behold
Those pleasures which my thoughts did then unfold:
Yet you (great Lady) Mistris of that Place,
From whose desires did spring this worke of Grace;
Vouchsafe to thinke upon those pleasures past,
As fleeting worldly Joyes that could not last:
Or, as dimme shadowes of celestiall pleasures,
Which are desir'd above all earthly treasures.
Oh how (me thought) against you thither came,
Each part did seeme some new delight to frame!
The House receiv'd all ornaments to grace it,
And would indure no foulenesse to deface it.
The Walkes put on their summer Liveries,
And all things else did hold like similies:
The Trees with leaves, with fruits, with flowers clad,
Embrac'd each other, seeming to be glad,
Turning themselves to beauteous Canopies,
To shade the bright Sunne from your brighter eies:
The cristall Streames with silver spangles graced,
While by the glorious Sunne they were embraced:
The little Birds in chirping notes did sing,
To entertaine both You and that sweet Spring.

189 Title *Cooke-ham* a village on the river Thames in Berkshire 2 *Grace* Margaret Clifford, Countess of Cumberland 6 *Storie* Lanyer's collection of poems *Salve deus rex Judæorum* 21 *Liveries* clothes

And *Philomela* with her sundry layes,
Both You and that delightfull Place did praise.
Oh how me thought each plant, each floure, each tree
Set forth their beauties then to welcome thee!
The very Hills right humbly did descend,
When you to tread upon them did intend.
And as you set your feete, they still did rise,
Glad that they could receive so rich a prise.
The gentle Windes did take delight to bee
Among those woods that were so grac'd by thee.
And in sad murmure utterd pleasing sound,
That Pleasure in that place might more abound:
The swelling Bankes deliver'd all their pride,
When such a *Phœnix* once they had espide.
Each Arbor, Banke, each Seate, each stately Tree,
Thought themselves honor'd in supporting thee.
The pretty Birds would oft come to attend thee,
Yet flie away for feare they should offend thee:
The little creatures in the Burrough by
Would come abroad to sport them in your eye;
Yet fearefull of the Bowe in your faire Hand,
Would runne away when you did make a stand.
Now let me come unto that stately Tree,
Wherein such goodly Prospects you did see;
That Oake that did in height his fellowes passe,
As much as lofty trees, low growing grasse:
Much like a comely Cedar streight and tall,
Whose beauteous stature farre exceeded all:
How often did you visite this faire tree,
Which seeming joyfull in receiving thee,
Would like a Palme tree spread his armes abroad,
Desirous that you there should make abode:
Whose faire greene leaves much like a comely vaile,
Defended *Phebus* when he would assaile:
Whose pleasing boughes did yeeld a coole fresh ayre,
Joying his happinesse when you were there.
Where beeing seated, you might plainely see,
Hills, vales, and woods, as if on bended knee

189 49 *Burrough* burrow 64 *Defended* kept off

They had appeard, your honour to salute,
Or to preferre some strange unlook'd for sute:
All interlac'd with brookes and christall springs,
A Prospect fit to please the eyes of Kings:
And thirteene shires appear'd all in your sight,
Europe could not affoard much more delight.
What was there then but gave you all content,
While you the time in meditation spent,
Of their Creators powre, which there you saw,
In all his Creatures held a perfit Law;
And in their beauties did you plaine descrie,
His beauty, wisdome, grace, love, majestie.
In these sweet woods how often did you walke,
With Christ and his Apostles there to talke;
Placing his holy Writ in some faire tree,
To meditate what you therein did see:
With *Moyses* you did mount his holy Hill,
To know his pleasure, and performe his Will.
With lovely *David* you did often sing,
His holy Hymnes to Heavens Eternall King.
And in sweet musicke did your soule delight,
To sound his prayses, morning, noone, and night.
With blessed *Joseph* you did often feed
Your pined brethren, when they stood in need.
And that sweet Lady sprung from *Cliffords* race,
Of noble *Bedfords* blood, faire steame of Grace;
To honourable *Dorset* now espows'd,
In whose faire breast true virtue then was hous'd:
Oh what delight did my weake spirits find
In those pure parts of her well framed mind:

189 73 *shires* districts, regions 85 *Moyses* Moses fetching the Ten Commandments from Mount Sinai (Exodus 24–34) 88 *Hymnes* the Psalms 91 *Joseph* cp. Genesis 47:12 'And Joseph nourished his father, and his brethren, and all his father's household, with bread, according to their families' 92 *pined* exhausted by hunger 93 *Lady* Anne Clifford (1590–1676), daughter of Margaret Clifford 94 *Bedfords blood* Margaret Clifford was the youngest daughter of Francis Russell, Earl of Bedford *steame* stem, offshoot 95 *Dorset* Anne Clifford married Richard Sackville, Lord Buckhurst, third Earl of Dorset, on 25 February 1609 *espows'd* married

And yet it grieves me that I cannot be
Neere unto her, whose virtues did agree
With those faire ornaments of outward beauty,
Which did enforce from all both love and dutie.
Unconstant Fortune, thou art most too blame,
Who casts us downe into so lowe a frame:
Where our great friends we cannot dayly see,
So great a diffrence is there in degree.
Many are placed in those Orbes of state,
Parters in honour, so ordain'd by Fate;
Neerer in show, yet farther off in love,
In which, the lowest alwayes are above.
But whither am I carried in conceit?
My Wit too weake to conster of the great.
Why not? although we are but borne of earth,
We may behold the Heavens, despising death;
And loving heaven that is so farre above,
May in the end vouchsafe us entire love.
Therefore sweet Memorie doe thou retaine
Those pleasures past, which will not turne againe:
Remember beauteous *Dorsets* former sports,
So farre from beeing toucht by ill reports;
Wherein my selfe did alwaies beare a part,
While reverend Love presented my true heart:
Those recreations let me beare in mind,
Which her sweet youth and noble thoughts did finde:
Whereof depriv'd, I evermore must grieve,
Hating blind Fortune, carelesse to relieve.
And you sweet Cooke-ham, whom these Ladies leave,
I now must tell the griefe you did conceave
At their departure; when they went away,
How every thing retaind a sad dismay:
Nay long before, when once an inkeling came,
Me thought each thing did unto sorrow frame:

189 102 *enforce* compel, oblige 108 *Parters* sharers (?); perhaps the correct reading should be 'Partners' 112 *conster* construe, explain, interpret 119 *Dorsets ... sports* Anne Clifford's 'sports' may have included masquing 130 *dismay* utter loss of resolution in the face of difficulty 131 *inkeling* hint, slight intimation

The trees that were so glorious in our view,
Forsooke both flowres and fruit, when once they knew
Of your depart, their very leaves did wither,
Changing their colours as they grewe together.
But when they saw this had no powre to stay you,
They often wept, though speechlesse, could not pray you;
Letting their teares in your faire bosoms fall,
As if they said, Why will ye leave us all?
This being vaine, they cast their leaves away,
Hoping that pitie would have made you stay:
Their frozen tops, like Ages hoarie haires,
Showes their disasters, languishing in feares:
A swarthy riveld ryne all over spread,
Their dying bodies halfe alive, halfe dead.
But your occasions call'd you so away,
That nothing there had power to make you stay:
Yet did I see a noble gratefull minde,
Requiting each according to their kind;
Forgetting not to turne and take your leave
Of these sad creatures, powrelesse to receive
Your favour, when with griefe you did depart,
Placing their former pleasures in your heart;
Giving great charge to noble Memory,
There to preserve their love continually:
But specially the love of that faire tree,
That first and last you did vouchsafe to see:
In which it pleas'd you oft to take the ayre,
With noble *Dorset*, then a virgin faire:
Where many a learned Booke was read and skand
To this faire tree, taking me by the hand,
You did repeat the pleasures which had past,
Seeming to grieve they could no longer last.
And with a chaste, yet loving kisse tooke leave,
Of which sweet kisse I did it soone bereave:
Scorning a sencelesse creature should possesse
So rare a favour, so great happinesse.

189 145 *riveld* wrinkled *ryne* rind, bark; frost 161 *skand* scanned

No other kisse it could receive from me,
For feare to give backe what it tooke of thee:
So I ingratefull Creature did deceive it,
Of that which you vouchsaft in love to leave it.
And though it oft had giv'n me much content,
Yet this great wrong I never could repent:
But of the happiest made it most forlorne,
To shew that nothing's free from Fortunes scorne,
While all the rest with this most beauteous tree,
Made their sad consort Sorrowes harmony.
The Floures that on the banks and walkes did grow,
Crept in the ground, the Grasse did weepe for woe.
The Windes and Waters seem'd to chide together,
Because you went away they knew not whither:
And those sweet Brookes that ranne so faire and cleare,
With griefe and trouble wrinckled did appeare.
Those pretty Birds that wonted were to sing,
Now neither sing, nor chirp, nor use their wing;
But with their tender feet on some bare spray,
Warble forth sorrow, and their owne dismay.
Faire *Philomela* leaves her mournefull Ditty,
Drownd in dead sleepe, yet can procure no pittie:
Each arbour, banke, each seate, each stately tree,
Lookes bare and desolate now for want of thee;
Turning greene tresses into frostie gray,
While in cold griefe they wither all away.
The Sunne grew weake, his beames no comfort gave,
While all greene things did make the earth their grave:
Each brier, each bramble, when you went away,
Caught fast your clothes, thinking to make you stay:
Delightfull Eccho wonted to reply
To our last words, did now for sorrow die:
The house cast off each garment that might grace it,
Putting on Dust and Cobwebs to deface it.
All desolation then there did appeare,
When you were going whom they held so deare.
This last farewell to *Cooke-ham* here I give,
When I am dead thy name in this may live,

189 178 *consort* accord, concert 187 *spray* twigs of a tree, shrub

Wherein I have perform'd her noble hest,
Whose virtues lodge in my unworthy breast,
And ever shall, so long as life remaines,
Tying my heart to her by those rich chaines.

BEN JONSON

190 TO PENSHURST

Thou art not, PENSHURST, built to envious show,
Of touch, or marble; nor canst boast a row
Of polish'd pillars, or a roofe of gold:
Thou hast no lantherne, whereof tales are told;
Or stayre, or courts; but stand'st an ancient pile,
And these grudg'd at, art reverenc'd the while.
Thou joy'st in better markes, of soyle, of ayre,
Of wood, of water: therein thou art faire.
Thou hast thy walkes for health, as well as sport:
Thy *Mount*, to which the *Dryads* doe resort,
Where PAN, and BACCHUS their high feasts have made,
Beneath the broad beech, and the chest-nut shade;
That taller tree, which of a nut was set,
At his great birth, where all the *Muses* met.
There, in the writhed barke, are cut the names
Of many a SYLVANE, taken with his flames.
And thence, the ruddy *Satyres* oft provoke
The lighter *Faunes*, to reach thy *Ladies oke*.
Thy copp's, too, nam'd of GAMAGE, thou hast there,
That never failes to serve thee season'd deere,

190 2 *touch* black marble 4 *lantherne* glazed turret on top of part of a building 5 *stayre* external staircase (?) *courts* courtyards, or the buildings within them; tennis-courts (?) *pile* castle, stronghold; imposing group of buildings 7 *markes* characteristic properties 10 *Mount* raised piece of ground *Dryads* classical wood nymphs 13 *tree* an oak 14 *his* Philip Sidney's 15 *writhed* contorted, twisting 16 *flames* passion 19 *Gamage* Barbara Gamage married Robert Sidney in 1584; she died in 1621

When thou would'st feast, or exercise thy friends.
 The lower land, that to the river bends,
Thy sheepe, thy bullocks, kine, and calves doe feed:
 The middle grounds thy mares, and horses breed.
Each banke doth yeeld thee coneyes; and the topps
 Fertile of wood, ASHORE, and SYDNEY'S copp's,
To crowne thy open table, doth provide
 The purpled pheasant, with the speckled side:
The painted partrich lyes in every field,
 And, for thy messe, is willing to be kill'd.
And if the high-swolne *Medway* faile thy dish,
 Thou hast thy ponds, that pay thee tribute fish,
Fat, aged carps, that runne into thy net.
 And pikes, now weary their owne kinde to eat,
As loth, the second draught, or cast to stay,
 Officiously, at first, themselves betray.
Bright eeles, that emulate them, and leape on land,
 Before the fisher, or into his hand.
Then hath thy orchard fruit, thy garden flowers,
 Fresh as the ayre, and new as are the houres.
The earely cherry, with the later plum,
 Fig, grape, and quince, each in his time doth come:
The blushing apricot, and woolly peach
 Hang on thy walls, that every child may reach.
And though thy walls be of the countrey stone,
 They'are rear'd with no mans ruine, no mans grone,
There's none, that dwell about them, wish them downe;
 But all come in, the farmer, and the clowne:
And no one empty-handed, to salute
 Thy lord, and lady, though they have no sute.
Some bring a capon, some a rurall cake,
 Some nuts, some apples; some that thinke they make

190 25 *coneyes* rabbits 29 *painted partrich* cp. Martial, *Epigrams* 3.58.15 'picta perdix' 30 cp. Juvenal, *Satires* 4.68–9 'and eat a turbot that has been kept to grace your reign. The fish himself was anxious to be caught' *messe* prepared serving of food; table 31 *Medway* river in Kent 34 *kinde* species 36 *Officiously* dutifully 40 *houres* Horae 48 *clowne* peasant, rustic 49 *empty-handed*** without a gift 51 *capon* castrated cock

The better cheeses, bring 'hem; or else send
By their ripe daughters, whom they would commend
This way to husbands; and whose baskets beare
An embleme of themselves, in plum, or peare.
But what can this (more then expresse their love)
Adde to thy free provisions, farre above
The neede of such? whose liberall boord doth flow,
With all, that hospitalitie doth know!
Where comes no guest, but is allow'd to eate,
Without his feare, and of thy lords owne meate:
Where the same beere, and bread, and selfe-same wine,
That is his Lordships, shall be also mine.
And I not faine to sit (as some, this day,
At great mens tables) and yet dine away.
Here no man tells my cups; nor, standing by,
A waiter, doth my gluttony envy:
But gives me what I call, and lets me eate,
He knowes, below, he shall finde plentie of meate,
Thy tables hoord not up for the next day,
Nor, when I take my lodging, need I pray
For fire, or lights, or livorie: all is there;
As if thou, then, wert mine, or I raign'd here:
There's nothing I can wish, for which I stay.
That found King JAMES, when hunting late, this way,
With his brave sonne, the Prince, they saw thy fires
Shine bright on every harth as the desires
Of thy *Penates* had beene set on flame,
To entertayne them; or the countrey came,
With all their zeale, to warme their welcome here.
What (great, I will not say, but) sodayne cheare
Did'st thou, then, make 'hem! and what praise was heap'd
On thy good lady, then! who, therein, reap'd
The just reward of her high huswifery;
To have her linnen, plate, and all things nigh,
When shee was farre: and not a roome, but drest,
As if it had expected such a guest!

190 56 *embleme* of sexual ripeness 67 *tells* counts 70 *below* below stairs, in the kitchen or servants' hall 73 *livorie* food, provisions 82 *sodayne* prompt, immediate 87 *drest* prepared

These, PENSHURST, are thy praise, and yet not all.
    Thy lady's noble, fruitfull, chaste withall.
His children thy great lord may call his owne:
    A fortune, in this age, but rarely knowne.
They are, and have beene taught religion: Thence
    Their gentler spirits have suck'd innocence.
Each morne, and even, they are taught to pray,
    With the whole houshold, and may, every day,
Reade, in their vertuous parents noble parts,
    The mysteries of manners, armes, and arts.
Now, PENSHURST, they that will proportion thee
    With other edifices, when they see
Those proud, ambitious heaps, and nothing else,
    May say, their lords have built, but thy lord dwells.

MICHAEL DRAYTON

191 [*from* Pastorals]

The Ninth Eglogue

Late 'twas in *June*, the Fleece when fully growne,
In the full compasse of the passed yeere,
The Season well by skilfull Shepheards knowne,
That them provide immediately to sheere.

Their Lambes late wax't so lusty and so strong,
That time did them their Mothers Teats forbid,
And in the fields the common flocks among,
Eate of the same Grasse that the greater did.

190 99 *proportion* compare, estimate 102 cp. Martial, *Epigrams* 12.1.8 'How well you are, not housed'

191 5 *lusty* vigorous

When not a Shepheard any thing that could,
But greaz'd his start-ups blacke as *Autumns* Sloe,
And for the better credit of the Wold,
In their fresh Russets every one doth goe.

Who now a Posie pins not in his Cap?
And not a Garland Baldricke-wise doth weare?
Some, of such Flowers as to his hand doth hap,
Others, such as a secret meaning beare:

He from his Lasse him Lavander hath sent,
Shewing her Love, and doth requitall crave,
Him Rosemary his Sweet-heart, whose intent,
Is that, he her should in remembrance have.

Roses, his youth and strong desire expresse,
Her Sage, doth shew his soverainty in all,
The *July*-Flowre declares his gentlenesse,
Time, Truth, the Pansie, Harts-ease Maydens call:

In Cotes such simples, simply in request,
Wherewith proud Courts in greatnesse scorne to mell,
For Countrey toyes become the Countrey best,
And please poore Shepheards, and become them well.

When the new-wash'd flocke from the rivers side,
Comming as white as *Januaries* Snow,
The Ram with Nose-gaies beares his Hornes in pride,
And no lesse brave, the Bell-wether doth goe.

After their faire flocks in a lusty rowt,
Came the gay Swaynes with Bag-pipes strongly blowne,
And busied, though this solemne sport about,
Yet had each one an eye unto his owne.

191 10 *start-ups* rustic labourer's boots *Sloe* blackthorn berry 12 *Russets* reddish-brown or grey clothes 14 *Baldricke* belt worn from one shoulder across the chest and under the other arm 25 *Cotes* humble country dwellings *simples* medicinal herbs 26 *mell* mix, get involved 28 *become* suit, fit 32 *brave* handsomely got up *Bell-wether* leading sheep of a flock

And by the ancient Statutes of the Field,
He that his Flocks the earlyest Lambe should bring,
(As it fell out then, ROWLANDS charge to yeeld)
Alwayes for that yeere was the Shepheards King.

And soone preparing for the Shepheards Boord,
Upon a Greene that curiously was squar'd,
With Country Cates be'ng plentifully stor'd:
And 'gainst their comming handsomely prepar'd:

New Whig, with Water from the cleerest streame,
Greene Plummes, and Wildings, Cherries chiefe of Feast,
Fresh Cheese, and Dowsets, Curds and clowted Creame,
Spic'd Syllibubs, and Sider of the best:

And to the same downe solemnely they sit,
In the fresh shaddow of their Summer Bowres,
With sundrie sweets them every way to fit,
The Neighb'ring Vale dispoyled of her Flowres.

And whil'st together merry thus they make,
The Sunne to West a little 'gan to leane,
Which the late fervour, soone againe did slake,
When as the Nymphs came forth upon the Plaine,

Here might you many a Shepheardesse have seene,
Of which no place, as *Cotswold*, such doth yeeld,
Some of it native, some for love I weene,
Thither were come from many a fertill Field.

There was the Widdowes Daughter of the *Glen*,
Deare ROSALYND, that scarsly brook'd compare,
The *Moreland*-Mayden, so admir'd of Men,
Bright GOLDY-LOCKS, and PHILLIDA the faire.

191 41 *Boord* table spread for a meal 42 *curiously* carefully, exactly *squar'd* divided into squares 43 *Cates* delicacies 45 *Whig* sour milk, buttermilk, whey 46 *Wildings* wild apples 47 *Dowsets* doucets, sweet dishes *clowted* clotted 48 *Syllibubs* syllabubs, cream dishes, mixed with wine and frothed up 58 *Cotswold* range of hills in Gloucestershire 61–2 cp. Edmund Spenser, *The shepheardes calender*, 'Aprill' l. 26, 'And woes the Widdowes daughter of the glenne'; neither Spenser's nor Drayton's Rosalind, nor any of the other maidens mentioned in Drayton's poem, has been convincingly identified with any known woman 63 *Moreland-Mayden* identified later in the poem as Sylvia

LETTICE and PARNEL, pretty lovely Peates,
CUSSE of the Fold, the Virgin of the Well,
Faire AMBRY with the Alablaster Teates,
And more, whose Names were here to long to tell.

Which now came forward following their Sheepe,
Their batning Flocks on grassy Leaes to hold,
Thereby from skathe, and perill them to keepe,
Till Evening come that it were time to fold.

When now, at last, as lik'd the Shepheards King,
(At whose command they all obedient were)
Was pointed, who the Roundelay should sing,
And who againe the under-Song should beare:

The first whereof he BATTE doth bequeath,
A wittier Wag on all the Wold's not found,
GORBO, the Man, that him should sing beneath,
Which his lowd Bag-pipe skilfully could sound.

Who amongst all the Nymphs that were in sight,
BATTE his daintie DAFFADIL there mist,
Which, to enquire of, doing all his might,
Him his Companion kindly doth assist.

BATTE.

GORBO, *as thou cam'st this way,*
By yonder little Hill,
Or, as thou, through the Fields didst stray,
Saw'st thou my DAFFADIL?

Shee's in a Frocke of Lincolne *greene,*
Which colour likes her sight,
And never hath her beautie seene,
But through a vale of white.

191 65 *Peates* pets, darlings 70 *batning* growing fat 71 *skathe* harm, danger 75 *pointed* appointed *Roundelay* short, simple song with a refrain 76 *under-Song* refrain, burden 84 *kindly* in this kind 89 *Lincolne greene* bright-green material made at Lincoln 90 *likes her sight* flatters her appearance

Then Roses richer to behold,
That trim up Lovers Bowres,
The Pansie and the Marigold,
Tho PHŒBUS *Paramours.*

GORBO. *Thou well describ'st the Daffadill,*
It is not full an houre,
Since, by the Spring, neere yonder Hill,
I saw that lovely Flowre.

BATTE. *Yet my faire Flowre thou didst not meet,*
Nor newes of her didst bring,
And yet my DAFFADIL'S *more sweet,*
Then that by yonder Spring.

GORBO. *I saw a Shepheard that doth keepe,*
In yonder Field of Lillies,
Was making (as he fed his Sheepe)
A Wreathe of Daffadillies.

BATTE. *Yet,* GORBO, *thou delud'st me still,*
My Flowre thou didst not see,
For, know, my pretty DAFFADIL
Is worne of none but mee.

To shew it selfe but neere her seate,
No Lilly is so bold,
Except to shade her from the heate,
Or keepe her from the cold.

GORBO. *Through yonder Vale as I did passe,*
Descending from the Hill,
I met a smerking bonny Lasse,
They call her DAFFADIL:

Whose presence, as along shee went,
The pretty Flowres did greet,
As though their Heads they downeward bent,
With homage to her feet.

191 119 *smerking* smiling, perhaps affectedly

And all the Shepheards that were nie,
From top of every Hill,
Unto the Valleyes lowd did crie,
There goes sweet DAFFADIL.

BATTE. *I, gentle Shepheard, now with joy*
Thou all my Flocks dost fill,
That's shee alone, kind Shepheards Boy,
Let us to DAFFADIL.

192 [*from* Poly-Olbion Song 6]

What spirit can lift you up, to that immortall praise
§. You worthilie deserve? by whom first *Gaul* was taught
Her knowledge: and for her, what Nation ever wrought
The conquest you atchiev'd? And, as you were most drad,
So yee (before the rest) in so great reverence had
Your Bards which sung your deeds, that when sterne hosts have stood
With lifted hands to strike (in their inflamed blood)
§. One Bard but comming in, their murd'rous swords hath staid;
In her most dreadful voice as thundring heaven had said,
Stay *Britans:* when he spake, his words so powrefull were.
So to her native Priests, the dreadlesse *Druides* here,

192 2–3 'Understand the knowledge of those great Philosophers, Priests, and Lawyers call'd *Druid's* . . . their [the Gauls'] youth were sent hither as to an University for instruction in their learned professions' Selden, citing Caesar, *De Bello Gallico* (Milton took up this point in *Areopagitica*, 1644). For Selden and his glosses, see the textual note 4 *drad* dreaded, feared 8 'with the amazing sweetnes of their delicious harmonies, not their own only, but withall their enemies armies have suddenly desisted from fierce encounters' Selden

The neerest neighboring *Gaul*, that wiselie could discerne
Th'effect their doctrine wrought, it for their good to learne,
Her apt and pregnant Youth sent hither yeere by yeere,
Instructed in our Rites with most religious feare.
And afterward againe, when as our ancient seat
Her surcrease could not keepe, growne for her soile too great
(But like to casting Bees, so rising up in swarmes)
§. Our *Cymbri* with the *Gaules*, that their commixed Armes
Joyn'd with the *German* powers (those Nations of the North
Which over-spread the world) together issued forth:
§. Where, with our brazen swords, we stoutly fought, and long;
And after Conquests got, residing them among,
First planted in those parts our brave courageous brood:
Whose natures so adher'd unto their ancient blood,
As from them sprang those Priests, whose praise so farre did sound,
Through whom that spacious *Gaul* was after so renown'd.
  Nor could the *Saxons* swords (which many a lingring yeere
Them sadlie did afflict, and shut us *Britans* heere
Twixt *Severne* and this Sea) our mightie minds deject;
But that even they which fain'st our weaknes would detect,

192 16 *ancient seat* the British settlements in Brittany 17 *surcrease* growth 18 *casting* swarming 19 *Cymbri* Cambrians, the Welsh: 'that *British* armie ... conducted under *Brennus* and *Belinus* ... through *Gaule*' Selden 22 *brazen swords* 'among the ancients, Brasse, not Iron, was the metall of most use' Selden 29 *sadlie* gravely, seriously 31 *fain'st* most readily

Were forced to confesse, our wildest beasts that breed
Upon our mightie wastes, or on our Mountaines feed,
Were farre more sooner tam'd, then heere our Welch-men were:
Besides, in all the world no Nation is so deere
As they unto their owne; that here within this Ile,
Or else in forraine parts, yea, forced to exile,
The noble *Britan* still his countryman releeves;
A Patriot, and so true, that it to death him greeves
To heare his *Wales* disgrac't: and on the *Saxons* swords
Oft hazardeth his life, ere with reprochefull words
His Language or his Leeke hee'le stand to heare abus'd.
Besides, the *Britan* is so naturallie infus'd
With true Poëtick rage, that in their [a]measures, Art
Doth rather seeme precise, then comlie; in each part
Their Metre most exact, in Verse of th'hardest kind.
And some to riming be so wondrouslie inclin'd,
Those Numbers they will hit, out of their genuine vaine,
Which many wise and learn'd can hardly ere attaine.
O memorable Bards, of unmixt blood, which still
Posteritie shall praise for your so wondrous skill,
That in your noble Songs, the long Descents have kept
Of your great Heroës, else in *Lethe* that had slept,
With theirs whose ignorant pride your labours have disdain'd;
How much from time, and them, how bravelie have you gain'd!

[a]See to the fourth Song.

192 44 side-note Song 4 ends with an account of the poetry and music of the British 45 *precise* formal, over-scrupulous

Musician, Herault, Bard, thrice maist thou be renown'd,
And with three severall wreathes immortallie be crown'd;
Who, when to *Penbrooke* call'd before the English King,
And to thy powerfull Harpe commaunded there to sing,
Of famous *Arthur* told'st, and where hee was interr'd;
In which, those retchlesse times had long and blindlie err'd,
And Ignorance had brought the world to such a pass
As now, which scarce beleeves that *Arthur* ever was.
But when King[b] *Henry* sent th'reported place to view,
He found that man of men: and what thou said'st was true.

[b] *Henry* the second.

193 To The Virginian Voyage

You brave Heroique Minds,
Worthy your Countries Name,
That Honour still pursue,
Goe, and subdue,
Whilst loyt'ring Hinds
Lurke here at home, with shame.

Britans, you stay too long,
Quickly aboord bestow you,
And with a merry Gale
Swell your stretch'd Sayle,
With Vowes as strong,
As the Winds that blow you.

192 56 *Herault* herald 61 *retchlesse* heedless, careless

193 9 *merry* favourable, fine

Your Course securely steere,
West and by South forth keepe,
  Rocks, Lee-shores, nor Sholes,
  When EOLUS scowles,
You need not feare,
So absolute the Deepe.

And cheerefully at Sea,
Successe you still intice,
  To get the Pearle and Gold,
  And ours to hold,
VIRGINIA,
Earth's onely Paradise.

Where Nature hath in store
Fowle, Venison, and Fish,
  And the fruitfull'st Soyle,
  Without your Toyle,
Three Harvests more,
All greater then your Wish.

And the ambitious Vine
Crownes with his purple Masse,
  The Cedar reaching hie
  To kisse the Sky
The Cypresse, Pine
And use-full Sassafras.

To whose, the golden Age
Still Natures lawes doth give,
  No other Cares that tend,
  But Them to defend
From Winters age,
That long there doth not live.

When as the Lushious smell
Of that delicious Land,
  Above the Seas that flowes,
  The cleere Wind throwes,
Your Hearts to swell
Approching the deare Strand.

193 36 *Sassafras* a North American tree of the laurel family 48 *Strand* shore

In kenning of the Shore
(Thanks to God first given,)
O you the happy'st men,
Be Frolike then,
Let Cannons roare,
Frighting the wide Heaven.

And in Regions farre
Such *Heroes* bring yee foorth,
As those from whom We came,
And plant Our name,
Under that Starre
Not knowne unto our North.

And as there Plenty growes
Of Lawrell every where,
APOLLO's Sacred tree,
You it may see,
A Poets Browes
To crowne, that may sing there.

Thy Voyages attend,
Industrious HACKLUIT,
Whose Reading shall inflame
Men to seeke Fame,
And much commend
To after-Times thy Wit.

SAMUEL DANIEL

194 [*from* Epistle. To Prince Henrie]

Theare be great Prince, such as will tell you howe
Renown'd a thing it is, for States t'inlardge
Their goverments abrode and to indowe
There Scepters with the stiles and with the chardg

193 49 *kenning* sight 68 *Hackluit* the geographer Richard Hakluyt (1552?–1616)

194 4 *stiles* titles

Of many wide dominions, and avere
How glorious theis discoveries and remote
Plantations are, how much our latter were
Blest, more then anncient times, by having gott
Possessions of a world, that never was
Knowne to our fathers, and how we were made
To have that glorie onlie, to transpass
Those bounds of th'ocean, hercules forbad;
Besides the inrichment, and the benefitt
That new detected world, hath brought with it.
But yet weigh you, with that discearning beame
Of inquisition, whither this be so
Or whither the effect confirme the same
And paie our reckonings currentlie, or noe:
Consider whither all the good that came
From that new world to this, acquits the some
Of th'ill events, which since hath by the same
Accrewd to theis our parts of Christendome,
Or wherein wee are bettred in our state
By that accession, and the excessive vayne
Of gould, which hath but here inhanc'd the rate
Of things that doe, but as they did, conteyne;
Or whither we, with what we had before
Produc'd not fairer actions to behold
Then since wee have performd, and had not more
Of men that time, when wee had less of gould.
Examin whither ever any state
Hath not miscarried, when dilisiousnes
The child of wealth was borne, that doth abate
Men by increasing of their substaunces,
Or what rich Treasorous state, hath not undone
The Conquerer, and wonne those, who hath wonne;
If Indea may not unto Christendome
As Fatall be, as Asia was to Rome.

194 11 *transpass*** pass beyond 15 *beame* balance 16 *inquisition* inquiry 20 *acquits* discharges, settles 25 *inhanc'd the rate* inflated the price 26 *doe . . . conteyne* consist only of what they did previously 32 *dilisiousnes* deliciousness, luxury, luxuriousness 33 *abate* diminish, lessen 35 *Treasorous*** full of treasure 37 *Indea* Asia, America

Weigh if greate Charles, had not more likely gain'd Charles 5.
The Empire of the west he sought t'infold,
Had not his powers disperc'd, his state constrain'd
To unman Spaine to furnish him with gould,
Who yet was still a borrower, even poore
Ingag'd in somes, he never could restore;
Whilst his Concurrent (without Indies) stood Francis. i.
Girt with home force, and made his partie good
And had, had not Pavia crost his day
Turn'd the whole Streame of things another way.
Enquire if that which lies abrod so farr
Out of the reach of healp in danger growne
Be able to continue as they are
Or be kept ours, come once to be their owne
Or if States doe not, wheare fitt meanes shall want,
Expose their people, rather then transplant.
And thereupon examyne, if by fate
The Pillors of Alsides, seem'd not sett
As bounds of heaven, to keepe us in our state
Least getting further, wee our ill should gett
And whither our presumption thus to taste
The goulden Apples of Hisperides
(Preserv'd for Dragons) was not wrought to cast
Us out of what we did possess with ease.
Since theis transgressions ever are repai'd
With sweate of travaile, and with miserie
When thus our longing lusts doe come betraid
By that intising Curiositie:
Superfluous wealth, as well as knowledg, doth
Deprive men of the Paradice of rest,
Whereas the moderation of them both
Would keepe them in the state they were possest.

194 39 side-note *Charles 5* (1500–58), Holy Roman Emperor; he abdicated in 1556 45 side-note *Francis.i* (1494–1547), King of France *Concurrent* rival, competitor 47 *Pavia* where in 1525 Charles V defeated Francis I 56 *Alsides* Hercules 66 *intising* enticing

But some may say, this worke yet glorious was
For that it did the christien faith extend
To Infidels, But that with men must pass
And was the fate thereof, and not our end.
I grannt that time, their turne must bring about
When the universall wheele of things shall move
Unto that point, and those rude lands throughout
Th'Europian arts and Customes shall approve;
And they shall curious grow, and delicate
(Which we call Civill) and enjoy their part
Of our vaine glories, putting of the state
Of nature to be suted unto art:
When we perhaps, arriv'd unto a more
Then Asiatique weaknes, by the trade
Of superfluities bred by their store
And our ymmoderate humors, may be made
A prey unto some Gothicq barbarous hand
That shall lay wast our glorie, ruynate
All these erected monuments, that stand
Fraile witnesses of our more fraile estate:
The earth being still the Center, as it was
About which all theis revolutions turne
Where we behould ruynes, and raisings pass
From East to west, succeeding in their turne.
Yet this dischardges not our greedines
And wide desires in breaking up the dore
To our confusion, when this sought access
To parts fore clos'd, may hasten it the more,
Since nature even herself did shutt us out
And sett the barrs of those huge fearefull seas
Betwixt us as the cherubines about
The bounds of Edonn, and hath lockt all theis
Procurements of our mischeife, Iron, silver, gould
Within her closet th'earth, as if they weare
Committed ill unto us, and shee would
Not have them found that thus confound us heere.

194 81–2 *state/Of nature*** 84 *Asiatique*** 87 *Gothicq*** barbarous, rude, uncouth (cp. no. 201 l. 13)

ANONYMOUS

195 On Francis Drake

Sir *Drake* whom well the world's end knew,
Which thou did'st compasse round,
And whom both Poles of heaven once saw
Which North and South do bound,
The stars above, would make thee known,
If men here silent were;
The Sun himself cannot forget
His fellow traveller.

W. TURNER

196 [*from* Turners dish of Lentten stuffe, or a Galymaufery]

To the tune of *Watton Townes end*

1 My Maisters all attend you,
if mirth you love to heare:
And I will tell you what they cry,
in London all the yeare.
Ile please you if I can,
I will not be too long,
I pray you all attend a while,
and lissen to my song.

195 Title *Drake* Sir Francis Drake (1540?–96), navigator and admiral, knighted in 1581 after he had sailed round the world 8 *fellow traveller*** companion in travel

196 Title *Galymaufery* a dish made up of odds and ends, a hotchpotch

2 The fish-wife first begins,
nye Musckles lylly white:
Hearings, Sprats, or Pleace,
or Cockles for delight.
Nye welflet Oysters:
then she doth change her note,
She had need to hane her tongue by grease
for she rattles in the throat.

3 For why they are but Kentish,
to tell you out of doubt:
Her measure is to little,
go beate the bottom out.
Halfe a Pecke for two pence,
I doubt it is a bodge,
Thus all the citty over,
the people they do dodge.

4 The wench that cries the Kitchin stuffe,
I marvell what she ayles:
She sings her note so merry,
but she has a dragle taile,
An empty Car came running,
and hit her on the bum,
Downe she threw her greasie tub,
and away that she did run.

5 But she did give a blessing,
to some but not to all:
To beare a loade to Tyburne,
and there to let it fall,

196 10 *nye* any (?); nigh, near here (?) 13 *welflet* Wallfleet or Allfleet, an island on the River Crouch near Foulness in Essex, famous for its oysters 15 *hane* restrain (?); smooth (?) 21 *Pecke* measure for dry goods, filling about two gallons 22 *bodge* half a peck 24 *dodge* play fast and loose with (?); haggle with (?) 25 *Kitchin stuffe* food, especially vegetables 26 *ayles* troubles 28 *dragle taile* wet, filthy skirt 29 *Car* cart 35 *Tyburne* the chief place of public executions in London, near where Marble Arch now stands

The miller with his golden thumbe,
  and his dusty necke:
If that he grind but two bushels,
  he needs must steale a peck.

6 The Weaver and the Tayler,
  cozens they be sure:
They cannot worke but they must steale,
  to keepe their hands in ure,
For it is a common proverbe,
  throughout all the towne,
The Taylor he must cut three sleeves,
  for every womans gowne.

7 Marke but the Water man,
  attending for his fare:
Of hot and could, of wet and dry,
  he alwaies takes a share.
He carrieth bony lasses,
  over to the plaies,
And here and there he gets a bit,
  and that his stomake staies.

8 There was a slinging boy,
  did write to ride to Rumford:
When I go to my close stoole,
  I will put him in a comfort:
But what I leave behind,
  shall be no private gaine:
But all is one when I am gone,
  let him take it for his paine.

196 37 millers proverbially had golden thumbs, either because of their dishonesty or because of their wealth 39 *bushels* a bushel contains four pecks, or eight gallons 42 *cozens* cousins; cozeners, frauds, cheats 44 *ure* use, practice 49 *Water man* boatman 57 *slinging* stone-throwing (?); flinging himself about (?) 58 *Rumford* Romford in Essex, famous for breeches-making; proverbially, but not certainly at this date, 'You might ride to Romford on it' was said of a blunt knife 59 *close stoole* chamber-pot enclosed in a stool or box

9 Ould shoes for new Broomes,
the broome man he doth sing:
For hats or caps or buskins,
or any ould Pooch rings.
Buy a Mat, a bed Mat,
a padlock or a Pas,
A cover for a close stoole,
a bigger or a lesse.

10 Ripe Chery ripe,
the Coster-monger cries,
Pipins fine, or Peares,
another after hies,
With basket on his head,
his living to advance,
And in his purse a paire of Dice,
for to play at Mumchance.

11 Hot Pippin pies,
to sell unto my friends:
Or puding pies in pans,
well stuft with Candles ends,
Will you buy any Milke,
I heare a wench to cry,
With a paile of fresh Cheese and creame,
another after hies.

12 Oh the wench went neately,
my thought it did me good:
To see her cheery cheakes,
so dimpled ore with blood,
Her wastecoate washed white:
as any lilly flower,
would I had time to talke with her
the space of halfe an houre.

196 67 *buskins* ankle boots 68 *Pooch rings* rings for closing up pouches or purses 70 *Pas* pess, hassock, cushion to kneel on 74 *Coster-monger* fruit-seller 75 *Pipins* a variety of apple 80 *Mumchance* a dice game 83 *puding pies* usually, a savoury pie baked in pastry

13 Buy blacke, saith the blacking man
the best that erė was seene:
Tis good for poore men Cittizens
to make their shooes to shine,
Oh tis a rare comodity,
it must not be for-got,
It wil make them glister gallantly
and quickly make them rot.

14 The world is ful of thredbare poets,
that live upon their pen:
But they will write too eloquent,
they are such witty men.
But the Tinker with his budget,
the begger with his wallet,
And *Turners* turnd a gallant man,
at making of a Ballet.

John Taylor

197 [*from* The Sculler]

Epigram 22.

As Gold is better that's in fire tride,
So is the Bankside *Globe* that late was burn'd:
For where before it had a thatched hide,
Now to a stately Theator 'tis turn'd.
Which is an Emblem, that great things are won,
By those that dare through greatest dangers run.

196 109 *budget* leather bag

William Browne

198 [*from* Britannia's Pastorals Book 2]

The Muses friend (gray-eyde *Aurora*) yet
Held all the Meadowes in a cooling sweat,
The milke-white *Gossamores* not upwards snow'd,
Nor was the sharpe and usefull steering goad
Laid on the strong-neckt Oxe; no gentle bud
The *Sun* had dryde; the cattle chew'd the cud
Low level'd on the grasse; no Flyes quicke sting
Inforc'd the Stonehorse in a furious ring
To teare the passive earth, nor lash his taile
About his buttockes broad; the slimy Snayle
Might on the wainscot, (by his many mazes
Winding *Meanders* and selfe-knitting traces)
Be follow'd, where he stucke, his glittering slime
Not yet wipt off. It was so earely time
The carefull *Smith* had in his sooty forge
Kindled no coale; nor did his hammers urge
His neighbours patience: *Owles* abroad did flye,
And day as then might plead his infancy.

198 2 *cooling sweat* dew 3 *Gossamores* cobwebs 8 *Stonehorse* stallion 11 *wainscot* wooden panelling for walls

EDWARD HERBERT, LORD HERBERT OF CHERBURY

199 Sonnet

You well compacted Groves, whose light and shade
   Mixt equally, produce nor heat, nor cold,
   Either to burn the young, or freeze the old,
But to one even temper being made,
Upon a greene embroidering through each Glade
   An Airy Silver, and a Sunny Gold,
   So cloath the poorest that they do behold
Themselves, in riches which can never fade,
   While the wind whistles, and the birds do sing,
While your twigs clip, and while the leaves do friss,
   While the fruit ripens which those trunks do bring,
   Sensless to all but love, do you not spring
Pleasure of such a kind, as truly is
A self-renewing vegetable bliss.

199 1 *compacted* pressed together 10 *clip* clasp together *friss* frisk, move about briskly, dance (?) 12 *spring* produce, bring forth 14 *vegetable* having the primary principle of life and growth (cp. no. 169 l.11)

RICHARD CORBETT

200 A PROPER NEW BALLAD INTITULED The FAERYES FAREWELL: Or GOD-A-MERCY WILL:

To be sung or whistled to the Tune of the *Meddow Brow* by the Learned; by the un Learned; To the Tune of *FORTUNE*

Farewell Rewards and *Faeries*
  Good Houswives now may say
For now foule Slutts in Daries
  Doe fare as well as they
And though they sweepe theyr Hearths no less
  Then Maydes were wont to doe
Yet who of late for Cleaneliness
  Finds *sixe-pence* in her Shoe?

Lament, lament old Abbies
  The *Faries* lost Command
They did but change Priests *Babies*
  But some have changd your *Land*.
And all your Children sprung from thence
  Are now growne *Puritanes*:
Who live as *Changelings* ever since
  For love of your Demaines.

At Morning and at Evening both
  You merry were and glad
So little Care of Sleepe or Sloth
  These Prettie ladies had
When *Tom* came home from labour
  Or *Ciss* to Milking Rose
Then merrily, merrily went theyre Tabor
  And nimbly went theyre Toes.

200 16 *Demaines* demesnes, lands, estates

Wittness those Rings and Roundelayes
Of theirs, which yet remaine
Were footed in Queene *Maries* dayes
On many a Grassy Playne
But since of late *Elizabeth*
And later *James* came in
They never daunc'd on any heath
As *when the Time hath bin.*

By which wee note the *Faries*
Were of the old Profession
Theyre Songs were *Ave Maryes*
Theyre Daunces were *Procession*
But now a las they all are dead,
Or gone beyond the Seas
Or Farther for Religion fled
Or elce they take theyre Ease.

A Tell-tale in theyre Company
They never could endure
And whoe so kept not secretly
Theyre Mirth was punisht sure
It was a just and Christian Deed
To pinch such blacke and blew
O how the Common welth doth need
Such Justices as you.

Now they have left our Quarters
A *Register* they have
Who looketh to theyre Charters
A Man both *Wise* and *Grave*
An hundred of theyre merry Prancks
By one that I could name
Are kept in Store conn twenty Thanks
To *William*, for the same.

200 34 *Profession* religion, faith 50 *Register* keeper of a register, registrar 55 *conn* offer 56 *William* William Chourne of Staffordshire, servant to Leonard Hutten, sub-dean of Christ Church, Oxford; Chourne's knowledge of the supernatural and the world of fairies is described by Corbett in his poem *Iter boreale*

I marvell who his Cloake would turne
When *Puck* had led him round
Or where those Walking Fires would burne
Where *Cureton* would be found
How *Broker* would appeare to be
For whom this Age doth mourne
But that theyre Spiritts live in Thee
In thee, old *William Chourne*.

To *William Chourne* of Stafford Shire
Give Laud and Prayses due
Who every Meale can mend your Cheare
With Tales both old and true,
To *William* all give Audience
And pray yee for his Noddle
For all the *Faries* Evidence
Were lost, if that were Addle.

SIR WILLIAM DAVENANT

201 The Countess of ANGLESEY lead Captive by the Rebels, at the Disforresting of *Pewsam*

SONG

1.

O Whither will you lead the Fair,
And spicy Daughter of the Morne?
Those Manacles of her soft Haire,
Princes, though free, would faine have worn.

200 59 *Walking Fires* 'ignes fatui', will-o'-the-wisps 60–1 *Cureton* ... *Broker* spirits, presumably friends from Staffordshire, conjured up by Chourne 70 *Noddle* head, mind 71 *Evidence* ground for belief 72 *Addle* empty, confused, muddled

201 Title *Disforresting*** changing the legal status of an area from being governed by the laws of the forest to being governed by the laws relating to ordinary land

2.

What is her crime? what has she done?
Did she, by breaking Beauty stay,
Or from his Course mislead the Sun;
So robb'd your Harvest of a Day?

3.

Or did her voyce, divinely clear!
(Since lately in your Forrest bred)
Make all the Trees dance after her,
And so your Woods disforrested?

4.

Run, Run! Pursue this Gothick Rout,
Who rudely Love in bondage keep;
Sure all old Lovers have the Goute,
The young are overwatcht and sleep.

George Wither

202 [*from* Britain's Remembrancer Canto 4]

If by mischance the people in the street,
A *Courtier*, or a Gentleman did meet,
They with as much amazement him did view,
As if they had beheld the wandring *Jew*.
And, many, seeing me to keepe this place,
Did looke as if they much bewaild my case,
And halfe belee'vd that I was doomed hither,
That (since close-prison, halfe a yeare together,

201 13 *Gothick*** barbarous, rude (cp. no. 194 l. 87) 16 *overwatcht* exhausted from being awake

202 4 *wandring Jew* a legendary figure who taunted Christ on the way to the Crucifixion, and was doomed to wander through the world until the Day of Judgement 5 *this place* London 8 *close-prison* prison with strict confinement; Wither had been imprisoned in 1613, 1621 and 1624

Nor private wrongs, nor publique dis-respect,
Could breake my heart, nor much the same deject)
This *Plague* might kill me, which is come to whip
Those faults which heretofore my pen did strip.
But here I walkt in safety to behold
What changes, for instruction, see I could.
And, as I wandred on, my eye did meet,
Those halfe-built *Pageants* which, athwart the street,
Did those triumphant Arches counterfeit,
Which heretofore in ancient *Rome* were set,
When their victorious *Generalls* had thither
The spoile of mighty kingdomes brought together.
The loyall Citizens (although they lost
The glory of their well-intended cost)
Erected those great Structures to renowne
The new receiving of the Sov'raigne Crowne
By hopefull *CHARLES* (*whose royall exaltation,*
Make thou oh! God, propitious to this Nation.)
But when those works, imperfect, I beheld,
They did new causes of sad musings yeeld,
Portending ruine. And, did seeme, me thought,
In honor of Deaths trophees to be wrought;
Much rather, then from purposes to spring
Which aymed at the honor of a King.
For, their unpolisht forme, did make them fit
For direfull *Showes*: yea, *DEATH* on them did sit.
His *Captives* passed under ev'ry *Arch*;
Among them, as in *Triumph* he did march;
Through ev'ry Street, upon mens backs were borne
His Conquests. His black Liveries were worne,
In ev'ry House almost. His spoyles were brought
To ev'ry Temple. Many Vaults were fraught

202 11–12 the first edition of Wither's popular *Abuses stript and whipt* had appeared in 1613 16 *Pageants* triumphal arches erected in preparation for the new king's ceremonial entry to London; Charles had unexpectedly cancelled the entry, leaving the city to foot the bill (see ll. 21–2) 34 *direfull* dreadful, terrible 38 *Liveries* servants' clothes, uniforms

With his new prizes. And his followers grew
To such a multitude, that halfe our Eugh,
And all our Cypresse trees, could hardly lend him
A branch for ev'ry one who did attend him.

JOHN MILTON

203 SONG

On *May* morning

Now the bright morning Star, Dayes harbinger,
Comes dancing from the East, and leads with her
The Flowry *May*, who from her green lap throws
The yellow Cowslip, and the pale Primrose.
  Hail bounteous *May* that dost inspire
  Mirth and youth, and warm desire,
  Woods and Groves, are of thy dressing,
  Hill and Dale, doth boast thy blessing.
Thus we salute thee with our early Song,
And welcom thee, and wish thee long.

204 *L'Allegro*

Hence loathed Melancholy
  Of *Cerberus*, and blackest midnight born,
In *Stygian* Cave forlorn
  'Mongst horrid shapes, and shreiks, and sights unholy,
Find out som uncouth cell,
  Wher brooding darknes spreads his jealous wings,
And the night-Raven sings;

202 42 *Eugh* yew

204 Title *L'Allegro* the cheerful, merry man 5 *uncouth* unknown, unfrequented 7 *night-Raven* unspecified nocturnal bird, perhaps an owl

There under *Ebon* shades, and low-brow'd Rocks,
As ragged as thy Locks,
In dark *Cimmerian* desert ever dwell.
But com thou Goddes fair and free,
In Heav'n ycleap'd *Euphrosyne*,
And by men, heart-easing Mirth,
Whom lovely *Venus* at a birth
With two sister Graces more
To Ivy-crowned *Bacchus* bore;
Or whether (as som Sager sing)
The frolick Wind that breathes the Spring,
Zephir with *Aurora* playing,
As he met her once a Maying,
There on Beds of Violets blew,
And fresh-blown Roses washt in dew,
Fill'd her with thee a daughter fair,
So bucksom, blith, and debonair.
Haste thee nymph, and bring with thee
Jest and youthful Jollity,
Quips and Cranks, and wanton Wiles,
Nods, and Becks, and Wreathed Smiles,
Such as hang on *Hebe*'s cheek,
And love to live in dimple sleek;
Sport that wrincled Care derides,
And Laughter holding both his sides.
Com, and trip it as ye go
On the light fantastick toe,
And in thy right hand lead with thee,
The Mountain Nymph, sweet Liberty;
And if I give thee honour due,
Mirth, admit me of thy crue
To live with her, and live with thee,
In unreproved pleasures free;

204 12 *ycleap'd* called; a Spenserian form, cp. no. 270 l. 155 15 *Graces* Aglaia and Thalia 24 *bucksom* yielding, soft *debonair* gentle, gracious 27 *Cranks* verbal tricks, turns of speech, conceits *Wiles* ruses, delusions 28 *Becks* beckonings, upwards nods of the head *Wreathed** contorted, twisted 33 *trip* caper, dance 34 *fantastick** making fantastic, extravagant movements 39 cp. Marlowe's 'Come live with mee, and be my love' (see no. 98) and cp. l. 152 below

To hear the Lark begin his flight,
And singing startle the dull night,
From his watch-towre in the skies,
Till the dappled dawn doth rise;
Then to com in spight of sorrow,
And at my window bid good morrow,
Through the Sweet-Briar, or the Vine,
Or the twisted Eglantine.
While the Cock with lively din,
Scatters the rear of darknes thin,
And to the stack, or the Barn dore,
Stoutly struts his Dames before,
Oft list'ning how the Hounds and horn,
Chearly rouse the slumbring morn,
From the side of som Hoar Hill,
Through the high wood echoing shrill.
Som time walking not unseen
By Hedge-row Elms, on Hillocks green,
Right against the Eastern gate,
Wher the great Sun begins his state,
Rob'd in flames, and Amber light,
The clouds in thousand Liveries dight,
While the Plowman neer at hand,
Whistles ore the Furrow'd Land,
And the Milkmaid singeth blithe,
And the Mower whets his sithe,
And every Shepherd tells his tale
Under the Hawthorn in the dale.
Streit mine eye hath caught new pleasures
Whilst the Lantskip round it measures,
Russet Lawns, and Fallows Gray,
Where the nibling flocks do stray,
Mountains on whose barren brest
The labouring clouds do often rest:

204 51 *stack* sheaf of hay, straw 54 *Chearly* cheerily 55 *Hoar* grey, misty 58 *Hedge-row** forming a hedge 59 *Eastern gate* cp. Shakespeare, *A Midsummer Night's Dream* III.2.391 ' . . . the eastern gate all fiery red' 60 *state* stately progress 62 *dight* clothed 67 *tells his tale* counts the number of his sheep; tells the story (of his life or love) 70 *Lantskip** landscape, country scenery

Meadows trim with Daisies pide,
Shallow Brooks, and Rivers wide.
Towers, and Battlements it sees
Boosom'd high in tufted Trees,
Wher perhaps som beauty lies,
The Cynosure of neighbouring eyes.
Hard by, a Cottage chimney smokes,
From betwixt two aged Okes,
Where *Corydon* and *Thyrsis* met,
Are at their savory dinner set
Of Hearbs, and other Country Messes,
Which the neat-handed *Phillis* dresses;
And then in haste her Bowre she leaves,
With *Thestylis* to bind the Sheaves;
Or if the earlier season lead
To the tann'd Haycock in the Mead,
Som times with secure delight
The up-land Hamlets will invite,
When the merry Bells ring round,
And the jocond rebecks sound
To many a youth, and many a maid,
Dancing in the Chequer'd shade;
And young and old com forth to play
On a Sunshine Holyday,
Till the live-long day-light fail,
Then to the Spicy Nut-brown Ale,
With stories told of many a feat,
How *Faery Mab* the junkets eat,
She was pincht, and pull'd she sed,
And he by Friars Lanthorn led
Tells how the drudging *Goblin* swet,
To ern his Cream-bowle duly set,

204 75 *trim* pretty, handsome *pide* variegated 78 *tufted** growing in a tuft, clustered 80 *Cynosure* centre of attraction, admiration 84 *savory* tasty, agreeable 85 *Messes* dishes 86 *neat-handed** deft, dextrous 90 *tann'd* tawny, sunburnt 91 *secure* free from care 94 *rebecks* fiddles, early violins 102 *Mab* 'the fairies' midwife' of Mercutio's speech in Shakespeare's *Romeo and Juliet* I.4.53–95 103–4 *She* ... *he* members of the story-telling group 104 *Friars Lanthorn** will-o'-the-wisp, 'ignis fatuus' 105 *Goblin* Puck, Robin Goodfellow

When in one night, ere glimps of morn,
His shadowy Flale hath thresh'd the Corn
That ten day-labourers could not end,
Then lies him down the Lubbar Fend.
And stretch'd out all the Chimney's length,
Basks at the fire his hairy strength;
And Crop-full out of dores he flings,
Ere the first Cock his Mattin rings.
Thus don the Tales, to bed they creep,
By whispering Windes soon lull'd asleep.
Towred Cities please us then,
And the busie humm of men,
Where throngs of Knights and Barons bold,
In weeds of Peace high triumphs hold,
With store of Ladies, whose bright eies
Rain influence, and judge the prise
Of Wit, or Arms, while both contend
To win her Grace, whom all commend.
There let *Hymen* oft appear
In Saffron robe, with Taper clear,
And pomp, and feast, and revelry,
With mask, and antique Pageantry,
Such sights as youthfull Poets dream
On Summer eeves by haunted stream.
Then to the well-trod stage anon,
If *Jonsons* learned Sock be on,
Or sweetest *Shakespear* fancies childe,
Warble his native Wood-notes wilde;
And ever against eating Cares,
Lap me in soft *Lydian* Aires,
Married to immortal verse
Such as the meeting soul may pierce
In notes, with many a winding bout
Of lincked sweetnes long drawn out,

204 110 *Lubbar* big, clumsy, loutish *Fend* fiend 113 *Crop-full** with stomach stuffed full 120 *weeds* clothes 121 *store* abundance 132 *Sock* the soft shoe worn by comic actors in ancient Greece and Rome 134 *Wood-notes** songs of a wild bird in a wood 135 *eating Cares* cp. Horace, *Odes* 2.11.18, 'curas edaces' 138 *meeting* welcoming, responsive 139 *bout* circuit, orbit

With wanton heed, and giddy cunning,
The melting voice through mazes running;
Untwisting all the chains that ty
The hidden soul of harmony.
That *Orpheus* self may heave his head
From golden slumber on a bed
Of heapt *Elysian* flowres, and hear
Such streins as would have won the ear
Of *Pluto*, to have quite set free
His half regain'd *Eurydice*.
These delights, if thou canst give,
Mirth with thee, I mean to live.

Robert Herrick

205 To *Dean-bourn*, a rude River in *Devon*, by which sometimes he lived

Dean-bourn, farewell; I never look to see
Deane, or thy warty incivility.
Thy rockie bottome, that doth teare thy streams,
And makes them frantick, ev'n to all extreames;
To my content, I never sho'd behold,
Were thy streames silver, or thy rocks all gold.
Rockie thou art; and rockie we discover
Thy men; and rockie are thy wayes all over.
O men, O manners; Now, and ever knowne
To be *A Rockie Generation!*
A people currish; churlish as the seas;
And rude (almost) as rudest Salvages.
With whom I did, and may re-sojourne when
Rockes turn to Rivers, Rivers turn to Men.

205 2 *warty** rocky, rough 9 *O ... manners* Cicero's repeated exclamation ('O tempora! O mores!') in his oration against Catiline 10 *Rockie Generation* cp. Jeremiah 5:3 'they have made their faces harder than a rock' 12 *Salvages* savages 13 *re-sojourne** live again

206 *Corinna's* going a Maying

Get up, get up for shame, the Blooming Morne
Upon her wings presents the god unshorne.
  See how *Aurora* throwes her faire
  Fresh-quilted colours through the aire:
  Get up, sweet-Slug-a-bed, and see
  The Dew-bespangling Herbe and Tree.
Each Flower has wept, and bow'd toward the East,
Above an houre since; yet you not drest,
  Nay! not so much as out of bed?
  When all the Birds have Mattens seyd,
  And sung their thankfull Hymnes: 'tis sin,
  Nay, profanation to keep in,
When as a thousand Virgins on this day,
Spring, sooner then the Lark, to fetch in May.

Rise; and put on your Foliage, and be seene
To come forth, like the Spring-time, fresh and greene;
  And sweet as *Flora*. Take no care
  For Jewels for your Gowne, or Haire:
  Feare not; the leaves will strew
  Gemms in abundance upon you:
Besides, the childhood of the Day has kept,
Against you come, some *Orient Pearls* unwept:
  Come, and receive them while the light
  Hangs on the Dew-locks of the night:
  And *Titan* on the Eastern hill
  Retires himselfe, or else stands still
Till you come forth. Wash, dresse, be briefe in praying:
Few Beads are best, when once we goe a Maying.

Come, my *Corinna*, come; and comming, marke
How each field turns a street; each street a Parke
  Made green, and trimm'd with trees: see how
  Devotion gives each House a Bough,

206 2 *god* Apollo 4 *Fresh-quilted** 22 *you come* your coming 24 *Dew-locks* dewy locks of hair 28 *Beads* prayers; beads of the rosary

Or Branch: Each Porch, each doore, ere this,
An Arke a Tabernacle is
Made up of white-thorn neatly enterwove;
As if here were those cooler shades of love.
Can such delights be in the street,
And open fields, and we not see't?
Come, we'll abroad; and let's obay
The Proclamation made for May:
And sin no more, as we have done, by staying:
But my *Corinna*, come, let's goe a Maying.

There's not a budding Boy, or Girle, this day,
But is got up, and gone to bring in May.
A deale of Youth, ere this, is come
Back, and with *White-thorn* laden home.
Some have dispatcht their Cakes and Creame,
Before that we have left to dreame:
And some have wept, and woo'd, and plighted Troth,
And chose their Priest, ere we can cast off sloth:
Many a green-gown has been given;
Many a kisse, both odde and even:
Many a glance too has been sent
From out the eye, Loves Firmament:
Many a jest told of the Keyes betraying
This night, and Locks pickt, yet w'are not a Maying.

Come, let us goe, while we are in our prime;
And take the harmlesse follie of the time.
We shall grow old apace, and die
Before we know our liberty.
Our life is short; and our dayes run
As fast away as do's the Sunne:
And as a vapour, or a drop of raine
Once lost, can ne'r be found againe:
So when or you or I are made
A fable, song, or fleeting shade;

206 35 *white-thorn* emblematic of joy and pain 40 the 'Book of Sports', issued nationally by James I in May 1618 and renewed by Charles I in 1633, defended rural festivities against Puritan attacks 48 *left to dreame* left off dreaming 51 *green-gown* the result of rolling women (in sport) in their clothes on the grass

All love, all liking, all delight
Lies drown'd with us in endlesse night.
Then while time serves, and we are but decaying;
Come, my *Corinna*, come, let's goe a Maying.

207 To Meddowes

1. Ye have been fresh and green,
Ye have been fill'd with flowers:
And ye the Walks have been
Where Maids have spent their houres.

2. You have beheld, how they
With *Wicker Arks* did come
To kisse, and beare away
The richer Couslips home.

3. Y'ave heard them sweetly sing,
And seen them in a Round:
Each Virgin, like a Spring,
With Hony-succles crown'd.

4. But now, we see, none here,
Whose silv'rie feet did tread,
And with dishevell'd Haire,
Adorn'd this smoother Mead.

5. Like Unthrifts, having spent,
Your stock, and needy grown,
Y'are left here to lament
Your poore estates, alone.

207 6 *Arks* baskets 10 *Round* circle

208 The Wassaile

1. Give way, give way ye Gates, and win
An easie blessing to your Bin,
And Basket, by our entring in.

2. May both with manchet stand repleat;
Your Larders too so hung with meat,
That though a thousand, thousand eat;

3. Yet, ere twelve *Moones* shall whirl about
Their silv'rie Spheres, ther's none may doubt,
But more's sent in, then was serv'd out.

4. Next, may your Dairies Prosper so,
As that your pans no Ebbe may know;
But if they do, the more to flow.

5. Like to a solemne sober Stream
Bankt all with Lillies, and the Cream
Of sweetest *Cow-slips* filling Them.

6. Then, may your Plants be prest with Fruit,
Nor Bee, or Hive you have be mute;
But sweetly sounding like a Lute.

7. Next may your Duck and teeming Hen
Both to the Cocks-tread say *Amen*;
And for their two egs render ten.

8. Last, may your Harrows, Shares and Ploughes,
Your Stacks, your Stocks, your sweetest Mowes,
All prosper by your Virgin-vowes.

9. Alas! we blesse, but see none here,
That brings us either Ale or Beere;
In a drie-house all things are neere.

208 Title *Wassaile* drinking-song, sung from house to house at Christmas 4 *manchet* finest kind of wheaten bread 16 *prest* crowded, thronged 20 *tread* sexual intercourse 23 *Mowes* stacks of hay, corn etc. 27 *neere* tight, mean

10. Let's leave a longer time to wait,
Where Rust and Cobwebs bind the gate;
And all live here with *needy Fate.*

11. Where Chimneys do for ever weepe,
For want of warmth, and Stomachs keepe
With noise, the servants eyes from sleep.

12. It is in vain to sing, or stay
Our free-feet here; but we'l away:
Yet to the Lares this we'l say,

13. The time will come, when you'l be sad,
And reckon this for fortune bad,
T'ave lost the good ye might have had.

RICHARD CRASHAW

209 [*from* Bulla]

Quid tu? quæ nova machina,
Quæ tam fortuito globo
In vitam properas brevem?
Qualis virgineos adhuc
Cypris concutiens sinus,
Cypris iam nova, iam recens,
Et spumis media in suis,
Promsit purpureum latus;
Conchâ de patriâ micas,
Pulchroque exsilis impetu;
Statim et millibus ebria
Ducens terga coloribus
Evolvis tumidos sinus
Sphærâ plena volubili.

208 28 *leave* leave off

209 Title *Bulla* bubble; a round ornament of gold or leather worn around the neck by the children of Roman freemen; it was laid aside when they arrived at maturity and consecrated to the Lares, the household gods 3 *vitam . . . brevem* emblematically, the bubble was often compared to the brevity and fragility of human life

Cuius per varium latus,
Cuius per teretem globum
Iris lubrica cursitans
Centum per species vagas,
Et picti facies chori
Circum regnat, et undique
Et se Diva volatilis
Iucundo levis impetu
Et vertigine perfidâ
Lascivâ sequitur fugâ
Et pulchrè dubitat; fluit
Tam fallax toties novis,
Tot se per reduces vias,
Erroŕesque reciprocos
Spargit vena Coloribus;
Et pompâ natat ebriâ.
Tali militiâ micans
Agmen se rude dividit;
Campis quippe volantibus,
Et campi levis æquore
Ordo insanus obambulans
Passim se fugit, et fugat;
Passim perdit, et invenit.
Pulchrum spargitur hîc Chaos.
Hîc viva, hîc vaga flumina
Ripâ non propriâ meant,
Sed miscent socias vias,
Communique sub alveo
Stipant delicias suas.
Quarum proximitas vaga
Tam discrimine lubrico,
Tam subtilibus arguit
Iuncturam tenuem notis,
Pompa ut florida nullibi
Sinceras habeat vias;
Nec vultu niteat suo.
Sed dulcis cumulus novos

209 17 *Iris* the rainbow, traditionally an efficient messenger, who is here celebrated for her resistance to delivering clear-cut messages

Miscens purpureos sinus
Flagrat divitiis suis,
Privatum renuens iubar.
Floris diluvio vagi,
Floris Sydere publico
Latè ver subit aureum,
Atque effunditur in suæ
Vires undique Copiæ.
Nempe omnis quia cernitur,
Nullus cernitur hîc color,
Et vicinia contumax
Allidit species vagas.
Illîc contiguis aquis
Marcent pallidulæ faces.
Undæ hîc vena tenellulæ,
Flammis ebria proximis
Discit purpureas vias,
Et rubro salit alveo.
Ostri Sanguineum iubar
Lambunt lactea flumina;
Suasu cærulei maris
Mansuescit seges aurea;
Et lucis faciles genæ
Vanas ad nebulas stupent;
Subque uvis rubicundulis
Flagrant sobria lilia.
Vicinis adeo rosis
Vicinæ invigilant nives,
Ut sint et niveæ rosæ,
Ut sint et roseæ nives;
Accenduntque rosæ nives,
Extinguuntque nives rosas.
Illîc cum viridi rubet,
Hîc et cum rutilo viret
Lascivi facies chori.
Et quicquid rota lubrica
Caudæ stelligeræ notat,
Pulchrum pergit in ambitum.

209 The Bubble

What are you? what new device, you who hurry in such a random globe into your brief life? What kind of Venus, shaking out her hitherto virginal curves, what kind of new, fresh-arrived Venus brought forth this purple body from the middle of her own foam? You flash out from your native shell, and with a beautiful rush spring forth; and at once, leading forth your back, intoxicatedly dazzling with a thousand colours, you unroll your swelling folds in a full spinning sphere. Through whose varying side, through whose smooth globe a shifting rainbow, running about through a hundred wandering images and facets of a painted dance, rules on all sides, and on all sides the shifting goddess, nimble in the pleasant attack, follows herself with a treacherous whirling in her wanton flight and beautifully hesitates; she flows so deceitfully and so often down new ways, and down so many ways she has followed before, and a vein sprinkles the wandering way back with colours; and swims in intoxicated pomp. Rushing forth on such military service, the army divides itself roughly; in battlefields that are actually flying, and on the sea-surface of a light field, the crazy troop, wandering about, runs away from itself and pursues itself in all directions; here and there it loses itself and finds itself. Here a beautiful chaos is scattered. Here living, here wandering rivers flow through banks not their own, but mix their allied ways, and pack together their pleasures in a common channel. Their wandering closeness asserts their tenuous connection with such a slippery separation, with such fine marks, that their flowering beauty nowhere has direct paths; nor does it shine with its own face. But the sweet swollen body, blending new rich-coloured curves, blazes with its own riches, denying its own brightness. With the deluge of a wandering flower, with the public star of a flower, far and wide the golden Spring appears, and is poured out into the strength of its own abundance in all directions. Just because every colour is seen, no colour is seen here, and the obstinate surroundings dash to pieces the wandering forms. There in neighbouring waters, pale torches die out. Here the vein of a delicate wave, drunk with the nearby flames, learns its purple paths and leaps up from a red channel. The milky rivers wash the blood-red shining of the purple; the golden cornfield grows mild at the urging of the blue sea; and the pliable cheeks of the light are stupefied by the deceptive clouds; and under the ruddy grapes, temperate lilies flame out. Neighbouring snows keep watch over neighbouring roses, so that there are snowy roses and rosy snow, and the roses set the snow on fire, and the snow extinguishes the roses. There the surface of the joyful dance reddens with green, here it greens with red. And whatever the gliding wheel of its starry tail marks, comes into its beautiful orbit.

ABRAHAM COWLEY

210 The Wish

1.

Well then; I now do plainly see,
This busie world and I shall ne'r agree;
The very *Honey* of all earthly joy
Does of all meats the soonest *cloy*,
And they (methinks) deserve my pity,
Who for it can endure the stings,
The *Crowd*, and *Buz*, and *Murmurings*
Of this great *Hive*, the *City*.

2.

Ah, yet, ere I descend to th'grave
May I a *small House*, and *large Garden* have!
And a *few Friends*, and *many Books*, both true,
Both wise, and both delightful too!
And since *Love* ne'r will from mee flee,
A *Mistress* moderately fair,
And good as *Guardian-Angels* are,
Onely belov'd, and loving mee!

3.

Oh, *Fountains*, when in you shall I
My self, eas'd of unpeaceful thoughts, espy?
Oh *Fields*! Oh *Woods*! when, when shall I be made
The happy *Tenant* of your shade?

Here's the Spring-head of *Pleasures* flood;
Here's wealthy Natures Treasury,
Where all the *Riches* lie, that she
Has coyn'd and stampt for good.

4.

Pride and *Ambition* here,
Onely in *far fetcht Metaphors* appear;
Here nought but *winds* can hurtful *Murmurs* scatter,
And nought but *Eccho flatter*.
The *Gods*, when they descended, hither
From heav'en did always choose their way;
And therefore we may boldly say,
That 'tis the *way* too *thither*.

5.

How happy here should I,
And one dear *Shee* live, and embracing dy?
She who is all the world, and can exclude
In *desarts Solitude*.
I should have then this onely feare,
Lest men, when they my pleasures see,
Should hither throng to live like Mee,
And so make a *City* here.

ANONYMOUS

211 [The Diggers' Song]

You noble diggers all stand up now
you noble diggers all stand up now
the wast land to maintaine seeing Cavaleirs by name
your digging does disdaine and persons all defame
Stand up now stand up now

210 27 *Murmurs* muttered, indistinct complaints

211 1 *diggers* an offshoot of the Levellers; believing in the common ownership of land, they began to dig and plant common land

Your houses they pull down: stand up now, stand up now
your houses they etc.
your houses they pull down to fright poore men in town
but the Gentry must come down, and the poor shall wear the
Crown.
Stand up now diggers all.

With spades and hoes and plowes: stand up now stand up now.
with spades and hoes etc.
your freedome to uphold seeing Cavaleirs are bold
to kill you if they could and rights from you to hold
Stand up now diggers all.

There self will is theire law, stand up now stand up now
there self will etc.
since Tyrany came in, they count it now no sin
to make a Goale a gin, to sterve poor men therein
Stand up now stand up now.

The Gentrye are all round, stand up now stand up now
the gentrie are all round etc.
the Gentrye are all round on each side they are found
there wisedomes so profound, to cheat us of our ground
Stand up now stand up now.

The Lawyers they conjoyne, stand up now stand up now
the Lawyers they etc.
To Arrest you they advise, such fury they devise
the devill in them lies, and hath blinded both their eyes
Stand up now stand up now.

The Clergy they come in, stand up now stand up now
the Clergy they etc.
the Clergy they come in, and say it is a sin
that we should now begin, our freedom for to win
Stand up now diggers all

211 19 *Goale* gaol *gin* trap 26 *conjoyne* combine, unite, ally with

The Tiths they yet will have, stand up now stand up now
the tiths they etc.
the tithes they yet will have, and Lawyers their fees crave
and this they say is brave, to make the poor their slave
Stand up now diggers all.

'Gainst Lawyers and the Priests, stand up now stand up now,
'gainst Lawyers etc.
for Tyrants they are both, even flatt against their oath
to grant us they are loth, free meat and drinke and cloth
Stand uppe now diggers all.

The Club is all their Law, stand uppe now, stand upp now
The Club is all their Law, stand uppe now,
The Club is all their Law to keepe men in awe,
but they noe vision saw to maintaine such a Law.
Stand uppe now diggers all.

The Cavaleers are foes, stand uppe now, stand uppe now,
The Cavaleers are foes stand uppe now
The Cavaleers are foes, themselves they do disclose,
by verses nott in prose, To please the singing boyes
Stand uppe now diggers all.

To conquer them by Love, come in now, come in now,
To conquer them by love, come in now,
To conquer them by Love, as itt does you behove,
for hee is Kinge above, and noe power like to Love.
Glory heere diggers all.

Henry Vaughan

212 [*from* To his retired friend, an Invitation to *Brecknock*]

The Town believes thee lost, and didst thou see
But half her suffrings, now distrest for thee,

212 1 *Town* Brecon, the nearest market-town to Vaughan's home in the Welsh borders

Thou'ldst swear (like *Rome*) her foule, polluted walls
Were sackt by *Brennus*, and the salvage *Gaules*.
Abominable face of things! here's noise
Of bang'd Mortars, blew Aprons, and Boyes,
Pigs, Dogs, and Drums, with the hoarse hellish notes
Of politickly-deafe Usurers throats,
With new fine *Worships*, and the old cast *teame*
Of Justices vext with the *Cough*, and *flegme*.
Midst these the *Crosse* looks sad, and in the *Shire-*
-Hall furs of an old *Saxon Fox* appear,
With brotherly Ruffs and Beards, and a strange sight
Of high Monumentall Hats ta'ne at the fight
Of *Eighty eight*; while ev'ry *Burgesse* foots
The mortall *Pavement* in eternall boots. . . .
  Come! leave this sullen state, and let not Wine
And precious Witt lye dead for want of thine,
Shall the dull *Market-land-lord* with his *Rout*
Of sneaking Tenants durtily swill out
This harmlesse liquor? shall they knock and beat
For Sack, only to talk of *Rye*, and *Wheat?*
O let not such prepost'rous tipling be
In our *Metropolis*, may I ne'r see
Such *Tavern-sacrilege*, nor lend a line
To weep the *Rapes* and *Tragedy* of wine!

212 6 *Mortars* vessels in which materials are pounded *blew Aprons*** tradesmen *Boyes* servants, apprentices 8 *politickly-deafe* cunningly, selectively deaf 9–10 these lines may refer to Walter Rumsey, Puisne Judge of the Brecon circuit, who suffered from phlegm 11 *Crosse* market cross 12 *Saxon Fox* this may refer to the Chief Justice of the Brecon circuit, a Lancashire man called Eltonhead, who replaced Sir Marmaduke Lloyd (for whom Vaughan may have worked as a clerk) 13 *brotherly* belonging to the select brethren of the '*Saxon Fox*' 15 *Eighty eight* the year of the Armada, 1588 16 *mortall* deadly, fatal *eternall* continuing endlessly 19 *Market-land-lord* landlord of a market tavern, landlord at a market (?) *Rout* crowd, rabble 20 *sneaking* creeping, skulking 22 *Sack* a type of white wine imported from Spain and the Canaries

RICHARD LOVELACE

213 The Snayl

Wise Emblem of our Politick World,
Sage Snayl, within thine own self curl'd;
Instruct me softly to make hast,
Whilst these my feet go slowly fast.
  Compendious Snayl! thou seem'st to me,
Large *Euclids* strickt Epitome;
And in each Diagram, dost Fling
Thee from the point unto the Ring.
A Figure now Triangulare,
An Oval now, and now a Square;
And then a Serpentine dost crawl
Now a straight Line, now crook'd, now all.
  Preventing Rival of the Day,
Th'art up and openest thy Ray,
And ere the Morn cradles the Moon,
Th'art broke into a Beauteous Noon.
Then when the Sun sups in the Deep,
Thy Silver Horns e're *Cinthia's* peep;
And thou from thine own liquid Bed
New *Phœbus* heav'st thy pleasant Head.
  Who shall a Name for thee create,
Deep Riddle of Mysterious State?
Bold Nature that gives common Birth
To all products of Seas and Earth,
Of thee, as Earth-quakes, is affraid,
Nor will thy dire Deliv'ry aid.
  Thou thine own daughter then, and Sire,
That Son and Mother art intire,

213 4 *feet* feet; metres, lines 5 *Compendious* concise, succinct 6 *strickt* close, exact, precise 8 *point . . . Ring* centre to the circumference (?) 13 *Preventing* going before, preceding 26 *Deliv'ry* birth

That big still with thy self dost go,
And liv'st an aged Embrio;
That like the Cubbs of *India*,
Thou from thy self a while dost play:
But frighted with a Dog or Gun,
In thine own Belly thou dost run,
And as thy House was thine own womb,
So thine own womb, concludes thy tomb.
  But now I must (analys'd King)
Thy Oeconomick Virtues sing;
Thou great stay'd Husband still within,
Thou, thee, that's thine dost Discipline;
And when thou art to progress bent,
Thou mov't thy self and tenement,
As Warlike *Scythians* travayl'd, you
Remove your Men and City too;
Then after a sad Dearth and Rain,
Thou scatterest thy Silver Train;
And when the Trees grow nak'd and old,
Thou cloathest them with Cloth of Gold,
Which from thy Bowels thou dost spin,
And draw from the rich Mines within.
  Now hast thou chang'd thee Saint; and made
Thy self a Fane that's cupula'd;
And in thy wreathed Cloister thou
Walkest thine own Gray fryer too;
Strickt, and lock'd up, th'art Hood all ore
And ne'r Eliminat'st thy Dore.
On Sallads thou dost feed severe,
And 'stead of Beads thou drop'st a tear,
And when to rest, each calls the Bell,
Thou sleep'st within thy Marble Cell;

213 29 *big* pregnant, swollen 31 *Cubbs of India* the sue, a wild animal, was thought to carry its young in a bag 36 *concludes* shuts up, encloses 37 *analys'd* resolved to its essential constituents 38 *Oeconomick* related to the management of the household 39 *stay'd* staid, grave, dignified *Husband* manager of his own business affairs 52 *Fane* temple, church *cupula'd* provided with a cupola 53 *wreathed* twisted, curled 56 *Eliminat'st** come out of, go beyond the threshold of 57 *severe* rigorously, strictly

Where in dark contemplation plac'd,
The sweets of Nature thou dost tast;
Who now with Time thy days resolve,
And in a Jelly thee dissolve.
Like a shot Star, which doth repair
Upward, and Rarifie the Air.

ANDREW MARVELL

214 Bermudas

Where the remote *Bermudas* ride
In th' Oceans bosome unespy'd,
From a small Boat, that row'd along,
The listning Winds receiv'd this Song.
What should we do but sing his Praise
That led us through the watry Maze,
Unto an Isle so long unknown,
And yet far kinder than our own?
Where he the huge Sea-Monsters wracks,
That lift the Deep upon their Backs.
He lands us on a grassy Stage;
Safe from the Storms, and Prelat's rage.
He gave us this eternal Spring,
Which here enamells every thing;
And sends the Fowle to us in care,
On daily Visits through the Air.
He hangs in shades the Orange bright,
Like golden Lamps in a green Night.
And does in the Pomgranates close,
Jewels more rich than *Ormus* show's.

213 65 *shot Star* on falling to earth, shooting stars were supposed to turn to jelly

214 1 *ride* lie at anchor; float 7 the Bermudas were discovered by Juan Bermudez in 1515 9 Edmund Waller's 'The battel of the Summer Islands', 1645, describes a fight between the Bermudans and two stranded whales 20 *Ormus* Hormuz in the Persian Gulf

He makes the Figs our mouths to meet;
And throws the Melons at our feet.
But Apples plants of such a price,
No Tree could ever bear them twice.
With Cedars, chosen by his hand,
From *Lebanon*, he stores the Land.
And makes the hollow Seas, that roar,
Proclaime the Ambergris on shoar.
He cast (of which we rather boast)
The Gospels Pearl upon our Coast.
And in these Rocks for us did frame
A Temple, where to sound his Name.
Oh let our Voice his Praise exalt,
Till it arrive at Heavens Vault:
Which thence (perhaps) rebounding, may
Eccho beyond the *Mexique Bay*.
Thus sung they, in the *English* boat,
An holy and a chearful Note,
And all the way, to guide their Chime,
With falling Oars they kept the time.

215 The Mower to the Glo-Worms

I.

Ye living Lamps, by whose dear light
The Nightingale does sit so late,
And studying all the Summer-night,
Her matchless Songs does meditate;

II.

Ye Country Comets, that portend
No War, nor Princes funeral,
Shining unto no higher end
Then to presage the Grasses fall;

214 23 *Apples* pineapples 28 *Proclaime* make known *Ambergris* the odoriferous secretion of the sperm whale, see Marvell's 'The Gallery' (no. 170), l. 38 39 *Chime* harmony, musical concord 40 the poem's forty lines may correspond to the Israelites' forty years in the wilderness

III.

Ye Glo-worms, whose officious Flame
To wandring Mowers shows the way,
That in the Night have lost their aim,
And after foolish Fires do stray;

IV.

Your courteous Lights in vain you wast,
Since *Juliana* here is come,
For She my Mind hath so displac'd
That I shall never find my home.

216 The Mower against Gardens

Luxurious Man, to bring his Vice in use,
  Did after him the World seduce:
And from the fields the Flow'rs and Plants allure,
  Where Nature was most plain and pure.
He first enclos'd within the Gardens square
  A dead and standing pool of Air:
And a more luscious Earth for them did knead,
  Which stupifi'd them while it fed.
The Pink grew then as double as his Mind;
  The nutriment did change the kind.
With strange perfumes he did the Roses taint.
  And Flow'rs themselves were taught to paint.
The Tulip, white, did for complexion seek;
  And learn'd to interline its cheek:
Its Onion root they then so high did hold,
  That one was for a Meadow sold.
Another World was search'd, through Oceans new,
  To find the *Marvel of Peru*.

215 9 *officious* dutiful, efficacious 12 *foolish Fires* will-o'-the-wisps, 'ignes fatui'

216 1 *Luxurious* voluptuous, lecherous *to ... use* to bring his vice into (more general) practice and establish it as the (universal) practice 6 *standing* stagnant 7 *luscious* cloying, sickly 9 *double* with a double bloom; fraudulent, deceiving 10 *nutriment* food, nourishment *kind* generic nature 13 *complexion* colour, colouring 14 *interline* mark with lines of various colours 15 *Onion root* bulb 18 *Marvel of Peru* tropical American plant, whose colourful flowers expand towards night

And yet these Rarities might be allow'd,
To Man, that sov'raign thing and proud;
Had he not dealt between the Bark and Tree,
Forbidden mixtures there to see.
No Plant now knew the Stock from which it came;
He grafts upon the Wild the Tame:
That the uncertain and adult'rate fruit
Might put the Palate in dispute.
His green *Seraglio* has its Eunuchs too;
Lest any Tyrant him out-doe.
And in the Cherry he does Nature vex,
To procreate without a Sex.
'Tis all enforc'd; the Fountain and the Grot;
While the sweet Fields do lye forgot:
Where willing Nature does to all dispence
A wild and fragrant Innocence:
And *Fauns* and *Faryes* do the Meadows till,
More by their presence then their skill.
Their Statues polish'd by some ancient hand,
May to adorn the Gardens stand:
But howso'ere the Figures do excel,
The *Gods* themselves with us do dwell.

217 The Garden

I.

How vainly men themselves amaze
To win the Palm, the Oke, or Bayes;
And their uncessant Labours see
Crown'd from some single Herb or Tree,

216 21 proverbial for foolish interference, meddling 22 cp. Leviticus 19:19 'thou shalt not sow thy field with mingled seed', Deuteronomy 22:9 'Thou shalt not sowe thy vineyard with divers seeds: lest the fruit of thy seed which thou hast sown, and the fruit of thy vineyard, be defiled' 24 *Tame* cultivated 27 *Seraglio* enclosure, place of confinement; harem 29 *vex* trouble, exercise 30 *procreate* produce offspring; here, by budding or grafting *Sex* male and female 31 *enforc'd* subjected to force, constraint; produced by force, constraint

217 1 *vainly* in vain; with vanity *amaze* bewilder, puzzle 2 leafy crowns associated with military, civic and poetic fame

Whose short and narrow verged Shade
Does prudently their Toyles upbraid;
While all Flow'rs and all Trees do close
To weave the Garlands of repose.

II.

Fair quiet, have I found thee here,
And Innocence thy Sister dear!
Mistaken long, I sought you then
In busie Companies of Men.
Your sacred Plants, if here below,
Only among the Plants will grow.
Society is all but rude,
To this delicious Solitude.

III.

No white nor red was ever seen
So am'rous as this lovely green.
Fond Lovers, cruel as their Flame,
Cut in these Trees their Mistress name.
Little, Alas, they know, or heed,
How far these Beauties Hers exceed!
Fair Trees! where s'eer your barkes I wound,
No Name shall but your own be found.

IV.

When we have run our Passions heat,
Love hither makes his best retreat.
The *Gods*, that mortal Beauty chase,
Still in a Tree did end their race.
Apollo hunted *Daphne* so,
Only that She might Laurel grow.
And *Pan* did after *Syrinx* speed,
Not as a Nymph, but for a Reed.

217 5 *verged* extended, stretched 6 *prudently* discreetly, wisely, judiciously *upbraid* censure 7 *close* unite, combine 15 *all but* very nearly, almost *rude* uncivilized, barbarous 18 *am'rous* loving, lovely 19 *Fond* foolish; affectionate 25 *run* ... *heat* spent ... ardour, fervour; run ... part of a race 26 *retreat* retirement from the world or battle 28 *Still* ever, always *race* running; house, family

V.

What wond'rous Life in this I lead!
Ripe Apples drop about my head;
The Luscious Clusters of the Vine
Upon my Mouth do crush their Wine;
The Nectaren, and curious Peach,
Into my hands themselves do reach;
Stumbling on Melons, as I pass,
Insnar'd with Flow'rs, I fall on Grass.

VI.

Mean while the Mind, from pleasure less,
Withdraws into its happiness:
The Mind, that Ocean where each kind
Does streight its own resemblance find;
Yet it creates, transcending these,
Far other Worlds, and other Seas;
Annihilating all that's made
To a green Thought in a green Shade.

VII.

Here at the Fountains sliding foot,
Or at some Fruit-trees mossy root,
Casting the Bodies Vest aside,
My Soul into the boughs does glide:
There like a Bird it sits, and sings,
Then whets, and combs its silver Wings;
And, till prepar'd for longer flight,
Waves in its Plumes the various Light.

217 37 *curious* dainty, delicate 41 *pleasure less* lesser pleasure 43–4 popularly, the animals and plants of the land were supposed to have their counterparts in the oceans 44 *streight* at once, immediately 47 *Annihilating* reducing to nothing, blotting out of existence 48 *green ... green* the colour green; young, youthful, raw, inexperienced, fresh, tender, immature, unripe; cp. Virgil, *Eclogues* 9.19–20 'Who would have strewn wild flowers on the ground or given our springs green cover from the sun ('viridi fontes induceret umbra')?' 51 *Vest* robe, gown 54 *whets** preens

VIII.

Such was that happy Garden-state,
While Man there walk'd without a Mate:
After a Place so pure, and sweet,
What other Help could yet be meet!
But 'twas beyond a Mortal's share
To wander solitary there:
Two Paradises 'twere in one
To live in Paradise alone.

IX.

How well the skilful Gardner drew
Of flow'rs and herbes this Dial new;
Where from above the milder Sun
Does through a fragrant Zodiack run;
And, as it works, th' industrious Bee
Computes its time as well as we.
How could such sweet and wholsome Hours
Be reckon'd but with herbs and flow'rs!

218 [*from* Upon Appleton House, to my Lord *Fairfax*]

XLVII.

And now to the Abbyss I pass
Of that unfathomable Grass,
Where Men like Grashoppers appear,
But Grashoppers are Gyants there:

217 60 *meet* suitable, fit 66 *Dial* sundial, possibly a floral sundial where a central marker or 'gnomon' cast shadows on flowers arranged in a circle 69–70 in the Latin version of this poem, 'Hortus', 'time' is represented by 'thymo', suggesting an allusion to Horace, *Odes* 4.2.27–9 and perhaps to the tag 'carpe diem' ('seize each day'): 'but I, very much in the manner of a Matine bee laboriously harvesting thyme ('carpentis thyma') from numerous groves and the banks of many-streamed Tibur, inconspicuously accrete my intricate verses' 70 *Computes* calculates, reckons

218 2 *unfathomable*** unmeasurable 3–4 cp. Numbers 13:33 'And there we saw the giants, the sons of Anak, which come of the giants: and we were in our own sight as grasshoppers, and so we were in their sight'

They, in there squeking Laugh, contemn
Us as we walk more low then them:
And, from the Precipices tall
Of the green spir's, to us do call.

XLVIII.

To see Men through this Meadow Dive,
We wonder how they rise alive.
As, under Water, none does know
Whether he fall through it or go.
But, as the Marriners that sound,
And show upon their Lead the Ground,
They bring up Flow'rs so to be seen,
And prove they've at the Bottom been. . . .

. . . LIII.

The Mower now commands the Field;
In whose new Traverse seemeth wrought
A Camp of Battail newly fought:
Where, as the Meads with Hay, the Plain
Lyes quilted ore with Bodies slain:
The Women that with forks it fling,
Do represent the Pillaging.

LIV.

And now the careless Victors play,
Dancing the Triumphs of the Hay;
Where every Mowers wholesome Heat
Smells like an *Alexanders sweat.*
Their Females fragrant as the Mead
Which they in *Fairy Circles* tread:
When at their Dances End they kiss,
Their new-made Hay not sweeter is.

218 12 *go* advances 18 *Traverse* way, path, track; possibly a curtain or screen used in a room or theatre for a play or masque 19 *Camp* field 21 *quilted* padded 25 *Hay* cut grass; country dance 29 *Fairy Circles* darker circles of grass where fairies were supposed to have danced; fairy dances

LV.

When after this 'tis pil'd in Cocks,
Like a calm Sea it shews the Rocks:
We wondring in the River near
How Boats among them safely steer.
Or, like the *Desert Memphis Sand*,
Short *Pyramids* of Hay do stand.
And such the *Roman Camps* do rise
In Hills for Soldiers Obsequies.

LVI.

This *Scene* again withdrawing brings
A new and empty Face of things;
A levell'd space, as smooth and plain,
As Clothes for *Lilly* strecht to stain.
The World when first created sure
Was such a Table rase and pure.
Or rather such is the *Toril*
Ere the Bulls enter at Madril.

LVII.

For to this naked equal Flat,
Which *Levellers* take Pattern at,
The Villagers in common chase
Their Cattle, which it closer rase;
And what below the Sith increast
Is pincht yet nearer by the Beast.
Such, in the painted World, appear'd
Davenant with th' Universal Heard.

218 38, 45, 54, 60 *such* similarly 38 *Roman Camps* tumuli, supposedly burial mounds for ancient Romans 43 *Clothes* canvases *Lilly* Sir Peter Lely (1618–80), best known as a portrait-painter, who had come to England from Holland in 1641 *stain* paint 45 *Table rase* 'tabula rasa', blank tablet from which writing has been erased, leaving it ready to be written on again 46 *Toril* bullring 47 *Madril* Madrid 48 *equal* level 49 *Levellers* perhaps the democratic party headed by John Lilburne and Richard Overton, or Winstanley's 'True Levellers' or Diggers (see no. 211), with whom Fairfax had conversed 50 *chase* drive 51 *rase* raze to the ground, shave, crop 52 *Sith* scythe *increast* grew 54–5 in Sir William Davenant's *Gondibert*, 1651 (Book 2, Canto 6), he describes a painting of creation, in which on the sixth day 'an universal Herd' appeared; Marvell joins the wits who satirized the strongly anti-Puritan poem (cp. no. 303) by making Davenant one of his own beasts

LVIII.

They seem within the polisht Grass
A Landskip drawen in Looking-Glass.
And shrunk in the huge Pasture show
As Spots, so shap'd, on Faces do.
Such Fleas, ere they approach the Eye,
In Multiplying Glasses lye.
They feed so wide, so slowly move,
As *Constellations* do above.

MARGARET CAVENDISH, DUCHESS OF NEWCASTLE

219 Of many *Worlds* in this *World*

Just like unto a *Nest* of *Boxes* round,
Degrees of *sizes* within each *Boxe* are found.
So in this *World*, may many *Worlds* more be,
Thinner, and lesse, and lesse still by degree;
Although they are not subject to our *Sense*,
A *World* may be no bigger then *two-pence*.
Nature is curious, and such *worke* may make,
That our dull *Sense* can never finde, but scape.
For *Creatures*, small as *Atomes*, may be there,
If every *Atome* a *Creatures Figure* beare.
If foure *Atomes* a *World* can make,* then see,
What severall *Worlds* might in an *Eare-ring* bee.
For *Millions* of these *Atomes* may bee in
The *Head* of one *small*, little, *single Pin*.
And if thus *small*, then *Ladies* well may weare
A *World* of *Worlds*, as *Pendents* in each *Eare*.

* As I have before shewed *they* do, in my *Atomes*.

218 60 *ere . . . Eye* before being brought into focus 61 *Multiplying Glasses* magnifying glasses 62 *They* the cattle

219 7 *curious* cunning, skilful 11 side-note *before shewed* in the poem 'The foure principall *Figur'd Atomes* make the foure *Elements*, as *Square*, *Round*, *Long*, and *Sharpe*'

220 A *Dialogue* betwixt *Man*, and *Nature*

Man. Tis strang,
How we do change.
First to live, and then to dye,
Is a great misery.

To give us sense, great paines to feele,
To make our lives to be *Deaths wheele*;
To give us *Sense*, and *Reason* too,
Yet know not what we're made to do.
Whether to *Atomes* turne, or *Heaven* up flye,
Or into new *Formes* change, and never dye.
Or else to *Matter Prime* to fall againe,
From thence to take new *Formes*, and so remaine.
Nature gives no such *Knowledge* to *Man-kind*,
But *strong Desires* to torment the *Mind*:
And *Senses*, which like *Hounds* do run about,
Yet never can the *perfect Truth* find out.
O *Nature! Nature!* cruell to *Man-kind*,
Gives *Knowledge* none, but *Misery* to find.
Nature. Why doth *Man-kind* complaine, and make such
Moane?
May not *I* work my *will* with what's my owne?
But *Men* among themselves contract, and make
A *Bargaine* for my *Tree*; that *Tree* will take:
Most cruelly do chop in peeces small,
And formes it as he please, then builds withall.
Although that *Tree* by me was made to stand,
Just as it growes, not to be cut by *Man*.
Man. *O Nature*, *Trees* are dull, and have no *Sense*,
And therefore feel not paine, nor take offence.
Nature. But *Beasts* have *life* and *Sense*, and *passion* strong,
Yet *cruell man* doth kill, and doth them wrong.

220 6 *wheele* emblem of fortune's mutability 11 *Matter Prime* first matter, matter without form

To take that *life*, I *gave*, before the time
I did ordaine, the *injury is mine*.
Man. What *Ill* man doth, *Nature* did make him do,
For he by *Nature* is prompt thereunto.
For it was in great *Natures power*, and *Will*,
To make him as *she* pleas'd, either *good*, or *ill*.
Though *Beast* hath *Sense*, feels paine, yet whilst they live,
They *Reason* want, for to dispute, or grieve.
Beast hath no paine, but what in *Sense* doth lye,
Nor troubled *Thoughts*, to think how they shall dye.
Reason doth stretch *Mans mind* upon the Rack,
With *Hopes*, with *Joyes*, pull'd up, with *Feare* pull'd back.
Desire whips him forward, makes him run,
Despaire doth wound, and pulls him back agen.
For *Nature*, thou mad'st *Man* betwixt *Extreames*,
Wants *perfect Knowledge*, yet thereof he dreames.
For had he bin like to a *Stock*, or *Stone*,
Or like a *Beast*, to live with *Sense* alone.
Then might he eate, or drink, or lye *stone*-still,
Nere troubled be, either for *Heaven*, or *Hell*.
Man knowledge hath enough for to inquire,
Ambition great enough for to aspire:
And *Knowledge* hath, that yet he knowes not all,
And that himselfe he knoweth least of all:
Which makes him wonder, and thinks there is mixt
Two severall *Qualities* in *Nature* fixt.
The one like *Love*, the other like to *Hate*,
By striving both hinders *Predestinate*.
And then sometimes, *Man* thinks, as *one* they be,
Which makes *Contrariety* so well agree;
That though the *World* were made by *Love and hate*,
Yet all is rul'd, and governed by *Fate*.
These are *Mans feares*; mans *hopes* run smooth, and high,
Which thinks his *Mind* is some *great Deity*.
For though the body is of *low* degree,
In *Sense* like *Beasts*, their *Soules* like *Gods* shall be.
Nature. Saies *Nature*, why doth *Man* complaine, and crye,
If he beleives his *Soule* shall never dye?

221 Similizing the *Sea* to *Meadowes*, and *Pastures*, the *Marriners* to *Shepheards*, the *Mast* to a *May-pole*, *Fishes* to *Beasts*

The *Waves* like *Ridges* of *Plow'd-land* lies high,
Whereat the *Ship* doth stumble, downe doth lye.
But in a *Calme*, levell* as *Meadowes* seem,
And by its *Saltnesse* makes it look as green.
When *Ships* thereon a slow, soft pace they walke,
Then *Mariners*, as *Shepheards* sing, and talke.
Some whistle, and some on their *Pipes* do play,
Thus merrily will passe their time away.
And every *Mast* is like a *May-pole* high,
Round which they dance, though not so merrily,
As *Shepheards* do, when they their *Lasses* bring,
Whereon are *Garlands* tied with *Silken string*.
But on their *Mast*, instead of *Garlands*, hung
Huge *Sailes*, and *Ropes* to tye those *Garlands* on.
Instead of *Lasses* they do dance with *Death*,
And for their *Musick* they have *Boreas Breath*.
Instead of *Wine*, and *Wassals*, drink salt *Teares*,
And for their *Meat* they feed on nought but *Feares*.
For *Flocks* of *Sheep* great sholes of *Herrings* swim,
As ravenous *Wolves* the *Whales* do feed on them.
As sportfull *Kids* skip over *Hillocks* green,
So dancing *Dolphines* on the *Waves* are seen.
The *Porpoyse*, like their watchfull *Dog* espies,
And gives them warning when great *Windes* will rise.
Instead of *Barking*, he his *Head* wil shew
Above the waters, where they rough do flow.
When showring *Raines* power downe, and *Windes* do blow:
Then fast *Men* run for *Shelter* to a *Tree*;
So *Ships* at *Anchor* lye upon the *Sea*.

* Here the *Ship* is taken for a *Horse*.

221 Title *Similizing* comparing, likening 27 *power* pour

Katherine Philips

222 Upon the graving of her Name upon a Tree in *Barnelmes* Walks

Alas how barbarous are we,
Thus to reward the courteous Tree,
Who its broad shade affording us,
Deserves not to be wounded thus;
See how the Yielding Bark complies
With our ungrateful injuries.
And seeing this, say how much then
Trees are more generous then Men,
Who by a Nobleness so pure
Can first oblige and then endure.

222 Title *Barnelmes* near Barnes outside London; both Sidney and Donne had lived there (see the textual note)

PART FOUR

FRIENDS, PATRONS AND THE GOOD LIFE

Sir Thomas Wyatt

223 [Myn owne John poyntz sins ye delight to know]

Myn owne John poyntz sins ye delight to know
   the cawsse why that homeward I me drawe
   and fle the presse of courtes wher soo they goo
Rathar then to lyve thrall under the awe
   of lordly lokes wrappid within my cloke
   to will and lust lerning to set a lawe
It is not for becawsse I skorne or moke
   the powar of them, to whome fortune hath lent
   charge over us, of Right to strike the stroke
But trwe it is, that I have allwais ment
   lesse to estime them then the comon sort
   off owtward thinges that Juge in their intent
Withowt Regarde what dothe inwarde resort
   I grawnt sumtime that of glorye the fyar
   dothe touche my hart, my lyst not to report
blame by honowr, and honour to desyar
   but how may I this honour now atayne
   that cannot dy the coloure blake a lyer
My poyntz I cannot frame my tongue to fayne
   to cloke the trothe for praisse withowt desart
   of them that lyst, all vice for to retayne
I cannot honour them that settes their part
   with venus and baccus all theire lyf long
   nor holld my pece, of them Allthoo I smart

223 3 *presse* crowd, throng; trouble, tribulation 5 *cloke* perhaps of virtue; cp. Horace, *Odes* 3.29.54–5 'and clad in my manhood pay court to honest Poverty, though she brings no dowry' 7 *moke* mock 10 *trwe* true 12 *intent* thought, way of looking 13 *resort* retire, withdraw; dwell 14 *fyar* fire 15 *my lyst not* I do not like to 15–16 *report/blame* talk censoriously 18 liars cannot be dyed any blacker than they already are (?) 19 *fayne* feign 20 *to . . . praisse* flatter

I cannot crowche nor knelle to do so grete a wrong
   to worship them lyke gode on erthe alone
   that ar as wollffes thes sely lambes among
I cannot with my wordes complaine and mone,
   and suffer nought: nor smart without complaynt:
   nor turne the worde that from my mouth is gone.
I cannot speke and loke lyke a saynct
   use willes for witt, and make deceyt a plesure
   ande call crafft counsell, for proffet styll to paint
I Cannot wrest the law, to fill the coffer
   with innocent blode to fede my sellff Fat
   ande doo most hurt, where most hellp I offer
I am not he that can, alow the state
   off him Cesar, and dam cato to dye
   that with his dethe, dyd skape owt off the gate
From Cesares handes if lyve donnot lye
   and wolld not lyve, whar lyberty was lost
   so dyd his hart the comonn wele aplye
I am not he such eloquence to boste
   to make the crow singing as the swane
   nor call the lyon, of Coward bestes the moste
That cannot take a mows, as the cat can
   ande he that dithe, for hungar of the golld
   call him alessaundre and say that pan
Passithe Apollo in musike manyfolld
   praysse syr thopias for a nobyll talle
   and skorne the story that the knyght tolld
Praise him for counceill that is droncke of ale
   grynne when he laugheth that bereth all the swaye
   frown when he frowneth and grone when he is pale
On othres lust to hang boeth nyght and daye
   none of these poyntes would ever frame in me
   my wit is nought I cannot lerne the waye

223 27 *sely* simple, innocent 32 *willes* wiles, tricks, deceits 33 *call ... counsell* call dishonest cunning sound advice *paint* fawn, flatter 37 *alow* praise, commend 38 *dam* condemn 39 *gate* way 40 *lyve* Livy 42 *aplye* devote himself to 48–9 *say ... manyfolld* as Midas did 50 *syr thopias* the narrator's own tale, a travesty of courtly romance, in Chaucer's *The Canterbury tales* 55 *lust* wish, desire, inclination 56 *poyntes* courses; Pointz *frame* suit

And much the lesse of thinges that greater be
 that asken helpe of colours of devise
 to Joyne the mene with eche extremitie
With the neryst vertue to cloke alwaye the vise
 and as to pourpose like wise it shall fall
 to presse the vertue that it may not rise
As dronkenes good felloweshipp to call
 the frendly Foo with his dowble face
 say he is gentill and courtois therewithall
And say that favell hath a goodly grace
 in eloquence and crueltie to name
 zele of Justice and chaunge in tyme and place
And he that sufferth offence withoute blame
 call him pitefull and him true and playn
 that raileth rekles to every mans shame
Say he is rude that cannot lye and fayn
 the letcher a lover and tirannye
 to be the right of a Prynces reigne
I cannot I, no no it will not be
 this is the cause that I could never yet
 hang on their slevis that way as thou maist se
A chipp of chaunce more then a pownde of witt
 this maketh me at home to hounte and to hawke
 and in fowle weder at my booke to sitt
In frost and snowe then with my bow to stawke
 no man doeth marke where so I ride or goo
 in lusty lees at libertie I walke
And of these newes I fele nor wele nor woo
 sauf that a clogg doeth hang yet at my hele
 no force for that, for it is ordered so
That I may lepe boeth hedge and dike full well
 I ame not now in Fraunce to Judge the wyne
 with saffry sauce the delicates to fele

223 59 *colours of devise* clever shifts; rhetorical figures (for this strategy, cp. *Rhetorica ad Herennium* III.3.6) 62 *pourpose* chance, opportunity 67 *favell* often a personification of flattery 72 *rekles to* heedless of 78 *hang . . . slevis*** to depend or rely upon *way* weigh 83 *goo* walk 84 *lusty* flourishing *lees* meadows 85 *newes* novelties 86 *clogg* block attached to a prisoner's leg; probably referring to restrictions placed on Wyatt's freedom of movement by the King 87 *no . . . that* it is no matter 90 *saffry* savoury *delicates* dainties, delicates *fele* taste

Nor yet in spaigne where oon must him inclyne
rather then to be owtewerdly to seme
I meddill not with wittes that be so fyne
Nor Flaunders chiere letteth not my sight to deme
of black and white nor taketh my wit awaye
with bestlynes, they beestes do so esteme
Nor I ame not where Christe is geven in pray
for mony poisen and traison at Rome
a comune practise used nyght and daie
But here I ame in Kent and christendome
emong the muses where I rede and ryme
Where if thou list my poynz for to com
Thou shalt be Judge how I do spend my tyme

George Gascoigne

224 [Upon the theme: *Magnum vectigal parcimonia*]

The common speech is, spend and God will send,
But what sends he? a bottell and a bagge.
A staffe, a wallet and a wofull ende,
For such as list in bravery so to bragge.
Then if thou covet coine enough to spend,
Learne first to spare thy budget at the brinke,
So shall the bottome be the faster bound:
But he that list with lavish hand to linke,
(In like expence) a pennie with a pound,
May chance at last to sitte aside and shrinke
His harbraind head without dame deinties dore.

223 94 *chiere* cheer, food, entertainment *letteth* hinders, stops *deme* judge 100 *Kent . . . christendome* proverbial, but the Wyatt family's home was at Allington Castle in Kent

224 Title *Magnum . . . parcimonia* 'Thrift is a great revenue', from Cicero, *Paradoxes* 6.3.49 2–3 *bottell . . . wallet* a beggar's possessions 4 *bravery* fine clothes *bragge* boast of their status 6 *budget* leather bag, wallet 11 *without* outside

Hick, Hobbe and Dick with cloutes uppon their knee,
Have many times more goonhole groates in store,
And change of crownes more quicke at call than he,
Which let their lease and tooke their rent before.
For he that rappes a royall on his cappe,
Before he put one pennie in his pursse,
Had neede turne quicke and broch a better tappe,
Or else his drinke may chance go downe the wursse.
I not denie but some men have good hap,
To climbe alofte by scales of courtly grace,
And winne the world with liberalitie:
Yet he that yerks old angells out apace,
And hath no new to purchase dignitie,
When orders fall, may chance to lacke his grace.
For haggard hawkes mislike an emptie hand:
So stiffely some sticke to the mercers stall,
Till sutes of silke have swet out all their land.
So ofte thy neighbours banquet in thy hall,
Till Davie *Debet* in thy parlor stande,
And bids thee welcome to thine owne decay.
I lyke a Lyons lookes not woorth a leeke
When every Foxe beguyles him of his praye:
What sauce but sorowe serveth him a weeke,
Whiche all his cates consumeth in one daye?
Fyrste use thy stomacke to a stonde of ale,
Before thy Malmesey come in Marchantes bookes,
And rather weare (for shifte) thy shirte of male,
Than teare thy silken sleeves with teynter hookes.
Put feathers in thy pillowes greate and small,

224 12 *cloutes* rags 13 *goonhole** of low value; gunhole, perhaps the corruption of a foreign proper name (?) *groates* silver coins worth four (old) pence 16 *rappes* claps *royall* a coin worth fifteen shillings 21 *scales* ladders 23 *yerks* chucks *angells* gold coins worth from six to ten shillings 25 *orders fall* ranks, positions fall vacant 26 cp. the proverb 'Empty hands no hawks allure' *haggard* wild, untamed 30 *Debet* the personification of Debt 32 *I lyke* like to 35 *cates* provisions, food 36 *use* accustom *stonde* stand, barrel 37 *Malmesey* sweet wine 39 *teynter hookes* metal hooks on which clothes were hung

Lette them bee princkt with plumes that gape for plummes,
Heape up bothe golde and silver safe in hooches,
Catche, snatche, and scratche for scrapings and for crummes,
Before thou decke thy hatte (on highe) with brooches.
Lette firste thyne one hande holde fast all that commes,
Before that other learne his letting flie:
Remember still that softe fyre makes sweete malte,
No haste but good (who meanes to multiplie:)
Bought wytte is deare, and drest with sowre salte,
Repentaunce commes to late, and then saye I,
Who spares the first and keepes the laste unspent,
Shall fynde that Sparing yeldes a goodly rent.

Sic tuli.

225 [Gascoignes wodmanship]

My worthy Lord, I pray you wonder not,
To see your wodman shoote so ofte awrie,
Nor that he stands amased like a sot,
And lets the harmlesse deare (unhurt) go by.
Or if he strike a doe which is but carren,
Laugh not good Lord, but favoure such a fault,
Take well in worth, he wold faine hit the barren,
But though his harte be good, his happe is naught:
And therefore now I crave your Lordships leave,
To tell you playne what is the cause of this:
First if it please your honour to perceive,
What makes your wodman shoote so ofte amisse,
Beleeve me Lord the case is nothing strange,
He shootes awrie almost at every marke,
His eyes have bene so used for to raunge,
That now God knowes they be both dimme and darke.

224 41 *princkt* dressed up *gape for plummes* long for rewards, perquisites 42 *hooches* hutches, chests, coffers [53] *Sic tuli* 'this is my burden'

225 Title *wodmanship** the business, or skill, of a woodman 5 *carren* a doe with young and hence unfit to eat 7 *barren* doe without fawns 8 *happe* luck, chance

For proofe he beares the note of follie nowe,
Who shotte sometimes to hit Philosophie,
And aske you why? forsooth I make avow,
Bycause his wanton wittes went all awrie.
Next that, he shot to be a man of lawe,
And spent some time with learned Litleton,
Yet in the end, he proved but a dawe,
For lawe was darke and he had quickly done.
Then could he wish Fitzharbert such a braine,
As *Tully* had, to write the law by arte,
So that with pleasure, or with litle paine,
He might perhaps, have caught a trewants parte.
But all to late, he most mislikte the thing,
Which most might helpe to guide his arrow streight,
He winked wrong, and so let slippe the string,
Which cast him wide, for all his queint conceit.
From thence he shotte to catch a courtly grace,
And thought even there to wield the world at will,
But out alas he much mistooke the place,
And shot awrie at every rover still.
The blasing baits which drawe the gazing eye,
Unfethered there his first affection,
No wonder then although he shot awrie,
Wanting the fethers of discretion.
Yet more than them, the marks of dignitie,
He much mistooke and shot the wronger way,
Thinking the purse of prodigalitie,
Had bene best meane to purchase such a pray.
He thought the flattring face which fleareth still,
Had bene full fraught with all fidelitie,
And that such words as courtiers use at will,
Could not have varied from the veritie.

225 22 *Litleton* Sir Thomas Littleton (1402–81), judge and author of *Tenures*, the first printed treatise on English law 23 *dawe* jackdaw, simpleton, fool 25 *Fitzharbert* Sir Anthony Fitzherbert (1470–1538), judge and author of standard legal reference works 26 *Tully* Cicero 31 *winked* aimed 33 *catch . . . grace* try to become a courtier 36 *rover* mark selected for shooting 45 *fleareth* grins, grimaces

But when his bonet buttened with gold,
His comelie cape begarded all with gay,
His bumbast hose, with linings manifold,
His knit silke stocks and all his queint aray,
Had pickt his purse of all the Peter pence,
Which might have paide for his promotion,
Then (all to late) he found that light expence,
Had quite quencht out the courts devotion.
So that since then the tast of miserie,
Hath bene alwayes full bitter in his bit,
And why? forsooth bicause he shot awrie,
Mistaking still the markes which others hit.
But now behold what marke the man doth find,
He shootes to be a souldier in his age,
Mistrusting all the vertues of the minde,
He trusts the power of his personage.
As though long limmes led by a lusty hart,
Might yet suffice to make him rich againe,
But flussing fraies have taught him such a parte,
That now he thinks the warres yeld no such gaine.
And sure I feare, unlesse your lordship deigne,
To traine him yet into some better trade,
It will be long before he hit the veine,
Whereby he may a richer man be made.
He cannot climbe as other catchers can,
To leade a charge before himselfe be led,
He cannot spoile the simple sakeles man,
Which is content to feede him with his bread.
He cannot pinch the painefull souldiers pay,
And sheare him out his share in ragged sheetes,
He cannot stop to take a gredy pray
Upon his fellowes groveling in the streetes.

225 49 *buttened ... gold* furnished with gold buttons 50 *begarded*** adorned with lace, embroidery 51 *bumbast* padded out 53 *Peter pence* a tax (abolished in 1534) of a penny per household payable to the See of St Peter, the Roman Church; money for bribery 58 *bit* bite 64 *personage* bodily frame, figure 67 *flussing* Flushing in the Low Countries, where Gascoigne fought in the spring of 1572 73 *catchers* cp. the proverb 'catch as catch can' 75 *sakeles* sackless, innocent 77 *pinch* stint *painefull* hard-working 78 *sheare* divide 79 *stop* stoop *pray* booty, plunder 80 *groveling* prone, because drunk

He cannot pull the spoile from such as pill,
And seeme full angrie at such foule offence,
Although the gayne content his greedie will,
Under the cloake of contrarie pretence:
And nowe adayes, the man that shootes not so,
Maye shoote amisse, even as your Woodman dothe:
But then you marvell why I lette them go,
And never shoote, but saye farewell forsooth:
Alas my Lorde, whyle I doe muze hereon,
And call to mynde my youthfull yeares myspente,
They give mee suche a boane to gnawe upon,
That all my senses are in silence pente.
My mynde is rapte in contemplation,
Wherein my dazeled eyes onely beholde,
The blacke houre of my constellation,
Whyche framed mee so lucklesse on the molde:
Yet therewithall I can not but confesse,
That vayne presumption makes my heart to swell,
For thus I thinke, not all the worlde (I guesse,)
Shootes bet than I, nay some shootes not so well.
In *Aristotle* somewhat did I learne,
To guyde my manners all by comelynesse,
And *Tullie* taught me somewhat to discerne
Betweene sweete speeche and barbarous rudenesse.
Olde *Parkyns, Rastall,* and *Dan Bractens* bookes,
Did lende mee somewhat of the lawlesse Lawe,
The craftie Courtyers with their guylefull lookes,
Muste needes put some experience in my mawe:
Yet can not these with manye maystries mo,
Make me shoote streyght at any gaynfull pricke,
Where some that never handled such a bow,
Can hit the white, or touch it neare the quicke,

225 81 *pill* pillage 95 *constellation* stars at birth 96 *molde* earth 105 *Parkyns* John Perkins (?–1545), author of a popular legal textbook on conveyancing *Rastall* John Rastell (1475–1536), legal author, printer, and publisher *Dan* master *Bractens* Henry de Bracton (?–1268), author of the first systematic statement of English law, which was published by Tottel (see no. 57) in 1569 108 *mawe* stomach 109 *maystries* mastery of arts and sciences 110 *pricke* bull's-eye 112 *white* white part of the target, near the centre

Who can nor speake, nor write in pleasant wise,
Nor leade their life by *Aristotles* rule,
Nor argue well on questions that arise,
Nor pleade a case more than my Lord Maiors mule,
Yet can they hit the marks that I do misse,
And winne the meane which may the man mainteine,
Nowe when my mynde dothe mumble upon this,
No wonder then although I pyne for payne:
And whyles myne eyes beholde this mirroure thus,
The hearde goeth by, and farewell gentle does:
So that your lordship quickely may discusse
What blyndes myne eyes so ofte (as I suppose.)
But since my Muse can to my Lorde reherse
What makes me misse, and why I doe not shoote,
Let me imagine in this woorthlesse verse:
If right before mee, at my standings foote
There stoode a Doe, and I shoulde strike hir deade,
And then shee prove a carrion carkas too,
What figure might I fynde within my head,
To scuse the rage whiche rulde mee so to doo?
Some myghte interprete by playne paraphrase,
That lacke of skill or fortune ledde the chaunce,
But I muste otherwyse expounde the case,
I saye *Jehova* did this Doe advaunce,
And made hir bolde to stande before mee so,
Till I had thrust myne arrowe to hir harte,
That by the sodaine of hir overthrowe,
I myght endevour to amende my parte,
And turne myne eyes that they no more beholde,
Suche guylefull markes as seeme more than they be:
And though they glister outwardely lyke golde,
Are inwardly but brasse, as men may see:
And when I see the milke hang in hir teate,
Me thinkes it sayth, olde babe nowe learne to sucke,

225 116 *mule* Lord Mayors traditionally rode mules 123 *discusse* decide 128 *standings* hunter's stand 139 *sodaine*** sudden, suddenness

Who in thy youthe couldst never learne the feate
To hitte the whytes whiche live with all good lucke.
Thus have I tolde my Lorde, (God graunt in season)
A tedious tale in rime, but little reason.

Haud ictus sapio.

Edward de Vere, Earl of Oxford

226 [Weare I a Kinge I coulde commande content]

Weare I a Kinge I coulde commande content;
Weare I obscure unknowne shoulde be my cares,
And weare I ded no thoughtes should me torment,
Nor wordes, nor wronges, nor loves, nor hopes, nor feares.
  A dowtefull choyse of these thinges one to crave,
  A Kingdom or a cottage or a grave.

Thomas Lodge

227 [*from* Scillaes Metamorphosis]

The minde through thee divines on endlesse things,
And formes a Heaven through others fond mislikes;
Time loathes thy haunt, yet lends thee many wings:
Refined wits against thy bulwarke strikes;
  And when their curious thoughts are overpast,
  They scorne their bookes, and like thy bent at last. . . .

225 [151] *Haud ictus sapio* 'I know nothing of shooting'; 'ictus' can mean 'stress' or 'beat' in poetry as well as 'shot'

227 1 *thee* Discontent *divines* conjectures, thinks, conceives by special inspiration 2 *fond* foolish, silly

How could the Heavens have retrograde aspects
Without thy helpe? How might the Plannets finde
Their oppositions, and their strange effects,
Unlesse thy powre assisted everie kinde?
The aire by thee at first invented voice,
Which once reverberate, straight yeelds a noice.
The pencile man that with a careles hand
Hath shaddowed *Venus*, hates his slack regard;
And all amaz'd doth discontented stand,
And mends the same that he before had mard:
Who sees not then that it was *Discontent*,
That sight to eie, and perfect judgement lent?
The schooleman that with heedlesse florish writes,
Refines his fault, if thou direct his eie:
And then againe with wonder he endites
Such sweete sententious lines, as never die:
Lost in my selfe in praising of thy might,
My speech yeelds up his office to delight.

JOHN DONNE

228 To Sir *Henry Wotton*

Sir, more then kisses, letters mingle Soules;
For, thus friends absent speake. This ease controules
The tediousnesse of my life: But for these
I could ideate nothing, which could please,
But I should wither in one day, and passe
To'a botle'of Hay, that am a locke of Grasse.

227 7 *retrograde* apparently moving against the order of the signs of the zodiac *aspects* the positions of the heavenly bodies as seen from the earth 9 *oppositions* relative positions of two heavenly bodies when exactly opposite each other, as seen from the earth 12 *reverberate** reverberated 13 *pencile man** man with a brush, artist 21 *endites* sets down, writes

228 2 *controules* relieves 4 *ideate*** imagine, conceive 6 *botle* bundle *locke* tuft

Life is a voyage, and in our lifes wayes
Countries, Courts, Towns are Rockes, or Remoraes;
They breake or stop all ships, yet our state's such,
That though then pitch they staine worse, wee must touch.
If in the furnace of the even line,
Or under th'adverse icy Poles thou pine,
Thou know'st two temperate Regions girded in,
Dwell there: But Oh, what refuge canst thou winne
Parch'd in the Court, and in the country frozen?
Shall cities, built of both extremes, be chosen?
Can dung and garlike be'a perfume? or can
A Scorpion and Torpedo cure a man?
Cities are worst of all three; of all three
(O knottie riddle) each is worst equally.
Cities are Sepulchers; they who dwell there
Are carcases, as if no such there were.
And Courts are Theaters, where some men play
Princes, some slaves, all to one end, and of one clay.
The Country is a desert, where no good,
Gain'd (as habits, not borne,) is understood.
There men become beasts, and prone to more evils;
In cities blockes, and in a lewd court, devills.
As in the first Chaos confusedly
Each elements qualities were in the'other three;
So pride, lust, covetize, being severall
To these three places, yet all are in all,
And mingled thus, their issue incestuous.
Falshood is denizon'd. Virtue is barbarous.
Let no man say there, Virtues flintie wall
Shall locke vice in mee, I'll do none, but know all.
Men are spunges, which to poure out, receive,
Who know false play, rather then lose, deceive.

228 8 *Remoraes*** impediments, hindrances; the remora or sucking-fish was believed to be able to stop any ship to which it attached itself 10 cp. the Apocryphal Ecclesiasticus 13:1, which became proverbial, 'He that toucheth pitch shall be defiled therewith' 11 *even line* equator 12 *adverse* opposite 18 *Torpedo* electric ray 22 *such* such people 28 *blockes* dullards, stupid men 31 *severall* particularly appropriate 34 *denizon'd* naturalized, made native *barbarous* wild, outside civilization

For in best understandings, sinne beganne,
Angels sinn'd first, then Devills, and then man.
Onely perchance beasts sinne not; wretched wee
Are beasts in all, but white integritie.
I thinke if men, which in these places live
Durst looke for themselves, and themselves retrive,
They would like strangers greet themselves, seeing then
Utopian youth, growne old Italian.
  Be then thine owne home, and in thy selfe dwell;
Inne any where, continuance maketh hell.
And seeing the snaile, which every where doth rome,
Carrying his owne house still, still is at home,
Follow (for he is easie pac'd) this snaile,
Bee thine owne Palace, or the world's thy goale.
And in the worlds sea, do not like corke sleepe
Upon the waters face; nor in the deepe
Sinke like a lead without a line: but as
Fishes glide, leaving no print where they passe,
Nor making sound, so, closely thy course goe,
Let men dispute, whether thou breath, or no.
Onely'in this one thing, be no Galenist: To make
Courts hot ambitions wholesome, do not take
A dramme of Countries dulnesse; do not adde
Correctives, but as chymiques, purge the bad.
But, Sir, I advise not you, I rather doe
Say o'er those lessons, which I learn'd of you:
Whom, free from German schismes, and lightnesse
Of France, and faire Italies faithlesnesse,
Having from these suck'd all they had of worth,
And brought home that faith, which you carried forth,
I throughly love. But if my selfe, I'have wonne
To know my rules, I have, and you have

DONNE

228 42 *integritie* innocence, sinlessness 46 *Utopian** impractically idealistic, from Sir Thomas More's humanist satire *Utopia* (1516) *Italian* degenerate, corrupt 48 *Inne* lodge *continuance* remaining, staying 52 *goale* gaol 59 *Galenist* a follower of Galen (129–99), who taught that imbalances in the body should be corrected by counterbalancing drugs 62 *Correctives*** things which counteract or neutralize what is harmful *chymiques* alchemists, physicians who follow Paracelsus (1493–1541) 69 *throughly* wholly, entirely

THOMAS DELONEY

229 The Weavers Song

When *Hercules* did use to spin,
and *Pallas* wrought upon the Loome,
Our Trade to flourish did begin,
While Conscience went not selling Broome.
Then love and friendship did agree,
To keepe the band of amitie.

When Princes sonnes kept sheep in field,
and Queenes made cakes of wheaten flower,
Then men to lucre did not yeeld,
which brought good cheare in every bower.
Then love and friendship did agree,
To hold the bands of amitie.

But when that Giants huge and hie,
did fight with speares like Weavers beames,
Then they in Iron beds did lie,
and brought poore men to hard extreames.
Yet love and friendship did agree,
To hold the bands of amitie.

Then *David* tooke his Sling and stone,
not fearing great *Golias* strength:
He pearc't his braines and broke the bone,
though he were fifty foote of length.
For love and friendship, etc.

229 4 *Broome* a common, yellow-flowering shrub 14 *Weavers beames* cp. 1 Samuel 17:7 'And the staff of his [Goliath's] spear was like a weaver's beam' 19–20 see 1 Samuel 17

But while the Greekes besieged *Troy*,
Penelope apace did spin,
And Weavers wrought with mickle joy,
though little gaines were comming in.
For love and friendship, etc.

Had *Helen* then sate carding wooll
(whose beautious face did breed such strife)
Shee had not been sir *Paris* trull,
nor caused so many lose their life.
Yet we by love did still agree, etc.

Or had King *Priams* wanton sonne,
beene making quils with sweet content,
He had not then his friends undone,
when he to *Greece* a gadding went.
For love and friendship did agree, etc.

The Cedar trees indure more stormes,
than little shrubs, that sprout on hie:
The Weavers live more voyd of harmes,
Than Princes of great dignitie,
While love and friendship doth agree, etc.

The Shepheard sitting in the field,
doth tune his pipe with hearts delight:
When Princes watch with speare and shield,
the poore man soundly sleepes all night.
While love and friendship doth agree, etc.

Yet this by proofe is daily tride,
for Gods good gifts wee are ingrate:
And no man through the World so wide,
lives well contented with his state.
No love and friendship wee can see,
To hold the bands of amitie.

229 26 *mickle* much, great 29 *carding* combing 31 *trull* prostitute, mistress
35 *quils* spools, bobbins

Thomas Dekker

230 [Art thou poore yet hast thou golden Slumbers]

The Song

Song. Art thou poore yet hast thou golden Slumbers:
Oh sweet content!
Art thou rich yet is thy minde perplexed?
Oh punnishment.
Dost thou laugh to see how fooles are vexed?
To ad to golden numbers, golden numbers.
O sweet content, o sweet etc.
Foote. Worke apace, apace, apace, apace:
Honest labour beares a lovely face,
Then hey noney, noney: hey noney, noney.

Canst drinke the waters of the Crisped spring,
O sweet content!
Swim'st thou in wealth, yet sinck'st in thine owne teares,
O punnishment.
Then hee that patiently wants burden beares,
No burden beares, but is a King, a King,
O sweet content, etc.
Foot. Worke apace, apace, etc.

230 8 *Foote* chorus, refrain 11*Crisped** with a surface curled into minute waves

Samuel Daniel

231 To The Lady Lucie, Countesse of Bedford

Though virtue be the same when low she stands
In th'humble shadowes of obscuritie
As when she either sweats in martiall bands,
Or sits in Court, clad with authoritie:
Yet Madame, doth the strictnesse of her roome
Greatly detract from her abilitie:
For as inwalld within a living tombe
Her handes and armes of action, labour not;
Her thoughts as if abortive from the wombe,
Come never borne, though happily begot.
But where she hath mounted in open sight
An eminent, and spacious dwelling got.
Where shee may stirre at will, and use her might,
There is she more her selfe, and more her owne:
There in the faire attyre of honour dight,
She sits at ease and makes her glory knowne,
Applause attends her hands, her deedes have grace,
Her worth new-borne is straight as if ful growne,
With such a goodly and respected face
Doth vertue looke, that's set to looke from hie,
And such a faire advantage by her place
Hath state and greatnesse to doe worthily.
And therefore well did your high fortunes meete
With her, that gracing you, comes grac't thereby,
And well was let into a house so sweete
So good, so faire; so faire, so good a guest,
Who now remaines as blessed in her seate,
As you are with her residencie blesst.

231 5 *strictnesse*** narrowness, tightness 15 *dight* dressed 18 *straight* immediately; not bending, erect

And this faire course of knowledge whereunto
Your studies, learned Lady, are addrest,
Is th'onely certaine way that you can goe
Unto true glory, to true happines:
All passages on earth besides, are so
Incumbred with such vaine disturbances,
As still we loose our rest, in seeking it,
Being but deluded with apparances.
And no key had you else that was so fit
T'unlocke that prison of your Sex, as this,
To let you out of weakenesse, and admit
Your powers into the freedome of that blisse
That sets you there where you may oversee
This rowling world, and view it as it is,
And apprehend how th'outsides do agree
With th'inward being of the things, we deeme
And hold in our ill-cast accounts, to be
Of highest value, and of best esteeme.
Since all the good we have rests in the mind,
By whose proportions onely we redeeme
Our thoughts from out confusion, and do finde
The measure of our selves, and of our powres.
And that all happinesse remaines confind
Within the Kingdome of this breast of ours.
Without whose bounds, all that we looke on, lies
In others Jurisdictions, others powres,
Out of the circuit of our liberties.
All glory, honor, fame, applause, renowne,
Are not belonging to our royalties,
But t'others wills, wherein th'are onely growne.
And that unlesse we finde us all within,
We never can without us be our owne:
Nor call it right our life, that we live in:

231 36 *apparances* appearances 42 *rowling* revolving 45 *ill-cast* badly reckoned 53 *Without* outside 55 *circuit* compass, limit *liberties* privileges, the areas over which those privileges extend 57 *royalties* personal prerogatives, rights

But a possession held for others use,
That seeme to have most int'rest therein.
Which we do so dissever, parte, traduce,
Let out to custome fashion and to shew
As we enjoy but onely the abuse,
And have no other Deed at all to shew.
How oft are we constrained to appeare
With other countenance then that we owe,
And be our selves farre off, when we are neere?
How oft are we forc't on a clowdie hart,
To set a shining face, and make it cleere.
Seeming content to put our selves apart,
To beare a part of others weaknesses:
As if we onely were compos'd by Arte,
Not Nature, and did all our deedes addresse
T'opinion, not t'a conscience what is right:
As fram'd b'example, not advisednesse
Into those formes that intertaine our sight.
And though Bookes, Madame, cannot make this minde,
Which we must bring apt to be set aright,
Yet do they rectifie it in that kinde,
And touch it so, as that it turnes that way
Where judgement lies: And though we cannot finde
The certaine place of truth, yet doe they stay,
And intertaine us neere about the same.
And give the Soule the best delights that may
Encheere it most, and most our spirits inflame
To thoughts of glory, and to worthy ends.
And therefore in a course that best became
The cleerenesse of your heart, and best commends
Your worthy powres, you runne the rightest way
That is on Earth, that can true glory give,
By which when all consumes, your fame shal live.

231 64 *dissever* sever, separate *parte* divide *traduce* defame, malign 69 *owe* own 71 *clowdie* gloomy, troubled 78 *advisednesse* caution, deliberation 88 *Encheere*** 90 *became* suited 91 *cleerenesse* purity, innocence

Ben Jonson

232 To Lucy, Countesse of Bedford, with Mr. Donnes Satyres

Lucy, you brightnesse of our spheare, who are
Life of the *Muses* day, their morning-starre!
If workes (not th'authors) their owne grace should looke,
Whose poemes would not wish to be your booke?
But these, desir'd by you, the makers ends
Crowne with their owne. Rare poemes aske rare friends.
Yet, *Satyres*, since the most of mankind bee
Their un-avoided subject, fewest see:
For none ere tooke that pleasure in sinnes sense,
But, when they heard it tax'd, tooke more offence.
They, then, that living where the matter is bred,
Dare for these poemes, yet, both aske, and read,
And like them too; must needfully, though few,
Be of the best: and 'mongst those, best are you.
Lucy, you brightnesse of our spheare, who are
The *Muses* evening, as their morning-starre.

233 Inviting a friend to supper

To night, grave sir, both my poore house, and I
Doe equally desire your companie:
Not that we thinke us worthy such a ghest,
But that your worth will dignifie our feast,
With those that come; whose grace may make that seeme
Something, which, else, could hope for no esteeme.
It is the faire acceptance, Sir, creates
The entertaynment perfect: not the cates.

232 1 *brightnesse* Lucy is derived as a name from the Latin 'lux', light 2 *morning-starre* Lucifer, 'light-bearing' 3 *looke* look to

233 8 *cates* food, provisions

Yet shall you have, to rectifie your palate,
An olive, capers, or some better sallade
Ushring the mutton; with a short-leg'd hen,
If we can get her, full of egs, and then,
Limons, and wine for sauce: to these, a coney
Is not to be despair'd of, for our money;
And, though fowle, now, be scarce, yet there are clarkes,
The skie not falling, thinke we may have larkes.
Ile tell you of more, and lye, so you will come:
Of partrich, pheasant, wood-cock, of which some
May yet be there; and godwit, if we can:
Knat, raile, and ruffe too. How so ere, my man
Shall reade a piece of VIRGIL, TACITUS,
LIVIE, or of some better booke to us,
Of which wee'll speake our minds, amidst our meate;
And Ile professe no verses to repeate:
To this, if ought appeare, which I not know of,
That will the pastrie, not my paper, show of.
Digestive cheese, and fruit there sure will bee;
But that, which most doth take my *Muse*, and mee,
Is a pure cup of rich *Canary*-wine,
Which is the *Mermaids*, now, but shall be mine:
Of which had HORACE, or ANACREON tasted,
Their lives, as doe their lines, till now had lasted.
Tabacco, Nectar, or the *Thespian* spring,
Are all but LUTHERS beere, to this I sing.
Of this we will sup free, but moderately,
And we will have no *Pooly*', or *Parrot* by;

233 9 *rectifie* in chemistry, to purify, refine 11 *Ushring* preceding 16 'If the sky falls we shall have larks' was proverbial 17 *lye* cp. Martial, *Epigrams* 11.52.13 'I'll lie to make you come' 19 *godwit* a marsh bird, like a curlew 20 *Knat* a bird of the snipe family *raile* corncrake *ruffe* a male bird of the sandpiper family 24 cp. Martial, *Epigrams* 11.52.16 'I also promise I'll recite nothing to you' *professe* promise 30 *Mermaids* the Mermaid Tavern in Bread Street, London, a meeting place for writers 34 *Luthers* from the German reformer Martin Luther: generally gloomy (?); German beer, and so weaker than English (?) 36 *Pooly', or Parrot* Robert Pooly or Poole was a government spy who betrayed Mary Queen of Scots' servant Anthony Babington (1561–86); Parrot was another informer

Nor shall our cups make any guiltie men:
But, at our parting, we will be, as when
We innocently met. No simple word,
That shall be utter'd at our mirthfull boord,
Shall make us sad next morning: or affright
The libertie, that wee'll enjoy to night.

[THOMAS RAVENSCROFT]

234 [Hey hoe what shall I say]

Hey hoe what shall I say,
Sir John hath carried my wife away,
They were gone ere I wist,
She will come when she list,
Hey trolly lolly,
Come againe ho, hey.

235 [Sing we now merily]

Sing we now merily
Our purses be empty
Hey ho,
Let them take care
That list to spare
For I will not doe so,
Who can sing so merry a note,
As he that cannot change a groat,
Hey hoe
Trolly lolly loe
Trolly lolly lo.

234 4 *list* pleases

235 5 *list to spare* choose to economize 8 *groat* coin worth four (old) pence

236 A Belmans Song

Maides to bed, and cover coale,
Let the Mouse Out of her hole:
Crickets in the Chimney sing,
Whil'st the little Bell doth ring.
If fast asleepe, who can tell
When the Clapper hits the Bell.

THOMAS CAMPION

237 [Now winter nights enlarge]

1 Now winter nights enlarge
  The number of their houres,
And clouds their stormes discharge
  Upon the ayrie towres,
Let now the chimneys blaze,
  And cups o'erflow with wine:
Let well-tun'd words amaze
  With harmonie divine.
Now yellow waxen lights
  Shall waite on hunny Love,
While youthfull Revels, Masks, and Courtly sights,
  Sleepes leaden spels remove.

2 This time doth well dispence
  With lovers long discourse;
Much speech hath some defence,
  Though beauty no remorse.
All doe not all things well;
  Some measures comely tread;
Some knotted Ridles tell;
  Some Poems smoothly read.

237 13–14 *dispence/With* permit, allow 18 *measures* dances; metres, verse forms

The Summer hath his joyes,
  And Winter his delights;
Though Love and all his pleasures are but toyes,
  They shorten tedious nights.

Anonymous

238 The Mode of France

1 Will you heare the Mode of france
to stopp the mouthe of those that done you
neatly Leade them in a dance
because wee are behind in mony
2 If your Lanlord chance to call
either for dyett or for rayment
Leade him in a dance withall
and forgett itt in your payment
3 If your taylor chance to strike you
with his bill and stay noe Leasure
Lead him in a dance that likes you
and in stead of coyne take measure
4 If your shoomaker come on
with his last and neatly Lead itt
lett this everlasting done
see his owne boots neatly tread itt
5 If your Landlady doe call
needs must satisfye her pleasure
shee despises your carrant
sheele be payd with standing measure
6 If your Lawer find you out
for fees for this devise or tother
let him dance for all his goute
and pay one Motion with another

238 1 *Mode*** way of doing things 2 *done* dun, pester for money 6 *dyett* daily allowance of food, board 12 *measure* dance 15 *done* dunner, debt-collector 19 *carrant* coranto, a kind of dance 20 *standing measure* stationary dance 24 *Motion* proposal, instigation

7 Thus wee range the world about
thus wee scape then all disasters
then Let all the world declare
that wee are nimble quicke paymasters.

MICHAEL DRAYTON

239 These verses weare made By Michaell Drayton Esquier Poett Lawreatt the night before hee dyed

Soe well I love thee, as without thee I
1 Love Nothing, yf I might Chuse, I'de rather dye
Then bee on day debarde thy companye

Since Beasts, and plantes doe growe, and live and move
2 Beastes are those men, that such a life approve
Hee onlye Lives, that Deadly is In Love

The Corne that in the grownd is sowen first dies
3 And of on seed doe manye Eares aRise
Love this worldes Corne, by dying Multiplies

The seeds of Love first by thy eyes weare throwne
4 Into A grownd untild, a harte unknowne
To beare such fruitt, tyll by thy handes t'was sowen

Looke as your Looking glass by Chance may fall
5 Devyde and breake in manye peyces smale
And yett shewes forth, the selfe same face In all

Proportions, Features Graces Just the same
6 And In the smalest peyce as well the name
Of Fayrest one deserves, as In the richest frame

Soe all my Thoughts are peyces but of you
Whiche put together makes a Glass soe true
As I therin noe others face but yours can Veiwe

239 3 *on* one 5 *approve* experience, commend 16 *Proportions* configurations, forms, shapes

EDMUND WALLER

240 At Pens-hurst

Had *Dorothea* liv'd when mortals made
Choice of their deities, this sacred shade
Had held an altar to her power that gave
The peace and glory, which these allays have
Embroydred so with flowers where she stood,
That it became a garden of the wood:
Her presence has such more then humane grace
That it can civilize the rudest place,
And beauty too, and order can impart
Where nature nere intended it, nor art.
The plants acknowledge this, and her admire
No less then those of old did *Orpheus* Lire:
If she sit downe with tops all toward her bow'd,
They round about her into arbours crowd:
Or if she walk, in even ranks they stand
Like some well marshall'd and obsequious band.
Amphion so made stones and timber leap
Into fair figures from a confus'd heap:
And in the symetry of her parts is found
A power like that of harmony in sound:
   —Yee lofty beeches tell this matchlesse dame
That if together ye feed all on one flame;
It could not equalize the hundred part
Of what her eyes have kindled in my heart.
Goe boy and carve this passion on the bark
Of yonder tree, which stands the sacred mark
Of noble *Sidneyes* birth; when such benigne,
Such more then mortall making stars did shine;

240 1 *Dorothea* Dorothy Sidney, known as 'Sacharissa' (see no. 159 1. 2) 3 *held* kept, maintained 4 *allays* alleys 8 *rudest* roughest 26 *tree* the tree supposedly planted at Sir Philip Sidney's birth (see no. 190 ll. 13–14)

That there they cannot but for ever prove
The monument and pledge of humble love:
His humble love whose hope shall nere rise higher
Then for a pardon that he dares admire.

Richard Lovelace

241 The Grasse-hopper.

To my Noble Friend, Mr. Charles Cotton. *Ode*

I.

Oh thou that swing'st upon the waving haire
Of some well-filled Oaten Beard,
Drunke ev'ry night with a Delicious teare
Dropt thee from Heav'n, where now th' art reard.

II.

The Joyes of Earth and Ayre are thine intire,
That with thy feet and wings dost hop and flye;
And when thy Poppy workes thou dost retire
To thy Carv'd Acron-bed to lye.

III.

Up with the Day, the Sun thou welcomst then,
Sportst in the guilt-plats of his Beames,
And all these merry dayes mak'st merry men,
Thy selfe, and Melancholy streames.

IV.

But ah the Sickle! Golden Eares are Cropt;
Ceres and *Bacchus* bid good night;
Sharpe frosty fingers all your Flowr's have topt,
And what sithes spar'd, Winds shave off quite.

241 8 *Acron-bed* acorn bed 10 *guilt-plats* gilded plaits, intertwined golden hair

V.

Poore verdant foole! and now green Ice, thy Joys
  Large and as lasting, as thy Peirch of Grasse,
Bid us lay in 'gainst Winter, Raine, and poize
  Their flouds, with an o'reflowing glasse.

VI.

Thou best of *Men* and *Friends*! we will create
  A Genuine Summer in each others breast;
And spite of this cold Time and frosen Fate
  Thaw us a warme seate to our rest.

VII.

Our sacred harthes shall burne eternally
  As Vestall Flames, the North-wind, he
Shall strike his frost-stretch'd Winges, dissolve and flye
  This *Ætna* in Epitome.

VIII.

Dropping *December* shall come weeping in,
  Bewayle th'usurping of his Raigne;
But when in show'rs of old Greeke we beginne
  Shall crie, he hath his Crowne againe!

IX.

Night as cleare *Hesper* shall our Tapers whip
  From the light Casements where we play,
And the darke Hagge from her black mantle strip,
  And sticke there everlasting Day.

X.

Thus richer then untempted Kings are we,
  That asking nothing, nothing need:
Though Lord of all what Seas imbrace; yet he
  That wants himselfe, is poore indeed.

241 19 *poize* balance, equal 28 *Ætna* Etna 29 *Dropping* rainy, wet 30 *usurping* Parliament's abolition of Christmas festivities, cp. no. 369 l. 80 34 *Casements* windows

ALEXANDER BROME

242 [*from* The Prisoners]

Written when *O.C.* attempted to be King

Come a *brimmer* (my bullies) drink whole ones or nothing,
  Now *healths* have been *voted* down,
'Tis *sack* that can *heat* us, we care not for *cloathing*,
  A gallon's as warm as a gown
    'Cause the Parliament sees,
    Nor the former nor these,
Could engage us to drink their health,
    They Vote that we shall
    Drink no healths at all
Nor to *King* nor to *Common-wealth*,
So that now we must venture to *drink* 'um by stealth.

JOHN MILTON

243 [To Edward Lawrence]

Lawrence of vertuous Father vertuous Son,
  Now that the Fields are dank, and ways are mire,
  Where shall we sometimes meet, and by the fire
  Help wast a sullen day; what may be won

242 Title *O.C.* Oliver Cromwell 1 *brimmer*** brimming cup *bullies* friends, fellows 3 *sack* Spanish wine 7 *engage* refers to the oath of loyalty demanded by the Republic

243 1 cp. Horace, *Odes* 1.16.1, 'O lovelier daughter of a lovely mother' 4 *wast* spend

From the hard Season gaining: time will run
On smoother, till *Favonius* re-inspire
The frozen earth; and cloth in fresh attire
The Lillie and Rose, that neither sow'd nor spun.
What neat repast shall feast us, light and choice,
Of Attick tast, with Wine, whence we may rise
To hear the Lute well toucht, or artfull voice
Warble immortal Notes and *Tuskan* Ayre?
He who of those delights can judge, And spare
To interpose them oft, is not unwise.

KATHERINE PHILIPS

244 Friendship's Mystery, To My Dearest *Lucasia*

1.

Come, my *Lucasia*, since we see
That Miracles Mens faith do move,
By wonder and by prodigy
To the dull angry world let's prove
There's a Religion in our Love.

2.

For though we were design'd t'agree,
That Fate no liberty destroyes,
But our Election is as free
As Angels, who with greedy choice
Are yet determin'd to their joyes.

243 6 *re-inspire* breathe new life into 8 cp. Matthew 6:28 'Consider the lilies of the field, how they grow; they toil not, neither do they spin' 10 *Attick* refined, elegant 12 *Tuskan* Florentine, Italian 13 *spare* spare time, afford; refrain

244 Title *Lucasia* Philips's name for her friend Anne Owen (1633–92) 8 *Election* choice, choosing 9 *greedy* hungry, voracious; eager, keen 10 *determin'd* restricted, limited

3.
Our hearts are doubled by the loss,
Here Mixture is Addition grown;
We both diffuse, and both ingross:
And we whose minds are so much one,
Never, yet ever are alone.

4.
We court our own Captivity
Than Thrones more great and innocent:
'Twere banishment to be set free,
Since we wear fetters whose intent
Not Bondage is, but Ornament.

5.
Divided joyes are tedious found,
And griefs united easier grow:
We are our selves but by rebound,
And all our Titles shuffled so,
Both Princes, and both Subjects too.

6.
Our Hearts are mutual Victims laid,
While they (such power in Friendship lies)
Are Altars, Priests, and Off'rings made:
And each Heart which thus kindly dies,
Grows deathless by the Sacrifice.

245 Friendship in Embleme, or the Seal. To my dearest *Lucasia*

1.
The Hearts thus intermixed speak
A Love that no bold shock can break;
For joyn'd and growing both in one,
Neither can be disturb'd alone.

244 13 *diffuse* disperse, disseminate, spread out *ingross* collect together, condense, concentrate 24 *shuffled* thrown together, jumbled up 29 *kindly* benevolently; naturally, according to its kind

245 1 *thus* on a seal symbolizing Philips's community of friends

2.

That means a mutual Knowledge too;
For what is't either heart can do,
Which by its panting Centinel
It does not to the other tell?

3.

That Friendship Hearts so much refines,
It nothing but it self designs:
The hearts are free from lower ends,
For each point to the other tends.

4.

They flame, 'tis true, and several wayes,
But still those Flames do so much raise,
That while to either they incline
They yet are noble and divine.

5.

From smoke or hurt those Flames are free,
From grossness or mortality:
The Heart (like *Moses* Bush presumed)
Warm'd and enlightned, not consumed.

6.

The Compasses that stand above
Express this great immortal Love;
For Friends, like them, can prove this true,
They are, and yet they are not, two.

7.

And in their posture is exprest
Friendship's exalted Interest:
Each follows where the other leans,
And what each does, this other means.

245 19 *Moses Bush* cp. Exodus 3:2 'And the angel of the Lord appeared unto him [Moses] in a flame of fire out of the midst of a bush: and he looked, and, behold, the bush burned with fire, and the bush was not consumed' 21 *Compasses* geometrical dividers; cp. John Donne's 'A Valediction forbidding mourning' (no. 137), l. 26

8.

And as when one foot does stand fast,
And t'other circles seeks to cast,
The steddy part does regulate
And make the wandrer's motion straight:

9.

So Friends are only two in this,
T'reclaim each other when they miss:
For whosoe're will grossly fall,
Can never be a Friend at all.

10.

And as that useful Instrument
For Even lines was ever meant;
So Friendship from good Angels springs,
To teach the world Heroick things.

11.

As these are found out in design
To rule and measure every Line;
So Friendship governs actions best,
Prescribing unto all the rest.

12.

And as in Nature nothing's set
So just as Lines in number met;
So Compasses for these b'ing made,
Do Friendship's harmony perswade.

13.

And like to them, so Friends may own
Extension, not Division:
Their Points, like Bodies, separate;
But Head, like Souls, knows no such fate.

14.

And as each part so well is knit,
That their Embraces ever fit:
So Friends are such by destiny,
And no third can the place supply.

245 34 *miss* go astray 50 *Extension* size, extent; spatial magnitude; extensiveness

15.

There needs no Motto to the Seal:
But that we may the mind reveal
To the dull Eye, it was thought fit
That *Friendship* only should be writ.

16.

But as there are Degrees of bliss,
So there's no Friendship meant by this,
But such as will transmit to Fame
Lucasia and *Orinda*'s Name.

246 To my Excellent *Lucasia*, on our Friendship

I did not live until this time
    Crown'd my felicity,
When I could say without a crime,
    I am not thine, but Thee.

This Carcass breath'd, and walkt, and slept,
    So that the World believ'd
There was a Soul the Motions kept;
    But they were all deceiv'd.

For as a Watch by art is wound
    To motion, such was mine:
But never had *Orinda* found
    A Soul till she found thine;

Which now inspires, cures and supplies,
    And guides my darkned Breast:
For thou art all that I can prize,
    My Joy, my Life, my Rest.

No Bridegrooms nor Crown-conquerors mirth
    To mine compar'd can be:
They have but pieces of this Earth,
    I've all the World in thee.

245 64 *Orinda's* Katherine Philips's name for herself

246 7 *Motions* movements, gestures, outward forms 13 *inspires* animates, breathes life into

Then let our Flames still light and shine,
And no false fear controul,
As innocent as our Design,
Immortal as our Soul.

PART FIVE

CHURCH, STATE AND BELIEF

JOHN SKELTON

247 [*from* Collyn Clout]

Over this the foresayd lay
Reporte howe the pope may
An holy anker call
Out of the stony wall
And hym a bysshop make
yf he on hym dare take
To kepe so harde a rule
To ryde upon a mule
With golde all be trapped
In purple and paule be lapped
Some hatted and some capped
Rychly be wrapped
God wotte to theyr great paynes
In rotchettes of fyne raynes
Whyte as mares mylke
Theyr tabertes of fyne sylke
Theyr styrops of myxt golde be gared
There may no cost be spared
Theyr moyles golde dothe eate
Theyr neyghbours dye for meate.

What care they thoughe gyll swete
Or Jacke of the nocke
The poore people they yoke
With sommons and citacyons
And excommunycacyons
Aboute churches and market
The bysshop on his carpet

247 3 *anker* anchorite, recluse, hermit 9 *be trapped* furnished with trappings 10 *paule* rich cloth *be lapped* enveloped 14 *rotchettes* cloaks, mantles, outer garments *raynes* fine Rennes cloth 16 *tabertes* tabards, sleeveless tunics 17 *be gared* faced, adorned 19 *moyles* mules 21 *gyll* Jill *swete* sweat 22 *Jacke of the nocke* John a-Nokes, any man

At home full softe dothe sytte
This is a farly fytte
To here the people jangle
Howe warely they wrangle....

And all the faute they lay
In you prelates, and say
Ye do them wronge and no ryght
To put them thus to flyght
No matyns at mydnyght
Boke and chalys gone quyte
Plucke away the leedes
Over theyr heedes
And sell away theyr belles
And all that they have elles
Thus the people telles
Rayles lyke rebelles
Rede shrewdly and spelles
And with foundacyons melles
And talke lyke tytyvylles
Howe ye breke the dedes wylles
Turne monasteries into water mylles,
Of an abbey ye make a graunge
Your workes they say are straunge
So that theyr founders soules
Have lost theyr bedde roules
The money for theyr masses
Spent among wanton lasses
Theyr dyriges are forgotten
Theyr founders lye there rotten
But where theyr soules dwell
Therwith I wyll nat mell
What coude the Turke do more
With all his false lore
Turke sarazyn or Jewe
I reporte me to you.

247 29 *farly fytte* dreadful, unpleasant experience 31 *warely* in a warlike manner (?); watchfully (?) 44 *Rede* advises, warns *spelles* talks 45 *melles* interferes, meddles 46 *tytyvylles* tattling tell-tales 47 *dedes wylles* dead's wills 52 *bedde roules* bead rolls, list of people to be prayed for 55 *dyriges* dirges 61 *sarazyn* Saracen

ANNE ASKEW

248 The Balade whych Anne Askewe made and sange whan she was in Newgate

Lyke as the armed knyght
Appoynted to the fielde
With thys world wyll I fyght
And fayth shall be my shielde.
Faythe is that weapon stronge
Whych wyll not fayle at nede
My foes therfor amonge
Therwith wyll I procede.
As it is had in strengthe
And force of Christes waye
It wyll prevayle at lengthe
Though all the devyls saye naye.
Faythe in the fathers olde
Obtayned ryghtwysnesse
Whych make me verye bolde
To feare no worldes dystresse.
I now rejoyce in hart
And hope byd me do so
For Christ wyll take my part
And ease me of my wo.
Thu sayst lorde, who so knocke
To them wylt thu attende
Undo therfor the locke
And thy stronge power sende.

248 Title *Newgate* a prison in the City of London to which Askew had been sent for her Protestant beliefs 14 *ryghtwysnesse* righteousness 21–2 cp. Matthew 7:7 'Ask, and it shall be given you; seek, and ye shall find; knock, and it shall be opened unto you'

More enmyes now I have
Than heeres upon my heed
Lete them not me deprave
But fyght thu in my steed.

On the my care I cast
For all their cruell spyght
I sett not by their hast
For thu art my delyght.

I am not she that lyst
My anker to lete fall
For everye dryslynge myst
My shyppe substancyall.

Not oft use I to wryght
In prose nor yet in ryme
Yet wyll I shewe one syght
That I sawe in my tyme.

I sawe a ryall trone
Where Justyce shuld have sytt
But in her stede was one
Of modye cruell wytt.

Absorpt was rygtwysnesse
As of the ragynge floude
Sathan in hys excesse
Sucte up the gyltelesse bloude.

Then thought I, Jesus lorde
Whan thu shalt judge us all
Harde is it to recorde
On these men what wyll fall.

Yet lorde I the desyre
For that they do to me
Lete them not tast the hyre
Of their inyquyte.

248 27 *deprave* vilify, defame 35 *dryslynge*** drizzling 44 *modye* angry, wrathful 55 *hyre* reward

LUKE SHEPHERD

249 [*from* The Upcheringe of the Messe]

Who hath not knowne or herd
How we were made a feard
That magre of our beard
Our messe shulde cleane awaye
That we did dayly saye
And utterly decaye
For ever and for aye
So were we brought in doubte
That all that are devout
Were like to go withoute
The messe that hath no peere
Which longe hath taried here
Yea many an hundreth yere
And to be destitute
Of that whiche constitute
Was of the highe depute
Of Christe and his apostles
Althoughe none of the Gospels
No mencion maketh or tells
We must beleve what ells?
Of things done by councells.
Wherin the high professours
Apostlique successours
Take holde to be possessours
And some wer made confessours
Some of them were no startars
But were made holi marters
Yet plowmen smythes and cartars
With such as be their hartars

249 Title *Upcheringe*** encouragement *Messe* mass 3 in defiance of, direct opposition to, our purpose 22 *professours* those who claim piety 26 *startars* deserters, inconstant turncoats 29 *hartars* hurters

Will enterprise to taxe
Thes auncyent mens actes
And holy fathers factes
Thoughe messe were made bi men
As popes nyne or ten
Or many more what then?
Or not of scripture grounded
Is yt therfore confounded
To be a supersticion?
Nay nay they mysse the quission
Make better Inquysicion
Ye have an evyll condicion
To make suche exposicion
Ye thinke nothing but scripture
Is only clene and pure
Yes yes I you ensure
The messe shalbe hir better
As light as ye do set hir
  The scripture hath nothing
Wher by profyte to bryng
But a lytyll preaching
With tattling and teaching
And nothing can ye espie
Nor se with outwarde eye
But must your ears applie
To learnyng inwardlye
And who so it will folowe
In goods though he may walow
If scripture once him swalowe
She wyll undo him holowe
Wherfore no good mes singers
Will come within hir fyngers
But are hir under styngers
For she wolde fayne undo
All such as lyveth so

249 30 *enterprise* undertake, attempt 32 *factes* deeds, course of conduct 39 *quission* question 40 *Inquysicion* inquiry; suppression of heresy 45 *ensure* assure 60 *mes* mass 62 *styngers*** sharp-tongued people

Anonymous

250 [A Lament for our Lady's Shrine at Walsingham]

In the wrackes of walsingam
  Whom should I chuse,
But the Queene of walsingam,
  to be guide to my muse
Then thou Prince of walsingam
  graunt me to frame,
Bitter plaintes to rewe thy wronge,
  bitter wo for thy name,
Bitter was it oh to see,
  The seely sheepe
Murdred by the raveninge wolves
  While the sheephardes did sleep,
Bitter was it oh to vewe
  the sacred vyne,
Whiles the gardiners plaied all close,
  rooted up by the swine
Bitter bitter oh to behould,
  the grasse to growe
Where the walles of walsingam
  so statly did sheue,
Such were the workes of walsingam:
  while shee did stand
Such are the wrackes as now do shewe
  of that holy land,
Levell Levell with the ground
  the towres doe lye
Which with their golden glitteringe tops
  Pearsed once to the skye,
Wher weare gates no gates ar nowe,
  the waies unknowen

250 1 *wrackes* destruction, devastation, ruin 10 *seely* simple, rustic 15 *plaied* worked

Wher the presse of peares did passe
  While her fame far was blowen
Oules do scrike wher the sweetest himnes
  lately weer songe
Toades and serpentes hold ther dennes,
  Wher the Palmers did thronge
Weepe weepe o walsingam
  Whose dayes are nightes
Blessinges turned to blasphemies
  Holy deedes to dispites,
Sinne is wher our Ladie sate
  Heaven turned is to Hell.
Sathan sittes wher our Lord did swaye
  Walsingam oh farewell.

John Heywood

251 [*from* Epygrams]

Of turnyng. 67.

Wilt thou use turners craft still? ye by my trouth.
Much thrift and most suretie in turners craft growth.
Halfe turne or whole turne, where turners be turning,
Turnyng keepes turners from hangyng and burning.

250 31 *peares* peers 36 *Palmers* pilgrims 40 *dispites* shameful injuries, outrages 43 *swaye* rule, hold sway

251 Title *turnyng* conversion, desertion to another side

GEORGE PUTTENHAM

252 [*from* Partheniades]

Partheniad 11 Urania

O mightye Muse
The mignionst mayde of mounte Parnasse
Ever verdurde with flowre and grasse
Of sundrye hews
Saye and not misse
How longe agone and whence yt was
The fayre rounde worlde first came to passe,
As yt now ys.

There be that saye
How yt was never otherwise,
Then as wee see it with our eyes,
This very daye,
There bee agayne
A secte of men somewhat precise
Beleeve a godd did yt devise
And not in vayne,

Nor longe agone
Onely to serve Adams linage
Some little while as for a stage
To playe upon
And by despighte
One daye agayne will in his rage
Crushe it all as a kicson cage
And spill it quite.

252 Title *Partheniad** a poem or song in honour of a virgin; a 'partheneion' is an ancient Greek choral lyric or hymn sung by a chorus of young women 2 *mignionst* most delicately formed, most prettily small 3 *verdurde*** clad with vegetation 5 *misse* fail 23 *kicson** kexen, made of the hollow stem of a plant

Some weene it must
Come by recourse of prety moates
Farr finer then the smallest groates
Of sand or dust
That swarme in sonne
Clinginge as faste as little clotes
Or burres uppon younge childrens cotes
That slise and runne.

Other suppose
A *νοῦς* approcht and by reason
Broughte it to shape and to season
From a Chaos
But some tech us
By playne proofes, whye yt were begone
Nor never more shalbe undone
But byde even thus,

Whoorlinge his whott
And endlesse roundell with a throwe
Swifter then shaft out of a bowe
Or cannon shott
O bootlesse carke
Of mortall men searchinge to knowe
Or this or that since he must rowe
The dolefull barke,

Which Charon guydes,
Fraught ful of shadows colde and starke
That ferrye to the coontryes darke
Tendinge theyr tydes
Since stoute nor stronge
Metall nor moulde of worldlye warke
Nor writt of any cunninge clarke
Can last soe longe,

252 30 *clotes* the prickly balls of the burdock 34 *νοῦς* 'nous' mind, intellect 41 *whott* hot 42 *roundell* small circular object 45 *bootlesse* pointless, useless, unprofitable *carke* distress, anxiety 50 *starke* stiff, incapable of movement

To outlast the skye
Honour empire nor erthly name
Save my princesse most woorthye fame
Which cannot dye.

Robert Southwell

253 The burning Babe

As I in hoarie Winters night stoode shivering in the snow,
Surpris'd I was with sodaine heate, which made my hart to glow;
And lifting up a fearefull eye, to view what fire was neare,
A pretty Babe all burning bright did in the ayre appeare;
Who scorched with excessive heate, such floods of teares did shed,
As though his floods should quench his flames, which with his teares were fed:
Alas (quoth he) but newly borne, in fierie heates I frie,
Yet none approach to warme their harts or feele my fire, but I;
My faultlesse breast the furnace is, the fuell wounding thornes:
Love is the fire, and sighs the smoake, the ashes, shame and scornes;
The fewell Justice layeth on, and Mercie blowes the coales,
The mettall in this furnace wrought, are mens defiled soules:
For which, as now on fire I am to worke them to their good,
So will I melt into a bath, to wash them in my blood.
With this he vanisht out of sight, and swiftly shrunk away,
And straight I called unto minde, that it was Christmasse day.

253 7 *frie* am tortured with fire 12 *wrought* fashioned, made

HENRY CONSTABLE

254 To St Mary Magdalen

Sweete Saynt: Thow better canst declare to me,
what pleasure ys obteyn'd by heavenly love,
then they which other loves, dyd never prove:
or which in sexe ar differyng from thee:
For lyke a woman spowse my sowle shalbee,
whom synfull passions once to lust did move,
and synce betrothed to goddes sonne above,
should be enamored with his dietye.
My body ys the garment of my spryght
whyle as the day tyme of my lyfe doth last:
when death shall brynge the nyght of my delight
My sowle uncloth'd, shall rest from labors past:
and clasped in the armes of God, injoye
by sweete conjunction, everlastyng joye.

SIR JOHN HARINGTON

255 A Groome of the Chambers religion in King *Henry* the eights time

One of King *Henries* Favorites beganne,
To move the King one day to take a man,
Whom of his Chamber he might make a Groome,
Soft, sayd the King, before I graunt that roome,
It is a question not to be neglected,
How he in his Religion stands affected.

254 3 *prove* experience

For his Religion, answered then the Minion,
I doe not certaine know whats his opinion:
But sure he may, talking with men of learning,
Conforme himselfe in lesse then ten days warning.

John Donne

256 Satyre 3

Kinde pitty chokes my spleene; brave scorn forbids
Those teares to issue which swell my eye-lids,
I must not laugh, nor weepe sinnes, and be wise,
Can railing then cure these worne maladies?
Is not our Mistresse faire Religion,
As worthy of all our Soules devotion,
As vertue was to the first blinded age?
Are not heavens joyes as valiant to asswage
Lusts, as earths honour was to them? Alas,
As wee do them in meanes, shall they surpasse
Us in the end, and shall thy fathers spirit
Meete blinde Philosophers in heaven, whose merit
Of strict life may be imputed faith, and heare
Thee, whom hee taught so easie wayes and neare
To follow, damn'd? O if thou dar'st, feare this;
This feare great courage, and high valour is.
Dar'st thou ayd mutinous Dutch, and dar'st thou lay
Thee in ships woodden Sepulchers, a prey
To leaders rage, to stormes, to shot, to dearth?
Dar'st thou dive seas, and dungeons of the earth?
Hast thou couragious fire to thaw the ice
Of frozen North discoveries? and thrise

255 7 *Minion* favourite

256 1 *spleene* the seat of laughter and of melancholy *brave* proud 7 *blinded* ignorant of Christian revelation 10 *meanes* revelation 11 *end* salvation 14 *neare* direct, straight 17 *mutinous* mutinying against the Spanish 22 *North discoveries* the search for the north-west passage

Colder then Salamanders, like divine
Children in th'oven, fires of Spaine, and the line,
Whose countries limbecks to our bodies bee,
Canst thou for gaine beare? and must every hee
Which cryes not, Goddesse, to thy Mistresse, draw,
Or eate thy poysonous words? courage of straw!
O desperate coward, wilt thou seeme bold, and
To thy foes and his (who made thee to stand
Sentinell in his worlds garrison) thus yeeld,
And for forbidden warres, leave th'appointed field?
Know thy foes: the foule Devill, whom thou
Strivest to please, for hate, not love, would allow
Thee faine, his whole Realme to be quit; and as
The worlds all parts wither away and passe,
So the worlds selfe, thy other lov'd foe, is
In her decrepit wayne, and thou loving this,
Dost love a withered and worne strumpet; last,
Flesh (it selfes death) and joyes which flesh can taste,
Thou lovest; and thy faire goodly soule, which doth
Give this flesh power to taste joy, thou dost loath.
Seeke true religion. O where? Mirreus
Thinking her unhous'd here, and fled from us,
Seekes her at Rome, there, because hee doth know
That shee was there a thousand yeares agoe,
He loves her ragges so, as wee here obey
The statecloth where the Prince sate yesterday.
Crants to such brave Loves will not be inthrall'd,
But loves her onely, who at Geneva is call'd

256 23 *Salamanders* lizardlike creatures, believed to be so cold that they could live in fire 24 *Children* Shadrach, Meshach and Abednego survived the fiery furnace in which the idol-worshipping Nebuchadnezzar threw them (see Daniel 3:11–30 and no. 28 l. 28) *fires* equatorial heat of the Spanish Main; the Spanish Inquisition 25 *limbecks* alembics used for chemical distillation 26 *for gaine beare* suffer for financial reward 27 *draw* draw his sword 28 *of straw* false, sham 30 *his* God's 32 abandon the legitimate struggle, because wars for gain are immoral 35 *to be quit* fully to discharge a debt or obligation 38 *wayne* waning, decay 43 *Mirreus* the name suggests myrrh, which is used in incense 47 *ragges* ceremonial trappings; few remaining truths 48 *statecloth* canopy over the throne of State 49 *Crants* a German name *brave* splendid, showy *inthrall'd* enthralled, captivated 50 *Geneva* Calvin's home

Religion, plaine, simple, sullen, yong,
Contemptuous, yet unhansome; As among
Lecherous humors, there is one that judges
No wenches wholsome, but course country drudges.
Graius stayes still at home here, and because
Some Preachers, vile ambitious bauds, and lawes
Still new like fashions, bid him thinke that shee
Which dwels with us, is onely perfect, hee
Imbraceth her, whom his Godfathers will
Tender to him, being tender, as Wards still
Take such wives as their Guardians offer, or
Pay valewes. Carelesse Phrygius doth abhorre
All, because all cannot be good, as one
Knowing some women whores, dares marry none.
Graccus loves all as one, and thinkes that so
As women do in divers countries goe
In divers habits, yet are still one kinde,
So doth, so is Religion; and this blind-
nesse too much light breeds; but unmoved thou
Of force must one, and forc'd but one allow;
And the right; aske thy father which is shee,
Let him aske his; though truth and falshood bee
Neare twins, yet truth a little elder is;
Be busie to seeke her, beleeve mee this,
Hee's not of none, nor worst, that seekes the best.
To adore, or scorne an image, or protest,
May all be bad; doubt wisely, in strange way
To stand inquiring right, is not to stray;
To sleepe, or runne wrong, is. On a huge hill,
Cragg'd, and steep, Truth stands, and hee that will

256 51 *sullen* obstinate; drab 53 *humors* longings, desires, tastes 55 *Graius* a Greek 56 *ambitious bauds* pimps who sell their mistress to anyone for advancement; prostituters of their office 58 *onely* alone, solely 62 *valewes* the fines (the value of the marriage) imposed on wards who would not marry their guardian's choice of partner *Phrygius* a Phrygian 65 *Graccus* from the name of a Roman family 67 *habits* clothes 68–9 *this ... breeds* his blindness to the real truth comes from being over-enlightened 69 *unmoved* unswayed 70 *Of force* by necessity *forc'd* when pressed 71 *aske ... shee* cp. Deuteronomy 32:7 'ask thy father, and he will shew thee; thy elders, and they will tell thee' 75 *none* no religion 77 *in strange way* on an unfamiliar road

Reach her, about must, and about must goe;
And what the hills suddennes resists, winne so;
Yet strive so, that before age, deaths twilight,
Thy Soule rest, for none can worke in that night,
To will, implyes delay, therefore now doe:
Hard deeds, the bodies paines; hard knowledge to
The mindes indeavours reach, and mysteries
Are like the Sunne, dazling, yet plaine to all eyes.
Keepe the truth which thou hast found; men do not stand
In so ill case here, that God hath with his hand
Sign'd Kings blanck-charters to kill whom they hate,
Nor are they Vicars, but hangmen to Fate.
Foole and wretch, wilt thou let thy Soule be tyed
To mans lawes, by which she shall not be tryed
At the last day? Will it then boot thee
To say a Philip, or a Gregory,
A Harry, or a Martin taught thee this?
Is not this excuse for mere contraries,
Equally strong? cannot both sides say so?
That thou mayest rightly obey power, her bounds know;
Those past, her nature, and name is chang'd; to be
Then humble to her is idolatrie;
As streames are, Power is; those blest flowers that dwell
At the rough streames calme head, thrive and prove well,
But having left their roots, and themselves given
To the streames tyrannous rage, alas are driven
Through mills, and rockes, and woods, and at last, almost
Consum'd in going, in the sea are lost:
So perish Soules, which more chuse mens unjust
Power from God claym'd, then God himselfe to trust.

256 81–2 gain in this way what the hill's abruptness or steepness (*suddennes**) prevents you from gaining 84 *for ... night* cp. John 9:4 'the night cometh, when no man can work' 86 *to* too 90 *here* on earth; in matters of religion 91 *blanck-charters* documents allowing the King's agents to do as they like 92 *Vicars* proxies, vicegerents 96–7 Roman Catholic and Protestant temporal and spiritual leaders: King Philip II of Spain; Gregory XIV, the then Pope; King Henry VIII of England; and Martin Luther

257 Goodfriday, *1613*. Riding Westward

Let mans Soule be a Spheare, and then, in this,
The intelligence that moves, devotion is,
And as the other Spheares, by being growne
Subject to forraigne motions, lose their owne,
And being by others hurried every day,
Scarce in a yeare their naturall forme obey:
Pleasure or businesse, so, our Soules admit
For their first mover, and are whirld by it.
Hence is't, that I am carryed towards the West
This day, when my Soules forme bends toward the East.
There I should see a Sunne, by rising set,
And by that setting endlesse day beget;
But that Christ on this Crosse, did rise and fall,
Sinne had eternally benighted all.
Yet dare I'almost be glad, I do not see
That spectacle of too much weight for mee.
Who sees Gods face, that is selfe life, must dye;
What a death were it then to see God dye?
It made his owne Lieutenant Nature shrinke,
It made his footstoole crack, and the Sunne winke.
Could I behold those hands which span the Poles,
And tune all spheares at once, peirc'd with those holes?
Could I behold that endlesse height which is
Zenith to us, and to our Antipodes,
Humbled below us? or that blood which is
The seat of all our Soules, if not of his,

257 1–10 *Let ... East* Donne moralizes contemporary astronomical theories to show that as the spheres are yearly deflected from their correct paths, so man's soul is 10 *East* the traditional location of Christ's, the Son's, resurrection and where the sun rises 17 cp. Exodus 33:20 'Thou canst not see my face: for there shall no man see me, and live' 19 *Nature shrinke* Nature shrank when Christ died on the Cross and when Adam fell 20 cp. Isaiah 66:1 'Thus saith the Lord, The heaven is my throne, and the earth is my footstool' 22 *tune* Platonically, sweetly harmonizes; the alternative reading 'turne' suggests that He, following Aristotle, is the prime mover of the spheres 24 our highest point and that of the people who live on the other side of the globe 26 *his* Christ's

Made durt of dust, or that flesh which was worne
By God, for his apparell, rag'd, and torne?
If on these things I durst not looke, durst I
Upon his miserable mother cast mine eye,
Who was Gods partner here, and furnish'd thus
Halfe of that Sacrifice, which ransom'd us?
Though these things, as I ride, be from mine eye,
They'are present yet unto my memory,
For that looks towards them; and thou look'st towards mee,
O Saviour, as thou hang'st upon the tree;
I turne my backe to thee, but to receive
Corrections, till thy mercies bid thee leave.
O thinke mee worth thine anger, punish mee,
Burne off my rusts, and my deformity,
Restore thine Image, so much, by thy grace,
That thou may'st know mee, and I'll turne my face.

258 Hymne to God my God, in my sicknesse

Since I am comming to that Holy roome,
   Where, with thy Quire of Saints for evermore,
I shall be made thy Musique; As I come
   I tune the Instrument here at the dore,
   And what I must doe then, thinke here before.

Whilst my Physitians by their love are growne
   Cosmographers, and I their Mapp, who lie
Flat on this bed, that by them may be showne
   That this is my South-west discoverie
   Per fretum febris, by these streights to die,

257 40 *rusts* moral corruptions

258 9 *South-west discoverie* the passage to the New World: the south is the zone of heat and fever, the west, where the sun sets, of decline and death 10 *Per . . . febris* by the strait, or raging heat, of fever

I joy, that in these straits, I see my West;
For, though theire currants yeeld returne to none,
What shall my West hurt me? As West and East
In all flatt Maps (and I am one) are one,
So death doth touch the Resurrection.

Is the Pacifique Sea my home? Or are
The Easterne riches? Is *Jerusalem?*
Anyan, and *Magellan*, and *Gibraltare*,
All streights, and none but streights, are wayes to them,
Whether where *Japhet* dwelt, or *Cham*, or *Sem*.

We thinke that *Paradise* and *Calvarie*,
Christs Crosse, and *Adams* tree, stood in one place;
Looke Lord, and finde both *Adams* met in me;
As the first *Adams* sweat surrounds my face,
May the last *Adams* blood my soule embrace.

So, in his purple wrapp'd receive mee Lord,
By these his thornes give me his other Crowne;
And as to others soules I preach'd thy word,
Be this my Text, my Sermon to mine owne,
Therfore that he may raise the Lord throws down.

259 [*from* Holy Sonnets]

10.

Batter my heart, three person'd God; for, you
As yet but knocke, breathe, shine, and seeke to mend;
That I may rise, and stand, o'erthrow mee,'and bend
Your force, to breake, blowe, burn and make me new.
I, like an usurpt towne, to'another due,
Labour to'admit you, but Oh, to no end,
Reason your viceroy in mee, mee should defend,
But is captiv'd, and proves weake or untrue,

258 18 *Anyan* perhaps Annam, the strait which was thought to divide America from Asia 20 *Japhet* ... *Sem* the sons of Noah who inherited Europe, Africa and Asia (see Genesis 10) 26 *purple* Christ's blood; His imperial robe 30 *Therfore that* in order that

Yet dearely'I love you', and would be lov'd faine,
But am betroth'd unto your enemie,
Divorce mee,'untie, or breake that knot againe,
Take mee to you, imprison mee, for I
Except you'enthrall mee, never shall be free,
Nor ever chast, except you ravish mee.

260 [Since she whome I lovd, hath payd her last debt]

Since she whome I lovd, hath payd her last debt
   To Nature, and to hers, and my good is dead,
   And her soule early into heaven ravished,
Wholy in heavenly things my mind is sett.
Here the admyring her my mind did whett
   To seeke thee God; so streames do shew the head,
   But though I have found thee, and thou my thirst hast fed,
A holy thirsty dropsy melts mee yett.
But why should I begg more love, when as thou
   Dost woe my soule for hers; offring all thine:
And dost not only feare least I allow
   My love to saints and Angels, things divine,
But in thy tender jealosy dost doubt
Least the World, fleshe, yea Devill putt thee out.

260 6 *head* source 8 *dropsy* insatiable thirst 10 *woe* woo *offring . . . thine* Christ as a dowry in the marriage between the poet's soul and that of his dead wife 14 *putt . . . out* exclude, displace, usurp God

261 [Show me deare Christ, thy spouse, so bright and cleare]

Show me deare Christ, thy spouse, so bright and cleare.
  What, is it she, which on the other shore
  Goes richly painted? or which rob'd and tore
Laments and mournes in Germany and here?
Sleepes she a thousand, then peepes up one yeare?
  Is she selfe truth and errs? now new, now outwore?
  Doth she,'and did she, and shall she evermore
On one, on seaven, or on no hill appeare?
Dwells she with us, or like adventuring knights
  First travaile we to seeke and then make love?
Betray kind husband thy spouse to our sights,
  And let myne amorous soule court thy mild Dove,
Who is most trew, and pleasing to thee, then
When she'is embrac'd and open to most men.

261 3–4 see the textual note 8 Solomon built the Temple at Jerusalem on Mount Moriah; Rome is built on seven hills, Geneva, the centre of Calvinism, on none 11 *Betray* reveal a secret, or a hidden person, against your will 12 *Dove* the Church; cp. Song of Solomon 5:2 'Open to me, my sister, my love, my dove, my undefiled'

FULKE GREVILLE, LORD BROOKE

262 [*from* Cælica]

SONNET 89.

The *Manicheans* did no Idols make,
Without themselves, nor worship gods of Wood,
Yet Idolls did in their *Idea's* take,
And figur'd *Christ* as on the crosse he stood.
  Thus did they when they earnestly did pray,
  Till clearer Faith this Idoll tooke away:

We seeme more inwardly to know the Sonne,
And see our owne salvation in his blood;
When this is said, we thinke the worke is done,
And with the Father hold our portion good:
  "As if true life within these words were laid,
  "For him that in life, never words obey'd.

If this be safe, it is a pleasant way,
The Crosse of Christ is very easily borne:
But *sixe dayes labour makes the sabboth day,*
The flesh is dead before grace can be borne.
  The heart must first beare witnesse with the booke,
  The earth must burne, ere we for Christ can looke.

262 1 *Manicheans* followers of the third-century dualist heretic Manes; they believed in the opposition of light and dark, brain and body, expressed in the struggle between Christ and Satan 2 *Without* outside

263 [*from* Cælica]

SONNET 99.

Downe in the depth of mine iniquity,
That ugly center of infernall spirits;
Where each sinne feeles her owne deformity,
In these peculiar torments she inherits,
Depriv'd of humane graces, and divine,
Even there appeares this *saving God* of mine.

And in this fatall mirrour of transgression,
Shewes man as fruit of his degeneration,
The errours ugly infinite impression,
Which beares the faithlesse downe to desperation;
Depriv'd of humane graces and divine,
Even there appeares this *saving God* of mine.

In power and truth, Almighty and eternall,
Which on the sinne reflects strange desolation,
With glory scourging all the Spr'its infernall,
And uncreated hell with unprivation;
Depriv'd of humane graces, not divine,
Even there appeares this *saving God* of mine.

For on this sp'rituall Crosse condemned lying,
To paines infernall by eternall doome,
I see my Saviour for the same sinnes dying,
And from that hell I fear'd, to free me, come;
Depriv'd of humane graces, not divine,
Thus hath his death rais'd up this soule of mine.

263 16 *unprivation** continuance of existence

264 [*from* Cælica]

SONNET 109.

Syon lyes waste, and thy *Jerusalem*,
O Lord, is falne to utter desolation,
Against thy Prophets, and thy holy men,
The sinne hath wrought a fatall combination,
Prophan'd thy name, thy worship overthrowne,
And made thee living Lord, a God unknowne.

Thy powerfull lawes, thy wonders of creation,
Thy Word incarnate, glorious heaven, darke hell,
Lye shadowed under Mans degeneration,
Thy Christ still crucifi'd for doing well,
Impiety, ô Lord, sits on thy throne,
Which makes thee living light, a God unknown.

Mans superstition hath thy truths entomb'd,
His Atheisme againe her pomps defaceth,
That sensuall unsatiable vaste wombe,
Of thy seene Church, thy unseene Church disgraceth;
There lives no truth with them that seem thine own,
Which makes thee living Lord, a God unknowne.

Yet unto thee, Lord, (mirrour of transgression)
Wee, who for earthly Idols, have forsaken
Thy heavenly Image (sinlesse pure impression)
And so in nets of vanity lye taken,
All desolate implore that to thine owne,
Lord, thou no longer live a God unknowne.

Yet Lord let *Israels* plagues not be eternall,
Nor sinne for ever cloud thy sacred Mountaines,
Nor with false flames spirituall but infernall,
Dry up thy mercies ever springing fountaines,
Rather, sweet *Iesus*, fill up time and come,
To yeeld the sinne her everlasting doome.

264 16 cp. the textual note to no. 261

GILES FLETCHER

265 [*from* Christs Victorie, and Triumph in Heaven, and Earth, over, and after death]

41

As when the cheerfull Sunne, elamping wide,
Glads all the world with his uprising raye,
And wooes the widow'd earth afresh to pride,
And paints her bosome with the flowrie Maye,
His silent sister steales him quite away,
Wrap't in a sable clowde, from mortall eyes,
The hastie starres at noone begin to rise,
And headlong to his early roost the sparrowe flies.

Appeased by Mercie, who is described by her cherfulnes to defend Man.

42

But soone as he againe dishadowed is,
Restoring the blind world his blemish't sight,
As though another day wear newely ris,
The cooz'ned birds busily take their flight,
And wonder at the shortnesse of the night:
So Mercie once againe her selfe displayes,
Out from her sisters cloud, and open layes
Those sunshine lookes, whose beames would dim a thousand dayes.

43

How may a worme, that crawles along the dust,
Clamber the azure mountaines, thrown so high,
And fetch from thence thy faire Idea just,
That in those sunny courts doth hidden lie,
Cloath'd with such light, as blinds the Angels eye;
How may weake mortall ever hope to file
His unsmooth tongue, and his deprostrate stile?
O raise thou from his corse, thy now entomb'd exile.

Our inabilitie to describe her.

265 1 *elamping** shining forth 9 *dishadowed* freed from shadow 23 *deprostrate** grovelling

44

One touch would rouze me from my sluggish hearse,
One word would call me to my wished home,
One looke would polish my afflicted verse,
One thought would steale my soule from her thicke lome,
And force it wandring up to heav'n to come,
 Thear to importune, and to beg apace
 One happy favour of thy sacred grace,
To see, (what though it loose her eyes?) to see thy face.

45

If any aske why roses please the sight,
Because their leaves upon thy cheekes doe bowre;
If any aske why lillies are so white,
Because their blossoms in thy hand doe flowre:
Or why sweet plants so gratefull odours shoure;
 It is because thy breath so like they be:
 Or why the Orient Sunne so bright we see;
What reason can we give, but from thine eies, and thee?

Her beautie, resembled by the creatures, which are all fraile shadows of her essentiall perfection.

46

Ros'd all in lively crimsin ar thy cheeks,
Whear beawties indeflourishing abide,
And, as to passe his fellowe either seekes,
Seemes both doe blush at one anothers pride:
And on thine eyelids, waiting thee beside,
 Ten thousand Graces sit, and when they moove
 To earth their amourous belgards from above,
They flie from heav'n, and on their wings convey thy love.

Her Attendants.

265 42 *indeflourishing** unfading 47 *belgards* loving looks

47

All of discolour'd plumes their wings ar made,
And with so wondrous art the quills ar wrought,
That whensoere they cut the ayrie glade,
The winde into their hollowe pipes is caught:
As seemes the spheres with them they down have brought:
  Like to the seaven-fold reede of Arcadie,
  Which Pan of Syrinx made, when she did flie
To Ladon sands, and at his sighs sung merily.

48

As melting hony, dropping from the combe, Her perswasive power.
So still the words, that spring between thy lipps,
Thy lippes, whear smiling sweetnesse keepes her home,
And heav'nly Eloquence pure manna sipps,
He that his pen but in that fountaine dipps,
  How nimbly will the golden phrases flie,
  And shed forth streames of choycest rhetorie,
Welling celestiall torrents out of poësie?

49

Like as the thirstie land, in summers heat,
Calls to the cloudes, and gapes at everie showre,
As though her hungry clifts all heav'n would eat,
Which if high God into her bosome powre,
Though much refresht, yet more she could devoure:
  So hang the greedie ears of Angels sweete,
  And every breath a thousand cupids meete,
Some flying in, some out, and all about her fleet.

50

Upon her breast, Delight doth softly sleepe,
And of eternall joy is brought abed,
Those snowie mountelets, through which doe creepe
The milkie rivers, that ar inly bred

265 75 *mountelets* mountainlets, small mountains

In silver cesternes, and themselves doe shed
To wearie Travailers, in heat of day,
To quench their fierie thrist, and to allay
With dropping nectar floods, the furie of their way.

51

If any wander, thou doest call him backe,
If any be not forward, thou incit'st him,
Thou doest expect, if any should growe slacke,
If any seeme but willing, thou invit'st him,
Or if he doe offend thee, thou acquit'st him,
Thou find'st the lost, and follow'st him that flies,
Healing the sicke, and quickning him that dies,
Thou art the lame mans friendly staffe, the blind mans eyes.

Her kind offices to Man.

52

So faire thou art that all would thee behold,
But none can thee behold, thou art so faire,
Pardon, O pardon then thy Vassall bold,
That with poore shadowes strives thee to compare,
And match the things, which he knowes matchlesse are;
O thou vive mirrhour of celestiall grace,
How can fraile colours pourtraict out thy face,
Or paint in flesh thy beawtie, in such semblance base?

53

Her upper garment was a silken lawne,
With needle-woorke richly embroidered,
Which she her selfe with her owne hand had drawne,
And all the world therein had pourtrayed,
With threads, so fresh, and lively coloured,
That seem'd the world she newe created thear,
And the mistaken eye would rashly swear
The silken trees did growe, and the beasts living wear.

Her Garments, wrought by her owne hands, wherwith shee cloaths her selfe, composd of all the Creatures,

265 77 *cesternes* cisterns 83 *expect* wait 94 *vive* reflecting life or reality

54

Low at her feet the Earth was cast alone, The Earth,
(As though to kisse her foot it did aspire,
And gave it selfe for her to tread upon)
With so unlike, and different attire,
That every one that sawe it, did admire
What it might be, was of so various hewe;
For to it selfe it oft so diverse grewe,
That still it seem'd the same, and still it seem'd a newe.

55

And here, and there few men she scattered,
(That in their thought the world esteeme but small,
And themselves great) but she with one fine thread
So short, and small, and slender wove them all,
That like a sort of busie ants, that crawle
About some molehill, so they wandered:
And round about the waving Sea was shed, Sea,
But, for the silver sands, small pearls were sprinkled.

56

So curiously the underworke did creepe,
And curling circlets so well shadowed lay,
That afar off the waters seem'd to sleepe,
But those that neere the margin pearle did play,
Hoarcely enwaved wear with hastie sway,
As though they meant to rocke the gentle eare,
And hush the former that enslumbred wear,
And here a dangerous rocke the flying ships did fear.

57

High in the ayrie element there hung Ayre,
Another clowdy sea, that did disdaine
(As though his purer waves from heaven sprung)
To crawle on earth, as doth the sluggish maine:

265 121 *underworke** undercurrent 125 *enwaved** formed into waves 127 *enslumbred*** lulled to sleep

But it the earth would water with his raine,
That eb'd, and flow'd, as winde, and season would,
And oft the Sun would cleave the limber mould
To alabaster rockes, that in the liquid rowl'd.

58

Beneath those sunny banks, a darker cloud,
Dropping with thicker deaw, did melt apace,
And bent it selfe into a hollowe shroude,
On which, if Mercy did but cast her face,
A thousand colours did the bowe enchace,
That wonder was to see the silke distain'd
With the resplendance from her beawtie gain'd,
And Iris paint her locks with beames, so lively feign'd.

59

About her head a cyprus heav'n she wore, The celestiall bodies,
Spread like a veile, upheld with silver wire,
In which the starres so burn't in golden ore,
As seem'd, the azure web was all on fire,
But hastily, to quench their sparkling ire,
A flood of milke came rowling up the shore,
That on his curded wave swift Argus bore,
And the immortall swan, that did her life deplore.

60

Yet strange it was, so many starres to see
Without a Sunne, to give their tapers light:
Yet strange it was not, that it so should be:
For, where the Sunne centers himselfe by right,
Her face, and locks did flame, that at the sight,
The heavenly veile, that else should nimbly moove,
Forgot his flight, and all incens'd with love,
With wonder, and amazement, did her beautie proove.

265 135 *limber* flexible, pliant 141 *enchace* decorate with engraved patterns 145 *cyprus* black, transparent cloth 152 *swan* the constellation Cygnus in the Milky Way

61

Over her hung a canopie of state, The third heaven.
Not of rich tissew, nor of spangled gold,
But of a substance, though not animate,
Yet of a heav'nly, and spirituall mould,
That onely eyes of Spirits might behold:
  Such light as from maine rocks of diamound,
  Shooting their sparks at Phebus, would rebound,
And little Angels, holding hands, daunc't all around.

62

Seemed those little sprights, through nimbless bold,
The stately canopy bore on their wings,
But them it selfe, as pendants, did uphold,
Besides the crownes of many famous kings,
Among the rest, thear David ever sings,
  And now, with yeares growne young, renewes his layes
  Unto his golden harpe, and ditties playes,
Psalming aloud in well tun'd songs his Makers prayse.

63

Thou self-Idea of all joyes to come,
Whose love is such, would make the rudest speake,
Whose love is such, would make the wisest dumbe,
O when wilt thou thy too long silence breake,
And overcome the strong to save the weake!
  If thou no weapons hast, thine eyes will wound
  Th'Almighties selfe, that now sticke on the ground,
As though some blessed object thear did them empound. Her Objects.

265 161 side-note *third heaven* the highest heaven, invisible to men 173 *David* King David the Psalmist

ÆMILIA LANYER

266 [*from* Salve Deus Rex Judæorum]

...
Our Mother *Eve*, who tasted of the Tree,
Giving to *Adam* what she held most deare,
Was simply good, and had no powre to see,
The after-comming harme did not appeare:
The subtile Serpent that our Sex betraide,
Before our fall so sure a plot had laide.

That undiscerning Ignorance perceav'd
No guile, or craft that was by him intended;
For, had she knowne of what we were bereavid,
To his request she had not condiscended.
But she (poore soule) by cunning was deceav'd,
No hurt therein her harmelesse Heart intended:
For she alleadg'd Gods word, which he denies
That they should die, but even as Gods, be wise.

But surely *Adam* cannot be excus'd,
Her fault, though great, yet he was most too blame;
What Weaknesse offerd, Strength might have refus'd,
Being Lord of all, the greater was his shame:
Although the Serpents craft had her abus'd,
Gods holy word ought all his actions frame:
For he was Lord and King of all the earth,
Before poore *Eve* had either life or breath.

Who being fram'd by Gods eternall hand,
The perfect'st man that ever breath'd on earth,
And from Gods mouth receiv'd that strait command,
The breach whereof he knew was present death:

266 3 *simply* ignorantly, artlessly 4 *after-comming* succeeding, following 9 *bereavid* deprived 14 cp. Genesis 3:3 'But of the fruit of the tree which is in the midst of the garden, God hath said, Ye shall not eat of it, neither shall ye touch it, lest ye die' and 3:6 '... a tree to be desired to make one wise ...' 25 *strait* strict

Yea having powre to rule both Sea and Land,
Yet with one Apple wonne to loose that breath,
Which God hath breathed in his beauteous face,
Bringing us all in danger and disgrace.

And then to lay the fault on Patience backe,
That we (poore women) must endure it all;
We know right well he did discretion lacke,
Beeing not perswaded thereunto at all;
If *Eve* did erre, it was for knowledge sake,
The fruit beeing faire perswaded him to fall:
No subtill Serpents falshood did betray him,
If he would eate it, who had powre to stay him?

Not *Eve*, whose fault was onely too much love,
Which made her give this present to her Deare,
That what shee tasted, he likewise might prove,
Whereby his knowledge might become more cleare;
He never sought her weakenesse to reprove,
With those sharpe words, which he of God did heare:
Yet Men will boast of Knowledge, which he tooke
From *Eves* faire hand, as from a learned Booke.

If any Evill did in her remaine,
Beeing made of him, he was the ground of all;
If one of many Worlds could lay a staine
Upon our Sexe, and worke so great a fall
To wretched Man, by Satans subtill traine;
What will so fowle a fault amongst you all?
Her weakenesse did the Serpents words obay,
But you in malice Gods deare Sonne betray.

Whom, if unjustly you condemne to die,
Her sinne was small, to what you doe commit;
All mortall sinnes that doe for vengeance crie,
Are not to be compared unto it:
If many worlds would altogether trie,
By all their sinnes the wrath of God to get;
This sinne of yours, surmounts them all as farre
As doth the Sunne, another little starre.

266 41 *prove* experience 48 *ground* basis, foundation

Then let us have our Libertie againe,
And challendge to your selves no Sov'raigntie;
You came not in the world without our paine,
Make that a barre against your crueltie;
Your fault beeing greater, why should you disdaine
Our beeing your equals, free from tyranny?
    If one weake woman simply did offend,
    This sinne of yours, hath no excuse, nor end.

WILLIAM DRUMMOND

267 [For the *Baptiste*]

The last and greatest Herauld of Heavens King,
Girt with rough Skinnes, hyes to the Desarts wilde,
Among that savage brood the Woods foorth bring,
Which hee than Man more harmlesse found and milde:
His food was Blossomes, and what yong doth spring,
With Honey that from virgine Hives distil'd;
Parcht Bodie, hollow Eyes, some uncouth thing
Made him appeare, long since from Earth exilde.
There burst hee foorth; All yee, whose Hopes relye
On GOD, with mee amidst these Desarts mourne,
Repent, repent, and from olde errours turne.

Who listned to his voyce, obey'd his crye?
Onelie the Ecchoes which hee made relent,
Rung from their Marble Caves, repent, repent.

268 [Content and Resolute]

As when it hapneth that some lovely Towne
Unto a barbarous Besieger falles,
Who there by Sword and Flame himselfe enstalles,
And (Cruell) it in Teares and Blood doth drowne;
Her Beauty spoyl'd, her Citizens made Thralles,
His spight yet so cannot her all throw downe,
But that some Statue, Arch, Phan of renowne,
Yet lurkes unmaym'd within her weeping walles:
So after all the Spoile, Disgrace, and Wrake,
That Time, the World, and Death could bring combind,
Amidst that Masse of Ruines they did make,
Safe and all scarre-lesse yet remaines my Minde:
  From this so high transcending Rapture springes,
  That I, all else defac'd, not envie Kinges.

Phineas Fletcher

269 [Vast Ocean of light, whose rayes surround]

Vast Ocean of light, whose rayes surround
The Universe, who know'st nor ebb, nor shore,
Who lend'st the Sun his sparkling drop, to store
With overflowing beams Heav'n, ayer, ground,
Whose depths beneath the Centre none can sound,
Whose heights 'bove heav'n, and thoughts so lofty soar,
Whose breadth no feet, no lines, no chains, no eyes survey,
  Whose length no thoughts can reach, no worlds can bound,
  What cloud can mask thy face? where can thy ray
Find an Eclipse? what night can hide Eternal Day?

268 7 *Phan* temple 12 *scarre-lesse** unblemished

Our Seas (a drop of thine) with arms dispread
Through all the earth make drunk the thirsty plains;
Our Sun (a spark of thine) dark shadows drains,
Guilds all the world, paints earth, revives the dead;
Seas (through earth pipes distill'd) in Cisterns shed,
And power their liver springs in river veins.
The Sun peeps through jet clouds, and when his face, and gleams
Are maskt, his eyes their light through ayers spread,
Shall dullard earth bury life-giving streams?
Earths foggs impound heav'ns light? hell quench heav'n-kindling beams?

How miss I then? in bed I sought by night,
But found not him in rest, nor rest without him.
I sought in Towns, in broadest streets I sought him,
But found not him where all are lost: dull sight
Thou canst not see him in himself: his light
Is maskt in light: brightness his cloud about him.
Where, when, how he'l be found, there, then, thus seek thy love:
Thy Lamb in flocks, thy Food with appetite,
Thy Rest on resting dayes, thy Turtle Dove
Seek on his cross: there, then, thus Love stands nail'd with love.

269 11 *dispread* spread out

John Milton

270 On the morning of Christs Nativity.

Compos'd 1629

I.

This is the Month, and this the happy morn
Wherin the Son of Heav'ns eternal King,
Of wedded Maid, and Virgin Mother born,
Our great redemption from above did bring;
For so the holy sages once did sing,
   That he our deadly forfeit should release,
And with his Father work us a perpetual peace.

II.

That glorious Form, that Light unsufferable,
And that far-beaming blaze of Majesty,
Wherwith he wont at Heav'ns high Councel-Table,
To sit the midst of Trinal Unity,
He laid aside; and here with us to be,
   Forsook the Courts of everlasting Day,
And chose with us a darksom House of mortal Clay.

III.

Say Heav'nly Muse, shall not thy sacred vein
Afford a present to the Infant God?
Hast thou no vers, no hymn, or solemn strein,
To welcom him to this his new abode,
Now while the Heav'n by the Suns team untrod,
   Hath took no print of the approching light,
And all the spangled host keep watch in squadrons bright?

270 5 *sages* Old Testament prophets 10 *wont* was accustomed 11 *Trinal Unity* three parts in one, the Trinity 15 *Heav'nly Muse* Urania 21 *host* stars; angels

IV.

See how from far upon the Eastern rode
The Star-led Wisards haste with odours sweet:
O run, prevent them with thy humble ode,
And lay it lowly at his blessed feet;
Have thou the honour first, thy Lord to greet,
  And joyn thy voice unto the Angel Quire,
From out his secret Altar toucht with hallow'd fire.

The Hymn.

I.

It was the Winter wilde,
While the Heav'n-born-childe,
  All meanly wrapt in the rude manger lies;
Nature in aw to him
Had doff't her gawdy trim,
  With her great Master so to sympathize:
It was no season then for her
To wanton with the Sun her lusty Paramour.

II.

Onely with speeches fair
She woo's the gentle Air
  To hide her guilty front with innocent Snow,
And on her naked shame,
Pollute with sinfull blame,
  The Saintly Vail of Maiden white to throw,
Confounded, that her Makers eyes
Should look so neer upon her foul deformities.

270 23 *Wisards* the Magi or Wise Men, cp. Matthew 2:1–12 24 *prevent* meet before, anticipate 28 cp. Isaiah 6:6–7 'Then flew one of the seraphims unto me, having a live coal in his hand, which he had taken with the tongs from off the altar: And he laid it upon my mouth, and said, Lo, this hath touched thy lips; and thine iniquity is taken away, and thy sin purged' 41 *Pollute* polluted *blame* for the Fall of Man

III.

But he her fears to cease,
Sent down the meek-eyd Peace,
She crown'd with Olive green, came softly sliding
Down through the turning sphear
His ready Harbinger,
With Turtle wing the amorous clouds dividing,
And waving wide her mirtle wand,
She strikes a universall Peace through Sea and Land.

IV.

No War, or Battails sound
Was heard the World around:
The idle spear and shield were high up hung;
The hooked Chariot stood
Unstain'd with hostile blood,
The Trumpet spake not to the armed throng,
And Kings sate still with awfull eye,
As if they surely knew their sovran Lord was by.

V.

But peacefull was the night
Wherin the Prince of light
His raign of peace upon the earth began:
The Windes with wonder whist,
Smoothly the waters kist,
Whispering new joyes to the milde Ocean,
Who now hath quite forgot to rave,
While Birds of Calm sit brooding on the charmed wave.

270 46 *meek-eyd** 48 *turning sphear* firmament which turned around the earth 50 *Turtle* dove 51 *mirtle* associated with Venus and so love 56 *hooked* armed with hooklike blades 59 *awfull* full of awe 64 *whist* silenced, hushed 68 *Birds of Calm* halcyons, kingfishers; their nesting-time at the winter solstice was traditionally associated with calm at sea

VI.

The Stars with deep amaze
Stand fixt in stedfast gaze,
Bending one way their pretious influence,
And will not take their flight,
For all the morning light,
Or *Lucifer* that often warn'd them thence;
But in their glimmering Orbs did glow,
Untill their Lord himself bespake, and bid them go.

VII.

And though the shady gloom
Had given day her room,
The Sun himself with-held his wonted speed,
And hid his head for shame,
As his inferiour flame,
The new-enlightn'd world no more should need;
He saw a greater Sun appear
Then his bright Throne, or burning Axletree could bear.

VIII.

The Shepherds on the Lawn,
Or ere the point of dawn,
Sate simply chatting in a rustick row;
Full little thought they than,
That the mighty *Pan*
Was kindly com to live with them below;
Perhaps their loves, or els their sheep,
Was all that did their silly thoughts so busie keep.

270 74 *Lucifer* the morning star, Venus 84 *Axletree* the axle around which the sun's chariot wheels revolve; the axis around which the earth and heavens revolve 86 *Or ere* before 90 *kindly* beneficently; as one of their kind 92 *silly* simple

IX.

When such musick sweet
Their hearts and ears did greet,
As never was by mortall finger strook,
Divinely-warbled voice
Answering the stringed noise,
As all their souls in blisfull rapture took:
The Air such pleasure loth to lose,
With thousand echo's still prolongs each heav'nly close.

X.

Nature that heard such sound
Beneath the hollow round
Of *Cynthia*'s seat, the Airy region thrilling,
Now was almost won
To think her part was don,
And that her raign had here its last fulfilling;
She knew such harmony alone
Could hold all Heav'n and Earth in happier union.

XI.

At last surrounds their sight
A Globe of circular light,
That with long beams the shame-fac't night array'd,
The helmed Cherubim
And sworded Seraphim,
Are seen in glittering ranks with wings displaid,
Harping in loud and solemn quire,
With unexpressive notes to Heav'ns new-born Heir.

270 100 *close* conclusion of a musical phrase, movement 103 *seat* the moon 110 *Globe* troop 116 *unexpressive* inexpressible

XII.

Such Musick (as 'tis said)
Before was never made,
But when of old the sons of morning sung,
While the Creator Great
His constellations set,
And the well-ballanc't world on hinges hung,
And cast the dark foundations deep,
And bid the weltring waves their oozy channel keep.

XIII.

Ring out ye Crystall sphears,
Once bless our human ears,
(If ye have power to touch our senses so)
And let your silver chime
Move in melodious time;
And let the Base of Heav'ns deep Organ blow,
And with your ninefold harmony
Make up full consort to th'Angelike symphony.

XIV.

For if such holy Song
Enwrap our fancy long,
Time will run back, and fetch the age of gold,
And speckl'd vanity
Will sicken soon and die,
And leprous sin will melt from earthly mould,
And Hell it self will pass away,
And leave her dolorous mansions to the peering day.

270 119–24 cp. Job 38:4–8 'Where wast thou when I laid the foundations of the earth . . . When the morning stars sang together, and all the sons of God shouted for joy? Or who shut up the sea with doors, when it brake forth?' 125 the music of the spheres, audible to the sinless and disembodied souls 135 *age of gold* described in Virgil's Messianic eclogue 4 and Ovid's *Metamorphoses* 1.89ff. 136 *speckl'd* blemished, sinful; cp. Horace, *Odes* 4.5.22 'maculosum nefas' ('spotted sin') 140 *peering*★ just appearing

XV.

Yea Truth, and Justice then
Will down return to men,
  Orb'd in a Rain-bow; and like glories wearing,
Mercy will sit between,
Thron'd in Celestiall sheen,
  With radiant feet the tissued clouds down stearing,
And Heav'n as at som festivall,
Will open wide the Gates of her high Palace Hall.

XVI.

But wisest Fate sayes no,
This must not yet be so,
  The Babe lies yet in smiling Infancy,
That on the bitter cross
Must redeem our loss;
  So both himself and us to glorifie:
Yet first to those ychain'd in sleep,
The wakefull trump of doom must thunder through the deep.

XVII.

With such a horrid clang
As on mount *Sinai* rang
  While the red fire, and smouldring clouds out brake:
The aged Earth agast
With terrour of that blast,
  Shall from the surface to the center shake;
When at the worlds last session,
The dreadfull Judge in middle Air shall spread his throne.

270 141 cp. Psalm 85:10 'Mercy and truth are met together; righteousness and peace have kissed each other' *Justice* Astraea 146 *tissued** woven with gold or silver thread 151 *Infancy*** speechlessness, silence 153 *redeem** make good 155 *ychain'd* a Spenserian form, cp. no. 204 l. 12 156 *wakefull** rousing, awaking 158 *Sinai* where Moses received the Ten Commandments, see Exodus 19:16–18

XVIII.

And then at last our bliss
Full and perfect is,
But now begins; for from this happy day
Th'old Dragon under ground
In straiter limits bound,
Not half so far casts his usurped sway,
And wrath to see his Kingdom fail,
Swindges the scaly Horrour of his foulded tail.

XIX.

The Oracles are dumm,
No voice or hideous humm
Runs through the arched roof in words deceiving.
Apollo from his shrine
Can no more divine,
With hollow shreik the steep of *Delphos* leaving.
No nightly trance, or breathed spell,
Inspire's the pale-ey'd Priest from the prophetic cell.

XX.

The lonely mountains o're,
And the resounding shore,
A voice of weeping heard, and loud lament;
From haunted spring, and dale
Edg'd with poplar pale,
The parting Genius is with sighing sent,
With flowre-inwov'n tresses torn
The Nimphs in twilight shade of tangled thickets mourn.

270 168 *Dragon* Satan 169 *straiter* narrower 172 *Swindges* lashes 185 *poplar pale* cp. Horace, *Odes* 2.3.9 'albaque poplus' 186 *Genius* local deity, spirit of the place 187 *flowre-inwov'n**

XXI.

In consecrated Earth,
And on the holy Hearth,
The *Lars*, and *Lemures* moan with midnight plaint,
In Urns, and Altars round,
A drear, and dying sound
Affrights the *Flamins* at their service quaint;
And the chill Marble seems to sweat,
While each peculiar power forgoes his wonted seat.

XXII.

Peor, and *Baalim*,
Forsake their Temples dim,
With that twise batter'd god of *Palestine*,
And mooned *Ashtaroth*,
Heav'ns Queen and Mother both,
Now sits not girt with Tapers holy shine,
The Libyc *Hammon* shrinks his horn,
In vain the *Tyrian* Maids their wounded *Thamuz* mourn.

XXIII.

And sullen *Moloch* fled,
Hath left in shadows dred,
His burning Idol all of blackest hue;
In vain with Cymbals ring,
They call the grisly king,
In dismall dance about the furnace blue;
The brutish gods of *Nile* as fast,
Isis and *Orus*, and the Dog *Anubis* hast.

270 193 *drear** dreary 196 *peculiar* own particular 197 *Peor* a mountain whose local deity, Baal, was worshipped by the Phoenicians as a sun-god (see Numbers 23:28 and 25:3) *Baalim* plural of Baal: the god in his other manifestations 199 *god* Dagon, the Philistine god who twice fell on his face before the Ark of the Lord (see 1 Samuel 5:3–4) 200 *Ashtaroth* plural of Ashtoreth, chief goddess of the Phoenicians, who linked her with the moon 203 *Hammon* Jove 204 *Tyrian* of the capital of Phoenicia *Thamuz* the Phoenician equivalent of Adonis 205 *Moloch* an idol worshipped by the Ammonites at Rabbah (see 2 Kings 23:10) 212 *Isis* Egyptian goddess of the earth *Orus* Egyptian god of the sun who was Isis's son *Anubis* son of Osiris; represented with the head of a dog or jackal

XXIV.

Nor is *Osiris* seen
In *Memphian* Grove, or Green,
  Trampling the unshowr'd Grasse with lowings loud:
Nor can he be at rest
Within his sacred chest,
  Naught but profoundest Hell can be his shroud,
In vain with Timbrel'd Anthems dark
The sable-stoled Sorcerers bear his worshipt Ark.

XXV.

He feels from *Juda*'s Land
The dredded Infants hand,
  The rayes of *Bethlehem* blind his dusky eyn;
Nor all the gods beside,
Longer dare abide,
  Not *Typhon* huge ending in snaky twine:
Our Babe to shew his Godhead true,
Can in his swadling bands controul the damned crew.

XXVI.

So when the Sun in bed,
Curtain'd with cloudy red,
  Pillows his chin upon an Orient wave,
The flocking shadows pale,
Troop to th'infernall jail,
  Each fetter'd Ghost slips to his severall grave,
And the yellow-skirted *Fayes*,
Fly after the Night-steeds, leaving their Moon-lov'd
  maze.

270 213 *Osiris* chief god of the Egyptians; represented as a bull 215 *unshowr'd* not moistened by showers 219 *Timbrel'd** accompanied by the playing of tambourines 220 *sable-stoled** black-robed 223 *eyn* eyes 226 *Typhon* the killer of Osiris 227 *Babe* the infant Christ is reminiscent of the infant Hercules 231 *Pillows** 234 *severall* own, particular 235 *Fayes* fairies 236 *Night-steeds** *Moon-lov'd**

XXVII.

But see the Virgin blest,
Hath laid her Babe to rest.
  Time is our tedious Song should here have ending:
Heav'ns youngest teemed Star,
Hath fixt her polisht Car,
  Her sleeping Lord with Handmaid Lamp attending.
And all about the Courtly Stable,
Bright-harnest Angels sit in order serviceable.

FRANCIS QUARLES

271 [*from* Pentelogia]

Fraus Mundi

  What is the *World*? A great *Exchange* of ware,
Wherein all *sorts*, and *sexes* cheapning are,
The *Flesh*, the *Divell* sit, and cry, *What lack ye*?
When most they fawne, they most intend to rack ye;
The wares, are Cups of *Joy*, and Beds of *Pleasure*,
Ther's goodly choice, downe weight, and flowing measure;
A Soul's the *price*, but they give time to pay,
Upon the *Death-bed*, on the dying *Day*.
  Hard is the Bargaine, and unjust the *Measure*,
When as the *Price* so much out-lasts the *Pleasure*:
The Joyes that are on earth are *Counterfeits*;
If ought be true, 'tis this, Th'are true *Deceits*;

270 239 *tedious* wearisome; late, tardy, slow 240 *youngest teemed* newest born 242 *Handmaid* handmaid-like 244 *harnest* armed, in armour *serviceable* ready, willing to do service

271 Title *Fraus mundi* the world's lie 2 *cheapning* bargaining 4 *rack* extort, overcharge 6 *downe weight* full, good weight 12 *ought* aught, anything

They flatter, fawne, and (like the *Crocadile*)
Kill where they laugh, and *murther* where they smile:
They daily dip within thy *Dish*, and Cry,
Who hath betrayd thee? Master, *Is it I*?

272 [*from* Divine Fancies]

On the contingencie of Actions

I saw him dead; I saw his Body fall
Before Deaths *Dart*; whom tears must not recall:
Yet is he not so dead, but that his *Day*
Might have been lengthen'd, had th'untrodden way
To life beene found: He might have rose agin,
If *something* had, or *somthing* had not bin:
What mine sees past, Heav'ns eye foresaw to come;
He saw, how that *contingent* Act should summe
The totall of his Dayes: His knowing Eye
(As mine doth see him dead) saw he should die
That very fatall howre; yet saw his death,
Not so so necessary, but his Breath
Might beene enlarg'd unto a longer date,
Had he neglected *This*, or taken *That:*
All times to Heav'n are *now*, both first and last;
He sees things *present*, as we see them *past*.

271 16 cp. Matthew 26:23–5 'He that dippeth his hand with me in the dish, the same shall betray me . . . Then Judas, which betrayed him, answered and said, Master, is it I? He said unto him, Thou hast said'

272 Title *contingencie* chance occurrence, fortuitousness 8 *contingent* liable, or not, to happen *summe* reckon, count, total up 13 *enlarg'd* freed, released

273 [*from* Divine Fancies]

On the Needle of a Sun-diall

Behold this needle; when the *Arctick* stone
Hath toucht it, how it trembles up and downe;
Hunts for the *Pole*; and cannot be possest,
Of peace, untill it finde that poynt, that rest:
Such is the *heart* of Man; which, when it hath
Attayn'd the virtue of a lively faith,
It findes no rest on earth, makes no abode
In any Object, but his *heav'n*, his *God*.

274 [*from* Divine Fancies]

On the Booke of Common Prayer

The Booke of *Common Pray'r* excels the rest;
For *Pray'rs* that are most *Common* are the best.

275 [*from* Divine Fancies]

On Christ and our selves

I wish a greater knowledge, then t'attaine
The knowledge of *my selfe:* A greater Gaine
Then to augment *my selfe*; A greater Treasure
Then to enjoy *my selfe*; A greater Pleasure
Then to content *my selfe:* How slight, and vaine
Is all selfe-Knowledge, Pleasure, Treasure, Gaine;

273 1 *Arctick* northern 6 *lively* living

Unlesse my better knowledge could retrive
My Christ; unles my better Gaine could thrive
In Christ; unles my better Wealth grow rich
In Christ; unles my better Pleasure pitch
On Christ; Or else my Knowledge will proclaime
To my owne heart how ignorant I am:
Or else my Gaine, so ill improv'd, will shame
My Trade, and shew how much declin'd I am;
Or else my Treasure will but blurre my name
With *Bankrupt*, and divulge how poore I am;
Or else my Pleasures, that so much *inflame*
My Thoughts, will blabb how full of sores I am:
Lord, keepe me from *my Selfe*; 'Tis best for me,
Never to owne my *Selfe*, if not in *Thee*.

GEORGE HERBERT

276 Perseverance

My God, the poore expressions of my Love
Which warme these lines, and serve them up to thee
Are so, as for the present, I did move
  Or rather as thou movedst mee.

But what shall issue, whither these my words
Shal help another, but my judgment bee;
As a burst fouling-peece doth save the birds
  But kill the man, is seald with thee.

For who can tell, though thou hast dyde to winn
And wedd my soule in glorious paradise;
Whither my many crymes and use of sinn
  May yet forbid the banes and bliss.

275 7 *retrive* retrieve, recover, bring back 15 *blurre* sully, defile

276 7 *fouling-peece* light gun for shooting fowl 12 *banes* banns

Onely my soule hangs on thy promisses
With face and hands clinging unto thy brest,
Clinging and crying, crying without cease
  Thou art my rock, thou art my rest.

277 Redemption

Having been tenant long to a rich Lord,
    Not thriving, I resolved to be bold,
    And make a suit unto him, to afford
A new small-rented lease, and cancell th' old.

In heaven at his manour I him sought:
    They told me there, that he was lately gone
    About some land, which he had dearly bought
Long since on earth, to take possession.

I straight return'd, and knowing his great birth,
    Sought him accordingly in great resorts;
    In cities, theatres, gardens, parks, and courts:
At length I heard a ragged noise and mirth

    Of theeves and murderers: there I him espied,
    Who straight, *Your suit is granted*, said, and died.

277 10 *resorts* gatherings, crowds

278 Easter wings

Lord, who createdst man in wealth and store,
　Though foolishly he lost the same,
　　Decaying more and more,
　　　Till he became
　　　　Most poore:
　　　　With thee
　　　O let me rise
　　As larks, harmoniously,
　And sing this day thy victories:
Then shall the fall further the flight in me.

My tender age in sorrow did beginne:
　And still with sicknesses and shame
　　Thou didst so punish sinne,
　　　That I became
　　　　Most thinne.
　　　　With thee
　　　Let me combine,
　　And feel this day thy victorie:
　For, if I imp my wing on thine,
Affliction shall advance the flight in me.

279 Prayer

Prayer the Churches banquet, Angels age,
　Gods breath in man returning to his birth,
　The soul in paraphrase, heart in pilgrimage,
The Christian plummet sounding heav'n and earth;

278 1 *store* plenty, abundance 10 *fall* Adam's fall, which resulted in Christ's coming 19 *imp* graft feathers on a damaged wing to improve or restore flight

279 1 *Angels age* ageless, timeless 3 *paraphrase* usually, a fuller and clearer version of a text, expressed in different words 4 *plummet* a lead weight used for measuring the depth of water

Engine against th' Almightie, sinners towre,
Reversed thunder, Christ-side-piercing spear,
The six-daies world-transposing in an houre,
A kinde of tune, which all things heare and fear;

Softnesse, and peace, and joy, and love, and blisse,
Exalted Manna, gladnesse of the best,
Heaven in ordinarie, man well drest,
The milkie way, the bird of Paradise,

Church-bels beyond the starres heard, the souls bloud,
The land of spices; something understood.

280 Deniall

When my devotions could not pierce
Thy silent eares;
Then was my heart broken, as was my verse:
My breast was full of fears
And disorder:

My bent thoughts, like a brittle bow,
Did flie asunder:
Each took his way; some would to pleasures go,
Some to the warres and thunder
Of alarms.

As good go any where, they say,
As to benumme
Both knees and heart, in crying night and day,
Come, come, my God, O come,
But no hearing.

279 7 *six-daies world* the world took six days to create *transposing* in music, putting into a different key 11 *in ordinarie* usual, not extraordinary 14 *understood* comprehended, thoroughly known

280 3 *verse* the final line of each verse is unrhymed, until the last line of the poem

O that thou shouldst give dust a tongue
To crie to thee,
And then not heare it crying! all day long
My heart was in my knee,
But no hearing.

Therefore my soul lay out of sight,
Untun'd, unstrung:
My feeble spirit, unable to look right,
Like a nipt blossome, hung
Discontented.

O cheer and tune my heartlesse breast,
Deferre no time;
That so thy favours granting my request,
They and my minde may chime,
And mend my ryme.

281 Jordan

When first my lines of heav'nly joyes made mention,
Such was their lustre, they did so excell,
That I sought out quaint words, and trim invention;
My thoughts began to burnish, sprout, and swell,
Curling with metaphors a plain intention,
Decking the sense, as if it were to sell.

Thousands of notions in my brain did runne,
Off'ring their service, if I were not sped:
I often blotted what I had begunne;
This was not quick enough, and that was dead.
Nothing could seem too rich to clothe the sunne,
Much lesse those joyes which trample on his head.

281 Title *Jordan* the river crossed by the Israelites to enter the promised land; the place of Christ's baptism 3 *trim* smart, fine *invention* the finding out of subjects about which to write (cp. no. 65 l. 6) 4 *burnish* spread out, grow in breadth 6 *Decking* adorning, ornamenting 8 *sped* getting on well, succeeding 10 *quick* lively

As flames do work and winde, when they ascend,
So did I weave my self into the sense.
But while I bustled, I might heare a friend
Whisper, *How wide is all this long pretence!*
There is in love a sweetnesse readie penn'd:
Copie out onely that, and save expense.

282 The Collar

I struck the board, and cry'd, No more.
I will abroad.
What? shall I ever sigh and pine?
My lines and life are free; free as the rode,
Loose as the winde, as large as store.
Shall I be still in suit?
Have I no harvest but a thorn
To let me bloud, and not restore
What I have lost with cordiall fruit?
Sure there was wine
Before my sighs did drie it: there was corn
Before my tears did drown it.
Is the yeare onely lost to me?
Have I no bayes to crown it?
No flowers, no garlands gay? all blasted?
All wasted?
Not so, my heart: but there is fruit,
And thou hast hands.
Recover all thy sigh-blown age
On double pleasures: leave thy cold dispute
Of what is fit, and not. Forsake thy cage,
Thy rope of sands,

281 13 *do work* are agitated, flicker 16 *wide* astray, mistaken

282 Title *Collar* band worn around the neck, hence restraint, discipline, duty; also a pun on 'choler' meaning 'anger', 'irascibility' 1 *board* table 5 *store* plenty, abundance 6 *in suit* in attendance by a tenant at a court; uniform with others; engaged in a lawsuit 9 *cordiall* reviving, restoring the heart 14 *bayes* laurels 19 *sigh-blown** 22 *rope of sands* something lacking coherence and the power to bind

Which pettie thoughts have made, and made to thee
Good cable, to enforce and draw,
And be thy law,
While thou didst wink and wouldst not see.
Away; take heed:
I will abroad.
Call in thy deaths head there: tie up thy fears.
He that forbears
To suit and serve his need,
Deserves his load.
But as I rav'd and grew more fierce and wilde
At every word,
Me thoughts I heard one calling, *Childe:*
And I reply'd, *My Lord.*

283 The Flower

How fresh, O Lord, how sweet and clean
Are thy returns! ev'n as the flowers in spring;
To which, besides their own demean,
The late-past frosts tributes of pleasure bring.
Grief melts away
Like snow in May,
As if there were no such cold thing.

Who would have thought my shrivel'd heart
Could have recover'd greennesse? It was gone
Quite under ground; as flowers depart
To see their mother-root, when they have blown;
Where they together
All the hard weather,
Dead to the world, keep house unknown.

282 24 *cable* strong, thick rope 26 *wink* close your eyes 29 *deaths head* skull, hence an emblem of mortality; a ring with the figure of a skull

283 3 *demean* demeanour, bearing; demesne, estate

These are thy wonders, Lord of power,
Killing and quickning, bringing down to hell
And up to heaven in an houre;
Making a chiming of a passing-bell.
We say amisse,
This or that is:
Thy word is all, if we could spell.

O that I once past changing were,
Fast in thy Paradise, where no flower can wither!
Many a spring I shoot up fair,
Offring at heav'n, growing and groning thither:
Nor doth my flower
Want a spring-showre,
My sinnes and I joining together:

But while I grow in a straight line,
Still upwards bent, as if heav'n were mine own,
Thy anger comes, and I decline:
What frost to that? what pole is not the zone,
Where all things burn,
When thou dost turn,
And the least frown of thine is shown?

And now in age I bud again,
After so many deaths I live and write;
I once more smell the dew and rain,
And relish versing: O my onely light,
It cannot be
That I am he
On whom thy tempests fell all night.

These are thy wonders, Lord of love,
To make us see we are but flowers that glide:
Which when we once can finde and prove,
Thou hast a garden for us, where to bide.
Who would be more,
Swelling through store,
Forfeit their Paradise by their pride.

283 16 *quickning* bringing to life 18 *chiming* harmonious ringing of bells *passing-bell* single bell rung to mark a death 25 *Offring* aiming, directing 44 *glide* pass, slip gently away 45 *prove* experience, try

284 The Forerunners

The harbingers are come. See, see their mark;
White is their colour, and behold my head.
But must they have my brain? must they dispark
Those sparkling notions, which therein were bred?
Must dulnesse turn me to a clod?
Yet have they left me, *Thou art still my God.*

Good men ye be, to leave me my best room,
Ev'n all my heart, and what is lodged there:
I passe not, I, what of the rest become,
So *Thou art still my God*, be out of fear.
He will be pleased with that dittie;
And if I please him, I write fine and wittie.

Farewell sweet phrases, lovely metaphors.
But will ye leave me thus? when ye before
Of stews and brothels onely knew the doores,
Then did I wash you with my tears, and more,
Brought you to Church well drest and clad:
My God must have my best, ev'n all I had.

Lovely enchanting language, sugar-cane,
Hony of roses, whither wilt thou flie?
Hath some fond lover tic'd thee to thy bane?
And wilt thou leave the Church, and love a stie?
Fie, thou wilt soil thy broider'd coat,
And hurt thy self, and him that sings the note.

284 Title *Forerunners* messengers sent before, to prepare the way and herald the arrival of a great man; harbingers; signs of things to follow 3 *dispark** disimpark, turn (deer) out of a park 6 *Thou . . . God* cp. Psalm 31:14 'But I trusted in thee, O Lord: I said, Thou art my God' 9 *passe* care 11 *dittie* theme, phrase, burden of a song 21 *tic'd* enticed *bane* ruin, destruction

Let foolish lovers, if they will love dung,
With canvas, not with arras, clothe their shame:
Let follie speak in her own native tongue.
True beautie dwells on high: ours is a flame
But borrow'd thence to light us thither.
Beautie and beauteous words should go together.

Yet if you go, I passe not; take your way:
For, *Thou art still my God*, is all that ye
Perhaps with more embellishment can say,
Go birds of spring: let winter have his fee,
Let a bleak palenesse chalk the doore,
So all within be livelier then before.

285 Love

Love bade me welcome: yet my soul drew back,
Guiltie of dust and sinne.
But quick-ey'd Love, observing me grow slack
From my first entrance in,
Drew nearer to me, sweetly questioning,
If I lack'd any thing.

A guest, I answer'd, worthy to be here:
Love said, you shall be he.
I the unkinde, ungratefull? Ah my deare,
I cannot look on thee.
Love took my hand, and smiling did reply,
Who made the eyes but I?

Truth Lord, but I have marr'd them: let my shame
Go where it doth deserve.
And know you not, sayes Love, who bore the blame?
My deare, then I will serve.
You must sit down, sayes Love, and taste my meat:
So I did sit and eat.

284 26 *canvas* coarse cloth *arras* fine cloth

285 2 *dust* man's mortal frame

286 [*from* The Church Militant]

Religion stands on tip-toe in our land,
Readie to passe to the *American* strand.
When height of malice, and prodigious lusts,
Impudent sinning, witchcrafts, and distrusts
(The marks of future bane) shall fill our cup
Unto the brimme, and make our measure up;
When *Sein* shall swallow *Tiber*, and the *Thames*
By letting in them both, pollutes her streams:
When *Italie* of us shall have her will,
And all her calender of sinnes fulfill;
Whereby one may fortell, what sinnes next yeare
Shall both in *France* and *England* domineer:
Then shall Religion to *America* flee:
They have their times of Gospel, ev'n as we.
My God, thou dost prepare for them a way
By carrying first their gold from them away:
For gold and grace did never yet agree:
Religion alwaies sides with povertie.
We think we rob them, but we think amisse:
We are more poore, and they more rich by this.
Thou wilt revenge their quarrell, making grace
To pay our debts, and leave our ancient place
To go to them, while that which now their nation
But lends to us, shall be our desolation.

286 1–2 according to Herbert's biographer Izaak Walton, the Vice-Chancellor of Cambridge University objected to these two lines, when he was reading *The temple* for its licence, but allowed them to stand   5 *bane* ruin, destruction

Anonymous

287 [Yet if his Majestie our Sovareigne lord]

Yet if his Majestie our Sovareigne lord,
Should of his owne accord
Freindly himselfe invite
And saye I'le be your guest to morrowe night
How should we stirr ourselves, Call and Comand
All hands to worke. Let no man idle stand.
Set me fine spanish Tables in the hall
See they be fitted all
Let there be rome to eate,
And order taken that there want no meate
See every sconce and Candlestick made bright,
That without Tapers they may give a light
Looke to the Presence. Are the Carpetts spred,
The Dazie o're the head
The Cushions in the Chayre
And all the Candles lighted on the stayres
Perfume the chambers and in any Case
Let each man give attendance in his place.
Thus if the King were Coming would wee doe
And 'twere good reason too,
For tis a duteous thing
To shew all honor to an earthly King,
And after all our travayle and our Cost,
So he be pleas'd, to think no labour lost.
But at the Coming of the King of heaven
All's set at six and seaven:
Wee wallow in our sinn
Christ cannot finde a Chamber in the Inn.
Wee entertaine him alwayes like a stranger
And as at first still lodge him in the manger.

287 14 *Dazie* dais, canopy

SIDNEY GODOLPHIN

288 [Lord when the wise men came from Farr]

Lord when the wise men came from Farr
Ledd to thy Cradle by A Starr,
Then did the shepheards too rejoyce,
Instructed by thy Angells voyce,
Blest were the wisemen in their skill,
And shepheards in their harmelesse will.

Wisemen in tracing Natures lawes
Ascend unto the highest cause,
Shepheards with humble fearefulnesse
Walke safely, though their light be lesse,
Though wisemen better know the way
It seemes noe honest heart can stray:

Ther is noe merrit in the wise
But love, (the shepheards sacrifice)
Wisemen all wayes of knowledge past,
To 'th shepheards wonder come at last,
To know, can only wonder breede,
And not to know, is wonders seede.

A wiseman at the Alter Bowes
And offers up his studied vowes
And is received, may not the teares,
Which spring too from a shepheards feares,
And sighs upon his fraylty spent,
Though not distinct, be eloquent.

288 1 *wise men* cp. Matthew 2:1–12 3 *shepheards* cp. Luke 2:8–20 8 *highest cause* in Aristotelian philosophy, the final cause: the end or purpose for which a thing is produced

Tis true, the object sanctifies
All passions which within us rise,
But since noe creature comprehends
The cause of causes, end of ends,
Hee who himselfe vouchsafes to know
Best pleases his creator soe.

When then our sorrowes wee applye
To our owne wantes and poverty,
When wee looke up in all distresse
And our owne misery confesse
Sending both thankes and prayers above
Then though wee doe not know, we love.

JOHN TAYLOR

289 [*from* Here followeth the unfashionable fashion, or the too too homely Worshipping of God]

Gods *Houses*, almost like *Troyes Ilion*,
Are also built of course and baser stone,
With broken *Pavement*, *Window*, *Wall* and *Dore*;
Well, if but White-lim'd, and then *Oaker'd* o're;
Drillings of Raine, make greene and yellow streakes,
And (Where they give him place) the Painter speakes
In Creed, Commands, and Prayer, and 'gainst his Will
To the Kings foes, puts *Dizzie Painter* still,
Sayes *Woodcock* was Church-warden, then cries Woe
Over the Pulpit, and in mind to show
Beggers at dore, how dreadfull to their trade
Death is, he sets him working with a *Spade*.
Nine dusty Seats, twelve Tressels, two crack'd Bels,
Three broken Halters. And what? Nothing else

289 Title *homely* familiar 4 *White-lim'd* whitewashed *Oaker'd* coloured ochre, orange-brown 5 *Drillings* tricklings, drippings 9 *Woodcock* generic name for a fool, simpleton 14 *Halters* rope nooses; bell-ropes (?)

Goes to a *Church*? The Chancell hath a Boord
Worth nine pence (most unworthy of the Lord)
With pretty home-spun Linsey-woolsey Spread
Under the Linnen, whither (scarce white) Bread
And cheape sowre wine, two hob-nail'd Wardens dragge
In *Gibeons* Bottles, and course Pudding-bagge.
All manners, and all decencie must be
Laid by; as much as bowing of the Knee,
Unlawfull is, though *Paul* commands it so,
Yet many new pure spirits doe say no.
That Kneeling, comes so neere Idolatry;
T'avoid which, they will be so mannerly
To be Christs fellow, and to sit at's Table,
And give his house like reverence as the stable.
Thus sawcie Mortals (vile and transitory)
Doe rob themselves of grace, and God of glory;
These rude behaviours every good man greeves,
When *Temples* are esteem'd like dens of Theeves.
Gods Worship this! The great Kings Service! see
How odly madly *God's* and *man's* agree.

EDMUND WALLER

290 Upon his MAJESTIES repairing of PAULS

That shipwrackt vessel which th'Apostle bore
Scarce suffer'd more upon Melitas shore,

289 17 *Linsey-woolsey* cheap material of wool and flax 19 *hob-nail'd* wearing hobnail boots; rustic, boorish 20 *Gibeons* cp. Joshua 9:27 'And Joshua made them that day hewers of wood and drawers of water for the congregation, and for the altar of the Lord, even unto this day, in the place which he should choose' *Pudding-bagge* a bag in which a pudding is boiled; dirty, used material 23 *Paul* cp. Philippians 2:10 '. . . at the name of Jesus every knee should bow' 26 *mannerly* polite

290 1 *Apostle* St Paul, cp. Acts 27 2 *Melitas shore* Malta, cp. Acts 28:1 'And when they were escaped, then they knew that the island was called Melita'

Then did his Temple in the sea of time
(Our Nations glory, and our Nations crime)
When the first Monarch of this happy Isle
Mov'd with the ruine of so brave a pile,
This worke of cost and piety begun
To be accomplish'd by his glorious Son;
Who all that came within the ample thought
Of his wise sire, has to perfection brought.
He like *Amphion* makes those quarries leap
Into fair figures from a confus'd heap:
For in his art of Regiment is found
A power like that of harmony in sound.

Those antique minstrels sure were *Charles* like Kings,
Cities their lutes, and subjects hearts their strings;
On which with so divine a hand they strook
Consent of motion from their breath they took.
So all our mindes with his conspire to grace
The Gentiles great Apostle, and deface
Those State-obscuring sheds, that like a chaine
Seem'd to confine and fetter him againe;
Which the glad Saint shakes off at his command
As once the viper from his sacred hand:
So joyes the aged Oake when we divide
The creeping Ivy from his injur'd side.

Ambition rather would affect the fame
Of some new structure, to have born her name;
Two distant vertues in one act we finde
The modesty, and greatness of his minde;
Which not content to be above the rage
And injury of all impairing age,
In its own worth secure, doth higher clime,
And things half swallow'd from the jaws of time

290 5 *Monarch* James I 13 *Regiment* royal rule, government 15 *minstrels* Amphion, Orpheus and others 18 *Consent* consort, harmony 21 *State* splendour, magnificence *sheds* shops and houses were pulled down from around the cathedral 24 cp. Acts 28:5 'And he shook off the beast into the fire, and felt no harm' 27 *affect* aspire to, aim at

Reduce; an earnest of his grand designe
To frame no new Church, but the old refine:
Which Spouse-like may with comly grace command
More then by force of argument or hand.
For doubtfull reason few can apprehend,
And war brings ruine, where it should amend.
But beauty with a bloodlesse conquest findes
A welcome sovereignty in rudest mindes.

Not ought which *Shebas* wondring Queen beheld
Amongst the works of *Solomon* excell'd,
His ships and building; emblems of a heart
Large both in magnanimity and art:
While the propitious heavens this worke attend,
Long wanted showres they forget to send;
As if they meant to make it understood
Of more importance then our vitall food.

The Sun which riseth to salute the quire,
Already finish'd, setting shall admire
How private bounty could so far extend:
The King built all, but *Charles* the Westerne end:
So proud a fabrick to devotion given,
At once it threatneth and obligeth heaven.

Laomedon that had the gods in pay,
Neptune, with him that rules the sacred day,
Could no such structure raise, Troy wall'd so high,
Th'Atrides might as well have forc'd the sky.

Glad, though amazed, are our neighbour Kings
To see such power employ'd in peacefull things.
They list not urge it to the dreadfull field,
The taske is easier to destroy, then build.

290 35 *Reduce* bring back, recall *earnest* token, pledge, instalment 36 Charles could not be said to be introducing Laudian innovations by restoring old St Paul's, but rather he was 'refining' the former Roman Catholic church 43 *Shebas ... Queen* her visit to Solomon is recorded in 1 Kings 10 and 2 Chronicles 9 45 *ships* at the same time as restoring St Paul's, Charles was, at an equally high cost, rebuilding the navy 51 *quire* choir, nave where Inigo Jones began work 54 since the work took place under a royal commission, the work was all Charles's, but he himself paid for the western end, including Jones's portico 63 *list* wish, desire

Richard Crashaw

291 A Hymne of the Nativity, sung by the Shepheards

Chorus. Come wee Shepheards who have seene
Dayes King deposed by Nights Queene.
Come lift we up our lofty song,
To wake the Sun that sleeps too long.

Hee in this our generall joy,
Slept, and dreampt of no such thing
While we found out the fair-ey'd Boy,
And kist the Cradle of our King;
Tell him hee rises now too late,
To shew us ought worth looking at.

Tell him wee now can shew him more
Then hee e're shewd to mortall sight,
Then hee himselfe e're saw before,
Which to be seene needs not his light:
Tell him *Tityrus* where th'hast been,
Tell him *Thyrsis* what th'hast seen.

Tityrus. Gloomy Night embrac't the place
Where the noble Infant lay:
The Babe lookt up, and shew'd his face,
In spight of Darknesse it was Day.
It was thy Day, Sweet, and did rise,
Not from the East, but from thy eyes.

Thyrsis. Winter chid the world, and sent
The angry North to wage his warres:
The North forgot his fierce intent,
And left perfumes, in stead of scarres:
By those sweet Eyes persuasive Powers,
Where he meant frosts, he scattered Flowers.

291 10 *ought* aught, anything 15–16 *Tityrus* ... *Thyrsis* traditional names for shepherds, both used by Virgil in the *Eclogues*

Both. We saw thee in thy Balmy Nest,
Bright Dawne of our *Eternall Day*;
Wee saw thine Eyes break from the East,
And chase the trembling shades away:
Wee saw thee (and wee blest the sight)
Wee saw thee by thine owne sweet Light.

Tityrus. I saw the curl'd drops, soft and slow
Come hovering o're the places head,
Offring their whitest sheets of snow,
To furnish the faire Infants Bed.
Forbeare (said I) be not too bold,
Your fleece is white, but 'tis too cold.

Thyrsis. I saw th'officious Angels bring,
The downe that their soft brests did strow,
For well they now can spare their wings,
When Heaven it selfe lyes here below.
Faire Youth (said I) be not too rough,
Thy Downe though soft's not soft enough.

Tityrus. The Babe no sooner 'gan to seeke,
Where to lay his lovely head,
But streight his eyes advis'd his Cheeke,
'Twixt Mothers Brests to goe to bed.
Sweet choise (said I) no way but so,
Not to lye cold, yet sleepe in snow.

All. Welcome to our wondring sight
Eternity shut in a span!
Summer in Winter! Day in Night!
Chorus. Heaven in Earth! and God in Man!
Great litle one, whose glorious Birth,
Lifts Earth to Heaven, stoops heaven to earth.

291 29 *Balmy* soft; fragrant 41 *officious* eager to serve, obliging, attentive 42 *strow* strew, cover 54 *span* of a hand

Welcome, though not to Gold, nor Silke,
    To more then *Cæsars* Birthright is.
Two sister-Seas of virgins Milke,
    With many a rarely-temper'd kisse,
That breathes at once both Maid and Mother,
Warmes in the one, cooles in the other.

Shee sings thy Teares asleepe, and dips
    Her Kisses in thy weeping Eye,
Shee spreads the red leaves of thy Lips,
    That in their Buds yet blushing lye.
Shee 'gainst those Mother-Diamonds tryes
The points of her young Eagles Eyes.

Welcome, (though not to those gay flyes
    Guilded i'th' Beames of Earthly Kings
Slippery soules in smiling eyes)
    But to poore Shepheards, simple things,
That use no varnish, no oyl'd Arts,
But lift clean hands full of cleare hearts.

Yet when young *Aprils* husband showres,
    Shall blesse the fruitfull *Maia*'s Bed,
Wee'l bring the first-borne of her flowers,
    To kisse thy feet, and crowne thy head.
To thee (Dread Lambe) whose Love must keepe
The Shepheards, while they feed their sheepe.

To thee meeke Majesty, soft King
    Of simple Graces, and sweet Loves,
Each of us his Lamb will bring,
    Each his payre of silver Doves.
At last, in fire of thy faire Eyes,
Wee'l burne, our owne best sacrifice.

291 60 *Cæsars Birthright* cp. Mark 12:17 'Render to Caesar the things that are Caesar's and to God the things that are God's' 62 *rarely* finely

292 TO THE Noblest and best of Ladyes, the Countesse of Denbigh. Perswading her to Resolution in Religion, and to render her selfe without further delay into the Communion of the Catholick Church

What heav'n-intreated HEART is This?
Stands trembling at the gate of blisse;
Holds fast the door, yet dares not venture
Fairly to open it, and enter.
Whose DEFINITION is a doubt
Twixt life and death, twixt in and out.
Say, lingring fair! why comes the birth
Of your brave soul so slowly forth?
Plead your pretences (o you strong
In weaknes!) why you choose so long
In labor of your selfe to ly,
Nor daring quite to live nor dy?
Ah linger not, lov'd soul! a slow
And late consent was a long no,
Who grants at last, long time tryd
And did his best to have deny'd.
What magick bolts, what mystick Barres
Maintain the will in these strange warres!
What fatall, yet fantastick, bands
Keep The free Heart from it's own hands!
So when the year takes cold, we see
Poor waters their owne prisoners be.
Fetter'd, and lockt up fast they ly
In a sad selfe-captivity.
The' astonisht nymphs their flood's strange fate deplore,
To see themselves their own severer shore.
Thou that alone canst thaw this cold,
And fetch the heart from it's strong Hold;
Allmighty LOVE! end this long warr,
And of a meteor make a starr.

292 11 *In . . . selfe* giving birth to yourself 30 meteors were held to be inconstant and passing, stars fixed and permanent

O fix this fair INDEFINITE.
And 'mongst thy shafts of soveraign light
Choose out that sure decisive dart
Which has the Key of this close heart,
Knowes all the corners of't, and can controul
The self-shutt cabinet of an unsearcht soul.
O let it be at last, love's houre.
Raise this tall Trophee of thy Powre;
Come once the conquering way; not to confute
But kill this rebell-word, IRRESOLUTE
That so, in spite of all this peevish strength
Of weaknes, she may write RESOLV'D AT LENGTH,
Unfold at length, unfold fair flowre
And use the season of love's showre,
Meet his well-meaning Wounds, wise heart!
And hast to drink the wholsome dart.
That healing shaft, which heavn till now
Hath in love's quiver hid for you.
O Dart of love! arrow of light!
O happy you, if it hitt right,
It must not fall in vain, it must
Not mark the dry regardles dust.
Fair one, it is your fate; and brings
Æternall worlds upon it's wings.
Meet it with wide-spread armes; and see
It's seat your soul's just center be.
Disband dull feares; give faith the day.
To save your life, kill your delay
It is love's seege; and sure to be
Your triumph, though his victory.
'Tis cowardise that keeps this feild
And want of courage not to yeild.
Yeild then, ô yeild, that love may win
The Fort at last, and let life in.
Yeild quickly. Lest perhaps you prove
Death's prey, before the prize of love.
This Fort of your fair selfe, if't be not won,
He is repulst indeed; But you'are undone.

292 61 *keeps this feild* stays to fight

293 [*from* The Flaming Heart]

For all the gallantry of him,
Give me the suffring SERAPHIM.
His be the bravery of all those Bright things,
The glowing cheekes, the glistering wings;
The Rosy hand, the radiant DART;
Leave HER alone THE FLAMING HEART.
Leave her that; and thou shalt leave her
Not one loose shaft but love's whole quiver.
For in love's feild was never found
A nobler weapon then a WOUND.
Love's passives are his activ'st part.
The wounded is the wounding heart.
O HEART! the æquall poise of love's both parts
Bigge alike with wounds and darts.
Live in these conquering leaves; live all the same;
And walk through all tongues one triumphant FLAME
Live here, great HEART; and love and dy and kill;
And bleed and wound; and yeild and conquer still.
Let this immortall life wherere it comes
Walk in a crowd of loves and MARTYRDOMES.
Let mystick DEATHS wait on't; and wise soules be
The love-slain wittnesses of this life of thee.
O sweet incendiary! shew here thy art,
Upon this carcasse of a hard, cold, hart,
Let all thy scatter'd shafts of light, that play
Among the leaves of thy larg Books of day,
Combin'd against this BREST at once break in
And take away from me my self and sin,
This gratious Robbery shall thy bounty be;
And my best fortunes such fair spoiles of me.
O thou undanted daughter of desires!
By all thy dowr of LIGHTS and FIRES;

293 3 *bravery* fineness, splendidness 5 *Rosy* seraphim were distinguished among angels for the burning fervour of their love and hence associated with the colour red 32 *dowr* dowry

By all the eagle in thee, all the dove;
By all thy lives and deaths of love;
By thy larg draughts of intellectuall day,
And by thy thrists of love more large then they;
By all thy brim-fill'd Bowles of feirce desire
By thy last Morning's draught of liquid fire;
By the full kingdome of that finall kisse
That seiz'd thy parting Soul, and seal'd thee his;
By all the heav'ns thou hast in him
(Fair sister of the SERAPHIM!)
By all of HIM we have in THEE;
Leave nothing of my SELF in me.
Let me so read thy life, that I
Unto all life of mine may dy.

ANONYMOUS

294 Upon Arch-bishop Laud, Prisoner in the Tower. 1641

Our Canterburye's great Cathedrall Bell
Seldome rings out, but makes a fatall knell.
Her loud unpleasing warring-jarring sound
The noyse of all our well-tun'd Bells hath drown'd.
Shee lately rang so loud, I am in doubt
Shee had almost struck Lincolne's clapper out.

It is reported by the men of Kent,
Shee sound's such discord, shee gives no content;
But that shee's ponderous, and so great, the People
Would very gladly pull her out o'th'steeple.

293 36 *thrists* thirsts

294 6 *Lincolne's* Lincoln Cathedral had a very large bell, Great Tom; the poet refers also to John Williams (1582–1650), Bishop of Lincoln, who had opposed Laud's policies and received a hero's welcome on his release from imprisonment in the Tower in 1640

Shee makes an hideous noyse with her Bum-Bom,
As did the roaring Bull that came from Rome.
Shee'le serve for nothing, shee's so full of brasse,
But for to ring the Catholicks to Masse.

Except the Parliament will take this Bell,
And cast her new agayne, or hang her well;
And make both her, and all the rest, that are
So bigge, more tuneable, though lesse by farre.

Then they, that wont to ring so seldome well,
May prove each one a constant Sermon-Bell.
So shall wee have good Musick, and lesse noyse;
And have our Church purg'd from new-fangled toyes.

Robert Wild

295 [*from* Alas poore Scholler, whither wilt thou goe]

To the tune of, *Halloo my Fancy, etc.*

In a melancholly studdy
None but my selfe,
Me thought my muse grew muddy,
After seaven yeares reading
And costly breeding,
I felt, but could finde no pelfe:

294 11 *Bum-Bom* Great Tom bell in Christ Church, Oxford, originally bore an inscription describing its sound as 'Bim Bom' 12 *Bull* punning on 'bull' in the sense of an injunction from Rome; Laud's reforming measures were widely seen as a reversion to Roman Catholicism 18 *lesse by farre* may refer to schemes for a 'reduced', modified episcopacy

295 3 *muddy* obscure, vague, confused 4 *seaven yeares* at university 6 *pelfe* money, riches

Into learned raggs
I've rent my Plush and Sattin,
And now am fit to begg
In *Hebrew*, *Greeke* and *Lattin*,
Instead of *Aristotle*,
would I had got a Patten:
Alasse poore Scholler whither wilt thou go?

Cambridge now I must leave thee
And follow Fate,
Colledge hopes doe deceive me,
I oft expected
To have beene elected,
But desert is reprobate:
Masters of *Colledges*
have no common graces,
And they that have *Fellowships*
have but common places,
And those that *Schollers* are,
they must have hansome faces:
Alas poore Scholler whither wilt thou goe?

I have bow'd, I have bended,
And all in hope,
One day to be befrended,
I have Preach'd, I have Printed
What ere I hinted,
To please our English *Pope*;
I worshipt towards the East,
but the Sunne doth now forsake me,

295 8 *Plush* rich cloth 12 *Patten* licence for a monopoly; wooden overshoe; communion plate, chalice cover (?) 21 *graces* favours; university dispensations 23 *common places* commonplaces, truisms 32 *Pope* Archbishop Laud 33 *East* the traditional position of the celebrant of the Eucharist, standing on the west side of the altar and facing east, was revived during the seventeenth century, especially among the Laudian wing of the Church

I finde that I am falling,
the Northerne winds doe shake me,
Would I had beene upright,
for bowing now will breake me:
Alas poore Scholler, whither wilt thou goe? . . .

Shipps, Shipps, Shipps I discover,
Crossing the Maine,
Shall I in and goe over
Turne *Jew* or Atheist,
Turke or *Papist*,
To *Geneva* or *Amsterdam*:
Bishoppricks are voyde
in *Scotland*, shall I thither,
Or follow *Windebanke*
and *Finch* to see if either
Doe want a Preist to shrive them,
O no tis blustring weather.
Alas poore Scholler whither wilt thou goe?

Ho, ho, ho, I have hit it,
Peace goodman foole,
Thou hast a trade will fit it,
Draw thy Indenture,
Be bound at adventure,
An Apprentice to a *Free-schoole*;
There thou may'st command
By *William Lillies* Charter,

295 45 *Geneva or Amsterdam* centres of Calvinism 48 *Windebanke* Sir Francis Windebank (1582–1646), Secretary of State, fled to Calais in 1640 having been accused of signing a letter in favour of Roman Catholic priests and Jesuits; he died in Paris 49 *Finch* Sir John Finch (1584–1660), Lord Keeper, widely unpopular for his severe sentences, including an extra cropping from the stumps of William Prynne's ears (see no. 296 l. 17); faced with impeachment in December 1640, he fled to the Low Countries 60 *William Lillies* William Lily (1468?–1522), first High Master of St Paul's School, London, and part-compiler of the standard English Renaissance Latin grammar

There thou mayst whipp, stripp
and hang and draw and quarter,
And commit to the red Rod,
both *Will.* and *Tom.* and *Arthur,*
I, I, 'tis thither, thither will I goe.

JOHN MILTON

296 On the new forcers of Conscience under the Long PARLIAMENT

Because you have thrown of your Prelate Lord,
And with stiff Vowes renounc'd his Liturgie
To seise the widdow'd whore Pluralitie
From them whose sin ye envi'd, not abhor'd,
Dare ye for this adjure the Civill Sword
To force our Consciences that Christ set free,
And ride us with a classic Hierarchy
Taught ye by meer *A. S.* and *Rotherford?*
Men whose Life, Learning, Faith and pure intent
Would have been held in high esteem with *Paul*
Must now be nam'd and printed Hereticks
By shallow *Edwards* and Scotch what d' ye call:
But we do hope to find out all your tricks,

296 1 the formal abolition of episcopacy, begun in 1643, was accomplished in September 1646 *Prelate Lord** 2 *Liturgie* the use of the Book of Common Prayer was prohibited in August 1645 3 *Pluralitie* the holding of more than one ecclesiastical living at the same time 5 *adjure* charge, entreat 7 *classic** classical, divided into classes, as parishes and congregations were divided under the Presbyterian system 8 *A. S.* Adam Stewart, Scottish Presbyterian divine; he wrote against the Independents who wished to maintain their own congregations *Rotherford* Samuel Rutherford, another, leading, Scottish Presbyterian 9 *Men* like the Independents 12 *Edwards* Thomas Edwards, an English Presbyterian *Scotch ... call* probably Robert Baillie

Your plots and packing wors then those of *Trent*,
That so the Parliament
May with their wholsom and preventive Shears
Clip your Phylacteries, though bauk your Ears,
And succour our just Fears
When they shall read this clearly in your charge
New Presbyter is but *Old Priest* writ Large.

MORGAN LLWYD

297 [*from* The Summer]

1. What? summer now? divisions ring
and subdivisions spring,
Errours and heresyes abound
And is it time to sing?

2. O yes. True members all are one
as Christ did preach and pray
The day the heaven and earth is burnt
is good mens wedding day.

3. As for opinions, weeds, and tares
Is trueth a feeble reed?
If the elect may bee deceav-d
I will even burne my creed.

296 14 *packing* fraudulent dealing *Trent* the Council of Trent (1545–63), called by the Roman Catholic Church after the Reformation to counter Protestantism 16 *preventive* able to keep off disease, prophylactic 17 *Phylacteries* Jewish ceremonial boxes; ostentatious, hypocritical displays of piety or rectitude *bauk* spare; in 1637 the Presbyterian pamphleteer William Prynne had the remains of his ears (first cut off in 1634) removed for attacking prelacy: see the MS version, quoted in the textual note on the poem 20 *Priest* derived etymologically from a contracted form of the Greek 'presbyter' ('an elder') *writ Large* written at length, expanded

4. Drowne not poore faith in faithlesse feares
walke Peter on the wave
Christ bears the earth, holds up the church
when men and devills do rave.

5. feare not the Pates of Jesuits
our Jesus them outwitts
now they are neere their journeyes end
lett satan tyre his titts.

6. Sing on a brittle sea of glasse
sing in a furne of fire
In flames wee leap for joy and find
a cave a singing quire.

7. Sight sense and reason, hold your peace
our Guides no longer bee,
word faith and spirit stand in stead
things (now) unseene wee see

8. Its true we differ in small points
as clocks in cittyes do
some travellers do lag behind
who yet to Salem go

9. Know that Christs army hath two wings
and diffring colours all
his house hath divers sorted roomes
his trees are short and tall

10. Mens faces, voices, differ much,
saincts are not all one size
flowers in one garden vary too
lett none monopolize.

297 14 cp. Matthew 14:22–33 17 *Pates* heads, skulls 20 *tyre his titts* exhaust his horses, nags (?) 21 cp. Revelation 15:2 'And I saw as it were a sea of glass mingled with fire' 22 *furne* the burning fiery furnace into which Shadrach, Meshach and Abednego were thrown for refusing to worship Nebuchadnezzar's golden statue; they miraculously survived: see Daniel 3 32 *Salem* Jerusalem, see Genesis 14:18

11. In our Gamaliels shcoole there are
and will bee many forms
and divers branches on one root
that clash in time of storms

12. In pronunciation of our tongue
some stammer lispe or tone
though sibboleth may cost us deare
in Christ wee are all one.

LAURENCE CLARKSON

298 [*from* A Single Eye All Light, no Darkness]

Behold, the King of glory now is come
T'reduce God, and Devil to their Doom;
For both of them are servants unto Me
That lives, and rules in perfect Majesty:
Though called God, yet that is not my Name,
True, I be both, yet am I not the same:
Therefore a wonder am I to you all,
So that to titul'd Gods ye pray and call.
Oh then my Creature, let me speak to thee;
Thy Worship, and thy God, shall dy truly.
Why dote ye Worldings? up and down being hurl'd,
As he is, so are we even in this World;
And so are all things perfect, just, and good;
Yea, all are sav'd by's Cross, his wounds, and blood.

297 41 *Gamaliels* a great Jewish rabbi, the teacher of St Paul; see Acts 22:3 46 *tone*** utter with a musical sound 47 *sibboleth* shibboleth, the Hebrew word Jephthah used to distinguish the fleeing enemy, the Ephraimites (who could not pronounce the 'sh'), from his men, the Gileadites; see Judges 12:4–6

298 1 cp. Psalm 24:7 'Lift up your heads, O ye gates; and be ye lift up, ye everlasting doors; and the King of glory shall come in' 8 *titul'd*** titled 11 *dote* be foolish, deranged

Where else is heaven, but in our present peace
From him? or hell, but when that this doth cease?
Fie then for shame, look not above the Skies
For God, or Heaven; for here your Treasure lies
Even in these Forms, *Eternal Will* will reigne,
Through him are all things, onely One, not Twain:
Sure he's the Fountain from which every thing
Bòth good and ill (so term'd) appears to spring.
Unto this *Single Eye,* though *Adams* two
Cannot perceive, to Such, to All

Adieu.

Henry Vaughan

299 The Retreate

Happy those early dayes! when I
Shin'd in my Angell-infancy.
Before I understood this place
Appointed for my second race,
Or taught my soul to fancy ought
But a white, Celestiall thought,
When yet I had not walkt above
A mile, or two, from my first love,
And looking back (at that short space,)
Could see a glimpse of his bright-face;
When on some *gilded Cloud*, or *flowre*
My gazing soul would dwell an houre,
And in those weaker glories spy
Some shadows of eternity;
Before I taught my tongue to wound
My Conscience with a sinfull sound,

299 4 *second race* this life, rather than the one which preceded it 5 *ought* aught, anything 8 cp. Revelation 2:4 'Nevertheless I have somewhat against thee, because thou hast left thy first love'

Or had the black art to dispence
A sev'rall sinne to ev'ry sence,
But felt through all this fleshly dresse
Bright *shootes* of everlastingnesse.
O how I long to travell back
And tread again that ancient track!
That I might once more reach that plaine,
Where first I left my glorious traine,
From whence th' Inlightned spirit sees
That shady City of Palme trees;
But (ah!) my soul with too much stay
Is drunk, and staggers in the way.
Some men a forward motion love,
But I by backward steps would move,
And when this dust falls to the urn
In that state I came return.

300 The World

1.

I saw Eternity the other night
Like a great *Ring* of pure and endless light,
All calm, as it was bright,
And round beneath it, Time in hours, days, years
Driv'n by the spheres
Like a vast shadow mov'd, In which the world
And all her train were hurl'd;
The doting Lover in his queintest strain
Did their Complain,

299 18 *sev'rall* different 20 *shootes* young branches or sprigs 23–6 cp. Deuteronomy 34:1–4 'And Moses went up from the plains ... And the Lord shewed him all the land ... and the plain of the valley of Jericho, the city of palm trees' 25 *Inlightned*** possessed of mental light

300 1–6 for the divine origins of the forms of time which imitate eternity and move in a circle, cp. Plato's *Timaeus* 37 8 *queintest* most ingenious, elegant, refined 9 *their* there

Neer him, his Lute, his fancy, and his flights,
Wits sour delights,
With gloves, and knots the silly snares of pleasure
Yet his dear Treasure
All scatter'd lay, while he his eys did pour
Upon a flowr.

2.

The darksome States-man hung with weights and woe
Like a thick midnight-fog mov'd there so slow
He did nor stay, nor go;
Condemning thoughts (like sad Ecclipses) scowl
Upon his soul,
And Clouds of crying witnesses without
Pursued him with one shout.
Yet dig'd the Mole, and lest his ways be found
Workt under ground,
Where he did Clutch his prey, but one did see
That policie,
Churches and altars fed him, Perjuries
Were gnats and flies,
It rain'd about him bloud and tears, but he
Drank them as free.

3.

The fearfull miser on a heap of rust
Sate pining all his life there, did scarce trust
His own hands with the dust,
Yet would not place one peece above, but lives
In feare of theeves.
Thousands there were as frantick as himself
And hug'd each one his pelf,
The down-right Epicure plac'd heav'n in sense
And scornd pretence

300 12 *knots* bows of ribbons 14 *pour* wept, cried; sent rays of light; pored, examined closely 16 *darksome* gloomy 25 *one* God 28 trivial matters, easily dealt with 34–5 cp. Matthew 6:20 'But lay up for yourselves treasures in heaven, where neither moth nor rust doth corrupt, and where thieves do not break through nor steal' 37 *hug'd* hugged

While others slipt into a wide Excesse
Said little lesse;
The weaker sort slight, triviall wares Inslave
Who think them brave,
And poor, despised truth sate Counting by
Their victory.

4.

Yet some, who all this while did weep and sing,
And sing, and weep, soar'd up into the *Ring*,
But most would use no wing.
O fools (said I,) thus to prefer dark night
Before true light,
To live in grots, and caves, and hate the day
Because it shews the way,
The way which from this dead and dark abode
Leads up to God,
A way where you might tread the Sun, and be
More bright than he.
But as I did their madnes so discusse
One whisper'd thus,
This Ring the Bride-groome did for none provide
But for his bride.

John Cap. 2. ver. 16, 17.

All that is in the world, the lust of the flesh, the lust of the Eys, and the pride of life, is not of the father, but is of the world.

And the world passeth away, and the lusts thereof, but he that doth the will of God abideth for ever.

300 43 *brave* handsome, fine   End quotation *John* John's first Epistle

301 Cock-crowing

Father of lights! what Sunnie seed,
What glance of day hast thou confin'd
Into this bird? To all the breed
This busie Ray thou hast assign'd;
Their magnetisme works all night,
And dreams of Paradise and light.

Their eyes watch for the morning-hue,
Their little grain expelling night
So shines and sings, as if it knew
The path unto the house of light.
It seems their candle, howe'r done,
Was tinn'd and lighted at the sunne.

If such a tincture, such a touch,
So firm a longing can impowre
Shall thy own image think it much
To watch for thy appearing hour?
If a meer blast so fill the sail,
Shall not the breath of God prevail?

O thou immortall light and heat!
Whose hand so shines through all this frame,
That by the beauty of the seat,
We plainly see, who made the same.
Seeing thy seed abides in me,
Dwell thou in it, and I in thee.

301 1 *Father of lights* cp. James 1:17 'Every good gift and every perfect gift is from above, and cometh down from the Father of lights, with whom is no variableness, neither shadow of turning' 2 *glance* flash, gleam 3 *bird* the cock 5 *magnetisme* the magnetic force which makes light attractive to the cock 11 *candle* instinctive faculty 12 *tinn'd* kindled 13 *tincture* in alchemy, a spiritual principle which can be infused into material substances, hence quintessence, spirit, soul; tinge, trace 14 *impowre* empower 15 *thy own image* Man, cp. Genesis 1:27 'So God created man in his own image' 17 *blast* puff of wind 18 cp. Genesis 2:7 'And the Lord God formed man of the dust of the ground, and breathed into his nostrils the breath of life; and man became a living soul'

To sleep without thee, is to die;
Yea, 'tis a death partakes of hell:
For where thou dost not close the eye
It never opens, I can tell.
In such a dark, Ægyptian border,
The shades of death dwell and disorder.

If joyes, and hopes, and earnest throws,
And hearts, whose Pulse beats still for light
Are given to birds; who, but thee, knows
A love-sick souls exalted flight?
Can souls be track'd by any eye
But his, who gave them wings to flie?

Onely this Veyle which thou hast broke,
And must be broken yet in me,
This veyle, I say, is all the cloke
And cloud which shadows thee from me.
This veyle thy full-ey'd love denies,
And onely gleams and fractions spies.

O take it off! make no delay,
But brush me with thy light, that I
May shine unto a perfect day,
And warme me at thy glorious Eye!
O take it off! or till it flee,
Though with no Lilie, stay with me!

302 The Water-fall

With what deep murmurs through times silent stealth
Doth thy transparent, cool and watry wealth
Here flowing fall,
And chide, and call,

301 29 *Ægyptian border* cp. Exodus 10:21 'And the Lord said unto Moses, Stretch out thine hand toward heaven, that there may be darkness over the land of Egypt, even darkness which may be felt' 37 *Veyle* the body 48 *Lilie* cp. Song of Solomon 2:16 'My beloved is mine, and I am his: he feedeth among the lilies'

As if his liquid, loose Retinue staid
Lingring, and were of this steep place afraid,
    The common pass
    Where, clear as glass,
    All must descend
    Not to an end:
But quickned by this deep and rocky grave,
Rise to a longer course more bright and brave.

    Dear stream! dear bank, where often I
    Have sate, and pleas'd my pensive eye,
    Why, since each drop of thy quick store
    Runs thither, whence it flow'd before
    Should poor souls fear a shade or night,
    Who came (sure) from a sea of light?
    Or since those drops are all sent back
    So sure to thee, that none doth lack,
    Why should frail flesh doubt any more
    That what God takes, hee'l not restore?

  O useful Element and clear!
  My sacred wash and cleanser here,
  My first consigner unto those
  Fountains of life, where the Lamb goes?
  What sublime truths, and wholesome themes,
  Lodge in thy mystical, deep streams!
  Such as dull man can never finde
  Unless that Spirit lead his minde,
  Which first upon thy face did move,
  And hatch'd all with his quickning love.
  As this loud brooks incessant fall
  In streaming rings restagnates all,
  Which reach by course the bank, and then
  Are no more seen, just so pass men.

302 11 *quickned* made to flow more quickly; restored to life 12 *brave* handsome, fine 16 water's cyclical movement from sea to clouds to rain to rivers to sea 24 *sacred wash* in baptism 30–2 cp. Genesis 1:2 'And the earth was without form, and void; and darkness was upon the face of the deep. And the spirit of God moved upon the face of the waters' 34 *restagnates** stagnates, becomes or remains stagnant; makes still as death will do 35 *by course* in due course; by flowing 36 *pass* die

O my invisible estate,
My glorious liberty, still late!
Thou art the Channel my soul seeks,
Not this with Cataracts and Creeks.

SIR WILLIAM DAVENANT

303 [*from* Gondibert Book 2]

84.

Praise, is devotion fit for mighty Mindes!
The diff'ring World's agreeing Sacrifice;
Where Heav'n divided Faiths united findes;
But Pray'r in various discord upward flies.

85.

For *Pray'r* the Ocean is, where diversly
Men steer their Course, each to a sev'ral Coast;
Where all our int'rests so discordant be,
That half beg windes by which the rest are lost.

86.

By *Penitence*, when we our selves forsake,
'Tis but in wise design on pitious Heav'n;
In Praise we nobly give, what God may take,
And are without a Beggers blush forgiv'n.

87.

Its utmost force, like Powder's is unknown!
And though weak Kings excess of Praise may fear,
Yet when tis here, like Powder, dang'rous grown,
Heav'n's Vault receives, what would the Palace tear.

302 38 *My ... liberty* cp. Romans 8:21 'Because the creature itself also shall be delivered from the bondage of corruption into the glorious liberty of the children of God'

303 6 *sev'ral* several, different, separate

Anna Trapnel

304 [*from* The Cry of a Stone]

O he is a rest that requires,
all his to draw him neer,
And they shal have ful sights of things
which in Creation are;
For he will shew that Sabbath and
first day he will bring out;
Unto his Saints, and he onely
shall draw the quintesence out
Of all things they shall draw the sap,
that runneth from the root,
And get up into the high tree,
where none shall go and pluck.
No, none shall be above to see
thine, when th'are in thy nest;
For they are closed in so round,
they lodge within that breast,
That none can scar, nor them afflict;
no musquet shot can come:
There is not any can draw their spears
or at all shoot their Canon.
Though nests in trees may shaken be,
yet thine shall e'r remaine;
They rest and nest in Jesus Christ,
his hand shall them sustain.

304 8 *quintesence* most essential part or feature

AN COLLINS

305 Another Song exciting to spirituall Mirth

The Winter being over
In order comes the Spring,
Which doth green Hearbs discover
And cause the Birds to sing;
The Night also expired,
Then comes the Morning bright,
Which is so much desired
By all that love the Light;
This may learn
Them that mourn
To put their Griefe to flight.
The Spring succeedeth Winter,
And Day must follow Night.

He therefore that sustaineth
Affliction or Distresse,
Which ev'ry member paineth,
And findeth no relesse;
Yet such therefore despaire not,
But on firm Hope depend
Whose Griefes immortall are not,
And therefore must have end;
They that faint
With complaint
Therefore are too blame,
They ad to their afflictions,
And amplify the same.

305 Title *exciting to* stirring up, inciting *Mirth* joy, happiness 16 *member* part of the body 17 *relesse* release

For if they could with patience
A while posesse the minde,
By inward Consolacions
They might refreshing finde,
To sweeten all their Crosses
That little time they 'dure;
So might they gain by losses,
And sharp would sweet procure;
But if the minde
Be inclinde
To Unquietnesse
That only may be called
The worst of all Distresse.

He that is melancolly
Detesting all Delight,
His Wits by sottish Folly
Are ruinated quite:
Sad Discontent and Murmors
To him are insident,
Were he posest of Honors,
He could not be content:
Sparks of joy
Fly away,
Floods of Cares arise,
And all delightfull Motions
In the conception dies.

But those that are contented
However things doe fall,
Much Anguish is prevented,
And they soon freed from all:
They finish all their Labours
With much felicity,
Theyr joy in Troubles savours
Of perfect Piety,

305 45 *insident* incidental

Chearfulnesse
Doth expresse
A setled pious minde
Which is not prone to grudging
From murmoring refinde.

Lascivious joy I prayse not,
Neither do it allow,
For where the same decayes not
No branch of peace can grow;
For why, it is sinister
As is excessive Griefe,
And doth the Heart sequester
From all good: to be briefe,
Vain Delight
Passeth quite
The bounds of modesty,
And makes one apt to nothing
But sensuality.

ANDREW MARVELL

306 The Coronet

When for the Thorns with which I long, too long,
   With many a piercing wound,
   My Saviours head have crown'd,
I seek with Garlands to redress that Wrong:
   Through every Garden, every Mead,
I gather flow'rs (my fruits are only flow'rs)
   Dismantling all the fragrant Towers
That once adorn'd my Shepherdesses head.

305 65 *murmoring* discontent, grumbling *refinde* freed, purified 70 *sinister* erring, wrong; unlucky, unfortunate 72 *sequester* seclude, keep apart 77 *apt* suited, fitted

306 7 *Towers* very high head-dresses

And now when I have summ'd up all my store,
    Thinking (so I my self deceive)
    So rich a Chaplet thence to weave
As never yet the king of Glory wore:
    Alas I find the Serpent old
    That, twining in his speckled breast,
    About the flow'rs disguis'd does fold,
    With wreaths of Fame and Interest.
Ah, foolish Man, that would'st debase with them,
And mortal Glory, Heavens Diadem!
But thou who only could'st the Serpent tame,
Either his slipp'ry knots at once untie,
And disintangle all his winding Snare:
Or shatter too with him my curious frame:
And let these wither, so that he may die,
Though set with Skill and chosen out with Care.
That they, while Thou on both their Spoils dost tread,
May crown thy Feet, that could not crown thy Head.

306 11 *Chaplet* wreath 14 *twining* writhing, winding *his . . . breast* cp. Edmund Spenser, *The Faerie Queene* 1.11.15 l. 2. 'Forelifting up aloft his speckled brest' 15 *fold* coil, wind 16 *wreaths* twisting, winding motions 22 *curious frame* elaborately wrought structure, the chaplet; cp. Sir Philip Sidney's *Astrophil and Stella* sonnet 28 l. 1 'You that with allegories curious frame . . .' 25 *Spoils* plunderings

And then, when I have [illegible] up all my [illegible],
[illegible]
[illegible]
A [illegible]
[illegible]
[illegible]
[illegible]
With sweets of flax and [illegible]
[illegible] with them
[illegible]
[illegible]
[illegible]
[illegible]
[illegible]
[illegible]
[illegible]
[illegible]

[illegible]

PART SIX

ELEGY AND EPITAPH

John Skelton

307 [*from* Phyllyp Sparowe]

Pla ce bo
Who is there who
Di le xi.
Dame Margery.
Fa re my my
Wherfore and why why
For the sowle of Philip sparowe
That was late slayn at carowe
Among the Nones blake
For that swete soules sake
And for all sparowes soules
Set in our bede rolles
Pater noster qui
With an Ave mari
And with the corner of a Crede
The more shalbe your mede.

Whan I remembre agayn
How mi philyp was slayn
Never halfe the payne
Was betwene you twayne
Pyramus and Thesbe
As than befell to me
I wept and I wayled
The tearys downe hayled
But nothynge it avayled
To call Phylyp agayne
Whom Gyb our cat hath slayne

307 1, 3 *Pla ce bo . . . Di le xi* the opening words of the antiphon and the Psalm of the Vespers for the Office of the Dead; the syllabic spacing may be meant to suggest plainsong 12 *bede rolles* lists of people to be prayed for 13 *Pater . . . qui* 'Our Father which' 14 *Ave mari* 'Hail Mary'

Gyb I saye our cat
Worrowyd her on that
Which I loved best
It can not be exprest
My sorowfull hevynesse
But all without redresse
For within that stounde
Halfe slumbrynge in a sounde
I fell downe to the grounde
Unneth I kest myne eyes
Towarde the cloudy skyes
But whan I dyd beholde
My sparow dead and colde
No creatuer but that wolde
Have rewed upon me
To behold and se
What hevynesse dyd me pange
Where with my handes I wrange
That my senaws cracked
As though I had ben racked
So payned and so strayned
That no lyfe well nye remayned
I syghed and I sobbed
For that I was robbed
Of my sparowes lyfe
O mayden, wydow, and wyfe
Of what estate ye be
Of hye or lowe degre
Great sorowe than ye myght se
And lerne to wepe at me
Such paynes dyd me frete
That myne hert dyd bete
My vysage pale and dead
Wanne, and blewe as lead
The panges of hatefull death
Well nye had stopped my breath

307 29 *Worrowyd* bit 34 *stounde* moment 35 *sounde* swoon, faint 37 *Unneth* scarcely, barely 42 *rewed* had pity

Heu heu me
That I am wo for the
Ad dominum cum tribularer clamavi
Of God nothynge els crave I

But phyllypes soule to kepe
From the marees depe
Of Acherontes well
That is a flode of hell
And from the great Pluto
The prynce of endles wo
And from foule Alecto
With vysage blacke and blo
And from Medusa that mare
That lyke a fende doth stare
And from Megeras edders
For rufflynge of phillips fethers
And from her fyry sparklynges
For burnynge of his wynges
And from the smokes sowre
Of Proserpinas bowre
And from the dennes darke
Wher Cerberus doth barke
Whom Theseus dyd afraye
Whom Hercules dyd outraye
As famous poetes say
From that hell hounde
That lyeth in cheynes bounde
With gastly hedes thre
To Jupyter pray we
That Phyllyp preserved may be
Amen say ye with me

307 64, 66 *Heu ... clamavi* 'Woe, woe is me ... In my distress, I cried unto the Lord', the opening of the second antiphon and Psalm of the Vespers 69 *marees* marsh 76 *mare* spectre, hag 87 *outraye* vanquish

Do mi nus.
Helpe nowe swete Jesus
Levavi oculos meos in montes
Wolde god I had zenophontes,

Or Socrates the wyse
To shew me their devyse
Moderatly to take
This sorow that I make
For Phyllip sparowes sake
So fervently I shake
I fele my body quake
So urgently I am brought
Into carefull thought
Like Andromach Hectors wyfe
Was wery of her lyfe
Whan she had lost her joye
Noble Hector of Troye
In lyke maner also
Encreaseth my dedly wo
For my sparowe is go
It was so prety a fole
It wold set on a stole
And lerned after my scole
For to kepe his cut
With Phyllyp kepe your cut
It had a velvet cap
And wold syt upon my lap
And seke after small wormes
And somtyme white bred crommes
And many tymes and ofte
Betwene my brestes softe
It wolde lye and rest
It was propre and prest

307 95, 97 *Do ... montes* 'Lord ... I lifted up my eyes to the hills'; the third antiphon and Psalm of the Vespers 98 *zenophontes* Xenophon 100 *devyse* advice 107 *carefull* sad, full of grief 118 *to kepe his cut* to know his place 127 *propre* pretty, handsome *prest* neat

Somtyme he wolde gaspe
Whan he sawe a waspe
A fly, or a gnat
He wolde flye at that
And prytely he wold pant
Whan he saw an ant
Lord how he wolde pry
After the butterfly
Lorde how he wolde hop
After the gressop
And whan I sayd, phyp, phyp
Than he wold lepe and skyp
And take me by the lyp
Alas it wyll me slo
That Phillyp is gone me fro
Si in i qui ta tes
Alas I was evyll at ease
De pro fun dis cla ma vi
Whan I sawe my sparowe dye

Nowe after my dome
Dame Sulpicia at Rome
Whose name regystred was
For ever in tables of bras
Because that she dyd pas
In poesy to endyte
And eloquently to wryte
Though she wolde pretende
My sparowe to commende
I trowe she coude not amende
Reportynge the vertues all
Of my sparowe royall
For it wold come and go
And fly so to and fro
And on me it wolde lepe
Whan I was aslepe

307 137 *gressop* grasshopper 141 *slo* slay 143, 145 *Si ... vi* 'If iniquities ... Out of the depths have I cried'; the fourth antiphon and Psalm of the Vespers 147 *dome* judgement 152 *endyte* write, compose 154 *pretende* attempt

And his fethers shake
Where with he wolde make
Me often for to wake
And for to take him in
Upon my naked skyn
God wot we thought no syn
What though he crept so lowe
It was no hurt I trowe
He dyd nothynge perde
But syt upon my kne
Phyllyp though he were nyse
In him it was no vyse
Phyllyp had leve to go
To pyke my lytell too
Phillip myght be bolde
And do what he wolde
Phillip wolde seke and take
All the flees blake
That he coulde there espye
With his wanton eye.

307 171 *perde* by God, truly, verily

Henry Howard, Earl of Surrey

308 [Norfolk sprang thee, Lambeth holds thee dead]

Norfolk sprang thee, Lambeth holds thee dead,
Clere of the County of Cleremont though hight.
Within the wombe of Ormondes race thou bread
And sawest thy cosin crowned in thy sight;
Shelton for love, Surrey for Lord thou chase,
Ay me, while life did last, that league was tender:
Tracing whose steps thou sawest Kelsall blaze,
Laundersey burnt, and battered Bullen render,
At Muttrell gates hopeles of all recure,
Thine Earle halfe dead gave in thy hand his will:
Which cause did thee this pining death procure,
Ere summers four times seaven, thou couldest fulfill.

Ah, Clere, if love had booted, care, or cost;
Heaven had not wonn, nor earth so timely lost.

309 [W. resteth here, that quick could never rest]

W. resteth here, that quick could never rest:
Whose heavenly giftes encreased by disdayn,
And vertue sank the deper in his brest.
Such profit he by envy could obtain.

308 1 *sprang* gave birth to 2 though called Clere, following a family tradition, after a Norman earldom 4 *cosin* Anne Boleyn, Henry VIII's second wife, was crowned in 1533 and executed in 1536 5 *Shelton* Clere married Mary Shelton *chase* chose 7–9 Kelsall in Scotland was burned by the English in 1542; Landrecy in France was besieged during 1543; Boulogne was captured by Surrey in 1544 after the fall of Montreuil 13 *booted* availed 14 *timely* early

309 1 *W.* Sir Thomas Wyatt *quick* alive, living

A hed, where wisdom misteries did frame:
Whose hammers bet styll in that lively brayn,
As on a stithe: where that some work of fame
Was dayly wrought, to turne to Britaines gayn.
A visage, stern, and myld: where bothe did grow,
Vice to contemne, in vertue to rejoyce:
Amid great stormes, whom grace assured so,
To lyve upright, and smile at fortunes choyce.
A hand, that taught, what might be sayd in ryme:
That reft Chaucer the glory of his wit:
A mark, the which (unparfited, for time)
Some may approche, but never none shall hit.
A toung, that served in forein realmes his king:
Whose courteous talke to vertue did enflame
Eche noble hart: a worthy guide to bring
Our English youth, by travail, unto fame.
An eye, whose judgement none affect could blinde,
Frendes to allure, and foes to reconcile:
Whose persing loke did represent a mynde
With vertue fraught, reposed, voyd of gyle.
A hart, where drede was never so imprest,
To hyde the thought, that might the trouth avance:
In neyther fortune loft, nor yet represt,
To swell in wealth, or yeld unto mischance.
A valiant corps, where force, and beawty met:
Happy, alas, to happy, but for foes:
Lived, and ran the race, that nature set:
Of manhodes shape, where she the molde did lose.
But to the heavens that simple soule is fled:
Which left with such, as covet Christ to know,
Witnesse of faith, that never shall be ded:
Sent for our helth, but not received so.
Thus, for our gilte, this jewel have we lost:
The earth his bones, the heavens possesse his gost.

309 5 *misteries* deep conceptions 7 *stithe* anvil 14 *reft* took away, deprived 15 *unparfited, for time* unfurnished for want of time 21 *affect** biased feeling, partiality 27 *loft* raised aloft, elevated 35–6 probably refer to Wyatt's translation of the seven penitential Psalms

NICHOLAS GRIMALD

310 [*from* A funerall song, upon the deceas of Annes his moother]

I, in your frutefull woomb conceyved, born was,
Whyle wanderyng moon ten moonths did overpasse.
Mee, brought to light, your tender arms sustaynd:
And, with my lips, your milky paps I straynd.
You mee embraced, in bosom soft you mee
Cherished, as I your onely chylde had bee.
Of yssue fayr with noombers were you blest:
Yet I, the bestbeloved of all the rest.
Good luck, certayn forereadyng moothers have,
And you of mee a speciall judgement gave.
Then, when firm pase I fixed on the ground:
When toung gan cease to break the lispyng sound:
You mee streightway did too the Muses send,
Ne suffered long a loyteryng lyfe to spend,
What gayn the wooll, what gayn the web had braught,
It was his meed, that me there dayly taught.
When with Minerve I had acquaintance woon:
And Phebus seemd to love mee, as his soon:
Brownshold I bad, at parents hest, farewell:
And gladly there in schools I gan to dwell:
Where Granta gives the ladies nyne such place,
That they rejoyse to see theyr blisfull case.
With joyes at hert, in this pernasse I bode,
Whyle, through his signes, five tymes great Titan glode:
And twyse as long, by that fayr foord, whereas
Swanfeeder Temms no furder course can passe.

310 4 *straynd* pressed, squeezed 9 *forereadyng** predestining, able to foresee the future 11 *pase* pace, foot 15 *web* woven fabric 16 *meed* reward 19 *Brownshold* probably Leighton-Bromswold in Huntingdonshire, where Grimald was born 21 *Granta* Cambridge *ladies nyne* Muses 23 *pernasse* Parnassus 24 *glode* glided 25 *foord* Oxford 26 *Swanfeeder**

O, what desire had you, therwhile, of mee?
Mid doutfull dreeds, what joyes were wont to bee?
Now linnen clothes, wrought with those fyngers fyne,
Now other thynges of yours dyd you make myne:
Tyll your last thredes gan Clotho to untwyne,
And of your dayes the date extreem assygne.
Hearyng the chaunce, your neybours made much mone:
A dearworth dame, they thought theyr coomfort gone.

Chidiock Tichborne

311 [My prime of youth is but a froste of cares]

My prime of youth is but a froste of cares:
My feaste of joy, is but a dishe of payne:
My cropp of corne, is but a field of tares:
And all my good is but vaine hope of gaine:
The daye is gone, and yet I sawe no sonn:
And nowe I live, and nowe my life is donn

The springe is paste, and yet it hath not sprong
The frute is deade, and yet the leaves are greene
My youth is gone, and yet I am but yonge
I sawe the woorld, and yet I was not seene
My threed is cutt, and yet it was not sponn
And nowe I lyve, and nowe my life is donn.

I saught my death, and founde it in my wombe
I lookte for life, and sawe it was a shade.
I trode the earth and knewe it was my Tombe
And nowe I die, and nowe I am but made
The glasse is full, and nowe the glass is rune
And nowe I live, and nowe my life is donn

310 34 *dearworth* dearly beloved

311 3 cp. the parable of the wheat and the tares, Matthew 13:24–30 17 *glasse* hourglass

WILLIAM SHAKESPEARE

312 [The Phoenix and Turtle]

Let the bird of lowdest lay,
On the sole *Arabian* tree,
Herauld sad and trumpet be:
To whose sound chaste wings obay.

But thou shriking harbinger,
Foule precurrer of the fiend,
Augour of the fevers end,
To this troupe come thou not neere.

From this Session interdict
Every foule of tyrant wing,
Save the Eagle feath'red King,
Keepe the obsequie so strict.

Let the Priest in Surples white,
That defunctive Musicke can,
Be the death-devining Swan,
Lest the *Requiem* lacke his right.

And thou treble dated Crow,
That thy sable gender mak'st,
With the breath thou giv'st and tak'st,
Mongst our mourners shalt thou go.

312 1 *bird* much disputed, but not certainly identified 2 *sole* unique 3 *trumpet* trumpeter 5 *shriking harbinger* screech-owl 6 *precurrer** forerunner 7 *Augour* augurer, prophet *fevers end* death 9 *interdict* exclude, forbid 12 *obsequie* funeral rite 13 *Surples* surplice 14 *defunctive** pertaining to death, funereal *can* knows, is skilful in 15 *death-devining* since it was thought swans sing before they die, they divine, know, when this will be 16 *his right* what is properly owing to him; his rite, liturgical ceremony (?) 17 *treble dated* living three times as long as man 18 *sable* black *gender* engendering, getting of children 19 crows, as well as living longer than men (l. 17), were traditionally thought to breed by their billing

Here the Antheme doth commence,
Love and Constancie is dead,
Phœnix and the *Turtle* fled,
In a mutuall flame from hence.

So they loved as love in twaine,
Had the essence but in one,
Two distincts, Division none,
Number there in love was slaine.

Hearts remote, yet not asunder;
Distance and no space was seene,
Twixt this *Turtle* and his Queene;
But in them it were a wonder.

So betweene them Love did shine,
That the *Turtle* saw his right,
Flaming in the *Phœnix* sight;
Either was the others mine.

Propertie was thus appalled,
That the selfe was not the same:
Single Natures double name,
Neither two nor one was called.

Reason in it selfe confounded,
Saw Division grow together,
To themselves yet either neither,
Simple were so well compounded,

That it cried, how true a twaine,
Seemeth this concordant one,
Love hath Reason, Reason none,
If what parts, can so remaine.

312 24 *mutuall* joint, common 26 *essence* life, existence 27 *distincts** separate things; merely verbal differences *Division* real difference 28 *Number* two become one and one is not a number (cp. no. 99 l. 255); the grammatical form expressing how many persons or things are spoken of 32 *But in them* except in their case 37 *Propertie* ownership, possession; essential quality 44 *Simple* unmixed, single 45 *it* Reason 46 *concordant* harmonious, unanimous 48 *parts* leaves; separates

Whereupon it made this *Threne*,
To the *Phœnix* and the *Dove*,
Co-supremes and starres of Love.
As *Chorus* to their Tragique Scene.

Threnos.

Beautie, Truth, and Raritie,
Grace in all simplicitie,
Here enclosde, in cinders lie.

Death is now the *Phœnix* nest,
And the *Turtles* loyall brest,
To eternitie doth rest.

Leaving no posteritie,
Twas not their infirmitie,
It was married Chastitie.

Truth may seeme, but cannot be,
Beautie bragge, but tis not she,
Truth and Beautie buried be.

To this urne let those repaire,
That are either true or faire,
For these dead Birds, sigh a prayer.

312 49 *Threne* threnos, funeral song, dirge 51 *Co-supremes** holders of joint supremacy 53 *Raritie* fineness of character 55 *Here* the urn of l. 65 60 *infirmitie* inability, impotence

JOHN DONNE

313 [*from* The Second Anniversarie]

OF THE PROGRES *of the Soule*

Nothing could make mee sooner to confesse — The entrance.
That this world had an everlastingnesse,
Then to consider, that a yeare is runne,
Since both this lower worlds, and the Sunnes Sunne,
The Lustre, and the vigor of this All,
Did set; 'twere Blasphemy, to say, did fall.
But as a ship which hath strooke saile, doth runne,
By force of that force which before, it wonne,
Or as sometimes in a beheaded man,
Though at those two Red seas, which freely ran,
One from the Trunke, another from the Head,
His soule be saild, to her eternall bed,
His eies will twinckle, and his tongue will roll,
As though he beckned, and cal'd backe his Soul,
He graspes his hands, and he puls up his feet,
And seemes to reach, and to step forth to meet
His soule; when all these motions which we saw,
Are but as Ice, which crackles at a thaw:
Or as a Lute, which in moist weather, rings
Her knell alone, by cracking of her strings:
So strugles this dead world, now shee is gone;
For there is motion in corruption.
As some Daies are, at the Creation nam'd,
Before the sunne, the which fram'd Daies, was
  fram'd,
So after this sunnes set, some show appeares,
And orderly vicisitude of yeares.

313 7 *strooke* lowered 24 *sunne* in Genesis 1:15 the sun was not named until the fourth day of creation

Yet a new Deluge, and of Lethe flood,
Hath drown'd us all, All have forgot all good,
Forgetting her, the maine Reserve of all,
Yet in this Deluge, grosse and generall,
Thou seest mee strive for life; my life shalbe,
To bee hereafter prais'd, for praysing thee,
Immortal Mayd, who though thou wouldst refuse
The name of Mother, be unto my Muse
A Father, since her chast Ambition is,
Yearely to bring forth such a child as this. . . .
But thinke that Death hath now enfranchis'd thee, Her liberty by death.
Thou hast thy'expansion now and libertee;
Thinke that a rusty Peece, discharg'd, is flowen
In peeces, and the bullet is his owne,
And freely flies: This to thy soule allow,
Thinke thy shell broke, thinke thy Soule hatch'd
 but now.
And thinke this slow-pac'd soule, which late did
 cleave
To'a body, and went but by the bodies leave,
Twenty, perchance, or thirty mile a day,
Dispatches in a minute all the way,
Twixt Heaven, and Earth: shee staies not in the
 Ayre,
To looke what Meteors there themselves prepare;
Shee carries no desire to know, nor sense,
Whether th'Ayrs middle Region be intense,
For th'Element of fire, shee doth not know,
Whether shee past by such a place or no;
Shee baits not at the Moone, nor cares to trie,
Whether in that new world, men live, and die.
Venus retards her not, to'enquire, how shee
Can, (being one Star) Hesper, and Vesper bee;
Hee that charm'd Argus eies, sweet Mercury,
Workes not on her, who now is growen all Ey;

313 29 *Reserve*** store 38 *expansion*** spreading out, unfolding 39 *Peece* firearm 40 *his owne* its own master 50 *intense* thick, dense 53 *baits* pauses, rests 58 *who* . . . *Ey* freed from the body, the soul perceives directly

Who, if shee meete the body of the Sunne,
Goes through, not staying till his course be runne;
Who finds in Mars his Campe, no corps of Guard;
Nor is by Jove, nor by his father bard;
But ere shee can consider how shee went,
At once is at, and through the Firmament.
And as these stars were but so many beades
Strunge on one string, speed undistinguish'd leades
Her through those spheares, as through the beades, a string,
Whose quicke succession makes it still one thing:
As doth the Pith, which, least our Bodies slacke,
Strings fast the little bones of necke, and backe;
So by the soule doth death string Heaven and Earth,
For when our soule enjoyes this her third birth,
(Creation gave her one, a second, grace,)
Heaven is as neare, and present to her face,
As colours are, and objects, in a roome
Where darknesse was before, when Tapers come.
This must, my soule, thy long-short Progresse bee;
To'advance these thoughts, remember then, that shee
Shee, whose faire body no such prison was,
But that a soule might well be pleas'd to passe
An Age in her; shee whose rich beauty lent
Mintage to others beauties, for they went
But for so much, as they were like to her;
Shee, in whose body (if wee dare prefer
This low world, to so high a mark, as shee,)
The Westerne treasure, Esterne spiceree,
Europe, and Afrique, and the unknowen rest
Were easily found, or what in them was best;
And when w'have made this large Discoveree,
Of all in her some one part then will bee

313 62 *father* Saturn 66 *undistinguish'd* too fast to be distinguished 69 *Pith* spinal cord 72 *third birth* death 77 *long-short Progresse* covering a long distance in a short time 82 *Mintage* coining (see no. 136 l. 4) 84 *prefer* raise to compare 90 *in . . . part* in any single part of her

Twenty such parts, whose plenty and riches is
Inough to make twenty such worlds as this;
Shee, whom had they knowne, who did first
    betroth
The Tutelar Angels, and assigned one, both
To Nations, Cities, and to Companies,
To Functions, Offices, and Dignities,
And to each severall man, to him, and him,
They would have given her one for every limme;
Shee, of whose soule, if we may say, 'twas Gold,
Her body was th'Electrum, and did hold
Many degrees of that; (we understood
Her by her sight, her pure and eloquent blood
Spoke in her cheekes, and so distinckly wrought,
That one might almost say, her bodie thought,)
Shee, shee, thus richly, and largely hous'd, is gone:
And chides us slow-pac'd snailes, who crawle upon
Our prisons prison, earth, nor thinke us well
Longer, then whil'st we beare our brittle shell.

BEN JONSON

314 ON MY FIRST SONNE

Farewell, thou child of my right hand, and joy;
  My sinne was too much hope of thee, lov'd boy,
Seven yeeres tho'wert lent to me, and I thee pay,
  Exacted by thy fate, on the just day.

313 94 *Tutelar* tutelary, guardian 100 *Electrum* an alloy of gold and silver, approaching perfection 102 *sight* appearance 105 *largely* at large, freely 107 *prisons prison* the soul imprisoned within the prison of the body

314 1 *right hand* Benjamin in Hebrew means 'fortunate' or 'dextrous' ('dexter' in Latin meaning 'right', or 'on the right-hand side')

O, could I loose all father, now. For why
   Will man lament the state he should envie?
To have so soone scap'd worlds, and fleshes rage,
   And, if no other miserie, yet age?
Rest in soft peace, and, ask'd, say here doth lye
   BEN. JONSON his best piece of *poetrie*.
For whose sake, hence-forth, all his vowes be such,
   As what he loves may never like too much.

315 To the immortall memorie, and friendship of that noble paire, Sir LUCIUS CARY, and Sir H. MORISON

The Turne.

Brave Infant of *Saguntum*, cleare
Thy comming forth in that great yeare,
When the Prodigious *Hannibal* did crowne
His rage, with razing your immortall Towne.
Thou, looking then about,
E're thou wert halfe got out,
Wise child, did'st hastily returne,
And mad'st thy Mothers wombe thine urne.
How summ'd a circle didst thou leave man-kind
Of deepest lore, could we the Center find!

The Counter-turne.

Did wiser Nature draw thee back,
From out the horrour of that sack?
Where shame, faith, honour, and regard of right
Lay trampled on; the deeds of death, and night,

314 10 *poetrie* since poets are makers, they make poetry and as men they make children 12 cp. Martial, *Epigrams* 6.29.8 'whatever you love, pray that you do not find it too pleasing'

315 *Turne, Counter-turne*, Stand** see the textual note 1–9 in Pliny, *Natural History* 7.3.39 'there is the case of a child of Saguntum who returned immediately to the womb, in the year in which Hannibal destroyed the city' 2 *yeare* 219 BC, when Hannibal began the second Punic War 3 *Prodigious* marvellous, amazing 9 *summ'd* collected into one sum *circle* figure, emblem of perfection

Urg'd, hurried forth, and horld
Upon th'affrighted world:
Sword, fire, and famine, with fell fury met;
And all on utmost ruine set;
As, could they but lifes miseries fore-see,
No doubt all Infants would returne like thee.

The Stand.

For, what is life, if measur'd by the space,
Not by the act?
Or masked man, if valu'd by his face,
Above his fact?
Here's one out-liv'd his Peeres,
And told forth fourescore yeares;
He vexed time, and busied the whole State;
Troubled both foes, and friends;
But ever to no ends:
What did this Stirrer, but die late?
How well at twentie had he falne, or stood!
For three of his foure-score, he did no good.

The Turne.

Hee entred well, by vertuous parts,
Got up and thriv'd with honest arts:
He purchas'd friends, and fame, and honours then,
And had his noble name advanc'd with men:
But weary of that flight,
Hee stoop'd in all mens sight
To sordid flatteries, acts of strife,
And sunke in that dead sea of life
So deep, as he did then death's waters sup;
But that the Corke of Title boy'd him up.

315 15 *horld* hurled 17 *fell* deadly 21–2 cp. Seneca, *Epistles* 93.4 'Let us measure acts not by their length but by their quality' 24 *fact* deeds 25–30 cp. Seneca, *Epistles* 93.2–3 'A life is really long if it is full ... What does the older man gain from his eighty years spent in idleness? A person like him has not lived; he has just loafed his life away. Nor has he died late; he has merely been dying for a long time' 30 *Stirrer* agitator 38 *stoop'd*** degraded himself morally

The Counter-turne.

Alas, but *Morison* fell young:
Hee never fell, thou fall'st, my tongue.
Hee stood, a Souldier to the last right end,
A perfect Patriot, and a noble friend,
But most, a vertuous Sonne.
All Offices were done
By him, so ample, full, and round,
In weight, in measure, number, sound,
As though his age imperfect might appeare,
His life was of Humanitie the Spheare.

The Stand.

Goe now, and tell out dayes summ'd up with feares,
And make them yeares;
Produce thy masse of miseries on the Stage,
To swell thine age;
Repeat of things a throng,
To shew thou hast beene long,
Not liv'd; for life doth her great actions spell,
By what was done and wrought
In season, and so brought
To light: her measures are, how well
Each syllab'e answer'd, and was form'd, how faire;
These make the lines of life, and that's her ayre.

315 43–52 cp. Seneca, *Epistles* 93.4 'Your other friend, however, died in his manhood's prime. But he had accomplished all the duties of a good citizen, a good friend, a good son. In no sense has he failed. His age may have been incomplete, but his life was complete' 44 *fell* fell morally *fall'st* fall short, fail 49 *round* complete 58–9 cp. Seneca, *Epistles* 93.4 'The other has lived eighty years. He has rather existed for eighty, unless, perhaps, by "he has lived" you mean what we mean when we talk of a tree living' 59 *spell* discover, reveal 62 *measures* criteria; with a reference to poetic and musical proportion or rhythm, cp. no. 345 title and no. 354 l. 5 64 *lines* lineaments, features; threads *ayre* manner; melody, tune

The Turne.

It is not growing like a tree
In bulke, doth make man better bee;
Or standing long an Oake, three hundred yeare,
To fall a logge at last, dry, bald, and seare:
A Lillie of a Day,
Is fairer farre, in May,
Although it fall, and die that night;
It was the Plant, and flowre of light.
In small proportions, we just beauties see:
And in short measures, life may perfect bee.

The Counter-turne.

Call, noble *Lucius,* then for Wine,
And let thy lookes with gladnesse shine:
Accept this garland, plant it on thy head,
And thinke, nay know, thy *Morison*'s not dead.
Hee leap'd the present age,
Possest with holy rage,
To see that bright eternall Day:
Of which we *Priests*, and *Poëts* say
Such truths, as we expect for happy men,
And there he lives with memorie; and *Ben.*

The Stand.

Johnson, who sung this of him, e're he went
Himselfe to rest,
Or taste a part of that full joy he meant
To have exprest,
In this bright *Asterisme:*
Where it were friendships schisme,

315 73–4 cp. Seneca, *Epistles* 93.7 'Just as a person of small stature can be a perfect figure of a man, so a short life can be a perfect one' 77 *garland* poem 89 *Asterisme* constellation

(Were not his *Lucius* Long with us to tarry)
To separate these twi-
Lights, the *Dioscuri*;
And keepe the one halfe from his *Harry*.
But fate doth so alternate the designe,
Whilst that in heav'n, this light on earth must shine.

The Turne.

And shine as you exalted are;
Two names of friendship, but one Starre:
Of hearts the union. And those not by chance
Made, or indentur'd, or leas'd out to'advance
The profits for a time.
No pleasures vaine did chime,
Of rimes, or ryots, at your feasts,
Orgies of drinke, or fain'd protests:
But simple love of greatnesse, and of good;
That knits brave minds, and manners, more then blood.

The Counter-turne.

This made you first to know the Why
You lik'd, then after, to apply
That liking; and approach so one the tother,
Till either grew a portion of the other:
Each stiled, by his end,
The Copie of his friend.
You liv'd to be the great surnames,
And titles, by which all made claimes
Unto the Vertue. Nothing perfect done,
But as a CARY, or a MORISON.

315 93 *Dioscuri* twin lights, Castor and Pollux 95 *alternate* change, reverse 97–8 cp. Persius, *Satires* 5.45–6 'I would not want you to doubt this, that there is a firm bond uniting our lives, and that both come from one star' 111 *stiled* named, called

The Stand.

And such a force the faire example had,
As they that saw
The good, and durst not practise it, were glad
That such a Law
Was left yet to Man-kind;
Where they might read, and find
Friendship, in deed, was written, not in words:
And with the heart, not pen,
Of two so early men,
Whose lines her rowles were, and records.
Who, e're the first downe bloomed on the chin,
Had sow'd these fruits, and got the harvest in.

SIR WALTER RALEGH

316 [Even suche is tyme that takes in trust]

Even suche is tyme that takes in trust
our youth, our joies and what we have
And paies us but with earth, and dust
which in the Darke and silent grave
when we have wandred all our waies
shutts up the storie of our daies:
  But from this earth, this grave this dust
  The Lord will raise me up I trust.

315 125 *early*** youthful, near the beginning of their lives 126 *rowles* rolls

WILLIAM BROWNE

317 On the Countesse *Dowager* of *Pembrooke*

Underneth this Marble Hearse;
Lyes the subject of all verse,
Sidneys sister; *Pembrookes* mother,
Death, ere thou hast kill'd another,
Faire, and learn'd, and good as shee,
Time shall throw a dart at thee.

Marble Pyles let no man rayse
To her name; for after dayes;
Some kinde woman borne as she
Reading this; (Like Niobe,)
Shall turne Marble, and become
Both her mourner and her Tombe.

HENRY KING

318 An Exequy To his matchlesse never to be forgotten Freind

Accept thou Shrine of my Dead Saint,
Instead of Dirges this Complaint,
And for sweet flowres to crowne thy Hearse
Receive a strew of weeping verse
From thy griev'd Friend; whome Thou mightst see
Quite melted into Teares for Thee
  Deare Losse, since thy untimely fate
My task hath beene to meditate

318 Title *Exequy* funeral ceremony, rites 2 *Dirges* mourning songs, lamentations *Complaint* plaintive poem 4 *strew* scattering

On Thee, on Thee: Thou art the Book
The Library whereon I look
Though almost blind. For Thee (Lov'd Clay)
I Languish out, not Live the Day,
Using no other Exercise
But what I practise with mine Eyes.
By which wett glasses I find out
How lazily Time creepes about
To one that mournes: This, only This
My Exercise and bus'nes is:
So I compute the weary howres
With Sighes dissolved into Showres.
  Nor wonder if my time goe thus
Backward and most præposterous;
Thou hast Benighted mee. Thy Sett
This Eve of blacknes did begett
Who wast my Day (though overcast
Before thou hadst thy Noon-tide past)
And I remember must in teares,
Thou scarce hadst seene so many Yeeres
As Day tells Howres; By thy cleere Sunne
My Love and Fortune first did run;
But Thou wilt never more appeare
Folded within my Hemispheare:
Since both thy Light and Motion
Like a fledd Starr is fall'n and gone,
And 'twixt mee and my Soules deare wish
The Earth now interposed is,
Which such a straunge Ecclipse doth make
As ne're was read in Almanake.
  I could allow Thee for a time
To darken mee and my sad Clime,
Were it a Month, a Yeere, or Ten,
I would thy Exile live till then;
And all that space my mirth adjourne
So Thou wouldst promise to returne,

318 22 *præposterous* in reversed order; monstrous, perverse, foolish 23 *Sett* setting 29 *tells* counts, measures 40 *Clime* climate, part of the earth

And putting off thy ashy Shrowd
At length disperse this Sorrowes Cloud.
But woe is mee! the longest date
To narrowe is to calculate
These empty hopes. Never shall I
Be so much blest as to descry
A glympse of Thee, till that Day come
Which shall the Earth to cinders doome,
And a fierce Feaver must calcine
The Body of this World like Thine,
(My Little World!) That fitt of Fire
Once off, our Bodyes shall aspire
To our Soules blisse: Then wee shall rise,
And view our selves with cleerer eyes
In that calme Region, where no Night
Can hide us from each others sight.
Meane time, thou hast Hir Earth: Much good
May my harme doe thee. Since it stood
With Heavens will I might not call
Hir longer Mine; I give thee all
My short liv'd right and Interest
In Hir, whome living I lov'd best.
With a most free and bounteous grief,
I give thee what I could not keep.
Be kind to Hir: and prethee look
Thou write into thy Doomsday book
Each parcell of this Rarity
Which in thy Caskett shrin'd doth ly:
See that thou make thy reck'ning streight,
And yeeld Hir back againe by weight.
For thou must Auditt on thy trust
Each Grane and Atome of this Dust,
As thou wilt answere Him that leant,
Not gave thee, my deare Monument.
So close the ground, and 'bout hir shade
Black Curtaines draw, My Bride is lay'd.

318 47 *longest* most distant 48 *narrowe* short, brief 53 *calcine* reduce, refine, by fire

Sleep on my Love in thy cold bed
Never to be disquieted.
My last Good-night! Thou wilt not wake
Till I Thy Fate shall overtake:
Till age, or grief, or sicknes must
Marry my Body to that Dust
It so much loves; and fill the roome
My heart keepes empty in Thy Tomb.
Stay for mee there: I will not faile
To meet Thee in that hollow Vale.
And think not much of my delay,
I am already on the way,
And follow Thee with all the speed
Desire can make, or Sorrowes breed.
Each Minute is a short Degree,
And e'ry Howre a stepp towards Thee.
At Night when I betake to rest,
Next Morne I rise neerer my West
Of Life, almost by eight Howres sayle,
Then when Sleep breath'd his drowsy gale.
Thus from the Sunne my Bottome steares,
And my Dayes Compasse downward beares.
Nor labour I to stemme the Tide
Through which to Thee I swiftly glide.
Tis true with shame and grief I yeild,
Thou like the Vann first took'st the Field,
And gotten hast the Victory
In thus adventuring to Dy
Before Mee; whose more yeeres might crave
A just præcedence in the Grave.
But hark! My Pulse like a soft Drum
Beates my Approach; Tells Thee I come;
And slowe howe're my Marches bee,
I shall at last sitt downe by Thee.
The thought of this bids mee goe on
And wait my dissolution

318 82 *disquieted* disturbed, deprived of peace, rest 97 *betake* go 101 *Bottome* ship, boat 102 *Compasse* extent, limit

With Hope and Comfort. Deare (forgive
The Crime) I am content to live
Divided, with but half a Heart,
Till wee shall Meet, and Never part.

George Herbert

319 [*from* Memoriae Matris Sacrum]

Ah Mater, quo te deplorem fonte? Dolores
  Quæ guttæ poterunt enumerare meos?
Sicca meis lacrymis Thamesis vicina videtur
  Virtutumque choro siccior ipse tuo.
In Flumen mærore nigrum si funderer ardens,
  Laudibus haud fierem sepia iusta tuis.
Tantùm istæc scribo gratus, ne tu mihi tantùm
  Mater: et ista Dolor nunc tibi Metra parit.

319 Sacred to the Memory of his Mother

Ah, mother, with what fountain may I weep for you? What drops could enumerate my sorrows? The Thames seems dry in comparison with my tears, and I myself seem even drier in comparison to the chorus of your virtues. If I were poured out burning into a river black with my grief, I would still not become ink that could do justice to your praises. In such gratitude I write these things, as indeed you were so much of a mother to me: and for you it is that my pain now gives birth to these poems.

Thomas Carew

320 Epitaph on the Lady *Mary Villers*

The Lady *Mary Villers* lyes
Under this stone; with weeping eyes
The Parents that first gave her birth,
And their sad Friends, lay'd her in earth:

If any of them (Reader) were
Knowne unto thee, shed a teare,
Or if thyselfe possesse a gemme,
As deare to thee, as this to them;
Though a stranger to this place,
Bewayle in theirs, thine owne hard case;
For thou perhaps at thy returne
Mayest find thy Darling in an Urne.

SIR HENRY WOTTON

321 Upon the death of Sir *Albert Morton's* Wife

He first deceas'd: She for a little tri'd
To live without Him: lik'd it not, and di'd.

ROBERT HERRICK

322 To the reverend shade of his religious Father

That for seven *Lusters* I did never come
To doe the *Rites* to thy Religious Tombe:
That neither haire was cut, or true teares shed
By me, o'r thee, *(as justments to the dead)*
Forgive, forgive me; since I did not know
Whether thy bones had here their Rest, or no.
But now 'tis known, Behold; behold, I bring
Unto thy Ghost, th'Effused Offering:

322 1 *Lusters* periods of five years 4 *justments** funeral rites 8 *Effused* poured out, shed

And look, what Smallage, Night-shade, Cypresse, Yew,
Unto the shades have been, or now are due,
Here I devote; And something more then so;
I come to pay a Debt of Birth I owe.
Thou gav'st me life, (but Mortall;) For that one
Favour, Ile make full satisfaction;
For my life mortall, Rise from out thy Herse,
And take a life immortall from my Verse.

323 Upon himselfe being buried

Let me sleep this night away,
Till the Dawning of the day:
Then at th' opening of mine eyes,
I, and all the world shall rise.

324 Upon a child

Here a pretty Baby lies
Sung asleep with Lullabies:
Pray be silent, and not stirre
Th'easie earth that covers her.

322 9 *Smallage* wild celery or water parsley

324 4 *easie* conducive to ease; insignificant; loose

JOHN MILTON

325 *Lycidas.*

In this Monody the Author bewails a learned Friend, unfortunatly drown'd in his Passage from *Chester* on the *Irish* Seas, 1637. And by occasion foretels the ruine of our corrupted Clergy then in their height.

Yet once more, O ye Laurels, and once more
Ye Myrtles brown, with Ivy never-sear,
I com to pluck your Berries harsh and crude,
And with forc'd fingers rude,
Shatter your leaves before the mellowing year.
Bitter constraint, and sad occasion dear,
Compels me to disturb your season due:
For *Lycidas* is dead, dead ere his prime
Young *Lycidas*, and hath not left his peer:
Who would not sing for *Lycidas?* he knew
Himself to sing, and build the lofty rhyme.
He must not flote upon his watry bear
Unwept, and welter to the parching wind,
Without the meed of som melodious tear.

325 Title *Lycidas* the name occurs in both Greek and Roman pastoral poetry *Monody** poem lamenting someone's death *learned Friend* Edward King 1 *Yet once more* cp. Hebrews 12:26–7 'Yet once more I shake not the earth only, but also heaven. And this word, Yet once more, signifieth the removing of those things that are shaken, as of things that are made, that those things which cannot be shaken may remain' 1–2 *Laurels . . . Myrtles . . . Ivy* evergreen leaves traditionally associated with poetic fame 2 *never-sear** never dry, never withered; evergreen 3 *crude* unripe, sour 4 *rude* unskilled, inexperienced 5 *mellowing** ripening, maturing 6 *dear* dire, hard, grievous 10 *Who . . . Lycidas?* cp. Virgil, *Eclogues* 10.3 'neget quis carmina Gallo?' ('who could refuse Gallo a little song?') 12 *bear* bier 13 *welter* be tossed, tumbled, rolled about *parching* scorching 14 *meed* reward, recompense *tear* elegiac verses were often collected under the title of *Lacrymae Musarum* ('The tears of the Muses')

Begin then, Sisters of the sacred well,
That from beneath the seat of *Jove* doth spring,
Begin, and somwhat loudly sweep the string.
Hence with denial vain, and coy excuse,
So may som gentle Muse
With lucky words favour my destin'd Urn,
And as he passes turn,
And bid fair peace be to my sable shrowd.
For we were nurst upon the self-same hill,
Fed the same flock, by fountain, shade, and rill.
Together both, ere the high Lawns appear'd
Under the opening eye-lids of the morn,
We drove a field, and both together heard
What time the Gray-fly winds her sultry horn,
Batt'ning our flocks with the fresh dews of night,
Oft till the Star that rose, at Ev'ning, bright
Toward Heav'ns descent had slop'd his westering wheel.
Mean while the Rural ditties were not mute,
Temper'd to th'Oaten Flute,
Rough *Satyrs* danc'd, and *Fauns* with clov'n heel,
From the glad sound would not be absent long,
And old *Damœtas* lov'd to hear our song.
But O the heavy change, now thou art gon,
Now thou art gon, and never must return!
Thee Shepherd, thee the Woods, and desert Caves,
With wilde Thyme and the gadding Vine o'regrown,
And all their echoes mourn.
The Willows, and the Hazle Copses green,
Shall now no more be seen,
Fanning their joyous Leaves to thy soft layes.
As killing as the Canker to the Rose,
Or Taint-worm to the weanling Herds that graze,

325 15 *Sisters* the Muses *well* Aganippe 19 *Muse* poet 22 *sable shrowd** black winding-sheet for corpses 24 *rill* brook, small stream 25 *Lawns* glades, open spaces between woods 27 *drove a field* drove animals to the fields 28 *Gray-fly** dung-beetle *winds* sounds 29 *Batt'ning* feeding, fattening 30 *Star* Hesperus 31 *westering** declining to the west 36 *Damœtas* a traditional name for a shepherd; no particular individual need be intended 40 *gadding* wandering, straggling 45 *Canker* canker-worm 46 *Taint-worm* worm that infects cattle *weanling** recently weaned

Or Frost to Flowers, that their gay wardrop wear,
When first the White thorn blows;
Such, *Lycidas,* thy loss to Shepherds ear.
Where were ye Nymphs when the remorseless deep
Clos'd o're the head of your lov'd *Lycidas?*
For neither were ye playing on the steep,
Where your old *Bards*, the famous *Druids* ly,
Nor on the shaggy top of *Mona* high,
Nor yet where *Deva* spreads her wisard stream:
Ay me, I fondly dream!
Had ye bin there—for what could that have don?
What could the Muse her self that *Orpheus* bore,
The Muse her self, for her inchanting son
Whom Universal nature did lament,
When by the rout that made the hideous roar,
His goary visage down the stream was sent,
Down the swift *Hebrus* to the *Lesbian* shore.
Alas! What boots it with uncessant care
To tend the homely slighted Shepherds trade,
And strictly meditate the thankles Muse,
Were it not better don as others use,
To sport with *Amaryllis* in the shade,
Or with the tangles of *Neæra*'s hair?

325 47 *wardrop* wardrobe 48 *White thorn* hawthorn 50–5 cp. Theocritus, *Idylls* 1.66–9 and Virgil, *Eclogues* 10.9–12 'Where were you, gentle Naiads, in what high woods or in what glades, while Gallus lay dying of unrequited love? Nothing detained you on Parnassus; nothing on any ridge of Pindus; and nothing at Aonian Aganippe's spring' 52 *steep* slope of a mountain 54 *shaggy* covered with rough, tangled growth *Mona* the island of Anglesey 55 *Deva* the river Dee; the rise and fall of its flow were supposed to presage good or ill fortune for England and Wales *wisard** magic, enchanted 56 *fondly* foolishly 58–63 for Milton's revisions to this passage, see the textual note on the poem 58 *Muse* Calliope 59 *inchanting* that enchants, lays under a spell 64 *boots* profits, avails 66 *meditate . . . Muse** occupy oneself in poetry, song, cp. Virgil, *Eclogues* 1.2 'musam meditaris' 67 cp. Virgil, *Eclogues* 2.14–15 'Would it not have been better to put up with the sulky moods of Amaryllis and the airs she gives herself?' *use* are wont to do 68 cp. Virgil, *Eclogues* 1.4–5 'and you lie sprawling in the shade, teaching the woods to echo back the charms of Amaryllis' 69 *with* withe, twist, wind, bind (?) *Neæra's* in classical and Renaissance literature, hair is frequently mentioned in connection with Neaera

Fame is the spur that the clear spirit doth raise
(That last infirmity of Noble mind)
To scorn delights, and live laborious dayes;
But the fair Guerdon when we hope to find,
And think to burst out into sudden blaze,
Comes the blind *Fury* with th'abhorred shears,
And slits the thin-spun life. But not the praise,
Phœbus repli'd, and touch'd my trembling ears;
Fame is no plant that grows on mortal soil,
Nor in the glistering foil
Set off to th'world, nor in broad rumour lies,
But lives and spreds aloft by those pure eyes,
And perfet witnes of all-judging *Jove*;
As he pronounces lastly on each deed,
Of so much fame in Heav'n expect thy meed.
   O Fountain *Arethuse*, and thou honour'd floud,
Smooth-sliding *Mincius*, crown'd with vocall reeds,
That strain I heard was of a higher mood:
But now my Oate proceeds,
And listens to the Herald of the Sea
That came in *Neptune*'s plea,
He ask'd the Waves, and ask'd the Fellon winds,
What hard mishap hath doom'd this gentle swain?
And question'd every gust of rugged wings
That blows from off each beaked Promontory;
They knew not of his story,
And sage *Hippotades* their answer brings,
That not a blast was from his dungeon stray'd,
The Ayr was calm, and on the level brine,
Sleek *Panope* with all her sisters play'd.
It was that fatall and perfidious Bark
Built in th'eclipse, and rigg'd with curses dark,
That sunk so low that sacred head of thine.

325 71 cp. Tacitus, *Histories* 4.6 'Even with wise men, the desire for glory is the last thing to be abandoned' 73 *Guerdon* reward 75 *Fury* Atropos 76 *thin-spun** 77 cp. Virgil, *Eclogues* 6.3–4 'Apollo plucked my ear and gave me his advice' 79 *foil* gold or silver leaf used to show off a jewel more brilliantly 84 *meed* reward, deserving 88 *Oate** pipe made of oaten straw 89 *Herald* Triton 90 *plea* apology, excuse 91 *Fellon* savage, wild, murderous 96 *Hippotades* Aeolus 101 *in th'eclipse* at an ill-omened time

Next *Camus*, reverend Sire, went footing slow,
His Mantle hairy, and his Bonnet sedge,
Inwrought with figures dim, and on the edge
Like to that sanguine flower inscrib'd with woe.
Ah! Who hath reft (quoth he) my dearest pledge?
Last came, and last did go,
The Pilot of the *Galilean* lake,
Two massy Keyes he bore of metals twain,
(The Golden opes, the Iron shuts amain)
He shook his Miter'd locks, and stern bespake,
How well could I have spar'd for thee young swain,
Anow of such as for their bellies sake,
Creep and intrude, and climb into the fold?
Of other care they little reck'ning make,
Then how to scramble at the shearers feast,
And shove away the worthy bidden guest;
Blind mouthes! that scarce themselves know how to hold
A Sheep-hook, or have learn'd ought els the least
That to the faithfull Herdmans art belongs!
What recks it them? What need they? They are sped;
And when they list, their lean and flashy songs
Grate on their scrannel Pipes of wretched straw,
The hungry Sheep look up, and are not fed,
But swoln with wind, and the rank mist they draw,
Rot inwardly, and foul contagion spread:

325 103 *Camus* the river Cam in Cambridge 105 *Inwrought** decorated 106 *flower* Hyacinth 107 *pledge* child as a token of married love 109 *Pilot* St Peter, the Galilean fisherman 110 cp. Matthew 16:19 'And I will give unto thee [Peter] the keys of the kingdom of heaven' *massy* massive, heavy 111 *amain* suddenly, with force 112 *Miter'd* wearing a mitre; traditionally, St Peter was the Church's first bishop 114 *Anow* enough 115 cp. John 10:1 'He that entereth not by the door into the sheepfold, but climbeth up some other way, the same is a thief and a robber' 118 *worthy ... guest* cp. Matthew 22:8 'The wedding is ready, but they which were bidden were not worthy' 119 *Blind* lacking spiritual light 122 *What ... them* what do they care about it? *sped* prospering, doing well 123 *list* please, choose *lean* poor, meagre *flashy* trashy, meaningless 124 *scrannel** harsh, unmelodious; thin, weak; cp. Virgil, *Eclogues* 3.27 'All you were good for was to stand at the crossroads and scrape a miserable tune out of one squeaking straw' 126 *rank* corrupt, stinking, foul *draw* inhale, breathe in

Besides what the grim Woolf with privy paw
Daily devours apace, and nothing sed,
But that two-handed engine at the door,
Stands ready to smite once, and smite no more.
  Return *Alpheus*, the dread voice is past,
That shrunk thy streams; Return *Sicilian* Muse,
And call the Vales, and bid them hither cast
Their Bels, and Flourets of a thousand hues.
Ye valleys low where the milde whispers use,
Of shades and wanton winds, and gushing brooks,
On whose fresh lap the swart Star sparely looks,
Throw hither all your quaint enameld eyes,
That on the green terf suck the honied showres,
And purple all the ground with vernal flowres.
Bring the rathe Primrose that forsaken dies,
The tufted Crow-toe, and pale Gessamine,
The white Pink, and the Pansie freakt with jeat,
The glowing Violet,
The Musk-rose, and the well attir'd Woodbine,
With Cowslips wan that hang the pensive hed,
And every flower that sad embroidery wears:
Bid *Amaranthus* all his beauty shed,
And Daffadillies fill their cups with tears,
To strew the Laureat Herse where *Lycid* lies.

325 128 *Woolf* the Roman Catholic Church, especially in its attempts to convert English Protestants 130–1 the exact meaning and significance of this 'engine' of God's justice are uncertain, but it is an emblem of apocalyptic justice; cp. Revelation 3:20 'Behold, I stand at the door, and knock', 1:16 'and out of his mouth went a sharp two-edged sword' and 19:15 'And out of his mouth goeth a sharp sword, that with it he should smite the nations' 130 *two-handed* wielded with two hands (cp. no. 356 l. 15) 133 *Sicilian Muse* Theocritus 135 *Bels* flowers with bell-shaped heads *Flourets* flowerets, little flowers 136 *use* frequent, haunt 138 *swart** producing swarthiness, darkness *Star* Sirius *sparely* sparingly, rarely 139 *quaint* beautiful, pretty *enameld* beautified with colours 142–50 a similar catalogue of flowers is in Spenser's *The shepheardes calender*, 'Aprill', ll. 136–44; for Milton's insertion and revision of this passage in the MS, see the textual note on this poem 142 *rathe* early *forsaken* deserted, left solitary 143 *tufted* growing in tufts *Crow-toe* wild hyacinth *Gessamine* jasmine 144 *freakt** flecked, streaked 146 *well attir'd** richly arrayed *Woodbine* honeysuckle 149 *Amaranthus* an imaginary flower which never fades 151 *Herse* hearse; tomb, grave

For so to interpose a little ease,
Let our frail thoughts dally with false surmise.
Ay me! Whilst thee the shores, and sounding Seas
Wash far away, where ere thy bones are hurld,
Whether beyond the stormy *Hebrides*,
Where thou perhaps under the whelming tide
Visit'st the bottom of the monstrous world;
Or whether thou to our moist vows deny'd,
Sleep'st by the fable of *Bellerus* old,
Where the great vision of the guarded Mount
Looks toward *Namancos* and *Bayona*'s hold;
Look homeward Angel now, and melt with ruth.
And, O ye *Dolphins*, waft the haples youth.
   Weep no more, woful Shepherds weep no more,
For *Lycidas* your sorrow is not dead,
Sunk though he be beneath the watry floar,
So sinks the day-star in the Ocean bed,
And yet anon repairs his drooping head,
And tricks his beams, and with new spangled Ore,
Flames in the forehead of the morning sky:
So *Lycidas* sunk low, but mounted high,
Through the dear might of him that walk'd the waves;
Where other groves, and other streams along,
With *Nectar* pure his oozy Lock's he laves,
And hears the unexpressive nuptiall Song,
In the blest Kingdoms meek of joy and love.
There entertain him all the Saints above,

325 153 *false surmise* since King's body was not recovered, his hearse cannot be covered with flowers; the flowers only appear to the mourner to be responding to King's death 157 *whelming** engulfing, submerging 158 *monstrous** full of monsters 159 *moist vows* tearful prayers 161 *Mount* St Michael's Mount, where St Michael was said to have appeared to monks 162 *Namancos* a district in north-west Spain *Bayona's* a fortress town in Spain 163 *Angel* St Michael *ruth* pity 164 the line is usually taken to allude to the story of Arion *waft* convey by water 168 *day-star* sun 170 *tricks* decks, adorns 173 *him* Christ; cp. Matthew 14:25–6 where He is described as 'walking on the sea' 175 *laves* washes 176 *unexpressive* inexpressible (cp. no. 270 l. 116) *nuptiall Song* cp. Revelation 19:9 'Blessed are they which are called unto the marriage supper of the Lamb'

In solemn troops, and sweet Societies
That sing, and singing in their glory move,
And wipe the tears for ever from his eyes.
Now *Lycidas* the Shepherds weep no more;
Henceforth thou art the Genius of the shore,
In thy large recompense, and shalt be good
To all that wander in that perilous flood.
  Thus sang the uncouth Swain to th'Okes and rills,
While the still morn went out with Sandals gray,
He touch'd the tender stops of various Quills,
With eager thought warbling his *Dorick* lay:
And now the Sun had stretch'd out all the hills,
And now was dropt into the Western bay;
At last he rose, and twitch'd his Mantle blew:
To morrow to fresh Woods, and Pastures new.

326 [Methought I saw my late espoused Saint]

Methought I saw my late espoused Saint
  Brought to me like *Alcestis* from the grave,
  Whom *Joves* great Son to her glad Husband gave,
  Rescu'd from death by force though pale and faint.
Mine as whom washt from spot of child-bed taint,
  Purification in the old Law did save,
  And such, as yet once more I trust to have
  Full sight of her in Heaven without restraint,

325 181 cp. Revelation 7:17 and 21:4 'And God shall wipe away all tears from their eyes' 183 *Genius* local deity 186 *uncouth* unknown 188 *stops* finger-holes *Quills* reed pipes 189 *Dorick* rustic, not refined 190 cp. Virgil, *Eclogues* 1.83 'shadows of the mountain crests are falling farther out'

326 3 *Son* Hercules *Husband* Admetus 6 *old Law* cp. Leviticus 12, which lays down that women who have boys 'shall be unclean seven days ... But if she bear a maid child, then she shall be unclean two weeks ... and she shall continue in the blood of her purifying three-score and six days'

Came vested all in white, pure as her mind:
  Her face was vail'd, yet to my fancied sight,
  Love, sweetness, goodness, in her person shin'd
So clear, as in no face with more delight.
  But O as to embrace me she enclin'd
  I wak'd, she fled, and day brought back my night.

'ELIZA'

327 To my Husband

When from the world, I shall be tane,
And from earths necessary paine,
Then let no blacks be worne for me,
Not in a Ring my dear by thee.
But this bright Diamond, let it be
Worn in rememberance of me.
And when it sparkles in your eye,
Think 'tis my shadow passeth by.
For why, more bright you shall me see,
Then that or any Gem can bee.
Dress not the house with sable weed,
As if there were some dismall deed
Acted to be when I am gone,
There is no cause for me to mourn.
And let no badge of Herald be
The signe of my Antiquity.
It was my glory I did spring
From heavens eternall powerfull King:
To his bright Palace heir am I.
It is his promise, hee'l not lye.

326 10 *fancied* existed only in fancy, imaginary

327 2 *necessary* inevitable 3 *blacks* black colours; black clothing as a sign of mourning 11 *sable weed* black mourning-garments 15 *badge of Herald* coat of arms

By my dear Brother pray lay me,
It was a promise made by thee,
And now I must bid thee adieu,
For I'me a parting now from you.

HENRY VAUGHAN

328 [They are all gone into the world of light]

They are all gone into the world of light!
And I alone sit lingring here;
Their very memory is fair and bright,
And my sad thoughts doth clear.

It glows and glitters in my cloudy brest
Like stars upon some gloomy grove,
Or those faint beams in which this hill is drest,
After the Sun's remove.

I see them walking in an Air of glory,
Whose light doth trample on my days:
My days, which are at best but dull and hoary,
Meer glimering and decays.

O holy hope! and high humility,
High as the Heavens above!
These are your walks, and you have shew'd them me
To kindle my cold love,

Dear, beauteous death! the Jewel of the Just,
Shining no where, but in the dark;
What mysteries do lie beyond thy dust;
Could man outlook that mark!

He that hath found some fledg'd birds nest, may know
At first sight, if the bird be flown;
But what fair Well, or Grove he sings in now,
That is to him unknown.

328 11 *hoary* grey 21 *fledg'd* with feathers large enough for flight

And yet, as Angels in some brighter dreams
    Call to the soul, when man doth sleep:
So some strange thoughts transcend our wonted theams,
        And into glory peep.

If a star were confin'd into a Tomb
    Her captive flames must needs burn there;
But when the hand that lockt her up, gives room,
        She'l shine through all the sphære.

O Father of eternal life, and all
    Created glories under thee!
Resume thy spirit from this world of thrall
        Into true liberty.

Either disperse these mists, which blot and fill
    My perspective (still) as they pass,
Or else remove me hence unto that hill,
        Where I shall need no glass.

KATHERINE PHILIPS

329 EPITAPH. On her Son *H. P.* at St. *Syth*'s Church where her body also lies Interred

What on Earth deserves our trust?
Youth and Beauty both are dust.
Long we gathering are with pain,
What one moment calls again.
Seven years childless marriage past,
A Son, a son is born at last:

328 38 *perspective* telescope

329 Title *H. P.* Hector Philips was born on 23 April and died on 2 May 1655, see the textual note to no. 330 *St. Syth's Church* the common name for St Benet Sherehog in the City of London

So exactly lim'd and fair,
Full of good Spirits, Meen, and Air,
As a long life promised,
Yet, in less than six weeks dead.
Too promising, too great a mind
In so small room to be confin'd:
Therfore, as fit in Heav'n to dwell,
He quickly broke the Prison shell.
So the subtle Alchimist,
Can't with *Hermes* Seal resist
The powerful spirit's subtler flight,
But t'will bid him long good night.
And so the Sun if it arise
Half so glorious as his Eyes,
Like this Infant, takes a shrowd,
Buried in a morning Cloud.

330 *Orinda* upon little *Hector Philips*

1.

Twice forty months of Wedlock I did stay,
Then had my vows crown'd with a Lovely boy,
And yet in forty days he dropt away,
O swift Visissitude of humane joy.

2.

I did but see him and he dis-appear'd,
I did but pluck the Rose-bud and it fell,
A sorrow unforeseen and scarcely fear'd,
For ill can mortals their afflictions spell.

3.

And now (sweet Babe) what can my trembling heart
Suggest to right my doleful fate or thee,
Tears are my Muse and sorrow all my Art,
So piercing groans must be thy Elogy.

329 7 *lim'd* limbed, having limbs 8 *Meen* mien, air, bearing, manner 16 *Hermes Seal* hermetic, airtight seal

330 1 *stay* wait

4.

Thus whilst no eye is witness of my mone,
I grieve thy loss (Ah boy too dear to live)
And let the unconcerned World alone,
Who neither will, nor can refreshment give.

5.

An Off'ring too for thy sad Tomb I have,
Too just a tribute to thy early Herse,
Receive these gasping numbers to thy grave,
The last of thy unhappy Mothers Verse.

James Shirley

331 [The glories of our blood and state]

The glories of our blood and state,
  Are shadows, not substantial things,
There is no armour against fate,
  Death lays his icy hand on Kings,
      Scepter and Crown,
      Must tumble down,
And in the dust be equal made,
With the poor crooked sithe and spade.

Some men with swords may reap the field,
  And plant fresh laurels where they kill,
But their strong nerves at last must yield,
  They tame but one another still;
      Early or late,
      They stoop to fate,
And must give up their murmuring breath,
When they pale Captives creep to death.

330 18 *Herse* coffin, grave

The Garlands wither on your brow,
  Then boast no more your mighty deeds,
Upon Deaths purple Altar now,
  See where the Victor-victim bleeds,
      Your heads must come,
      To the cold Tomb,
Onely the actions of the just
Smell sweet, and blossom in their dust.

331 19 *purple* bloody, blood-stained; the colour was associated with mourning, especially royal mourning 20 *Victor-victim**

PART SEVEN

TRANSLATION

Henry Howard, Earl of Surrey

332 [*from* Virgil's Aeneid Book 4]

Then from the seas, the dawning gan arise,
The Sun once up, the chosen youth gan throng
Out at the gates: the hayes so rarely knit,
The hunting staves with their brod heads of steele
And of Masile the horsemen fourth they brake
Of senting houndes a kenel huge likewise.
And at the threshold of her chaumber dore,
The Carthage Lords did on the Quene attend.
The trampling steede with gold and purple trapt,
Chawing the fomie bit, there fercely stood.
Then issued she, awayted with great train,
Clad in a cloke of Tyre embradred riche.
Her quyver hung behinde her back, her tresse
Knotted in gold, her purple vesture eke
Butned with gold, the Troyans of her train
Before her go, with gladsome Iulus.
Aeneas eke the goodliest of the route
Makes one of them, and joyneth close the throngs:
Like when Apollo leaveth Lycia,
His wintring place, and Xanthus floods likewise:
To viset Delos his mothers mansion:
Repairing eft and furnishing her quire
The Candians, and folkes of Driopes,
With painted Agathyrsies shoute, and crye:
Environing the altars roundabout
When that he walks upon mount Cynthus top:
His sparkled tresse represt with garlandes soft
Of tender leaves, and trussed up in gold:
His quivering dartes clattring behinde his back:
So fresh and lustie did Aeneas seme:
Such lordly port in countenaunce present.

332 3 *hayes* nets for catching animals 27 *represt* held back 30 *lustie* youthful, vigorous, strong

But to the hils, and wilde holtes when they came:
From the rocks top the driven savage rose,
Loe from the hill above on thother side,
Through the wyde lawnds, they gan to take their course
The harts likewise, in troupes taking their flight,
Raysing the dust, the mountain fast forsake.
The childe Iulus, blithe of his swift steede
Amids the plain now pricks by them, now thes:
And to encounter wisheth oft in minde
The foming Bore in steede of ferefull beasts,
Or Lion brown might from the hill descend.
In the meane while the skies gan rumble sore:
In tayle therof, a mingled showr with hayle.
The Tyrian folk, and eke the Troyans youth,
And Venus nephew the cotages for feare
Sought round about: the floods fell from the hils.
Dido a den, the Troyan prince the same,
Chaunced upon. Our mother then the earth,
And Juno that hath charge of mariage,
First tokens gave with burning gledes of flame,
And privie to the wedlock lightning skies:
And the Nymphes yelled from the mountains top.
Ay me, this was the first day of their mirth,
And of their harmes the first occasion eke.
Respect of fame no longer her witholdes:
Nor museth now to frame her love by stelth.
Wedlock she cals it: under the pretence
Of which fayre name she cloketh now her faut.

332 32 *holtes* woods, copses 33 *rose* roes, young deer 35 *lawnds* open spaces among woods 38 *childe* young gentleman, not yet a knight *blithe* glad, well-pleased 39 *pricks* spurs, rides fast 48 *den* cavern 51 *gledes* live coals, embers 54 *mirth* joy, happiness

RICHARD STANYHURST

333 [*from* Virgil's Aeneid Book 4]

Thee whilst thee dawning Aurora fro the Ocean hastned,
And the May fresh yooncker to the gates doo make there asemblye
With nets and catch toyls, and huntspears plentiful yrond:
With the hounds quicksenting, with pricking galloper horsman.
Long for thee Princesse thee Moors gentilitye wayted,
As yet in her pincking not pranckt with trinckerye trinckets:
As they stood attending thee whilst her trapt genet hautye
Deckt with ritche scarlet, with gould stood furniture hanging,
Praunseth on al startling, and on byt gingled he chaumpeth.
At leingth foorth she fleeth with swarming coompanye circled,
In cloke Sidonical with rich dye brightlye besprinckled.
Her locks are broyded with gould, her quiver is hanging
Backward: with gould tache thee vesture purple is holden.
Thee band of Troians lykewise, with wanton Iülus
Doo marche on forward: but of al thee Lucifer hevnlye
In bewty Æneas hymself to the coompanye rancketh.
Lyke when as hard frozen Lycia and Zanth floods be relinquisht
By Pheebe, to Delos, his native contrye seat, hastning.
Hee poinctes a dawnsing, foorthwith thee rustical hoblobs
Of Cretes, of Dryopes, and payncted clowns Agathyrsi
Dooe fetch theyre gambalds hopping neere consecrat altars.

333 2 *yooncker* young noblemen, men 3 *catch toyls* toils, nets for catching wild animals 6 *pincking* decorating clothes with punched holes to make patterns; the correct reading may be *prinking*** smart dressing up *pranckt* showing off, ostentatiously displaying *trinckerye** ornamental 7 *trapt* adorned with trappings *genet* jennet, small Spanish horse 8 *furniture* harness, trappings 9 *gingled* jingled 12 *broyded* braided 13 *tache* buckle, clasp 15 *Lucifer* the morning star 19 *poinctes a dawnsing* appoints, orders, a dance *hoblobs** rustics, peasants 21 *gambalds* gambols, friskings, caperings

Hee trips on Zanthus mountayn, with delicat hearelocks
Trayling: with greene shrubs and pure gould neatly becrampound
His shafts on shoulder rattle: the lyke hautye resemblaunce
Carried Æneas with glistring coomlines hevnlye.
  When they toe thee mountayns and too layrs uncoth aproched,
Then, loa, behold ye, breaking thee goats doo trip fro the rocktops
Neere toe the playne: the heard deare dooth stray from mounten unharbourd.
Thee chase is ensued with passadge dustye bepowdred.
But the lad Ascanius, with praunsing courser hye mounted,
Dooth manage in valley, now theym, now theese overambling.
Hee scornes theese rascal tame games, but a sounder of hogsteers,
Or thee brownye lion too stalck fro the mounten he wissheth.
  Thee whilst in the skye seat great bouncing rumbelo thundring
Ratleth: downe powring too sleete thick hayle knob is added.
Thee Tyrian feloship with yoouthful Troian asemblye
And Venus hautye nephew doo run too sundrye set houses.
Hudge fluds lowdlye freaming from mountayns loftye be trowlling,
Dido and thee Troian captayne doo jumble in one den.
Then the earth crav's the banes, theare too watrye Juno, the chaplayne,
Seams up thee bedmatch, the fyre and ayre testifie wedlock.
And Nymphs in mountayns high typ doe squeak, hullelo, yearning.
That day cros and dismal was cause of mischief al after,
And bane of her killing; her fame for sleight she regarded.
No more dooth she laboure too mask her Phansye with hudwinck,
With thee name of wedlock her carnal leacherye cloaking,
Straight through towns Lybical this fame with an infamye rangeth.

333 22 *hearelocks* hair-locks 23 *becrampound*★ set with jewels; bound 26 *uncoth* unknown, little-used 28 *unharbourd* dislodged from shelter 30 *courser* swift horse 31 *manage* put a horse through its paces *overambling*★ ambling surpassingly, excellingly 32 *sounder* herd *hogsteers* hoggasters, boars in their third year 34 *rumbelo*★ rumbling 35 *knob* stone 37 *set* prescribed, prearranged (?) 38 *freaming* roaring, raging *trowlling* trolling, rolling 39 *jumble*★ have sexual intercourse (?); come together *den* cavern 40 *crav's* calls for, demands *banes* banns, formal announcement of marriage 41 *Seams*★ fastens together with seams *bedmatch*★ marriage 44 *sleight* unimportant, trifling 45 *hudwinck*★ a hoodwink, a blind, something to hide sight

ARTHUR GOLDING

334 [*from* Ovid's Metamorphoses Book 6]

. . . This Damsell was not famous for the place
In which she dwelt, nor for hir stocke, but for hir Arte. Hir Sier
Was *Idmon* one of *Colophon* a pelting Purple Dier.
Hir mother was deceast: but she was of the baser sort,
And egall to hir Make in birth, in living, and in port.
But though this Maide were meanly borne, and dwelt but in a shed
At little *Hypep*: yet hir trade hir fame abrode did spred
Even all the Lydian Cities through. To see hir wondrous worke
The Nymphes that underneath the Vines of shadie *Tmolus* lurke
Their Vineyards oftentimes forsooke. So did the Nymphes also
About *Pactolus* oftentimes their golden streames forgo.
And evermore it did them good not only for to see
Hir clothes already made, but while they eke a making bee
Such grace was in hir workmanship. For were it so that shee
The newshorne fleeces from the sheepe in bundels deftly makes,
Or afterward doth kemb the same, and drawes it out in flakes
Along like cloudes, or on the Rocke doth spinne the handwarpe woofe,
Or else embroydreth, certenly ye might perceive by proofe
She was of *Pallas* bringing up: which thing she nathelesse
Denyeth, and disdaining such a Mistresse to confesse,
Let hir contend with me she saide: and if she me amend
I will refuse no punishment the which she shall extend.
    Minerva tooke an olde wives shape and made hir haire seeme gray,
    And with a staffe hir febled limmes pretended for to stay.
Which done, she thus began to speake. Not all that age doth bring
We ought to shonne. Experience doth of long continuance spring.

334 1 *This Damsell* Arachne 3 *pelting* paltry, insignificant 5 *egall* equal *Make* mate *port* demeanour; social rank 16 *kemb* comb *flakes* like snowflakes 17 *Rocke* distaff *handwarpe* cloth 21 *amend* improve on, surpass

Despise not mine admonishment. Seeke fame and chiefe report
For making cloth, and Arras worke, among the mortall sort.
But humbly give the Goddesse place: and pardon of hir crave
For these thine unadvised wordes. I warrant thou shalt have
Forgivenesse, if thou aske it hir. *Arachne* bent hir brewes
And lowring on hir, left hir worke: and hardly she eschewes
From flying in the Ladies face. Hir countnance did bewray
Hir moodie minde: which bursting forth in words she thus did say.
Thou commest like a doting foole: thy wit is spent with yeares:
Thy life hath lasted over long as by thy talke appeares.
And if thou any daughter have, or any daughtrinlawe,
I would she heard these wordes of mine: I am not such a Daw,
But that without thy teaching I can well ynough advise
My selfe. And least thou shouldest thinke thy words in any wise
Availe, the selfe same minde I keepe with which I first begonne.
Why commes she not hirselfe I say? this matche why doth she shonne?
Then said the Goddesse: here she is. And therewithall she cast
Hir oldewives riveled shape away, and shewde hir selfe at last
Minerva like. The Nymphes did streight adore hir Majestie,
So did the yong newmaried wives that were of *Migdonie*.
The Maiden only unabasht woulde nought at all relent.
But yet she blusht and sodenly a ruddynesse besprent
Hir cheekes which wanzd away againe, even like as doth the Skie
Looke sanguine at the breake of day, and turneth by and by
To white at rising of the Sunne. As hote as any fire
She sticketh to hir tackling still. And through a fond desire
Of glorie, to hir owne decay all headlong forth she runnes.
For *Pallas* now no lenger warnes, ne now no lenger shunnes
Ne seekes the chalenge to delay. Immediatly they came
And tooke their places severally, and in a severall frame
Eche streynde a web, the warpe whereof was fine. The web was tide
Upon a Beame. Betweene the warpe a slay of reede did slide.

334 31 *brewes* brows 33 *bewray* reveal 34 *moodie* angry 38 *Daw* jackdaw; simpleton, fool 44 *riveled* wrinkled, shrivelled 48 *besprent* spread over 49 *wanzd** faded away 52 *tackling* ground, attitude *fond* foolish 56 *severally* separately *severall* separate, different 58 *slay* a reed instrument used to beat up the weft

The woofe on sharpened pinnes was put betwixt the warp, and
wrought
With fingars. And as oft as they had through the warpe it brought,
They strake it with a Boxen combe. Both twayne of them made
hast:
And girding close for handsomnesse their garments to their wast
Bestirde their cunning handes apace. Their earnestnesse was such
As made them never thinke of paine. They weaved verie much
Fine Purple that was dide in *Tyre*, and colours set so trim
That eche in shadowing other seemde the very same with him.
Even like as after showres of raine when *Phebus* broken beames
Doe strike upon the Cloudes, appeares a compast bow of gleames
Which bendeth over all the Heaven: wherein although there shine
A thousand sundry colours, yet the shadowing is so fine,
That looke men nere so wistly, yet beguileth it their eyes:
So like and even the self same thing eche colour seemes to rise
Whereas they meete, which further off doe differ more and more.
Of glittring golde with silken threede was weaved there good
store,
And stories put in portrayture of things done long afore.
Minerva painted *Athens* towne and *Marsis* rocke therein,
And all the strife betweene hirselfe and *Neptune*, who should
win
The honor for to give the name to that same noble towne.
In loftie thrones on eyther side of *Jove* were settled downe
Six Peeres of Heaven with countnance grave and full of Majestie,
And every of them by his face discerned well might be.
The Image of the mightie *Jove* was Kinglike. She had made
Neptunus standing striking with his long threetyned blade
Upon the ragged Rocke: and from the middle of the clift
She portrayd issuing out a horse, which was the noble gift
For which he chalengde to himselfe the naming of the towne.
She picturde out hirselfe with shielde and Morion on hir crowne
With Curet on hir brest, and Speare in hand with sharpened ende.
She makes the Earth (the which hir Speare doth seeme to strike) to
sende

334 61 *Boxen* made of boxwood 62 *handsomnesse* convenience 65 *trim* beautifully, smartly 68 *compast* round, arched, curved 71 *wistly* closely, intently 83 *threetyned* three-pronged 87 *Morion* helmet 88 *Curet* cuirass, breastplate

An Olyf tree with fruite thereon: and that the Gods thereat
Did wonder: and with victorie she finisht up that plat.
Yet to thintent examples olde might make it to be knowne
To hir that for desire of praise so stoutly helde hir owne,
What guerdon she shoulde hope to have for hir attempt so madde,
Foure like contentions in the foure last corners she did adde.
The Thracians *Heme* and *Rodope* the formost corner hadde:
Who being sometime mortall folke usurpt to them the name
Of *Jove* and *Juno*, and were turnde to mountaines for the same.
A *Pigmie* womans piteous chaunce the second corner shewde,
Whome *Juno* turned to a Crane (bicause she was so lewde
As for to stand at strife with hir for beautie) charging hir
Against hir native countriefolke continuall war to stir.
The thirde had proude *Antigone* who durst of pride contende
In beautie with the wife of *Jove*: by whome she in the ende
Was turned to a Storke, no whit availed hir the towne
Of *Troy*, or that *Laomedon* hir father ware a crowne,
But that she clad in feathers white hir lazie wings must flap
And with a bobbed Bill bewayle the cause of hir missehap.
The last had chyldelesse *Cinyras*: who being turnde to stone,
Was picturde prostrate on the grounde, and weeping all alone,
And culling fast betweene his armes a Temples greeces fine
To which his daughters bodies were transformde by wrath divine.
The utmost borders had a wreath of Olyf round about,
And this is all the worke the which *Minerva* portrayd out.
For with the tree that she hirselfe had made but late afore
She bounded in hir Arras cloth, and then did worke no more.
The Lydian maiden in hir web did portray to the full
How *Europe* was by royall *Jove* beguilde in shape of Bull.
A swimming Bull, a swelling Sea, so lively had she wrought,
That Bull and Sea in very deede ye might them well have thought.
The Ladie seemed looking backe to landwarde and to crie
Upon hir women, and to feare the water sprinkling hie,
And shrinking up hir fearfull feete. She portrayd also there
Asteriee struggling with an *Erne* which did away hir beare.

334 91 *plat* plot, design 94 *guerdon* reward 100 *lewde* stupid, ignorant *Crane* bird 108 *bobbed*** cut short 111 *culling* embracing *fast* tightly *greeces* steps, flight of steps 119 *lively* in a lifelike way 124 *Erne* eagle

And over *Leda* she had made a Swan his wings to splay.
She added also how by *Jove* in shape of *Satyr* gaye
The faire *Antiope* with a paire of children was besped:
And how he tooke *Amphitrios* shape when in *Alcmenas* bed
He gate the worthie *Hercules*: and how he also came
To *Danae* like a shoure of golde, to *Aegine* like a flame,
A sheepeherd to *Mnemosyne*, and like a Serpent sly
To *Proserpine*. She also made *Neptunus* leaping by
Upon a Maide of *Aeolus* race in likenesse of a Bull,
And in the streame *Enipeus* shape begetting on a trull
The Giants *Othe* and *Ephialt*, and in the shape of Ram
Begetting one *Theophane Bisalties* ympe with Lam,
And in a lustie Stalions shape she made him covering there
Dame *Ceres* with the yellow lockes, and hir whose golden heare
Was turnde to crawling Snakes: on whome he gate the winged horse.
She made him in a Dolphins shape *Melantho* to enforce.
Of all these things she missed not their proper shapes, nor yit
The full and just resemblance of their places for to hit.
In likenesse of a Countrie cloyne was *Phebus* picturde there,
And how he now ware Gossehaukes wings, and now a Lions heare.
And how he in a shepeherdes shape was practising a wile
The daughter of one *Macarie* dame *Issa* to beguile.
And how the faire *Erygone* by chaunce did suffer rape
By *Bacchus* who deceyved hir in likenesse of a grape.
And how that *Saturne* in the shape of Genet did beget
The double *Chiron*. Round about the utmost Verdge was set
A narrow Traile of pretie floures with leaves of Ivie fret.
Not *Pallas*, no nor spight it selfe could any quarrell picke
To this hir worke: and that did touch *Minerva* to the quicke.
Who thereupon did rende the cloth in pieces every whit,
Bicause the lewdnesse of the Gods was blased so in it.
And with an Arras weavers combe of Box she fiercely smit
Arachne on the forehead full a dosen times and more.
The Maide impacient in hir heart, did stomacke this so sore,

334 125 *splay* spread open 127 *besped*** prospered, favoured 134 *trull* girl, wench; Aloeus's wife 136 *ympe* implant, engraft 138 *hir* Medusa 139 *horse* Pegasus 140 *enforce* ravish 143 *cloyne* clown, peasant, rustic 149 *Genet* jennet, small Spanish horse 155 *blased* emblazoned, depicted 158 *stomacke* resent

That by and by she hung hirselfe. Howbeit as she hing,
Dame *Pallas* pitying hir estate, did stay hir in the string
From death, and said lewde Callet live: but hang thou still for mee.
And least hereafter from this curse that time may set thee free,
I will that this same punishment enacted firmely bee,
As well on thy posteritie for ever as on thee.
And after when she should depart, with juice of *Hecats* flowre
She sprinkled hir: and by and by the poyson had such powre,
That with the touch thereof hir haire, hir eares, and nose did fade:
And verie small it both hir heade and all hir bodie made.
In steade of legs, to both hir sides sticke fingars long and fine:
The rest is bellie. From the which she nerethelesse dooth twine
A slender threede, and practiseth in shape of Spider still
The Spinners and the Websters crafts of which she erst had skill.

EDMUND SPENSER

335 [*from* Ruines of Rome: by Bellay]

5

Who lists to see, what ever nature, arte,
And heaven could doo, O *Rome*, thee let him see,
In case thy greatnes he can gesse in harte,
By that which but the picture is of thee.
Rome is no more: but if the shade of *Rome*
May of the bodie yeeld a seeming sight,
It's like a corse drawne forth out of the tombe
By Magicke skill out of eternall night:

334 161 *Callet* strumpet 172 *Websters* weaver's

335 1 *lists* likes, pleases 5 *shade* shadow 6 *seeming* apparent; fitting, appropriate 7 *corse* body

The corpes of *Rome* in ashes is entombed,
And her great spirite rejoyned to the spirite
Of this great masse, is in the same enwombed;
But her brave writings, which her famous merite
In spight of time, out of the dust doth reare,
Doo make her Idole through the world appeare.

MARY SIDNEY, COUNTESS OF PEMBROKE

336 Quid gloriaris? Psalm 52

Tyrant whie swel'st thou thus,
of mischief vanting?
since helpe from god to us,
is never wanting?

Lewd lies thy tongue contrives,
lowd lies it soundeth:
sharper then sharpest knives
with lies it woundeth.

Falshood thy witt approves,
all truth rejected:
thy will all vices loves,
vertue neglected.

Not wordes from cursed thee,
but gulphes are powred.
Gulphes wherin daily bee
good men devoured.

335 12 *brave* splendid, fair 14 *Idole* image, effigy, likeness

336 14 *gulphes* abysses, yawning chasms

Think'st thou to beare it soe?
God shall displace thee
God shall thee overthrow,
crush thee, deface thee.

The Just shall fearing see
theis fearefull chaunces:
and laughing shoote at thee
with scornfull glaunces.

Loe, loe, the wretched wight,
who god disdaining,
his mischief made his might,
his guard his gaining.

I as an Olive tree,
still greene shall flourish:
Gods howse the soile shall bee
my rootes to nourish.

My trust on his true love
truly attending,
shall never thence remove,
never see ending.

Thee will I honor still
lord for this justice:
There fix my hopes I will
where thy saincts trust is.

Thy saincts trust in thy name,
therin they joy them:
protected by the same
nought can anoy them.

336 20 *deface* blot out, extinguish

337 [*from* Psalm 89 Misericordias]

Gods boundles bownties gods promise ever abyding
shall bee my songs eternall them still gladly recording
of fowloing ages, while ranged in absolute order
gold armed squadrons of stares shall muster in heaven
yea this soaner I think that stares best ordered order
shall to disorder fall, confusd in contrary courses
then that league be reverst, that sacred treatye repealed
thus by thy selfe sometime confirmd, thus sworn to thy David
while earth, while waters, while palace of heev'n abideth
stablish I will thy elected seed and loftily seated
on throne will hold them, till endles eternities ending
O father highe heavens at thee most worthily wonder
O father earth dwellers, whose hearts al on god bee reposed
Bend to thy thruthe their praise, when so their company meteth
who is above that may compare with mighty Jehova?
who can among th'exalted train of gloriows angells
like to Jehova be fownd? all him with an awfull obeisance
terrible acknowledge, and flock affrighted abowt him,
thow comander of hosts, indeed most mighty Jehova
seest not a match in powr in verity knowst not an equall
Thow of foaming seas, dost still the tumultuows outcries
thow their high swelling, dost coole with lowly residing
prowd Phæroa hath felt thee: all enemies all thy resisters
felt thy revendging hand, disperst and bloudily wounded
thow thow only the fownder of earth, and former of heaven
framer of all this vawted rownd, which hanged on hindges
north and south sustain thie benignity, Thabor and hermon
that where sunn falleth, this where his charrit ariseth
testify with praises: thee, thee, all oly belongeth
all powre, all pusiance, makes earth with wonder amazed

337 2 *them* theme 14 *thruthe* truth 26 *vawted* vaulted 27 *Thabor and hermon* Tabor and Hermon, mountains in the north of Palestine and the south of Lebanon

338 Voce mea ad Dominum Psalm 142

My voice to thee it self extreamly strayning,
cries prayeng, lord; againe it cryeng praieth.
before thy face the cause of my complayning,
before thy face my cases mapp it laieth
wherein my soule is painted
in doubtfull way a stranger:
but, Lord, thou art acquainted,
and knowst each path, where stick the toiles of danger:
for me, mine ey to ev'ry coast directed
lights, not on one that will so much as know me:
my life by all neglected,
ev'n hope of help is now quight perish'd from me.

Then with good cause to thee my spiritt flieth,
flieth, and saith: ô lord my safe abiding
abides in thee: in thee all-only lieth
lott of my life, and plott of my residing.
alas then yeeld me heiring,
for wearing woes have spent me:
and save me from their tearing,
who hunt me hard, and daily worse torment me.
ô change my state, unthrall my soule enthralled:
of my escape then will I tell the story:
and with a crown enwalled
of godly men, will glory in thy glory.

338 1 *extreamly* to the uttermost degree 4 *mapp** detailed account of the state of things 8 *toiles** nets 16 *lott* fate, destiny *plott* place, site 21 *unthrall** set free

Christopher Marlowe

339 [*from* Ovids Elegies Book 1]

ELEGIA. 13.

Ad Auroram ne properet

Now ore the sea from her old Love comes she
That drawes the day from heavens cold axletree.
Aurora whither slidest thou? downe againe
And birdes from *Memnon* yearely shal be slaine.
Now in her tender armes I sweetly bide
If ever, now well lies she by my side.
The aire is cold, and sleepe is sweetest now
And birdes send forth shrill notes from every bough:
Whither runst thou, that men, and women love not?
Hold in thy rosy horses that they move not.
Ere thou rise, starres teach sea-men where to saile
But when thou commest they of their courses faile.
Poore travailers though tierd, rise at thy sight,
And souldiours make them ready to the fight.
The painefull hinde by thee to field is sent,
Slowe Oxen early in the yoake are pent.
Thou cousenst boyes of sleepe, and doest betray them
To *Pedants* that with cruell lashes pay them.
Thou mak'st the surety to the Lawyer runne,
That with one word hath nigh himselfe undone.
The Lawyer and the client hate thy view,
Both whom thou raisest up to toyle anew.
By thy meanes women of their rest are bard,
Thou setst their labouring hands to spin and card.
All could I beare, but that the wench should rise,
Who can endure save him with whom none lyes?

339 1 *Love* Tithonus 2 *axletree* the line around which the earth revolves 10 *Hold in* restrain, rein in 15 *painefull* industrious *hinde* labourer 16 *pent* penned 17 *cousenst* cozen, cheat 24 *card* comb wool

How oft wisht I, night would not give thee place,
Nor morning starres shunne thy uprising face.
How oft that either winde would breake thy coach,
Or steeds might fall forc'd with thick clouds approach.
Whether goest thou hatefull Nimph? *Memnon* the elfe
Receiv'd his cole-black colour from thy selfe.
Say that thy love with *Cæphalus* were not knowne,
Then thinkest thou thy loose life is not showne.
Would *Tithon* might but talke of thee a while,
Not one in heaven should be more base and vile.
Thou leavest his bed, because hee's faint through age,
And early mountest thy hatefull carriage.
But heldst thou in thine armes some *Cephalus*,
Then wouldst thou cry, stay night and runne not thus.
Doest punish me, because yeares make him waine?
I did not bid thee wed an aged swaine.
The Moone sleepes with *Endymion* every day,
Thou art as faire as she, then kisse and play.
Jove that thou shouldst not hast but waite his leasure,
Made two nights one to finish up his pleasure.
I chide no more, she blusht and therefore heard me
Yet lingered not the day, but morning scard me.

340 [*from* Lucan's Pharsalia Book 1]

This said, the restles generall through the darke
(Swifter then bullets throwne from Spanish slinges,
Or darts which *Parthians* backward shoot) marcht on
And then (when *Lucifer* did shine alone,
And some dim stars) he *Arriminum* enter'd:
Day rose and viewde these tumultes of the war;
Whether the gods, or blustring south were cause
I know not, but the cloudy ayre did frown;
The soldiours having won the market place,
There spred the colours, with confused noise
Of trumpets clange, shril cornets, whistling fifes;

340 1 *generall* Julius Caesar 4 *Lucifer* the morning star 11 *clange* ringing sound

The people started; young men left their beds;
And snatcht armes neer their household gods hung up
Such as peace yeelds; wormeaten leatherne targets,
Through which the wood peer'd, headles darts, olde swords
With ugly teeth of blacke rust fouly scarr'd:
But seeing white Eagles, and Roomes flags wel known,
And lofty *Cæsar* in the thickest throng,
They shooke for feare, and cold benumm'd their lims,
And muttering much, thus to themselves complain'd.
O wals unfortunate too neere to France,
Predestinate to ruine; all lands else
Have stable peace, here wars rage first begins,
We bide the first brunt, safer might we dwel,
Under the frosty beare, or parching East,
Wagons or tents, then in this frontire towne,
We first sustain'd the uproares of the *Gaules*,
And furious *Cymbrians* and of *Carthage* moores,
As oft as Roome was sackt, here gan the spoile:
Thus sighing whispered they, and none durst speake
And shew their feare, or griefe: but as the fields
When birds are silent thorough winters rage;
Or sea far from the land, so all were whist.

SIR JOHN HARINGTON

341 [*from* Ariosto's Orlando Furioso Book 34]

68

Thus all that day, they spent in divers talke,
With sollace great, as never wanteth there,
But when the sunne began this earth to balke,
And passe into the tother hemispheare,

340 14 *targets* shields 25 *beare* the constellation of the bear; in the north 27 in the third and fourth centuries BC 28 *Cymbrians . . . moores* German invaders and Hannibal's Moorish army 33 *whist* silenced

341 1 *they* Astolfo and St John (see the textual note) 3 *balke* pass by, shun

Then they prepard to fetch a further walke,
And strait the firie charret that did beare
Elyas, when he up to heav'n was caryd,
Was readie in a trise, and for them taryd.

69

Foure horses fierce as red as flamming fire,
Th'Apostle doth into the charret set,
Which when he framed had to his desire,
Astolfo in the Carre by him he set;
Then up they went and still ascending hyer,
Above the firie region they did get,
Whose nature so th'Apostle then did turne,
That though they went through fire, they did
not burne.

70

I say although the fire were wondrous hot,
Yet in their passage they no heat did feele,
So that it burnd them, nor offends them not;
Thence to the moone he guids the running
wheele,
The Moone was like a glasse all voyd of spot,
Or like a peece of purelie burnisht steele,
And lookt, although to us it seemes so small,
Well nye as bigg as earth, and sea and all.

71

Here had *Astolfo* cause of double wonder,
One, that that region seemeth there so wyde,
That unto us that are so far a sunder,
Seems but a litle circle, and beside,
That to behold the ground that him lay under,
A man had need to have been sharply eyd,
And bend his brows, and marke ev'n all they
might,
It seemd so small, now chiefly wanting light.

341 7 Elias or Elijah was carried up to heaven in a fiery chariot, see 2 Kings 2:11

72

Twere infinit to tell what wondrous things
He saw, that passed ours not few degrees,
What towns, what hills, what rivers and what springs
What dales, what Pallaces, what goodly trees:
But to be short, at last his guide him brings,
Unto a goodlie vallie, where he sees,
A mightie masse of things straungely confused,
Things that on earth were lost, or were abused.

This fiction is agreeing with an English proverb we use: that mens wits are beyond the moone and they have layd up things in the circle of the moone.

73

A store house straunge, that what on earth is lost,
By fault, by time, by fortune, there is found,
And like a marchaundise is there engrost,
In straunger sort then I can well expound:
Nor speake I sole of wealth, or things of cost,
In which blind fortunes powre doth most abound,
But ev'n of things quite out of fortunes powre,
Which wilfullie we wast each day and houre.

Looke in the Allegorie.

74

The precious time that fools mispend in play,
The vaine attempts that never take effect,
The vows that sinners make, and never pay,
The counsells wise that carelesse men neglect,
The fond desires that lead us oft astray,
The prayses that with pride the heart infect,
And all we loose with follie and mispending,
May there be found unto this place ascending.

75

Now, as *Astolfo* by those regions past,
He asked many questions of his guide,
And as he on tone side his eye did cast,

341 42 side-note *Looke ... Allegorie* 'All those things that he [Ariosto] faynes to have been showed *Astolfo* in the circle of the moone, are but similitudes, and likenesse of such follies, as he that will marke them well, shall easely discerne' 43 *engrost* bought up wholesale

A wondrous hill of bladders he espyde;
Pride of Princes and vanitie of their titles.
And he was told they had been in time past,
The pompous crowns and scepters, full of pride,
Of Monarks of Assiria, and of Greece,
Of which now scantlie there is left a peece.

76

He saw great store of baited hookes with gold,
Gifts geven to Princes in hope of reward.
And those were gifts that foolish men prepard,
To give to Princes covetous and old,
With fondest hope of future vaine reward:
Then were there ropes all in sweet garlands
rold,
Cunning flatterers.
And those were all false flatteries he hard,
Then hard he crickets songs like to the verses,
Base flatterers.
The servant in his masters prayse reherses.

77

There did he see fond loves, that men pursew,
Fond loves.
To looke like golden gives with stones all set,
Then things like Eagles talents he did vew,
Favorites rewards.
Those offices that favorites do get:
Then saw he bellows large that much winde
blew,
Great mens promises.
Large promises that Lords make, and forget,
Unto their Ganimeds in flowre of youth,
But after nought but beggerie insewth.

78

He saw great Cities seated in fayre places,
Treasons and conspiracies.
That overthrown quite topsie turvie stood,
He askt and learnd, the cause of their defaces
Was treason, that doth never turne to good:
He saw fowle serpents, with fayre womens faces,
Of coyners and of thieves the cursed brood,
He saw fine glasses, all in peeces broken,
Of service lost in court, a wofull token.
Poore courtiers.

341 74 *gives* gyves, shackles, fetters 79 *Ganimeds* male favourites 83 *defaces* defacements

79

Of mingled broth he saw a mightie masse,
That to no use, all spilt on ground did lye,
He askt his teacher, and he heard it was,
The fruitlesse almes that men geve when they dye:
Then by a fayre green mountain he did passe,
That once smelt sweet, but now it stinks perdye,
This was that gift (be't said without offence)
That *Constantin* gave *Silvester* long since.

Almes and charitable deeds done to late.

By that gift is understood the Citie of Rome, which Constantin gave Pope Silvester, which he saith now stinketh because of their sinnes.

80

Of birdlymd rodds, he saw no litle store,
And these (O Ladies fayre) your bewties be,
I do omit ten thousand things and more
Like unto these, that there the Duke did see
For all that here is lost, there evermore
Is kept, and thither in a trise doth flee,
Howbeit more nor lesse there was no folly,
For still that here with us remaineth wholly.

The bewtie of women.

81

He saw some of his own lost time and deeds,
But yet he knew them not to be his own,
They seemd to him disguisd in so straunge weeds,
Till his instructer made them better known:
But last, the thing which no man thinks he needs,
Yet each man needeth most, to him was shown,
By name mans wit, which here we leese so fast,
As that one substance, all the other past.

82

It seemd to be a body moyst and soft,
And apt to mount by ev'ry exhalation,
And when it hither mounted was aloft,
It there was kept in potts of such a fashion,

341 96 by the medieval forgery, the Donation of Constantine, Pope Sylvester I (314–35) was supposed to have given lands to the Church and initiated its temporal power 97 *birdlymd* limed to trap birds 111 *leese* lose

As we call Jarrs, where oyle is kept in oft:
The Duke beheld with no small admiration,
The Jarrs of wit, amongst which one had writ,
Upon the side thereof, *Orlandos wit.*

Mans wit kept in Jarrs like oyle.

83

This vessell bigger was then all the rest,
And ev'ry vessell had ingrav'n with art,
His name, that earst the wit therein possest:
There of his own, the Duke did finde a part,
And much he musd, and much him selfe he blest,
To see some names of men of great desart,
That thinke they have great store of wit, and bost it,
And here it playne appeard they quite had lost it.

84

Some loose their wit with love, some with ambition,
Some running to the sea, great wealth to get,
Some following Lords, and men of high condition,
And some in fayre jewells ritch and costlie set,
One hath desire to prove a rare Magicion,
And some with Poetrie their wit forget,
An other thinks to be an Alcumist,
Till all be spent, and he his number mist.

85

Astolfo takes his own before he goes,
For so th'Evangelist did him permit;
He set the vessels mouth but to his nose,
And to his place, he snuft up all his wit:
Long after wise he liv'd as *Turpin* shows,
Untill one fault he after did commit,
By name, the love of one fayre Northern lasse,
Sent up his wit unto the place it was.

This is written in the fourth booke of the five Cantos added to Ariosto, which many thinke were none of his doing, and are verie unperfet.

341 141 *Turpin* legendary Archbishop of Rheims; a *Life of Charlemagne* was ascribed to him which Ariosto frequently cites as his source

Edward Fairfax

342 [*from* Tasso's Godfrey of Bulloigne Book 4]

3

The drearie trumpet blew a dreadfull blast,
And rombled through the lands and kingdomes under,
Through wastnes wide it roard, and hollowes vast,
And fild the deepe, with horror, feare and wonder,
Not halfe so dreadfull noise the tempests cast,
That fall from skies, with storms of haile and thunder,
  Nor halfe so lowd the whistling winds doe sing,
  Broke from the earthen prisons of their king.

4

The Peeres of *Plutoes* realme assembled beene
Amid the pallace of their angrie king,
In hideous formes and shapes, tofore unseene,
That feare, death, terror and amasement bring,
With ouglie pawes some trample on the greene,
Some gnaw the snakes that on their shoulders hing,
  And some their forked tailes stretch forth on hie,
  And teare the twinkling stars from trembling skie.

5

There were *Cilenos* foule and loathsome rout,
There Sphinges, Centaures, there were *Gorgons* fell,
There howling Scillaes, yawling round about,
There serpents hisse, there sev'n-mouth'd Hydraes yell,
Chimera there spues fire and brimstone out,
And *Poliphemus* blinde supporteth hell,
  Besides ten thousand monsters therein dwels
  Mis-shapt, unlike themselves, and like nought els.

342 8 *king* Aeolus 11 *tofore* before 18 *Sphinges* sphinxes *fell* deadly 19 *yawling* wailing, screaming

6

About their Prince each tooke his wonted seat
On thrones red hot, ibuilt of burning brasse,
Pluto in middest heav'd his trident great,
Of rustie iron huge that forged was,
The rockes, on which the salt sea billowes beat,
And Atlas tops, the clouds in height that passe,
  Compar'd to his huge person, mole-hils be,
  So his rough front, his hornes so lifted he.

7

The tyrant proud frown'd from his loftie cell,
And with his lookes made all his monsters tremble,
His eies, that full of rage and venome swell,
Two beacons seeme, that men to armes assemble,
His feltred lockes, that on his bosome fell,
On rugged mountaines briers and thornes resemble,
  His yawning mouth, that fomed clotted blood,
  Gapte like a whirlepoole wide in Stygian flood.

8

And as mount Etna vomits sulphur out,
With clifts of burning crags, and fire and smoke,
So from his mouth flew kindled coales about,
Hot sparks and smels, that man and beast would choke,
The gnarring porter durst not whine for dout,
Still were the Furies, while their soveraigne spoke,
  And swift *Cocytus* staid his murmur shrill,
  While thus the murdrer thundred out his will.

9

Ye powres infernall, worthier far to sit
Above the sunne, whence you your ofspring take,
With me that whilome, through the welkin flit,
Downe tombled headlong to this emptie lake,
Our former glorie, still remember it,
Our bold attemptes and war we once did make
  Gainst him, that rules above the starrie sphere,
  For which like traitors we lie damned here.

342 37 *feltred* tangled, matted 45 *gnarring* growling *porter* Cerberus *dout* fear 51 *welkin* sky

10

And now in stead of cleere and gladsome skie,
Of *Titans* brightnes, that so glorious is,
In this deepe darknes loe we helplesse lie,
Hopelesse againe to joy our former blis,
And more (which makes my grieves to multiplie)
That sinfull creature man, elected is,
  And in our place, the heavens possesse he must,
  Vile man, begot of clay, and borne of dust.

11

Nor this suffis'd, but that he also gave
His only sonne, his darling to be slaine,
To conquer so, hell, death, sinne and the grave,
And man condemned to restore againe,
He brake our prisons and would algates save
The soules that here should dwell in woe and paine,
  And now in heav'n with him they live alwaies
  With endlesse glorie crown'd, and lasting praise.

12

But why recount I thus our passed harmes?
Remembrance fresh makes weak'ned sorrowes strong,
Expulsed were we with injurious armes
From those due honours, us of right belong.
But let us leave to speake of these alarmes,
And bend our forces gainst our present wrong,
  Ah see you not, how he attempted hath
  To bring all lands, all nations to his faith?

13

Then, let us carelesse spend the day and night,
Without regard what haps, what comes or goes.
Let Asia subject be to Christians might,
A pray be Sion to her conquering foes,
Let her adore againe her Christ aright,
Who her before all nations whilome choes,
  In brasen tables be his lore iwrit,
  And let all tongues and lands acknowledge it.

342 69 *algates* entirely, altogether 84 *pray* prey *Sion* Zion, Jerusalem, the heavenly city, see Revelation 14:1 86 *choes* chose

14

So shall our sacred altars all be his,
Our holie Idols tombled in the mold,
To him the wretched man, that sinfull is,
Shall pray, and offer incense, myrrhe and gold;
Our temples shall their costly deckings mis,
With naked walles and pillars freezing cold,
Tribute of soules shall end, and our estate,
Or *Pluto* raigne in kingdoms desolate.

15

Oh, be not than the courage perisht cleene,
That whilome dwelt within your haughtie thought,
When, arm'd with shining fire and weapons keene,
Against the Angels of proud heav'n we fought,
I grant we fell on the Phlegrean greene,
Yet good our cause was, though our fortune nought;
For chance assisteth oft th'ignobler part,
We lost the field, yet lost we not our hart.

16

Goe then my strength, my hope, my spirits, goe,
These westren rebels, with your power withstand,
Plucke up these weedes, before they overgroe
The gentle garden of the Hebrewes land,
Quench out this sparke, before it kindle soe
That Asia burne, consumed with the brand.
Use open force, or secret guile unspied;
For craft is vertue gainst a foe defied.

17

Among the knights and worthies of their traine,
Let some like out-lawes wander uncouth waies,
Let some be slaine in field, let some againe
Make oracles of womens yeaes and naies,
And pine in foolish love, let some complaine
On *Godfreyes* rule, and mutines gainst him raise,
Turne each ones sword, against his fellowes hart,
Thus kill them all, or spoile the greatest part.

342 90 *mold* earth, dust 114 *uncouth* unknown

18

Before his words the tyrant ended had,
The lesser devils arose with gastlie rore,
And thronged foorth about the world to gad,
Each land they filled, river, streame and shore,
The Goblins, Fairies, Feends and Furies mad,
Ranged in flowrie dales, and mountaines hore,
  And under everie trembling leafe they sit,
  Betweene the solid earth and welkin flit.

19

About the world they spread both far and wide,
Filling the thoughts of each ungodly hart,
With secret mischiefe, anger, hate and pride,
Wounding lost soules with sinnes impoyson'd dart.
But say (my muse) recount whence first they tride
To hurt the Christian Lords, and from what part,
  Thou know'st of things perform'd so long agone,
  This later age heares little troath or none.

JOSUAH SYLVESTER

343 [*from* Saluste du Bartas' Devine Weekes]

  The cunning Painter, that with curious care,
Limning a Land-scape, various, rich, and rare,
Hath set a Worke in all and every part,
Invention, Judgement, Nature, Use, and Art;
And hath at length (t'immortalize his name)
With wearie Pencill perfected the same;

By an excellent Similitude of a Painter delighted with the sight of a curious table which hee hath lately finished: our Poet showeth how God Resteth the seaventh Day: and saw (as saith the Scripture) that all that he had made was Good.

342 126 *hore* frosty; ancient 128 *welkin* sky

343 1 side-note *curious* carefully, skilfully made *table* picture *God Resteth* cp. Genesis 2:2 'And on the seventh day God ended his work which he had made; and he rested on the seventh day from all his work which he had made' *Scripture* cp. Genesis 1.31 'And God saw every thing that he had made, and, behold, it was very good' 2 *Limning* painting *Land-scape*★ 3 *a Worke* at work 6 *Pencill* brush

Forgets his paines; and inly fill'd with glee,
Still on his Picture gazeth greedilie.
  First, in a Mead he marks a frisking Lambe,
Which seemes (though dumb) to bleat unto the Dam:
Then he observes a Wood, seeming to wave:
Then th'hollow bosome of some hideous Cave:
Heere a High-way, and there a narrow Path:
Heere Pines, there Oakes, torne by tempestuous wrath:
Heere, from a craggie Rocks steep-hanging bosse
(Thrumb'd halfe with Ivie, halfe with crisped Mosse)
A silver Brooke in broken streames doth gush,
And head-long downe the horned Cliffe doth rush;
Then winding thence above and under ground,
A goodly Garden it be-moateth round:
There on his knee, behind a Box-Tree shrinking,
A skilfull Gunner, with his left eye winking,
Levells directly at an Oake hard by,
Whereon a hundred groaning Culvers crie;
Downe falls the Cock, up from the Touch-pan flies
A ruddie flash that in a moment dies,
Off goes the Gunne, and through the Forrest rings
The thundering bullet borne on fierie wings.
Heere, on a Greene, two Striplings, stripped light,
Runne for a prize with laboursome delight;
A dustie Cloud about their feet doth floe
(Their feet, and head, and hands, and all doo goe)
They swelt in sweat; and yet the following Rout
Hastens their hast with many a cheerefull shout.
Heere, sixe pyed Oxen under painfull yoake
Rip up the folds of *Ceres* Winter Cloake.
Heere, in the shade, a prettie Sheppardesse
Drives softly home her bleating happinesse;

343 15 *bosse** knoll, mass of rock 16 *Thrumb'd* fringed, clothed *crisped* closely, stiffly curled 20 *be-moateth** surround with a moat 22 *winking* closed 24 *Culvers* woodpigeons 25 *Touch-pan** pan holding the gunpowder 33 *swelt* swelter, melt 36 plough the hard ground

Still as she goes, she spinnes; and as she spinnes,
A man would thinke some Sonnet she beginnes.
Heere runnes a River, there springs forth a
Fountaine,
Heere vailes a Valley, there ascends a Mountaine,
Heere smoakes a Castle, there a Citie fumes,
And heere a Shipp upon th'Ocean Loomes.
In briefe, so lively, Art hath Nature shap't,
That in his Worke the Work-mans selfe is rapt,
Unable to looke off; for looking still,
The more he lookes, the more he findes his skill:
So th'Architect (whose glorious Workmanships,
My cloudie Muse doth but too-much eclipse)
Having, with pain-lesse paine, and care-lesse care,
In these *Sixe Dayes*, finisht the Table faire
And infinite of th'*Universall Ball*,
Resteth *This Day*, t'admire himselfe in All:
And, for a season, eying nothing els,
Joyes in his Worke, sith all his Worke excells.
(If my dull, stutting, frozen eloquence
May dare conjecture of his high Intents).

God rested the seaventh Day, and contemplates on his Works.

George Chapman

344 [*from* Homer's Iliad Book 12]

... Through the wall, uprore
stood up on end.
Nor had great *Hector* and his friends, the rampire
overrun,
If heavens great Counsellour, high *Jove*, had not
inflam'd his sonne

343 39 *spinnes* protracts, prolongs, draws out her way 42 *vailes* descends, sinks 52 *Table* picture, plan 53 *Universall Ball* the world 57 *stutting* stuttering

344 2 *rampire* rampart

Sarpedon (like the forrests king, when he on Oxen flies)
Against the *Grecians:* his round targe, he to his arme applies
Brasse-leav'd without: and all within, thicke Oxe-hides quilted hard:
The verge nail'd round with rods of gold, and with two darts prepard;
He leades his people: as ye see, a mountaine Lion fare,
Long kept from prey: in forcing which, his high mind makes him dare,
Assault upon the whole full fold: though guarded never so
With well-arm'd men, and eager dogs; away he will not go,
But venture on, and either snatch, a prey, or be a prey:
So far'd divine *Sarpedons* mind, resolv'd to force his way
Through all the fore-fights, and the wall: yet since he did not see
Others, as great as he, in name, as great in mind as he:
He spake to *Glaucus*: Glaucus, say, why are we honord more
Then other men of *Lycia*, in place? with greater store
Of meates and cups? with goodlier roofes? delightsome gardens? walks?
More lands, and better? so much wealth, that Court and countrie talks
Of us, and our possessions; and every way we go,
Gaze on us as we were their Gods? this where we dwell, is so:

Sarpedons speech to Glaucus, never equalled by any (in this kind) of all that have written.

344 4 *forrests king* the lion, the king of beasts 7 *verge* rim 14 *fore-fights** foremost defences

The shores of *Xanthus* ring of this; and shall not we exceed,
As much in merit, as in noise? Come, be we great in deed
As well as looke; shine not in gold, but in the flames of fight;
That so our neat-arm'd-*Lycians*, may say; See, these are right
Our kings, our Rulers; these deserve, to eate, and drinke the best;
These governe not ingloriously: these, thus exceed the rest,
Do more then they command to do. O friend, if keeping backe
Would keepe backe age from us, and death; and that we might not wracke
In this lifes humane sea at all: but that deferring now
We shund death ever; nor would I, halfe this vaine valour show,
Nor glorifie a folly so, to wish thee to advance:
But since we must go, though not here; and that, besides the chance
Proposd now, there are infinite fates, of other sort in death,
Which (neither to be fled nor scap't) a man must sinke beneath:
Come, trie we, if this sort be ours: and either render thus,
Glorie to others, or make them, resigne the like to us.

JOHN MILTON

345 The Fifth Ode of *Horace*. Lib. *I*

Quis multa gracilis te puer in Rosa, Rendred almost word for word without Rhyme according to the Latin Measure, as near as the Language will permit.

What slender Youth bedew'd with liquid odours
Courts thee on Roses in some pleasant Cave,
Pyrrha for whom bindst thou
In wreaths thy golden Hair,
Plain in thy neatness; O how oft shall he
On Faith and changed Gods complain: and Seas
Rough with black winds and storms
Unwonted shall admire:
Who now enjoyes thee credulous, all Gold,
Who alwayes vacant alwayes amiable
Hopes thee; of flattering gales
Unmindfull. Hapless they
To whom thou untry'd seem'st fair. Me in my vow'd
Picture the sacred wall declares t' have hung
My dank and dropping weeds
To the stern God of Sea.

345 Title *Measure* metre 8 *shall admire* 'emirabitur', shall marvel, wonder at 9 *all Gold* 'aurea', 'your worth is golden' 10 *vacant* 'vacuam', not taken up by any one 11 *flattering* 'fallacis', delusively promising 13–16 'My votive plaque on the temple wall shows me as having hung up my damp clothes to Neptune'

PART EIGHT

WRITER, LANGUAGE AND PUBLIC

John Skelton

346 [*from* A Replycacion]

Than, if this noble kyng
Thus can harpe and syng
With his harpe of prophecy
And spyrituall poetry
As saynt Jerome saythe
To whom we must gyve faythe
Warblyng with his strynges
Of suche Theologicall thynges
Why have ye than disdayne
At poetes. And complayne
Howe poetes do but fayne.
  Ye do moche great outrage
For to disparage
And to discorage
The fame matryculate
Of poetes laureate.
  For if ye sadly loke
And wesely rede the boke
Of good advertysement
With me ye must consent
And infallibly agre
Of necessyte
Howe there is a spyrituall
And a mysteriall
And a mysticall
Effecte Energiall
As Grekes do it call

346 1 *kyng* David the Psalmist 5 *Jerome* in a letter prefacing his translation of the Bible into Latin, St Jerome compares the Psalms with the poems of classical writers 11 *fayne* invent stories 15 *matryculate* entered in a register or official list 17 *sadly* seriously 18–19 *the boke ... advertysement* one of Skelton's lost works 26 *Effecte Energiall* efficacious power

Of suche an industry
And suche a pregnacy
Of hevenly inspyracion
In laureate creacyon
Of poetes commendacion
That of divyne myseracion
God maketh his habytacion
In Poetes whiche excelles
And sojourns with them and dwelles

Thomas Churchyard

347 [*from* A Musicall Consort]

That humor now, declines for age drawes on,
The full tide is, of fine invention gon:
Ebbe followes floud, when vitall vaines waxe dead,
Wit weares and wastes, as torch consumes with winde,
When water turnes, drie growes a flowing head:
In age ech thing, decaies by course of kinde:
Yet whiles the oyle, in lampe may make a blaze,
Or candell in, the socket shewes a light,
On sparkling flame, the cleerest eies will gaze,
And comfort finde, thereby in darkest night:
I yeeld to time, that like a sithe cuts cleane,
All that doth grow, in spring or fall of leafe,
And wish in world, my treble were a meane,
That I might sing, to eares that are not deafe,
A note should sinke, as deepe in jugging brest,
As ever yet, in sea did ancker rest:

346 29 *pregnacy** pregnancy, productiveness 33 *myseracion* mercy, compassion

347 2 *invention* the finding out of subjects to write about 6 *kinde* nature 8 *socket* candle-holder 13 *treble* treble voice 15 *jugging*** making a noise like 'jug' which is associated with nightingales (?); judging (?)

Songs are but likt, as fancies gives them leave,
Both well and ill, as sounds of trumpets are,
Though Syrens voice, the hearers doth deceave,
Mine hath no charme, but open plaine and bare,
As I was borne, so speake I English still,
To lose my paines, and win the worlds good will,
No losse so much, as credit crackt with pen,
Nor gaine so great, as love of honest men.

EDMUND SPENSER

348 [*from* The Faerie Queene Book 6]

Unto this place when as the Elfin Knight
  Approcht, him seemed that the merry sound
  Of a shrill pipe he playing heard on hight,
  And many feete fast thumping th'hollow ground,
  That through the woods their Eccho did rebound.
  He nigher drew, to weete what mote it be;
  There he a troupe of Ladies dauncing found
  Full merrily, and making gladfull glee,
And in the midst a Shepheard piping he did see.

He durst not enter into th'open greene,
  For dread of them unwares to be descryde,
  For breaking of their daunce, if he were seene;
  But in the covert of the wood did byde,
  Beholding all, yet of them unespyde.
  There he did see, that pleased much his sight,
  That even he him selfe his eyes envyde,
  An hundred naked maidens lilly white,
All raunged in a ring, and dauncing in delight.

347 23 *credit crackt* completely ruined, damaged utterly

348 1 *place* Mount Acidale *Elfin* elvish 3 *on hight* aloud; on high 5 cp. the refrain from Spenser's *Epithalamion*, no. 88 6 *weete* know, discover 12 *For breaking* for fear of breaking

All they without were raunged in a ring,
And daunced round; but in the midst of them
Three other Ladies did both daunce and sing,
The whilest the rest them round about did hemme,
And like a girlond did in compasse stemme:
And in the middest of those same three, was placed
Another Damzell, as a precious gemme,
Amidst a ring most richly well enchaced,
That with her goodly presence all the rest much graced.

Looke how the Crowne, which *Ariadne* wore
Upon her yvory forehead that same day,
That *Theseus* her unto his bridale bore,
When the bold *Centaures* made that bloudy fray
With the fierce *Lapithes*, which did them dismay;
Being now placed in the firmament,
Through the bright heaven doth her beams display,
And is unto the starres an ornament,
Which round about her move in order excellent.

Such was the beauty of this goodly band,
Whose sundry parts were here too long to tell:
But she that in the midst of them did stand,
Seem'd all the rest in beauty to excell,
Crownd with a rosie girlond, that right well
Did her beseeme. And ever, as the crew
About her daunst, sweet flowres, that far did smell,
And fragrant odours they uppon her threw;
But most of all, those three did her with gifts endew.

Those were the Graces, daughters of delight,
Handmaides of *Venus*, which are wont to haunt
Uppon this hill, and daunce there day and night:
Those three to men all gifts of grace do graunt,

348 19 *without* on the outside 21 *Ladies* the classical Graces 23 *in compasse* all round *stemme** encircle 26 *enchaced* set as a jewel 30 *bridale* wedding 32 *dismay** defeat by sudden onslaught 42 *beseeme* become *crew* company 44 *odours* perfumes, odoriferous flowers 45 *endew* invest, endow

And all, that *Venus* in her selfe doth vaunt,
Is borrowed of them. But that faire one,
That in the midst was placed paravaunt,
Was she to whom that shepheard pypt alone,
That made him pipe so merrily, as never none.

She was to weete that jolly Shepheards lasse,
Which piped there unto that merry rout,
That jolly shepheard, which there piped, was
Poore *Colin Clout* (who knowes not *Colin Clout?*)
He pypt apace, whilest they him daunst about.
Pype jolly shepheard, pype thou now apace
Unto thy love, that made thee low to lout;
Thy love is present there with thee in place,
Thy love is there advaunst to be another Grace.

Much wondred *Calidore* at this straunge sight,
Whose like before his eye had never seene,
And standing long astonished in spright,
And rapt with pleasaunce, wist not what to weene;
Whether it were the traine of beauties Queene,
Or Nymphes, or Faeries, or enchaunted show,
With which his eyes mote have deluded beene.
Therefore resolving, what it was, to know,
Out of the wood he rose, and toward them did go.

But soone as he appeared to their vew,
They vanisht all away out of his sight,
And cleane were gone, which way he never knew;
All save the shepheard, who for fell despight

348 50 *vaunt* boast of 52 *paravaunt* before the rest, pre-eminently 54 *as never none* as nobody had ever piped before 55 *to weete* to wit, namely 58 *Colin Clout* the pastoral name Spenser had used for himself in *The shepheardes calender* and in his poem 'Colin Clouts come home againe'; it was a name that Skelton had used in his poem (see no. 247), suggesting a poor man of lowly birth: 'Colin' from Latin 'colonnus' meaning a farmer and 'Clout' meaning a rag or patch (cp. no. 177 l. 33) 60 *apace* quickly 61 *lout* bow, stoop 63 *advaunst* promoted, preferred 67 *pleasaunce* pleasure, joy 68 *traine* attendants, followers *Queene* Venus 76 *fell* fierce, savage *despight* scorn, outrage, anger

Of that displeasure, broke his bag-pipe quight,
And made great mone for that unhappy turne.
But *Calidore*, though no lesse sory wight,
For that mishap, yet seeing him to mourne,
Drew neare, that he the truth of all by him mote learne.

And first him greeting, thus unto him spake,
Haile jolly shepheard, which thy joyous dayes
Here leadest in this goodly merry make,
Frequented of these gentle Nymphes alwayes,
Which to thee flocke, to heare thy lovely layes;
Tell me, what mote these dainty Damzels be,
Which here with thee doe make their pleasant playes?
Right happy thou, that mayst them freely see:
But why when I them saw, fled they away from me?

Not I so happy answerd then that swaine,
As thou unhappy, which them thence didst chace,
Whom by no meanes thou canst recall againe,
For being gone, none can them bring in place,
But whom they of them selves list so to grace.
Right sory I, (saide then Sir *Calidore*,)
That my ill fortune did them hence displace.
But since things passed none may now restore,
Tell me, what were they all, whose lacke thee grieves so sore.

Tho gan that shepheard thus for to dilate;
Then wote thou shepheard, whatsoever thou bee,
That all those Ladies, which thou sawest late,
Are *Venus* Damzels, all within her fee,
But differing in honour and degree:
They all are Graces, which on her depend,
Besides a thousand more, which ready bee
Her to adorne, when so she forth doth wend:
But those three in the midst, doe chiefe on her attend.

348 77 in 'Januarye' in *The shepheardes calender* Spenser makes Colin break his pipe 78 *turne* event 84 *merry make* merry-making 86 *lovely layes* lays, songs of love 94 *in place* back again 95 *But whom* except for the person whom *grace* be gracious to 100 *dilate* relate at length 103 *fee* service 105 *on her depend* are dependants of her

They are the daughters of sky-ruling Jove,
By him begot of faire *Eurynome*,
The Oceans daughter, in this pleasant grove,
As he this way comming from feastfull glee,
Of *Thetis* wedding with *Æacidee*,
In sommers shade him selfe here rested weary.
The first of them hight mylde *Euphrosyne*,
Next faire *Aglaia*, last *Thalia* merry:
Sweete Goddesses all three which me in mirth do cherry.

These three on men all gracious gifts bestow,
Which decke the body or adorne the mynde,
To make them lovely or well favoured show,
As comely carriage, entertainement kynde,
Sweete semblaunt, friendly offices that bynde,
And all the complements of curtesie:
They teach us, how to each degree and kynde
We should our selves demeane, to low, to hie;
To friends, to foes, which skill men call Civility.

Therefore they alwaies smoothly seeme to smile,
That we likewise should mylde and gentle be,
And also naked are, that without guile
Or false dissemblaunce all them plaine may see,
Simple and true from covert malice free:
And eeke them selves so in their daunce they bore,
That two of them still forward seem'd to bee,
But one still towards shew'd her selfe afore;
That good should from us goe, then come in greater store.

348 109 *sky-ruling*** 112 *feastfull* feasting, festive 117 *cherry** cheer, delight 118 *gracious gifts* gifts of grace 121 *carriage* deportment, behaviour *entertainement* social behaviour, treatment 122 *semblaunt* demeanour, favour *friendly ... bynde* acts of friendship which forge links between friends 123 *complements* accomplishments; perfections 124 *kynde* nature, estate 126 *Civility* culture, refinement 127 *smoothly* gently 130 *dissemblaunce*** dissimulation, dissembling 133 *forward* going forward from the viewer 134 *towards* coming towards the viewer *afore* before, in front 135 *store* abundance

Such were those Goddesses, which ye did see;
But that fourth Mayd, which there amidst them traced,
Who can aread, what creature mote she bee,
Whether a creature, or a goddesse graced
With heavenly gifts from heven first enraced?
But what so sure she was, she worthy was,
To be the fourth with those three other placed:
Yet was she certes but a countrey lasse,
Yet she all other countrey lasses farre did passe.

So farre as doth the daughter of the day,
All other lesser lights in light excell,
So farre doth she in beautyfull array,
Above all other lasses beare the bell,
Ne lesse in vertue that beseemes her well,
Doth she exceede the rest of all her race,
For which the Graces that here wont to dwell,
Have for more honor brought her to this place,
And graced her so much to be another Grace.

Another Grace she well deserves to be,
In whom so many Graces gathered are,
Excelling much the meane of her degree;
Divine resemblaunce, beauty soveraine rare,
Firme Chastity, that spight ne blemish dare;
All which she with such courtesie doth grace,
That all her peres cannot with her compare,
But quite are dimmed, when she is in place.
She made me often pipe and now to pipe apace.

Sunne of the world, great glory of the sky,
That all the earth doest lighten with thy rayes,
Great *Gloriana*, greatest Majesty,
Pardon thy shepheard, mongst so many layes,

348 137 *traced* danced 138 *aread* tell, say 140 *enraced* inborn, inbred 145 *daughter* Venus 147 *array* attire, dress; presence 148 *beare the bell* take first place, be the best 156 *meane* average 160 *peres* equals, rivals 165 *Gloriana* the Queen of Fairyland; one of the names in the poem by which Spenser refers to Queen Elizabeth

As he hath sung of thee in all his dayes,
To make one minime of thy poore handmayd,
And underneath thy feete to place her prayse,
That when thy glory shall be farre displayd
To future age of her this mention may be made.

Sir John Harington

349 Of honest Theft. To my good friend Master *Samuel Daniel*

Proud *Paulus* late my secrecies revealing,
Hath told I got some good conceits by stealing.
But where got he those double Pistolets,
With which good clothes, good fare, good land he gets?
Tush, those, he saith, came by a man of warre,
That brought a Prize of price, from countries farre.
Then, fellow Thiefe, let's shake together hands,
Sith both our wares are filcht from forren lands.
You'le spoile the Spaniards, by your writ of Mart:
And I the Romanes rob, by wit, and Art.

John Donne

350 The triple Foole

I am two fooles, I know,
For loving, and for saying so
In whining Poëtry;
But where's that wiseman, that would not be I,
If she would not deny?

348 168 *minime* traditionally, a musical note of the shortest duration

349 2 *conceits* ideas 3 *Pistolets* a Spanish gold coin worth just under a pound 9 *writ of Mart* licence to fit out an armed vessel to raid an enemy's merchant shipping 10 *Romanes* classical writers

Then as th'earths inward narrow crooked lanes
Do purge sea waters fretfull salt away,
I thought, if I could draw my paines,
Through Rimes vexation, I should them allay,
Griefe brought to numbers cannot be so fierce,
For, he tames it, that fetters it in verse.

But when I have done so,
Some man, his art and voice to show,
Doth Set and sing my paine,
And, by delighting many, frees againe
Griefe, which verse did restraine.
To Love, and Griefe tribute of Verse belongs,
But not of such as pleases when'tis read,
Both are increased by such songs:
For both their triumphs so are published,
And I, which was two fooles, do so grow three;
Who are a little wise, the best fooles bee.

William Shakespeare

351 [*from* Sonnets]

108

What's in the braine that Inck may character,
Which hath not figur'd to thee my true spirit,
What's new to speake, what now to register,
That may expresse my love, or thy deare merit?
Nothing sweet boy, but yet like prayers divine,
I must each day say ore the very same,
Counting no old thing old, thou mine, I thine,
Even as when first I hallowed thy faire name.

350 6–7 the theory that the salt in sea-water was lost through the earth's filtration in winding rivers 10 *numbers* poetry, verse, metrical forms

351 1 *character* write 2 *figur'd* represented 3 *register* list, record 7 *old thing* familiar phrase 8 *hallowed ... name* cp. the Lord's Prayer, 'hallowed be Thy name'

So that eternall love in loves fresh case,
Waighes not the dust and injury of age,
Nor gives to necessary wrinckles place,
But makes antiquitie for aye his page,
  Finding the first conceit of love there bred,
  Where time and outward forme would shew it dead.

JOHN MARSTON

352 [*from* The Scourge of Villanie]

In Lectores prorsus indignos

Fy Satyre fie, shall each mechanick slave,
Each dunghill pesant, free perusall have
Of thy well labor'd lines? Each sattin sute,
Each quaint fashion-monger, whose sole repute
Rests in his trim gay clothes, lye slavering
Taynting thy lines with his lewd censuring?
Shall each odd puisne of the Lawyers Inne,
Each barmy-froth, that last day did beginne
To reade his little, or his *nere a whit*,
Or shall some greater auncient, of lesse wit,
(That never turnd but browne Tobacco leaves)
Whose sences some damn'd *Occupant* bereaves,
Lye gnawing on thy vacant times expence?
Tearing thy rimes, quite altering the sence?

351 9 *case* condition, circumstances; covering; subject for poetry 10 *Waighes* considers, values, balances 13 *conceit* flush; literary conceit

352 Title *In ... indignos* 'Directly to unworthy readers' 3 *sattin sute* courtier, dandy 4 *fashion-monger** follower, student, of fashion 7 *puisne* junior, novice *Inne* Inns of Court 8 *barmy-froth** empty-headed fellow 9 *nere a whit* never a whit, none at all; the *little* and the *nere a whit* may refer to elementary law books (?) 10 *auncient* ancient, senior member of the Inns of Court or Chancery division 12 *Occupant* whore, harlot 13 *thy* the satirist's *expence* expenditure

Or shall perfum'd *Castilio* censure thee?
Shall he oreview thy sharpe-fang'd poesie?
(Who nere read farther then his Mistris lips)
Nere practiz'd ought, but som spruce capring skips
Nere in his life did other language use,
But, *Sweete Lady, faire Mistres, kind hart, deare couse,*
Shall this *Fantasma*, this *Colosse* peruse
And blast with stinking breath, thy budding Muse?
Fye, wilt thou make thy wit a Curtezan
For every broking hand-crafts artizan?
Shall brainles Cyterne heads, each jubernole,
Poket the very *Genius* of thy soule?
  I *Phylo*, I, I'le keepe an open hall,
A common, and a sumptuous festivall,
Welcome all eyes, all eares, all tongues to me,
Gnaw pesants on my scraps of poesie.
Castilios, Cyprians, court-boyes, spanish blocks,
Ribanded eares, granado-netherstocks,
Fidlers, Scriveners, pedlers, tynkering knaves,
Base blew-coats, tapsters, brod-cloth minded slaves,
Welcome I-fayth, but may you nere depart,
Till I have made your gauled hides to smart.
Your gauled hides? avaunt base muddy scum.
Thinke you a Satyres dreadfull sounding drum
Will brace it selfe? and daine to terrefie,
Such abject pesants basest rogary?

352 15 *Castilio* a generic name for a courtier, from Castiglione's *The book of the courtier* 16 *sharpe-fang'd** caustic, sarcastic 18 *capring** dancing, leaping 20 *couse* coz, cousin 21 *Fantasma* illusion, vision; apparition, spectre *Colosse* vast, but empty, rotten figure 24 *broking* dealing as a broker, fraudulently 25 *Cyterne* cithern, a plucked musical instrument of the guitar kind which often had a grotesque human head carved at one end *jubernole* jobbernowl, blockhead 27 *Phylo* a generic name (from the Greek) for a friend 28 *common* common table, shared by, open to, all 31 *Cyprians* prostitutes *court-boyes* pages; rent-boys *spanish blocks* wooden moulds for Spanish hats: those who wear such hats; blockheads from, or affecting to be from, Spain 32 *Ribanded** *granado-netherstocks* silk stockings from Granada 33 *Scriveners* legal writers, money-lenders 34 *blew-coats* servants; beadles *brod-cloth... slaves* servants who can think of nothing but selling good-quality cloth; citizens who are slaves to the social and fashionable status of wearing such cloth 37 *gauled* sore, rubbed 39 *brace* stretch, tighten 40 *rogary* roguery

No, no, passe on ye vaine fantasticke troupe
Of puffie youthes; Know I doe scorne to stoupe
To rip your lives. Then hence lewd nags, away,
Goe read each post, view what is plaid to day.
Then to *Priapus* gardens. You *Castilio*,
I pray thee let my lines in freedome goe,
Let me alone, the Madams call for thee
Longing to laugh at thy wits povertie.
Sirra, livorie cloake, you lazie slipper slave,
Thou fawning drudge, what would'st thou Satyres have?
Base mind away, thy master calls, begon,
Sweet *Gnato* let my poesie alone.
Goe buy some ballad of the Faiery King,
And of the begger wench, some rogie thing
Which thou maist chaunt unto the chamber-maid
To some vile tune, when that thy Maister's laid.
  But will you needs stay? am I forc'd to beare,
The blasting breath of each lewd Censurer?
Must naught but clothes, and images of men
But sprightles truncks, be Judges of my pen?
Nay then come all, I prostitute my Muse,
For all the swarme of Idiots to abuse.
Reade all, view all, even with my full consent,
So you will know that which I never meant;
So you will nere conceive, and yet dispraise,
That which you nere conceiv'd, and laughter raise:
Where I but strive in honest seriousnes,
To scourge some soule-poluting beastlines.
So you will raile, and finde huge errors lurke
In every corner of my Cynick worke.
Proface, reade on, for your extreamst dislikes
Will add a pineon, to my praises flights.

352 43 *rip* expose or reveal something bad *nags** ponies, as a term of abuse 44 *post* plays were advertised on posts 45 *Priapus gardens* perhaps intended to suggest the Paris Garden, near the theatres, where bears were baited 49 *livorie cloake** as a gentleman, Gnato wears a cloak, but he is really a servant in livery *slipper* slippery 52 *Gnato* from the plays of Terence and Plautus, a generic name for a parasite 54 *rogie** roguy, roguish 60 *sprightles* spiritless 71 *Proface* an Old French greeting at the beginning of a meal, 'may it do you good' 72 *pineon* pinion, the outermost feather of a bird's wing

O, how I bristle up my plumes of pride,
O, how I thinke my Satyres dignifi'd,
When I once heare some quaint *Castilio*,
Some supple mouth'd slave, some lewd *Tubrio*,
Some spruce pedant, or some span-new come fry
Of Innes a-court, striving to vilefie
My darke reproofes. Then doe but raile at me,
No greater honor craves my poesie.

1. But yee diviner wits, celestiall soules,
Whose free-borne mindes no kennel thought controules,
Ye sacred spirits, *Mayas* eldest sonnes.

2. Yee substance of the shadowes of our age,
In whom all graces linke in marriage,
To you how cheerfully my poeme runnes.

3. True judging eyes, quick sighted censurers,
Heavens best beauties, wisedoms treasurers,
O how my love embraceth your great worth.

4. Yee Idols of my soule, yee blessed spirits,
How shold I give true honor to your merrits,
Which I can better thinke, then here paint forth.

You sacred spirits, *Maias* eldest sonnes,
To you how cheerfully my poeme runnes.
O how my love, embraceth your great worth,
Which I can better think, then here paint forth.

O rare!

352 76 *supple mouth'd** obsequious or flattering in speech *Tubrio* generic name for a braggart soldier 77 *span-new** brand-new *fry* junior, young person 82 *kennel* gutter 83 *Mayas . . . sonnes* those most skilled in eloquence

Samuel Daniel

353 [*from* Musophilus]

Philocosmus.

Fond man *Musophilus*, that thus dost spend
In an ungainefull arte thy deerest daies,
Tyring thy wits and toiling to no end,
But to attaine that idle smoake of praise;
Now when this busie world cannot attend
Th'untimely musicke of neglected layes.
Other delights then these, other desires
This wiser profit-seeking age requires. . . .

[Philocosmus]

Men find that action is another thing
Then what they in discoursing papers reade,
The worlds affaires require in managing
More arts then those wherin you Clearks proceed,
Whilst timorous knowledge stands considering,
Audacious ignorance hath done the deed.
For who knowes most, the more he knows to doubt,
The least discourse is commonly most stout.
This sweet inchaunting knowledge turnes you cleene
Out from the fields of naturall delight,
And makes you hide unwilling to be seene
In th'open concourse of a publike sight:
This skill wherewith you have so cunning beene,
Unsinewes all your powres, unmans you quite.

353 1 *Fond* foolish 2 *ungainefull** 8 *profit-seeking** 10 *discoursing* abstract, philosophical 16 *least* shortest 22 *Unsinewes** weakens, enfeebles

Publike societie and commerce of men
  Require another grace, another port:
  This eloquence, these rymes, these phrases then
  Begot in shades, do serve us in no sort,
  Th'unmateriall swellings of your pen
  Touch not the spirit that action doth import:
A manly stile fitted to manlie eares
  Best grees with wit, not that which goes so gay,
  And commonly the gaudie liv'rie weares
  Of nice corruptions which the times do sway,
  And waites on th'humor of his pulse that beares
  His passions set to such a pleasing kay;
  Such dainties serve onely for stomacks weake,
  For men do fowlest when they finest speake. ...

[Musophilus]

Powre above powres, O heavenly *Eloquence*,
  That with the strong reine of commanding words,
  Dost manage, guide, and master th'eminence
  Of mens affections, more then all their swords:
  Shall we not offer to thy excellence
  The richest treasure that our wit affoords?
Thou that canst do much more with one poor pen
  Then all the powres of princes can effect:
  And draw, divert, dispose, and fashion men
  Better then force or rigour can direct:
  Should we this ornament of glorie then
  As th'unmateriall fruits of shades, neglect?
Or should we carelesse come behind the rest
  In powre of wordes, that go before in worth,
  When as our accents equall to the best
  Is able greater wonders to bring forth:
  When all that ever hotter spirits exprest
  Comes bettered by the patience of the North?

353 24 *port* disposition 32 *nice* precise, exact 34 *kay* key 39 *eminence*** eminent quality, excellence; pride (?) 51 *accents* speech, language

And who in time knowes whither we may vent
The treasure of our tongue, to what strange shores
This gaine of our best glorie shal be sent,
T'inrich unknowing Nations with our stores?
What worlds in th'yet unformed Occident
May come refin'd with th'accents that are ours?
Or who can tell for what great worke in hand
The greatnes of our stile is now ordain'd?
What powres it shall bring in, what spirits command,
What thoughts let out, what humors keep restrain'd
What mischiefe it may powrefully withstand,
And what faire ends may thereby be attain'd.
And as for Poesie (mother of this force)
That breeds, brings forth, and nourishes this might,
Teaching it in a loose, yet measured course,
With comely motions how to go upright:
And fostring it with bountifull discourse
Adorns it thus in fashions of delight,
What should I say? since it is well approv'd
The speech of heaven, with whom they have commerce
That only seeme out of themselves remov'd,
And do with more then humane skils converse:
Those numbers wherewith heaven and earth are mov'd,
Shew, weakenes speaks in prose, but powre in verse.

BEN JONSON

354 A Fit of Rime against Rime

Rime, the rack of finest wits,
That expresseth but by fits,
True Conceipt,

353 55 *vent* vend, sell 77 *numbers* poems, verses

354 1 *rack* instrument of torture; wreck 2 *fits* spasms; sections of poems

Spoyling Senses of their Treasure,
Cosening Judgement with a measure,
                But false weight.
Wresting words, from their true calling;
Propping Verse, for feare of falling
                To the ground.
Joynting Syllabes, drowning Letters,
Fastning Vowells, as with fetters
                They were bound!
Soone as lazie thou wert knowne,
All good Poëtrie hence was flowne,
                And Art banish'd.
For a thousand yeares together,
All *Pernassus* Greene did wither,
                And wit vanish'd.
Pegasus did flie away,
At the Wells no Muse did stay,
                But bewail'd
So to see the Fountaine drie,
And *Apollo's* Musique die,
                All light failed!
Starveling rimes did fill the Stage,
Not a Poët in an Age,
                Worth crowning.
Not a worke deserving Baies,
Nor a lyne deserving praise,
                Pallas frowning.
Greeke was free from Rimes infection,
Happy Greeke by this protection!
                Was not spoyled.
Whilst the Latin, Queene of Tongues,
Is not yet free from Rimes wrongs,
                But rests foiled.

354 5 *measure* metrical unit 10 *Joynting* dividing up into parts, between lines or verses 20 *Wells* Aganippe and Hippocrene 25 *Starveling* weak, hungry 28 *Baies* poetic laurels 34–5 Humanists deplored the medieval custom of using rhyme in Latin verse

Scarce the hill againe doth flourish,
Scarce the world a Wit doth nourish,
To restore
Phœbus to his Crowne againe;
And the Muses to their braine;
As before.
Vulgar Languages that want
Words, and sweetnesse, and be scant
Of true measure,
Tyran Rime hath so abused,
That they long since have refused
Other ceasure.
He that first invented thee,
May his joynts tormented bee,
Cramp'd forever;
Still may Syllabes jarre with time,
Stil may reason warre with rime,
Resting never.
May his Sense, when it would meet
The cold tumor in his feet,
Grow unsounder.
And his Title be long foole,
That in rearing such a Schoole,
Was the founder.

355 An Ode. To himselfe

Where do'st thou carelesse lie,
Buried in ease and sloth?
Knowledge, that sleepes, doth die;
And this Securitie,
It is the common Moath,
That eats on wits, and Arts, and oft destroyes them both.

354 37 *hill* Parnassus 43 *Vulgar* ordinary, vernacular, not learned 48 *ceasure* caesura 56 *tumor* swelling, turgidity, bombast *feet* metre

355 1–2 cp. Ovid, *Amores* 1.15.1 'Why, devouring Envy, do you accuse me of wasting my years and call a poem of genius an idler's work?' 4 *Securitie* complacency, carelessness 5 *Moath* moth

Are all th'*Aonian* springs
Dri'd up? lyes *Thespia* wast?
Doth *Clarius* Harp want strings,
That not a Nymph now sings!
Or droop they as disgrac't,
To see their Seats and Bowers by chattring Pies defac't?

If hence thy silence be,
As 'tis too just a cause;
Let this thought quicken thee,
Minds that are great and free,
Should not on fortune pause,
'Tis crowne enough to vertue still, her owne applause.

What though the greedie Frie
Be taken with false Baytes
Of worded Balladrie,
And thinke it Poësie?
They die with their conceits,
And only pitious scorne, upon their folly waites.

Then take in hand thy Lyre,
Strike in thy proper straine,
With *Japhets* lyne, aspire
Sols Chariot for new fire,
To give the world againe:
Who aided him, will thee, the issue of *Joves* braine.

And since our Daintie age,
Cannot indure reproofe,
Make not thy selfe a Page,
To that strumpet the Stage,
But sing high and aloofe,
Safe from the wolves black jaw, and the dull Asses hoofe.

355 9 *Clarius* Apollo's 12 *chattring Pies* saucy, gossiping people (magpies) 15 *quicken* stimulate, excite 19 *Frie* young fish; young people 21 *worded*** wordy (?) 27 *lyne* Prometheus *aspire* inspire; aspire to 30 *issue* Minerva 35–6 also used by Jonson in the last two lines of the 'Apologetic Dialogue' to *Poetaster*, 1602

GEORGE CHAPMAN

356 [*from* Homer's Iliad, To the Reader]

Our English language, above all others, for Rhythmicall Poesie.

And, for our tongue, that still is so empayr'd
  By travailing linguists; I can prove it cleare,
That no tongue hath the Muses utterance heyr'd
  For verse, and that sweet Musique to the eare
Strooke out of rime, so naturally as this;
  Our Monosyllables, so kindly fall
And meete, opposde in rime, as they did kisse:
  French and Italian, most immetricall;
Their many syllables, in harsh Collision,
  Fall as they brake their necks; their bastard Rimes
Saluting as they justl'd in transition,
  And set our teeth on edge; nor tunes, nor times
Kept in their falles. And me thinkes, their long words
  Shew in short verse, as in a narrow place,
Two opposites should meet, with two-hand swords
  Unweildily, without or use or grace.

356 2 *travailing* travelling; toiling 3 *heyr'd* made heir 8 *immetricall** unmetrical 15 *opposites* enemies 16 *Unweildily** in an unwieldy way

SIR WALTER RALEGH

357 To the Translator

Had *Lucan* hid the truth to please the time,
He had beene too unworthy of thy Penne:
Who never sought, nor ever car'd to clime
By flattery, or seeking worthlesse men.
For this thou hast been bruis'd: but yet those scarres
Do beautifie no lesse, then those wounds do
Receiv'd in just, and in religious warres;
Though thou hast bled by both, and bearst them too.
Change not, to change thy fortune tis too late.
Who with a manly faith resolves to dye,
May promise to himselfe a lasting state,
Though not so great, yet free from infamy.
Such was thy *Lucan*, whom so to translate
Nature thy Muse (like LUCANS) did create.

WILLIAM BROWNE

358 [*from* Britannia's Pastorals Book 2]

Happyer those times were, when the Flaxen clew
By faire *Arachne's* hand the *Lydians* knew,
And sought not to the worme for silken threds,
To rowle their bodies in, or dresse their heads.
When wise *Minerva* did th'*Athenians* learne
To draw their milke-white fleeces into yarne;

357 Title *Translator* Sir Arthur Gorges 7 *just* joust, tournament; righteous

358 1 *clew* ball of thread

And knowing not the mixtures which began
(Of colours) from the *Babilonian*,
Nor wooll in *Sardis* dyde, more various knowne
By hues, then *Iris* to the world hath showne:
The bowels of our mother were not ript
For *Mader-pits*, nor the sweet meadowes stript
Of their choise beauties, nor for *Ceres* loade
The fertile lands burd'ned with needlesse *Woade*.
Through the wide Seas no winged Pine did goe
To Lands unknowne for staining *Indico*;
Nor men in scorching clymates moar'd their Keele
To trafficke for the costly *Coucheneele*.
Unknowne was then the *Phrygian* brodery,
The *Tyrian* purple, and the Scarlet dye,
Such as their sheepe clad, such they wove and wore,
Russet or white, or those mixt, and no more:
Except sometimes (to bravery inclinde)
They dyde them yealow caps with *Alder* rynde.
The *Græcian* mantle, *Tuscan* robes of state,
Tissue nor *Cloth of gold* of highest rate,
They never saw; onely in pleasant woods,
Or by th'embrodered margin of the floods,
The dainty *Nymphs* they often did behold
Clad in their light silke robes, stitcht oft with gold.
The Arras hangings round their comely Hals,
Wanted the *Cerites* web and minerals:
Greene boughes of trees which fatning Acornes lade,
Hung full with flowres and Garlands quaintly made,
Their homely *Cotes* deck'd trim in low degree,
As now the *Court* with richest *Tapistry*. . . .
The *Pansie*, *Thistle*, all with prickles set,
The *Cowslip*, *Honisuckle*, *Violet*,
And many hundreds more that grac'd the Meades,
Gardens and Groves, (where beauteous *Flora* treads)

358 8 *Babilonian* the confusion of languages began with the building of the Tower of Babel; see Genesis 11:1–9 12 *Mader-pits** a pit dug in connection with the madder plant which was used in dyeing 15 *Pine* ship 16 *Indico* indigo 18 *trafficke* bargain, trade *Coucheneele* cochineal, a dye 19 *brodery* embroidery 23 *bravery* fine, showy clothes 32 *Cerites* a precious stone, mentioned by Pliny; its identity is now unknown 35 *Cotes* cottages

Were by the Shepheards Daughters (as yet are
Us'd in our Cotes) brought home with speciall care:
For bruising them they not alone would quell
But rot the rest, and spoile their pleasing smell.
Much like a Lad, who in his tender prime
Sent from his friends to learne the use of time,
As are his mates, or good or bad, so he
Thrives to the world, and such his actions be.
  As in the *Rainbowes* many coloured hewe
Here see wee watchet deepned with a blewe,
There a darke tawny with a purple mixt,
Yealow and flame, with streakes of greene betwixt,
A bloudy streame into a blushing run
And ends still with the colour which begun,
Drawing the deeper to a lighter staine,
Bringing the lightest to the deep'st againe,
With such rare Art each mingleth with his fellow,
The blewe with watchet, greene and red with yealow;
Like to the changes which we daily see
About the Doves necke with varietie,
Where none can say (though he it strict attends)
Here one begins; and there the other ends:
So did the Maidens with their various flowres
Decke up their windowes, and make neate their bowres:
Using such cunning as they did dispose
The ruddy *Piny* with the lighter *Rose*,
The *Moncks-hood* with the *Buglosse*, and intwine
The white, the blewe, the flesh-like *Columbine*
With *Pinckes*, *Sweet-williams*; that farre off the eye
Could not the manner of their mixtures spye.
  Then with those flowres they most of all did prise,
(With all their skill and in most curious wise
On tufts of Hearbs or Rushes) would they frame
A daintie border round their Shepheards name.
Or *Poesies* make, so quaint, so apt, so rare,
As if the *Muses* onely lived there:

358 43 *bruising* crushing 50 *watchet* a light blue colour; cloth or a garment of the colour 66 *Piny* peony

And that the after world should strive in vaine
What they then did to counterfeit againe.
Nor will the Needle nor the Loome e're be
So perfect in their best embroderie,
Nor such composures make of silke and gold,
As theirs, when Nature all her cunning told.

Rachel Speght

359 [*from* The Dreame]

Disswasion hearing her assigne my helpe,
(And seeing that consent I did detect)
Did many remoraes to me propose,
As dulnesse, and my memories defect;
The difficultie of attaining lore,
My time, and sex, with many others more.

Which when I heard, my minde was much perplext,
And as a horse new come into the field,
Who with a Harquebuz at first doth start,
So did this shot make me recoyle and yeeld.
But of my feare when some did notice take,
In my behalfe, they this reply did make.

First quoth *Desire*, *Disswasion*, hold thy peace,
These oppositions come not from above:
Quoth *Truth*, they cannot spring from reasons roote,
And therefore now thou shalt no victor prove.
No, quoth *Industrie*, be assured this,
Her friends shall make thee of thy purpose misse.

358 81 *composures* compositions

359 1 *her* Experience *helpe* Industry 2 *detect* uncover, display 3 *remoraes* obstacles, hindrances 8 *field* of battle 9 *Harquebuz* arquebus, gun

For with my sickle I will cut away
All obstacles, that in her way can grow,
And by the issue of her owne attempt,
I'le make thee *labor omnia vincet* know.
Quoth *Truth*, and sith her sex thou do'st object,
Thy folly I by reason will detect.

Both man and woman of three parts consist,
Which *Paul* doth bodie, soule, and spirit call: I.Thess. 5.23.
And from the soule three faculties arise,
The mind, the will, the power; then wherefore shall
A woman have her intellect in vaine,
Or not endevour *Knowledge* to attaine.

The talent, God doth give, must be imploy'd, Luke 19.23.
His owne with vantage he must have againe:
All parts and faculties were made for use; I Sam. 2.3.
The God of *Knowledge* nothing gave in vaine.
'Twas *Maries* choyce our Saviour did approve, Luke 10.42.
Because that she the better part did love.

Cleobulina, and *Demophila*,
With *Telesilla*, as Historians tell,
(Whose fame doth live, though they have long bin dead)
Did all of them in Poetrie excell.
A Roman matron that *Cornelia* hight,
An eloquent and learned style did write.

Hypatia in Astronomie had skill,
Aspatia was in Rheth'ricke so expert,
As that Duke *Pericles* of her did learne;
Areta did devote her selfe to art:
And by consent (which shewes she was no foole)
She did succeed her father in his schoole.

359 22 *labor ... vincet* work will overcome all things, cp. Virgil, *Georgics* 1.145; it is traditionally love ('amor') which overcomes all obstacles 26 'I pray God your whole spirit and soul and body be preserved blameless unto the coming of our Lord Jesus Christ' 31 the parable of the talents, Luke 19:11–27 33 'for the Lord is a God of knowledge' 35 'Mary hath chosen that good part, which shall not be taken away from her'

And many others here I could produce,
Who were in Science counted excellent;
But these examples which I have rehearst,
To shew thy error are sufficient.
Thus having sayd, she turn'd her speech to mee,
That in my purpose I might constant bee.

My friend, quoth she, regard not vulgar talke;
For dung-hill Cocks at precious stones will spurne,
And swine-like natures prize not cristall streames,
Contemned mire, and mud will serve their turne.
Good purpose seldome oppositions want:
But constant mindes *Disswasion* cannot daunt.

Shall every blast disturbe the Saylors peace?
Or boughes and bushes Travellers affright?
True valour doth not start at every noyse;
Small combates must instruct for greater fight.
Disdaine to bee with every dart dismayd;
'Tis childish to be suddenly affrayd.

Michael Drayton

360 [*from* Idea]

25.

O, why should Nature niggardly restraine!
That Foraine Nations rellish not our Tongue,
Else should my Lines glide on the Waves of *Rhene*,
And crowne the *Piren's* with my living Song:
But bounded thus, to *Scotland* get you forth,
Thence take you Wing unto the *Orcades*,
There let my Verse get glory in the North,
Making my Sighes to thaw the Frozen Seas;

359 56 *spurne* tread on, come across; scorn, despise

360 4 *Piren's* the Pyrenees 6 *Orcades* Orkneys

And let the *Bards* within that *Irish* Ile,
To whom my Muse with fierie Wings shall passe,
Call backe the stiffe-neck'd Rebels from Exile,
And mollifie the slaught'ring *Galliglasse*;
  And when my flowing Numbers they rehearse,
  Let Wolves and Beares be charmed with my Verse.

361 To my most dearely-loved friend Henery Reynolds Esquire, of *Poets and Poesie*

My dearely loved friend how oft have we,
In winter evenings (meaning to be free,)
To some well chosen place us'd to retire;
And there with moderate meate, and wine, and fire,
Have past the howres contentedly with chat,
Now talk'd of this, and then discours'd of that,
Spoke our owne verses 'twixt our selves, if not
Other mens lines, which we by chance had got,
Or some Stage pieces famous long before,
Of which your happy memory had store;
And I remember you much pleased were,
Of those who lived long agoe to heare,
As well as of those, of these latter times,
Who have inricht our language with their rimes,
And in succession, how still up they grew,
Which is the subject, that I now pursue;
For from my cradle (you must know that) I,
Was still inclin'd to noble Poesie,
And when that once *Pueriles* I had read,
And newly had my *Cato* construed,
In my small selfe I greatly marveil'd then,
Amongst all other, what strange kinde of men
These Poets were; And pleased with the name,
To my milde Tutor merrily I came,
(For I was then a proper goodly page,
Much like a Pigmy, scarse ten yeares of age)

360 12 *Galliglasse* Irish soldiers or retainers

361 Title *Henery Reynolds* see the textual note

Clasping my slender armes about his thigh.
O my deare master! cannot you (quoth I)
Make me a Poet, doe it; if you can,
And you shall see, Ile quickly be a man,
Who me thus answered smiling, boy quoth he,
If you'le not play the wag, but I may see
You ply your learning, I will shortly read
Some Poets to you; *Phœbus* be my speed,
Too't hard went I, when shortly he began,
And first read to me honest *Mantuan*,
Then *Virgils Eglogues*, being entred thus,
Me thought I straight had mounted *Pegasus*,
And in his full Careere could make him stop,
And bound upon *Parnassus* by-clift top.
I scornd your ballet then though it were done
And had for Finis, *William Elderton*.
But soft, in sporting with this childish jest,
I from my subject have too long digrest,
Then to the matter that we tooke in hand,
Jove and *Apollo* for the *Muses* stand.
  That noble *Chaucer*, in those former times,
The first inrich'd our *English* with his rimes,
And was the first of ours, that ever brake,
Into the *Muses* treasure, and first spake
In weighty numbers, delving in the Mine
Of perfect knowledge, which he could refine,
And coyne for currant, and asmuch as then
The *English* language could expresse to men,
He made it doe; and by his wondrous skill,
Gave us much light from his abundant quill.
  And honest *Gower*, who in respect of him,
Had only sipt at *Aganippas* brimme,
And though in yeares this last was him before,
Yet fell he far short of the others store.

361 36 *Mantuan* Johannes Baptista Spagnolo of Mantua (1448–1516), whose Latin eclogues were widely read in Renaissance schools (see no. 174) 40 *by-clift* bicleft, split in two 42 *William Elderton* (?–1592?) ballad-writer 47 *Chaucer* Geoffrey Chaucer (1343?–1400), author of *The Canterbury tales*, *Troilus and Criseyde* etc. 57 *Gower* John Gower (1330?–1408), author of the *Confessio amantis* and other poems

When after those, foure ages very neare,
They with the Muses which conversed, were
That Princely *Surrey*, early in the time
Of the Eight *Henry*, who was then the prime
Of *Englands* noble youth; with him there came
Wyat; with reverence whom we still doe name
Amongst our Poets, *Brian* had a share
With the two former, which accompted are
That times best makers, and the authors were
Of those small poems, which the title beare,
Of songs and sonnets, wherein oft they hit
On many dainty passages of wit.
Gascoine and *Churchyard* after them againe
In the beginning of *Eliza's* raine,
Accoumpted were great Meterers many a day,
But not inspired with brave fier, had they
Liv'd but a little longer, they had seene,
Their workes before them to have buried beene.
Grave morrall *Spencer* after these came on
Then whom I am perswaded there was none
Since the blind *Bard* his *Iliads* up did make,
Fitter a taske like that to undertake,
To set downe boldly, bravely to invent,
In all high knowledge, surely excellent.
The noble *Sidney*, with this last arose,
That *Heroe* for numbers, and for Prose.
That throughly pac'd our language as to show,
The plenteous *English* hand in hand might goe
With *Greeke* and *Latine*, and did first reduce
Our tongue from *Lillies* writing then in use;

361 63 *Surrey* Henry Howard, Earl of Surrey, see Appendix 4 66 *Wyat* Sir Thomas Wyatt, see Appendix 4 67 *Brian* Sir Francis Bryan (?–1550), courtier and diplomat; the nature of his contribution to Tottel's *Songes and sonettes* is uncertain 69 *makers* poets 71 *songs and sonnets* the title of the important collection of poems published by Richard Tottel in 1557 73 *Gascoine* George Gascoigne, see Appendix 4 *Churchyard* Thomas Churchyard, see Appendix 4 79 *Spencer* Edmund Spenser, see Appendix 4 81 *blind Bard* Homer 85 *Sidney* Sir Philip Sidney, see Appendix 4 86 *numbers* poetry, metrical compositions 90 *Lillies* John Lyly (1554?–1606), playwright whose prose romance *Euphues* (1578 and 1580) made the euphuistic style popular

Talking of Stones, Stars, Plants, of fishes, Flyes,
Playing with words, and idle Similies,
As th'*English*, Apes and very Zanies be
Of every thing, that they doe heare and see,
So imitating his ridiculous tricks,
They spake and writ, all like meere lunatiques.
Then *Warner* though his lines were not so trim'd,
Nor yet his Poem so exactly lim'd
And neatly joynted, but the Criticke may
Easily reproove him, yet thus let me say;
For my old friend, some passages, there be
In him, which I protest have taken me,
With almost wonder, so fine, cleere, and new
As yet they have bin equalled by few.
Neat *Marlow* bathed in the *Thespian* springs
Had in him those brave translunary things,
That the first Poets had, his raptures were,
All ayre, and fire, which made his verses cleere,
For that fine madnes still he did retaine,
Which rightly should possesse a Poets braine.
And surely *Nashe*, though he a Proser were
A branch of Lawrell yet deserves to beare,
Sharply *Satirick* was he, and that way
He went, since that his being, to this day
Few have attempted, and I surely thinke
Those words shall hardly be set downe with inke;
Shall scorch and blast, so as his could, where he,
Would inflict vengeance, and be it said of thee,
Shakespeare thou hadst as smooth a Comicke vaine,
Fitting the socke, and in thy naturall braine,
As strong conception, and as Cleere a rage,
As any one that trafiqu'd with the stage.

361 93 *Apes* unthinking imitators *Zanies* mimics 97 *Warner* William Warner (1558?–1609), poet most famous for his long poem *Albions England*, 1586 98 *lim'd* given limbs, articulated 105 *Marlow* Christopher Marlowe, see Appendix 4 106 *translunary** beyond or above the moon, ethereal, visionary 111 *Nashe* Thomas Nashe, see Appendix 4 *Proser** writer of prose 119 *Shakespeare* William Shakespeare, see Appendix 4 120 *socke* light shoe worn by comic actors in ancient Greece and Rome, comedy 122 *trafiqu'd* had dealings

Amongst these *Samuel Daniel*, whom if I
May spake of, but to sensure doe denie,
Onely have heard some wisemen him rehearse,
To be too much *Historian* in verse;
His rimes were smooth, his meeters well did close
But yet his maner better fitted prose:
Next these, learn'd *Johnson*, in this List I bring,
Who had drunke deepe of the *Pierian* spring,
Whose knowledge did him worthily prefer,
And long was Lord here of the Theater,
Who in opinion made our learn'st to sticke,
Whether in Poems rightly dramatique,
Strong *Seneca* or *Plautus*, he or they,
Should beare the Buskin, or the Socke away.
Others againe here lived in my dayes,
That have of us deserved no lesse praise
For their translations, then the daintiest wit
That on *Parnassus* thinks, he highst doth sit,
And for a chaire may mongst the Muses call,
As the most curious maker of them all;
As reverent *Chapman*, who hath brought to us,
Musæus, *Homer*, and *Hesiodus*
Out of the Greeke; and by his skill hath reard
Them to that height, and to our tongue endear'd,
That were those Poets at this day alive,
To see their bookes thus with us to survive,
They would think, having neglected them so long,
They had bin written in the *English* tongue.
And *Silvester* who from the *French* more weake,
Made *Bartas* of his sixe dayes labour speake
In naturall *English*, who, had he there stayd,
He had done well, and never had bewraid,
His owne invention, to have bin so poore
Who still wrote lesse, in striving to write more.

361 123 *Samuel Daniel* see Appendix 4 129 *Johnson* Ben Jonson, see Appendix 4 136 *Buskin* thick-soled boot worn by actors in ancient Greece in tragedies 151 *Silvester* Josuah Sylvester, see Appendix 4 152 *Bartas* Guillaume de Salluste, Seigneur du Bartas (1544–90), French poet most famous for his epic of the creation *La semaine*, 1578, which Sylvester translated (see no. 343)

Then dainty *Sands* that hath to *English* done,
Smooth sliding *Ovid*, and hath made him run
With so much sweetnesse and unusuall grace,
As though the neatnesse of the *English* pace,
Should tell the Jetting *Lattine* that it came
But slowly after, as though stiffe and lame.
So *Scotland* sent us hither, for our owne
That man, whose name I ever would have knowne,
To stand by mine, that most ingenious knight,
My *Alexander*, to whom in his right,
I want extreamely, yet in speaking thus
I doe but shew the love, that was twixt us,
And not his numbers which were brave and hie,
So like his mind, was his cleare Poesie,
And my deare *Drummond* to whom much I owe
For his much love, and proud I was to know,
His poesie, for which two worthy men,
I *Menstry* still shall love, and *Hauthorne-den*,
Then the two *Beamounts* and my *Browne* arose,
My deare companions whom I freely chose
My bosome friends; and in their severall wayes,
Rightly borne Poets, and in these last dayes,
Men of much note, and no lesse nobler parts,
Such as have freely tould to me their hearts,
As I have mine to them; but if you shall
Say in your knowledge, that these be not all
Have writ in numbers, be inform'd that I
Only my selfe, to these few men doe tye,
Whose workes oft printed, set on every post,
To publique censure subject have bin most;

361 157 *Sands* George Sandys (1578–1644); the first five books of his translation of Ovid's *Metamorphoses* were published in 1621, the complete work in 1626 161 *Jetting* strutting, boastful, vain 166 *Alexander* Sir William Alexander of Menstry (1567?–1640), Earl of Stirling, Scottish poet and friend of Drayton's; author of *Aurora*, 1604 and *Doomsday*, 1614 171 *Drummond* William Drummond, see Appendix 4 175 *two Beamounts* Francis Beaumont (1584–1616), playwright (often with John Fletcher), and his brother Sir John Beaumont (1583–1627), author of *The metamorphosis of tobacco*, 1602, and *Bosworth Field*, 1629 *Browne* William Browne, see Appendix 4

For such whose poems, be they nere so rare,
In private chambers, that incloistered are,
And by transcription daintyly must goe;
As though the world unworthy were to know,
Their rich composures, let those men that keepe
These wonderous reliques in their judgement deepe,
And cry them up so, let such Peeces bee
Spoke of by those that shall come after me,
I passe not for them: nor doe meane to run,
In quest of these, that them applause have wonne,
Upon our Stages in these latter dayes,
That are so many, let them have ther bayes
That doe deserve it; let those wits that haunt
Those publique circuits, let them freely chaunt
Their fine Composures, and their praise pursue,
And so my deare friend, for this time adue.

362 [*from* The Muses Elizium]

THE DESCRIPTION of ELIZIUM

A paradice on earth is found,
Though farre from vulgar sight,
Which with those pleasures doth abound
That it *Elizium* hight.

Where, in Delights that never fade,
The Muses lulled be,
And sit at pleasure in the shade
Of many a stately tree,

Which no rough Tempest makes to reele
Nor their straight bodies bowes,
Their lofty tops doe never feele
The weight of winters snowes;

361 188 *incloistered* shut in, confined 189 *transcription* copying 191 *composures* compositions 193 *cry them up* praise them 195 *passe* care 198 *bayes* laurel wreaths

362 2 *vulgar* common

In Groves that evermore are greene,
No falling leafe is there,
But *Philomel* (of birds the Queene)
In Musicke spends the yeare.

The *Merle* upon her mertle Perch,
There to the *Mavis* sings,
Who from the top of some curld Berch
Those notes redoubled rings;

There Daysyes damaske every place
Nor once their beauties lose,
That when proud *Phœbus* hides his face
Themselves they scorne to close.

The Pansy and the Violet here,
As seeming to descend,
Both from one Root, a very payre,
For sweetnesse yet contend,

And pointing to a Pinke to tell
Which beares it, it is loath,
To judge it; but replyes, for smell
That it excels them both,

Wherewith displeasde they hang their heads
So angry soone they grow
And from their odoriferous beds
Their sweets at it they throw.

The winter here a Summer is,
No waste is made by time,
Nor doth the Autumne ever misse
The blossomes of the Prime.

The flower that July forth doth bring
In Aprill here is seene,
The Primrose that puts on the Spring
In July decks each Greene.

362 17 *Merle* blackbird 18 *Mavis* song thrush 21 *damaske* ornament with a pattern 40 *Prime* spring

The sweets for soveraignty contend
And so abundant be,
That to the very Earth they lend
And Barke of every Tree:

Rills rising out of every Banck,
In wilde Meanders strayne,
And playing many a wanton pranck
Upon the speckled plaine,

In Gambols and lascivious Gyres
Their time they still bestow
Nor to their Fountaines none retyres,
Nor on their course will goe

Those Brooks with Lillies bravely deckt,
So proud and wanton made,
That they their courses quite neglect:
And seeme as though they stayde,

Faire *Flora* in her state to viewe
Which through those Lillies looks,
Or as those Lillies leand to shew
Their beauties to the brooks.

That *Phœbus* in his lofty race,
Oft layes aside his beames
And comes to coole his glowing face
In these delicious streames;

Oft spreading Vines clime up the Cleeves,
Whose ripned clusters there,
Their liquid purple drop, which drives
A Vintage through thee yeere.

Those Cleeves whose craggy sides are clad
With Trees of sundry sutes,
Which make continuall summer glad,
Even bending with their fruits,

362 50 *strayne* flow 53 *Gyres* twistings, circles 61 *in her state* with great pomp and solemnity, in her splendid trappings 69 *Cleeves* cliffs

Some ripening, ready some to fall,
Some blossom'd, some to bloome,
Like gorgeous hangings on the wall
Of some rich princely Roome:

Pomegranates, Lymons, Cytrons, so
Their laded branches bow,
Their leaves in number that outgoe
Nor roomth will them alow.

There in perpetuall Summers shade,
Apolloes Prophets sit
Among the flowres that never fade,
But flowrish like their wit;

To whom the Nimphes upon their Lyres,
Tune many a curious lay,
And with their most melodious Quires
Make short the longest day.

The *thrice three Virgins* heavenly Cleere,
Their trembling Timbrels sound,
Whilst the three comely *Graces* there
Dance many a dainty Round,

Decay nor Age there nothing knowes,
There is continuall Youth,
As Time on plant or creatures growes,
So still their strength renewth.

The Poets Paradice this is,
To which but few can come;
The Muses onely bower of blisse
Their Deare *Elizium*.

Here happy soules, (their blessed bowers,
Free from the rude resort
Of beastly people) spend the houres,
In harmelesse mirth and sport,

362 81 *Cytrons* citron-, lemon-, lime-trees 90 *curious* skilful, intricate 93 *Virgins* Muses 94 *Timbrels* tambourines 103 cp. Spenser's *The Faerie Queene*, 2.12 (see no. 80)

Then on to the *Elizian* plaines
Apollo doth invite you
Where he provides with pastorall straines,
In *Nimphals* to delight you.

JOHN MILTON

363 [*from* At a Vacation Exercise]

Anno Æetatis 19. At a Vacation Exercise in the Colledge, part *Latin,* part *English.* The *Latin* speeches ended, the *English* thus began.

Hail native Language, that by sinews weak
Didst move my first endeavouring tongue to speak,
And mad'st imperfect words with childish tripps,
Half unpronounc't, slide through my infant-lipps,
Driving dum silence from the portal dore,
Where he had mutely sate two years before:
Here I salute thee and thy pardon ask,
That now I use thee in my latter task:
Small loss it is that thence can come unto thee,
I know my tongue but little Grace can do thee:
Thou needst not be ambitious to be first,
Believe me I have thither packt the worst:
And, if it happen as I did forecast,
The daintest dishes shall be serv'd up last.
I pray thee then deny me not thy aide
For this same small neglect that I have made:
But haste thee strait to do me once a Pleasure,
And from thy wardrope bring thy chiefest treasure;

362 112 *Nimphals** a meeting, gathering of nymphs; the name for each division of the poem which follows

363 Title *Anno Ætatis* aged *Exercise* an academic debate or dissertation forming part of the requirements for a degree 8 *latter* later 12 *thither* into the first, the Latin, part

Not those new fangled toys, and triming slight
Which takes our late fantasticks with delight,
But cull those richest Robes, and gay'st attire
Which deepest Spirits, and choicest Wits desire:
I have some naked thoughts that rove about
And loudly knock to have their passage out;
And wearie of their place do only stay
Till thou hast deck't them in thy best aray;
That so they may without suspect or fears
Fly swiftly to this fair Assembly's ears;
Yet I had rather, if I were to chuse,
Thy service in some graver subject use,
Such as may make thee search thy coffers round,
Before thou cloath my fancy in fit sound:
Such where the deep transported mind may soare
Above the wheeling poles, and at Heav'ns dore
Look in, and see each blissful Deitie
How he before the thunderous throne doth lie,
Listening to what unshorn *Apollo* sings
To th'touch of golden wires, while *Hebe* brings
Immortal Nectar to her Kingly Sire:
Then passing through the Spherse of watchful fire,
And mistie Regions of wide air next under,
And hills of Snow and lofts of piled Thunder,
May tell at length how green-ey'd *Neptune* raves,
In Heav'ns defiance mustering all his waves;
Then sing of secret things that came to pass
When Beldam Nature in her cradle was;
And last of Kings and Queens and *Hero's* old,
Such as the wise *Demodocus* once told

363 19 *toys* ornaments, trinkets; fantastic, mocking speeches *triming* trimming, adornment 20 *fantasticks* those who wear fine or showy clothes; perhaps Donne and his imitators 21 *richest Robes* perhaps Spenser and his followers 24 *to … out* get their way 27 *suspect* suspicion 33 *deep* high 34 *wheeling* turning, revolving 37 *unshorn* a traditional epithet for Apollo 40 between the spheres of the moon and of the air cosmologists believed there was a sphere of fire; the sun, moon and planets were thought to guard the numbers of time 42 *lofts* layers, strata 46 *Beldam* great mother

In solemn Songs at King *Alcinous* feast,
While sad *Ulisses* soul and all the rest
Are held with his melodious harmonie
In willing chains and sweet captivitie.

John Taylor

364 [*from* A comparison betwixt a *Whore* and a *Booke*]

Me thinks I heare some Cavillers object,
That 'tis a name absurd and indirect,
To give a Booke the Title of a *Whore*:
When sure I thinke no Name befits it more.
For like a *Whore* by day-light, or by Candle,
'Tis ever free for every knave to handle:
And as a new *whore* is belov'd and sought,
So is a new *Booke* in request and bought.
When *whores* wax old and stale, they're out of date,
Old Pamphlets are most subject to such fate.
As *whores* have Panders to emblaze their worth,
So these have Stationers to set them forth.
And as an old *whore* may be painted new
With borrowed beauty, faire unto the view,
Whereby shee for a fine fresh *whore* may passe,
Yet is shee but the rotten *whore* shee was.
So Stationers, their old cast Bookes can grace,
And by new Titles paint a-fresh their face.
Whereby for currant they are past away,
As if they had come forth but yesterday.
A *Booke* is dedicated, now and than
To some great worthy, or unworthy man:
Yet for all that, 'tis common unto mee,
Or thee, or hee, or all estates that bee.

364 11 *emblaze* celebrate 17 *cast* abandoned, discarded, worn-out

THOMAS CAREW

365 An Elegie upon the death of the Deane of Pauls, Dr. John Donne

Can we not force from widdowed Poetry,
Now thou art dead (Great DONNE) one Elegie
To crowne thy Hearse? Why yet dare we not trust
Though with unkneaded dowe-bak't prose thy dust,
Such as the uncisor'd Churchman from the flower
Of fading Rhetorique, short liv'd as his houre,
Dry as the sand that measures it, should lay
Upon thy Ashes, on the funerall day?
Have we no voice, no tune? Did'st thou dispense
Through all our language, both the words and sense?
'Tis a sad truth; The Pulpit may her plaine,
And sober Christian precepts still retaine,
Doctrines it may, and wholesome Uses frame,
Grave Homilies, and Lectures, But the flame
Of thy brave Soule, that shot such heat and light,
As burnt our earth, and made our darknesse bright,
Committed holy Rapes upon our Will,
Did through the eye the melting heart distill;
And the deepe knowledge of darke truths so teach,
As sense might judge, what phansie could not reach;
Must be desir'd for ever. So the fire,
That fills with spirit and heat the Delphique quire,
Which kindled first by thy Promethean breath,
Glow'd here a while, lies quench't now in thy death;
The Muses garden with Pedantique weedes
O'rspred, was purg'd by thee; The lazie seeds
Of servile imitation throwne away;
And fresh invention planted, Thou didst pay

365 4 *dowe-bak't* imperfect, badly finished, like doughy bread 5 *uncisor'd* unscissored, with hair uncut 9 *dispense* deal out, distribute 13 *Uses* religious services, rites 28 *invention* subject for poetry, poetical composition

The debts of our penurious bankrupt age;
Licentious thefts, that make poëtique rage
A Mimique fury, when our soules must bee
Possest, or with Anacreons Extasie,
Or Pindars, not their owne; The subtle cheat
Of slie Exchanges, and the jugling feat
Of two-edg'd words, or whatsoever wrong
By ours was done the Greeke, or Latine tongue,
Thou hast redeem'd, and open'd Us a Mine
Of rich and pregnant phansie, drawne a line
Of masculine expression, which had good
Old Orpheus seene, Or all the ancient Brood
Our superstitious fooles admire, and hold
Their lead more precious, then thy burnish't Gold,
Thou hadst beene their Exchequer, and no more
They each in others dust, had rak'd for Ore.
Thou shalt yield no precedence, but of time,
And the blinde fate of language, whose tun'd chime
More charmes the outward sense; Yet thou maist claime
From so great disadvantage greater fame,
Since to the awe of thy imperious wit
Our stubborne language bends, made only fit
With her tough-thick-rib'd hoopes to gird about
Thy Giant phansie, which had prov'd too stout
For their soft melting Phrases. As in time
They had the start, so did they cull the prime
Buds of invention many a hundred yeare,
And left the rifled fields, besides the feare
To touch their Harvest, yet from those bare lands
Of what is purely thine, thy only hands
(And that thy smallest worke) have gleaned more
Then all those times, and tongues could reape before;
But thou art gone, and thy strict lawes will be
Too hard for Libertines in Poetrie.
They will repeale the goodly exil'd traine
Of gods and goddesses, which in thy just raigne

365 35 *two-edg'd* ambiguous 43 *Exchequer* treasury

Were banish'd nobler Poems, now, with these
The silenc'd tales o'th'Metamorphoses
Shall stuffe their lines, and swell the windy Page,
Till Verse refin'd by thee, in this last Age,
Turne ballad rime, Or those old Idolls bee
Ador'd againe, with new apostasie;
Oh, pardon mee, that breake with untun'd verse
The reverend silence that attends thy herse,
Whose awfull solemne murmures were to thee
More then these faint lines, A loud Elegie,
That did proclaime in a dumbe eloquence
The death of all the Arts, whose influence
Growne feeble, in these panting numbers lies
Gasping short winded Accents, and so dies:
So doth the swiftly turning wheele not stand
In th'instant we withdraw the moving hand,
But some small time maintaine a faint weake course
By vertue of the first impulsive force:
And so whil'st I cast on thy funerall pile
Thy crowne of Bayes, Oh, let it crack a while,
And spit disdaine, till the devouring flashes
Suck all the moysture up, then turne to ashes.
I will not draw the envy to engrosse
All thy perfections, or weepe all our losse;
Those are too numerous for an Elegie,
And this too great, to be express'd by mee.
Though every pen should share a distinct part,
Yet art thou Theme enough to tyre all Art;
Let others carve the rest, it shall suffice
I on thy Tombe this Epitaph incise.

Here lies a King, that rul'd as hee thought fit
The universall Monarchy of wit;
Here lie two Flamens, and both those, the best,
Apollo's first, at last, the true Gods Priest.

365 66 *Metamorphoses* Ovid's epic poem 82 *impulsive* impelling, propelling 85 *flashes* blazing flames 87 *engrosse* write, copy, out 89 *numerous* copious, plentiful; harmonious, metrically rhythmical 97 *Flamens* priests

366 A Fancy

Marke how this polisht Easterne sheet,
Doth with our Northerne tincture meet,
For though the paper seeme to sinke,
Yet it receives, and bears the Inke;
And on her smooth soft brow these spots,
Seeme rather ornaments then blots;
Like those you Ladies use to place
Mysteriously about your face:
Not only to set off and breake
Shaddowes and Eye beames, but to speake
To the skild Lover, and relate
Unheard, his sad or happy Fate:
Nor doe their Characters delight,
As carelesse workes of black and white:
But 'cause you underneath may find
A sence that can enforme the mind;
Divine, or moral rules impart
Or Raptures of Poetick Art:
So what at first was only fit,
To fold up silkes, may wrap up wit.

Robert Herrick

367 To the Detracter

Where others love, and praise my Verses; still
Thy long-black-Thumb-nail marks 'em out for ill:
A fellon take it, or some Whit-flaw come
For to unslate, or to untile that thumb!

366 7 *those* beauty spots 13 *Characters* letter forms

367 3 *fellon* inflamed sore *Whit-flaw* whitlow, a sore or swelling in finger or thumb 4 *untile**

But cry thee Mercy: Exercise thy nailes
To scratch or claw, so that thy tongue not railes:
Some numbers prurient are, and some of these
Are wanton with their itch; scratch, and 'twill please.

368 Posting to Printing

Let others to the Printing Presse run fast,
Since after death comes glory, *Ile not haste.*

GEORGE WITHER

369 [*from* Vox Pacifica]

The *Sun* hath run his course through all the Signes,
And, thirteen times the *Moone* renew'd her light,
Since last I limb'd my thoughts in measur'd lines,
Or, felt my heart for *Numbers* tun'd aright;
For, ever since my *Musings in the Field*,
The close whereof, a *Voice* of *PEACE* fore-tells,
With such disord'red thoughts I have been fild
As use to thrive where sad distemper dwells:
And, we have, *All*, so broken that Condition,
On which our wished Comforts founded are,
That, of accomplishing our hopes fruition,
Not many certaine symptomes, yet, appear;
  Though, therefore, I have silent been till now,
  My slownesse blame not, neither murmure you.

367 7 *numbers* people; poems, verses *prurient* itching

368 Title *Posting* hurrying, hastening

369 3 *limb'd* limned, painted *measur'd* metrical 4 *Numbers* poetry, poems 5 *Musings . . . Field* in 1643 Wither had published *Campo-musae: or the field-musings of Captain George Wither*

The *Muses* are not still at my command,
Whereby those Informations are acquir'd,
Which many have expected at my hand;
(And somwhat out of season too, desir'd.)
The VOICE, there mentioned, was but a *Sound*,
Not then, articulated into words;
The perfect Forme thereof I had not found,
Nor what interpretation it affords.
If I had spoken, e're I had mine *Arrant*,
Beyond my wit, my forward tongue had went;
If I had run, before I had my *Warrant*,
Well might I, for my labour, have been shent.
  There is, for all things an appointed houre;
  And, *Times*, and *Seasons*, are not in my power.
My *Vessell* stirreth not, till that *Wind* blowes
Which never blowes but when, and where it list:
Drie is my *Cisterne*, till that *Fountain* flowes,
Whose flowings-forth, I cannot then resist.
Somtimes, in me, so low the *Waters* lie,
That every Childe and Beast is trampling on me;
Somtime againe, they rise, they swell so high,
That Princes cannot make a Bridge upon me.
Had *King*, and *Parliament*, the other day,
Commanded from me that which now I write,
To save my life, I knew not what to say
Of that, which was inspired yesternight:
  And, being, now, as full as I can hold,
  Though none they please, my *Musings* must be told.
Mistake not tho, as if it should be thought,
That by *Enthusiasme*, now, I write;
Or, that the matter which to me is brought,
By GODS immediate dictates, I indite.
Far is that Arrogancie from my Pen:
The Objects of my *Contemplation*, be
The same which GOD affords to other men,
Who use aright, the Guifts bestow'd on me.

369 16 *Informations* instructions, communications 23 *Arrant* errand, message 26 *shent* blamed, reproved 31 *Cisterne* reservoir, tank; the fourth ventricle of the brain 44 *Enthusiasme* possession by a god, supernatural inspiration, poetic frenzy

The *Muses* challenge a peculiar phrase
And freedomes, not so well becoming those,
Who are confined to observe the lawes
Of common speech, and tell their minds in prose:
  For, whereas these have but one worke to do,
  I have, in my Intentions, often two.
To reason out a *Truth*, is their perfection;
That, so, mens judgements rectifie they might:
Thereat, I aime: But, how to move *Affection*,
And set the motions of the *Will* aright,
Is my chiefe work: And; to that end, I catch
At all advantages of *Place* and *Time*,
Of *Actions*, or *Expressions*; and, I watch
For ev'ry meanes of well improving them.
By which endeavours (and, for ought I know,
By some aid, more then ordinary too)
Mixt with mine own Conjectures, I fore-show
Some things, which GOD requires, or means to do.
  And, when I apprehend such things as these,
  They neither are conceall'd, nor told with ease.
As when a portion of new spritly-wine,
Is in a close, and crazie Vessell pent,
Which neither can sufficiently confine
The working Liquour, nor well give it vent;
Ev'n so I far'd: For, (though I felt my breast
With matter fully stor'd) seaven daies I strove
My swelling *Thoughts*, in *Words*, to have exprest,
Yet neither could desist, nor forward move.
But, on that night in which our *Monethly-Fast*
Had swallow'd up our greatest *Festivall*,
My *Muse* broke loose: And, now the stop is past,
Will run her Course, what ever may befall;
  And (since to speak her mind she hath begun)
  Resolves, She will be heard, e're She hath done.

369 65 *ought* aught, anything 72 *crazie* old, broken 74 *working* lively 80 *Festivall* Parliament had abolished Christmas festivities and in 1644 one of the prescribed monthly fasts was held on 25 December

Once more therefore, yee BRITAINS lend an eare;
KING, PRIEST, AND PEOPLE mark what now I say,
And, if you shall be pleas'd this VOICE to heare,
Take heed, you harden not your hearts to day.
For, if your pride, and follie, shall despise
The gentle VOICE, that now salutes your eare,
Ere long, there shall another VOICE arise,
Which will not such a peacefull note preferre.
It shall not move with so becalm'd a Breath,
Nor be dilated through so milde an ayre,
But, from the wombe of *Hell*, and Jawes of *Death*,
Be thund'red forth, with horrours and despaire:
  And, few shall hear that VOICES dreadfull sound,
  Without a smarting, and a curelesse wound.
Though you my former *Warnings* did abuse,
It brookes excuse: Because, I so fore-told
Ensuing things, as yet, no *Moderne-Muse*
Hath done the like; and few in times of old:
But, now, by seeing those *Predictions* true,
You, as it were, an *Earnest* have receiv'd,
And an assurance, tendred unto you,
That, what is here declar'd, may be believ'd.
By vertue, therefore, of that *Seal*, and *Signe*,
I challenge that beleefe, and that respect,
Which appertaineth to this VOICE of mine,
Till, thence, I seeke to draw some ill effect;
  By making that, which hath fulfilled bin,
  An Argument to warrantize a sin.

369 94 *dilated* spread abroad 98 *curelesse* incurable 112 *warrantize* sanction, authorize

SIR WILLIAM DAVENANT

370 [*from* Gondibert Book 2]

37.

There, when they thought they saw in well sought Books,
Th'assembled soules of all that Men held wise,
It bred such awfull rev'rence in their looks,
As if they saw the bury'd writers rise. . . .

39.

They saw *Egyptian* Roles, which vastly great,
Did like faln Pillars lie, and did display
The tale of Natures life, from her first heat,
Till by the Flood o're-cool'd, she felt decay.

40.

And large as these (for Pens were Pencils then)
Others that *Egypts* chiefest Science show'd;
Whose River forc'd Geometry on Men,
Which did distinguish what the *Nyle* o're-flow'd.

41.

Neer them, in Piles, *Chaldean* Cous'ners lie;
Who the hid bus'nesse of the Stars relate;
Who make a Trade of worship'd Prophesie;
And seem to pick the Cabinet of Fate.

42.

There *Persian Magi* stand; for wisdom prais'd;
Long since wise Statesmen, now *Magicians* thought;
Altars and Arts are soon to fiction rais'd,
And both would have, that miracles are wrought.

370 8 *o're-cool'd* over-cooled, chilled 9 *Pencils* paintbrushes 13 *Chaldean Cous'ners* Babylonian tricksters, astrologers, soothsayers 16 *pick* pick the lock, rob 17 *Magi* wise men 19 *Altars and Arts* religion and scientific knowledge

43.

In a dark Text, these States-men left their Mindes;
For well they knew, that Monarch's Mistery
(Like that of Priests) but little rev'rence findes,
When they the Curtain op'e to ev'ry Eie.

44.

Behinde this Throng, the talking *Greeks* had place;
Who Nature turn to Art, and Truth disguise,
As skill does native beauty oft deface;
With *Termes* they charm the weak, and pose the wise.

45.

Now they the *Hebrew*, *Greek*, and *Roman* spie;
Who for the Peoples ease, yoak'd them with Law;
Whom else, ungovern'd lusts would drive awry;
And each his own way frowardly would draw.

46.

In little Tomes these grave first Lawyers lie,
In Volumes their Interpreters below;
Who first made Law an Art, then Misterie;
So cleerest springs, when troubled, cloudy grow.

47.

But here, the Souls chief Book did all precede;
Our Map tow'rds Heav'n; to common Crowds deny'd;
Who proudly aim to teach, ere they can read;
And all must stray, where each will be a Guide.

48.

About this sacred little Book did stand
Unwieldy Volumes, and in number great;
And long it was since any Readers hand
Had reach'd them from their unfrequented Seat.

370 21 *dark* hard to understand 25 *talking* loquacious 28 *Termes* technical expressions *pose* confuse, perplex 32 *frowardly* perversely 34 *Interpreters* commentators

49.

For a deep Dust (which Time does softly shed,
   Where only Time does come) their Covers beare;
On which, grave Spyders, streets of Webbs had spred;
   Subtle, and slight, as the grave Writers were.

50.

In these, Heav'ns holy fire does vainly burn;
   Nor warms, nor lights, but is in Sparkles spent;
Where froward Authors, with disputes, have torn
   The Garment seamlesse as the Firmament.

MARGARET CAVENDISH, DUCHESS OF NEWCASTLE

371 The Claspe

Give *Mee* the *Free*, and *Noble Stile*,
Which seems *uncurb'd*, though it be *wild:*
Though *It* runs wild about, *It* cares not where;
It shewes more *Courage*, then *It* doth of *Feare*.
Give me a *Stile* that *Nature* frames, not *Art*:
For *Art* doth seem to take the *Pedants* part.
And that seemes *Noble*, which is *Easie*, *Free*,
Not to be bound with ore-nice *Pedantry*.

372 [The Common Fate of Books]

The *worst Fate Bookes* have, when they are once read,
They're laid aside, forgotten like the *Dead*:
Under a heap of *dust* they buried lye,
Within a *vault* of some small *Library*.

371 Title *Claspe* fastening (of a book); embrace 5 *frames* shapes, creates
8 *ore-nice* overprecise, niggling

But *Spiders* they, for honour of that *Art*
Of *Spinning*, which by *Nature* they were taught;
Since *Men* doe spin their *Writings* from the *Braine*,
Striving to make a lasting *Web* of *Fame*,
Of *Cobwebs* thin, *high Altars* doe they raise,
There offer *Flyes*, as sacrifice of *praise*.

Abraham Cowley

373 The Muse

1.

Go, the rich *Chariot* instantly prepare;
    The *Queen*, my *Muse*, will take the aire;
Unruly *Phansie* with strong *Judgement* trace,
    Put in nimble-footed *Wit*,
    Smooth-pac'ed *Eloquence* joyn with it,
Sound *Memory* with young *Invention* place,
    Harness all the *winged race*.
Let the *Postillian Nature* mount, and let
    The *Coachman Art* be set.
And let the airy *Footmen* running all beside,
    Make a long row of *goodly pride*.
Figures, Conceits, Raptures, and *Sentences*
        In a well-worded *dress*.
And *innocent Loves*, and *pleasant Truths*, and *useful Lies*,
        In all their gaudy *Liveries*.
    Mount, glorious *Queen*, thy *travelling Throne*,
        And bid it to put on;
    For *long*, though *chearful*, is the *way*,
And *Life*, alas, allows but one ill *winters Day*.

373 3 *trace* tread, travel 8 *Postillian* rider of the near horse of the leaders in a coach-and-four 17 *put on* ascend

2.

Where never *Foot* of *Man*, or *Hoof* of *Beast*,
The passage prest,
Where never *Fish* did *fly*,
And with short silver *wings* cut the low liquid *Sky*.
Where *Bird* with painted *Oars* did n'ere
Row through the trackless *Ocean* of the *Air*.
Where never yet did pry
The busie *Mornings* curious *Ey*.
The *Wheels* of thy bold *Coach* pass quick and free;
And all's an *open Road* to *Thee*.
Whatever *God* did *Say*,
Is all thy plain and smooth, uninterrupted *way*.
Nay ev'n beyond his *works* thy *Voyages* are known,
Thou'hast thousand *worlds* too of thine *own*.
Thou speakst, great *Queen*, in the same *stile* as *He*,
And a *New world* leaps forth when *Thou* say'st, *Let it Be*.

3.

Thou fadom'est the deep *Gulf* of *Ages* past,
And canst pluck up with ease
The *years* which Thou dost please,
Like shipwrackt *Treasures* by rude *Tempests* cast
Long since into the *Sea*,
Brought up again to *light* and publique *Use* by Thee.
Nor dost thou only *Dive* so low,
But *Fly*
With an unwearied *Wing* the other way on high,
Where *Fates* among the *Stars* do grow;
There into the close *Nests* of *Time* do'est peep,
And there with piercing *Eye*,
Through the firm *Shell*, and the thick *White* do'st spie,
Years to come a forming lie,

373 24 *n'ere* never 25 *trackless** pathless, untrodden 27 the sun 35 cp. Genesis 1:3 'Let there be light' 36 *fadom'est* fathom, measure the depths

Close in their *sacred Secundine* asleep,
Till *hatcht* by the *Suns* vital heat
Which ore them yet does *brooding* set
They *Life* and *Motion* get,
And *ripe* at last with vigorous might
Break through the *Shell*, and take their everlasting *Flight*.

4.

And sure we may
The same too of the *Present* say,
If *Past*, and *Future Times* do thee obey.
Thou stopst this *Current*, and dost make
This running *River* settle like a *Lake*,
Thy certain hand holds fast this slippery *Snake*.
The *Fruit* which does so quickly waste,
Men scarce can see it, much less *taste*,
Thou *Comfitest* in *Sweets* to make it *last*.
This shining piece of *Ice*
Which melts so soon away
With the *Suns* ray,
Thy *Verse* does solidate and *Chrystallize*,
Till it a lasting *Mirror* be;
Nay thy *Immortal Rhyme*
Makes this one short *Point* of *Time*,
To fill up half the *Orb* of *Round Eternity*.

373 50 *Secundine* womb: correctly, the afterbirth; 'The thin *Film* with which an *Infant* is covered in the *womb*' Cowley 61 *Snake* 'the ancient *Hieroglyphique* of the *year*' Cowley 64 *Comfitest* preserve 68 *solidate* make solid *Chrystallize** give a permanent or definite shape

HENRY VAUGHAN

374 The Book

Eternal God! maker of all
That have liv'd here, since the mans fall;
The Rock of ages! in whose shade
They live unseen, when here they fade.

Thou knew'st this *papyr*, when it was
Meer *seed*, and after that but *grass*;
Before 'twas *drest* or *spun*, and when
Made *linen*, who did *wear* it then:
What were their lifes, their thoughts and deeds
Whither good *corn*, or fruitless *weeds*.

Thou knew'st this *Tree*, when a green *shade*
Cover'd it, since a *Cover* made,
And where it flourish'd, grew and spread,
As if it never should be dead.

Thou knew'st this harmless *beast*, when he
Did live and feed by thy decree
On each green thing; then slept (well fed)
Cloath'd with this *skin*, which now lies spred
A *Covering* o're this aged book,
Which makes me wisely weep and look
On my own dust; meer dust it is,
But not so dry and clean as this.
Thou knew'st and saw'st them all and though
Now scatter'd thus, dost know them so.

374 2 *mans* Adam's 5–8 paper was made from linen, which was made from flax 11–12 some bookbindings were made by covering wooden boards with leather

O knowing, glorious spirit! when
Thou shalt restore trees, beasts and men,
When thou shalt make all new again,
Destroying onely death and pain,
Give him amongst thy works a place,
Who in them lov'd and sought thy face!

Notes to the Text

1 Text: London, Public Record Office, E36/228, f. 7r–v; facsimile in P. J. Croft, *Autograph Poetry in the English Language*, 2 vols., 1973, i.6–7. Edition: ed. John Scattergood, *John Skelton: The Complete English Poems*, Harmondsworth 1983, pp. 110–11, ll. 1–28. This, the only known autograph poem by Skelton, was probably presented to King Henry VIII on his accession, 22 April 1509. It was not printed until 1843. The poem's title is not in Skelton's hand.

7 dolowrs.] dolowrs *MS*

2 Text: Thomas More, *Epigrammata clarissimi disertissimique viri Thomae Mori*, Basel 1520, sig. g2r. Edition: ed. Clarence H. Miller, Leicester Bradner, Charles A. Lynch and Revilo P. Oliver, *The Complete Works of St. Thomas More*, vol. 3, part 2, *Latin Poems*, New Haven and London 1984, no. 115, p. 164. The epigram was first printed in 1518 and translated into English by Timothy Kendall in *Flowers of epigrammes*, 1577. The poem is written in elegiac couplets – a quantitative hexameter followed by a pentameter.

1 princeps? Canis] princeps, canis *1518, 1520* gregis] *1518* gregis, *1520*
2 lupos. Quid] lupos, quid *1518, 1520*

3 Text: Thomas More, *Epigrammata*, 1520, see no. 2, sigs. l1v.–2v. Edition: ed. Clarence H. Miller etc., see no. 2, no. 198, pp. 228–30. The title of this poem clearly relates it to More's *Utopia*, whose full Latin title was *De optimo reipublicae statu deque nova insula Utopia*: it was written and published at about the same time as More's Latin poems. There appears to be no English translation of this poem published before 1660. It is written in elegiac couplets.

4 Text: Sir David Lindsay, *The testament and complaynt of Papyngo, The dreme of Sir David Lindsay*, [1559], sig. F3r–v, appended to his *Ane dialogue betwixt experience and a courteour*, [1559]. Edition: ed. Douglas Hamer, *The Works of Sir David Lindsay of the Mount 1490–1555*, Scottish Text Society, 4 vols., 1931–6, i.32, ll. 918–45. The text of the poem survives in one MS; a lost edition of the *Dreme* was probably printed at Edinburgh between 1528 and 1530 and it was reprinted frequently in editions of Lindsay's works during the sixteenth century, including in one published at London in 1566.

5 Text: Trinity College, Dublin, MS 160, f. 183r. Edition: ed. R. A. Rebholz, *Sir Thomas Wyatt: The Complete Poems*, Harmondsworth 1978, p. 155. Attributed from its unique text in this MS (known from its owner in about 1545–6, Sir George Blage (1512–51), as the Blage MS) by Kenneth Muir and Patricia Thomson, *Collected Poems of Sir Thomas Wyatt*, Liverpool 1969, pp. 187–8. The Latin motto is in a different hand from that of the rest of the poem. The poem was probably written during or after 1536.

6 Text: British Library, MS Egerton 2711, f. 69r; facsimile in P. J. Croft, see no. 1, i.9. Edition: ed. R. A. Rebholz, see no. 5, p. 98. The Egerton MS was compiled during the 1530s, with much of the work probably dating from 1537–9; some of the poems in the MS are in Wyatt's own hand and others contain his autograph corrections and revisions and those of Nicholas Grimald (see no. 310). The MS later passed into the hands of the Harington family. This autograph poem was probably written shortly before Wyatt returned to England in June 1539. It was first printed in Tottel's *Songes and sonettes*, 1557, see no. 57, where it was headed 'Of his returne from Spaine'.

6 doth lend] that leanes *Tottel*
7 alone for whome I] for whome only alone I *unrevised MS*
8 winges] windes *Tottel*

7 Text: Duke of Norfolk, Arundel-Harington MS, f. 60v. Edition: ed. R. A. Rebholz, see no. 5, p. 86. Adapted from Petrarch (*Rime* 269), this sonnet may lament the death of Thomas Cromwell in 1540. The Arundel-Harington MS (ed. Ruth Hughey, 2 vols., Columbus, Ohio, 1960) is an important collection of poetry compiled by Sir John Harington and his father from the mid to the late sixteenth century. This poem was first printed in Tottel's *Songes and sonettes*, 1557, see no. 57, where it was headed 'The lover laments the death of his love'.

8 Dearlye] Daily *Tottel*
11 wofull] carefull *Tottel*
14 ease] *Tottel* cause *MS* cease *Rebholz*

8 Text: British Library, MS Additional 36529, f. 56v. Edition: ed. Emrys Jones, *Henry Howard Earl of Surrey: Poems*, Oxford 1964, p. 29. The poem survives in a MS miscellany once owned by the family of Sir John Harington. It was first published in Tottel's *Songes and sonettes*, 1557, see no. 57, with the heading 'Of Sardinapalus dishonorable life, and miserable death'.

9 Text: T. R., *John Arm-strongs last good night*, [1658], single-sheet broadside. Edition: ed. F. J. Child, *The English and Scottish Popular Ballads*, 3 vols., Boston 1882–98, iii. 368–9. At least five seventeenth-century printed versions of the ballad survive. The unique Bodleian copy (Wood 401, ff. 93v–94r), from which the text here is taken, was probably printed about thirty or so years earlier than any of the other extant texts. A version from the 1670s survives in the Euing Collection (see no. 127) and one from the second half of the 1680s in the Pepys Library at Magdalene College, Cambridge. Like the Bodleian text, this edition is also signed with the initials T. R., whose significance is uncertain. The historical John Armstrong was a border raider who lived near Langholme; he and his followers were hanged in 1528.

22 valiantly] gallantly *Pepys*
30 sore] fast *Euing and Pepys*
56 body] fair body *Euing*
70 hurt] wounded *Euing*
96 blood] death *Euing and Pepys*

10 Text: Robert Crowley, *One and thyrtye epigrammes*, 1550, sigs. E2v–3r. Edition: ed. J. M. Cowper, *The Select Works of Robert Crowley*, Early English Text Society, Extra Series, vol. 15 (1872), pp. 48–9. The collection of epigrams was reprinted in 1573.

11 Text: John Heywood, *A balade specifienge partly the maner, partly the matter, in the mariage betwene our soveraigne lord, and our soveraigne lady*, [1554], single-sheet broadside. Edition: ed. Burton A. Milligan, *John Heywood's Works and Miscellaneous Short Poems*, Urbana, Ill., 1956, pp. 269–70, ll. 1–35. The unique surviving copy of this ballad, celebrating the marriage of Mary Tudor to Philip II of Spain on 25 July 1554, belongs to the Society of Antiquaries in London. It was not reprinted in the later editions of Heywood's works.

12 Text: William Birch, *A songe betwene the quenes majestie and Englande*, [1564], single-sheet broadside, stanzas 1–12, 17–18. Edition: ed. Thomas Park, *The Harleian Miscellany*, 10 vols., 1808–13, x.260–1. The song was entered in the Stationers' Register in 1558–9 and survives in a unique copy in the library of the Society of Antiquaries in London. A version of the song's burden was quoted by William Wager in *The longer thou livest, the more foole thou art*, [1569], which may date from as early as 1559; Edgar sings a line from it in Shakespeare's *King Lear*, III.6.25. There is a copy of part of the poem in the Bodleian Library, Oxford, MS Ashmole 176.

48 tirably] ticably *[1564]*

13 Text: Bodleian Library, Oxford, MS Rawlinson poetical 108, f. 44v. Edition: ed. Leicester Bradner, *The Poems of Queen Elizabeth I*, Providence, RI, 1964, p. 4. In the Rawlinson MS the poem is headed 'Verses made by the Quenes Majestie'. The poem relates to the conspiracies of Mary, Queen of Scots, in the late 1560s and had some MS circulation later in the Queen's reign, including in the Arundel-Harington MS (see no. 7) and in the Inner Temple MS Petyt 538, vol. 10 (see no. 20). Puttenham printed it in *The arte of English poesie*, 1589 (ed. Willcock and Walker, see no. 16, p. 248), as an example of 'Exargasia', 'Expolitio' or 'The Gorgious', calling it 'passing sweete and harmonicall . . . most sweet and sententious'.

1 dowbt] dread *Arundel-Harington MS*
5 joyes] tois *Puttenham*
6 raigne] *Puttenham* raige *Rawlinson and Arundel-Harington MSS*
7 upreard] of Rue *Arundel-Harington MS* of ruth *Puttenham*
11 doth] *Arundel-Harington MS and Puttenham* do ye *Rawlinson MS*
14 seditious sects] strangers force *Puttenham*

14 Text: Sir Philip Sidney, *The Countesse of Pembrokes Arcadia*, 1590, f. 91r–v; Kent State University Press facsimile, intro. Carl Dennis, 1970. Edition: ed. William A. Ringler, Jr., *The Poems of Sir Philip Sidney*, Oxford 1962, pp. 100–1, ll. 43–77 of OA66. The poem circulated in the ten extant MS copies of the *Old Arcadia* and was incorporated in the *New Arcadia* published in 1590. The *New Arcadia* was printed, combined with the *Old Arcadia*, in 1593 and 1598, being frequently reprinted. In his *Old Arcadia* Sidney made his pastoral persona Philisides sing this song, which, he says, he had been taught on the banks of the river Ister (Danube) by his friend the Huguenot statesman Hubert Languet in 1573 or 1574. The political beast-fable, written in an ancient, rustic language, has links with Spenser's 'Maye' eclogue (see no. 182). It may date from the political crisis of 1579–80, when the Queen's negotiations to marry the French King's brother, the Duc d'Alençon, combined with repressive measures against Puritans (cp. footnote to no. 182 l. 75), aroused fears of a drift to absolutism. The passage alludes to 1 Samuel 8, a text with possible republican interpretations in which God warns the Israelites against being ruled by a king.

4 builden] *some MSS* builded *1590, 1593 and some MSS*
18 dammes] *1593* dames *1590*

15 Text: Chetham's Library, Manchester, MS 8012 (A.4.15), f. 96r. Edition: ed. Alexander B. Grosart, *The Dr. Farmer Chetham MS.*, Chetham Society, 2 vols., 1873, ii.180. The Chetham MS is a MS miscellany compiled during the 1620s by someone connected with the Inns of Court. Sir Francis Walsingham died in 1590, Sir Philip Sidney in 1586 and Sir Christopher Hatton in 1591. All three men were buried in St Paul's Cathedral: Sidney after a magnificent state funeral but without a monument; Walsingham, because of his debts, with the minimum of ceremony; and Hatton with great pomp in a magnificent tomb. A variant of the poem circulated in MS and was first printed by John Stowe in his *A survay of London*, 1598:

> *Philip* and *Francis* have no Tombe,
> For great *Christopher* takes all the roome.

16 Text: [George Puttenham], *The arte of English poesie*, 1589, p. 80; Scolar Press facsimile, Menston 1968. Edition: ed. Gladys Doidge Willcock and Alice Walker, *The Arte of English Poesie by George Puttenham*, Cambridge 1936, p. 97. Although *The arte* was published anonymously, Puttenham's authorship of it is generally accepted. In the section on pattern poems, Puttenham uses this poem to illustrate the 'Piller', by which 'figure is signified stay, support, rest, state and magnificence'.

17 Text: Anne Dowriche, *The French historie. That is; a lamentable discourse of three bloodie broiles in France for the gospell of Jesus Christ*, 1589, sig. I1r. This episode from the recent French wars of religion, in which opponents of the Crown articulated theories of resistance to tyrants, describes part of the events of the massacre of Protestants in Paris on St Bartholomew's Day in 1572.

18 Text: ed. R. S., *The phœnix nest*, 1593, p. 69; Scolar Press facsimile, London and Menston 1973. Edition: ed. Agnes M. C. Latham, *The Poems of Sir Walter Ralegh*, 1951, pp. 10–11. The poem was not assigned an author in *The phoenix nest*; it was reprinted in 1600 in *Englands Helicon* (see no. 98), under the heading 'The Sheepheards praise of his sacred *Diana*'. It was assigned there to 'S. W. R.' but this attribution was replaced in some copies of the book by a cancel slip bearing the word 'Ignoto'.

19 Text: Archbishop Marsh's Library, Dublin, MS Z.3.5.21, f. 30v. Edition: L. G. Black, 'A lost poem by Queen Elizabeth I', *Times Literary Supplement*, 23 May 1968, p. 535, ll. 13–24. This poem is found, together with its probable reply by Queen Elizabeth (see no. 20), in a MS of the 1620s in the Wiltshire Record Office. In a heavily reworked version the two poems were printed together in a single-sheet broadside called *A sweet sonnet, wherein the lover exclaimeth against fortune* in about 1650. Extracts from Ralegh's poem (including ll. 9–10) were first printed in Puttenham's *The arte of English poesie*, 1589, (ed. Willcock and Walker, see no. 16, pp. 198, 201). Another copy of the poem survives in a Phillipps MS and is reproduced in facsimile by Walter Oakeshott in *The Queen and the Poet*, 1960, opposite p. 156. 'Fortune my foe' was a popular tune, referred to by Falstaff in Shakespeare's *The Merry Wives of Windsor* III.3.60–1.

1, 2 Thus now I] Then will I *Phillipps MS* 2 fortunes] worldlinges *Phillipps MS*
5 I joy in this] And only joye *Phillipps MS*
7 Cupids] vertues *Phillipps MS*
8 dame] goddes *Phillipps MS* cupid] vertue *Phillipps MS*
9 Cupid] fortune *Phillipps MS, Puttenham*
12 shal ever] nor frayle shall *Phillipps MS*

20 Text: Inner Temple Library, MS Petyt 538, vol. 10, f. 3r. Edition: L. G. Black, see no. 19. In the MS, the poem is ascribed to the Queen as an answer to one by Ralegh, probably 'Fortune hath taken the away my love', see no. 19. In the Petyt MS, where the poem is divided into ten and a half long lines, three lines are missing between ll. 15 and 16. Puttenham in *The arte of English poesie*, 1589 (ed. Willcock and Walker, see no. 16, p. 236), quotes ll. 11–12 in a slightly different version:

> Never thinke you fortune can beare the sway,
> Where vertues force, can cause her to obay

as an example of 'that which our soveraigne Lady wrate in defiance of fortune'.

21 Text: Marquess of Salisbury, Hatfield House, Cecil Papers, 144, ff. 240r–7r. Edition: ed. Agnes M. C. Latham, see no. 18, pp. 25–43. This autograph poem may date either from Ralegh's first imprisonment under Queen Elizabeth in 1592 or his second under James I. Of the rest of the poem, only the beginning of the twenty-second book is known to survive, also in this autograph MS at Hatfield House. '21th' has been read as '11th' and 'VIth'. The punctuation of the poem is sometimes uncertain due to Ralegh's use of a point for a comma.

50 joyes] joes *MS*
59 transferde] fashond *MS corrected to* transferde
182 fliinge] flowinge *MS corrected to* fliinge
244 + and onn thos withered stalkes no signe remayneth
  of thos incarnate bewties erst so pleasinge *deleted in MS*
330 + *three lines deleted and mostly illegible in MS; the second ends* so late abydinge
339 sence] ought *MS corrected to* sence
421 the] yet *MS corrected to* the
449 + though all her thoughts be drawne back to her brest
  and noon remayne that call thee to her *deleted in MS*
522 hath end] is gone *MS corrected to* hath end

22 Text: ed. Francis Davison, *A poetical rapsodie*, 1608, pp. 17–19. Edition: ed. Agnes M. C. Latham, see no. 18, pp. 45–7. This poem of the early to mid 1590s circulated widely in MS (there are late-sixteenth-century texts in the British Library, MS Harleian 6910, and in a MS in the Henry E. Huntington Library, HM 198) and provoked several replies. It was also known as 'Sir Walter Ralegh's farewell', 'The soul's errand' or 'Satyra volans' ('The flying satire', from its opening word). In the table of contents to the 1608 edition the poem is described as one 'wherein is glaunced some generall vices in sundry states of men'.

14 by] *1608 and Harleian MS* but *most MSS*
16 affection] their factions *some MSS*
20 manage the] in affaires of *Harleian MS*
28 seek] *most MSS* like *1608*
31 it wants] it's blinde *Harleian MS*
39 beauty] truth *Harleian MS* blasteth] boasteth *Huntington MS*
46 in ... wisenesse] by much precisenes *Harleian MS*
51 charity of] mercye of her *Huntington MS*
62 esteeming] contryvynge *Huntington MS*
64 seeming] stryvynge *Huntington MS*
70 least] none *Huntington MS* preferreth] *MSS* preferred *1608*
75 Because] although *MSS*

23 Text: Edinburgh University Library, MS De.3.70, f. 68r. Edition: ed. James Cranstoun, *The Poems of Alexander Montgomerie*, Scottish Text Society, 1887, pp. 102–3. This sonnet is no. 28 in the collection preserved in the unique MS known, after its owner Margaret Kerr, as the Kerr MS. It was one of a group of five addressed to Robert Hudson, a musician of the Chapel Royal, when Montgomerie faced banishment for his Catholic sympathies in 1593. On account of damage to the MS, the last words in ll. 9, 11, 12 (all but the first letter), 13 and 14 (all but the first two letters) are editorial conjectures.

24 Text: Sir John Harington, *The most elegant and witty epigrams of Sir John Harrington*, 1618, Book 4, no. 82, sig. M6r; Scolar Press facsimile, Menston 1970. Edition: ed. Norman Egbert McClure, *The Letters and Epigrams of Sir John Harington*, Philadelphia 1930, no. 336, pp. 280–1. As well as making several MS collections of his epigrams for his own use and for presentation (including ones in the British Library, the Folger Shakespeare Library and Cambridge University Library), Harington allowed many of the epigrams to circulate in MS before he collected them in print. This epigram was first published in *Epigrams both pleasant and serious*, 1615. 'Headless' applied to a woman could mean 'unmarried'. In the Folger MS of the *Epigrams*, which was presented to Prince Henry probably in 1605, Harington brought out the hit at Queen Elizabeth by preceding this poem with an attack on monsters, culminating in headless women, and by 'Of Treason' (see no. 25).

1 Peeres and Judges] death by judgement *most MSS*
2 racking] strayning *Cambridge MS*
8 noblenesse] nobles *Cambridge MS*

25 Text: Sir John Harington, *Epigrams*, 1618, see no. 24, Book 4, no. 5, sig. K4v. Edition: ed. Norman Egbert McClure, see no. 24, no. 259, p. 255. The epigram is also quoted by Harington in a letter of 1609 to Prince Henry (McClure, p. 136). First published in *Epigrams*, 1615.

26 Text: Fulke Greville, Lord Brooke, *Certaine learned and elegant workes of the Right Honorable Fulke Lord Brooke, written in his youth, and familiar exercise with Sir Philip Sidney*, 1633, pp. 225–6. Edition: ed. Geoffrey Bullough, *Poems and Dramas of Fulke Greville first Lord Brooke*, 2 vols., Edinburgh and London [1939], i.129–30. A scribal manuscript of this and other poems from *Cælica* with Greville's autograph revisions is in the British Library, MS Additional 54570. In the MS there are 108 poems, the same number as in Greville's friend Sidney's *Astrophil and Stella* (see no. 65). The numbering of the poems differs between the MS, 1633 and Bullough's edition. This poem about servile courtiers may have been written in the last years of Queen Elizabeth's reign. The 1633 edition marks ll. 7–24 as sententiae. In the textual notes, revisions in italics are in Greville's own hand.

2 Move] More *1633*
6 Staple-rate] staple rate *MS* Staple-rates *1633*
12 Where shyne they doe by hiding others light *MS, later revised*

22 Tempt man to] Make man first *MS, later revised*
24 To sore the higher uppon *princes* winges *MS, later revised*
26 which they see] *of supremacie MS, later revised*
27 all States] the publique *MS, later revised to* the *monarches later revised*
28 Transforming truth and right to flatterie *MS, later revised*
30 Tyrants] Princes *MS, later revised*

27 Text: British Library, MS Additional 21432, ff. 2v–3v. Edition: ed. David H. Horne, *The Life and Minor Works of George Peele*, New Haven 1952, pp. 265–6, ll. 17–54. The autograph MS of this poem was damaged by a corrosive substance in the nineteenth century, so that some readings have had to be restored from its first publication (by its then owner W. Stevenson Fitch) in about 1830. From the 1580s, the anniversary of the Queen's accession to the throne on 17 November was marked by tilts and elaborate entertainments. This poem, Peele's last known work, celebrates 'Englandes hollydayes' on 17 November 1595; Peele had marked the anniversary in 1590 with another poem, *Polyhymnia*, which he published in the same year.

28 Text: John Donne, *Poems by J. D.*, 1633, pp. 59–61; Scolar Press facsimile, Menston 1969. Edition: ed. A. J. Smith, *John Donne: The Complete English Poems*, Harmondsworth 1971, pp. 199–200. There were further editions of Donne's poems printed in 1635, 1639, 1649, 1650, 1654 and 1669. The poems also circulated widely in MS: some sixty-nine collections are known to contain more than ten of his poems. Many of these MSS were copied or owned by members of the Inns of Court and the universities; they were particularly popular in those circles during the 1620s, 1630s and 1640s. On account of the large number of MSS, in the textual notes unattributed emendations are generally those of one or more MSS. With its companion-piece 'The storm', this poem commemorates Donne's involvement in the 'Islands Expedition' to the Azores against the Spanish in the summer of 1597. Of the many MS versions of it, none is thought to be earlier than the 1620s.

9 those] *some MSS* the *1633*
21 lost] left *some MSS*
37 Sea-goales] sea gulls *later prints and some MSS* sea snails *some MSS*
38 venices] pinnaces *some MSS*
55 no ... sense] nor will, nor power, nor sense *some MSS*

29 Text: John Donne, *Poems*, 1633, see no. 28, pp. 339–45. Edition: ed. A. J. Smith, see no. 28, pp. 165–70, ll. 61–187, 229–44. Although this satire probably dates from 1597, only one of the many MSS of it predates the 1620s. Two MSS of the 1630s identify it as a satire 'Of' or 'against' the court. The dialogue between the speaker and courtier relies on the speaker's 'crossing' (l. 31), or deliberate misunderstanding, of what the courtier says: the poem's narrator's speeches begin at lines 3, 7, 14, 23,

27, 83; the courtier's at lines 6, 13, 21, 25, 33, 83, 84.

2 wonders] words *1633 and some MSS*
7, 8 lonenesse] lonelinesse *1633 and some MSS*
9 last] taste *a few MSS*
23 Mine?] Fine, *1633*
32 addresse] dresse *a few MSS*
38 trash he] trash; He *1633*
46 shall] they *most MSS*
51 on] me *a few MSS*
56 sigh] belch *a few MSS*
57 talke: In] talke in *1633*
73 in; . . . him,] in, . . . him. *1633*
74–6 That . . . free] *1635; omitted in 1633 and replaced by dashes*
74 venom'd] venome *1635*
81 mercy] redemption *some MSS*
94 make] hast *1633 and some MSS*
96 precious] piteous *later prints and some MSS*
104 th'] *omitted in 1633*
110 Transported] Transplanted *some MSS* stand] Strand *some MSS*
111 Presence] Court here *a few MSS* Courtiers *later prints and one MS*
125 players;] players, *1633*
129 which] *omitted in 1633*
131 sinnes?); Being] sinnes) being *1633*
135 Living,] Living *1633* wine;] wine. *1633*
136 Spie.] Spie; *1633*
137 Wit] Wits *1633*

30 Text: Robert Dowland, *A musicall banquet*, 1610, sigs. B2v–C1r; Scolar Press facsimile, Menston 1969. Edition: ed. Steven W. May, *The Poems of Edward DeVere, Seventeenth Earl of Oxford and of Robert Devereux, Second Earl of Essex*, Studies in Philology 77, no. 5 (1980), pp. 45–6. This is one of several lyrics in which Essex lamented the fickleness of women at a time when he was falling from favour with the Queen. The poem had some limited circulation in MS, but all extant texts apart from Dowland's are unattributed. In Dowland's collection the poem was printed with music by Richard Martin, who may have been a Gentleman of the Queen's Chapel. The poem, which was headed 'The Right Honourable *Robert*, Earle of Essex: Earle Marshall of England' in Dowland's collection, was probably written shortly after his appointment as Earl Marshal in December 1597. Bodleian Library, Oxford, MS Rawlinson poetical 85 (see no. 89) preserves a different ending for ll. 23–30 of the poem:

They enjoy whats but theyr owne
happyer lyfe to lyve alone

Yet thus much to ease my mynd
Lett her know what she hath gotten
She who tyme hath provd unkynde
havyng changd is quytt forgotten
Fortune now hath done her worst
Would she had done so had fyrst

10 deceiv'd] betrayed *most MSS*

31 Text: Headington, Oxford, Dr B. E. Juel-Jensen MS, ff. 1r–2r. Edition: ed. G. F. Waller, *The Triumph of Death and Other Unpublished and Uncollected Poems by Mary Sidney, Countess of Pembroke (1561–1621)*, Salzburg Studies in English Literature, Elizabethan and Renaissance Studies, 65, Salzburg 1977, pp. 88–91. The unique copy of this poem, which is in the Juel-Jensen MS, is dated 1599 at its end with the '5' written over a '6'. The poem is one of two by the Countess of Pembroke written in front of a copy of her and her brother, Sir Philip Sidney's, translation of the Psalms. The Juel-Jensen MS was copied from another MS of their translation of the Psalms owned by Viscount De L'Isle (see no. 336) and was probably prepared for presentation to the Queen in expectation of her visit to Wilton in 1599.

22 reft] rest *MS*
44 others, woold] other woold, *MS*

32 Text: Edmund Spenser, *The Faerie Queene*, 2 vols., 1596, ii.342–9, Book 5, Canto 12, verses 4–27; Scolar Press facsimile, London 1976. Edition: ed. Thomas P. Roche, Jr., and C. Patrick O'Donnell, Jr., *Edmund Spenser: The Faerie Queene*, Harmondsworth 1978, pp. 865–70. The first three books of *The Faerie Queene* were published in 1590; they were reprinted with Books 4 to 6 when they were first published in 1596. The whole poem was reprinted in 1609 and 1611. The defeat of Grantorto, the climax of Book 5, runs parallel in the poem's allegorical structure to the defeat of Acrasia in Book 2 (see no. 80): the public virtue of justice complements the private virtue of temperance. Artegall is accompanied on his quest to rescue Irena, who is under sentence of death, by Talus, his iron henchman, and Sir Sergis. Irena's name associates her with peace but also more specifically with Ireland. Artegall's struggle with Grantorto is generally taken to represent the struggle of the English, and perhaps in particular Spenser's patron Lord Grey of Wilton, against the Irish rebels.

114 sight] *1609, 1611* fight *1596*

33 Text: Dublin, Royal Irish Academy, MS 23.L.17, f. 113v. Edition: ed. Osborn Bergin, *Irish Bardic Poetry*, Dublin 1970, pp. 124–7. There is another copy of the poem in MS 23.F.16. The poem describes the hardships endured by Ó Heóghusa's patron Hugh Maguire, Lord of Fermanagh. Maguire had joined the forces of the leader of the Irish rebellion, Hugh O'Neill, who marched southward from Ulster into Munster threatening to plunder all who refused to join him. Maguire was killed in March 1600; this setback heralded the gradual triumph of the English forces which culminated in the flight of the earls in 1607, opening the way to the extensive Protestant settlement of Ulster. The punctuation of the poem follows Bergin's text.

34 Text: Ben Jonson, *The workes of Benjamin Jonson*, 1616, p. 770; Scolar Press facsimile, London 1976. Edition: ed. George Parfitt, *Ben Jonson: The Complete Poems*, Harmondsworth 1975, p. 36. This poem is the fifth in the collection of *Epigrammes*, which were entered in the Stationers' Register on 15 May 1612. It celebrates the union of England and Scotland; it was written in 1604 and circulated in MS of which none extant is earlier than the 1620s. James himself compared the union of the two countries to a marriage: 'I am the Husband, and all the whole Isle is my lawfull Wife.'

1 Never was bargaine better driven by fate *some MSS*
Never was marriage better driven by fate *MS*
Never was Union better driven by fate *some MSS*
Was ever contract driven by better fate *some MSS*
Was ever contract better driven by fate *some MSS*
2 celebrated ... truth of] solemnized ... Royall *MS*
4 spoused ... realmes] married ... Nations *MS*

35 Text: British Library, MS Egerton 3165, f. 110r. Edition: ed. Helen Estabrook Sandison, *The Poems of Sir Arthur Gorges*, Oxford 1953, p. 130. Although this poem is in a scribe's hand, the volume contains MS corrections to other poems in Gorges's own hand.

1–3 No praise for Poesie doe I affect
Nor flatteries hoped meed doth me incyte:
Such base borne thoughts as servile I reject *MS deleted and the present ll. 1–3 substituted*

36 Text: Sir Henry Wotton, *Reliquiæ Wottonianæ*, 1651, p. 522. Edition: Ted-Larry Pebworth, 'Sir Henry Wotton's "Dazel'd Thus, with Height of Place" and the Appropriation of Political Poetry in the Earlier Seventeenth Century', *Papers of the Bibliographical Society of America*, 71 (1977), 151–69. The first edition of *Reliquiæ Wottonianæ* was edited by Izaak Walton; a second, enlarged edition appeared in 1654 and was reprinted in 1672 and with further additions in 1685. James I's favourite, Robert Carr, Earl of Somerset, was tried and sentenced to death in 1616 with his wife Frances Carr for the murder of Sir Thomas Overbury in 1613. The executions were never carried out and, after six years' imprisonment in the Tower, Carr and his wife were released. The poem has also been associated with the falls of Francis Bacon and George Villiers, Duke of Buckingham. It circulated quite widely in MS, where it often has an additional verse (from Bodleian Library, Oxford, MS Rawlinson poetical 166; transcribed by Pebworth, pp. 154–5):

> All things falle, that stande by Arte,
> nought is free from fumes of swaye,
> One manne acted ill his parte,
> Lette another mende the playe.

Title] Upon the sudden restraint of a favourite *some MSS*
Of Favourites *MS*
1 thus, with] with the *all MSS*
5 favours] children *MS*
13 darkned, you shall] broken, he may *MS*
14 faile] sink *some MSS*
15 roughest] hardest *all MSS*

37 Text: William Browne, *Britannia's pastorals. The second booke*, 1616, Song 1, pp. 22–4; Scolar Press facsimile, Menston 1969. Edition: ed. Gordon Goodwin, *Poems of William Browne of Tavistock*, 2 vols., 1894, i.219–21, ll. 825–85. The first book of *Britannia's pastorals* was published in 1613 and reissued in 1616 when the second book appeared. The two were reprinted together in 1623. The third book was never finished and remained in MS until the nineteenth century.

38 Text: British Library, MS Sloane 826, f. 197r. Edition: ed. F. W. Fairholt, *Poems and Songs Relating to George Villiers, Duke of Buckingham; and his Assassination*, Percy Society, vol. 90 (1850), p. 78. The Sloane MS, which probably dates from the 1630s, contains an extensive collection of poems on Buckingham and his assassin, John Felton, who was hanged in 1628. First printed in *Wit restor'd in severall select poems, not formerly publish't*, 1658, this epitaph circulated very widely in MS. Bodleian Library, Oxford, MS Ashmole 38 attributes the poem to Donne; British Library MS Additional 15226 attributes it to Henry Cholmley. The epitaph is sometimes succeeded by the motto 'Coelo tegitur qui non habet urnam' ('He who does not have a monument is covered by the heavens'), from Lucan's condemnation of Julius Caesar for failing to give the defeated republicans due burial (*Pharsalia* 7.819).

6 I . . . himself] I dare not say; by hym *Ashmole MS*
13 yf] *Ashmole MS* oft *BL MS*
15 last] live *Ashmole MS* till] *Ashmole MS* And *BL MS*

39 Text: British Library, MS Sloane 826, see no. 38, f. 181v. Edition: ed. F. W. Fairholt, see no. 38, p. 63.

40 Text: Richard Fanshawe, *Il Pastor Fido The faithfull shepheard with an addition of divers other poems*, 1648, pp. 225–7, ll. 1–4, 33–80. Edition: ed. N. W. Bawcutt, *Sir*

Richard Fanshawe: Shorter Poems and Translations, Liverpool 1964, pp. 5–7. The poem, which exists in two MSS (British Library, MS Additional 15228, and Bodleian Library, Oxford, MS Firth c. 1), relates to a proclamation of 9 September 1630, one of a series issued in the early years of the century, urging country gentlemen with no particular business at court to return to their rural estates. It is the first among the 'Other Poems' printed in 1648.

Title: reside upon] repaire to *Bodleian MS*
12 nest] West *Bodleian MS*
13 usurping] in's brazen *BL MS*
23 come] seeke *BL MS*
30 his Realmes] our State *BL and Bodleian MSS*
33–6 Therefore the happy Lords of Land
Sends to their Vine and Figgtree home
(I would not stay the kings command
If I were one.) *BL MS deleted*

41 Text: John Cleveland, *The character of a London-diurnall: with severall select poems: by the same author*, 1647, p. 45. Edition: ed. Brian Morris and Eleanor Withington, *The Poems of John Cleveland*, Oxford 1967, p. 66. The poem circulated widely in MS, but its attribution to Cleveland is by no means certain. It was, however, included in the many editions of Cleveland's *Poems* published in 1651 and later.

6 yet] and *MSS*

42 Text: Sir John Denham, *Poems and translations*, 1668, pp. 1–22. Edition: ed. Brendan O Hehir, *Expans'd Hieroglyphicks: A Critical Edition of Sir John Denham's Coopers Hill*, Berkeley and Los Angeles 1969, pp. 139–62. The origins of Denham's famous topographical poem probably go back to 1640; an edition of this version of the poem (known as the 'A' text) was printed at London in 1642. Further reprints of it were published in 1643, 1650 and 1653. In 1655 a revised edition (known as the 'B' text) appeared which is generally regarded, because of the claim that it was 'obtained from the Author's owne papers', as the first 'authorized' one. The text of the poem in 1655 is, however, largely taken from the same setting of type used in 1653. Furthermore, there exists a unique copy of the 1653 edition (now at Yale) described on its title-page as 'Now Printed from a perfect Copy; And a Corrected Impression'. It contains three corrections in Denham's own hand, supplying omitted words. The 1655 edition was the basis for a slightly revised version of the poem, with four new lines, included in the collected edition of Denham's *Poems and translations* which he published in 1668 (reprinted in 1671 and 1684). Some copies of these early prints contain MS corrections and revisions; in particular, as well as the Yale copy of 1653 mentioned above, a copy of 1668 (also at Yale, in the Osborn Collection) has corrections and an important addition between ll. 188 and 189 in

Denham's own hand. Several early texts of the poem bear witness to its MS circulation, usually in forms close to the 'A' text.

The present version of the poem probably dates from Denham's work on it while staying at Wilton during 1653–4. Only variants between 1655 and 1668 (and within different copies of them) are given below. It is not certain whether 1668 represents Denham's revision of the poem as it stood in 1655, or whether 1655 represents a mildly corrupt form of the poem.

1 Sure there are] If there be *1655*
3 therefore] justly *1655*
18 descending] a falling *1655*
19 M. W.] Master Waller *1655*
109 Nor . . . Emblemes] He, who not needs that Embleme *1655*
118 Christian King] Christian *1655*
188 + Rome only conquerd halfe the world, but trade
One commonwealth of that and her hath made
And though the sunn his beame extends to all
Yet to his neighbour sheds most liberall
Least God and Nature partiall should appeare
Commerse makes everything grow everywhere *1668 Yale Osborn*
193–6 *omitted in 1655*
197 The Forrest.] *omitted in 1655*
242 Give] Gave *1671*

43 Text: S. N., *The loyal garland, containing choice songs and sonnets of our late unhappy revolutions*, 4th edn, 167[3?], sig. A3r–v. Edition: ed. H. J. C. Grierson and G. Bullough, *The Oxford Book of Seventeenth Century Verse*, Oxford 1934, no. 408. This popular ballad exists in several forms. At least three early single-sheet broadside versions survive: one, in the British Library among the Roxburghe Ballads (see no. 157), was published in about 1660–5; its refrain is 'When the King comes home in Peace again'. The date of publication of another version in the British Library (1876.f.1(3)) cannot be precisely determined, but it has the same refrain as the Roxburghe text and like it also represents a pre-Restoration version of the poem. In the Euing Collection in Glasgow (see no. 127) is a post-Restoration version of the ballad published in about 1660–1 under the title *Englands great prognosticator*, with the refrain 'Now the King injoyes his own again'. There is also at least one early MS version of the poem, in the British Library, MS Additional 27879 (see no. 238), with the refrain 'When the King enjoyes his rights againe'. The ballad continued being adapted for contemporary political uses in the early eighteenth century as a Jacobite song. The earliest known edition of *The loyal garland*, in which this poem is the first in the volume, survives in a unique copy in the Bodleian Library, Oxford, dated either 1673 or 1678 (an earlier edition dated 1671 recorded in Wing's *Short-Title Catalogue* appears to be a ghost); the collection was reprinted several times. If the reference to forty years' reign (l. 17) in this text of the poem is taken literally, the ballad must originally have dated from around 1643; it is referred to in the opening issue of *Mercurius melancholicus*, 4 September 1647, a newspaper to which Parker contributed. In the 1640s Parker's ballads grew increasingly politicized and he became involved, like many ballad-writers, in the emergent public press. Like the other pre-Restoration versions, the one printed here is later than the 1640s: the glossing of the Dove in l. 43 as General Monck is probably a post-Restoration annotation.

In the MS version the fifth and sixth verses are omitted; in the Roxburghe and Euing texts verse 4 precedes verse 3, verse 5 is omitted, but there are seven further verses to the poem. Since the different versions of the poem vary to a large degree, with one emendation, no textual variants have been recorded.

41 Till then upon Ararats-hill] *Roxburghe, Euing* Then avaunt upon thy hill *167[3?]*

44 Text: Robert Herrick, *Hesperides: or, the works both humane and divine of Robert Herrick Esq.*, 1648, p. 393; Scolar Press facsimile, Menston 1969. Edition: ed. L. C. Martin, *The Poetical Works of Robert Herrick*, Oxford 1956, p. 331. This epigram renders a comment by the tyrant Atreus in Seneca's play *Thyestes*.

45 Text: Andrew Marvell, *Miscellaneous poems. By Andrew Marvell, Esq;*, 1681, pp. 115–18; Scolar Press facsimile, Menston 1969. Edition: ed. Elizabeth Story Donno, *Andrew Marvell: The Complete Poems*, Harmondsworth 1972, pp. 55–8. The poem was first printed in the 1681 collection of Marvell's poems. In all but two of the extant copies of 1681 (in the British Library and the Henry E. Huntington Library, San Marino, California) it was cancelled, along with two other poems on Cromwell (see also no. 50). A copy in the Bodleian Library, Oxford, of 1681 (MS English poetical d. 49) contains MS corrections to the text and supplements the volume with several additional poems in MS (the corrections and MS poems are reproduced in the Scolar Press facsimile; they are referred to as 1681MS). In the MS this poem is divided into thirty four-line verses. Cromwell returned from Ireland in May 1650; since he did not invade Scotland until 22 July (see ll. 105–8), the poem can probably be dated to the early summer of 1650. The works most usually cited as important influences on the poem are Horace's *Odes* 1.35, 1.37, 4.4, 5, 14 and 15, and Book 1 of Lucan's *Pharsalia* (cp. the extract from Marlowe's translation, no. 340), which he may also have read in Thomas May's translation of 1631, 1635 or 1650.

Title Horatian] *1681MS* Horation *1681*
15 thorough] *1681MS* through *1681*
35 Kingdome] *1681* Kingdoms *1681MS*
85 Commons] commons *1681MS* Common *1681*
100 crown] crowns *1681MS*

46 Text: Sir William Mure, *The cry of blood, and of a broken covenant*, Edinburgh 1650, pp. 1–2. Edition: ed. William Tough, *The works of Sir William Mure of*

Rowallan, Scottish Text Society, 2 vols., 1898, ii.33–4, ll. 9–24. This extract is taken from what was probably Mure's last poem; it was addressed to Charles II, condemned the execution of Charles I, and called on Mure's fellow-countrymen to rise against Parliament.

47 Text: Katherine Philips, *Poems by Mrs. Katherine Philips the Matchless Orinda*, 1667, pp. 13–14. Edition: ed. Patrick Thomas, *The Collected Works of Katherine Philips The Matchless Orinda, Volume I The Poems*, Stump Cross, Essex, 1990, pp. 82–3. Philips's poems were first published in an unauthorized edition with a corrupt text in 1664; the posthumous edition of 1667 presents a better text, which was reprinted in 1669, 1678 and 1710. As well as circulating in MS during her lifetime, Philips's poems also survive in several MSS. In what is now National Library of Wales MS 775, she kept fair copies of her poems; MS 776, in the same collection, contains transcripts of poems, apparently made sometime between 1664 and 1667; a MS in the Harry Ransom Humanities Research Center, the University of Texas at Austin, contains copies of her poems in the hand of her friend Sir Edward Dering.

18 else attend] wait upon *775, Texas*
24 bear] keep *Texas*

48 Text: Trinity College, Cambridge, MS R. 34, f. 47r; Scolar Press facsimile, Menston 1970; all of Milton's poetical works were reproduced in facsimile ed. H. F. Fletcher, 4 vols., Urbana, Ill., 1943–8. Edition: ed. John Carey and Alastair Fowler, *The Poems of John Milton*, 1968, pp. 326–7. The Trinity MS represents Milton's own fair copies and working drafts of his earlier poems written before he went blind: many contain important revisions and corrections. The copy of this sonnet in the Trinity MS, like that of several other later poems, is in the hand of a scribe. The poem was first printed in Edward Phillips's edition of Milton's *Letters of state*, 1694, in what appears to be a corrupt form. The Committee, on which Cromwell sat, was in favour of an established Church and of limits to dissent. Milton's sonnet voices his opposition to establishment.

5–6 And fought God's Battels, and his Work pursu'd *1694*
9 And ... wreath] And twentie battles more *deleted in MS*

49 Text: Trinity College, Cambridge, MS R. 34, see no. 48, f. 47v. Edition: ed. John Carey and Alastair Fowler, see no. 48, pp. 328–9. The copy in the Trinity MS is in the hand of the same scribe as the sonnet to Cromwell which it follows, see no. 48. The poem was first printed in George Sikes, *The life and death of Sir Henry Vane*, 1662, where it is said that the sonnet was sent to Vane by 'a learned Gentleman' on 3 July 1652. Vane (1613–62), who was appointed Treasurer to the Navy in 1639, served on the Council of State, to which Milton was secretary, and was opposed to an established Church; he was executed by the restored government.

1 counsell] counsells *MS, corrected to* counsell
6 drift] drifts *MS corrected to* drift
8 by] on *MS corrected to* by
10–11 What powre the Church and what the civill meanes
Thou teachest best, which few have ever don
MS corrected to
Both spirituall powre and civill, what it meanes *corrected to* each meanes
Thou hast learnt well, a praise which few have won
corrected to present form
13 firme] right *MS corrected to* firme

50 Text: Andrew Marvell, *Miscellaneous poems*, 1681, see no. 45, p. 128. Edition: ed. Elizabeth Story Donno, see no. 45, pp. 135–6, ll. 349–66. The poem was first published, anonymously, in January 1655 and reprinted from that text in the 1681 collection. It was one of the poems cancelled from that edition in most of the extant copies: the text of the poem in the Bodleian MS (1681MS) was probably copied from 1655. Two other early MSS attribute the poem's authorship to Edmund Waller and it was reprinted in 1707 supposedly as his in the collection *Poems on affairs of state*. Cromwell celebrated his first anniversary as Protector on 16 December 1654. The extract is part of a speech by an unnamed foreign prince about the state of the country under Cromwell.

4 their] *MS* our *1655, 1681*

51 Text: Alexander Brome, *Songs and other poems*, 1661, pp. 103–6. Edition: ed. Roman R. Dubinski, *Alexander Brome: Poems*, 2 vols., Toronto, Buffalo and London 1982, i.166–8. Brome's poems were reprinted in 1664 and 1668. This poem was also included in the collection by W. N., C. B., R. S. and J. G., *The second part of merry drollery*, [1661].

Title] The Contented *Merry drollery*
5 has oft] *Merry drollery* has *1661–1668*
14 dust] th'ground *1664, 1668* ground *Merry drollery*
15 Whose] Their *Merry drollery* they] their *Merry drollery*
must] down *Merry drollery, 1664, 1668*
16 Fall down] Must fall *Merry drollery, 1664, 1668*
34 Lambert] Monck *Merry drollery*
38 blowes] Swords *Merry drollery*
41 Luck] Such *Merry drollery* rule] root *Merry drollery*

52 Text: British Library, MS Royal, Appendix 58, f. 5r; facsimile in Anthony G. Petti. Edition: Anthony G. Petti, *English Literary Hands from Chaucer to Dryden*, 1977, no. 11. The only MS of this late-fifteenth-century lyric is a tenor part-book; it is possible that this text is only a fragment of a longer poem.

53 Text: British Library, MS Egerton 2711, see no. 6, f. 26v; facsimile in Muir and Thomson, see no. 5, opposite p. 68. Edition: ed. R. A. Rebholz, see no. 5, pp. 116–17. There is another copy of the poem in the British Library, MS Additional 17492, a courtly miscellany of the 1530s and 1540s, known from its later owners as the Devonshire MS. The poem was first printed in Tottel's *Songes and sonettes*, 1557, (see no. 57), where it was headed 'The lover sheweth how he is forsaken of such as he somtime enjoyed'.

17 straunge] bitter *Tottel*
18 goo] parte *Devonshire MS*
20 kyndely] gentillye *Devonshire MS*
21 What think you bye this that she hat deserved *Devonshire MS*
How like you this, what hath she now deserved *Tottel*

54 Text: British Library, MS Egerton 2711, see no. 6, f. 7v; facsimile in Ruth Hughey, 'The Harington Manuscript at Arundel Castle and Related Documents', *The Library*, 4th series, 15 (1934–5), opposite p. 414. Edition: ed. R. A. Rebholz, see no. 5, p. 77. Attributed to Wyatt by Muir and Thomson (see no. 5), the poem is also found in the Blage and Arundel-Harington MSS (see nos. 5 and 7). The copy in the Egerton MS contains alterations in the hand of Nicholas Grimald (see no. 310) and the heading in another hand 'Sonet'. Adapted from Petrarch (*Rime* 190), and probably written in, or before, 1527, the poem seems to allude to Henry VIII's winning of Anne Boleyn.

9 her] to *Arundel-Harington MS*

55 Text: British Library, MS Egerton 2711, see no. 6, f. 17r. Edition: ed. R. A. Rebholz, see no. 5, pp. 120–1. The poem is also found in the Blage MS (see no. 5) and was first printed in Tottel's *Songes and sonettes*, 1557 (see no. 57), where it was headed 'The lover taught, mistrusteth allurementes'.

5 The wordes, that from your mouth last came *Tottel*
18 hath founde] yet proved *Blage MS*
19 great] but *Blage MS*

56 Text: British Library, MS Egerton 2711, see no. 6, ff. 43v–4r. Edition: ed. R. A. Rebholz, see no. 5, pp. 144–5. The poem is also found in the Blage and Devonshire MSS (see nos. 5 and 53). A religious imitation of the poem was printed in the collection *The courte of vertue*, 1565, where it appears it should be sung to the same tune supplied for another poem 'My pen obey my wyll a whyle'. Included in Tottel's *Songes and sonettes*, 1557 (see no. 57), it was headed 'The lover complayneth the unkindnes of his love'.

9 sigh or syng] syng or walle *Blage MS*
26 the lye] *Egerton MS corrected from* they lay
27 nyghts] *Blage and Devonshire MSS* nyght *Egerton MS*
36 Now . . . lute] My lute be styll *Blage MS*
39 now . . . song] For when this song ys *Blage MS*

57 Text: Richard Tottel (ed.?), *Songes and sonettes*, 1557, sig. A2v; Scolar Press facsimile, Menston and London 1970. Edition: ed. Emrys Jones, see no. 8, p. 2. Tottel's miscellany is the most important of the earlier Tudor collections of printed verse. It is uncertain whose work it was; Richard Tottel was its publisher and the poet Nicholas Grimald (see no. 310) may have had a hand in the editing. The collection was reprinted in 1559, 1565, 1567, 1574, 1585 and 1587. Tottel gives the poem the heading, 'Description of Spring, wherin eche thing renewes, save onelie the lover'. The poem imitates Petrarch (*Rime* 310).

58 Text: National Library of Scotland, MS Advocates 1.1.6, f. 256r–v; Scolar Press facsimile, London 1980. Edition: ed. James Cranstoun, *The Poems of Alexander Scott*, Scottish Text Society, 1896, pp. 73–4. The Bannatyne MS, in which the unique MS text of this poem survives, is a large collection of Scottish poems. It was compiled at Edinburgh in about 1568 by George Bannatyne (1545–1608). The poem is subscribed in the MS as being written by Scott 'quhen his wyfe left him'.

59 Text: George Turbervile, *Epitaphes, epigrams, songs and sonets*, 1567, sig. L6v; Scholars' Facsimiles & Reprints, intro. Richard J. Panofsky, Delmar, NY, 1977. Edition: ed. [John Payne Collier], [1867], p. 141. There was a second edition of Turbervile's work published in 1570. The motto or a variant 'Let reason rule affection' is found on some surviving rings, see Joan Evans, *English Posies and Posy Rings*, Oxford 1931, p. 67.

60 Text: Isabella Whitney, *The copy of a letter, lately written in meeter, by a yonge gentilwoman: to her unconstant lover* [1567?], sigs. A2r–5v.

61 Text: George Gascoigne, *A hundreth sundrie flowres bounde up in one small poesie*, [1573], p. 306; Scolar Press facsimile, Menston 1970. Edition: ed. C. T. Prouty, *George Gascoigne's A Hundreth Sundrie Flowres*, Columbia, Mo., 1942, pp. 115–16. The poem was reprinted in further collections of Gascoigne's works in 1575 and 1587. Writers often refer to the unattractiveness of women with dark complexions; in the last line of the poem Gascoigne alludes to the famous fifteenth-century ballad of 'The nutbrown maid'. In the [1573] collection the poem is one of 'The devises of sundrie Gentlemen', presented as though they had come into Gascoigne's hands. It is introduced with the following paragraph, from which the present title has been taken:

> Enough of this Dame. And let us peruse his other doings which have come to my hands, in such disordred order, as I can best set them down. I will now then present you with a Sonet written in prayse of the brown beautie, which he compyled for the love of Mistresse E. P. as foloweth.

Title] A Sonet written in prayse of the browne beautie, compiled for the love of Mistresse E. P. as foloweth *1575*

62 Text: *A handefull of pleasant delites newly devised to the newest tunes by Clement Robinson and divers others*, 1584, sigs. B2r–3v; Scolar Press facsimile, Ilkley and London 1973. Edition: ed. H. E. Rollins, *A Handful of Pleasant Delights (1584) by Clement Robinson and Divers Others*, Cambridge, Mass., 1924, pp. 19–22. The 1584 edition is the earliest complete one to survive: fragments of other editions survive from about 1575 and 1595. The collection preserves poems originally printed as ballads, probably from before 1566. In September 1580 two works which may have been ballads, 'A newe northern Dittye of ye Ladye Greene Sleves' and 'Greene Sleves moralised to the Scripture Declaringe the manifold benefites and blessinges of God bestowed on sinfull manne', were entered in the Stationers' Register. The popular tune of 'Greensleeves' is referred to in Shakespeare's *The Merry Wives of Windsor*, II.1.59 and V.5.19.

44 grassie] grossie *1584*

63 Text: Sir Philip Sidney, *The Countesse of Pembrokes Arcadia*, 1598, pp. 473–4, *Certain Sonnets*, no. 4; Scholars' Facsimiles & Reprints, intro. A. J. Colaianne, 2 vols., New York 1983. Edition: ed. William A. Ringler, Jr., see no. 14, p. 137. The collection of *Certain Sonnets* circulated with some *Old Arcadia* MSS; it was first printed in 1598. The poem and the one preceding it, 'The fire to see my wrongs for anger burneth', are set 'To the tune of *Non credo gia che piu infelice amante*', whose origins are not known. The poem is based on the story of the rape of Philomela by Tereus and her transformation into a nightingale (Ovid, *Metamorphoses* 6.424ff.).

64 Text: Sir Philip Sidney, *Arcadia*, 1590, see no. 14, ff. 95v–96v. Edition: ed. William A. Ringler, Jr., see no. 14, pp. 111–13; OA71. The poem circulated among the *Old Arcadia* MSS and in one MS miscellany, Bodleian Library, Oxford, MS Rawlinson poetical 85 (see no. 89). This double-sestina is sung by the two shepherds in the *Old Arcadia* as a lament for their love Urania.

1, 2 Yee] *1593* You *1590 and Rawlinson MS*
3 Ye] *1593* You *1590 and Rawlinson MS*
14 sporte] *most MSS* sports *1590, 1593*   in] *MSS* at *1590, 1593*
59 hate] *1593 and MSS* have *1590*
62 beawties] *most MSS* beautie *1590, 1593 and Rawlinson MS*
67 with] *most MSS* to *1590, 1593 and Rawlinson MS*

69 rase] *most MSS* rose *1590, 1593 and some MSS*
75 this is] *MSS* is this *1590, 1593*

65 Text: Sir Philip Sidney, *Arcadia*, 1598. see no. 63, p. 519. Edition: ed. William A. Ringler, Jr., see no. 14, p. 165. Several MSS of the sequence or parts of it are known to have circulated at an early date. The sequence was first printed in *Syr P. S. His Astrophel and Stella. Wherein the excellence of sweete poesie is concluded*, an unauthorized edition in 1591 (1591a) and again in the same year in a better text (1591b). The first five lines of this sonnet were printed in Abraham Fraunce's *The Arcadian rhetorike* [1588], as an example of gradatio or climax. Early textual witnesses and allusions to the sequence are divided between calling the hero 'Astrophel' and 'Astrophil'; since the name is intended to mean 'star-lover', Stella being the star, the form 'Astrophil' has been adopted here. Sidney's sonnet sequence (the earliest in the English language) was probably written during 1581–2, when Sidney seems to have been in love with Penelope Devereux, the sister of the Earl of Essex. She married Robert, Lord Rich, on 1 November 1581.

2 she (deare she)] the deare She *MSS, 1591a and 1591b*
13 trewand] tongue and *some MSS and 1591a*

66 Text: Sir Philip Sidney, *Arcadia*, 1598, see no. 63, p. 519. Edition: ed. William A. Ringler, Jr., see no. 14, pp. 165–6.

1 at] *MSS, 1591a and 1591b* at the *1598*
3 mine] tract *1591a*
13 my] *most MSS, 1591a and 1591b* me *1598 and MS*

67 Text: Sir Philip Sidney, *Arcadia*, 1598, see no. 63, p. 522. Edition: ed. William A. Ringler, Jr., see no. 14, p. 169.

2 chiefest] *MSS, 1591a and 1591b* choisest *1598 and MS*
13 myne] *MSS, 1591a and 1591b* mind *1598*

68 Text: Sir Philip Sidney, *Arcadia*, 1598, see no. 63, p. 544. Edition: ed. William A. Ringler, Jr., see no. 14, p. 202.

14 alas how shall] within my call *1591a*

69 Text: Sir Philip Sidney, *Arcadia*, 1598, see no. 63, p. 547. Edition: ed. William A. Ringler, Jr., see no. 14, p. 207.

70 Text: Sir Philip Sidney, *Arcadia*, 1598, see no. 63, p. 548. Edition: ed. William A. Ringler, Jr., see no. 14, p. 208.

71 Text: Sir Philip Sidney, *Arcadia*, 1598, see no. 63, pp. 555–8. Edition: ed. William A. Ringler, Jr., see no. 14, pp. 217–21. 1591a omits ll. 69 to 100.

3 pide] new *some MSS*
4 fresh] sweetly *MS*
5 *etc.* Astrophil] Astrophel *1598*
94 In . . . smart] The torment in my selfe *MS*
95 Tyran] Tyran, *1598*
102 so] *1591b* to *1598*

72 Text: Sir Philip Sidney, *Arcadia*, 1598, see no. 63, pp. 567–8. Edition: ed. William A. Ringler, Jr., see no. 14, pp. 233–5. This song was omitted in both quartos of 1591. Stella speaks in the first two lines of each verse.

23 theye] *MSS* thy *1598*
40 there] *MSS* thee *1598*
43 unjustest] *MSS* unjust *1598*

73 Text: Fulke Greville, Lord Brooke, *Workes*, 1633, see no. 26, p. 174. Edition: ed. Geoffrey Bullough, see no. 26, i.84–5.

74 Text: Fulke Greville, Lord Brooke, *Workes*, 1633, see no. 26, pp. 177–8. Edition: ed. Geoffrey Bullough, see no. 26, i.87.

75 Text: Fulke Greville, Lord Brooke, *Workes*, 1633, see no. 26, pp. 187–8. Edition: ed. Geoffrey Bullough, see no. 26, i.96. This poem is number 40 in Bullough's edition.

76 Text: Fulke Greville, Lord Brooke, *Workes*, 1633, see no. 26, pp. 192–3. Edition: ed. Geoffrey Bullough, see no. 26, i.99–100. This is a paradoxical praise of absence; in the last verse Greville changes his mind about the pleasures of absence. This poem is number 45 in Bullough's edition.

35 Presence] Pleasures *1633* Pleasure *MS*

77 Text: Fulke Greville, Lord Brooke, *Workes*, 1633, see no. 26, p. 234. Edition: ed. Geoffrey Bullough, see no. 26, i.134–5.

78 Text: Mark Alexander Boyd, *Sonet*, [La Rochelle? *c.* 1590], single sheet. Edition: ed. Helen Gardner, *The New Oxford Book of English Verse 1250–1950*, Oxford 1972, no. 98. The sonnet is known only from this printing, which survives in a unique copy pasted to the flyleaf of a copy of David Chalmers, Lord Ormond's *Histoire abregee de tous les roys de France, Angleterre et Escosse*, Paris 1579, in the National Library of Scotland. Boyd's name is written in MS at the foot of the poem. In the original printed version of the poem, the printer seems to have used the letter 'v' for 'w' as well as for 'u': in the version printed here, the 'w' has been restored where appropriate.

79 Text: Robert Greene, *Menaphon Camillas alarum to slumbering Euphues*, 1589, sig. D3v. Edition: ed. G. B. Harrison, *Menaphon by Robert Greene and A Margarite of America by Thomas Lodge*, Oxford 1927, pp. 45–6. Greene's popular romance was reprinted in 1599, 1605, 1610 and 1616.

80 Text: Edmund Spenser, *The Faerie Queene*, 1596, see no. 32, i.382–7, Book 2, Canto 12, verses 70–87. Edition: ed. Thomas P. Roche, Jr., and C. Patrick O'Donnell, Jr., see no. 32, pp. 378–82. These verses, in which Sir Guyon and his companion the Palmer complete the quest of destroying the Bower of Blisse and overthrowing its creator Acrasia, conclude the second book of *The Faerie Queene*.

124 spoyle] *1590* spoyld *1596*

81 Text: Edmund Spenser, *The Faerie Queene*, 1596, see no. 32, i.486–90, Book 3, Canto 6, verses 29–43. Edition: ed. Thomas P. Roche, Jr., and C. Patrick O'Donnell, Jr., see no. 32, pp. 469–72. The episode tells of the raising of Amoret by Venus in the Garden of Adonis, which is to be contrasted with the Bower of Blisse (see no. 80). It evokes comparisons with the Garden of Eden, as described in Genesis 1, and the myths of the golden age and of the earthly paradise, described by Ovid and Ariosto. The passage ends with a stanza ('Right in the middest of that Paradise') which comes at the exact centre of Book 3 (excluding Proems and Arguments) in 1590.

122 heavy] heavenly *1590*

82 Text: Edmund Spenser, *The Faerie Queene*, 1596, see no. 32, i.568–74, Book 3, Canto 11, verses 28–49. Edition: ed. Thomas P. Roche, Jr., and C. Patrick O'Donnell, Jr., see no. 32, pp. 543–8. Britomart enters the House of the enchanter Busirane to rescue Amoret. The source for the tapestries she sees there is the one woven by Arachne in her tapestry-weaving competition with Minerva, which Ovid describes in *Metamorphoses* 6.103–28 (see no. 334).

139 prove)] *1609* prove. *1590* prove.) *1596*
197 ever more] *1609* evermore *1590 and 1596*

83 Text: Edmund Spenser, *Amoretti and Epithalamion. Written not long since by Edmunde Spenser*, 1595, sig. B5r; Scolar Press facsimile, Menston 1968. Edition: ed. William A. Oram, Einar Bjorvand, Ronald Bond, Thomas H. Cain, Alexander Dunlop and Richard Schell, *The Yale Edition of the Shorter Poems of Edmund Spenser*, New Haven and London 1989, p. 614. The sonnet sequence *Amoretti* ('little loves') and the marriage poem *Epithalamion* (see no. 88), which were published together in the same volume, are generally thought to celebrate Spenser's love for Elizabeth Boyle, whom he married on 11 June 1594. They were reprinted in the 1611 collection of Spenser's works.

84 Text: Edmund Spenser, *Amoretti and Epithalamion*, 1595, see no. 83, sig. E1v. Edition: ed. William A. Oram etc., see no. 83, pp. 638–9.

12 Jessemynes.] Jessemynes, *1595*

85 Text: Edmund Spenser, *Amoretti and Epithalamion*, 1595, see no. 83, sig. E3r. Edition: ed. William A. Oram etc., see no. 83, pp. 640–1.

4 pray:] pray. *1595*

86 Text: Edmund Spenser, *Amoretti and Epithalamion*, 1595, see no. 83, sig. E4v. Edition: ed. William A. Oram etc., see no. 83, pp. 642–3.

2 displayd] displayd, *1595*

87 Text: Edmund Spenser, *Amoretti and Epithalamion*, 1595, see no. 83, sig. E5r. Edition: ed. William A. Oram etc., see no. 83, p. 643.

9 above] about *1595*
13 see,] see. *1595*

88 Text: Edmund Spenser, *Amoretti and Epithalamion*, 1595, see no. 83, sigs. G4r–H7v. Edition: ed. William A. Oram etc., see no. 83, pp. 662–79. The wedding poem, celebrating Spenser's marriage to Elizabeth Boyle on 11 June 1594, was published in the same volume as the *Amoretti* (see no. 83). Each verse of the *Epithalamion* was printed on its own page and, following the Greek etymology of its title, the poem forms a progression to the bridal chamber. St Barnabas's day (l. 266), 11 June, was reckoned by the calendar in Spenser's time to be the longest day of the year. It has been observed that the poem consists of 365 long lines (the number of days in a year) and 68 short lines (the total of weeks, months and seasons in a year) and is divided into 24 stanzas (the number of hours in a day).

24 dove,] dove *1595*
61 take,] take. *1595*
67 dere] dore *1595*
116 see.] see *1595*
129 aloud] aloud, *1595*
158 Queene.] Queene, *1595*
209 you.] you, *1595*
214 faces.] faces *1595*
215 may] may, *1595*

218 play] play; *1595*
220 throates] throates. *1595*
237 unsownd.] unsownd, *1595*
239 band?] band, *1595*
272 weare:] weare. *1595*
304 coverlets.] coverlets, *1595*
310 brooke.] brooke *1595*
385 thy] they *1595*
411 clods] clods: *1595*

89 Text: Bodleian Library, Oxford, MS Rawlinson poetical 85, f. 123r–v. Edition: ed. Agnes M. C. Latham, see no. 18, pp. 22–3. The first known printing of this poem is in the earliest extant copy of Thomas Deloney's *The garland of good will*, 1628; but the work had been entered in the Stationers' Register as early as 5 March 1593 and, although no copy survives from around this time, Ralegh's poem may have been in print during the 1590s. The poem also survives in the Percy MS (see no. 238) and one late-sixteenth-century Huntington MS (see no. 22). The poem draws on the ballad tradition; its attribution to Ralegh rests on the ascription in the Rawlinson MS. In the MS, ll. 1–4 as printed here replace the following lines, which have been deleted:

As you went to Walsingam
To that holy lande
Met you not with my true love
By the waye as you went:

11 form] *written over* powre
26 now] no *MS*
30 forgets] forgett *MS*
39 many chyldysh desyres] there ungratefull sex *Huntington MS*
40 conceytes] hard harttes *Huntington MS*

90 Text: Samuel Daniel, *The works of Samuel Daniel newly augmented*, 1601, 'To Delia', p. 7. Edition: ed. Arthur Colby Sprague, *Samuel Daniel: Poems and A Defence of Ryme*, Chicago and London 1965, p. 17. The poem was first printed in the first (unauthorized) edition of Sir Philip Sidney's *Astrophil and Stella*, 1591, see no. 65, where it was numbered sonnet 7 in an untitled group of twenty-seven sonnets attributed to 'S. D.'. In 1592 it was printed as sonnet 13 in Daniel's collection *Delia. Contayning certayne sonnets: with the complaint of Rosamond*; there were further editions in 1594, 1595 and 1598.

2 proper griefe] griefe himselfe *1591*
7 fairest forme] goodliest shape *1591*   that all the world] the worldes eye *1592*
10 sweetest . . . do] sweete *Idea* I *1591*
13 happie] blessed *1591*   joy'd] joyes *1591*

91 Text: Samuel Daniel, *The works*, 1601, see no. 90, 'To Delia', p. 20. Edition: ed. Arthur Colby Sprague, see no. 90, p. 27. This sonnet was first printed in 1592.

1 sable] golden *1592–1598*
2 beauties] flowers *1592–1598*

92 Text: Samuel Daniel, *The works*, 1601, see no. 90, 'To Delia', p. 26. Edition: ed. Arthur Colby Sprague, see no. 90, p. 33. This sonnet was first printed in 1592.

13 in . . . appeare] they shall discover *1592–1598*
14 lov'd . . . deare] was thy lover *1592–1598*

93 Text: Chetham's Library, Manchester, MS 8012 (A.4.15), see no. 15, f. 49r. Edition: ed. Robert Krueger, *The Poems of Sir John Davies*, Oxford 1975, p. 166. This is the sixth of the *Gullinge Sonnets*, which may date from about 1594; the Chetham MS, the unique witness to their text, may date from the 1620s. Davies's blazon of Cupid is related to Spenser's (see no. 82), but the clothes Cupid wears bear no connection with the attributes he gives him apart from alliteration.

94 Text: John Davies and Christopher Marlowe, *Epigrammes and elegies. By J. D. and C. M.*, Middleborugh [*c.* 1599?], sig. D4r–v. Edition: ed. Robert Krueger, see no. 93, p. 180. Two editions exist, both undated with false Middelburg imprints: one of these may be as early as 1595–6, but their order of printing is disputed. The text here is taken from the British Library copy ([1599?a]), with some readings from the Henry E. Huntington copy ([1599?b]). In both editions this poem appeared under the heading of 'Ignoto' and the second, third and fourth stanzas were printed as one. It may date from about 1594 or 1595, and had some limited circulation in MS. It has sometimes been compared to Richard's opening speech in Shakespeare's *Richard III*, I.1.12–17.

1 sprightly] piercing *MS*
13 fist] *MS and [1599?b]* fill *[1599?a]* cheeks *MS*
14 Jove] love *[1599?a and b]*
15 by Cock] by God *[1599?b]* by Jove *MS* in fayth *MS*   I tel] *MSS and [1599?b]* tel *[1599?a]*

95 Text: London, Inner Temple Library, MS Petyt 538, vol. 43, ff. 295v–8v. Editions: ed. Ronald B. McKerrow, *The Works of Thomas Nashe*, rev. F. P. Wilson, 5 vols., Oxford 1958, iii.403–16; ed. J. B. Steane, *Thomas Nashe: The Unfortunate Traveller and Other Works*, Harmondsworth 1972, pp. 458–68. The exact date of the poem is unknown, but it must certainly have been written before 1597, when it was referred to in the anonymous pamphlet *The trimming of Thomas Nashe*; Ferdinando Stanley (1559?–94) succeeded his father as Earl of Derby in 1593. In the previous year Nashe had praised Stanley in his *Pierce Penilesse*. Six MSS of the poem are known, two of which (Rosenbach Foundation, MS 1083/15, and London, Victoria and Albert Museum, MS Dyce 44) present it in a much abbreviated form of 161 or 162 lines. None of the four longer MS versions of the poem (the Petyt MS; Bodleian Library, Oxford, MS Rawlinson poetical 216; British Library MS Additional 10309, which has only ll. 1–232; and Folger Shakespeare Library MS V.a.399) belongs before the early seventeenth century: the Folger and Rosenbach MSS have not been collated for this edition.

Title] Nash his Dildo *MSS and in contemporary allusions*
Sonnet title] To the right Honourable Lord Straing*e* *Folger MS*
4 so . . . gaie] as fresh as May *BL MS*
7 At] As *Petyt MS*
11–14 *omitted in BL MS*
13 Whereto] Where, to *Petyt MS*
48 venus . . . vestalls] never-daunted venus *BL MS*
50 prettie Trulls] wenches straight *Bodleian MS*
61 swive] cope *Dyce MS*
72 Provided you procure me my request *BL MS*
106 For pearles, and Jewells, they are idle toyes *BL MS*
Oh . . . all] all earthly pleasures seeme to this *Bodleian MS*
110 silver streame] Christall Jem *BL and Bodleian MSS*
115 loftie] lusty *BL, Bodleian and Dyce MSS*
117 stype] gripe *Bodleian MS*
129 clap] clip *BL and Bodleian MSS*
144 did . . . foyne] laboured and foamed *Bodleian MS*
145 rubd'] firkt *BL MS*
147 stryking] frigging *BL MS*
171 icie limmes] verry mappe *Bodleian MS*
172 And] A *Petyt MS*
183–4 *text from Bodleian MS; omitted in Petyt MS*
186 consumed] dissolved *BL MS* blandishment] languishment *BL and Bodleian MSS*
192 blisse . . . sorrow] course of pleasure *BL MS*
195 trilling] drisling *Bodleian MS*
198 As is the balme that all her woombe destraynes *Bodleian MS*
199 itching . . . hipps] trickling . . . lippes *Bodleian MS*
201 sprauleth] fresketh *Bodleian MS*
202 solace] pleasures *Bodleian MS*
203 I faint . . . death] I Come I come sweete death *Bodleian MS* yeald] dye *BL MS*
208 Withould] *Bodleian MS* Without *Petyt MS* flood] abode *BL MS*
211 is fleeting] in stealing *Bodleian MS*
212 fleshie] earthly *Bodleian MS*
214 fade] dye *BL MS*

240 knave] youth *Bodleian MS*
247 whose . . . now] thy kingdome needes *Bodleian MS*
270 plumb] plump *Bodleian MS*
274 whott] warme *Bodleian MS*
275 Arm'd otherwhile] Running sometymes *Bodleian MS*
283 clammie] Clayey *Bodleian MS*
285 jollie] royall *Bodleian MS*
287 Bedasht bespotted and beplotted foule *Bodleian MS*
He dasht, and spurted, and he plodded foule *Petyt MS*
294 If Illian queene knewe of thy bravery heere *Bodleian MS*
299 nurserie] mistery *Bodleian MS*
300 penurie] misery *Bodleian MS*
315 eve'rie one] every one *Bodleian MS* eve'rie each one *Petyt MS*

96 Text: John Donne, *Poems*, 1669, pp. 97–9. Edition: ed. A. J. Smith, see no. 28, pp. 124–6. The poem, usually numbered as Elegy 19, was not published in the 1633 edition and was first included (in what seems to be a slightly corrupt text) in editions of Donne's poems from 1669. It was extremely popular among collectors of MS verse and was first printed in *The harmony of the Muses: or the gentlemans and ladies choisest recreation, by C. R.*, 1654. The end of the first half of the poem at l. 24 suggests the man's erection. The variant reading of l. 46 suggests different interpretations of the poem's ending.

14 from] through *1669* shadow] shadows *1669*
16 on you] on your head *1669*
17 safely] softly *1669 and some MSS*
20 Receavd by] Reveal'd to *1669*
26 Behind, before, above, between, below *most MSS*
28 kingdome, safeliest] Kingdom's safest, *1669*
30 How . . . this] How am I blest in thus *1669*
32 be.] be, *1669*
36 balls] ball *1669*
38 covet] court *1669* theirs] that *1669 and some MSS*
41 Themselves are only mystick books, which we, *1669*
44 a] thy *1669*
46 There is no pennance due to innocence: *1669 and some MSS*

97 Text: Barnabe Barnes, *Parthenophil and Parthenophe. Sonnettes, madrigals, elegies and odes*, [1593], p. 18. Edition: ed. Victor A. Doyno, *Barnabe Barnes: Parthenophil and Parthenophe, A Critical Edition*, Carbondale and Edwardsville 1971, p. 18.

98 Text: *Englands Helicon*, 1600, sigs. Aa1v–2r; Scolar Press facsimile, Menston and London 1973. Edition: ed. Stephen Orgel, *Christopher Marlowe: The Complete Poems and Translations*, Harmondsworth 1971, p. 211. *Englands Helicon* is the most important Elizabethan printed miscellany of lyric and pastoral poetry; a second edition with some additional poems was issued in 1614. The poem was first published in a four-stanza version in the anthology *The passionate pilgrim*, 1599. It circulated in this form in MS, being attributed to both Sidney and Ralegh, whose reply often appeared with Marlowe's version in both print and MS. The shorter version of the poem generally omits ll. 13–16 and 20–4, substituting l. 23 for l. 18.

8 sing] sings *1600*

99 Text: Christopher Marlowe, *Hero and Leander*, 1598; Folger facsimile, intro. Louis L. Martz, New York and Washington 1972. Edition: ed. Stephen Orgel, see no. 98, pp. 17–40. The poem was first entered in the Stationers' Register to John Wolfe on 28 September 1593; the first extant edition was published by Edward Blount in 1598 (1598a). On 2 March 1598 Blount assigned his rights in the poem to another publisher, Paul Lynley, who later in the same year printed a second edition in which Marlowe's poem was divided into two sestiads and completed by four more translated by George Chapman (see no. 124). This second edition printed in 1598 (1598b) was reprinted from Blount's text: nine further editions before 1640 testify to the poem's popularity: these appeared in 1600, 1606, 1609, 1613, 1616, 1617, 1622, 1629 and 1637. The text printed here is from 1598a. Critical opinion is divided as to whether this is one of Marlowe's first or one of his last works and whether its fragmentary state was planned from the start or not. The principal sources for the poem are Ovid's *Heroides* 18 and 19, an exchange of letters between Hero and Leander, and Musaeus's fifth-century poem about the lovers, a favourite and important Renaissance text.

Chapman's arguments to the two sestiads (the name is derived from the place-name Sestos) read:

The Argument of the First Sestyad.

Heros description and her Loves,
The Phane of *Venus*; where he moves
His worthie Love-suite, and attaines;
Whose blisse the wrath of Fates restraines,
For *Cupids* grace to *Mercurie*,
Which tale the Author doth implie.

The Argument of the Second Sestyad

Hero of love takes deeper sence,
And doth her love more recompence.
Their first nights meeting, where sweet kisses
Are th'only crownes of both their blisses.

He swims t'*Abydus*, and returnes;
Cold *Neptune* with his beautie burnes,
Whose suite he shuns, and doth aspire
Heros faire towre, and his desire.

The second sestiad begins in 1598b at l. 485.

3 Seaborderers] *1622* Seaborders *1598a*
72 eies,] eies. *1598a*
134 spye.] spye, *1598a*
184 dissembled.] dissembled, *1598a*
186 stands.] stand, *1598a*
191 day.)] day) *1598a*
247 sweet in] sweet, in *1598a*
320 done.] done, *1598a*
330 before.] before, *1598a*
442, 452, 652 Jove] *not italicized in 1598a*
477 inaspiring] in aspiring *1598a*
516 pais'd.)] pais'd) *1598a*
650 abode.] abode, *1598a*
674 swim,] swim. *1598a*
676 I.] I, *1598a*
679 faire] lovely faire *1629*
730 Through] Though *1598b*
763–74 *in all the early prints these lines follow l. 784*
774 wing,] wing. *1598a*
782 Th'] *italicized in 1598a*
788 night,] night. *1598a*
800 One] And *1598b*
818 Dang'd] Hurld *1598b*

100 Text: William Shakespeare, *Venus and Adonis*, 1593, sigs. B1r–4v; Scolar Press facsimile, Menston 1968. Edition: ed. Maurice Evans, *William Shakespeare: The Narrative Poems*, Harmondsworth 1989, pp. 71–6, ll. 1–180. Shakespeare's poem, dedicated to Henry Wriothesley, Earl of Southampton, was entered in the Stationers' Register on 18 April 1593; it was reprinted in 1594 and frequently thereafter. Most scholars believe that it dates from the closing of the theatres in July 1592.

111 obayed,] obayed. *1593*

101 Text: William Shakespeare, *Lucrece*, 1594, sigs. K1v–L1v; Scolar Press facsimile, Menston 1968. Edition: ed. Maurice Evans, see no. 100, pp. 148–53, ll. 1366–547. In contrast to the title-page, the book's head-title and running titles call the poem *The Rape of Lucrece*. The poem was entered in the Stationers' Register on

9 May 1594 and was several times reprinted. Like *Venus and Adonis* (see no. 100), which was probably written a year or two before, *Lucrece* was dedicated to the Earl of Southampton. No specific source or model for the painting of Troy has been found, but the general shape of the description may derive from Virgil's *Aeneid* 1.455–93.

110 Thy] Thine *some edns*
121 sounds,] sounds; *1594; the reading is uncertain*
133 borrow.] borrow, *1594*
172 tooke.] tooke *1594*
179 armed, to] armed to *1594*
181 vice: ... cherish,] *1616* vice, ... cherish: *1594*

102 Text: Richard Barnfield, *Cynthia. With certaine sonnets, and the legend of Cassandra*, 1595, sig. C1v. Edition: ed. George Klawitter, *Richard Barnfield: The Complete Poems*, Selinsgrove, London and Toronto 1990, p. 126. Barnfield's twenty sonnets to Ganymede in *Cynthia* helped to inaugurate a fashion for homoerotic poetry in the 1590s.

6 sucke] sucke, *1595*

103 Text: Richard Barnfield, *Cynthia*, 1595, see no. 102, sig. C3r. Edition: ed. George Klawitter, see no. 102, p. 127.

104 Text: William Shakespeare, *Shake-speares sonnets. Never before imprinted*, 1609, sigs. B4v–C1r; Scolar Press facsimile, Menston 1968. Edition: ed. John Kerrigan, *William Shakespeare: The Sonnets and A Lover's Complaint*, Harmondsworth 1986, p. 86. Although there is some evidence that a few of Shakespeare's sonnets circulated in MS (for example, 2, 8, 106, 128, 138 and 144), the 1609 quarto is the only authoritative text of them. If Shakespeare did not himself authorize their publication in 1609, there is nothing to show that the book was a literary piracy: the text of the sonnets is on the whole accurate and their order is almost certainly that in which Shakespeare wished them to be arranged. Their date of composition cannot be fixed, but they were probably begun sometime around 1593 and work continued on them for perhaps as much as a decade. In 1598 a reference appeared in print to Shakespeare's 'sugred Sonnets among his private friends' and two sonnets had appeared in the miscellany *The passionate pilgrim* by 1599.

13 Time;] Time *1609*

105 Text: William Shakespeare, *Sonnets*, 1609, see no. 104, sig. C1r. Edition: ed. John Kerrigan, see no. 104, p. 86.

106 Text: William Shakespeare, *Sonnets*, 1609, see no. 104, sigs. C2v–3r. Edition: ed. John Kerrigan, see no. 104, p. 91.

107 Text: William Shakespeare, *Sonnets*, 1609, see no. 104, sig. C4r. Edition: ed. John Kerrigan, see no. 104, p. 94.

8 thy . . . thy] their . . . their *1609*

108 Text: William Shakespeare, *Sonnets*, 1609, see no. 104, sig. C4r–v. Edition: ed. John Kerrigan, see no. 104, p. 94. The same concluding couplet completes Sonnet 96.

109 Text: William Shakespeare, *Sonnets*, 1609, see no. 104, sig. D4r–v. Edition: ed. John Kerrigan, see no. 104, p. 104. The poem is indebted to the opening of Horace, *Odes* 3.30 and the last lines of Ovid's *Metamorphoses*.

1 monuments] monument, *1609*
7 burne] burne: *1609*

110 Text: William Shakespeare, *Sonnets*, 1609, see no. 104, sig. D4v. Edition: ed. John Kerrigan, see no. 104, p. 104.

11 see] see: *1609*

111 Text: William Shakespeare, *Sonnets*, 1609, see no. 104, sig. E2v. Edition: ed. John Kerrigan, see no. 104, p. 109.

112 Text: William Shakespeare, *Sonnets*, 1609, see no. 104, sig. E4r–v. Edition: ed. John Kerrigan, see no. 104, p. 113.

113 Text: William Shakespeare, *Sonnets*, 1609, see no. 104, sig. F4v. Edition: ed. John Kerrigan, see no. 104, p. 123.

114 Text: William Shakespeare, *Sonnets*, 1609, see no. 104, sig. H2r. Edition: ed. John Kerrigan, see no. 104, p. 137.

11 bevel.] bevel *1609*

115 Text: William Shakespeare, *Sonnets*, 1609, see no. 104, sig. H2v. Edition: ed. John Kerrigan, see no. 104, p. 138.

116 Text: William Shakespeare, *Sonnets*, 1609, see no. 104, sig. H3v. Edition: ed. John Kerrigan, see no. 104, p. 141. The elliptical reading produced by 1609's comma in l. 10 has been strongly defended by some editors; in this edition, two difficult readings from 1609 have been retained in ll. 9 and 11.

10 quest] quest, *1609*
11 a] and *1609*

117 Text: William Shakespeare, *Sonnets*, 1609, see no. 104, sig. I1r. Edition: ed. John Kerrigan, see no. 104, p. 144.

118 Text: William Shakespeare, *Sonnets*, 1609, see no. 104, sig. I1v. Edition: ed. John Kerrigan, see no. 104, p. 145. A version of the poem was first published in *The passionate pilgrim*, 1599.

4 Unlearned] Unskilful *1599* subtilties] forgeries *1599*
6 she . . . dayes] I know my yeares *1599*
7 Simply I] I smiling, *1599*
8 Outfacing faults in love, with loves ill rest. *1599*
9 she . . . unjust] my love that she is young *1599*
11 habit . . . trust] habit's in a soothing toung *1599*
12 to have] *1599* t'have *1609*
13 I . . . she] I'le lye with Love, and love *1599*
14 Since that our faultes in love thus smother'd be *1599*

119 Text: William Shakespeare, *Sonnets*, 1609, see no. 104, sigs. I2v–3r. Edition: ed. John Kerrigan, see no. 104, p. 148. A version of the poem was first published in *The passionate pilgrim*, 1599.

3–4 The] My *1599*
6 side] *1599* sight *1609*
8 fowle] faire *1599*
9 finde] feend *1599*
11 But . . . from] For . . . to *1599*
13 Yet . . . nere] The truth I shall not *1599*

120 Text: British Library, MS Additional 58435, f. 24r. Edition: ed. P. J. Croft, *The Poems of Robert Sidney*, Oxford 1984, p. 216. Robert Sidney's poems survive only in the British Library MS, which is autograph and contains the author's own corrections and revisions. This poem and no. 122 may date from around 1597 and reflect Sidney's frustrations as Governor of Flushing, in the Low Countries.

121 Text: British Library, MS Additional 58435, see no. 120, f. 26r. Edition: ed. P. J. Croft, see no. 120, p. 224.

4 and Triumphs leade in my captivity *MS deleted*
11 made, these] composd *MS deleted*
13 Sunn] heaven *MS deleted*

122 Text: British Library, MS Additional 58435, see no. 120, f. 33v. Edition: ed. P. J. Croft, see no. 120, p. 254.

123 Text: British Library, MS Additional 58435, see no. 120, f. 41r. Edition: ed. P. J. Croft, see no. 120, p. 284.

124 Text: Christopher Marlowe and George Chapman, *Hero and Leander: begun by Christopher Marloe; and finished by George Chapman*, 1598, sigs. F1r–4r; Scolar Press facsimile, Menston 1968. Edition: ed. Stephen Orgel, see no. 98, pp. 43–7, ll. 1–160. The first two sestiads of Marlowe's poem were published in 1598 on their own (see no. 99); later in the same year they were reprinted with four further sestiads by Chapman which completed the poem. Chapman may have written his part of the poem in 1598. The 'Argument' of the third sestiad reads:

Leander to the envious light
Resignes his night-sports with the night,
And swims the *Hellespont* againe;
Thesme the Deitie soveraigne
Of Customes and religious rites
Appeares, improving his delites
Since Nuptiall honors he neglected;
Which straight he vowes shall be effected.
Faire *Hero* left Devirginate
Waies, and with furie wailes her state:
But with her love and womans wit
She argues, and approveth it.

6 became] became, *1598*

125 Text: John Marston, *The metamorphosis of Pigmalions image. And certaine satyres*, 1598, sigs. A6r–8v. Edition: ed. Arnold Davenport, *The Poems of John Marston*, Liverpool 1961, pp. 52–4, ll. 1–72. The book was entered in the Stationers' Register on 27 May 1598; the title poem was reprinted several times in I. or J. C.'s *Alicilia*, 1613, 1619 and 1628. Marston took the story from Ovid's *Metamorphoses* 10.243ff.; the anachronistic reference by Pygmalion to Ovid within the poem (l. 68) was deliberate on Marston's part.

126 Text: Thomas Deloney, *Thomas of Reading*, 1612, sig. C4r–v; Scolar Press facsimile, Menston 1969. Edition: ed. Merritt E. Lawless, *The Novels of Thomas Deloney*, Bloomington, Ind., 1961, p. 289. The earliest extant text of Deloney's novel is described on its title-page as the fourth edition: it probably was written in 1598 or 1599. The poem is 'one of my country Jigges' which Cuthbert sings to the hostess of 'Bosomes Inne'; the refrain is probably meant to imitate the twanging sound made by a musical instrument.

127 Text: *The wanton wife of Bath*, [1641–81?], single-sheet broadside. Edition: intro. John Holloway, *The Euing Collection of English Broadside Ballads in the Library of the University of Glasgow*, Glasgow 1971, no. 374, pp. 623–4. The date of the ballad's composition is unknown, but it may go back to the beginning of the seventeenth century: on 25 June 1600 the Stationers' Company ordered that a 'Disorderly ballad' of this title should be 'brought in and burnt'. There are copies of the earliest extant version preserved in the Euing Collection and in the Bodleian Library, Oxford; five further editions of the ballad are recorded up to about 1700, one of which, probably from the 1690s, in the Roxburghe Ballads in the British Library, is printed in ed. W. Chappell and J. W. Ebsworth, see no. 157, vii.213–15. All these early versions of the ballad differ from each other. The ballad is to be sung to the tune of 'Flying Fame', which is the tune of Thomas Churchyard's poem (part of which is attributed to Edward de Vere, Earl of Oxford) 'In peascod time', best known from the version in *Englands Helicon*, 1600; it is also the same tune as 'Chevy Chase'.

7 soul . . . Heavens] Soul came to Elizium's *Roxburghe*
37 starts] rose *Roxburghe*
39 Fond fool] Sinner *Roxburghe*
40 Christ] us *Roxburghe*
43 my Christ] the Faith *Roxburghe*
45 Saviour Christ] Saviour *Roxburghe*
49 crave] cry *Roxburghe*
57 amend] forsake *Roxburghe*
59 at . . . silly] when he had said these *Roxburghe*
63–4 in any . . . ye] no notice took/as I did plainly see *Roxburghe*
65 I . . . Lord] Do thou forgive me now *Roxburghe*
71 So come enter into my Rest *Roxburghe*

128 Text: John Dowland, *The second booke of songs or ayres*, 1600, sig. G2v; Scolar Press facsimile, Menston 1970. Edition: ed. E. H. Fellowes, *English Madrigal Verse 1588–1632*, 3rd edn, rev. Frederick W. Sternfeld and David Greer, Oxford 1967, pp. 471–2. The authorship of this pedlar's song is unknown.

17 But in] But *1600*

129 Text: Philip Rosseter, *A booke of ayres, set foorth to be song*, 1601, sig. C1r; Scolar Press facsimile, Menston 1970. Edition: ed. Walter R. Davis, *The Works of Thomas Campion*, 1969, p. 24. *A book of ayres* is divided into two parts: Campion was the author of those songs in the first part and has sometimes had those in the second part attributed to him.

130 Text: Thomas Campion, *Observations in the art of English poesie*, 1602, p. 31; Scolar Press facsimile, Menston 1968. Edition: ed. Walter R. Davis, see no. 129, p. 310. The poem is an example of the dimeter, which Campion says 'is voluble and fit to expresse any amorous conceit'.

131 Text: Thomas Campion, *The third and fourth booke of ayres*, [1617?], sig. H2r; Scolar Press facsimile, Menston 1969. Edition: ed. Walter R. Davis, see no. 129, p. 174. The poem had been set by Robert Jones in *Ultimum vale, with a triplicity of musicke*, 1605, and by Richard Alison in *An howres recreation in musicke*, 1606. There are several MS copies of the poem in songbooks and part-books as well as MS miscellanies.

15 frownes] shaftes *1605*
16 attempt] presume *1605* approch *1606*

132 Text: John Donne, *Poems*, 1633, see no. 28, pp. 51–2. Edition: ed. A. J. Smith, see no. 28, pp. 100–1. The poem is usually numbered Elegy 5. The picture in the poem is probably intended to be a miniature portrait.

Title] *1635* Travelling he leaves his Picture with his mystris *MS*
8 hoarinesse] stormes, being *1633*
16 now] like and *some MSS*

133 Text: John Donne, *Poems*, 1633, see no. 28, pp. 199–200. Edition: ed. A. J. Smith, see no. 28, pp. 80–1. This aubade may be contrasted with no. 339. The reference to courtiers hunting with the King suggests the poem was written after 1603 when James I, a passionate enthusiast for the sport, came to the throne.

Title] To the Sunne *some MSS*
8 offices;] offices, *1633*
23 us;] us, *1633*

134 Text: John Donne, *Poems*, 1633, see no. 28, pp. 202–4. Edition: ed. A. J. Smith, see no. 28, pp. 47–8. The poem's title refers to making love's martyrs saints after they have sacrificed their lives for love.

4 improve,] improve *1633*
15 more] man *most MSS*
22 dove;] dove, *1633*
25 fit,] fit. *1633*
30 legend] legends *1633*
39 rage;] rage, *1633*
40 contract] extract *MSS*
45 your] our *1633 and some MSS*

135 Text: John Donne, *Poems*, 1633, see no. 28, pp. 223–4. Edition: ed. A. J. Smith, see no. 28, p. 69.

Title] The Spring *some MSS*
6–7 *space between lines in 1633*

9 painING] vexing *some MSS*
10 working] active *some MSS*
23 so] to *most MSS*
28 the] this *some MSS*

136 Text: John Donne, *Poems*, 1633, see no. 28, pp. 228–9. Edition: ed. A. J. Smith, see no. 28, p. 89.

Title] A Valediction of teares *some MSS*
6 thee;] thee, *1633*
8 thou falls] thou falst *1633*
22 soone;] soone, *1633*
25 purposeth;] purposeth, *1633*

137 Text: John Donne, *Poems*, 1633, see no. 28, pp. 193–4. Edition: ed. A. J. Smith, see no. 28, pp. 84–5. The date and occasion of this poem are unknown.

Title] Upon the parting from his Mistresse *some MSS*
3 Whilst] And *most MSS*
4 no:] no. *1633*
8 layetie our] layetie of our *some MSS*
20 lips, and] lips, *1633*
32 that] it *some MSS*
34 runne;] runne. *1633*
35 makes] draws *some MSS*

138 Text: Michael Drayton, *Poems: by Michael Drayton, Esquire*, 1619, p. 256; Scolar Press facsimile, Menston 1969. Edition: ed. J. William Hebel, Kathleen Tillotson and Bernard Newdigate, *The Works of Michael Drayton*, 5 vols., Oxford 1931–41 (reprinted Oxford 1961), ii.315. Drayton's sonnet sequence *Idea* was first printed in 1594; it was revised and added to in 1599, 1600, 1602, 1605 and 1619, when it more or less reached its final form. There were also editions printed in 1603, 1608, 1610, 1613, [1616?] and 1630. This sonnet was first printed in 1599.

6 doth . . . spend] and . . . spends *1599–[1616?]*
8 lend] send *1602–1608*

139 Text: Michael Drayton, *Poems*, 1619, see no. 138, p. 273. Edition: ed. J. William Hebel etc., see no. 138, ii.341. This sonnet was first printed in 1619.

140 Text: Michael Drayton, *Poems*, 1619, see no. 138, p. 303. Edition: ed. J. William Hebel etc., see no. 138, ii.372. This poem, included among the 'Odes. With other lyrick poesies', was first printed in 1619. Unlike most of Drayton's poems, it had some circulation in MS: of the fifteen copies known, all are later than 1616 and three survive with musical settings.

Title] On Tantalized by his Mistriss *MS*

141 Text: Ben Jonson, *The workes*, 1616, see no. 34, p. 819. Edition: ed. George Parfitt, see no. 34, p. 95. The poem is the first in the collection called 'The Forrest': no MS copies of it are known. It was probably written in 1611–12, when Jonson was about forty.

142 Text: Ben Jonson, *The workes of Benjamin Jonson. The second volume*, 1640, sig. Aa4v. Edition: ed. George Parfitt, see no. 34, p. 140. The poem is the ninth in the collection called 'The Under-wood'. Jonson gave an autograph fair copy (Scottish Record Office, GD18/4312; facsimile in Peter Beal, *Index of English Literary Manuscripts, Volume I: 1450–1625*, 2 parts, London and New York 1980, ii.237) to his friend William Drummond of Hawthornden, signed and dated 19 January 1619, and headed:

> Yet, that Love when it is at full, may admit heaping,
> Receive another; and this a picture of my selfe.

In his conversations with Jonson, Drummond preserves another text of the poem (with the same date as the autograph), 'which is (as he [Jonson] said) a picture of himselfe'. The poem circulated in MS from the 1620s and was printed in the quarto edition of Jonson's poems (*Ben Jonson's execration against Vulcan. With divers epigrams*: 1640q) and in the duodecimo edition (*Q.Horatius Flaccus: his art of poetry. Englished by Ben: Jonson. With other workes of the author*: 1640d), which were published in 1640. Most modern editions start a new stanza with l. 11, but not the autograph MS nor the 1640 *Workes*.

5 love] suite *autograph MS and 1640q and 1640d*
7 every close did] all my closes *autograph MS*
8 sentence] numbers *autograph MS*
9 hath] makes *autograph MS*
13 Tell] Prompt *autograph MS*
15 seven] sixe *autograph MS and 1640q and 1640d* yeares,] *autograph MS* yeares. *1640*

143 Text: Folger Shakespeare Library, MS V.a.104, f. 14r. Edition: ed. Josephine A. Roberts, *The Poems of Lady Mary Wroth*, Baton Rouge and London 1983, pp. 99–100. The autograph Folger MS of *Pamphilia to Amphilanthus* may date from the first decade of the seventeenth century, but includes authorial corrections perhaps made in 1618–20. A revised version of the sequence was appended to the printed edition of Lady Mary Wroth's romance *The Countesse of Mountgomeries Urania*, [1621].

4 prise.] *[1621]* prise *MS*
12 is theyr] choose as *[1621]* grace.] *[1621]* grace *MS*
14 deere] sweet *[1621]*

144 Text: Folger Shakespeare Library, MS V.a.104, see no. 143, f. 20v. Edition: ed. Josephine A. Roberts, see no. 143, p. 106.

8 with] for *[1621]*
13 my] mine *[1621]*

145 Text: Folger Shakespeare Library, MS V.a.104, see no. 143, ff. 43r–6v. Edition: ed. Josephine A. Roberts, see no. 143, pp. 127–34. Among those English poets who had written or attempted a crown of sonnets – Sir Philip Sidney, Samuel Daniel, George Chapman and John Donne – Lady Mary Wroth's sequence is probably most closely related to the incomplete one begun by her father, Robert Sidney. The third sonnet imitates the '-ight/-ite' rhyme-words of Philip Sidney's *Old Arcadia* sonnet 'Howe is my Sunn, whose beames are shining bright' (OA42).

7 with] which *[1621]*
16 line] path *MS corrected to* line
25 that] The *[1621]*
26 increase.] *[1621]* increase *MS*
27 delight,] *[1621]* delight *MS*
68 deserne.] *[1621]* deserne *MS*
70–1 profitt] Prophet *[1621]*
75 with much] which must *[1621]*
91 respire] aspire *[1621]*
110 intise.] *[1621]* intise *MS*
116 binn.] *[1621]* binn *MS*
117 sunn] Sonne *[1621]*
118 space;] *[1621]* space *MS*
144 dearth.] *[1621]* dearth *MS*
152 desires.] *[1621]* desires *MS*
162 night.] night *MS* might. *[1621]*
176 directnes] directions *[1621]*
186 stay.] *[1621]* stay *MS*
194 see.] *[1621]* see *MS*

146 Text: Folger Shakespeare Library, MS V.a.104, see no. 143, f. 25r. Edition: ed. Josephine A. Roberts, see no. 143, p. 139. This is the second sonnet in the final sequence.

12 him safe] *[1621]* him *MS*

147 Text: Lady Mary Wroth, *The Countesse of Mountgomeries Urania*, [1621], p. 428. Edition: ed. Josephine A. Roberts, see no. 143, p. 178. This is the last of seven poems, 'Lindamara's Complaint' ending Book 3, in which the semi-autobiographical figure Lindamira complains against her betrayal in love.

148 Text: Robert Herrick, *Hesperides*, 1648, see no. 44, p. 28. Edition: ed. L. C. Martin, see no. 44, p. 28. The theme of the poem has classical and contemporary analogues in, for example, the song 'Still to be neat' in Jonson's play *Poetaster*, 1602.

149 Text: Robert Herrick, *Hesperides*, 1648, see no. 44, pp. 54–5. Edition: ed. L. C. Martin, see no. 44, p. 51.

150 Text: Robert Herrick, *Hesperides*, 1648, see no. 44, p. 133. Edition: ed. L. C. Martin, see no. 44, p. 116.

151 Text: Robert Herrick, *Hesperides*, 1648, see no. 44, p. 160. Edition: ed. L. C. Martin, see no. 44, p. 139.

1 See'st] Sec'st, *1648*

152 Text: Robert Herrick, *Hesperides*, 1648, see no. 44, p. 210. Edition: ed. L. C. Martin, see no. 44, p. 181.

153 Text: Robert Herrick, *Hesperides*, 1648, see no. 44, p. 236. Edition: ed. L. C. Martin, see no. 44, p. 203. Scaliger (see Appendix 1) classified the epigram into categories of honey, gall, vinegar and salt; Herrick is best known for his sweetness, but this poem illustrates his technique of juxtaposing sweetness with a much tarter note.

154 Text: Thomas Carew, *Poems. By Thomas Carew Esquire*, 1640, pp. 1–2; Scolar Press facsimile, Menston 1969. Edition: ed. Rhodes Dunlap, *The Poems of Thomas Carew with his Masque Coelum Britannicum*, Oxford 1949, p. 3. A second edition of the *Poems* of 1640 was published in 1642 containing eight new poems, and a third with three new poems in 1650. Like most of Carew's poems this one circulated widely in MS, some fifteen copies being known.

Title] On a Lady of exquisite beauty but most inexcrable of disposition *MS*
A faire yet hard mistress *MS*
6 sacred] second *some MSS*
8 Humble-Bee.] Humble-Bee, *1640*

155 Text: Thomas Carew, *Poems*, 1640, see no. 154, p. 28. Edition: ed. Rhodes Dunlap, see no. 154, pp. 17–18. Twenty-three MS copies of this poem are known.

Title] A Lover that had made divers coppies of verses to his mistress that cared not for him *several MSS*
Upon Caelia growne proud *a few MSS*

156 Text: Thomas Carew, *Poems*, 1640, see no. 154, p. 83–4. Edition: ed. Rhodes Dunlap, see no. 154, pp. 49–50, ll. 1–44. Twenty-nine MS copies of this poem, which may date from before 1624, are known.

Title] A Lovers Rapture *some MSS*
7 Lovers] souldiers *corrected in errata*
11 Only tame] *many MSS* Only to tame *1640*
25 Queens] Queene *many MSS*

157 Text: Martin Parker, ... *Or, Cupids wrongs vindicated*, [1633], single-sheet broadside. Edition: ed. W. Chappell and J. W. Ebsworth, *The Roxburghe Ballads*, 9 vols., 1869–97, i.160–4, ll. 23–126. The Roxburghe Ballads in the British Library are a collection of over two thousand ballads of the sixteenth to eighteenth centuries collected by John Ker (1740–1804), third Duke of Roxburghe. Many of the ballads, like this one, are unique copies. The top of its title has been cropped; it was entered in the Stationers' Register on 29 May 1633 as 'The faire Maides appology or Cupids wronges vindicated'. The ballad is introduced by the lines:

> Wherein he that *Cupids* wiles did discover,
> Is proved a false dissembling Lover.
> The Mayd shewes such cause that none can her condemne,
> But on the contrary the fault's layd on him.

158 Text: Martin Parker, *Well met neighbour: or, a dainty discourse betwixt Nell and Sisse*, [1640?], single-sheet broadside. Edition: *The Euing Collection of Broadside Ballads*, see no. 127, no. 383, pp. 639–40, ll. 1–48, 109–20. There is another copy of the ballad in the British Library among the Roxburghe Ballads (ed. W. Chappell and J. W. Ebsworth, see no. 157, iii.98–100, 102–3). The ballad is introduced by the lines:

> A dainty discourse betwixt Nell and Sisse,
> of men that doe use their wives amisse:
> Then all you good women their cases pitty,
> the cause you shall heare if you list to this ditty.

159 Text: Edmund Waller, *Poems, etc. written by Mr Ed. Waller*, 1645, p. 32; Scolar Press facsimile, Menston 1971. Edition: ed. G. Thorn Drury, *The Poems of Edmund Waller*, 2 vols., [1905], i.52. There were three editions of the poems published in 1645 and these were reprinted regularly during the rest of the century, including two issues in 1686, the year before Waller died. This poem had some circulation in MS: the Scolar Press edition also includes a facsimile of Bodleian Library, Oxford, MS Don. d. 55, a contemporary copy of several of the poems.

9 Invoked] *MS* Invoke *1645*
12 now] *MS* none *1645*

160 Text: Edmund Waller, *Poems*, 1645, see no. 159, pp. 48–9. Edition: ed. G. Thorn Drury, see no. 159, i.128. This poem had some circulation in MS.

7 graces] *MS* grace *1645*

161 Text: Edmund Waller, *Poems*, 1645, see no. 159, pp. 80–1. Edition: ed. G. Thorn Drury, see no. 159, i.98. This poem circulated in MS.

5 I] *MS* And *1645*

162 Text: Sir John Suckling, *The last remains of Sir John Suckling*, 1659, p. 2. Edition: ed. Thomas Clayton, *The Works of Sir John Suckling: The Non-dramatic Works*, Oxford 1971, pp. 55–6. Several MSS of the poem survive; it was first printed in the collection *Wit and drollery* in 1656. That and some of the other later prints of this poem give it the title 'Song'. In 1659, whose text may have been toned down (see the variant in l. 9), the poem is the first in the book after 'The Invocation'.

4 prove] hold *most MSS*
9 the . . . is] a pox upon't *most MSS*
10 Is] There is *most MSS*
11 staies] stay *most MSS*
14 very] very very *most MSS*

163 Text: John Cleveland, *Poems by J. C., with additions*, 1651, pp. 15–16. Edition: ed. Brian Morris and Eleanor Withington, see no. 41, pp. 54–6. The poem had some MS circulation and was frequently reprinted in collections of Cleveland's poems.

2 never fall] *MSS* never falling *1651*

164 Text: Richard Lovelace, *Lucasta: epodes, odes, sonnets, songs, etc*, 1649, p. 3; Scolar Press facsimile, Menston 1972. Edition: ed. C. H. Wilkinson, *The Poems of Richard Lovelace*, Oxford 1930, p. 18. The sheet in which this and the next poem appear was reset in the 1649 edition, without producing any significant variants. The texts above reproduce the first state; the Scolar Press facsimile the second state. John Lanier, who died in 1650, was a descendant of the family of court musicians who had served Queen Elizabeth; his setting of this song is not known to be extant.

165 Text: Richard Lovelace, *Lucasta*, 1649, see no. 164, pp. 13–14. Edition: ed. C. H. Wilkinson, see no. 164, pp. 25–6.

166 Text: Richard Lovelace, *Lucasta*, 1649, see no. 164, pp. 97–8. Edition: ed. C. H. Wilkinson, see no. 164, pp. 78–9. This poem is usually thought to have been written by Lovelace in 1642, when he was imprisoned in the Gatehouse Prison, Westminster (for which, see also no. 316). It circulated in at least nine MS versions and provoked several replies and imitations. John Wilson's setting of the poem was first printed in his *Select ayres and dialogues for one, two, and three voices*, 1659.

Title] Captaine Loveles made this poem in his duresse at the Gatehouse *MS*
4 To whisper] Spic'd whispers *MS*
7 Gods] birds *most MSS*
8 Know] Enjoyes *MS*
10 With no allaying] Like to the posting *MS*
11 Roses] chapplets *MS* bound] crown'd *most MSS*
14 and draughts go] in Bowles runne *MS*
18 throat] notes *some MSS*
19 sweetnes] glory *MS* Mercy] virtue *MS* might *MS*
20 glories] mildnesse *MS* goodnes *MS*
26 bars] grates *MS*
27–8 A spotles minde, and Innocent
Calls that an hermitage *most MSS*

167 Text: Richard Lovelace, *Lucasta. Posthume poems*, 1659, pp. 7–8. Edition: ed. C. H. Wilkinson, see no. 164, pp. 128–9.

1 receive] deceive *1659*
12 Bore,] Bore; *1659*
13 Herse;] Herse, *1659*

168 Text: Richard Lovelace, *Lucasta*, 1659, see no. 167, pp. 79–80. Edition: ed. C. H. Wilkinson, see no. 164, pp. 195–6, ll. 89–111. Lovelace's translation of Jacopo Sannazaro's poem of six lines was printed (with the original Latin) in the same volume as this poem on the subject. Sannazaro's Latin works were published at Venice in 1535 and often reprinted. Lovelace's satire probably dates from 1645 or slightly later.

5 high,] high *1659*

169 Text: Andrew Marvell, *Miscellaneous poems*, 1681, see no. 45, pp. 19–20. Edition: ed. Elizabeth Story Donno, see no. 45, pp. 50–1. A shorter version of the poem, copied in the hand of Sir William Haward, probably in 1672, is contained in Bodleian Library, Oxford, MS Don. b. 8 (reproduced in Hilton Kelliher, *Andrew Marvell Poet & Politician. An Exhibition to Commemorate the Tercentenary of his Death*, British Library 1978, p. 53); it may represent an earlier version of the poem than that printed in 1681, but the text is, in parts, corrupt.

Title] Poeme amorous *MS*
1, 3 we . . . We] I . . . I *MS*

15 each Breast:] each Breast. *1681* your eyes *MS*
16 the rest] your Thighes *MS*
25–32 Your beauty will stand neede of Salt,
For in the hollow Marble Vault
Will my Songs Eccho, Wormes must try
Your longe preserv'd Virginity *MS*
33 glew] *1681MS, MS* hew *1681*
34 Sits on thy skin] Stickes on your Cheeke *MS* dew] *1681MS, MS* glew *1681*
35–46 Or like the amorous Bird of prey,
Scorning to admitt delay,
Lett us att once our selves devoure,
Not linger in Tymes slow-Chop't power,
And synce Wee cannot make the Sun
Goe backe, nor stand, wee'l make him run. *MS*
44 gates] grates *1681MS*

170 Text: Andrew Marvell, *Miscellaneous poems*, 1681, see no. 45, pp. 22–4. Edition: ed. Elizabeth Story Donno, see no. 45, pp. 40–1.

42 do] *1681MS* dost *1681*

171 Text: Andrew Marvell, *Miscellaneous poems*, 1681, see no. 45, pp. 32–3. Edition: ed. Elizabeth Story Donno, see no. 45, pp. 49–50.

172 Text: James Harrington, *An essay upon two of Virgil's Eclogues, and two books of his Æneis (if this be not enough) towards the translation of the whole*, 1658, p. 45. This is the first of two short poems appended to the translation.

173 Text: Katherine Philips, *Poems*, 1667, see no. 47, p. 155. Edition: ed. Patrick Thomas, see no. 47, i.227–8. This poem survives only in 1667.

16 his] this *1667*

174 Text: *Certayne egloges of Alexander Barclay* appended to his translation of Sebastian Brant, *The ship of fooles*, 1570, sig. D2r–v. Edition: ed. Beatrice White, *The Eclogues of Alexander Barclay*, Early English Text Society, Original Series, vol. 175 (1928), pp. 182–5, ll. 63–116. Barclay's fifth eclogue, translated from Mantuan's sixth, 'Cornix, De disceptatione rusticorum et civium', was 'entituled Amintas and Faustus, of the disputation of Citizens and men of the Countrey': this was probably the first eclogue Barclay translated, early in the 1510s and perhaps revised in 1514. It was first published in [1518?] as *The fyfte eglog of Alexandre Barclay of the cytezen and uplondyshman*.

24 As] At *[1518?], 1570*

175 Text: George Buchanan, *Opera omnia*, ed. Thomas Ruddiman and Peter Burmann, 2 vols., Leiden 1725, ii.415. Edition: ed. Fred J. Nichols, *An Anthology of Neo-Latin Poetry*, New Haven and London 1979, pp. 482–5. This poem, which survives in at least one early Continental collection of Buchanan's verse, was first printed in the collection *Selectorum carminum ex doctissimis poetis collectorum, libri quatuor*, [Geneva?] 1590. The poem, written in alcaics, may date from the late 1540s or early 1550s.

176 Text: British Library, MS Harley 367, ff. 132v–4r. Edition: ed. F. J. Furnivall and W. R. Morfill, *Ballads from Manuscripts*, Ballad Society, 2 vols., 1868–73, i.128–30, ll. 170–237. *Vox populi vox Dei* is preserved in two MSS: it is attributed to John Skelton in Cambridge University Library, MS Nn. 4.5, but is anonymous in the Harleian MS. The Harleian MS has some additions in a later hand (Harleian MS add.). The poem, of which this extract is from the fourth section, criticizes a wide range of social abuses. It is addressed to the King, who may be Henry VIII or Edward VI, and probably dates from around 1547.

5 reght . . . to] highe tyme for to *Harleian MS add.*
7 *omitted in Cambridge MS*
16 powr man he] *Harleian MS add.* powr man *Harleian MS* povertye *Cambridge MS*
20 + I meane the playne true man *Cambridge MS*
21 vytalyng] vylyng *Harleian MS* victualing *Cambridge MS*
25–6 *omitted in Cambridge MS*
40 wadde] vade *Cambridge MS*
51 comenes] poremen *Harleian MS add.*

177 Text: Corpus Christi College, Cambridge, MS 106, pp. 312–13. Edition: ed. C. H. Cooper, *Annals of Cambridge*, 5 vols., Cambridge 1842–1908, ii.40–2. This poem about enclosures of common land probably dates from about 1549.

178 Text: *The jolly pinder of Wakefield*, [*c*. 1650–60], single-sheet broadside. Edition: ed. F. J. Child, see no. 9, iii.131. The first extant printed version of the ballad survives in a chapbook of 1632, *The pinder of Wakefield*, which prints a shortened version of it. Although probably corrupt, the unique Bodleian copy of this ballad (Wood 402, f. 42r) is the earliest of several broadside versions which survive from the mid seventeenth century. They probably derive ultimately from versions which circulated at least a century earlier. A ballad 'of Wakefylde and agrene' was entered in the Stationers' Register in 1557–8. The original text of this ballad has probably been shortened after l. 27, since in other versions of the story the Pinder of Wakefield fights his adversaries one by one, not all at once.

179 Text: Barnabe Googe, *Eglogs, epytaphes, and sonettes*, 1563, sig. H1r–v. Edition: ed. Judith M. Kennedy, *Barnabe Googe: Eclogues, Epitaphs, and Sonnets*, Toronto,

Buffalo and London 1989, pp. 100–1. Googe travelled abroad to France and Spain in 1561–2.

13 pynch] pych *1563*

180 Edition: ed. Thomas Parry, *The Oxford Book of Welsh Verse*, Oxford 1962, no. 118, pp. 237–8, ll. 1–32. Many MSS of this love-poem survive from the seventeenth century onwards: the text printed here is an eclectic one prepared by Parry for his anthology. The poem is a 'cywydd', made up of seven-syllable couplets rhyming alternately on stressed and unstressed syllables.

181 Text: Sir Philip Sidney, *The Countesse of Pembrokes Arcadia*, 1593, f. 43r. Edition: ed. William A. Ringler, Jr., see no. 14, p. 35, ll. 102–15 of OA13. The poem circulated in the MSS of the *Old Arcadia* and in extracts in one miscellany MS. This is part of a hexameter poem sung by the disguised princes Pyrocles and Musidorus; the extract is sung by the latter and prefaces a catalogue of trees.

4 juices] *most MSS* joyces *1593*
10 heavens] *MSS* heav'n *1593*
14 estate] *some MSS* state *1593 and some MSS*

182 Text: Edmund Spenser, *The shepheardes calender conteyning twelve æglogues proportionable to the twelve monethes*, 1579, sigs. D4v–E2v; Scolar Press facsimile, Menston 1968. Edition: ed. William A. Oram etc., see no. 83, pp. 87–93, ll. 1–169. Four more separate editions were published after 1579, in 1581, 1586, 1591 and 1597; the poem was included in the collected edition of 1611. The 'Argument' prefixed to the poem explains that:

> under the persons of two shepheards Piers and Palinodie, be represented two formes of pastoures or Ministers, or the protestant and the Catholique: whose chiefe talke standeth in reasoning, whether the life of the one must be like the other ...

The work was published with glosses to each poem said to have been written by 'E. K.' whose identity has never been firmly established; they are quoted selectively in the footnotes to the text.

36 swinck?] swinck. *1579*

183 Text: Alexander Hume, *Hymnes. Or sacred songs, wherein the right use of poësie may be espied*, Edinburgh 1599, pp. 13–16. Edition: ed. Alexander Lawson, *The Poems of Alexander Hume*, Scottish Text Society, 1902, pp. 25–9, ll. 1–112. The poem may date from 1587–9; there is one contemporary MS of it.

24 As] And *1599*

184 Text: John Davies and Christopher Marlowe, *Epigrammes and elegies*, [*c.* 1599?], see no. 94, sigs. B2v–3r. Edition: ed. Robert Krueger, see no. 93, pp. 135–6. The poem was included in several MS collections of Davies's *Epigrams*. The *Epigrams* date from about 1594–5.

2 Jove] *MSS* love *[1599?a] and [1599?b]*
7 whores,] *[1599?b]* whores *[1599?a]*
11 forwarde] ready *some MSS*
12 passage] issue *some MSS*

185 Text: Joseph Hall, *Virgidemiarum. The three last bookes. Of byting satyres*, 1599, sigs. E7r, E8r–F1r. Edition: ed. A. Davenport, *The Collected Poems of Joseph Hall*, Liverpool 1949, pp. 79–81, Book 5, satire 2, ll. 1–4, 35–76. The first three books of Hall's satires, containing 'Tooth-lesse Satyrs' were published in 1597 and reprinted in 1598; in that year the second three books were published for the first time and reprinted in 1599 as being 'Corrected and amended with some Additions'. This satire, concerned with the decay of hospitality and its causes, takes as its motto 'Hic quærite Troiam' ('Look here for your Troy'), from Virgil's *Aeneid* 5.637.

186 Text: Everard Guilpin, *Skialetheia. Or, a shadow of truth, in certaine epigrams and satyres*, 1598, sig. D5r–v, Satire 5; Shakespeare Association facsimile, no. 2, 1931, with an introduction by G. B. Harrison. Edition: ed. D. Allen Carroll, *Skialetheia or A Shadowe of Truth, in Certaine Epigrams and Satyres*, Chapel Hill 1974, pp. 83–4, ll. 37–71. This satire on vanity takes the form of a city walk through London.

187 Text: British Library, MS Additional 38599, ff. 142r–3r. Edition: ed. Hyder E. Rollins, *Old English Ballads 1553–1625*, Cambridge 1920, pp. 372–5. This MS version of the ballad probably dates from about 1624; there is a longer version of it among the Roxburghe Ballads (see no. 157), printed in about 1635. For Protestant attacks on Christmas festivities, cp. nos. 241 and 369.

188 Text: John Donne, *Poems*, 1633, see no. 28, pp. 187–8. Edition: ed. A. J. Smith, see no. 28, pp. 72–3. St Lucy's Day, 13 December, was popularly thought to be the shortest day of the year and the winter solstice, when the sun entered Capricorn (l. 39). From the Latin, *lux, lucis*, Lucy means light, and attempts have been made to link this poem with the illness in 1612–13 or the death in 1627 of Donne's patroness Lucy, Countess of Bedford. Other editors and commentators have sought to associate it with the illness of Donne's wife, Ann, in 1611–12 or her death in 1617 (see no. 260).

7 beds-feet,] beds-feet *1633*
20 have;] have, *1633*
31 know;] know, *1633*
34 love;] love, *1633*   invest;] invest, *1633*
41 all;] all, *1633*

189 Text: Æmilia Lanyer, *Salve deus rex Judæorum. Containing, 1 The passion of*

Christ. 2 Eves apologie in defence of women. 3 The teares of the daughters of Jerusalem. 4 The salutation and sorrow of the Virgine Marie. With divers other things not unfit to be read, 1611, sigs. H2r–I1r. Edition: ed. A. L. Rowse, *The Poems of Shakespeare's Dark Lady: Salve Deus Rex Judæorum by Emilia Lanier*, 1978, pp. 137–43. The poem was written in honour of Margaret Clifford (1560?–1616), Countess of Cumberland, whose brother is known to have stayed at the royal manor of Cookham near Maidenhead in 1603. This, the last poem in the volume (whose title means 'Hail Lord, King of the Jews'), probably dates from 1609–10 (see ll. 95 and 119).

190 Text: Ben Jonson, *The workes*, 1616, see no. 34, pp. 819–21. Edition: ed. George Parfitt, see no. 34, pp. 95–8. The poem is the second in the collection called 'The Forrest' and dates from before the death of Prince Henry (see l. 77) in November 1612. It is not known to have circulated in MS. Penshurst in Kent was the home of the Sidney family; at the time of the poem's composition its 'great lord' (l. 91) was Robert Sidney, Viscount L'Isle, later Earl of Leicester (see nos. 120–3).

31 high-swolne] *1640* high swolne *1616*

191 Text: Michael Drayton, *Poems*, 1619, see no. 138, pp. 467–70. Edition: ed. J. William Hebel etc., see no. 138, ii.564–7, ll. 1–132. Two songs from this eclogue (of which only the first is printed here) were first published in *Englands Helicon* in 1600 (see no. 98), without the speakers' names and under the title 'The Sheepheards *Daffadill*'; they were reprinted, without any variants, in the second edition of *Englands Helicon* of 1614. The eclogue was first published in its complete form by Drayton among the 'Eglogs' in the volume *Poemes lyrick and pastorall* of [1606?]. It was reprinted in the 1619 volume among the 'Pastorals. Contayning Eglogues'.

9 When] Now *[1606?]*
39 then,] now *[1606?]*
43 be'ng] that *[1606?]*
48 Spic'd] Spice *[1606?]*
51 them] which *[1606?]*
52 The . . . dispoyled] Which . . . not spoiled *[1606?]*
82 His best belov'd Daffadill he mis'd *[1606?]*
90 The colour Maydes delight *Englands Helicon and [1606?]*
94 trim] dresse *Englands Helicon*
96 Tho] Are *Englands Helicon*
101 my faire] with my *Englands Helicon*
127 lowd] lowe *[1606?]*
129 Batte] Gorbo *[1606?] and 1619*

192 Text: Michael Drayton, *Poly-Olbion. Or a chorographicall description of tracts, rivers, mountaines, forests and other parts of this renowned isle of Great Britaine*, 1622, pp. 92–3. Edition: ed. J. William Hebel etc., see no. 138, iv.116–18, ll. 210–74. The first part of *Poly-Olbion* was published in 1612 and reissued in 1613; the second part was first published in 1622, when the remaining sheets of the first part were once again issued. Drayton had a particular interest in Welsh antiquities and included in the volume a prefatory address 'To my friends, the Cambro-Britans'. This extract is spoken by the River Wye on reaching the middle of Wales. Drayton's assertion of the literal truth of the myth of King Arthur was already old-fashioned. The passage is succeeded by an attack on iconoclastic assaults on old beliefs and churches. The notes written for the poem by the lawyer John Selden (signalled in the text by a section mark) are quoted selectively in the footnotes to the text.

193 Text: Michael Drayton, *Poems*, 1619, see no. 138, pp. 295–6. Edition: ed. J. William Hebel etc., see no. 138, ii.363–4. The poem was first printed in *Poemes lyrick and pastorall* of [1606?] and was included among the 'Odes' in 1619. Three ships left London for Virginia at the end of 1606. Drayton's poem owes something to Richard Hakluyt's descriptions of the voyages to Virginia in 1584–6 (for example, ll. 31–6 and 43–4).

41 age] rage *[1606?]*
64 You it] Your dayes *[1606?]*

194 Text: University of Leeds, Brotherton Collection, MS Lt q 36, ff. 1r–2r; facsimile in Pitcher, pp. 105–7. Edition: ed. John Pitcher, *Samuel Daniel: The Brotherton Manuscript: A Study in Authorship*, Leeds Texts and Monographs 7, Leeds 1981, pp. 131–3, ll. 1–106. The unique MS of this poem dates from about 1620; the poem itself, whose authorship is unattributed in the MS, may date from about 1609–10 and discusses the question of whether Prince Henry should support colonial expansion. The text has been repunctuated (for details, see Pitcher, p. 152).

49 if] of *MS*
102 Edonn] Edom *MS*

195 Text: *Wits recreations. Selected from the finest fancies of moderne muses*, 1640, sig. D7r–v; facsimile, ed. Colin Gibson, Aldershot and Vermont 1990. Edition: ed. H. J. C. Grierson and G. Bullough, see no. 43, no. 201. This epigram was no. 146 in the collection.

196 Text: W. Turner, *Turners dish of lentten stuffe, or a galymaufery*, [1612?], single-sheet broadside. Edition: ed. Hyder E. Rollins, *A Pepysian Garland: Black-Letter Broadside Ballads of the Years 1595–1639 Chiefly from the Collection of Samuel Pepys*, Cambridge 1922, pp. 31–4, first part only. Three other ballads by Turner, which are not known to have survived, were entered in the Stationers' Register on 19 November 1612. Although this version is extant only in the unique copy in the Pepys Library at Magdalene College, Cambridge, the ballad was reprinted in 1662 as 'The common cries of London Town, Some go up street, some go down. With

Turners dish of stuff, or a gallymaufery': this also survives only in an unique copy, now in the John Rylands Library, Manchester. Thomas Ravenscroft had set 'City Rounds' of the cries of London in his collection *Melismata*, 1611; see no. 236.

10 nye] Anye *1662*
15 She had need to have her tongue be greas'd *1662*
32 that] straight *1662*
38 dusty] dirty *1662*
57 slinging] singing *1662*
58 did write to] who did *1662*
59 close stoole] own school *1662*
69 Buy] *1667; Pepys defective*
70 a Pas] *Rollins; Pepys defective* a hassock or a presse *1667*

197 Text: John Taylor, *All the workes of John Taylor the water-poet. Beeing sixty and three in number. Collected into one volume by the author*, 1630, sig. [2]3C5r; Scolar Press facsimile, Menston and London 1973. Edition: *Works of John Taylor the Water-Poet Comprised in the Folio Edition of 1630*, Spenser Society, vol. 4, 1869, p. 515. The epigram appears in the collection *The sculler* (first printed in 1612), to which it was added in 1614. The Globe theatre burned down during a performance of Shakespeare's play *Henry VIII* on 29 June 1613.

198 Text: William Browne, *Britannia's pastorals*, 1616, see no. 37, Book 2, Song 2, pp. 29–30. Edition: ed. Gordon Goodwin, see no. 37, i.228–9, ll. 1–18.

199 Text: Edward Herbert, Lord Herbert of Cherbury, *Occasional verses of Edward Lord Herbert, Baron of Cherbery*, 1665, p. 54; Scolar Press facsimile, Menston 1969. Edition: ed. G. C. Moore Smith, *The Poems English & Latin of Edward Lord Herbert of Cherbury*, Oxford 1923, p. 54. The printed text adds that the sonnet was 'Made upon the Groves near *Merlow* Castle'; in the copy of the poem which has Herbert's autograph corrections (British Library, MS Additional 37157), he adds the date 1620. Merlou or Mello, thirty miles north of Paris, was owned by the Duc de Montmorenci, whose daughter was a friend of Herbert's.

5 greene] Grave *1665*
10 friss] kisse *MS*
13 Pleasure ... truly is] Pleasures ... never misse *MS revised by Herbert to* Pleasure ... truely is

200 Text: Richard Corbett, *Poëtica stromata or a collection of sundry peices in poetry: drawne by the known and approved hand of R. C.*, [Holland? France?] 1648, pp. 91–5. Edition: ed. J. A. W. Bennett and H. R. Trevor-Roper, *The Poems of Richard Corbett*, Oxford 1955, pp. 49–52. The poem was first printed in a version omitting ll. 57–64 in *Certain elegant poems, written by Dr. Corbet, Bishop of Norwich*, 1647. The poem, which may have been written in the early 1620s, survives in four MSS, the earliest of which dates from about the 1630s.

13 sprung] stolne *1647*
23 merrily, merrily] merrily *1647*
39 for] from *1647*
47 need] *1647* want *1648*
51 Who looketh to] Who can preserve *1647*
63 Spiritts] Spritts *1648*

201 Text: Sir William Davenant, *The works of Sir William Davenant Kt*, 1673, p. 288. Edition: ed. A. M. Gibbs, *Sir William Davenant: The Shorter Poems, and Songs from the Plays and Masques*, Oxford 1972, p. 125. This is one of the *Poems on several occasions.* Elizabeth Sheldon became the wife of Christopher Villiers (1593?–1630; see no. 320), Earl of Anglesey, the younger brother of George Villiers, Duke of Buckingham. Villiers was created Earl of Anglesey in 1623, in which year he was granted the remaining forests and lands at Pewsham, or Chippenham Forest, in Wiltshire. For small farmers the disafforestment of Chippenham, completed in 1624, was highly unpopular; Davenant's poem, one of his earliest, probably dates from 1623–4.

202 Text: George Wither, *Britain's remembrancer containing a narration of the plague lately past; a declaration of the mischiefs present; and a prediction of judgments to come*, 1628, sigs. K2r–3r. Edition: *Britain's Remembrancer. By George Wither*, Spenser Society, vols. 28, 29, 1880, pp. 219–21. Extracts from the work were reprinted in 1642 and 1643. This extract from the poem describes the effects of the plague in London in 1625.

203 Text: John Milton, *Poems of Mr. John Milton, both English and Latin, compos'd at several times*, 1645, pp. 26–7; Scolar Press facsimile, Menston 1970. Edition: ed. John Carey and Alastair Fowler, see no. 48, pp. 90–1. A second edition of 1645 was published in 1673. The poem may date from 1629–31.

204 Text: John Milton, *Poems*, 1645, see no. 203, pp. 30–6. Edition: ed. John Carey and Alastair Fowler, see no. 48, pp. 132–9. The poem and its partner '*Il Penseroso*' may date from 1631.

33 ye] you *1673*
62 dight,] *1673* dight. *1645*
134 wilde;] wilde, *1645, 1673*

205 Text: Robert Herrick, *Hesperides*, 1648, see no. 44, p. 29. Edition: ed. L. C. Martin, see no. 44, p. 29. Herrick was ejected from his living at Dean Prior in 1647.

206 Text: Robert Herrick, *Hesperides*, 1648, see no. 44, pp. 74–6. Edition: ed. L. C. Martin, see no. 44, pp. 67–9. The poem, especially its last stanza, is one of the most famous evocations of the 'carpe diem' ('seize each day') theme; see Horace, *Odes* 1.11.

207 Text: Robert Herrick, *Hesperides*, 1648, see no. 44, p. 125. Edition: ed. L. C. Martin, see no. 44, p. 110.

208 Text: Robert Herrick, *Hesperides*, 1648, see no. 44, pp. 206–8. Edition: ed. L. C. Martin, see no. 44, pp. 178–9.

209 Text: Richard Crashaw, *Steps to the temple, sacred poems. With the delights of the muses. The second edition wherein are added divers pieces not before extant*, 1648, *The delights of the muses*, pp. 54–6. Edition: ed. L. C. Martin, *The Poems, English Latin and Greek of Richard Crashaw*, 2nd edn, Oxford 1957, pp. 216–18, ll. 5–93. For translations of Crashaw's Latin poems, see ed. George Walton Williams, *The Complete Poetry of Richard Crashaw*, New York 1972. The poem was first published at the end of Daniel Heinsius' *Crepundia Siliana*, Cambridge 1646; a MS exists in Bodleian Library, Oxford, MS Tanner 465, copied by William Sancroft (according to his own inscription in the volume) 'from his own [Crashaw's] Copie, before they were printed'. The soap-bubble was a traditional emblem for the frailty of human life, although Crashaw confines his moralizations to introductory and concluding passages which are omitted in this extract. Heinsius noted that his own linguistic commentaries were similar toys or bubbles. The metre of the poem is glyconic (see Appendix 2). In 1646 the poem is divided into paragraphs beginning at ll. 15, 31, 44, 55, 70 and 84.

20 regnat,] regnat; *1646* undique] undique. *1646 and MS*
33 Campis] Castris *MS*
52 purpureos] *1646* purpureus *1648*
53 Flagrat] *1646* Flagrant *1648*
81 roseæ] *1646* rosæ *1648*
89 in] *1646* et in *1648*

210 Text: Abraham Cowley, *Poems*, 1656, *The Mistress*, pp. 22–3; Scolar Press facsimile, Menston 1971. Edition: ed. John Sparrow, *The Mistress and Other Select Poems of Abraham Cowley*, 1926, pp. 85–6. The poem was first published in the collection *The mistresse*, 1647, and was included in the many posthumous editions of the *Works* published from 1668 onwards.

17 Fountains,] Founts! *1647*
22 *omitted in 1656; text from 1647*
39 hither . . . like] all come, im'itate *1647*

211 Text: Worcester College, Oxford, MS Clarke 18, ff. 32r–3v. Edition: ed. C. H. Firth, *Clarke Papers: Selections from the Papers of William Clarke*, Camden Society, 4 vols., 1891–1901, ii.221–4. The poem probably dates from around 1649. It is unattributed in the unique MS in which it survives, but the same MS contains several pieces and letters by Gerrard Winstanley. In 1649 Winstanley, Henry Bickerstaffe and Thomas Star were taken to court for cultivating common land, without paying rent, at St George's Hill, Walton-on-Thames in Surrey; their cows were attacked with clubs. The Surrey clergy preached against the Diggers.

56 Love] Land *MS*

212 Text: Henry Vaughan, *Olor Iscanus. A collection of some select poems, and translations, formerly written by Mr. Henry Vaughan Silurist*, 1651, pp. 9–10. Edition: ed. Alan Rudrum, *Henry Vaughan: The Complete Poems*, Harmondsworth 1976, pp. 77–9, ll. 11–26, 55–64. The identity of the friend is not known; the poem has been dated to the winter of 1645 (the year in which the town walls at Brecon were pulled down to avoid military involvement) and to 1649.

213 Text: Richard Lovelace, *Lucasta*, 1659, see no. 167, pp. 15–17. Edition: ed. C. H. Wilkinson, see no. 164, pp. 136–7.

22 State?] State: *1659*

214 Text: Andrew Marvell, *Miscellaneous poems*, 1681, see no. 45, pp. 10–11. Edition: ed. Elizabeth Story Donno, see no. 45, pp. 116–17. Marvell went to live at Eton in July 1653 to act as tutor to William Dutton, later a ward of Cromwell's. While there he stayed in the house of John Oxenbridge, a Fellow of the College. Driven by Laud's persecution of his Puritanism (cp. l. 12), Oxenbridge had made two visits to the Bermudas. In 1612 a party of Englishmen landing in the Bermudas sang a Psalm of thanksgiving as they rowed to the shore.

15 Fowle] *1681MS* Fowl's *1681*

215 Text: Andrew Marvell, *Miscellaneous poems*, 1681, see no. 45, pp. 44–5. Edition: ed. Elizabeth Story Donno, see no. 45, p. 109. The glow-worm is called 'the husbandman's star' in Pliny's *Natural history*.

216 Text: Andrew Marvell, *Miscellaneous poems*, 1681, see no. 45, pp. 40–1. Edition: ed. Elizabeth Story Donno, see no. 45, pp. 105–6.

217 Text: Andrew Marvell, *Miscellaneous poems*, 1681, see no. 45, pp. 48–51. Edition: ed. Elizabeth Story Donno, see no. 45, pp. 100–2. The poem may belong to the early 1650s. It is closely related to a Latin poem, 'Hortus', on the same subject, which immediately follows it in 1681; however, 'Hortus' omits the material contained in stanzas V to VIII.

33 in] is *Donno*

218 Text: Andrew Marvell, *Miscellaneous poems*, 1681, see no. 45, pp. 89, 91–2. Edition: ed. Elizabeth Story Donno, see no. 45, pp. 87–9, ll. 369–84, 418–64. Marvell acted as tutor to Mary, daughter of Thomas, third Baron Fairfax, at Nun Appleton in Yorkshire from 1650 to 1652. In this extract from the central part of the poem, the poet has moved from a consideration of the house and its history into the landscape surrounding it.

53 Beast] *1681MS* Breast *1681*

219 Text: Margaret Cavendish, Duchess of Newcastle, *Poems, and fancies*, 1653, pp. 44–5; Scolar Press facsimile, Menston 1972. A second, revised edition of the poems was published in 1664 and a third, which introduced a few more changes to the text, in 1668. All the variant readings below are substantially shared by 1664 and 1668, except for that in l. 11.

3 Worlds more] others
7 make] shape
8 Which our dull *Senses* easily escape:
10 Atome] one
11 foure Atomes] *1653, 1664* Atoms Four *1668* side-note] *omitted in 1664, 1668*
13 these] those

220 Text: Margaret Cavendish, Duchess of Newcastle, *Poems*, 1653, see no. 219, pp. 58–9. All the variant readings below are substantially shared by 1664 and 1668, except for those to l. 32.

1 Tis] It is most
4 a great] the greatest
5 great] for nought but
6 lives] Lives only
7–8 To give us Reason, and yet not to know
What we are made for, or what we must do,
9 Heaven up] to Heav'n
12 so] so always
14 to . . . Mind] which do torment his Mind
22 will] they
23 Most] Which
24 formes] form he] they builds] Build
25 was . . . stand] to stand, was grac'd
26 not . . . Man] by none to be Defac'd

29 Nature.] *omitted in 1653*
32 the . . . mine] 's to me an Injury *1664* to me's an Injury *1668*
33 Man.] *omitted in 1653*
43 Desire doth Whip and makes him run amain;
46 yet] though
49 or lye . . . still] and all be well
54–5 He hath this Knowledge, that he knows not all,
And of himself his Knowledge is but small,
58 And striving both they do shut out wise Fate;
60 Contrariety] that Contraries
64 Which] Who
67 Nature.] *omitted in 1653*

221 Text: Margaret Cavendish, Duchess of Newcastle, *Poems*, 1653, see no. 219, pp. 146–7. All the variant readings below are substantially shared by 1664 and 1668.

Title Similizing the Sea] The Sea Similized Fishes] the Fish
1 lies] are
2 doth stumble] oft Stumbling
3 levell . . . seem,] the Sea's like Meadows, seen
4 And by] Level, its
5 they] do
8 Thus merrily] And thus with Mirth they
12–13 Garlands, to May-poles ty'd with a Silk-string;
Instead of Garlands they hang on their Mast
14 those . . . on] these . . . fast
20 As . . . Whales] The Whales as Ravenous Wolves
25 wil] doth
26 rough do] Roughly
27–8 And like as Men in time of showring Rain
And Wind, do not in open Fields remain,
But quickly run for shelter to a Tree,

222 Text: Katherine Philips, *Poems*, 1667, see no. 47, p. 137. Edition: ed. Patrick Thomas, see no. 47, i. 208. The poem is not in the Texas MS, nor in the 1664 edition; it may date from a visit to Abraham Cowley at Barn Elms in or after 1663.

2 reward] requite 776

223 Texts: British Library, MS Egerton 2711, see no. 6, f. 49r–v (ll. 52–103); British Library, MS Additional 17492, see no. 53, ff. 85v–7r (ll. 1–27, 31–51); Duke of Norfolk, Arundel-Harington MS, see no. 7, ff. 64r–5r (l. 28); Tottel, *Songes and sonettes*, 1557, see no. 57, sigs. L3r–4r (ll. 29–30). Edition: ed. R. A. Rebholz, see no. 5, pp. 186–9. Ideally, this epistolary satire would be printed from the Egerton

MS; unfortunately, the leaf with the first 51 lines is missing in the MS and these have to be taken from the Devonshire MS. This MS in turn lacks three lines (28–30), the first of which is found in the Arundel-Harington MS, but this lacks the next two, which have to be taken from Tottel's miscellany. There is a further MS copy of the poem in Corpus Christi College, Cambridge. Tottel first printed the poem, where it was headed 'Of the Courtiers life written to John Poins'. Both the Egerton and Additional MSS retain the poem's functional indentation: in this composite version functional indentation and Egerton's pattern of initial capitalization have been imposed on the whole poem. The poem, which imitates the tenth satire of Luigi Alamanni, was probably written after Wyatt's first (1536) or second (1541) imprisonment in the Tower; little is known about the poem's addressee.

8 fortune] powre *Arundel-Harington MS*
15 touche] twyche *Devonshire MS*
18–19 *omitted in Arundel-Harington and Cambridge MSS*
19 frame my tongue] from me tune *Devonshire MS* frame my tune *Tottel*
28 *omitted in Devonshire MS* my wordes] *Tottel* wordes *Arundel-Harington MS*
29–30 *omitted in Devonshire, Arundel-Harington and Cambridge MSS*
33 proffet] lucre *Tottel*
38 him] highe *Arundel-Harington MS and Tottel*
45 Coward] *Arundel-Harington and Cambridge MSS* cowardes *Devonshire MS*
54 he is] is *Egerton MS*
97 Christe] truth *Tottel*
98 at Rome] of some *Tottel*
99 practise] plague *Arundel-Harington MS*

224 Text: George Gascoigne, *A hundreth sundrie flowres*, [1573], see no. 61, pp. 359–60. Edition: ed. C. T. Prouty, see no. 61, pp. 154–5. The poem was reprinted in 1575 and 1587. In [1573] among 'The devises of sundrie Gentlemen', the poem's full title is '*John Vaughan* delivered him this theame. *Magnum vectigal parcimonia*, whereuppon he wrote thus'. John Vaughan was a fellow member of Gascoigne's at Gray's Inn.

15 tooke] take *1575*

225 Text: George Gascoigne, *A hundreth sundrie flowres*, [1573], see no. 61, pp. 394–8. Edition: ed. C. T. Prouty, see no. 61, pp. 181–4. The poem was reprinted in 1575 and 1587. It celebrates events from the winter of 1572–3. Among 'The devises of sundrie Gentlemen' in [1573], the poem is introduced with the following paragraph, from which its title has been taken:

> Gascoignes wodmanship written to the L. Grey of wilton uppon this occasion, the sayde L. Grey delighting (amongst many other good qualities) in chusing of his winter deare, and killing the same with his bowe, did furnishe master Gascoigne with a crossebowe cum Pertinenciis ['with appurtenances'], and vouchsafed to use his company in the said exercise, calling him one of his wodmen. Now master

> Gascoigne shooting very often, could never hitte any deare, yea and often times he let the heard passe by as though he had not seene them. Whereat when this noble Lord tooke some pastime, and had often put him in remembrance of his good skill in choosing, and redinesse in killing of a winter deare, he thought good thus to excuse it in verse.

Arthur, Lord Grey of Wilton, (1536–93) was later to succeed Sir Henry Sidney as Lord Deputy in Ireland and employ Spenser as his secretary, see no. 32.

67 flussing] Flushyng *1575*

226 Text: British Library, MS Additional 22583, f. 95v. Edition: ed. Steven W. May, see no. 30, p. 37. The text is taken from the collection of the Oxford don and neo-Latin dramatist William Gager (1555–1632); he probably copied it there during the 1580s. As well as being in the Farmer Chetham manuscript (see no. 15), which alone attributes it to Oxford and which supplies an answer wrongly attributed to Sidney, the poem also survives in two contemporary MSS (British Library, MS Harleian 6910, and a Folger Shakespeare Library MS) and was printed with a musical setting in John Mundy's *Songs and Psalmes*, 1594.

2 Weare I obscure] If I were base *Harleian MS* unknowne] hidden *Chetham MS*
3 no thoughtes] no cares *Chetham MS* my sorrowes *Harleian MS* should me torment] would relent *Harleian MS*
4 Nor hopes nor hates nor loves nor grefes nor feares *Chetham MS*
But death, nor lucke, will lend me such a share, *Harleian MS*
5 Thus of the three, the choyse is harde to have *Harleian MS*
6 or . . . grave] Cottage, or a wished grave *Harleian MS*

227 Text: Thomas Lodge, *Scillaes metamorphosis: enterlaced with the unfortunate love of Glaucus, with sundrie other poems and sonnets*, 1589, sigs. D2v–3r. Edition: ed. Edmund Gosse, *The Complete Works of Thomas Lodge*, Hunterian Club, Glasgow 1883 (reprinted New York 1963), i. 32–3. The speaker is a satyr.

228 Text: John Donne, *Poems*, 1633, see no. 28, pp. 61–3. Edition: ed. A. J. Smith, see no. 28, pp. 214–16. For Sir Henry Wotton, see no. 36; Wotton and Donne were at Oxford together, but Wotton became a successful lawyer, courtier and diplomat. He worked for the Earl of Essex, as his secretary, and like Donne went on the Cadiz and Islands expeditions of 1596–7 (see no. 28). The poem, which contributes to a debate among members of the Essex circle about the merits of life at court, in the city and in the country, probably dates from 1597 or 1598, before Wotton's knighthood in 1603.

11 even] raging *1633*
12 Poles] pole *1633*
16 cities,] cities *1633* extremes,] extremes *1633*

17 dung] dung, *1633*
18 Scorpion and] Scorpion, or *1633*
22 there] they *1633*
26 Gain'd (... borne,)] Gain'd, ... borne, *1633*
27 more] meere *some MSS*
44 for] in *1633*
47 then] thou *1633*
50 home,] home. *1633*
52 goale.] goale; *1633*
57 sound,] sound; *1633*
58 no.] no: *1633*
59 Galenist:] Galenist. *1633*
64 you:] you. *1633*

229 Text: Thomas Deloney, *The pleasant history of John Winchcomb, in his younger yeares called Jack of Newberie*, 1619, sigs. F1v–2v. Edition: ed. Merritt E. Lawless, see no. 126, pp. 40–2. The earliest extant edition of 1619 claims to be the eighth; the book was first entered in the Stationers' Register in 1597. In the novel, this poem is sung by two hundred weavers to King Henry VIII and Catherine of Aragon.

230 Text: Thomas Dekker, *The pleasant comodie of Patient Grissill*, 1603, sigs. A4v–B1r. Edition: ed. Fredson T. Bowers, *The Dramatic Works of Thomas Dekker*, 4 vols., Cambridge 1953–61, i. 218. The play, in which Henry Chettle and Thomas Haughton also had a part, was entered in the Stationers' Register on 28 March 1600. The song comes in I.2.

231 Text: Samuel Daniel, *A panegyrike congratulatory to the kings majesty. Also certaine epistles*, [1603], sigs. E3v–4v; Scolar Press facsimile, Menston 1969. Edition: ed. Arthur Colby Sprague, see no. 90, pp. 116–18. Daniel had probably come into contact with his important patron the Countess of Bedford (see no. 188) by 1600. The poem was reprinted in 1603, in 1607 and in Daniel's *Workes* of 1623.

19 goodly] godly *1623*
44 th'inward ... things,] th'inward, being of the things *1607, 1623*
61 right ... we] *1603 reprint* right, our life we *[1603]* in:] *1607, 1623* in. *[1603] and reprint*
87 delights] delight *1603 reprint – 1623*

232 Text: Ben Jonson, *The workes*, 1616, see no. 34, p. 796. Edition: ed. George Parfitt, see no. 34, p. 66. The poem is number 94 of the 'Epigrammes'. It may date from 1607 (the year in which Donne came into contact with the Countess of Bedford and in which he contributed a Latin poem for the first publication of Jonson's play *Volpone*) and was printed with editions of Donne's poems in 1650, 1654 and 1669: only one mid-seventeenth-century MS of it is known.

233 Text: Ben Jonson, *The workes*, 1616, see no. 34, pp. 799–800. Edition: ed. George Parfitt, see no. 34, pp. 70–1. The poem is number 101 of the 'Epigrammes'. The poem derives from several on the subject by Martial (5.78, 10.48 and 11.52). The identity of the classically minded friend is unknown, and the poem may date from some time between about 1605 and 1612. A mid- and a late-seventeenth-century MS of it are known.

25 not know] know not *1616 and 1640*

234 Text: Thomas Ravenscroft, *Pammelia. Musicks miscellanie*, 1609, sig. G4v; facsimile, The English Experience, no. 412, Amsterdam and New York 1971. Edition: ed. E. H. Fellowes, see no. 128, p. 219. This and the following two poems were first published in Ravenscroft's collections of songs; the music is his work, but not necessarily the words.

235 Text: Thomas Ravenscroft, *Pammelia*, 1609, see no. 234, sig. H1r. Edition: ed. E. H. Fellowes, see no. 128, p. 219. This is the last song in the collection. Lines 7–8 are sung by Merrythought in Francis Beaumont's *The Knight of the Burning Pestle*, 1613, and by Ver in Nashe's *Summers last will and testament*, 1600: they were proverbial.

236 Text: Thomas Ravenscroft, *Melismata. Musicall phansies*, 1611, sig. D4v; facsimile, The English Experience, no. 411, Amsterdam and New York 1971. Edition: ed. E. H. Fellowes, see no. 128, p. 238. The bellman acted as night-watchman and called the hours.

237 Text: Thomas Campion, *The third and fourth booke of ayres*, [1617?], see no. 131, sig. C2r. Edition: ed. Walter R. Davis, see no. 129, p. 147.

238 Text: British Library, MS Additional 27879, ff. 96v–7r. Edition: ed. J. W. Hales and F. J. Furnivall, *British Percy's Folio Manuscript*, 4 vols., 1867–9, iv. 45–6. Although it is written in a hand of the mid seventeenth century, the Percy MS contains pieces which date from the Middle Ages. This poem may date from the 1620s.

15 this] his *MS*

239 Text: Bodleian Library, Oxford, MS Ashmole 38, pp. 77–8. Edition: ed. J. William Hebel etc., see no. 138, i. 507. The unique MS of this poem was copied by Nicholas Burghe in about 1638.

240 Text: Edmund Waller, *Poems*, 1645, see no. 159, pp. 22–3. Edition: ed. G. Thorn Drury, see no. 159, i. 46–7. The poem had some circulation in MS.

3 her] the *MS and later prints*
6 the] a *MS and later prints*
22 on one] on *MS and later prints*

241 Text: Richard Lovelace, *Lucasta*, 1649, see no. 164, pp. 34–6. Edition: ed. C. H. Wilkinson, see no. 164, pp. 38–40. Charles Cotton (1630–87) was a poet, on whose marriage in 1656 Lovelace wrote an epithalamium.

242 Text: Alexander Brome, *Songs*, 1661, see no. 51, p. 83. Edition: ed. Roman R. Dubinski, see no. 51, i.150, ll. 1–11. The poem probably dates from 1657, when there was a campaign for Cromwell to accept the Crown.

243 Text: John Milton, *Poems, etc. upon several occasions*, 1673, p. 60. Edition: ed. John Carey and Alastair Fowler, see no. 48, p. 410. This sonnet to Edward Lawrence (1633–57), an MP and son of the President of Cromwell's Council, may date from about 1653–5.

244 Text: Katherine Philips, *Poems*, 1667, see no. 47, pp. 21–2. Edition: ed. Patrick Thomas, see no. 47, i.90–1. This poem was first printed in Henry Lawes's *Second book of ayres and dialogues*, 1655; it was published in 1664 and survives in both the MSS in the National Library of Wales, MSS 775 and 776, as well as in the Texas MS. This is the only one of Philips's poems for which Lawes's setting survives: Lawes (1596–1662) was tutor to Philips's friend Lady Dering.

Title] Mutuall Affection betweene Orinda and Lucatia *1655*
Mystery] Mysterys *775*
4 dull angry] fierce angry *1655* enraged *776*
16 court] count *1664*
17 Thrones . . . and] greatest thrones more *1664*
19 Since] When *1655* While *Texas*

245 Text: Katherine Philips, *Poems*, 1667, see no. 47, pp. 36–9. Edition: ed. Patrick Thomas, see no. 47, i.106–8.

28 this] each *1664*
44 unto] law to *775, Texas*
46 in] and *775, Texas*

246 Text: Katherine Philips, *Poems*, 1667, see no. 47, pp. 51–2. Edition: ed. Patrick Thomas, see no. 47, i.121–2. This poem was first printed in 1664 and survives in both the MSS in the National Library of Wales, MSS 775 and 776, as well as in the Texas MS. In both 775 and 776 the poem is not divided into stanzas.

Title] To My ... friendship. 17th July 1651 [*or* 1653] *775* To my ... mutuall friendship promis'd. 17. July 1651 *776* 17 July 1652. To the ... Friendship *Texas*
17 Crown-conquerors] crown'd conquerors *775, 776, Texas*
22 false] bold *775* damp *776*

247 Text: John Skelton, *Here after foloweth a lytell boke called Collyn Clout, compyled by mayster Skelton poete laureate*, [1531?], sigs. A8v–B1v, B3r–4r. Edition: ed. John Scattergood, see no. 1, pp. 254–7, ll. 301–31, 402–32. The poem was probably written in 1521–2 and was included in John Stowe's edition of Skelton's *Workes* published in 1568. It was reprinted in editions which date from about 1545, 1554 and 1558. A version of the poem was copied in British Library MS Harley 2252 by John Colyns of the parish of St Mary Woolchurch, London, in about 1530.

6 dare] can *MS*
12 Rychely and warme wrappyd *MS*
15 mares] morowes *[1545?], 1568*
17 be gared] be gloryd *MS*
23 yoke] choke *MS*
25 excommunycacyons] extermynacions *MS*
29 farly] fearfull *[1545?]*
31 And them all to mangyll *MS*
32 the faute] *omitted in [1545?], 1568*
33 you prelates] your presepte *MS*
43 lyke] and *MS*
47 dedes] dethes *MS*
57–8 *omitted in MS*
60 false] hole *MS*
61–2 *omitted in MS*

248 Text: Anne Askew, *The lattre examinacyon of Anne Askewe, with the elucydacyon of Johan Bale*, Marpurg [Wesel] 1547, sigs. H7r–8r. Edition: ed. Betty Travitsky, *The Paradise of Women: Writings by Englishwomen of the Renaissance*, rev. edn, New York 1989, pp. 185–6. John Bale's two accounts of Anne Askew's examinations were printed in 1546 and 1547; the first may have been reprinted as late as about 1585.

15 bolde] bolde. *1547*
21 knocke] knocke. *1547*
25 have] have. *1547*
47 excesse] excesse. *1547*

249 Text: Luke Shepherd, *The upcheringe of the messe*, [1548?], sigs. A1v–2v. Edition: ed. Friedrich Germann, *Luke Shepherd: ein Satirendichter der englischen Reformationszeit*, Augsburg 1911, pp. 97–8, ll. 1–64. The poem, spoken by a corrupt churchman, is attributed to Shepherd by the contemporary writer John Bale.

250 Text: Bodleian Library, Oxford, MS Rawlinson poetical 219, f. 16r–v. Edition: ed. Louise Imogen Guiney, *Recusant Poets with a Selection from their Work*, 1938, pp. 355–6. The shrine at Walsingham in Norfolk containing a replica of the Holy House of Nazareth, said to have been built in the eleventh or twelfth century, and attached to the Priory of the Blessed Virgin, was destroyed in 1538. The MS of this possibly unique text of the poem contains other Catholic works and may date from about 1600.

251 Text: John Heywood, *John Heywoodes woorkes*, 1562, sig. Aa3v. Edition: ed. Burton A. Milligan, see no. 11, p. 217. This epigram was included among 'The fifth hundred of Epygrams'. Heywood's works were reprinted for the fifth time in 1598.

252 Text: British Library, MS Cotton Vespasian E. VIII, ff. 173r–4r. Edition: ed. F. J. Furnivall and W. R. Morfill, see no. 176, ii. 81–3. Extracts from the *Partheniades*, presented as a New Year's gift to Queen Elizabeth on 1 January 1579, first appeared in the anonymous work *The arte of English poesie* (1589), which is usually attributed to Puttenham (see no. 16). This eleventh section of the poem is addressed in the manuscript to Urania, the Muse of Divine Poetry, and is headed:

> That her Majesties most woorthye renowne can not perishe while the worlde shall laste, with certayne philosophicall opinions touchinge the beginninge and durabilitye of the worlde.

253 Text: Robert Southwell, *Saint Peters complaint. Newlie augmented with other poems*, 1602, p. 74. Edition: ed. James H. McDonald and Nancy Pollard Brown, *The Poems of Robert Southwell, S.J.*, Oxford 1967, pp. 15–16. The poem exists in six early MSS and, like Southwell's other English verse, probably dates from between 1586 and 1592. Three of the MSS present the poem in eight four-line stanzas. The collection of poems, *Saint Peters complaint*, was first printed in 1595 and frequently reprinted during the 1590s; in 1602 a new edition appeared adding seven poems of which 'The burning Babe' was one. It was included in the collected editions of the works published in 1620, 1630 and 1636.

6 fed] *MSS* bred *1602*
10 shame] *MSS* shames *1602*

254 Text: British Library, MS Harleian 7553, f. 40r. Edition: ed. Joan Grundy, *The Poems of Henry Constable*, Liverpool 1960, p. 192. This is the last of the *Spirituall sonnettes* written 'to the honour of God and hys Sayntes'; the authorship of the poems is not given in the manuscript, but they must have been written after Constable's conversion to Roman Catholicism, which took place in about 1590.

255 Text: Sir John Harington, *Epigrammes*, 1618, see no. 24, Book 2, no. 35, sig. E8v. Edition: ed. Norman Egbert McClure, see no. 24, no. 131, pp. 198–9.

256 Text: John Donne, *Poems*, 1633, see no. 28, pp. 333–6. Edition: ed. A. J. Smith, see no. 28, pp. 161–4. In two MSS this satire is said to be 'Of Religion' or 'Uppon Religion'. It may date from the mid-1590s.

7 to] in *1633 and some MSS*
15 this;] this. *1633*
16 is.] is; *1633*
17 and dar'st] darest *most MSS*
22–3 discoveries? . . . Salamanders,] discoveries, . . . Salamanders? *1633*
28 words?] words, *1633*
31 Sentinell] Souldier *some MSS*
33 foes:] foe, *1633* Devill] devill h'is *1633*
34 please,] please: *1633*
35 quit] ridde *some MSS*
40 selfes] selfe *1633*
42 loath.] loath; *1633*
47 her] the *1633 and some MSS*
51 sullen] solemne *a few MSS*
52 unhansome;] unhansome. *1633*
54 drudges.] drudges: *1633*
57 bid] bids *1633 and some MSS*
67 kinde,] kinde; *1633*
79 is. On] is: on *1633* huge] high *some MSS*
80 Cragg'd] Ragged *some MSS* stands] dwells *some MSS*
84 Soule] mynde *some MSS*
85 doe:] doe *1633*
88 eyes.] eyes; *1633*
90 case here] case *1633 and a few MSS*
95 Will] Oh will *some MSS*
99 strong?] strong *1633*
101 chang'd; to be] chang'd to be, *1633*
103 is;] is, *1633*
104 prove] do *1633 and some MSS*
107 and rockes] Rockes *some MSS*

257 Text: John Donne, *Poems*, 1633, see no. 28, pp. 170–1. Edition: ed. A. J. Smith, see no. 28, pp. 329–31. The occasion of this poem is generally thought to be the journey on Good Friday, 3 April 1613, which Donne undertook between Sir Henry Goodyer's house at Polesworth in Warwickshire and Sir Edward Herbert's house at Montgomery, some seventy miles west. Three MSS call the poem a 'Meditation on Good Friday'.

Title] Goodfryday. 1613. Ridinge towards Wales *some MSS* Goodfriday Made as I was Rideing westwards that daye *some MSS* Mr. J. Dun goeinge from Sir H. G.: on good fryday sent him back this Meditacon, on the Waye *one MS*

4 motions] motion *1633*
22 tune] turne *some MSS* once,] once *1633*
24 and to] and *1633*
27 Made] Make *some MSS*

258 Text: John Donne, *Poems*, 1635, pp. 387–8. Edition: ed. A. J. Smith, see no. 28, pp. 347–8. In his *Life of Dr John Donne*, 1640, Izaak Walton claimed that Donne wrote this poem on his deathbed in March 1631, only a few days before he died. In a volume of his papers of *c.* 1623–5 (British Library, MS Additional 34324), the judge Sir Julius Caesar (1558–1636) described this poem as 'D. Dun Deane of Paules his verses in his greate sicknes in Decemb. 1623'; from other sources, Donne is known to have been ill during the winter of 1623–4.

5 here] now *MSS*
12 theire] those *1635*
19 streights,] streights *1633*

259 Text: John Donne, *Poems*, 1633, see no. 28, p. 38. Edition: ed. A. J. Smith, see no. 28, pp. 314–15. This is the tenth of the *Holy Sonnets*; they may date from 1609 to 1611.

260 Text: New York Public Library, Berg Collection, Westmoreland MS. Edition: ed. A. J. Smith, see no. 28, p. 316. The Westmoreland MS is written in the hand of Rowland Woodward (1573–1636/7), secretary to Francis Fane (1582/3–1628), first Earl of Westmoreland; it contains three Holy Sonnets, of which this is the first, not found in any other MS or printed source. This poem commemorates the death of Donne's wife, Ann, who died in August 1617, aged thirty-three, seven days after giving birth to their twelfth child (see no. 188).

2 dead,] dead *MS*
12 Angels, . . . divine,] Angels . . . divine *MS*

261 Text: New York Public Library, Berg Collection, Westmoreland MS, see no. 260. Edition: ed. A. J. Smith, see no. 28, p. 316. This is the second of the Holy Sonnets found only in the Westmoreland MS. The poem has been associated with several periods: the time of Satire 3 (see no. 256); before Donne's ordination in 1615; the time of his wife's death in 1617 (see no. 260); and with the year 1620 from the political events, the collapse of the Protestant cause in Bohemia after the defeat of the Elector Palatine outside Prague in October 1620, apparently alluded to in ll. 3–4. The poem presents contending images of the Church as a female figure. The Church visible was often represented as female in Catholic symbolism. For many Protestants, the true Church was the Church invisible of the faithful, whom they identified with the woman wandering in the wilderness in Revelation 12:6; Revelation 19:7–8 prophesies her marriage with Christ. The growing corruption of the Roman Church was identified by many commentators with Satan's thousand-year captivity in the abyss, see Revelation 20:3 and cp. l. 5.

2 What,] What *MS*

262 Text: Fulke Greville, Lord Brooke, *Workes*, 1633, see no. 26, p. 237. Edition: ed. Geoffrey Bullough, see no. 26, i.137.

263 Text: Fulke Greville, Lord Brooke, *Workes*, 1633, see no. 26, pp. 245–6. Edition: ed. Geoffrey Bullough, see no. 26, i.144.

10 downe] *MS* doome *1633*

264 Text: Fulke Greville, Lord Brooke, *Workes*, 1633, see no. 26, pp. 255–6. Edition: ed. Geoffrey Bullough, see no. 26, i.152–3. This is the last poem in the sequence.

19–24 *omitted in MS*
30 yeeld] give *MS*

265 Text: Giles Fletcher the younger, *Christs victorie, and triumph in heaven, and earth, over and after death*, Cambridge 1610, pp. 12–19, Book 1, stanzas 41–63. Edition: ed. Frederick S. Boas, *Giles and Phineas Fletcher: Poetical Works*, 2 vols., Cambridge 1908–9, i.28–33. The poem was reprinted in 1632 and reissued in 1640. This religious allegory opens with a debate between Justice, who condemns man for his sin, and Mercy, who here replies. The passage draws on the Song of Solomon and reveals Fletcher's great admiration for du Bartas and Spenser.

4 paints] *1632* paint *1610*

266 Text: Æmilia Lanyer, *Salve deus rex Judæorum*, 1611, see no. 189, sigs. D1r–2r. Edition: ed. A. L. Rowse, see no. 189, pp. 103–5. This apology for Eve is spoken by Pontius Pilate's wife.

267 Text: William Drummond, *Flowres of Sion*, Edinburgh 1630, p. 7. Edition: ed. L. E. Kastner, *The Poetical Works of William Drummond of Hawthornden*, 2 vols., Manchester 1913, ii.12. The collection of poems *Flowres of Sion*, with its accompanying piece *A cypresse grove*, was first published in 1623; it was reprinted in the collected editions of Drummond's poems published at London in 1656 and 1659. This was the eleventh sonnet in the sequence. The titles of the poems were first printed in the table of contents in 1630.

5 His food was Locusts, and what there doth spring *1623*
14 Marble] flintie *1623*

268 Text: William Drummond, *Flowres of Sion*, 1630, see no. 267, p. 27. Edition: ed. L. E. Kastner, see no. 267, ii.31. This sonnet, the twenty-fourth in the sequence, is an imitation of one by the Italian poet Guglia.

4 Cruell] shamelesse *1623*

269 Text: Phineas Fletcher, *A fathers testament. Written long since for the benefit of the particular relations of the authour*, 1670, pp. 91–2. Edition: ed. Frederick S. Boas, see no. 265, ii.322–3. *A fathers testament* is a prose tract interspersed with poems.

270 Text: John Milton, *Poems*, 1645, see no. 203, pp. 1–12. Edition: ed. John Carey and Alastair Fowler, see no. 48, pp. 101–13. The poem is the first in the 1645 volume and if it does date, as Milton claimed, from the Christmas of 1629, was begun soon after his twenty-first birthday.

143–4 *1673* Th'enameld *Arras* of the Rainbow wearing,
And Mercy set between, *1645*
185 pale,] *1673* pale. *1645*
207 hue;] *1673* hue, *1645*
210 blue;] *1673* blue, *1645*
231 wave,] *1673* wave. *1645*
239 ending:] *1673* ending, *1645*
241 Car,] *1673* Car. *1645*

271 Text: Francis Quarles, *A feast for wormes. Set forth in a poeme of the history of Jonah*, 1620, sig. N3r. Edition: ed. Alexander B. Grosart, *The Complete Works in Prose and Verse of Francis Quarles*, Chertsey Worthies' Library, 3 vols., 1880, ii.35. This is the third poem in *Pentelogia: or the quintessence of meditation*, which was the fourth part of *A feast for wormes*; the whole collection was reprinted in 1626.

272 Text: Francis Quarles, *Divine fancies: digested into epigrammes, meditations, and observations*, 1632, pp. 2–3. Edition: ed. Alexander B. Grosart, see no. 271, ii.201. This is the second poem in Book 1. *Divine fancies* was reprinted in 1633, 1636, 1638 and 1641. The poem touches on the contentious issue of predestination.

273 Text: Francis Quarles, *Divine fancies*, 1632, see no. 272, p. 13. Edition: ed. Alexander B. Grosart, see no. 271, ii.204. This is the twenty-fifth poem in Book 1.

274 Text: Francis Quarles, *Divine fancies*, 1632, see no. 272, p. 104. Edition: ed. Alexander B. Grosart, see no. 271, ii.227. This is the eighty-first poem in Book 2.

275 Text: Francis Quarles, *Divine fancies*, 1632, see no. 272, pp. 145–6. Edition: ed. Alexander B. Grosart, see no. 271, ii.238. This is the sixty-sixth poem in Book 3.

276 Text: Dr Williams's Library, London, MS Jones B. 62, f. 76r; intro. Amy M. Charles, Scholars' Facsimiles & Reprints, Delmar, NY, 1977. Edition: ed. F. E. Hutchinson, *The Works of George Herbert*, Oxford 1941, pp. 204–5. The poem is the last of six found only in the Williams MS, once owned by Nicholas Ferrar, which contains autograph corrections and revisions in Herbert's own hand. The MS probably dates from the 1620s.

277 Text: George Herbert, *The temple. Sacred poems and private ejaculations*, Cambridge 1633, pp. 31–2; Scolar Press facsimile, Menston 1968. Edition: ed. F. E. Hutchinson, see no. 276, p. 40. As well as being copied in the Williams MS, the poem is also transcribed in Bodleian Library, Oxford, MS Tanner 307, which was probably prepared in about 1633, from Herbert's own MS of his poems, to obtain a licence for the edition of 1633. There were many reprints of 1633 throughout the seventeenth century.

Title The Passion *Williams MS*
10–11 Sought him in Citties, Theaters, resorts
In grottos, gardens, Palaces and Courts
Williams MS, later revised in Herbert's autograph

278 Text: George Herbert, *The temple*, 1633, see no. 277, pp. 34–5. Edition: ed. F. E. Hutchinson, see no. 276, p. 43. The poem is in both the Williams MS (facsimile in Petti, see no. 52, no. 57) and the Tanner MS.

8 harmoniously] doe by degree *Williams MS, later revised in Herbert's autograph to* harmoniouslie
9 victories] sacrifice *Williams MS, later revised in Herbert's autograph to* victories
10 the fall] my fall *Williams MS*
12 And still] Yet thou *Williams MS, later revised in Herbert's autograph to* And still
13 Thou didst so] Dayly didst *Williams MS, later revised in Herbert's autograph to* Thou didst so
14 That] Till *Williams MS, later revised in Herbert's autograph to* That
18 this day] *omitted in Williams MS*

279 Text: George Herbert, *The temple*, 1633, see no. 277, p. 43. Edition: ed. F. E. Hutchinson, see no. 276, p. 51. The poem is in both the Williams and Tanner MSS. This is the first poem in the 1633 collection with this title.

5 towre] fort *Williams MS*
7 Transposer of the world, wonders ressort, *Williams MS*

280 Text: George Herbert, *The temple*, 1633, see no. 277, pp. 71–2. Edition: ed. F. E. Hutchinson, see no. 276, pp. 79–80. The poem is in both the Williams and Tanner MSS.

13 knees and heart] hart and knees *Williams MS*
20 But] Yet *Williams MS*
29 minde] hart *Williams MS, later revised in Herbert's autograph to* soule
30 mend] meet *Williams MS*

281 Text: George Herbert, *The temple*, 1633, see no. 277, p. 95. Edition: ed. F. E. Hutchinson, see no. 276, pp. 102–3. The poem is in both the Williams and Tanner MSS. This is the second poem in the 1633 collection with this title.

Title] Invention *Williams MS*
1 lines] verse *Williams MS*
4 sprout] spredd *Williams MS*
6 Decking] Praising *Williams MS*
14 So I bespoke me much insinuation: *Williams MS*
16 long pretence] preparation *Williams MS*
18 Coppy out that: there needs no alteration. *Williams MS*

282 Text: George Herbert, *The temple*, 1633, see no. 277, p. 147. Edition: ed. F. E. Hutchinson, see no. 276, pp. 153–4. The poem is only in the Tanner MS.

21 not. Forsake] *Tanner MS* not forsake *1633*

283 Text: George Herbert, *The temple*, 1633, see no. 277, pp. 160–1. Edition: ed. F. E. Hutchinson, see no. 276, pp. 165–7. The poem is only in the Tanner MS.

284 Text: George Herbert, *The temple*, 1633, see no. 277, pp. 170–1. Edition: ed. F. E. Hutchinson, see no. 276, pp. 176–7. The poem is only in the Tanner MS.

26 arras,] arras *1633*

285 Text: George Herbert, *The temple*, 1633, see no. 277, p. 183. Edition: ed. F. E. Hutchinson, see no. 276, pp. 188–9. The poem is in both the Williams and Tanner MSS. This, the third poem in the collection with this title, is the last of the shorter poems in 1633, before 'The Church Militant' (see no. 286), the concluding work in the volume.

286 Text: George Herbert, *The temple*, 1633, see no. 277, pp. 190–1. Edition: ed. F. E. Hutchinson, see no. 276, pp. 196–7, ll. 235–58. The poem is in both the Williams and Tanner MSS. The poem may date from the early 1620s; Herbert placed it in the last section of *The temple*, immediately after 'Love' (see no. 285). It records the steady emigration of religion from east to west.

22 leave our] leave her *MSS*

287 Text: Christ Church, Oxford, MSS 736–8, ff. 2v–3r. Edition: ed. H. J. C.

Grierson and G. Bullough, see no. 43, no. 308. A setting of this poem for three voices was composed by Thomas Ford, a musician to both Prince Henry and Prince Charles. The setting probably dates from after 1620; Ford died in 1648.

288 Text: Bodleian Library, Oxford, MS Malone 13, pp. 85–6. Edition: ed. William Dighton, *The Poems of Sidney Godolphin*, Oxford 1931, pp. 28–9. At least one other MS of this poem is known to exist.

36 know, we] know we, *MS*

289 Text: John Taylor, *Differing worships, or, the oddes, betweene some knights service and God's. Or Tom Nash his ghost*, 1640, pp. 3–4. Edition: *Works of John Taylor the Water Poet not Included in the Folio Volume of 1630: First Collection*, Spenser Society, vol. 7, 1870, no. 5, pp. 9–10. It has been suggested that, since a shorter version (dated 1638) was written in MS by Thomas Pestell (1584?–1659?), this may indicate that the poem is by him: see Allan Pritchard, 'Unpublished Poems by Thomas Pestell', *English Literary Renaissance*, 10 (1980), 129–47. Many anti-Puritan poems were published under Taylor's name in the 1640s.

290 Text: Edmund Waller, *Poems*, 1645, see no. 159, pp. 3–5. Editions: ed. G. Thorn Drury, see no. 159, i.16–18; ed. Brendan O Hehir, see no. 42, pp. 279–83. Under the influence of the then Bishop of London, William Laud, Charles I issued a proclamation to raise funds for the rebuilding of the decrepit medieval cathedral of St Paul's, which had lost its steeple during a fire in 1561. Work began in 1633 and continued until it was brought to a sudden end by Parliament in 1643. The new Corinthian portico, designed by Inigo Jones, was probably erected in 1637 or 1638, and Waller's poem may date from about then. It circulated in MSS, of which several survive, and was an important influence on Denham's *Coopers Hill*, see no. 42. The 1686 edition ends with an adaptation of ll. 404–5 of Horace's *Ars poetica*, '... Sic gratia regum/Pieriis tentata modis ...', 'the favour of kings was sought in Pierian strains'.

4 crime)] *1686* crime.) *1645*
13 Regiment] *1686 and MS* Regiments *1645*
21 State-obscuring] *1686 and MS* State observing *1645*
27 affect] *1686 and MS* effect *1645*
28 structure, ... name;] *1686* structure; ... name *1645*
35 Reduce;] *1686* Reduce *1645*

291 Text: Richard Crashaw, *Steps to the temple. Sacred poems, with other delights of the muses*, 1646, pp. 28–31; Scolar Press facsimile, Menston 1970. Edition: ed. L. C. Martin, see no. 209, pp. 106–8. The poem appeared in a revised form in the second edition of *Steps to the temple*, 1648, and again in a further revised form in *Carmen Deo nostro, te decet hymnus. Sacred poems, collected, corrected, augmented*, Paris 1652, see no. 292. Three MS copies of the poem are known: one (reproduced in the Scolar Press facsimile) in the Sancroft MS, see no. 209; extracts in British Library MS Sloane 1925; and extracts in Folger MS V.a.148. Since the revisions involve substantial rewriting and rearranging of the poem, only variants between 1646 and the Sancroft MS are noted below. The poem derives from Luke 2:15–20.

4 sleeps] lies *MS, 1648 and 1652*
31 Eyes break] *MS, 1648 and 1652* Eyes-break *1646*
37 whitest] white *MS*
50 Twixt] Twixt's *MS, 1648 and 1652*

292 Text: Richard Crashaw, *Carmen Deo nostro, te decet hymnus. Sacred poems, collected, corrected, augmented,* Paris 1652, sigs. a3v–4r. Edition: ed. L. C. Martin, see no. 209, pp. 236–8. The poem was first printed in the 1652 volume which was dedicated to Susan Feilding, first Countess of Denbigh, the sister of the Duke of Buckingham (cp. nos. 38–9). Like Cowley, she joined Queen Henrietta Maria in exile in Paris and in 1651 she became a Catholic. A second, revised, version of the poem was published on its own in London in 1653 as *A letter from Mr. Crashaw to the Countess of Denbigh, against irresolution and delay in matters of religion.* Since 1653 represents a quite different version of the poem, its readings (with one exception) are not collated below.

In 1652 the poem appears below an engraving (possibly by Crashaw himself) of an emblem of a heart with a hinge on its left side and on its right a combination lock with letters on it. Beneath the emblem is the inscriptional motto 'NON VI' ('Not by force') and the following lines:

'Tis not the work of force but skill
To find the way into man's will.
'Tis love alone can hearts unlock.
Who knowes the WORD, he needs not knock.

10 weaknes!)] weaknes! *1652*
16 deny'd.] *1653* deny'd, *1652*

293 Text: Richard Crashaw, *Carmen Deo nostro*, 1652, see no. 292, pp. 105–7. Edition: ed. L. C. Martin, see no. 209, pp. 326–7, ll. 63–108. The poem was first printed in 1648, in a shorter version, in the second edition of *Steps to the temple*; there are brief extracts from the poem in one MS. The full title of the poem is 'The Flaming Heart upon the Book and Picture of the seraphicall saint Teresa, (as she is usually expressed with a Seraphim biside her)': the poem objects to the unflattering portrait of Teresa and the angel which usually appeared in editions of her works.

3 things,] *1648* things. *1652*
4 glistering] glittering *1648*
12 heart.] *1648* heart *1652*

14 wounds] *1648* wound *1652*
23–42 *omitted in 1648*

294 Text: Bodleian Library, Oxford, MS Rawlinson poetical 26, f. 131r. Edition: ed. Mary Anne Everett Green, *Diary of John Rous, Incumbent of Salton Downham, Suffolk, from 1625 to 1642*, Camden Society, 1856, p. 117, taken from the shorter text in British Library MS Additional 22959, see no. 295. The anonymous poet satirizes William Laud (1573–1645), Archbishop of Canterbury, through the figure of church bells. The poem probably dates from 1640–1, when Parliament was starting to undo Laud's changes.

5–6 She lately rung so loud without all doubt,
She strooke good Tom of Lincones clapper out. *BL MS*
10–11 Would gladly plucke her quite out of the steeple;
She makes such hideous noise with her *Boom Boom. BL MS*
13–14 But seeing that she's made o'the Romish dresse
She'll serve the Papists for to ring to Masse. *BL MS*

295 Text: Robert Wild, *Alas poore scholler, whither wilt thou goe: or strange alterations which at this time be, there's many did thinke they never should see*, [1641?], single-sheet broadside. Edition: ed. John Hunt, *Poems by Robert Wilde*, 1870, pp. 46–7, 49–50, verses 1–3, 7–8. The ballad was published anonymously, but reprinted in Robert Wild's collection *Iter boreale*, 1668. With a shorter version of the preceding poem, it was copied by John Rous in his MS volume (see no. 294), between entries dated March 1641 and April 1642. The poem is also preserved in Bodleian Library, Oxford, MS Malone 21 and MS English Miscellaneous e. 13. None of these MS texts gives the author's name.

Title] The schollers complaint in these latter ages *Malone*
8 rent] read *BL MS* turnd *Malone*

296 Text: John Milton, *Poems*, 1673, see no. 243, p. 69. Edition: ed. John Carey and Alastair Fowler, see no. 48, pp. 296–8. The poem is copied in the Trinity MS in the same scribal hand as the sonnets to Vane and Cromwell, see nos. 48 and 49. Milton probably wrote the poem in the summer of 1646, after Parliament had established the Presbyterian system.

Title] On the forcers of Conscience *MS*
3 widdow'd] vacant *MS corrected to* widow'd
6 our] the *MS corrected to* our
12 shallow] hare braind *MS corrected to* shallow
17 Cropp yee as close as marginall P——s eares *MS corrected to*
Clip your Phylacteries though bauke your eares
19 they] you *MS corrected to* they
20 Large] at large *MS corrected to* large

297 Text: Cardiff Central Library, MS 1.6, ff. 13v–14r. Edition: ed T. E. Ellis, *Gweithiau Morgan Llwyd, o Wynedd*, Bangor 1899, pp. 23–5, stanzas 1–12. The extract is taken from a sequence of poems about the seasons in which historical events are compared to the cycle of the seasons, with the reigns of James and Charles as winter, the reforms of the 1640s as summer, and the harvest as the approaching apocalypse. Like Milton, Llwyd rejects the idea that sects and divisions in the Church are a sign of weakness. The poem is dated 1648.

298 Text: Laurence Clarkson, *A single eye all light, no darkness; or light and darkness one*, [1650], sig. A1v. Edition: ed. Nigel Smith, *A Collection of Ranter Writings from the Seventeenth Century*, 1983, p. 162. The short pamphlet to which this poem is prefixed questioned conventional moral categories and was ordered to be burned by the common hangman.

299 Text: Henry Vaughan, *Silex scintillans: or sacred poems and private ejaculations by Henry Vaughan Silurist*, 1650, p. 34; Scolar Press facsimile, Menston 1968. Edition: ed. Alan Rudrum, see no. 212, pp. 172–3. The unsold sheets (slightly changed) of the first part of *Silex scintillans* were bound up and sold with the second part when it was published in a second edition in 1655 (see no. 301). The poem mixes Platonic and Christian ideas about childhood's innocence and perfection.

300 Text: Henry Vaughan, *Silex scintillans*, 1650, see no. 299, pp. 91–3. Edition: ed. Alan Rudrum, see no. 212, pp. 227–8.

301 Text: Henry Vaughan, *Silex scintillans: sacred poems and private ejaculations. The second edition, in two books; by Henry Vaughan, Silurist*, 1655, part 2, pp. 10–11. Edition: ed. Alan Rudrum, see no. 212, pp. 251–2.

302 Text: Henry Vaughan, *Silex scintillans*, 1655, see no. 301, pp. 76–7. Edition: ed. Alan Rudrum, see no. 212, pp. 306–7.

16 before] before. *1655*

303 Text: Sir William Davenant, *Gondibert: an heroick poem*, 1651, p. 197, Book 2, Canto 6, verses 84–7; Scolar Press facsimile, Menston 1970. Edition: ed. David F. Gladish, *Sir William Davenant's Gondibert*, Oxford 1971, p. 169. *Gondibert* was first published in a quarto edition in 1651 (1651a); in the same year a reprint of it in octavo was issued (1651b). The poem was reprinted with some revisions in the 1673 edition of Davenant's *Works*. Apparently, every known copy of the first edition of 1651 contains MS corrections to the text: these are thought to have been made by Davenant himself. The lines are introduced as Gondibert's 'inward' singing of 'high Heav'ns praise in musick of the heart'. Davenant quotes these verses in his 'Author's Preface' to the poem, which is addressed to the philosopher Thomas Hobbes, as part of his defence of poetry.

304 Text: *The cry of a stone: or a relation of something spoken in Whitehall, by Anna Trapnel, being in the visions of God. Relating to the governors, army, churches, ministry, universities: and the whole nation*, 1654, p. 49. The poem is preceded by the statement: 'Here she seemed to have over-flowings of joy and delight in spirit, and poured out her heart in a Song, as follows.' Trapnel, a Fifth Monarchist, uttered this poem during her twelve-day visionary seizure at Whitehall in January 1654. The title of her collection of poems comes from Habbakuk 2:11–12: 'For the stone shall cry out of the wall . . . Woe to him that buildeth a town with blood, and stablisheth a city by iniquity!'

305 Text: An Collins, *Divine songs and meditacions composed by An Collins*, 1653, pp. 50–2; Augustan Reprint Society facsimile, no. 94, ed. Stanley N. Stewart, 1961.

34 sharp] harp *1653*

306 Text: Andrew Marvell, *Miscellaneous poems*, 1681, see no. 45, pp. 7–8. Edition: ed. Elizabeth Story Donno, see no. 45, p. 54. The coronet of the poem has been taken as a metaphorical garland of poetry.

307 Text: John Skelton, *Here after foloweth the boke of Phyllyp Sparowe compyled by mayster Skelton poete laureate*, [1545?], sigs. A2r–5r. Edition: ed. John Scattergood, see no. 1, pp. 71–6, ll. 1–182. There were further editions of the poem published in about 1554 and 1558; it was included in Skelton's *Workes* of 1568. The poem is a mock elegy for the death of Jane Scrope's sparrow at Carrow Abbey, a Benedictine house near Norwich; the main part was completed by 1509.

89 From] For *[1545?]–1568*
98 zenophontes,] zenophontes. *[1545]*
163 fethers] fether *[1545?]*

308 Text: William Camden, *Remaines of a greater worke concerning Britaine*, 1605, sig. g1v. Edition: ed. Emrys Jones, see no. 8, p. 32. Surrey and Clere were both wounded, or fell ill, during the siege of Montreuil in northern France. Related by marriage to the Howard family, Thomas Clere, who died in 1545, was buried in their chapel in Lambeth and this epitaph, partly modelled on the one ascribed to Virgil, was provided for his tomb. The tomb had been destroyed by 1769 and Camden's collection of antiquarian matters, including early versions of several poems, is the only contemporary source for this epitaph.

2 hight] high *Camden*
12 four times seaven] seaven times seaven *Camden*

309 Text: Richard Tottel (ed.?), *Songes and sonettes*, 1557, see no. 57, sig. D2v. Edition: ed. Emrys Jones, see no. 8, pp. 27–8. The poem was published during Surrey's lifetime in *An excellent epitaffe of Syr Thomas Wyat, with two other compendious dytties*, [1545?]; there are a few minor variants.

18 enflame] enflame. *Tottel*
32 manhodes shape,] manhodes, shape *Tottel*

310 Text: Richard Tottel (ed.?), *Songes and sonettes*, 1557, see no. 57, sig. O4v. Edition: ed. L. R. Merrill, *The Life and Poems of Nicholas Grimald*, New Haven 1925, pp. 398–9, ll. 27–60. Tottel's edition of 1557 contains the unique text of this poem mourning the death of Grimald's mother Agnes, who died sometime after January 1552, when her son left Oxford.

15 web] wed *Tottel*

311 Text: Bodleian Library, Oxford, MS Tanner 169, f. 79r; facsimile in Hirsch, p. 314. Edition: Richard S. M. Hirsch, 'The Works of Chidiock Tichborne (text)', *English Literary Renaissance*, 16 (1986), 309–10. Tichborne was executed in 1586; these verses, which are generally attributed to him, are among the most popular of poems extant in MS, being preserved in at least thirty texts. They were first printed in 1586 in *Verses of prayse and joye, written upon her majesties preservation. Whereunto is annexed Tychbornes lamentation* and appeared again set to music in John Mundy's *Songs and Psalmes*, 1594, (verse one only; ed. E. H. Fellowes, see no. 128, p. 171), Michael East's *Madrigalles*, 1604, (verses one and two only; ed. E. H. Fellowes, p. 86) and Richard Alison's *An howres recreation in musicke*, 1606, (verses one and two only; ed. E. H. Fellowes, p. 11). The owner of the Tanner MS, Sir Stephen Powle, noted that Tichborne's verses were 'made by him selfe not three dayes before his execution' and that he had 'the originall written with his owne hande'.

Title] The map of man *MS*
7–9 My tale was heard, and yet it was not told,
    My fruite is falne, and yet my leaves are greene:
  My youth is spent, and yet I am not old, *1586*
16 am] was *1586*

312 Text: Robert Chester, *Love's martyr: or Rosalins complaint. Allegorically shadowing the truth of love, in the constant fate of the phoenix and turtle*, 1601, pp. 170–2. Edition: ed. Maurice Evans, see no. 100, pp. 164–5. The untitled but signed poem was contributed to a volume celebrating the love of Chester's patron, Sir John Salusbury, for his wife Ursula, the natural daughter of Henry Stanley, fourth Earl of Derby. The phoenix and the turtle also appear in Chester's own poem. Salusbury married Ursula Stanley in 1586, and the poem may date from any time after then. Many different allegorical interpretations have been offered of Chester's and Shakespeare's poems.

313 Text: John Donne, *The second anniversarie. Of the progres of the soule*, 1612, pp. 1–4, 17–24. Edition: ed. A.J. Smith, see no. 28, pp. 287–8, 292–4, ll. 1–36, 179–250. Neither of the two *Anniversary* poems circulated widely in MS; the second has only one MS witness, a copy made late in the seventeenth century. The first poem was published on its own in 1611 and the second in 1612: they are the only substantial poems printed during Donne's life with whose publication he was certainly concerned. They were reprinted together in 1621 and 1625, as well as being collected in the *Poems* of 1633. The *Anniversaries* were written to commemorate the death of Elizabeth Drury in December 1610, when she was fourteen. She was the only child of a wealthy London landowner and, if Donne did not personally know the girl or her family when he wrote the *First Anniversary*, which was published in 1611, he soon came to be a family friend, accompanying them on a Continental tour in 1611–12. On the second anniversary of Elizabeth's death, Donne and the Drurys were in Amiens, where this poem was probably written.

1 confesse] confesse. *1612*
10 Though] Through *1612 corrected in errata*
16 meet] meet. *1612*
17 soule;] soule, *1612*
20 strings:] strings. *1612*
34–5 Muse . . . Father,] Muse, . . . Father *1612*
43 cleave] cleave, *1612*
56 bee;] bee, *1612*
104 thought,)] thought, *1612*

314 Text: Ben Jonson, *The workes*, 1616, see no. 34, pp. 780–1. Edition: ed. George Parfitt, see no. 34, p. 48. The poem is number 45 of the 'Epigrammes'. Jonson's son, also called Benjamin, died of the plague in 1603. The only MS of the poem is a late-seventeenth-century one.

315 Text: Ben Jonson, *The workes*, 1640, see no. 142, sigs. Hh4v–Ii2r. Edition: ed. George Parfitt, see no. 34, pp. 211–15. The poem is the seventieth in the collection called 'The Under-wood'; it circulated in MS from the 1630s and was printed in the quarto and duodecimo editions of Jonson's poems which were published in 1640 (1640q and 1640d: see no. 142). Sir Lucius Cary (1610?–43), second Viscount Falkland of Great Tew in Oxfordshire, was a poet and statesman of great learning. Sir Henry Morison died at Carmarthen in 1629 when he was about twenty-one years old (cp. l. 31); he had been knighted about two years before. Jonson's poem attempts to imitate the Pindaric ode, his terms 'Turne', 'Counter-turne' and 'Stand' being intended to represent the Greek 'strophe', 'anti-strophe' and 'epode'. The 1640 duodecimo text notes the number of lines in each section of the poem. The poem is much indebted to Seneca's *Epistles* 93.

Title] To Sir Lucius Carey, on the death of his Brother Morison *MS*
Ode Pindarique *MS*
ODE PINDARICK To the Noble Sir *Lucius Cary 1640d*
ODE PINDARICK On the Death of Sir *Hen. Morison 1640q*

10 deepest] secret *MS*
11 wiser] wisest *some MSS*
12 sack?] *1640q and 1640d* sack, *1640*
15 hurried] harried *MS*
17 and famine] famine *1640q and 1640d and some MSS* fell] full *1640q and 1640d*
20 thee.] thee? *1640*
44 fall'st,] fall'st *1640* tripst *1640q and 1640d and most MSS*
45 right] night *1640q and 1640d*
47 most,] *MS* most *1640*
50 in] and *1640q and 1640d* measure] fashion *MS*
68 logge] logge, *1640* bald] bold *1640*
71 that] at *1640q and 1640d*
73 beauties] beauty *1640q and 1640d and some MSS*
84 Ben.] Ben *1640q* Ben: *1640d* Ben- *MS*
90 were] was *1640q and 1640d*
97 And shine] Shine then *MS*
100 indentur'd] *1640q and 1640d and MS* indenture *1640* to'] t' *1640*
111 stiled,] stiled *1640*
123 in deed] *MS* indeed *1640*
126 lines] lives *some MSS*

316 Text: Bodleian Library, Oxford, MS Don. c. 54, f. 3v. Edition: ed. Agnes M. C. Latham, see no. 18, p. 72. The poem was frequently reprinted after its first publication in Richard Brathwait's *Remains after death*, 1618, and circulated very widely in MS (at least ninety texts survive), often with copies of Ralegh's speech on the scaffold at his execution in 1618: the Bodleian MS dates from the 1620s. Some MSS claim that the verses were written in the Gatehouse Prison in Westminster on the night before his execution or were found in his Bible.

1 in] *most MSS* on *Bodleian MS*

317 Text: William Camden, *Remaines, concerning Britaine: the third impression reviewed, corrected, and encreased*, 1623, p. 340. Edition: ed. Gordon Goodwin, see no. 37, ii.294. The third edition of Camden's *Remaines* (see no. 308) was published in 1623, the year of his death. Numerous copies of the epitaph, with and without the second verse, circulated in MS. The Countess died on 25 September 1621.

1 Marble] sable *some MSS*
4 kill'd] slaine *some MSS*

318 Text: Bodleian Library, Oxford, MS Malone 22, ff. 17v–19v. Edition: ed. Margaret Crum, *The Poems of Henry King*, Oxford 1965, pp. 68–72. The circulation of King's poems in MS centred around his amanuensis Thomas Manne, Chaplain of Christ Church, Oxford, where King was a canon. Of the seven important MS collections of King's verse which are extant, Manne had a hand in two and an unidentified imitator of his script had a hand in three. The Malone MS is in the imitator's hand, as are the Houghton MS (British Library, MS Additional 62134) and the Stoughton MS (owned privately); his hand is also found in the Hannah MS (Bodleian Library, Oxford, MS English poetical e. 30), which is principally in Manne's hand but also contains corrections by King himself. Manne was also mainly responsible for the Manne MS (British Library, MS Additional 58215) and for a stray copy of the poem in the British Library, MS Additional 27408. Of the many MSS of the poem, the earliest date from the 1630s and some copies bear witness to King's revisions (especially in ll. 65–70) before its printing in the unauthorized edition of his poetical works published in 1657. In the variants below, 'most MSS' refers to some or all of the group discussed above; 'some MSS' refers to the many other copies of the poem. Henry King's wife, Anne, was buried in London on 5 January 1624.

21 *no new paragraph in Malone MS; new paragraph in most MSS*
24 blacknes] darkness *some MSS*
33 Since ... thy] For now both *MS Additional 62134*
36 The] An *most MSS*
43 And ... space] Would willingly *some MSS*
53 must] shall *most MSS*
89 *Stoughton MS begins a new paragraph*
106 Vann] Vaunt *MS Additional 62134, Manne MS*
111 *Houghton MS begins a new paragraph*

319 Text: John Donne, *A sermon of commemoration of the Lady Danvers. By John Donne. Together with other commemorations of her; by her sonne G. Herbert*, 1627, sig. H9r. Edition: ed. F. E. Hutchinson, see no. 276, p. 422. For translations of Herbert's Latin poems, see ed. Mark McCloskey and Paul R. Murphy, *The Latin Poetry of George Herbert*, Athens, Ohio, 1965. Herbert contributed a sequence of nineteen Latin and Greek poems, of which this is the first, to the memorial volume of verse for his mother. They contain some of his most personal, as well as most hyperbolical, writing. Herbert's mother Magdalen, a close friend of Donne's, remarried in 1609. At the time of her death, Herbert still seems to have been hesitating about finally becoming a priest.

320 Text: Thomas Carew, *Poems*, 1640, see no. 154, p. 90. Edition: ed. Rhodes Dunlap, see no. 154, pp. 53–4. Three MS copies of this poem survive. The poem may commemorate the death of Mary, the daughter of Carew's patrons the Earl and Countess of Anglesey (see no. 201). She died in 1630 aged two, her father having predeceased her by a few months. Carew wrote two further epitaphs on the same girl.

321 Text: Sir Henry Wotton, *Reliquiæ Wottonianæ*, 1651, see no. 36, p. 529. Edition: ed. Logan Pearsall Smith, *The Life and Letters of Sir Henry Wotton*, Oxford 1907, ii.311. The couplet had first appeared in print in Sir John Mennis's and James Small's anthology *Wits recreations*, 1641. Wotton quotes it in a letter (first printed in the third edition of *Reliquiæ Wottonianæ*, 1672) written from London on 13 November 1628 to John Dynely in The Hague, as an epitaph for Albertus Morton and his wife, praising it for its 'passionate plainness'. In the first edition of *Reliquiæ Wottonianæ*, 1651, it appears with the ascription 'H. Wotton'. The poem circulated widely in MS and at least one copy calls the poem Wotton's epitaph on his wife (he was unmarried). Sir Albertus Morton (1584?–1625) was Wotton's half-nephew and became Secretary of State on 9 February 1625; he died on 6 September, having married his wife Elizabeth Apsley on 13 January 1624.

322 Text: Robert Herrick, *Hesperides*, 1648, see no. 44, p. 27. Edition: ed. L. C. Martin, see no. 44, p. 27. Herrick's father, Nicholas, died on 7 November 1592, it was suspected by his own hand; hence, perhaps, the poet's uncertainty as to the precise location of his father's grave in St Vedast's, Foster Lane, London, (ll. 5–6) and the feeling that his father had not had the proper funeral rites, for which Herrick coins the unique usage of '*justments*' (l. 4). If the 'seven *Lusters*' are taken literally for thirty-five years, the poem would date from 1627, before Herrick went to the Isle of Rhé as Buckingham's chaplain. The exact sense of 'religious' in the poem – revered, sacred, pious, scrupulous – is hard to determine.

323 Text: Robert Herrick, *Hesperides*, 1648, see no. 44, p. 232. Edition: ed. L. C. Martin, see no. 44, p. 199.

324 Text: Robert Herrick, *Hesperides*, 1648, see no. 44, p. 263. Edition: ed. L. C. Martin, see no. 44, p. 224.

325 Text: John Milton, *Poems*, 1645, see no. 203, pp. 57–65. Edition: ed. John Carey and Alastair Fowler, see no. 48, pp. 239–54. 'Lycidas' was first published as the last English poem in a Cambridge University memorial volume, *Justa Edouardo King*, Cambridge 1638 (ed. Ernest C. Mossner, Facsimile Text Society, no. 45, New York 1939); two copies survive with MS corrections in Milton's hand – one in Cambridge University Library and one in the British Library, referred to as 1638C and 1638L. An autograph version of the poem (with another copy of its opening lines and several other passages, which are referred to here as MS*) survives in the Trinity MS (see no. 48). Edward King, a fellow of Milton's Cambridge College, Christ's, was drowned on 10 August 1637; in the Trinity MS the poem is dated November 1637.

MS and 1645 share the same arrangement of paragraphs; 1638 begins new paragraphs at ll. 15, 37, 132, 165 and 186

Title] In . . . height *omitted in 1638*   And . . . height *omitted in MS*

4–5 before the mellowing yeare
and crop your young *MS* corrected to present text*
8 For] young *MS* corrected to* for
10 he knew] he well knew *MS*, MS, 1638L, 1638C*
21 passes turn,] passes, turn *1638*
22 And bid] to bid *MS corrected to* and bid
26 opening] glimmering *MS corrected to* opening
30 oft till the ev'n starre bright *MS, 1638; MS corrected to* oft till the starre that rose in Evning bright
31 westering] burnisht *MS, 1638; MS corrected to* westring
47 wardrop wear] buttons weare *MS corrected to* buttons beare *corrected to* wardrope weare
51 lov'd] youn[g] *MS corrected to* lov'd lord *1638 corrected to* lov'd *1638L, 1638C*
53 your] the *1638 corrected to* your *1638C*
56 Ay] Ah *1638*
58–63 what could the golden hayrd Calliope
for her inchaunting son
when shee beheld (the gods farre sighted bee)
his goarie scalpe rowle downe the Thracian lee
MS corrected to
what could the golden hayrd Calliope
for her inchaunting son
whome universal nature might lament
and heaven and hel deplore
when his divine head downe the streame was sent
downe the swift Hebrus to the Lesbian shore.
recopied in MS as*
whome universal nature did lament *corrected from* might lament
when by the rout that made the hideous roare
his goarie *corrected from* divine visage downe the streame was sent
downe the swift Hebrus to the Lesbian shoare.
67 use] do *1638 corrected to* use *1638L, 1638C*
69 Or with] hid in *MS, 1638; corrected in MS to* or with
85 honour'd] smooth *MS corrected to* fam'd *corrected to* honour'd
86 Smooth-sliding] soft-sliding *MS corrected to* smooth-sliding
94 Promontory;] *1673* Promontory, *1645*
114 Anow] anough *MS* Enough *1638*
118 guest;] *1673* guest. *1638, 1645*
121 Herdmans] heardsmans *MS*
129 nothing] little *1638* nothing *MS corrected to* little *with the intention of restoring* nothing
131 and smite] and smites *1638*
138 sparely] sparely *MS corrected to* faintly *corrected to* sparely

139 Throw] bring *MS corrected to* throw
142 dies,] *1638* dies. *1645, 1673*
142–50 *omitted in MS, but marked to be inserted from MS**
Bring the rathe primrose that unwedded dies
colouring the pale cheeke of uninjoyd love
and that sad floure that strove
to write his owne woes on the vermeil graine
next adde Narcissus that still weeps in vaine
the woodbine and the pancie freak't with jet
the glowing violet
the cowslip wan that hangs his pensive head
and every bud that sorrows liverie weares
let Daffadillies fill thire cups with teares
bid Amaranthus all his beautie shed
to strew the laureat herse etc.
deleted and rewritten as
Bring the rathe primrose that forsaken dies
the tufted crowtoe and pale Gessamin
the white pinke, and the pansie *corrected from* and pansie freakt with jet
the glowing violet
the muske rose and the garish columbine *corrected to* the well-attir'd woodbine
with cowslips wan that hang the pensive head
and every flower that sad escutcheon beares *corrected to* weare *corrected to* imbroidrie beares *corrected to* weares
2 and *corrected from* let daffadillies fill thire cups with teares
1 bid Amaranthus all his beauties shed
to strew etc
145 Violet,] violet, *1638* Violet. *1645, 1673*
151 Lycid] Lycid' *MS*
153 frail] sad *MS corrected to* fraile
154 shores] floods *MS corrected to* shoars
157 whelming] humming *1638* whelming *1638L, 1638C*
160 Bellerus] Corineus *MS corrected to* Bellerus
176 And hears] listening *MS corrected to* and heares
177 *omitted in 1638; present in 1638L, 1638C*

326 Text: John Milton, *Poems*, 1673, see no. 243, p. 61. Edition: ed. John Carey and Alastair Fowler, see no. 48, pp. 415–16. It is the last poem copied in the Trinity MS (see no. 48) and is not in Milton's hand. Scholars who assume the sonnet contains autobiographical elements are divided as to whether it refers to the death of Milton's second wife, Katherine Woodcock, whom he married on 12 November 1656 and who died on 3 February 1658, or to the death of his first wife, Mary Powell, in May 1652. Both women had given birth to daughters.

327 Text: *Eliza's babes: or the virgins-offering. Being divine poems, and meditations. Written by a Lady, who onely desires to advance the glory of God, and not her own*, 1652, pp. 46–7. Edition: ed. Germaine Greer, Susan Hastings, Jeslyn Medoff and Melinda Sansone, *Kissing the Rod: An Anthology of Seventeenth-Century Women's Verse*, 1988, pp. 144–5. The identity of the husband, as of the poet, is unknown.

328 Text: Henry Vaughan, *Silex scintillans*, 1655, see no. 301, part 2, pp. 4–6. Edition: ed. Alan Rudrum, see no. 212, pp. 246–7.

329 Text: Katherine Philips, *Poems*, 1667, see no. 47, p. 134. Edition: ed. Patrick Thomas, see no. 47, i.205. The poem is not in the Texas MS, nor in 1664, but is preserved in National Library of Wales MS 776.

5 childless] childless, *1667*
13 as fit] fit *776*
19 And so] So *776*

330 Text: Katherine Philips, *Poems*, 1667, see no. 47, pp. 148–9. Edition: ed. Patrick Thomas, see no. 47, i.220. The first eight lines of the poem are preserved in National Library of Wales MS 775; the poem is not in the Texas MS, nor in 1664. Lawes's music for the poem does not survive. Katherine Philips was married in August 1648.

Title] On the death of my first and dearest childe, Hector Philipps, borne the 23d of April, and dy'd the 2d of May 1655. Set by Mr Lawes *775*
6 pluck] touch *775*
8 For] Soe *775*

331 Text: James Shirley, *Honoria and Mammon. Whereunto is added the contention of Ajax and Ulisses, for the armour of Achilles*, 1659, pp. 127–8. Edition: ed. Ray Livingstone Armstrong, *The Poems of James Shirley*, New York 1941, p. 54. The play at the end of which this poem was printed may date from the mid 1640s; the poem circulated separately in MS, and several settings for it survive. In the printed edition the song was said to have been set by Edward Coleman and was intended to be sung by Calchas 'before the body of Ajax, supported by six Princes ... following the Hearse, as going to the Temple'. There is no contemporary evidence that this poem should be associated with the execution of Charles I.

Title] The vanitye of greatnesse *MS*
1 blood] birth *some MSS*

332 Text: *Certain bokes of Virgiles Aenæis turned into English meter by Henry [Howard] Earle of Surrey*, 1557, sig. E1r–v. Edition: ed. Emrys Jones, see no. 8, pp. 67–9, ll. 164–222. The lines are a version of *Aeneid* 4.129–72. Surrey translated Books 2 and 4 of the *Aeneid*. Apart from the 1557 edition published by Richard Tottel, there are two other texts of Surrey's translation of *Aeneid* 4: an earlier one printed by John Day for William Owen in [1554], which was dedicated to Surrey's son, Thomas Howard the fourth Duke of Norfolk, and a MS version, probably copied in about 1568, in the British Library, MS Hargrave 205. All three editions differ from each other in various ways.

2 once] hoist *MS*
4 steele] yron *MS*
8 attend] awayte *[1554], MS*
9 trapt] deckt *[1554], MS*
11 awayted] backed *[1554]* train] route *[1554]*
14 Knotted in] Wownde up wyth *[1554]*
21 viset] se *MS*
22 *omitted in [1554]*
23 Candians] Cretians *MS*
24 shoute] do howle *MS*
25 *omitted in [1554]*
28 leaves] bowes *MS*
31 countenaunce present] *[1554]* present countenaunce *1557*
33 driven] wild *MS*
34 Loe . . . above] availe the hill, and on *MS*
41 ferefull] tymerous *[1554]*
45 eke the] skattred *MS*
46 cotages] cotage? *1557* coltage *[1554]*
48–9 Dido . . . upon] Quene Dido with the Trojane prince alone chanst on a denn. *MS*
53 yelled] wayled *MS* wayted *[1554]*
54 first . . . their] formest day of *[1554], MS*
55 their harmes] myshappe *[1554]* mischief *MS*

333 Text: *Thee first foure bookes of Virgil his Aeneis translated intoo English heroical verse by Richard Stanyhurst*, Leiden 1582, pp. 68–70. Edition: ed. Edward Arber, *Richard Stanyhurst. Translation of the first Four Books of the Aeneis of P. Virgilius Maro*, 1880, pp. 99–100. This extract is a version of *Aeneid* 4.129–73. This translation was reprinted in 1583 at London. Stanyhurst tries to indicate metrical quantity by his reformed spelling.

19 foorthwith] *1583* foorth with *1582*

334 Text: *The .xv. bookes of P. Ovidius Naso, entytuled Metamorphosis, translated into English meeter, by Arthur Golding*, 1567, sigs. K3v–5v; facsimile, The English Experience, no. 881, Amsterdam and Norwood, NJ, 1977. Edition: ed. W. H. D. Rouse, *Shakespeare's Ovid: Being Arthur Golding's Translation of the Metamorphoses*, 1904, pp. 119–22, Book 6, ll. 10–182. Golding's translation of Ovid was frequently reprinted, with editions in 1575, 1584, 1587, 1593, 1603 and 1612; his translation of the first four books of the *Metamorphoses* had appeared first in 1565.

68 appeares] there commes *1575*
137 covering] *1575* hovering *1567*
162 hereafter . . . may] that tyme may from this curse hereafter *1575*

335 Text: Edmund Spenser, *Complaints. Containing sundrie small poemes of the worlds vanitie*, 1591, sig. R2r; facsimile, The English Experience, no. 278, Amsterdam and New York 1970. Edition: ed. William A. Oram etc., see no. 83, pp. 387–8. The *Complaints* were included in the collected edition of Spenser's poems published in 1611. Spenser's thirty-three sonnets comprising the *Ruines of Rome* are based on Joachim du Bellay's sequence *Les antiquitez de Rome* published in 1558. Like other members of his poetic school, the Pléiade, the French writer du Bellay championed the literary possibilities of the vernacular, seeking to revive the classical traditions of poetry.

336 Text: Penshurst Place, Kent, Viscount De L'Isle MS. Edition: ed. J. C. A. Rathmell, *The Psalms of Sir Philip Sidney and the Countess of Pembroke*, New York 1963, pp. 122–3. The Penshurst MS (known to Sidney scholars as A) was written by John Davies of Hereford and was intended for presentation to Queen Elizabeth I; it preserves an intermediate state of the Countess's revisions of the Psalms. Some seventeen MSS survive of the translation of the Psalms by Sir Philip Sidney and his sister the Countess of Pembroke; Sidney translated the first forty-three Psalms and his sister completed the rest, frequently revising his as well as her own work. On account of the textual complexity of the Psalms, no variants between MSS have been noted.

39 will] will. *MS*

337 Text: British Library, MS Additional 12047, ff. 44v–45r. Edition: Derek Attridge, *Well-weighed Syllables: Elizabethan Verse in Classical Metres*, Cambridge 1974, pp. 205–6. Attridge considers this version of the Countess's revision, which differs considerably from the text printed by Rathmell (see no. 336) of the same Psalm, 'the most successful Elizabethan attempt to naturalise the hexameter'.

5 think] thing *MS*
13 hearts] heares *MS* reposed] repose *MS*

338 Text: Penshurst Place, Kent, Viscount De L'Isle MS, see no. 336. Edition: ed. J. C. A. Rathmell, see no. 336, p. 326.

4 laieth] laieth. *MS*
10 not on] *most MSS* not *Penshurst MS*

339 Text: *All Ovids elegies: 3. bookes. By C. M. Epigrams by J. D.*, Middlebourgh [London, after 1602], sigs. B4v–5v. Edition: ed. Stephen Orgel, see no. 98, pp. 131–2. At least three other undated editions of Marlowe's translations were issued, all with false Middelburg imprints, before 1640. The second half of the poem's last line is Marlowe's addition to Ovid.

9 not?] not *[1602]*
10 not.] not? *[1602]*
41 waine?] waine, *[1602]*
42 swaine.] swaine? *[1602]*

340 Text: *Lucans first booke translated line for line, by Chr. Marlow*, 1600. sig. C1r–v. Edition: ed. Stephen Orgel, see no. 98, pp. 195–6, ll. 230–62. Only one edition of Marlowe's translation was published: it is mentioned in the Stationers' Register on 28 September 1593 at the same time as his version of *Hero and Leander* was entered, see no. 99. The date of Marlowe's translation is not known. The extract begins just after Caesar has crossed the Rubicon into Italy.

341 Text: *Orlando Furioso in English heroical verse, by John Harington*, 1591, Book 34, stanzas 68–85, pp. 286–7; facsimile, The English Experience, no. 259, Amsterdam and New York 1970. Edition: ed. Robert McNulty, *Ludovico Ariosto's Orlando Furioso Translated into English Heroical Verse by Sir John Harington*, Oxford 1972, pp. 395–7. Two important MSS, both partly autograph, of Harington's Ariosto survive: one in the Bodleian Library, Oxford, contains a version of Books 1–24 and the other in the British Library (MS Additional 18920) consists of the printers' copy for the 1591 edition of Books 14–46. The romance *Orlando Furioso* by the Italian poet Ludovico Ariosto (1474–1535) was published in its final form in 1532. Harington's translation, which included his important allegorical commentary, was reprinted in a revised form in 1607 and 1634. In this extract, the English knight Astolfo leaves the Earthly Paradise with St John and they fly by chariot to the moon, where he collects his cousin Orlando's lost wits.

31 ev'n . . . they] *1607* all that he *1591 and MS*
60 bladders] potsherds *deleted and corrected MS*
66 prepard] prefard *1607*
74 To looke] *1607* Looking *1591 and MS*
91–6 side-note] The Sin of roome maketh yt stink thus and other great citties will savor as ill yf they bee not the better kept with devocion and relligion *MS deleted and corrected*
103 Howbeit] *1607* Onlie nor *1591 and MS*
109 But last] *1607* Lastlie *1591 and MS*
111 By name] *1607* Namely *1591 and MS*
114 And . . . mount] *1607* Apt to ascend *1591 and MS*
116 It there] *1607* There it *1591 and MS*

132 And some] *1607* Some *1591 and MS*
134 And some] *1607* Others *1591 and MS*
143 By name,] *1607* Namelie *1591 and MS*

342 Text: *Godfrey of Bulloigne, or the recoverie of Jerusalem. Done into English heroicall verse, by Edward Fairefax*, 1600, pp. 55–9. Edition: ed. Kathleen M. Lea and T. M. Gang, *Godfrey of Bulloigne: A Critical Edition of Edward Fairfax's Translation of Tasso's Gerusalemme Liberata, together with Fairfax's Original Poems*, Oxford 1981, pp. 162–7, Book 4, stanzas 3–19. *La Gerusalemme liberata*, an epic of the crusades, by the Italian poet Torquato Tasso, was first published in 1580–1. This extract describes Satan's rallying of his followers.

343 Text: *Bartas his devine weekes and workes translated by Josuah Sylvester*, 1605, Week 1, Day 7, pp. 231–3. Edition: ed. Susan Snyder, *The Divine Weeks and Works of Guillaume de Saluste Sieur du Bartas Translated by Josuah Sylvester*, 2 vols., Oxford 1979, i.294–6, Week 1, Day 7, ll. 1–58. Du Bartas's biblical epic was published in 1578; Sidney is said to have translated part of it. Sylvester's translations from du Bartas's poem began to appear in 1592 and were first collected in 1605; Sylvester continued to add to the work in 1608, 1611 and 1613; more material was included in the posthumous edition of 1621. The part of the poem from which this extract is taken was first printed in 1605.

38 Drives] *1611, 1613, 1621* Brings *1605*
42 ascends] *1611, 1613, 1621* doth rise *1605*

344 Text: *The Iliads of Homer; prince of poets. Never before in any language truely translated. With a comment uppon some of his chiefe places; donne according to the Greeke by Geo: Chapman*, [1611], pp. 165–6. Edition: ed. Allardyce Nicoll, *Chapman's Homer*, 2 vols., 1957, i.247–8, ll. 296–332. Chapman published his translation of seven books of the *Iliad* in 1598; to these he added a further five books in an undated volume probably issued in 1609 and reprinted in 1611. In the same year he published a complete translation in which the first two books had been revised, from which the text printed here is taken. The collected translation of all of Homer's works was published probably in 1616. Chapman goes beyond Homer in emphasizing his protagonists' high rank and political skill (see ll. 14–15 and 25–7).

1 on] an *[1611]*
5 arme] armes *[1609]*
34 sort] sorts *[1609]*

345 Text: John Milton, *Poems*, 1673, see no. 243, p. 62. Edition: ed. John Carey and Alastair Fowler, see no. 48, pp. 96–7. In 1673 the translation was printed with the Latin original in a text which differs slightly from modern editions; it was headed 'Horatius ex Pyrrhæ illecebris tanquam è naufragio enataverat, cuius amore irretitos, affirmat esse miseros' (translated by Carey and Fowler: 'Horace, having escaped from Pyrrha's charms, as from a shipwreck, declares that those who are ensnared by her love are in a wretched state'). The date of the translation is unknown and may belong to any time between the 1620s and 1650s. Translations from Horace were common in the seventeenth century, but this is the only unrhymed example.

346 Text: John Skelton, *A replycacion agaynst certayne yong scolers, abjured of late*, [1528], sig. B3r–v. Edition: ed. John Scattergood, see no. 1, p. 384, ll. 343–78. This attack on two Cambridge scholars, Thomas Arthur and Thomas Bilney, who renounced their heretical attacks on Roman Catholic practices, was probably written in 1528. The marginal Latin notes and references have been omitted.

347 Text: Thomas Churchyard, *A musicall consort of heavenly harmonie called Churchyards charitie*, 1595, sig. A4v. This extract is taken from the address 'To the generall Readers', in which Churchyard has been discussing the vein in which he wrote about women, especially about 'Shores wife' for *A myrrour for magistrates*, in which various historical characters relate their downfall, in verse.

348 Text: Edmund Spenser, *The Faerie Queene*, 1596, see no. 32, ii.482–7, Book 6, Canto 10, verses 10–28. Edition: ed. Thomas P. Roche, Jr., and C. Patrick O'Donnell, Jr., see no. 32, pp. 990–5. Calidore, having abandoned his quest to capture the Blatant Beast, stays in the country, where he dresses up as a shepherd, falls in love with Pastorella and comes across Mount Acidale. The identity of the woman at the centre of the hundred dancing maidens is disputed: she has been variously identified with Queen Elizabeth; the Rosalind of *The shepheardes calender*; Elizabeth Boyle, whose marriage with the poet in 1594 Spenser celebrated in *Amoretti and Epithalamion* (see nos. 83–8); and with the muse of his poetry.

103 within] *1609* with in *1596*
113 Æacidee,] Æcidee. *1596* Aecidee, *1609*
133 forward] froward *most modern edns*

349 Text: Sir John Harington, *Epigrams*, 1618, see no. 24, Book 2, no. 30, sig. E7r. Edition: ed. Norman Egbert McClure, see no. 24, no. 126, p. 196. For Samuel Daniel, see no. 90.

350 Text: John Donne, *Poems*, 1633, see no. 28, pp. 204–5. Edition: ed. A. J. Smith, see no. 28, p. 81.

20 triumphs] trials *some MSS*

351 Text: William Shakespeare, *Sonnets*, 1609, see no. 104, sig. G3r–v. Edition: ed. John Kerrigan, see no. 104, p. 130.

352 Text: John Marston, *The scourge of villanie. Three bookes of satyres*, 1598, sigs. B1r–3v. Edition: ed. Arnold Davenport, see no. 125, pp. 96–9. Two further editions appeared in 1599, the first of which (1599a) contains revisions to the text which appear to be authorial.

3 Each] *1599a and 1599b* Shal each *1598*
22 thy] my *1599a and 1599b*
60 my] thy *1598, 1599a and 1599b*

353 Text: Samuel Daniel, *The poeticall essayes*, 1599, *Musophilus*, sigs. A2r, D1v–2r, F2r–3r. Edition: ed. Arthur Colby Sprague, see no. 90, pp. 69, 83, 96–7, ll. 1–13, 481–518, 934–75. *Musophilus: containing a generall defence of learning*, was dedicated to Fulke Greville. It was reprinted in 1601–2 with minor changes and in a revised form in 1607, which was reprinted in 1611 when the poem was given the title *Musophilus or a defence of poesie*. The poem takes the form of a dialogue between Philocosmus, 'lover of the world', and Musophilus, 'lover of the Muses' (especially Poetry).

15 doubt,] *1601–2* doubt *1599*

354 Text: Ben Jonson, *The workes*, 1640, see no. 142, sigs. Dd2v–3r. Edition: ed. George Parfitt, see no. 34, pp. 166–7. The poem is the twenty-ninth in the collection called 'The Under-wood': it is not known to have circulated in MS. As he told Drummond of Hawthornden, Jonson's favourite metre was the couplet. He had written against both Campion and Daniel in their debate about rhyme, proving 'couplets to be the bravest sort of Verses'.

1 Rime,] Rime *1640*
3 Conceipt,] Conceipt *1640*
15 Art] are *1640*
21 bewail'd] bewail'd. *1640*
30 frowning.] frowning; *1640*
39 restore] restore, *1640*
47 refused] refused, *1640*
48 ceasure.] ceasure; *1640*
55 Sense, . . . meet] Sense . . . meet, *1640*

355 Text: Ben Jonson, *The workes*, 1640, see no. 142, sig. Cc4v. Edition: ed. George Parfitt, see no. 34, pp. 160–1. The poem is the twenty-third in the collection called 'The Under-wood'. It had some circulation in MS from the 1620s; one MS of the 1630s (British Library MS Egerton 923) ends the poem with the motto 'Virtus vera nobilitas' ('virtue is true nobility').

1 lie,] lie *1640*
4 Securitie] obscuritie *Egerton MS*

6 and oft] *most MSS* and *1640*
12 defac't] displact *Egerton MS*
16 great] quicke *Egerton MS*
23 die] drincke *MS*
29 give] guide *Egerton MS*
32 reproofe,] reproofe. *1640*

356 Text: George Chapman, *The Iliads of Homer*, [1611], see no. 344, sig. ²A1v. Edition: ed. Allardyce Nicoll, see no. 344, i.11, ll. 163–78. The extract comes from Chapman's address 'To the Reader', which was first published probably in [1609].

357 Text: *Lucans Pharsalia translated into English verse by Sir Arthur Gorges knight*, 1614, sig. A4v. Edition: ed. Agnes M. C. Latham, see no. 18, p. 54. For Gorges, who was Ralegh's first cousin, see no. 35. This was the first complete English translation of Lucan's epic; for Marlowe's version of Book 1, see no. 340.

358 Text: William Browne, *Britannia's pastorals*, 1616, see no. 37, Book 2, Song 3, pp. 59–62. Edition: ed. Gordon Goodwin, see no. 37, i.272–3, 275–7, ll. 287–322, 379–424.

359 Text: Rachel Speght, *Mortalities memorandum, with a dreame prefixed, imaginarie in manner; reall in matter*, 1621, pp. 4–6. Edition: ed. Germaine Greer etc., see no. 327, pp. 70–2, ll. 103–68, (ll. 157–68 are omitted). The poem from which this extract is taken is an allegorical dream vision written to support Speght's plea for the education of women.

360 Text: Michael Drayton, *Poems*, 1619, see no. 138, p. 261. Edition: ed. J. William Hebel etc., see no. 138, ii.323. This sonnet was first printed in 1599.

2 That Foraine] The Sotherne *1599–[1616?]*
4 living] lovely *1613–[1616?]*

361 Text: Michael Drayton, *The battaile of Agincourt*, 1627, pp. 204–8; Scolar Press facsimile, Menston 1972. Edition: ed. J. William Hebel etc., see no. 138, iii.226–31. The poem is the eighth among the group of 'Elegies'. Henry Reynolds (1563/4–1632) was a Suffolk man, a schoolmaster and poet; his few publications, including a translation of Tasso's *Aminta*, 1628, and a theoretical work, *Mythomystes wherein a short survay is taken of the nature and value of true poesy, and depth of the ancients above our moderne poets*, [1632], reveal his interest in poetry. This poem may date from 1621, the year of the publication of the first part of Sandys's translation of Ovid (see ll. 157–62).

201 pursue,] pursue *1627*

362 Text: Michael Drayton, *The muses Elizium, lately discovered, by a new way over Parnassus*, 1630, pp. 1–4. Edition: ed. J. William Hebel etc., see no. 138, iii.248–51. This is the first poem in Drayton's last volume of verse.

363 Text: John Milton, *Poems*, 1673, see no. 243, pp. 64–6. Edition: ed. John Carey and Alastair Fowler, see no. 48, pp. 76–8, ll. 1–52. The Latin part of the exercise, the speeches, form Milton's sixth Prolusion, which was printed in 1674. The English poem dates from the summer vacation of 1623.

364 Text: John Taylor, *All the workes*, 1630, see no. 197, sig. Kk4v. Edition: Spenser Society, see no. 197, vol. 3, 1868, p. 274, ll. 1–24. This extract is taken from one of the poems first printed in the collection *A common whore with all these graces grac'd*, 1622, which was reprinted in 1625 and 1635.

365 Text: John Donne, *Poems, by J. D. With elegies on the authors death*, 1633, see no. 28, pp. 385–8. Edition: ed. Rhodes Dunlap, see no. 154, pp. 71–4. The poem was reprinted in the collections of Donne's poems published in 1635 and 1639; it was included in the 1640 edition of Carew's poems, but in a slightly different form. Three MS copies of the poem survive. Donne died on 31 March 1631.

3 dare] did *1640*
5 Churchman] Lect'rer *1640*
7 should] might *1640*
44 dust, had rak'd] dung had search'd *1640*
50 stubborne] troublesome *1640*
58 is purely] was onely *1640*
61 *new paragraph in 1640*
63 repeale] recall *1640*
71 *new paragraph in 1640*
74 faint] rude *1640*
81 small] short *1640*   maintaine] retaine *1640*
87 *new paragraph in 1640*

366 Text: Thomas Carew, *Poems by Thomas Carew Esquire. The second edition revised and enlarged*, 1642, p. 222. Edition: ed. Rhodes Dunlap, see no. 154, p. 117. This is one of eight poems added to the second edition of Carew's *Poems* two years after the majority of them first appeared in print. Two settings (1642a and 1642b) of the text exist in 1642. One mid-seventeenth-century MS copy of the poem survives.

1 polisht] peevish *1642a*
19 fit,] fit. *1642a and 1642b*
20 silkes,] silkes *1642a*

367 Text: Robert Herrick, *Hesperides*, 1648, see no. 44, p. 72. Edition: ed. L. C. Martin, see no. 44, p. 66.

368 Text: Robert Herrick, *Hesperides*, 1648, see no. 44, p. 372. Edition: ed. L. C. Martin, see no. 44, p. 314.

369 Text: George Wither, *Vox pacifica: a voice tending to the pacification of God's wrath*, 1645, pp. 2–5. Edition: *Miscellaneous Works of George Wither: Second Collection*, Spenser Society, vol. 13, 1872, pp. 16–19. John Lilburne and other Levellers admired this poem in which Wither called for democratic reforms.

58 rectifie] terrific *1645*

370 Text: Sir William Davenant, *Gondibert*, 1651, see no. 303, pp. 172–5, Book 2, Canto 5, verses 37, 39–50. Edition: ed. David F. Gladish, see no. 303, pp. 155–7. Gondibert has been brought to the House of Astragon by old Ulfin; he is being shown 'The Monument of vanish'd Mindes'.

1 There] *press correction in 1651a* Where *1651a uncorrected, 1651b and 1673*
33 Tomes] *1651b and 1673; corrected in MS in 1651a from* Tombs

371 Text: Margaret Cavendish, Duchess of Newcastle, *Poems*, 1653, see no. 219, p. 110. The title may refer to the poem's position as the first within a group of poems in this part of the book. The variant readings below are substantially shared by 1664 and 1668.

1–3 Give me a free and noble Style, that goes
In an Uncurbed Strain, though Wild it shows;
For though it Runs about it cares not where,
8 Not . . . bound] And not bound up

372 Text: Margaret Cavendish, Duchess of Newcastle, *Poems*, 1653, see no. 219, p. 213. The variant readings below are substantially shared by 1664 and 1668.

Title] The Common Fate of Books
1 Books have the worst Fate, when they once are Read,
5–10 But *Spiders*, which Nature has taught to Spin,
For th'Love and Honour of this Art, since Men
Spin likewise all their Writings from their Brain,
A lasting *Web* of *Fame* thereby to Gain,
They do high *Altars* of thin *Cobwebs* raise,
Their Off'rings *Flies*, a *Sacrifice* of *Praise*.

373 Text: Abraham Cowley, *Poems*, 1656, see no. 210, *Pindarique Odes*, pp. 23–4. Edition: ed. John Sparrow, see no. 210, pp. 159–61. Cowley's notes to this Ode are quoted selectively in the commentary.

68 Chrystallize,] Chrystallize. *1656*

374 Text: Henry Vaughan, *Silex scintillans,* 1655, see no. 301, part 2, pp. 80–1. Edition: ed. Alan Rudrum, see no. 212, pp. 309–10. This is the last poem in the volume apart from 'To the Holy Bible' and 'L'Envoy'. In Romans 8:21, St Paul declares that 'the creature' will be delivered. Vaughan aligns himself with the small minority who believed that this implied the possibility of universal salvation not only for humans but for all sentient beings.

APPENDICES

APPENDIX 1: INDEX OF GENRES

Renaissance writers were highly conscious of poetic kinds; but there was no single coherent system of generic classification. One form of classification derived from classical rhetoric. Of the three traditional kinds of rhetorical discourse – demonstrative, dealing with praise and dispraise; deliberative, dealing with persuasion; and forensic, dealing with legal proof – the poetic genres were generally aligned with the first. At the head of the hierarchy, epic praised heroic deeds. A huge array of complimentary forms celebrated State occasions – births, marriages, deaths and voyages. Love-poetry of course praised or dispraised the loved one. Pastoral celebrated rural life, while satire dispraised the vicious. Elegy involved praise of the deceased. Poets would, however, freely draw on persuasive and forensic strategies to complicate the picture; much Renaissance love-poetry has a strong persuasive element, while elegy might involve consolatory argument as well as emotional release. In theory, each category had an appropriate style: poetry dealing with princes and court affairs needed a high style, while a low style was appropriate for the base-born. This classically based system of genres became increasingly dominant in the Renaissance, but it did not displace other genres which were rooted in popular culture and did not fit neatly into the neoclassical hierarchy. The 'complaint', with its loose accumulation of denunciations of social and religious abuses, was never entirely displaced by the more poised and controlled classical satire; the medieval 'bergerie', portraying everyday rural work and recreation, maintained its hold despite the vogue for classicizing pastoral set in a distant past and in a Mediterranean landscape.

As well as *functional* definitions of genre, based on the acts the poem was considered as performing, there were also various *formal* definitions which often overlapped with considerations of metrical pattern. Thus the ode could be considered a separate genre, though its different variants could perform differing generic functions. Roman poets applied the term 'elegy' to poems of lamentation written in a specific metre which included love-complaints – as one critic explained, the loved one was 'dead' to the unrequited lover. 'Elegy' was still used for love-poetry in the Renaissance (nos. 96, 132). Today the term 'sonnet' tends to be used both as a generic and as a formal description, while the Renaissance used it to describe a short love-poem without restricting it to a fourteen-line verse form (cp. no. 62).

Renaissance poets were not rigidly bound by generic categories but enjoyed mixing and varying genres. For example, the pastoral, concerned with the leisurely life of shepherds, and the georgic, concerned with the cycle of agrarian labour, were originally distinct, but their boundaries became blurred in the English Renaissance. Popular songs and street-cries would be reworked for a different audience (cp. no.

196 with nos. 128, 131); vernacular generic traditions would be fused with classical ones. *The Faerie Queene* is a veritable anthology of literary kinds, with its overall framework of Arthurian romance accommodating elements of the Homeric and Virgilian epic, the pastoral, the complaint, the love-lyric, the *epyllion*, and the topographical poem. If the name of the villainness of Book 2, Acrasia, means 'bad mixture', the possibility of good kinds of mixture is left open. At the opposite end of the generic scale, there was a growing fondness for concentrating the elements of large-scale genres in the humble epigram (cp. Sir John Harington's 'A Tragicall Epigram', no. 24); epigrammatic formulations became popular in love-poetry, most notably in Shakespeare's sonnets; Herrick's collection of epigrams forms an encyclopaedia of different genres. The sonnet was often seen as a subspecies of the epigram, a classification stressing its economy; yet it could take on a heroic tone, as in Milton's sonnet to Cromwell (no. 48). One genre might be inset within another: thus Shakespeare's *Lucrece* (no. 101), while focusing on the personal aspect of the rape which led to the fall of the Roman monarchy, and while closely linked with the genre of the complaint, incorporates a narrative of the fall of Troy in the description of the painting. The poetic effect of such mixtures, however, depended on the audience's having some prior assumptions and expectations: abrupt departures from expectation would have all the more force. Thus several of Shakespeare's sonnets gain tension from the speaker's ambivalent refusal to utter the complaints to which his situation would conventionally entitle him.

In the list below, some allowance is made for the Renaissance hierarchy of genres in which heroic poetry and the poetry of ceremonial praise required a high style and love-poetry a middle style, while more 'plain' or 'low' styles were appropriate for less elevated genres such as the verse epistle, pastoral and satire. Such generic hierarchies were never rigid, however, and within these broad categories there is much room for disagreement over the classification of individual poems; in the list that follows, some poems may be found in more than one category, while others have been found too problematic to be classified under these headings. The 'love-poetry' classification contains poems addressed to patrons, illustrating the overlapping of discourses in this area. These qualifications made, the list does offer some primary generic distinctions as a starting-point for comparison and contrast.

For fuller historical discussion, see Rosalie Colie, *The Resources of Kind: Genre Theory in the Renaissance*, ed. Barbara K. Lewalski, Berkeley 1973, and Alastair Fowler, *Kinds of Literature: An Introduction to the Theory of Genres and Modes*, Oxford 1982; on the broader social aspects of genre, see Mikhail Bakhtin, *Speech Genres and Other Late Essays*, translated by Vern W. McGee, ed. Caryl Emerson and Michael Holquist, Austin 1986, pp. 60–102. Julius Caesar Scaliger gave the fullest Renaissance treatment of genre theory in his *Poetices libri septem*, Lyon 1562; see F. M. Padelford, *Select Translations from Scaliger's Poetics*, Yale Studies in English, 26 (1905).

Narrative poetry

epic and romance: 32, 80–2, 332–3, 340–2, 344, 348
hexameral poem (narrative based on Genesis): 343
mythological narrative (a short, self-contained narrative is sometimes labelled an *epyllion*): 99–100, 124–5, 334
other narratives: 17, 101

Poetry of praise

anniversary poem: 27, 50, 313
coronation poem: 1
dedication: 31
epibaterion, *prosphonetikon* (greeting to returned traveller): 45
festivals, poems marking:
religious: 187–8, 253, 257, 270, 278
secular: 27, 88, 95, 175, 182, 191, 203, 206, 208
hymn: 18, 175, 214 (ll. 5–36), 258, 270, 278, 291, 336–7
ode:
epithalamium: 11, 34 (political), 88
Horatian: 40, 45, 210, 241, 252, 345, 355
Partheniad: 252
Pindaric: 315, 373
prothalamion (betrothal song): 12 (political)
other: 193, 270
paradoxical encomium: 61, 76, 172, 227, (354, dispraise)
paraenesis (praise combined with persuasion): 48
syntaktikon (speech by a departing traveller): 6, 179
other: 16, 21, 49–50, 189–90, 192, 290, 357

Elegiac poetry

anniversary poem: 313
consolation: 315
elegy: 7, 35, 307, 310, 312, 314, 318–19, 322–3, 325, 365
epitaph: 15, 38–9, 41, 308–9, 317, 320, 323 (anticipatory), 324, 329–30
farewell to the world: (22, satirical), 239, 311, 316, 327
threnos: 312 (ll. 53–67)
other: 260, 321, 326, 328, 331

Love-poetry

aubade (poetry of the dawn): 133, 339
basium (poem on a kiss): 69, 102
blazon (praise of parts of body): 61, 67, 84, 88 (ll. 148–203), 93 (parody), 96, 99 (ll. 9–90), 105, 125 (ll. 13–72), 131, 142 (of self), 149, 169–170, 265 (ll. 17–96) (religious allegory), 309, 313 (ll. 84–105) (elegiac)
comparison of sensual and spiritual love: 68, 135, 145, 163
complaint: 21, 30, 53–8, 60, 62–4, 66, 73–4, 78, 83, 89–90, 97, 105, 107, 113, 117–19, 120–3, 129, 138, 140, 154–5, 157, 170–1, 215
concealment of love: 108, 144, 147
defence of love: 114–15, 133–5, 143, 239
definition of love: 116, 171
dialogue: 71–2, 126, 158
elegy, erotic poem: 94–6, 156, 339
female friendship: 244–6
mythological allegory: 19, 68, 74, 78, 81–2, 90, 145–6, 149, 159
palinode, farewell to love: 19, 21, 30, 54–6, 77, 139, 141, 345
poem on separation: 52, 108, 110, 171

Love-poetry–contd
promise of immortality: 91–2, 104, 109, 112
suasio (persuasion to love): 80 (ll. 38–54), 86, 94, 96, 98, 99 (ll. 199–310), 100 (ll. 95–174), 156, 160–1, 163, 169, 173 (refusal of *suasio*), 206
valediction: 132, 136–7, 139, 164

Descriptive poetry

description of place (*topographia*): 28, 42, 57, 80–1, 122, 154, 174–222, 240, 290, 302, 348, 362, 370
eclogue, pastoral: 21, 37, 174, 182, 191, 198, 216–17, 325, 348, 358, 362
estate poem: 189–90, 218, 240
georgic: 37, 42, 192
of a work of art (*ekphrasis*): 82, 87, 99 (ll. 135–57), 101 (ll. 1–91), 125, 132, 142, 170, 265 (ll. 97–160), 334, 343

Discursive (deliberative) poetry

allegory, emblem and *exemplum*: 11, 14, 16, 23, 26, 42 (ll. 241–326), 182, 213, 225, 241, 245, 259, 265, 268, 271, 273, 277, 300, 302, 306, 325, 359
biblical narrative: 267, 343
complaint: 4, 33, 176, 181, 247
dialogue: 12, 177, 182, 220, 282, 285, 353, 359
epistle: 28, 60, 194, 212, 223, 225, 228, 231–3, 243, 292, 361
invitation: 212, 233, 243
meditation:
moral and political: 3, 5, 13, 15, 20, 36, 47, 111, 113, 166, 202, 209, 213, 219, 222, 224–6, 241, 244–6, 331, 335
religious: 248, 250, 252–4, 257, 262–3, 266, 269, 272, 274–5, 279, 282–4, 287–8, 297–303, 305–6, 328, 374
persuasion: to battle, 45–6, 342 (ll. 49–120); to religious conversion, 292
poems on writing poetry: 65, 141, 155, 159, 192, 281, 284, 306, 319, 346–74
prayer, supplication: 259, 261, 264, 276, 278, 280, 293, 338

Satirical poetry

dying words: 22
epigram: 2, 3, 10, 24–5, 34, 44, 148–53, 184, 195, 197, 251, 255, 271–5, 321, 349, 364, 367–8, 371–2
fable: 14, 23, 26
formal satire (classical models): 29, 168, 185–6, 223, 256, 352
pastoral satire: 37, 182, 325
other: 8, 37, 51, 168, 205, 247, 249, 289, 294–6, 335

Other

beast-fable: 11, 14, 23, 312
prophecy: 1, 43, 202, 286, 304, 325, 369
songs and ballads:
festive and drinking songs: 234–8, 242
of love: 62, 79, 123, 126–31, 140, 157–8, 162, 164, 166
political and historical: 9, 12, 43, 51, 177–8, 187, 195–6, 200–1, 211, 250, 295, 297
work songs: 229–30
(dream) vision: 4, 32, 149, 253, 265, 270, 300, 304, 326, 348, 359, 362

Appendix 2: Index of Metrical and Stanzaic Forms

Renaissance literary theorists tended to be characteristically confident that their own age was bringing new light to former darkness. Their confidence has sometimes been shared by later literary historians, who have seen the Renaissance as establishing a firm basis for the theory and practice of English metre after the clumsiness of earlier centuries. In typical humanist fashion, Renaissance theorists adapted classical terminology to English verse. This immediately raised problems, given that classical verse was based on the length of syllables – a feature not easily perceived in English, where stress is a far more significant factor. Some attempts were made to establish quantitative metre in English, but eventually a compromise was reached in which stress was substituted for quantity but the classical names were retained and attention was paid to the number of syllables in a line. A unit with an unstressed followed by a stressed syllable was labelled an iamb, the opposite stressed–unstressed pattern formed a trochee, and two syllables of equal stress formed a spondee; a stressed syllable followed by two unstressed syllables was a dactyl, two unstressed followed by a stressed syllable formed an anapaest. The line that became the dominant form in English poetry, the iambic pentameter, was in theory made up of five iambs.

This classically based terminology did not readily apply to a great deal of earlier English verse, where the basic line tended to involve four stresses bound together by alliteration, without a consistent number of syllables; this kind of metre was seen by the Renaissance as rough and rustic and hence appropriate for forms like the pastoral (cp. no. 182). Editors of the mid sixteenth century saw their immediate predecessors as groping towards iambic regularity: hence Tottel's emendation of Wyatt's 'I would fain knowe what she hath deserved' (no. 53 l. 21) to 'How like you this, what hath she now deserved.' Today's readers tend to prefer the earlier version, which is more forceful and can be seen as consistent with the traditional four-stress metre; and they may see the growing metrical regularity of the later sixteenth century as a sign of rigidity. Modern linguists question the Renaissance idea of metrical progress and point out that the classical formulae do not really apply to a great deal of English poetry; in many ways their adoption served to heighten a separation between popular and élite culture.

These large questions, and the vexed question of the metrical basis of fifteenth-century poetry, cannot be explored here; the purpose of the index below is not to provide definitive analyses but to see the period in something like its own terms and to throw light on its interest in metrical experimentation. Renaissance poets' general concern with language and rhetoric extended to a keen interest in verbal patterning and syllabic proportions. Wyatt's sonnets do tend to have a ten-syllable pattern, even though the distribution of stresses is very uneven. By the latter part of the century the formal experiments of Sidney and Spenser were drawing readers' attention to the pleasures to be gained by a strict sense of formal control, with each syllable playing a clearly marked part in the overall effect. The Elizabethans attempted to emulate in their poetry the more directly syllabic procedures of Continental as well as of classical languages, especially when trying to achieve musical effects. The index below tries to register such effects by classifying line lengths according to the number of syllables, indicating the main points where such a classification breaks down; the metre is iambic unless otherwise indicated. Letters indicate rhyme words, numbers indicate the count of syllables (rather than feet: this makes it possible to indicate prominent occurrences of such phenomena as lines with a 'feminine' ending, an extra unstressed syllable in an iambic line). Thus aa_{10} indicates a ten-syllable couplet. In the classification of stanza forms, the basic criterion used is the minimum unit before repetition, but where the poet was clearly aiming at a distinctive look on the page, as in Marvell's eight-line stanzas of octosyllabic couplets, the poems have sometimes been classified separately. It should be emphasized that, as with genres, such patterns are ideal types which were necessarily subject to wide variation in practice.

John Hollander's *Rhyme's Reason: A Guide to English Verse*, enlarged edn, New Haven and London 1989, gives an excellent, and witty, introduction to metrics; for fuller historical and theoretical discussion, see Derek Attridge, *Well-Weighed Syllables: Elizabethan Verse in Classical Metres*, Cambridge 1974, and *The Rhythms of English Poetry*, 1982; Anthony Easthope, *Poetry as Discourse*, 1983; Susanne Woods, *Natural Emphasis: English Versification from Chaucer to Dryden*, San Marino 1984. For an Elizabethan view, George Puttenham's *The arte of English poesie* (see no. 16), with its diagrams of different stanza forms, gives a useful indication of the visual aspect of poetry.

Two-line units (*couplets*)

aa_7: 39; 236, 323–4, 329 (trochaic)
iambic tetrameter aa_8: 41, 141, 148–50, 169, 172, 204, 213–14, 222, 292–3, 299, 318, 320, 327, 366, 374
four-stress couplet: 182
$a_{10}a_8$: 216
pentameter couplet $aabb_{10}$: 19–20, 25, 28–9, 34, 37–8, 42, 44, 46–7, 50, 94–6, 99, 124, 132, 153–4, 156, 159, 168, 185–6, 189–90, 198, 202, 205, 212, 219, 220 (irregular), 221, 228, 232–3, 240, 255–7, 271–5, 286, 289–90, 294, 298, 310, 313–14, 321–2, 339, 343, 349, 352, 358, 361, 363–5, 367–8, 371–2
aa_{12} (alexandrine): 192
$a_{12}a_{14}$ ('poulter's measure'): 13, 17, 179
aa_{14} ('fourteeners'): 253, 334, 344
five-stress couplets: 174, 251

elegiac couplet (quantitative hexameter succeeded by pentameter): 2–3, 319
irregular iambic couplets: 287

Three-line units (tercets)

aaa_7: 312 (ll. 53–67) (trochaic)
aaa_8: 151, 208
aaa_{10}: 239
ababcbcdc . . . $_{10}$ (*terza rima*): 223, 231

Four-line units (quatrains)

$a_6b_4a_6b_4$: 152
$a_6b_5a_6b_5$: 336
$abab_6$: 157, 207, 248
$a_7b_6c_7b_6$: 162 (trochaic)
$aabb_7$: 71
$abab_7$: 36 (trochaic)
$abba_7$: 312 (trochaic)
$a_7b_8a_7b_8$: 238 (trochaic)
$a_8b_4a_8b_4$: 123
aba_8b_4: 40
aa_8bb_6: 45
ballad stanza, 'common measure' (variously $a_8b_6a_8b_6$, $a_8b_7a_8b_7$, $a_8b_6c_8b_6$ and variants based on four and three stresses): 9–10, 52, 60, 89, 126–7, 140, 158, 164, 166, 173, 178, 183, 191 (ll. 85–132), 195–6, 200, 246, 250, 297, 304, 362
$abab_8$ ('long measure'): 62, 137, 171, 201, 215
$aabb_8$: 98, 245
$a_{10}b_8a_{10}b_6$: 328
$a_{10}b_4a_{10}b_6$: 282 (ideal pattern, realized only in final stanza)
$aba_{10}b_6$: 276
$a_{10}b_8a_{10}b_8$: 241
$a_{10}bb_8a_{10}$: 129
$abab_{10}$ (pentameter quatrain, heroic stanza): 21, 184, 191 (ll. 1–84), 194 (modified), 225, 303, 309, 330, 347 (modified), 356, 370
alcaics (stanza of two lines of eleven syllables, one of nine and one of ten, with varying feet): 175
$ab_{10}cd_6$, unrhymed: 345
$a_5b_8c_8d_4$, unrhymed trochaics: 130
assonantal seven- or eight-syllable lines: 33

Five-line units (cinquains)

$a_4b_8a_4bb_8$: 160
$a_7b_8a_7b_8a_7$: 72 (trochaic)

ababb$_8$: 244
aabab$_8$: 5, 56
aa$_8$b$_9$a$_8$b$_9$: 58
a$_8$b$_4$a$_{10}$b$_6$b$_4$: 280 (final stanza)
aa$_{10}$bb$_8$b$_{10}$: 167
ababb$_{10}$: 258
ababa$_{10}$: 224

Six-line units (sixains)

aabccb (two- and three-stress lines): 12
abc$_6$ca$_4$b$_6$: 193
ababcc$_6$: 22
abaab$_6$b$_{12}$: 355
aa$_7$b$_3$cc$_7$b$_3$: 354
aabbcc$_7$: 317 (trochaic)
a$_7$b$_8$a$_7$b$_8$cc$_7$: 30 (trochaic)
ababcc$_8$: 131, 155, 161, 229, 291, 301
aabbcc$_8$: 288
aabccb$_8$: 165
ab$_{10}$c$_5$ab$_{10}$c$_5$: 79
a$_{10}$b$_6$a$_{10}$b$_6$c$_{10}$c$_6$: 285
abab$_{10}$c$_8$c$_{10}$: 284
ababab$_{10}$: 281
abcbdd$_{10}$: 359
ababcc$_{10}$: 26, 59, 73, 100, 125, 197, 226–7, 262–4, 311
abcdef$_{10}$ faebdc$_{10}$ (double sestina): 64

Seven-line units

ababbcc$_6$: 1
ababbcc$_8$: 11, 55
ababa$_{10}$aa$_4$: 128
a$_8$b$_{10}$a$_8$b$_{10}$cc$_4$b$_8$: 283
ababbcc$_{10}$ (rhyme royal): 4, 14, 53, 101
ababbc$_{10}$c$_{12}$: 270 (proem)

Eight-line units

a$_4$bb$_8$a$_4$c$_4$dd$_8$c$_4$: 252
aa$_8$b$_7$ccdd$_8$b$_7$: 51
abab$_8$cc$_4$dd$_8$: 331
aabbccdd$_8$: 170, 217–18

$ababccaa_8$: 316
$a_8a_{10}b_{10}b_8c_8dd_8c_{6-8}$: 210
$aabbcc_8dd_{10}$: 163
$ababccdd_{10}$: 15
$ababbcc_{10}c_{12}$: 265
$abababcc_{10}$ (*ottava rima*): 6, 266, 341–2, 353 (modified)
$ababbcbc_{10}$ (*ballade* stanza): 31
$aa_6b_{10}cc_6b_{10}d_8d_{12}$: 270 (Hymn)

Nine-line units

$a_4bba_{10}cc_4dd_{10}d_{14}$: 136
$ab_{10}ba_8c_6ccdd_{10}$: 188
$a_{10}b_8ba_{10}cc_8c_{10}a_8a_6$: 134
$ababbcbc_{10}c_{12}$ (Spenserian stanza): 32, 80–2, 348

Ten-line units

$a_6b_4a_6b_4cc_7d_4ee_7d_4$: 76
$aabb_8cc_5d_8ee_5f_8$ (mixed metre): 43
$a_{10}b_8a_6b_4a_2c_2d_4c_6d_8c_{10}$: 278
$a_8b_4b_{10}a_{10}cd_8c_{10}dee_{10}$: 133
$aabb_{10}c_8c_7dd_8e_{10}e_8$: 203
$abbaab_{10}c_{12}ac_{10}c_{12}$: 269

Eleven-line units

ababccdeedd (four- and three-foot anapaestic lines): 242
$a_6a_8b_6b_{10}b_6cd_{10}c_8dee_{10}$: 350

Twelve-line units

$ababcdcdef_6e_{10}f_6$: 237
$ababcdcdeeff_{10}$: 24
$abab_{11}cdd_7cee_{11}f_7f_{11}$: 63
$abab_{11}cdc_7def_{11}e_7f_{11}$: 338

Thirteen-line units

$a_7b_6a_7b_6c_7d_6c_7d_6ee_3f_6g_7f_6$: 305

Fourteen-line units

$\mathrm{aa_{10}bbcc_8dd_{10}eeff_8gg_{10}}$: 206
$\mathrm{a_{10}ba_6bccdeedffgg_{10}}$: 135
Sonnet (basic paradigms: Petrarchan abbaabbacdecde, Shakespearean ababcdcdefefgg, Spenserian ababbcbccdcdee): 7–8, 18 (extended), 23, 35, 48–9, 54, 57, 61, 65–70, 74–5, 77–8, 83–7, 90–3, 95 (prologue and epilogue), 97 (extended), 102–22, 138–9, 143–7, 199, 243, 254, 259–61, 267–8, 277, 279, 296 (*codata* – with tail), 308, 326, 335, 351, 357, 360, 369
corona (a group of sonnets linked by closing and opening lines): 145

Others

$\mathrm{aa_{10}a_6b_{10}b_4c_{10}c_6d_{10}d_4e_{10}e_4f_{10}f_4g_{10}g_4}$: 300
$\mathrm{a_{10}b_6b_2b_{10}a_6c_{10}c_6c_8b_6b_{10}deedd_6ffd_{10}}$: 142
$\mathrm{a_{10}bb_6a_{10}c_8d_{10}d_8ce_{10}ff_8e_{10}ghgh_8iijkljklmm_{10}}$: 306
Iambic pentameter (five iambic feet: 'blank verse'): 27, 332, 340
Canzone (a poem made up of lyric stanzas divided into two *piedi* (feet) and a concluding *coda* (tail) culminating in a *commiato* or valediction. A sonnet can be seen as a condensed *canzone*): 88, 325 (irregular)
Cywydd (seven-syllable couplets rhyming alternately on stressed and unstressed syllables): 180
Glyconics (a metre of mixed feet, generally forming eight syllables): 209
Hexameter (six dactylic or spondaic feet): 181, 333, 337
Pattern poem: 16, 278, 302
Pindaric ode: 315, 373
Skeltonics (verse with two or three stresses and varying numbers of sequential rhymes): 176–7, 247, 249, 307, 346
Songs with miscellaneous forms: 187, 211, 230, 234–5, 295

Appendix 3: Glossary of Classical Names

This glossary is intended to provide only a brief identification of classical allusions in the poems in this anthology. Fuller and further accounts of most of the entries here will be found in Eric Smith, *A Dictionary of Classical Reference in English Poetry*, Woodbridge, Suffolk, and Totowa, NJ, 1984, and ed. M. C. Howatson, *The Oxford Companion to Classical Literature*, 2nd edn, Oxford 1989. This glossary is much indebted to both of these works. The poems richest in classical allusions are nos. 82, 88, 99, 101, 270, 325 and 332–4.

Usually, only the first occurrence of a classical name in a poem is indexed here. The numbers of poems which are largely devoted to the subject in question are printed in bold. Latin and Greek forms of names have not been distinguished: most entries begin with the form which the name takes most frequently in the texts in which it occurs. Cross-references within entries are selective.

Abydos A town on the Hellespont, opposite Sestos; Leander's birthplace. 99.4

Acheron A river in Hades. 99.189, 307.70

Achilles The Greek hero who killed Hector during the siege of Troy. 35.9, 101.59

Acidale A fountain, where the Graces bathed, and hill sacred to Venus. 88.310, 348.1

Actaeon A hunter, turned into a stag and killed by hounds for seeing Diana and her nymphs bathing naked. 99.745

Admetus The husband of Alcestis. 82.103, 326.3

Adonis The beautiful son of the King of Cyprus; loved by Venus, he was killed by a boar and turned into an anemone. See also Thammuz. **81**, 99.14, **100**

Adrastus The aged King of Argos, leader of the seven against Thebes. 1.14

Aeacidee Peleus, King of Thessaly, son of Aeacus; he married Antigone and Thetis. See also Aegina. 348.113

Aegina Impregnated by Jove, in the form of a flame, she became mother of King Aeacus. 82.65, 334.130

Aeneas A Trojan prince, son of Anchises and Venus, born on Mount Ida; the hero of Virgil's *Aeneid*; the founder of Rome. 60.33, **332, 333**

Aeolus The god of the winds. 60.57, 82.128, 193.16, 325.96, 334.133, 342.8

Aesop (6th? century BC) The name traditionally given to the author of fables. 3.19, **23**, 26.25, 28.3, 42.137–8, 99.535

Aganippe A fountain at the foot of Mount Helicon, sacred to the Muses. 325.15, 354.20, 361.58

Agarthyrsi A tribe in Thrace, north of Greece. 332.24, 333.20

Aglaia One of the Graces. 204.15, 348.116
Ajax One of the Greeks who besieged Troy. 101.29
Albanact According to Geoffrey of Monmouth, third son of Brutus and ruler of Albany or Scotland. 42.67
Alcestis The wife of Admetus, in whose place she agreed to die to assuage her brother's fury; Hercules rescued her from death. 326.2
Alcides Hercules, named after his grandfather, Alcaeus. 99.604, 194.56
Alcinous King of the island of Phaeacia, where he entertained Ulysses. See also Demodocus. 363.49
Alcmena The mother of Hercules, wife of Amphitryon, whom she cuckolded by sleeping with Jove. 82.51, 88.328, 334.128
Alecto One of the Furies. 307.74
Alexander the Great (356–323 BC) King of Macedonia and ruler of Greece, conqueror of most of the east. His sweat was said to be perfumed. 218.27, 223.48
Aloeus The husband of the woman by whom Neptune fathered the giants Othe and Ephialt. 334.134
Alpheus A river in Arcadia in which Arethusa bathed. The two were invoked as muses of pastoral poetry. 325.132
Amphion By the power of his music he moved stones to build Thebes' walls. 240.17, 290.11
Amphitrio Amphitryon, husband of Alcmena. 334.128
Anacreon (*c.* 570–? BC) A Greek lyric love-poet. 233.31, 365.32
Andromache The wife of Hector, whose death she mourns in Homer's *Iliad* Book 24. 307.108
Antigone The daughter of Laomedon, turned into a crane. 334.103
Antiope The mother of Amphion and Zethus, pursued by Jove in the form of a satyr. 82.64, 334.127
Aonia The country in which Mount Helicon stood. 355.7
Aphrodite The Greek goddess of love, Venus. 88.103
Apollo Phoebus, god of poetry, music, light, archery, prophecy and healing; son of Jove. He was associated with driving the chariot of the sun, playing a golden lyre and wearing a laurel wreath because of his seduction of Daphne. See also Clarius, Sol. 27.15, 95.166, 95 (end sonnet).2, 99.6, 142.10, 165.24, 193.63, 206.2, 217.29, 223.49, 270.176, 332.19, 354.23, 361.46, 362.86, 363.37, 365.98
Arachne A Lydian woman who hanged herself after Minerva tore up her perfect weaving and needlework; she was turned into a spider. 80.70, **82, 334,** 358.2
Arcadia The centre of the Peloponnese, inhabited by Pan and by musical shepherds; later it was thought of as a paradisal land of nymphs and shepherds. See also Alpheus, Ladon. **14, 64, 181,** 265.54
Archimedes (*c.* 287–212 BC) A Greek mathematician and inventor. 74.11
Areta The daughter of Aristippus of Cyrene, himself a pupil of Socrates; the

Cyrenaic school taught the importance of the immediate moment and pleasure. 359.46

Arethusa A nymph of Diana's train who, pursued to Sicily by the god of the river Alpheus, was transformed into a fountain. 79.5, 325.85

Argus A herdsman with a hundred eyes who was set to watch Io; killed by Mercury, his eyes were placed in the peacock's tail. 72.42, 73.19, 99.388, 265.151, 313.57

Ariadne Married to Theseus, whom she helped out of the Minotaur's labyrinth, she was later given a crown by Bacchus, which turned into a constellation after her death. 145.1, 348.28

Arion A Greek lyric poet whose song moved a dolphin to save him from drowning. 99.718, 325.164

Aristotle (384–322 BC) A Greek philosopher. 225.101, 295.11

Arne The daughter of Aeolus, loved by Neptune when he took the form of a bull. 82.128

Arriminum Rimini in modern Italy. 340.5

Ascanius The son of Aeneas. See also Iulus. 333.30

Ashtaroth The Syrian Astarte, goddess of love, associated with Venus. 270.200

Aspatia A Greek teacher of rhetoric, said to have been a friend of Socrates; mistress of Pericles. 359.44

Asteria The daughter of the Titans and mother of Hecate; pursued by Jove, she turned into a quail and became the island Delos. 82.57, 334.124

Astraea Goddess of justice; she lived on earth during the golden age but fled to the heavens because of man's wickedness. 1.15, 270.141

Athens The chief city of Greece. 334.76

Atlanta Atalanta, a virgin huntress who outran her suitors until, in a race, Hippomenes dropped the golden apples of the Hesperides in her path and she could not resist stopping to pick them up. 96.36

Atlas One of the Titans, he held up the heavens, or the world, on his shoulders; he was identified with the Atlas mountains in North Africa. 42.52, 165.10, 182.142, 342.30

Atrides The sons of Atreus: Agamemnon and Menelaus, the theft of whose wife, Helen, began the wars between the Greeks and the Trojans. 290.60

Atropos The oldest of the Fates; she was blind and with scissors cut the threads of life which her sisters had spun; Milton conflates her with the avenging Furies. 325.75

Augustus (63 BC–AD 14) The first Roman emperor, the peace of whose reign after a long period of civil war was praised by many poets. 40.50

Aurora Goddess of dawn, married to Tithonus. See also Caephalus. 79.7, 88.75, 99.571, 170.18, 198.1, 204.19, 206.3, 333.1, 339.3

Bacchus The Roman name for the Greek god Dionysus, god of wine and ecstasy. 82.141, 88.255, 99.139, 190.11, 204.16, 223.23, 241.14, 334.148

Bellerus The name invented by Milton for the ruler of Cornwall, supposedly a descendant of Brutus. 325.160

Bellona The goddess of war and wife of Mars. 42.79

Berenice (*c.* 273–? BC) Pledged her hair to the gods for the safe return of her husband; the hair disappeared and Jove or Venus was said to have turned it into a constellation. 168.14

Bisaltis Theophane's family name. 82.126

Boreas The north wind. 221.16

Brennus Leader of the Gauls and invader of Italy; his failure to capture the Capitol in Rome in 390 BC was attributed to the warning given by the geese that lived there. 212.4

Brutus First King of Britain, great-grandson of Aeneas. See also Albanact. 6.5, 42.67, 179.2

Caephalus The husband of Procris; he resisted Aurora's advances after she had abducted him. 339.33

Caesar Gaius Julius Caesar (100–44 BC), conqueror of Gaul and of Britain in 55–54 BC. The name 'Caesar' subsequently came to be used as a title. 42.67, 45.23, 101, 54.13, 223.38, 340.18

Calliope The Muse of epic poetry, said to be the mother of Orpheus. 325.58

Candia The Renaissance name for Crete. 332.23

Capitol One of the hills on which Rome was built. 45.68

Carthage A city in North Africa. 332.7, 340.28

Cassandra A prophetess (the daughter of Priam and Hecuba) who foretold the fall of Troy. 60.114

Cassiopeia As a punishment for her pride, after her death she was placed in the heavens on her back with her feet in the air as a constellation. 168.15

Castor The brother of Pollux; together they form the Gemini or Dioscuri. 315.93

Cato, Marcus Porcius (234–149 BC) A politician and writer, to whom the *Dicta Catonis* ('Sayings of Cato'), a collection of moral maxims, were attributed; they were much used in schools during the Middle Ages and the Renaissance. 361.20

Cato of Utica (95–46 BC) A Stoic and opponent of Julius Caesar; he committed suicide. 223.38

Centaurs Creatures, half man and half horse, who tried to rape the women of their neighbours in Thessaly, the Lapiths. 82.140, 342.18, 348.31

Cerberus Pluto's dog, the guardian of Hades, who lived by the river Styx. 204.2, 307.85, 342.45

Ceres The goddess of corn and harvest, she often bore a cornucopia of fruit and flowers. 187.22, 241.14, 334.138, 343.36, 358.13

Charon The ferryman who took the souls of the dead across the river Styx in Hades. 252.49

Chimera A three-headed monster made out of lion, goat and dragon; the sister of Hydra. 342.21

Chiron A centaur. 334.150
Cicero, Marcus Tullius (106–43 BC) A Roman orator and statesman. 225.26
Cileno Silenos were satyrs, companions of Bacchus. 342.17
Cimbrians Inhabitants of northern Germany. 340.28
Cimmeria A people thought to live on the edge of the world in permanent darkness and mist, or in caves. 204.10
Cinyras King of Cyprus and father of Adonis. 334.109
Circe A magician, enchantress and seductress who turned Ulysses' men into swine. 18.18, 29.69, 80.140, 99.61
Clarius Apollo, named after a grove and oracle in Ionia. 355.9
Cleobulina The daughter of Cleobis of Lindus, and writer of verse riddles. 359.37
Climene The mother of Phaethon. 82.92
Clio The Muse of history. 27.4
Cloris Chloris, the Greek name for Flora. 154.21
Clotho One of the Fates – the 'spinner', who held the distaff. 310.31
Cocytus One of the rivers of Hades, its name meant 'weeping'. 342.47
Colchos A country at the eastern end of the Black Sea, the home of Medea and the Golden Fleece. See also Jason. 99.56
Colophon A town in Lydia, near the sea. 334.3
Colossus A gigantic statue of the sun-god, Helios, that stood astride the entrance to the harbour at Rhodes. 156.8, 352.21
Corinna A woman, the subject of many of Ovid's *Amores*. 125.69
Cornelia The daughter of Scipio Africanus and mother of the Gracchi, she was famous as a letter-writer. 359.41
Coronis The sister of Ixion and mother by Jove of Aesculapius; she was transformed into a sweet-briar. 82.83
Cretes Cretans, inhabitants of Crete. 333.20
Croesus The extraordinarily wealthy King of Lydia. 60.130
Cupid The god of love, son of Venus, usually represented either as a warrior or as being blind, with a bow and arrows: the golden arrows are of love, the leaden ones of scorn or disdain. 19.7, 59.2, 61.12, 67.13, 68.8, 71.34, 73.12, **74**, 76.2, 77.13, 78.5, 82.14, 94.6, 95.174, 99.37, 125.51, **141**, 145.88, **146**, 156.35, 163.21
Cybele The goddess of nature and fertility, mother of a hundred gods. 42.60
Cyclops One-eyed giants who helped Vulcan forge his iron net. 99.152
Cynick Cynic, an adherent of a loosely held set of beliefs of the 4th century BC, that the pleasures of life were unimportant and that self-sufficiency brought contentment. 352.70
Cynthia A name for Diana, goddess of the moon, from her birthplace at Cynthus. **21**, 88.374, 99.59, 213.18, 270.103
Cynthus A hill on the island of Delos. See also Zanthus. 332.26
Cytheron An island where Venus landed after she was born from the sea. 81.4

Danae The daughter of the King of Argos, who imprisoned her in a bronze tower;

Jove came to her in the form of a golden shower and she became the mother of Perseus. 82.29, 95.193, 99.146, 334.130

Daphne A nymph who, pursued by Apollo, prayed for her deliverance and was transformed into a laurel tree. 82.79, **159**, 217.29

Dardan Dardania – Troy and its lands. 101.71

Delos An island in the Aegean, the birthplace of Apollo and Diana. 332.21, 333.18

Delphos, Delphic The location and name of the oracle of Apollo. 270.178, 365.22

Demodocus A bard at the court of King Alcinous. 363.48

Demophila A lyric poet of Pamphylia and friend of the Greek lyric poet Sappho. 359.37

Deucalion King of Thessaly, father of Melantho. 82.131

Diana The virgin goddess of chastity, the moon, woods, hunting and childbirth; she was often represented with her train of nymphs (with whom she might be bathing), or with hounds and carrying a bow and arrows. See also Cynthia, Phoebe. **18**, 64.8, 68.6, 79.1, 99.284, 149.13

Dido Queen of Carthage, who killed herself after she was deserted by her lover Aeneas. 60.34, **332, 333**

Dioscuri Castor and Pollux. 315.93

Dis The ruler of Hades. See also Pluto. 99.810

Doric In architecture, the oldest style of column, fluted and tapering towards a plain, square, capital; in poetry, a rustic style suitable for pastoral. 185.5, 325.189

Dryopes Inhabitants of Epirus. 332.23, 333.20

Elysium The Elysian Fields, originally the Isles of the Blest where the gods' favourite heroes enjoyed a blissful afterlife; later, part of Hades where souls rested before being reborn. 99.411, 156.2, 175.17, 204.147, **362**

Endymion A shepherd, loved by Diana, famous for his eternal youth and eternal sleep on Mount Latmus. 88.380, 99.59, 339.43

Enipeus A river god. 334.134

Ephialt A giant, son of Neptune; attacker of the gods with his brother Othe. 334.135

Ericyne A name for Venus, from her shrine on Mount Eryx. 99.789

Eridanus The amber-bearing river into which Phaethon fell. Later identified with the River Po. 42.193

Erigone The daughter of Icarius of Attica; she hanged herself on his death caused by peasants to whom he had given wine. 82.139 (probably for Philyra), 334.147

Erinnys The Furies. 40.2

Etna A volcano on Sicily, the site of Vulcan's forge. 241.28, 342.41

Euclid (*c*. 300 BC) A Greek mathematician. 213.6

Euphrosyne Mirth – one of the Graces. 204.12, 348.115

Europa Loved by Jove in the form of a bull; she climbed on its back and the two swam to Crete. 82.24, 99.149, 334.118

Eurydice The dead wife of Orpheus, whose charmed lyre allowed him to rescue her from Hades as long as he did not look back at her; he did so and lost her for ever. 88.16, 204.150

Eurynome The mother of the Graces. 348.110

Fates The Destinies or Parcae – three goddesses who ruled over the life of man; Clotho and Lachesis spun the thread of human life and Atropos cut it with her scissors or knife. 99.377

Faunus A god of the country, especially of agriculture. 42.235

Favonius The west wind, Zephyr. 243.6

Flamens Roman priests. 270.194

Flora Goddess of flowers and gardens. See also Chloris, Zephyr. 182.31, 206.17, 358.40, 362.61

Furies The Eumenides – the merciless avengers and punishers of human wrong-doing and crimes; they were Alecto, Megera and Tisiphone; snakes were entwined in their hair. 342.46

Ganymede The beautiful cup-bearer to Jove who took the form of an eagle to snatch him from Mount Ida. 82.58, 99.62, 341.79

Gemini The heavenly twins or Dioscuri, Castor and Pollux. 128.18

Genius A man's guardian spirit; the spirit of a place. 270.186, 325.183

Glaucus One of the leaders of the Trojan's allies. 344.16

Gnidus Cnidus, a hill and town sacred to Venus. 81.5

Gorgons Three sisters, of whom at least one, Medusa, had serpents for hair and turned those who looked on her to stone. 342.18

Graces Three daughters of Jove – Aglaia, Euphrosyne and Thalia; companions of Venus and the Muses, they gave pleasure to life and were often represented as naked and holding hands while dancing in a circle. See also Acidale, Aglaia, Euphrosyne, Eurynome. 88.103, 99.501, 124.142, 165.24, 175.4, 204.15, 348.21, 362.95

Hades The underworld, the realm of the dead. See Acheron, Charon, Cocytus, Dis, Elysium, Eurydice, Hecate, Lethe, Orpheus, Proserpina, Pluto, Sisyphus, Stygia, Tantalus.

Hammon The name in Libya, where he was worshipped as a ram, for Jove. 270.203

Hannibal (247–182 BC) Leader of the Carthaginian forces against Rome. 45.102, 49.4, 315.3

Harpy A monstrous winged creature with the body of a vulture and the face of a woman, it defiled the food it preyed on. 99.754

Hebe The beautiful goddess of youth, Ganymede's predecessor as cup-bearer to Jove. 88.405, 99.434, 204.29, 363.38

Hebrus A river in Thrace. 325.63

Hecate A goddess of Hades, especially associated with magic and sorcery. 334.165

Hector A son of Priam and leader of the Trojans against the Greeks. 101.65, 307.108, 344.2

Hecuba Priam's wife. 101.82

Helen The beautiful wife of Menelaus, her seduction by Paris began the wars between the Trojans and the Greeks. 60.97, 101.4, 229.29

Helicon A mountain, one of the favourite seats of the Muses. See also Pegasus. 42.3

Helle In flight from her father's house, on the back of a ram provided by Neptune, she fell into the sea which was named the Hellespont after her. 82.23, 99.663

Hellespont The Dardanelles – straits named after Helle, with the towns Sestos and Abydos on either side. 99.1, 124.20

Heme Haemus, King of Thrace; he and his wife Rhodope were turned into mountains as a punishment for their pride. 334.96

Hercules, Heracles The heroic son of Jove and Alcmena, grandson of Alcaeus. Brought up at Thebes, he completed the twelve labours imposed on him by his brother with the help of the gods. Other stories tell of his strangling two snakes sent to kill him while he was still in his cradle and of his capture by the Amazon Omphale, who made him wear women's clothes and perform women's tasks. The Pillars of Hercules, at the straits of Gibraltar, marked the limits of the western world. See also Alcides. 88.329, 95.301, 99.781, 194.12, 229.1, 270.227, 307.87, 326.3, 334.129

Hermes Mercury. 99.421, 329.16

Hero A priestess of Venus at Sestos, loved by Leander. 21.488, **99**, **124**

Hesiod (*c.* 700 BC) One of the earliest Greek poets. 361.144

Hesper, Hesperus Vesper, the evening star, the planet Venus. 88.95, 99.813, 241.33, 313.56, 325.30

Hesperides Guardians of the golden apples which Juno gave Jove on their wedding day; they were also guarded by a dragon which never slept. One of Hercules' labours was to get three of the apples. 99.782, 194.60

Hippocrene A fountain at the foot of Mount Helicon, sacred to the Muses. 354.20

Hippolitus The son of Theseus, he rejected the advances of his stepmother Phaedra. 99.77

Homer (8th century BC) The reputedly blind author of the *Odyssey* and *Iliad*; seven cities claimed his birthplace. 42.70, **344**, **356**, 361.81

Horace (65–8 BC) A Roman poet. **45**, 233.31, **345**

Hours, Horae Three daughters of Jove and attendants of Venus and the Muses, representing the seasons spring, summer and winter. 88.98, 124.142, 190.40

Hyacinth, Hyacinthus A Spartan youth loved by Jove; jealous of his love, Zephyrus killed him and Jove transformed him into a light-blue flower bearing the letters '*ai, ai*' – 'alas, alas'. 82.82, 325.106

Hydra A many-headed monster, sister of Chimera. 342.20

Hymen The god of marriage; he is often represented as carrying flowers and a torch and wearing a purple robe. 88.25, 99.258, 204.125

Hypatia (AD ?–415) A female Greek mathematician and philosopher. 359.43
Hypep Hypaepae, a village in Lydia. 334.7

Ida A mountain near Troy, where Jove snatched Ganymede. 82.59
Idalia A region in Cyprus. 99.148
Idmon The father of Arachne. 334.3
Ilion A fortress or town of Troy. 101.5, 289.1
Io One of Jove's loves, transformed into a cow and watched over by Argus. 99.388
Ionic In architecture, a thin, fluted style of column tapering towards a capital decorated with spiral scrolls. 185.6
Iphimedia A lover of Neptune, by whom she had Othe and Ephialt. 82.127
Iris A messenger to Juno; associated with the rainbow, she severed the thread that kept soul and body together. 82.179, 209.17, 265.144, 358.10
Isse A shepherdess loved by Jove, who dressed up as a shepherd to win her. 82.100, 334.146
Iulus Ascanius, son of Aeneas: the form of the name indicated the descent of the Julian family from Aeneas; his grandmother was supposedly Venus. 332.16, 333.14
Ixion The father by Juno of the race of Centaurs. 99.114

Japhet A Titan, father of mankind. 355.27
Jason Won the Golden Fleece with the help of Medea, for whom he abandoned Hypsipyle, the mother of his twins. See also Colchos. 60.41
Jove Jupiter, Zeus, chief of the gods. See also Hammon. 40.13, 42.195, 82.19, 88.99, 94.14, 99.62, 184.2, 187.62, 313.62, 325.16, 326.3, 334.79, 339.45, 344.3, 355.30, 361.46
Juno The wife of Jove, goddess of marriage and childbirth. 79.20, 82.47, 88.390, 124.104, 332.50, 333.40, 334.98
Jupiter Jove. 99.464, 307.92

Ladon A river in Arcadia. 265.56
Laomedon Priam's treacherous father; he refused to pay Apollo and Poseidon (Neptune), who, as a punishment, had been made to build Troy for him. 290.57, 334.106
Lapiths A Greek tribe of Thessaly. See also Centaurs. 348.32
Lares, Lars Roman gods of the household. 208.36, 270.191
Latmus The mountain where Diana slept with Endymion. 99.109
Leander The lover of Hero. 21.487, **99, 124**
Leda The mother of Helen and the Dioscuri, loved by Jove in the form of a swan. 82.38, 334.125
Lemures Malignant spirits of the dead in households. 270.191
Lesbos An island in the Aegean. 325.63
Lethe A river of forgetfulness and oblivion in Hades. 175.23, 192.53, 313.27

Livy (59 BC – AD 17) A Roman historian. 223.40, 233.22

Lucan (AD 39–65) A Roman poet. He committed suicide after being implicated in a conspiracy to kill the emperor Nero. **38, 340, 357**

Lucifer The morning star, the planet Venus. 64.9, 270.74, 333.15, 340.4

Lucretia The wife of L. Tarquinius Collatinus, she was raped by Sextus, the son of Tarquinius Superbus, and, having revealed this to her husband, took her own life. 60.101, **101**

Lybical Of Libya in North Africa. 333.47

Lycia An area in south-west Asia Minor, where Jove was the principal god; its inhabitants were famous for their archery. 332.19, 333.17, 344.18

Lydia A wealthy country in Asia Minor, famous for its gentle music. 204.136, 334.8, 358.2

Macarie Macareus, father of Isse and a follower of Ulysses. 334.146

Maia May, mother of Mercury by Jove. 88.307, 291.78, 352.83

Mars The god of war and lover of Venus. 42.39, 82.77, 99.151, 100.98, 109.7, 141.6, 313.61, 334.76

Masile Massylia, an area inhabited by a north-African tribe. 332.5

Medea An enchantress who helped her lover Jason win the Golden Fleece. See also Colchos. 60.45

Medusa One of the Gorgons, her child by Poseidon (Neptune), Pegasus, emerged out of her neck. 82.134, 88.190, 307.76, 334.138

Megera One of the Furies. 307.78

Melantho The daughter of Deucalion. 82.131, 334.140

Memnon The son of Aurora and Tithonus, killed in the Trojan war; a flight of birds issued from his funeral pyre, half of which were consumed in it: they returned to his tomb each year and the process was repeated. 339.4

Memphis The former capital of Egypt, famous for its temples dedicated to Osiris. 218.36, 270.214

Mercury The messenger of the gods, god of oratory, patron of thieves and pick-pockets, son of Jove; he was often represented carrying a caduceus, a baton entwined with snakes, with which he put men to sleep and conducted them to Hades. See also Hermes. 64.7, 99.386, 313.57

Midas A Phrygian king for whom everything he touched turned to gold; unwisely judging the playing of Pan to be superior to the music of Apollo, he became a type of the rich philistine. 99.475, 223.48

Migdonie Mygdonia, a country in Asia Minor. 334.46

Mincius A tributary of the river Po; Virgil was born by it at Mantua. 325.86

Minerva Pallas Athene, goddess of war, wisdom, arts and trades, and justice; she sprang fully formed from Jove's head and was one of the contenders in the judgement of Paris. 310.17, **334**, 355.30, 358.5

Minotaur A monster with a man's body and a bull's head, kept in a maze or labyrinth on Crete and fed on young men and women; it was killed by Theseus. 145.1

Mnemosyne The goddess of memory, the mother by Jove of the Muses. 82.66, 334.131

Morpheus The god of sleep. 99.349

Musaeus (5th century AD) The author of an epic poem about Hero and Leander. 99.52, 361.144

Muses The nine daughters of Jove and Mnemosyne; they presided over literature, music and dance from their seats at Pieria and Mount Helicon. See also Aganippe, Calliope, Clio, Graces, Hours, Orpheus, Parnassus, Thalia, Thespia, Urania. 42.6, 88.1, 99.476, 310,13, 325.15, 354.41, 356.3, 358.76, 361.46, 362.93, 365.25, 369.15

Narcissus Tried to kiss his own reflection in water and either drowned or eventually killed himself and was turned into a flower. 42.214, 99.73, 100.161

Neptune The god of the sea, usually represented with a trident and sometimes riding a chariot drawn by dolphins. See also Laomedon, Medusa, Pegasus. 60.58, 79.11, 82.109, 99.3, 180.12, 290.58, 325.90, 334.77, 363.43

Nestor The ancient elder statesman of the Greeks in the Trojan war. 60.126, 101.36

Nilus The river Nile. 27.12

Niobe The wife of Amphion; when her children were killed, she was changed into a stone and wept constantly. 163.12, 317.10

Olympus A mountain, the seat of the gods. 99.454

Ops The goddess of abundance. 99.456

Orpheus The son of one of the Muses, perhaps Calliope; his playing of the lyre could charm wild animals and his music could make stones and trees move. He failed on his mission to rescue Eurydice from Hades. 88.16, 204.145, 240.12, 290.15, 325.58, 365.40

Othe A giant son of Neptune; attacker of the gods with his brother Ephialt. 334.135

Ovid (43 BC – AD 17) A Roman poet. 95.124, 125.68, **334**, **339**, 361.158, 365.66

Pactolus A river in Lydia whose sands were supposed to be golden. 42.165, 334.11

Pallas Minerva. 61.6, 79.22, 99.321, 184.2, 229.2, 334.19, 354.30

Pan The god of shepherds, the country and huntsmen, son of Jove or Mercury, but brought up by Bacchus; usually represented with the body of a man and the ears, legs and horns of a goat and playing a pipe of seven reeds. See also Arcadia, Midas, Syrinx. 182.54, 187.21, 190.11, 217.31, 223.48, 265.55, 270.89

Panope A water-nymph, called upon by sailors in storms or after safe voyages. 325.99

Paphos A city in Cyprus where Venus was born. 81.4

Paris A son of Priam, his elopement with Helen began the war between the Greeks and the Trojans. 60.74, 101.108, 229.31

Parnassus A mountain sacred to Jove and the Muses. 42.2, 310.23, 354.17, 361.40

Parthians A warrior nation of western Asia. 340.3

Pegasus A winged horse, sprung from the blood of Medusa when she was pregnant by Poseidon (Neptune); the fountain Hippocrene on Mount Helicon was started by a blow from his hoof, and his flight was associated with the composition of poetry. 82.135, 334.139, 354.19, 361.38

Pelops The son of Tantalus, who served his body to the gods; all refused the food except Ceres, who ate his shoulder. Jove restored him to life, replacing the missing part with ivory. 99.65

Penates Roman household gods. 190.79

Penelope The wife of Ulysses; during his twenty years' absence, she maintained she could not remarry until she had finished weaving a shroud for her husband's father: every night she unravelled the day's work. 60.99, **83**, 229.25

Pericles (*c.* 495–429 BC) A ruler of Athens. 359.45

Phaethon The son of Apollo; when he asked to drive his father's chariot of the sun for one day, the horses got out of control, the earth was nearly burned up and Phaethon fell into the river Eridanus. 82.91, 99.101, 183.109

Phebus See Phoebus.

Philemon With his wife, Baucis, he was visited by the disguised Jove and Mercury; although poor, they entertained the gods well and were rewarded by seeing their cottage transformed into a rich temple. 187.61

Philomela, Philomel Raped by her brother-in-law Tereus, King of Thrace, her tongue was also cut out; she depicted her ordeal in a tapestry and was eventually transformed into a swallow or nightingale. 21.28, 35.11, 63.9, 189.31, 362.15

Philyra Caught by Saturn's wife with her husband, she was changed into a horse and eventually into a lime-tree. 82.142 (probably for Erigone)

Phlegrea The place in Macedonia where the giants attacked the gods and were repulsed by Hercules. 342.101

Phoebe Diana, the moon. 88.149

Phoebus Apollo. 21.97, 82.73, 88.77, 95.160, 124.24, **159**, 183.98, 189.64, 191.96, 213.20, 265.167, 310.18, 325.77, 333.18, 334.67, 354.40, 361.34, 362.23

Phoenix A hermaphroditic, solitary and unique Arabian bird said to make its nest in a palm-tree every five hundred years and then die being consumed by fire; from its funeral pyre a new phoenix rises and flies off to the sun. The bird's ambiguous sexual nature made it a useful emblem of duality. 104.4, 134.23, 189.44, **312**

Phrygia A pastoral country in Turkey, invaded by the Lydians and famous for its invention of the reed-pipe. 101.137, 256.62, 358.19

Pieria The birthplace of the Muses and Orpheus near Mount Olympus. 361.130

Pindar (518 – *c.* 446 BC) A Greek lyric poet. **315**, 365.33, **373**

Plato (427–347 BC) A Greek philosopher. **163**, 185.34

Plautus (*c.* 250–184 BC) A Roman writer of comedies. 352.52, 361.135

Pluto King of Hades. See also Dis, Plutus. 204.149, 307.72, 342.9

Plutus The god of wealth. See also Pluto. 99.810

Pollux The brother of Castor: together they form the Gemini or Dioscuri. 315.93

Polyphemus A one-eyed giant, strongest of the Cyclops, blinded by Ulysses. 342.22

Pompey (106–48 BC) A Roman general, the opponent of Caesar. 47.23

Priam King of Troy, married to Hecuba and father to Hector and Paris; he was murdered by Neoptolemus. 101.2, 229.34

Priapus The god of gardens and fertility, his symbol was a phallus. 95.247, 352.45

Prometheus The son of Japetus (Japhet), he restored fire to the earth from the sun after Jove had taken it from man as a punishment; Jove condemned him to be chained to a rock and have his liver eaten by an eagle for thirty thousand years. 99.438, 355.27, 365.23

Proserpina Queen of Hades and the wife of Pluto, who carried her off while she was gathering flowers; she spent half the year with Pluto and half with Demeter on earth. 82.67, 307.83, 334.132

Proteus Neptune's son; he was able to change his shape at will. 99.137

Pueriles A collection of proverbial Latin phrases used as a school textbook. 361.19

Pygmalion King of Cyprus who, finding all women fell short of his ideal, made a marble statue with which he fell in love; Venus answered his prayer, gave it life and he married it. **90**, 163.10

Pyramus The tragic lover of Thisbe. 307.21

Pyrrhus (319–272 BC) King of Epirus, he defeated the Romans but failed to take advantage of his victory. 49.4

Pyrrhus Neoptolemus, son of Achilles, the Greek warrior who killed Priam. 101.84

Pythagoras (6th century BC) A Greek philosopher and mathematician; among the stories told about him was one that he had a golden thigh. 124.60

Rodope Rhodope, a mountain range in Thrace named after the wife of Haemus (Heme). 334.96

Sabaea Sheba, famous for its gold and spices. 168.11

Saguntum A city in Spain which Hannibal besieged in 219 BC, precipitating war with Rome; according to the Roman writer on natural history Pliny the elder, a child returned to its mother's womb immediately after birth during the siege. 315.1

Salmacis A nymph who, hugging her beloved Hermaphroditus, had her prayer for lasting union answered and the two were transformed into a hermaphrodite. 99.530

Sardanapalus The last King of the Assyrians. 8.1

Sardis The ancient capital of Lydia. 358.9

Sarpedon One of the leaders of the Trojans' allies. 344.4

Saturn The god of Time, father of Jove, Pluto, Neptune, Juno and Ceres as well as of other children that he devoured; the golden age of his reign gave way to that of Jove. 82.136, 99.452, 313.62, 334.149

Scilla Scylla; she was changed by Circe, whose love for Scylla's lover Glaucus was unrequited, into a hideous sea-monster and eventually into a rock opposite the whirlpool Charybdis. **227**, 342.19

Scythians A barbarous and warlike northern nation famous for their mounted archers. 213.43

Semele Was killed by her lover Jove's lightning when she wanted to see him in his real form. 82.46

Seneca (*c*. 4 BC – AD 65) A Roman philosopher and writer of tragedies. **44**, 361.135

Sestos The birthplace of Hero. 21.487, 99.4

Sidonical From a Phoenician city near Tyre, famous for its purple dye. 333.11

Simois A Trojan river. 101.72

Sinon The deviser of the wooden horse of Troy and so usually associated with treachery. 60.28, 101.136

Sirius The dog-star, associated with heat or drought and a presage of destruction. 325.138

Sisyphus Punished in Hades with eternally having to roll a large stone to the top of a hill; whenever he reached the top, it rolled back down again. 99.761

Socrates (469–399 BC) A Greek philosopher. 307.99

Sol The sun, Apollo. 355.28

Spartans Inhabitants of Laconia in the Peloponnese, famous for the simple austerity of their way of life and their fierceness as fighters. 29.8, 149.8

Sphinx A monster made up of parts of a woman, a dog, a serpent, a bird and a lion; it ate those unable to answer its riddles. 342.18

Stygia The river Styx, which encircled Hades. 95.272, 99.458, 204.3, 342.40

Sulpicia (1st century BC) A Roman woman poet. 307.148

Sybarite An inhabitant of the Greek colony Sybaris, famous for its luxury and wealth. 185.28

Sylvanus A wood god who loved Cyparissus; she changed into a cypress tree, of which Sylvanus often carries a bough. 42.235, 99.154

Syrens Sirens, sea-nymphs whose singing was so seductive that men listening to them forgot to eat and died. 347.19

Syrinx A nymph changed into a reed while being pursued by Pan, who later used the reed in his pipes. 217.31, 265.55

Tacitus (AD *c*. 56 – *c*. 117) A Roman historian. 233.21

Tagus A river in Spain whose sands were supposed to be golden. 6.1, 42.165

Tanais The river Don. 27.14

Tantalus Was tormented in Hades by fruit just out of his reach and water that went away whenever he tried to drink it. 99.559, 140.13

Tarquinius Superbus, Sextus Son of the King of Rome. His rape of Lucretia led to the expulsion of his family from the city. 101.171

Telesilla A woman poet of the fifth century BC; she armed the women of Argos after the men had been defeated by the Spartans. 359.38

Tempe A paradisal valley in Thessaly. 88.308

Terence (193 or 183–159 BC) A writer of Roman comedies. 352.52

Thalia The Muse of comic and pastoral poetry. 204.15, 348.116

Thammuz Adonis. 270.204

Theocritus (3rd century BC) Greek poet born in Sicily, the founder of pastoral poetry. 325.133

Theophane Bisaltis A woman loved by Neptune; to keep her other suitors away, he turned her into a ewe and himself into a ram. See also Bisaltis. 334.136

Thereus Tereus, the husband of Procne the sister of Philomel. 63.8

Theseus King of Athens; husband of Ariadne, Antiope and Phaedra; killer of the Minotaur; he sought Proserpina in Hades. See also Hippolitus. 60.37, 145.1, 307.86, 348.30

Thespia A town near the foot of Mount Helicon. 233.33, 355.8, 361.105

Thetis A goddess of the sea, wife of Peleus (son of Aeacus) and mother of Achilles; the origins of the Trojan war were laid at her wedding. See also Aeacidee. 27.9, 79.10, 99.687, 348.113

Thisbe Killed herself when she found her lover Pyramus dead. 60.102, 307.21

Thrace A warlike country. 99.81

Time Saturn. 88.281

Titan Hyperion, the sun; one of the Titans, who were the children of heaven and earth. They rebelled against the gods and were eventually overthrown by Jove. See also Asteria, Japhet. 100.177, 206.25, 310.24, 342.58

Tithonus Begged Aurora for immortality, which she granted without adding youth and beauty; he grew immensely old but did not die and was eventually transformed into a cicada. See also Memnon. 88.75, 339.1

Tmolus A mountain in Lydia. 334.9

Triton A merman, usually represented blowing on a conch shell. 99.640, 325.89

Troilus The Trojan lover of Cressida. 60.77, 101.121

Troy The town where the Trojans were besieged by the Greeks. 60.75, 99.153, **101**, 229.24, 334.106

Tyre, Tyrian (Of) a city on the coast of Phoenicia, famous for its purple dyes which were extracted from a local shellfish. 270.204, 332.12, 333.36, 334.65, 358.20

Ulysses Odysseus, joined the Greeks in the siege of Troy; his adventures on the way home to his wife Penelope are the subject of Homer's *Odyssey*. 83.1, 101.29, 363.50

Urania The Muse of astronomy, and later of Christian inspiration and heavenly poetry. 270.15

Venus The goddess of gardens, love, beauty and fertility. Daughter of Jove, she was born emerging from the sea. Married to Vulcan, she loved, among others

Adonis and was Cupid's mother. See also Aeneas, Aphrodite, Ashtaroth, Ericyne, Graces, Hesper, Iulus, Vesper. 42.39, 68.6, 79.19, 81.102, 82.70, 88.108, 95.43, 99.12, **100**, 125.52, 141.6, 145.114, 149.6, 156.38, 163.4, 170.34, 204.14, 209.5, 223.23, 227.14, 313.55, 332.46, 333.37, 348.47

Vesper Venus as the evening star. 313.56

Virgil (70–19 BC) A Roman poet. 40.48, 233.21, **332**, **333**, 361.37

Vulcan The god of fire, who, with the help of the Cyclops, forged a net in which he caught his wife Venus and her lover Mars. See also Cyclops, Etna. 73.24, 99.152

Xanthus A river on the plain of Troy. See also Zanth. 332.20, 344.22

Xenophon (*c.* 428 – *c.* 354 BC) A Greek historian, a disciple of Socrates. 307.98

Xerxes (5th century BC) A Persian king, reputed to have decorated a plane-tree with gold. 60.129

Zanth See Xanthus. 333.17

Zanthus See Cynthus. 333.22

Zephyr The west wind, husband of Flora. See also Favonius. 204.19

Zeus Jove. 28.3, 42.137–8

Appendix 4: Biographical Notes on Authors

These brief notes draw heavily on the *Dictionary of National Biography* and ed. Margaret Drabble, *The Oxford Companion to English Literature*, 5th edn, Oxford 1985; further information can be found in the standard editions referred to in the textual notes. References at the end of entries are to poem numbers.

Anne **Askew** (1521–46), Protestant martyr, came from a Lincolnshire family and was well educated and deeply read in the Bible. In 1545 she was investigated in London for heretical views about the sacraments, imprisoned in Newgate and the Tower and tortured. She was burned at the stake at Smithfield. The Protestant bishop John Bale (1495–1563) published two accounts of her examination and execution, which were first printed at Wesel in 1546 and 1547; she is one of the martyrs whose sufferings are described in John Foxe's *Acts and monuments*. Ballads about her survive from 1624 and later than 1692. 248

Alexander **Barclay** (1475?–1552) was probably of Scottish birth. Having been a priest in Devon and a monk in Ely and Canterbury, he ended his religious career as rector of All Hallows, Lombard Street in London. He translated Sebastian Brant's popular satire *The ship of fools*, 1509. 174

Barnabe **Barnes** (1571–1609), the son of Richard Barnes, Bishop of Durham, was educated at Brasenose College, Oxford. In 1591 he joined the Earl of Essex against the Duke of Parma, and in 1598 he avoided being sentenced for the attempted murder of the Recorder of Berwick with poisoned claret. His play *The divils charter* was published in 1607. 97

Richard **Barnfield** (1574–1620) was educated at Brasenose College, Oxford. As well as a collection of sonnets, *Cynthia*, 1595, he claimed the authorship of *The affectionate shepheard*, 1594, and *The encomion of Lady Pecunia*, 1598. Two of his poems appeared in the volume *The passionate pilgrim*, 1599, whose authorship is attributed to Shakespeare on its title-page. See Harry Morris, *Richard Barnfield, Colin's Child*, Tampa 1963. 102–3

William **Birch** (fl. 1558–71). Five ballads published under his name and printed between 1563 and 1571 survive. Nothing appears to be known about his life. 12

Mark Alexander **Boyd** (1563–1601) was educated in Glasgow. Most of his work is in Latin and reflects his travels abroad in France and the Low Countries. He published volumes of poems and letters at Bordeaux in 1590 and a further collection of letters and poems at Antwerp in 1592. 78

Alexander **Brome** (1620–66) was an attorney in London and a royalist writer. As well as satires and a play, *The cunning lovers*, published in 1654, he was involved in the collaborative translation of Horace's poems of 1666. 51, 242

William **Browne** (1590?–1645?) was born at Tavistock and educated at Exeter College, Oxford. He entered the Inner Temple in 1611. As well as teaching for a time at Oxford, he also attached himself to the Herberts at Wilton, dedicating Book 2 of *Britannia's pastorals* to William Herbert, the third Earl, in 1616. He was a notable collector of medieval MSS. 37, 198, 317, 358

George **Buchanan** (1506–82) studied at St Andrews and in Paris. As a teacher, his pupils included the French essayist Montaigne and James VI of Scotland. He was perhaps the most important Latin poet and playwright from the British Isles in the Renaissance. See I. D. McFarlane, *Buchanan*, 1981. 175

Thomas **Campion** (1567–1620), musician and doctor, was born in London and educated at Peterhouse, Cambridge, and Gray's Inn. Later in life he studied medicine, receiving his MD from the University of Caen in 1605. As well as Latin poems, he wrote five volumes of airs, court entertainments under James I and poems on the death of Prince Henry. He may have been the author of five poems included in the first edition of Sidney's *Astrophil and Stella*, 1591. In his *Observations in the art of English poesie*, 1602, he defended the use of classical metres in English verse, thus provoking Samuel Daniel's reply in *A defence of ryme*, [1603]. See Edward Lowbury, Timothy Salter and Alison Young, *Thomas Campion: Poet, Composer, Physician*, 1970. 129–31, 237

Thomas **Carew** (1595?–1640), son of Sir Matthew Carew, a master in Chancery, was educated at Merton College, Oxford, and the Middle Temple. He acted as secretary to his cousin by marriage Sir Dudley Carleton at Venice and later The Hague, 1613–16, and in 1619 accompanied Edward Herbert, Lord Herbert of Cherbury (q.v.), on a diplomatic mission to France. He was a successful courtier; his important masque *Cœlum Britannicum* was performed before the King in 1634. See John Kerrigan, 'Thomas Carew', *Proceedings of the British Academy*, 74 (1988), 311–50. 154–6, 320, 365–6

Margaret **Cavendish** (1623–73), Duchess of Newcastle, daughter of Sir Thomas Lucas, was the second wife of William Cavendish (1592–1676). They married in 1645 in Paris, where Margaret Cavendish had accompanied Queen Henrietta Maria as a maid of honour, and lived in exile abroad until the Restoration. Returning to England, they lived quietly at Welbeck Abbey. Her unacted, closet-drama plays were published in 1662; her poems and *Philosophical letters*, 1664, reveal her interest in chemistry and natural philosophy. See Douglas Grant, *Margaret the First: A Biography of Margaret Cavendish Duchess of Newcastle*, 1957. 219–21, 371–2

George **Chapman** (1559?–1634) was born near Hitchin in Hertfordshire. He may have been educated at Oxford and may have fought as a soldier in France and the Low Countries. His earliest publications were non-dramatic poems, *The shadow of night*, 1594, and *Ovids banquet of sence*, 1595. From about 1596 to 1608 he worked in the theatre and then, with the patronage of Prince Henry and Robert Carr, Earl of Somerset, undertook his translations from Homer. See ed. Phyllis Brooks Bartlett, *The Poems of George Chapman*, New York and London 1941. 124, 344, 356

Thomas **Churchyard** (1520?–1604) was one of the most prolific of Elizabethan poets, starting his career as a page to Henry Howard, Earl of Surrey (q.v.). He served as a soldier in France and the Low Countries. His earliest extant works date from 1552; he contributed *Shores wife* to the collection *A myrrour for magistrates*, 1563, wrote much occasional verse and mourned Sidney's death; his verse paraphrase of Sidney's *A defence of poetry* was published in 1595. He was buried in St Margaret's, Westminster, near to John Skelton. 347

Laurence **Clarkson** (1615–67), born at Preston in Lancashire, served in the parliamentarian army; he was at various times a Presbyterian, Independent, Antinomian, Anabaptist, Seeker, Ranter and Muggletonian. He moved between East Anglia, Lincolnshire and London, where he died in prison for debt. He published several tracts between 1646 and 1660, one of which was condemned by order of the Commons to be burned by the hangman. His name is sometimes given as Claxton. 298

John **Cleveland** (1613–58) was born at Loughborough and educated at Christ's College, Cambridge; he stayed at Cambridge as a fellow of St John's from 1634 until about 1643, when, as a royalist, he left to join the King's camp at Oxford. After the fall in 1646 of Newark, where he was Judge Advocate to the garrison, he may have lived in London and Norwich, where he was arrested in 1655. He seems then to have spent some time living in Gray's Inn, before dying of fever. His poems were extremely popular throughout the seventeenth century. 41, 163

An **Collins** (fl. 1653), from her *Divine songs and meditacions*, seems to have sought consolation in religion from lifelong physical and mental afflictions. See ed. Germaine Greer etc., *Kissing the Rod*, 1988, p. 148. 305

Henry **Constable** (1562–1613) was educated at St John's College, Cambridge, and Lincoln's Inn. From 1583 to 1588, as Sir Francis Walsingham's emissary, he was in Scotland and Paris, from where he travelled throughout Europe. On his return to England he became friendly with Penelope Rich (Sir Philip Sidney's 'Stella'). By 1590 he had converted to Roman Catholicism and had probably abandoned writing secular poetry: his collection *Diana* was printed in 1592 and in an enlarged version in [1594]. He spent the next few years in Rome and Paris, with a visit to Scotland in 1599. Returning to England in 1603, he was imprisoned and lived in poverty until he went back to Paris in 1610. He died in Liège. 254

Richard **Corbett** (1582–1635) was educated at Westminster School and Christ Church, Oxford. He was a chaplain to James I, Dean of Christ Church, 1620–8, and successively Bishop of Oxford and, from 1632, of Norwich. He had a considerable contemporary reputation as a wit. 200

Abraham **Cowley** (1618–67) was the seventh, posthumous son of a London stationer. Educated at Westminster School and Trinity College, Cambridge, in 1643 he left Cambridge for Oxford and in 1644 went from there to Paris, where he was in the service of Henry Jermyn, one of Queen Henrietta Maria's courtiers. He returned to England in 1654, was briefly imprisoned, but was disappointed of some reward at the Restoration. A precociously gifted poet, he also wrote plays, an epic on the Civil War, essays and Latin verses. See Arthur H. Nethercot, *Abraham Cowley: The Muse's Hannibal*, Oxford 1931. 210, 373

Richard **Crashaw** (1612/13–49) was the son of the Puritan divine William Crashaw. Educated at Charterhouse and Pembroke Hall, Cambridge, he was a fellow of Peterhouse from 1635 to 1643. Crashaw came under the influence of the Anglican community at Little Gidding and subsequently converted to Roman Catholicism. In Paris, where Crashaw had fled by 1646, Abraham Cowley (q.v.) interested Queen Henrietta Maria in his career. With her help he went to Italy as attendant on Cardinal Palotta and then held a minor post at the Santa Casa of Loreto, where he died. Crashaw published a volume of Latin poems at Cambridge in 1634; the engravings in the collection *Carmen Deo nostro, te decet hymnus. Sacred poems*, Paris 1652, may be by his own hand. See Thomas F. Healy, *Richard Crashaw*, Leiden 1986. 209, 291–3

Robert **Crowley** (1518?–88) came from Gloucestershire and was educated at Magdalen College, Oxford. He was briefly a publisher, issuing three editions of *Piers Plowman* in 1550. A Protestant, under Queen Mary he went into exile, but returned to a rather troubled career in the Church of England. He published a verse translation of the Psalms in 1549, a collection of epigrams in 1550 and many controversial works. 10

Samuel **Daniel** (1563–1619) was educated at Magdalen Hall, Oxford. After Continental travels he gained the patronage first of the Countess of Pembroke and then of Fulke Greville (qq.v.) and the Earl of Devonshire. His command of genres from the sonnet sequence (*Delia*, 1592) through neoclassical tragedy (*Cleopatra*, 1594, revised 1607) to the historical poem (*The civile warres*, 1595, revised 1609) led to his being regarded by some as the *de facto* Poet Laureate on Spenser's death in 1599. Despite a *Panegyrike* of James I (1603), however, he came under suspicion early in his reign for alleged sympathy with the rebellious Earl of Essex in his tragedy *Philotas*, 1605, and, though the Queen continued to patronize him, he never fully regained favour with the King. A prose history of England occupied much of his later life.

See Joan Rees, *Samuel Daniel: A Critical and Biographical Study*, Liverpool 1964. 90–2, 194, 231, 353

Sir William **Davenant** (1606–68) served as page to the Duchess of Richmond and to Fulke Greville (q.v.). He made a career as dramatist and masque-writer and became effective Poet Laureate on the death of Ben Jonson (q.v.) in 1637. He fought for the royalists in the 1640s. While in exile in Paris he worked on his epic *Gondibert*, 1651, whose ambition of formulating a truly modernized poetic in the light of the latest thinking was greeted with respect by his friend Thomas Hobbes, and with ridicule by the wits. Captured by the parliamentarians in 1650, he made his peace with the regime after a period of imprisonment and was allowed to experiment with dramatic performances. On the Restoration, he became head of one of the two licensed theatrical companies. See Mary Edmond, *Rare Sir William Davenant: Poet Laureate, Playwright, Civil War General, Restoration Theatre Manager*, Manchester 1987. 201, 303, 370

Sir John **Davies** (1569–1626) was educated at Winchester and Queen's College, Oxford, and also studied on the Continent. He was one of a group of notoriously rowdy and irreverent wits at the Middle Temple; his poem *Orchestra*, 1596, may have been connected with Inns of Court revels. In 1598 he was expelled for assaulting a colleague. To regain favour he turned to didactic (*Nosce teipsum*, 1599) and panegyrical verse. In 1603 he was made Solicitor-General for Ireland, and he played a leading role in the Ulster plantation. 93–4, 184

Thomas **Dekker** (*c.* 1572–1632) was a prolific pamphleteer and professional dramatist; his works present the life of the city with a partly satirical and partly affectionate eye. See M.-T. Jones-Davies, *Un peintre de la vie londonienne, Thomas Dekker*, 2 vols., Paris 1958. 230

Thomas **Deloney** (*c.* 1543–1607?) began as a silk-weaver and became a prolific author of ballads and of prose narratives. 126, 229

Sir John **Denham** (1615–69) was educated at Trinity College, Oxford, and Lincoln's Inn. His play *The Sophy* and the celebrated political poem *Coopers Hill* appeared in 1642. He served the royalist cause as a soldier, as a satirical poet and, during the 1650s, in negotiations for the King's restoration; he was rewarded in 1660 by being appointed Charles II's Surveyor of the Works. See Brendan O Hehir, *Harmony From Discords: A Life of Sir John Denham*, Berkeley and Los Angeles 1968. 42

Robert **Devereux**, (1565–1601), second Earl of Essex, was the heir to the strongly Protestant political and cultural patronage network built up by the Earl of Leicester and Sir Philip Sidney (q.v.). His dashing but unstable career in the 1590s indicated the difficulties of sustaining this political alliance; disgraced after a disastrous campaign in Ireland, he staged a *coup d'état* in 1601 and was executed. See Robert Lacey, *Robert Earl of Essex, an Elizabethan Icarus*, 1971. 30

John **Donne** (1572–1631) was the son of a London ironmonger; his mother, a lifelong Catholic, was the daughter of John Heywood (q.v.). He was educated at Hart Hall, Oxford, and Lincoln's Inn. He sailed on the expeditions to Cadiz and the Azores (see no. 28). He entered the service of Sir Thomas Egerton, the Lord Keeper, but was dismissed when his secret marriage to Ann More, Lady Egerton's niece, was revealed. After many years of fruitless quests for office and scruples about taking holy orders, he entered the Church in 1615 and in 1621 was made Dean of St Paul's; his sermons were very popular. Though his poetry circulated in manuscript, the bulk of it remained unprinted until after his death. See ed. Helen Gardner, *John Donne: The Elegies and the Songs and Sonnets*, Oxford 1965, *John Donne: The Divine Poems*, 2nd edn, Oxford 1978; ed. W. Milgate, *John Donne: The Satires, Epigrams and Verse Letters*, Oxford 1967, *John Donne: The Epithalamions, Anniversaries and Epicedes*, Oxford 1978; R. C. Bald, *John Donne: A Life*, Oxford 1970. 28–9, 96, 132–7, 188, 228, 256–61, 313, 350

Anne **Dowriche** (fl. 1589–96) came from a prominent West Country family. Her father, Sir Richard Edgcumbe, and her brother Piers were both MPs. In 1580 she married Hugh Dowriche of Lapford, Devon, and she wrote commendatory verses for a treatise by him. See W. H. Edgcumbe, *Records of the Edgcumbe Family*, 1888. 17

Michael **Drayton** (1563–1631) was born in Warwickshire, served in the Nottinghamshire household of Thomas Goodere and had come to London by 1591. A lifelong professional poet, he published poetry in every major genre: pastoral (*Idea: the shepheards garland*, 1593), the sonnet (*Ideas mirrour*, 1594), the historical poem (*Mortimeriados*, 1596, revised as *The barrons wars*, 1603) and the Ovidian epistle (*Englands heroicall epistles*, 1597). He also wrote for the public stage. He became alienated from James's court and joined with Browne and Wither in attacking its abuses; his bitterness was increased by the poor sales of his huge topographical poem *Poly-Olbion*, 1612–22, which seemed old-fashioned to many readers. He found favour in his last years from Edward Sackville, fourth Earl of Dorset, at whose home he may have composed *The muses Elizium*. See Jean R. Brink, *Michael Drayton Revisited*, Boston 1990. 138–40, 191–3, 239, 360–2

William **Drummond** (1585–1649) studied at Edinburgh University. After extensive travels, he retired to his home at Hawthornden and lived as an independent gentleman of letters. His poetry reflected the very wide, if somewhat academic, interests in European and English literature that gained Milton's admiration. He also wrote a history of Scotland from James I to James V. His record of his conversations with Ben Jonson (q.v.) throws revealing light on both men. A strong monarchist, though a believer in religious toleration, he was deeply saddened by the political crises of the 1640s. See Robert H. MacDonald, *The Library of Drummond of Hawthornden*, Edinburgh 1971. 267–8

'Eliza' (fl. 1652) is known only from her volume *Eliza's babes*, 1652, in which she describes herself as 'a Lady', says that she has committed some unspecified sin in the past and that she has a spiritual adviser called 'Mr. C.' and a 'Brother' who was ill and died. See ed. Germaine Greer etc., *Kissing the Rod*, 1988, pp. 141–2. 327

Elizabeth Tudor (1533–1603), Queen of England, was educated by the humanist Roger Ascham; she produced translations from Plutarch, Horace, Boethius, Petrarch and Marguerite of Navarre as well as some original lyrics. See J. E. Neale, *Queen Elizabeth*, 1934. 13, 20

Essex, Robert Devereux, second Earl of, *see* Robert **Devereux**.

Edward **Fairfax** (?–1635) came from a branch of the same Yorkshire family as Marvell's patron Sir Thomas Fairfax. He may have studied at Clare Hall, Cambridge. His translation of Tasso's *Gerusalemme liberata*, 1600, became celebrated as a contribution to the 'refining' of English metre later perfected by Waller and Denham (qq.v.). He also wrote some allegorical eclogues. 342

Sir Richard **Fanshawe** (1608–66) was educated at Thomas Farnaby's school in London, Jesus College, Cambridge, and the Inner Temple. In the 1630s he travelled widely; in the 1640s he served the royalist cause. Captured in 1651, he made his peace with the republic and in 1655 published his translation of Camoëns's Portuguese epic the *Lusiads*. After the Restoration he served as ambassador to Portugal and then to Spain. His wife gave an account of his life in her autobiography: see ed. John Loftis, *The Memoirs of Anne, Lady Halkett and Ann, Lady Fanshawe*, Oxford 1979. 40

Giles **Fletcher** the younger (1586?–1623) was the son of a minor poet and cousin of the dramatist John Fletcher. He was educated at Westminster School and at Trinity College, Cambridge. His *Christs victorie, and triumph* appeared in 1610. About 1618 he left the University to become a minister in Sussex. 265

Phineas **Fletcher** (1582–1650), Giles's brother, was educated at Eton and at King's College, Cambridge. Plans for a court or academic career having failed, he eventually became a minister in Norfolk. Most of his poetry was written fairly early in his life but was not published until Charles's reign: most notably *The locusts, or Apollyonists*, 1627, and *The purple island*, 1633. See A. B. Langdale, *Phineas Fletcher: Man of Letters, Science and Divinity*, New York 1937. 269

George **Gascoigne** (1534?–77) was probably educated at Trinity College, Cambridge, and entered Gray's Inn in 1555; he represented Bedford as an MP in the late 1550s. In 1561 he became by his marriage stepfather to the poet Nicholas Breton. He served as a soldier in the Low Countries from 1572 to 1574 and played a notable part in the entertainment written for Queen Elizabeth's visit to Woodstock in 1575. He benefited from the patronage of the Earl of Leicester. See C. T. Prouty, *George Gascoigne: Elizabethan Courtier, Soldier and Poet*, New York 1942. 61, 224–5

Sidney **Godolphin** (1610–43) was educated at Exeter College, Oxford, and the Inns of Court. A member of Viscount Falkland's circle at Great Tew, he was elected to

Parliament in 1628 and again in 1640. He left London to serve with the King and became one of the first casualties of the Civil War. Thomas Hobbes was so moved by his death that he dedicated *Leviathan*, 1651, to his brother in his memory. 288

Arthur **Golding** (1536?–1606) was educated at Jesus College, Cambridge; his half-sister was married to John de Vere, sixteenth Earl of Oxford. In the dedication to the Earl of Leicester of his translation of Philippe de Mornay's *A woorke concerning the trewnesse of the Christian religion*, 1587, he claimed that it was begun by Sir Philip Sidney (q.v.), who had entrusted his work to him. See Louis Thorn Golding, *An Elizabeth Puritan: Arthur Golding the Translator of Ovid's Metamorphoses and also of John Calvin's Sermons*, New York 1937. 334

Barnabe **Googe** (1540–94) was educated at Christ's College, Cambridge. He was a government servant in Ireland for some years and an MP and may have been a gentleman-pensioner at court. Besides his original verse, he published a number of translations. See William E. Sheidley, *Barnabe Googe*, Boston 1981. 179

Sir Arthur **Gorges** (1557–1625) was educated at Oxford. He took part in a number of naval voyages and was a close friend of Sir Walter Ralegh (q.v. and see no. 357). He twice incurred royal disapproval for impolitic marriages and won little favour at the Elizabethan and Jacobean courts, though he gained a place in Prince Henry's household. In *Daphnaida*, 1591, Spenser mourned the death of Gorges' wife, Douglas Howard. 35

Robert **Greene** (*c.* 1558–92) was educated at Cambridge and also gained an MA from Oxford. He travelled in Italy and Spain. In 1586 he left his wife and embarked on a flamboyant literary life in London, writing many plays and romances. During his final illness he wrote a pious recantation of his earlier life. See René Pruvost, *Robert Greene et ses romans (?1558–1592): Contribution à l'histoire de la Renaissance en Angleterre*, Paris 1938. 79

Fulke **Greville** (1554–1628), first Lord Brooke, attended Shrewsbury School, with his lifelong friend Sir Philip Sidney (q.v.), and Jesus College, Cambridge. He served as an MP and held various public offices under Elizabeth; falling from favour in James's first years, he expressed his political disillusion in a work posthumously published as *The life of the renowned Sir Philip Sidney*, 1652. He regained favour in 1614 and held various State offices. In 1628 he was stabbed to death by a servant. Besides the lyric sequence *Cælica*, he wrote the closet dramas *Mustapha* and *Alaham* and a number of versified political treatises. See Ronald A. Rebholz, *The Life of Fulke Greville, First Lord Brooke*, Oxford 1971. 26, 73–7, 262–4

Nicholas **Grimald** (1519?–62?) was educated at Christ's College, Cambridge, and became chaplain to Nicholas Ridley, Bishop of Rochester and subsequently of London: he later recanted his Protestant faith. He was involved in the publication of Richard Tottel's *Songes and sonettes*, 1557, to which he contributed. As well as writing two Latin plays, he also made translations from Virgil and Cicero. 310

Everard **Guilpin** (1572?–?). Apart from his presumed authorship of *Skialetheia*, 1598, and *The whipper of the satyre his pennance in a white sheet*, 1601, little about Guilpin is known for certain. In 1588 he entered Emmanuel College, Cambridge; in 1591 he became a member of Gray's Inn. He may have known Donne (q.v.), who had been at Cambridge at the same time as Guilpin and was a member of Lincoln's Inn. 186

Joseph **Hall** (1574–1656) came from a Puritan background and was educated at Emmanuel College, Cambridge. Besides his verse satires, he wrote a prose satire in Latin, *Mundus alter et idem*, [1605?], a treatise on meditation and a collection of prose 'characters'. He became Bishop of Exeter, in which capacity his Calvinist views left him at odds with Archbishop Laud, but he was still too conservative for radicals like Milton, who made him his butt in his anti-episcopal tracts. See Richard A. McCabe, *Joseph Hall: A Study in Satire and Meditation*, Oxford 1982. 185

Sir John **Harington** (1560–1612) was educated at Eton, Christ's College, Cambridge, and Lincoln's Inn. As the Queen's godson he attended the court, though he risked her disfavour by such indiscretions as his Rabelaisian treatise on the water-closet *The metamorphosis of Ajax*, 1596. He served with Essex in Ireland and advocated conciliatory approaches to the Catholic rebels. On James's accession he was appointed tutor to Prince Henry. See D. H. Craig, *Sir John Harington*, Boston 1985. 24–5, 255, 341, 349

James **Harrington** (1611–77) was educated at Trinity College, Oxford. Though he is now known as a leading theorist of republicanism (*Oceana*, 1656), he had youthful ambitions of becoming a poet; he was a friend of Milton, and Marvell composed an epitaph for him. See ed. J. G. A. Pocock, *The Political Works of James Harrington*, Cambridge 1977. 172

Edward **Herbert** (1582–1648), first Lord Herbert of Cherbury, elder brother of George Herbert (q.v.), studied at University College, Oxford, and travelled widely. In 1619 he became ambassador to France, but he fell from royal favour in 1624 and did not fully regain it. He tried to remain neutral in the Civil War. He published a sceptical treatise on religion, *De veritate*, in 1624; his poems and his autobiography were published posthumously. See Eugene D. Hill, *Lord Herbert of Cherbury*, Boston 1982. 199

George **Herbert** (1593–1633) was educated at Westminster School and Trinity College, Cambridge, where he became public orator. In 1624 he was elected to Parliament. He was already contemplating a career in the Church, however, and in 1630 he became rector of Bemerton near Salisbury, a living in the gift of William Herbert, third Earl of Pembroke. He died three years later, having entrusted the publication of his poems to his close friend Nicholas Ferrar. See Amy M. Charles, *A Life of George Herbert*, Ithaca, NY, and London 1977. 276–86, 319

Mary **Herbert**, Countess of Pembroke, *see* Mary **Sidney**, Countess of Pembroke.

Robert **Herrick** (1591–1674) was apprenticed as a goldsmith before attending St John's College, Cambridge. In 1623 he was ordained priest; he accompanied the Duke of Buckingham as his chaplain on the disastrous Isle of Rhé expedition in 1627. In 1629 he was appointed to the living of Dean Prior in Devonshire. An attempt to publish his poems in 1640 seems to have been abandoned. In 1647, on his ejection from his living, he went to London and arranged for the publication of *Hesperides*, 1648. He returned to Devon in 1660. See George Walton Scott, *Robert Herrick 1591–1674*, 1974. 44, 148–53, 205–8, 322–4, 367–8

John **Heywood** (*c.* 1497–*c.* 1580) may have studied at Oxford; he served as a court dramatist and musician under Henry VIII, Edward VI and Mary. A strong Catholic, he left for the Continent on Elizabeth's accession. 11, 251

Henry **Howard** (1517?–47), Earl of Surrey, was the son of Thomas Howard (later third Duke of Norfolk). During the war with France of 1544–6 he was present at the siege of Montreuil, and was Commander of Boulogne. Accused of minor offences, he was executed on the charge of treasonably quartering the royal arms. He married Frances Vere in 1532, but the Elizabethans, especially Nashe and Drayton (qq.v.), liked on very slender evidence to imagine him as the lovelorn worshipper of 'Geraldine' (Elizabeth, daughter of the ninth Earl of Kildare). See W. A. Sessions, *Henry Howard, Earl of Surrey*, Boston 1986. 8, 57, 308–9, 332

Alexander **Hume** (*c.* 1556–1609) was educated at St Andrews and in France; in 1597 he became a minister, and most of his poetry was strongly didactic. 183

Ben **Jonson** (1572?–1637) was educated at Westminster School. He worked for a time at his stepfather's trade of bricklaying and fought in the Low Countries before turning to the public stage, first as actor then as playwright. Converted to Catholicism in 1598, he returned to the Anglican Church in 1610. Under James I he effectively became Poet Laureate, devising a long series of court masques with the designer Inigo Jones. He also received patronage from such leading nobles as the third Earl of Pembroke. The publication of his *Workes* in 1616 was a major claim for the social and intellectual respectability of the professions of poet and dramatist. His relations with Charles I were less close, and his last years were clouded by poverty. See ed. C. H. Herford, Percy and Evelyn Simpson, *Ben Jonson*, 11 vols., Oxford 1925–52; David Riggs, *Ben Jonson: A Life*, Cambridge, Mass., 1989. 34, 141–2, 190, 232–3, 314–15, 354–5

Henry **King** (1592–1669), son of John King, Bishop of London, was educated at Westminster School and Christ Church, Oxford. In 1642, after a successful ecclesiastical career, he was appointed Bishop of Chichester. Donne, Jonson (qq.v.) and Izaak Walton were among his friends. See Ronald Berman, *Henry King and the Seventeenth Century*, 1964. 318

Æmilia **Lanyer** (1569–1645) was of Italian Jewish descent. She may have served in the Duchess of Kent's household. Her husband Alfonso was a musician. Her volume of poems *Salve deus rex Judæorum*, 1611, was in part a bid for support from a number of prominent women patrons. 189, 266

Leicester, Robert Sidney, Earl of, *see* Robert **Sidney**.

Sir David **Lindsay** (1490?–1555) spent his life at the Scottish court. In his later years he joined the reforming party and gained great influence, particularly through his ambitious morality play *Ane satire of the thrie estaitis*, 1540. See William Murison, *Sir David Lyndsay*, Cambridge 1938. 4

Morgan **Llwyd** (1619–59) served with Parliament in the Civil War and in 1650 was appointed a Propagator of the Gospel in Wales. He was a Fifth Monarchist, but his interests shifted from activism to an internally oriented mysticism influenced by Jacob Boehme. He wrote several treatises which are regarded as landmarks in Welsh prose. See M. Wynn Thomas, *Morgan Llwyd*, Cardiff 1984. 297

Thomas **Lodge** (1558–1625) was educated at Merchant Taylors' School, at Oxford and at Lincoln's Inn. He made several naval voyages and published prose romances before becoming a doctor; he continued to write, notably translations of Josephus and of Seneca. As a Catholic he frequently found himself in difficulties with the authorities. See Charles J. Sisson et al., *Thomas Lodge and Other Elizabethans*, Cambridge, Mass., 1933. 227

Richard **Lovelace** (1618–57/8) was educated at Charterhouse and at Gloucester Hall, Oxford. He served in the Bishops' Wars in 1639–40. In 1642 he was imprisoned for presenting Parliament with a royalist petition that had been banned. He does not seem to have fought in the King's forces, though he did see military service on the Continent. He was again imprisoned in 1648–9. He seems to have died in poverty. See Gerald Hammond, 'Richard Lovelace and the Uses of Obscurity', *Proceedings of the British Academy*, 71 (1985), 203–34. 164–8, 213, 241

Christopher **Marlowe** (1564–93) was educated at the King's School, Canterbury, and Corpus Christi College, Cambridge. He seems to have served as a government spy on Continental missions. After experimenting with the academic drama in *Dido Queen of Carthage*, he took the London stage by storm with the two parts of *Tamburlaine*, *c.* 1587, a success followed up with *The Jew of Malta, Doctor Faustus, Edward II* and *The Massacre at Paris*. His official contacts helped to shield him in his recurrent brushes with the law – in 1592 he was arrested in the Netherlands for coining, and in May 1593 he was arrested on suspicion of dangerous religious opinions. He was stabbed to death in a tavern quarrel in circumstances that remain mysterious. *Hero and Leander* and his translation from Lucan were published posthumously. See John Bakeless, *The Tragicall History of Christopher Marlowe*, 2 vols., Cambridge, Mass., 1942. 98–9, 339–40

John **Marston** (1576–1634) was educated at Brasenose College, Oxford, and the Middle Temple. In 1599 his satires *The metamorphosis of Pigmalions image* and *The scourge of villanie* were ordered to be burned by the common hangman. He wrote a series of satirical plays, mostly for the boys' companies, of which the best-known is *The malcontent.* He was briefly imprisoned in 1608, possibly because of a satirical play, after which he left London and was ordained as a clergyman. See Philip J. Finkelpearl, *John Marston of the Middle Temple: An Elizabethan Dramatist in his Social Setting*, Cambridge, Mass., 1969. 125, 352

Andrew **Marvell** (1621–78) was educated at Hull Grammar School and Trinity College, Cambridge. He spent the years of the Civil War travelling on the Continent, returning to England by 1647. Under the republic and the protectorate he became increasingly aligned with the Cromwellian party; he was elected MP for Hull in that interest in 1659. Under the Restoration he continued to serve as an MP and fought vigorously for toleration of dissenters in verse and prose satires, most notably *The rehearsal transpros'd*, 1672–3. See ed. H. M. Margoliouth, *The Poems and Letters of Andrew Marvell*, 3rd edn, rev. Pierre Legouis and E. E. Duncan-Jones, 2 vols., Oxford 1971; Pierre Legouis, *Andrew Marvell: Poet, Puritan, Patriot*, 2nd edn, Oxford 1968. 45, 50, 169–71, 214–18, 306

John **Milton** (1608–74) was educated at St Paul's School and Christ's College, Cambridge. Instead of entering the Church as originally planned, he undertook a prolonged period of private study, supported by his father. Commissions for the entertainment *Arcades*, [1633?], and the masque now known as *Comus*, 1634, indicate an early reputation as a poet. In 1638–9 he travelled in Italy. On his return he earned his living as a private tutor. In 1641 he published the first of a series of tracts calling for reforms in Church government, the divorce laws and restrictions on the press. A strong supporter of the regicide, in 1649 he was appointed Secretary for Foreign Tongues and defended the republic in pamphlets that brought him international fame. By 1652 he was totally blind. Despite the defiant affirmation of his republican principles in *The readie and easy way to establish a free commonwealth* just before the Restoration, he was released after a brief period of imprisonment and published *Paradise lost* in 1667 and *Paradise regained* and *Samson agonistes* in 1671. See William Riley Parker, *Milton: A Biography*, 2 vols., Oxford 1968. 48–9, 203–4, 243, 270, 296, 325–6, 345, 363

Alexander **Montgomerie** (1545?–98) attended the court of James VI. He converted to Catholicism and his career became entangled in James's vacillations between Catholic and Protestant alignments; in 1597 he was involved in a Catholic plot to support Tyrone's rebellion in Ireland and was outlawed. His allegorical poem *The cherrie and the slaye*, 1597, became very popular. See R. D. S. Jack, *Alexander Montgomerie*, Edinburgh 1985. 23

Sir Thomas **More** (1477/8–1535) was educated at St Antony's School, London, Canterbury College, Oxford, and the Inns of Court. He became a lawyer, MP and City official while maintaining contact with Erasmus and other humanist scholars. After some hesitation, he entered the royal service in 1517. In 1529 he became Lord Chancellor, becoming celebrated both for incorruptibility and for the determination with which he opposed heretics. He resigned in 1532, disliking Henry VIII's elevation of himself as head of the Church and his plans for a divorce; his consistent opposition led to his eventual execution for high treason. See Richard Marius, *Thomas More: A Biography*, 1985. 2–3

Sir William **Mure** (1594–1657) was the nephew of Alexander Montgomerie (q.v.); he was probably educated at Glasgow University. He voiced the resentment of the Scots against Laud's regime in prophetic sonnets of the 1630s and fought against the royalists in the 1640s, but like most Scots he strongly opposed the English government's unilateral decision to execute Charles I. 46

Thomas **Nashe** (1567–*c.* 1601) was educated at St John's College, Cambridge. He became a professional writer and besides numerous controversial pamphlets produced the dramatic entertainment *Summers last will and testament* in 1592–3 and the picaresque narrative *The unfortunate traveller*, 1594. Recurrent skirmishes with the City authorities culminated in the scandal caused by the play *The isle of dogs*, 1597, which he co-authored, and Nashe had to flee London for a time. Little is known of his last years. See Charles Nicholl, *A Cup of News: The Life of Thomas Nashe*, 1984. 95

Newcastle, Margaret Cavendish, Duchess of, *see* Margaret **Cavendish**.

Eochaidh **Ó Heóghusa (O'Hussey)** (fl. 1593) was poet to the Maguires of Fermanagh; his surviving poems date from the late sixteenth and early seventeenth centuries. 33

Oxford, Edward de Vere, seventeenth Earl of, *see* Edward de **Vere**.

Martin **Parker** (1600?–?) was the best-known ballad-writer of the age. In the political crisis of the 1640s he rallied strongly behind Church and King and was attacked by parliamentarians as 'the prelates' poet'. He fell victim to the censorship of royalist ballads; he probably died in the early 1650s. See Hyder E. Rollins, 'Martin Parker, Ballad-Monger', *Modern Philology*, 16 (1919), 449–74. 43, 157–8

George **Peele** (1556–96) was educated at Christ's Hospital and Christ Church, Oxford. He earned his living as the author of plays, pageants and occasional poems. 27

Pembroke, Mary Sidney, Countess of, *see* Mary Sidney.

Katherine **Philips** (1632–64) came from a Puritan family and in 1648 married James Philips, a parliamentarian, but she also had contacts with royalist literary circles. Her poems were already circulating in 1651 when Henry Vaughan wrote in her praise. Her translation of Corneille's *La mort de Pompée* was staged in Dublin in 1663 and brought her widespread fame, which was consolidated by editions of her poems in 1664 and 1667. See P. W. Souers, *The Matchless Orinda*, Cambridge, Mass., 1931. 47, 173, 222, 244–6, 329–30

Siôn **Phylip** (1543?–1620) belonged to a family of professional bards and wrote prolifically in many different genres. One of his patrons was Sir John Salusbury, whose wedding was celebrated by Shakespeare's 'The Phoenix and Turtle' (no. 312). See William Ll. Davies, 'Phylipiaid Ardudwy: A Survey and a Summary', *Y Cymmrodor*, 42 (1931), 155–268. 180

George **Puttenham** (*c.* 1529–90/91) was educated at Christ's College, Cambridge, and the Middle Temple. He wrote numerous court poems and a defence of the execution of Mary Queen of Scots. Puritans suspected him of Catholic or atheistic tendencies, and he was accused of plotting to assassinate Archbishop Grindal. 16, 252

Francis **Quarles** (1592–1644) was educated at Christ's College, Cambridge, and Lincoln's Inn. He gained enormous popularity with his religious and didactic poetry, particularly with his *Emblemes*, 1635. He was strongly hostile to Laud but wrote pamphlets for the royalists in the 1640s. See Karl Josef Höltgen, *Francis Quarles 1592–1644: meditativer Dichter, Emblematiker, Royalist. Eine biographische und kritische Studie*, Tübingen 1978. 271–5

Sir Walter **Ralegh** (*c.* 1552–1618) was educated at Oriel College, Oxford. Beginning his career as a soldier, he became a royal favourite. He was given a royal patent for colonization in North America and journeyed to Virginia and Guiana. He was imprisoned in 1592 for marrying Elizabeth Throckmorton, a royal maid of honour, against the Queen's will. James I imprisoned him in 1603 for allegedly conspiring against his succession. His *The history of the world*, 1614, which became immensely popular, was published from prison. He was released to take part in an expedition to Orinoco in 1616, but the mission was a failure and he broke a promise not to attack the Spanish. In 1618 he was executed. The canon of his works is disputed. See Pierre Lefranc, *Sir Walter Ralegh écrivain*, Paris 1968. 18–19, 21–2, 89, 316, 357

Alexander **Scott** (1515?–83?) was a poet at the Scottish court; little is known of his life. See John MacQueen, 'Alexander Scott and Scottish Poetry of the Middle Sixteenth Century', *Proceedings of the British Academy*, 54 (1968), 93–116. 58

William **Shakespeare** (1564–1616) was born in Stratford-upon-Avon and probably left his wife and three children to come to London towards the end of the 1580s. His theatrical career as playwright, actor and share-owner in the Lord Chamberlain's Men and later the King's Men appears to have been extremely successful. Both of his narrative poems, *Venus and Adonis*, 1593, and *Lucrece*, 1594, were dedicated to Henry Wriothesley, Earl of Southampton; the meaning of the dedication to the *Sonnets*, 1609, is uncertain. None of Shakespeare's poems was printed in the folio collection of his plays published in 1623, which was dedicated to William Herbert, third Earl of Pembroke, and his brother Philip, the future fourth Earl. See E. K. Chambers, *William Shakespeare: A Study of Facts and Problems*, 2 vols., Oxford 1930, and Samuel Schoenbaum, *William Shakespeare: A Documentary Life*, 1975. 100–1, 104–19, 312, 351

Luke **Shepherd** (fl. 1548) is known only from a series of prophetic poems published in the mid sixteenth century. It is possible that his name was a pseudonym alluding to St Luke and the Good Shepherd. See John N. King, *English Reformation Literature*, Princeton 1982. 249

James **Shirley** (1596–1666) was educated at Merchant Taylors' School and Catherine Hall, Cambridge. He became a convert to Catholicism. He wrote many successful plays for the London stage and in 1636–40 managed a theatre at Dublin. During the Civil War he seems to have lived as a schoolmaster; in 1651 his property was sequestrated for royalist activities. See Georges Bas, *James Shirley (1596–1666): dramaturge caroléen*, Lille 1973. 331

Mary **Sidney** (1561–1621), Countess of Pembroke, sister of Sir Philip Sidney (q.v.), married Henry Herbert, second Earl of Pembroke, in 1577. Her poetical interests mostly took the form of translations; she collaborated with her brother Sir Philip Sidney in translating the Psalms and also translated some of Petrarch's *Trionfi* and Robert Garnier's neoclassical play *Antonie*. Samuel Daniel (q.v.), one of many poets whom she patronized, dedicated his *Cleopatra* to her. Her son William, the third Earl, continued the family tradition of literary and political patronage. See Margaret P. Hannay, *Philip's Phoenix: Mary Sidney, Countess of Pembroke*, Oxford 1990. 31, 336–8

Sir Philip **Sidney** (1554–86) was born at Penshurst, the eldest son of Sir Henry Sidney and his wife Mary, the sister of Robert Dudley, Earl of Leicester. Sidney was educated at Shrewsbury School with his friend Fulke Greville (q.v.), at Christ Church, Oxford, and probably for a time at Cambridge. From 1572 to 1575 he travelled throughout Europe, and he was abroad again in 1577. His career as a writer probably dates from then, and in the next few years he wrote two versions of his pastoral romance the *Arcadia*, his sonnet sequence *Astrophil and Stella* and his treatise *A defence of poetry*. He was knighted for reasons of protocol in 1583, the year in which he married Frances, daughter of Sir Francis Walsingham. In 1585 he went to the Low Countries as part of the force led by Leicester against the Spanish. There he was appointed Governor of Flushing; he was wounded in a skirmish outside Zutphen and died three weeks later. None of his major works was printed during his lifetime. See Katherine Duncan-Jones, *Sir Philip Sidney: Courtier Poet*, London 1991. 14, 63–72, 181

Robert **Sidney** (1563–1626), Earl of Leicester, Philip Sidney's younger brother, was educated at Christ Church, Oxford, and travelled abroad during 1579–82. He married Barbara Gamage in 1584 and in the next year followed his brother to the Low Countries, where he was knighted in 1586. He succeeded his brother as Governor of Flushing in 1589 and held the appointment until 1616. He was created

Baron Sidney of Penshurst in 1603, when he was appointed Lord Chamberlain to Queen Anne; Viscount L'Isle in 1605; and Earl of Leicester in 1618. He published nothing during his lifetime, but was a patron of composers. See Millicent V. Hay, *The Life of Robert Sidney Earl of Leicester (1563–1626)*, Washington, London and Toronto 1984. 120–3

John **Skelton** (1460?–1529) seems to have studied both at Cambridge and Oxford. He became a court poet for Henry VII. About 1503 he left the court to become rector of Diss, Norfolk. About 1512 he returned to court but seems to have fallen foul of the King's powerful minister Cardinal Wolsey, whom he attacked in the courtly allegory *Speke parott* and a series of satires adopting a popular voice; he succeeded in regaining favour in his last years. See Greg Walker, *John Skelton and the Politics of the 1520s*, Cambridge 1988. 1, 247, 307, 346

Robert **Southwell** (1561?–95) was educated at Douai and became a Jesuit priest. He arrived in England in 1586; in 1592 he was arrested and underwent a long period of imprisonment and torture. He was executed at Tyburn in 1595. See Christopher Devlin, *The Life of Robert Southwell, Poet and Martyr*, 1956. 253

Rachel **Speght** (1597–?) was the daughter of a clergyman from Yorkshire. She may have been related to Thomas Speght, the editor of Chaucer. In 1617 she published *A mouzell for Melastomus*, in reply to a misogynistic treatise by Joseph Swetnam. In *Mortalities memorandum*, 1621, which she dedicated to her godmother Mary Moundeford, she refuted claims that the book had been written by her father. Nothing is known of her after her marriage to William Procter in 1621. See Simon Shepherd, *The Women's Sharp Revenge: Five Women's Pamphlets from the Renaissance*, 1985. 359

Edmund **Spenser** (1552?–99) was educated at Merchant Taylors' School and Pembroke Hall, Cambridge. The publication of *The shepheardes calender* in 1579 with a dedication to Sidney brought him in contact with the Sidney–Leicester patronage network. In 1580 he went to Ireland as secretary to Arthur, Lord Grey of Wilton. He served as a government official and gained extensive Irish lands. The publication of the first three books of *The Faerie Queene* in 1590 gained him an official pension, and many of his minor poems were published in the following year. *Amoretti and Epithalamion* and *Colin Clouts come home againe* were published in 1595. The second part of *The Faerie Queene* appeared in 1596, as did the *Fowre hymnes* and *Prothalamion*. In his later years he was disillusioned by what he considered to be the government's irresolute conduct of Irish affairs; his *A view of the present state of Ireland* was refused a licence in 1598. In that year rebels burned down his castle at Kilcolman. He died in London; the Earl of Essex (q.v.) paid for his funeral. See A. C. Judson, *The Life of Edmund Spenser*, Baltimore 1945. 32, 80–8, 182, 335, 348

Richard **Stanyhurst** (1547–1618) was born in Dublin and was educated at University College, Oxford. After studying at Lincoln's Inn for a time, he returned to Ireland

and wrote a description of Ireland for the first edition of Holinshed's *Chronicles*. After his first wife's death in 1579 he went to the Low Countries and he seems to have become a Catholic while staying at Leiden, where he worked on his translation of Virgil. He later published other historical and theological works and eventually became a priest. 333

Sir John **Suckling** (1609–41) was educated at Trinity College, Cambridge, and Gray's Inn. Living as a well-to-do wit, he wrote several plays and many lyrics. He served in the Bishops' Wars against the Scots. His part in a plot to free Strafford from the Tower in 1641 was discovered and he fled to Paris. See Charles L. Squier, *Sir John Suckling*, Boston 1978. 162

Surrey, Henry Howard, Earl of, *see* Henry **Howard**.

Josuah **Sylvester** (1562/3–1618) was educated at Southampton Grammar School and entered the Society of Merchant Adventurers, dividing his time between London and the Netherlands. In 1590 he published the first of many translations from the French Protestant poet du Bartas, and he increasingly sought literary patronage. He gained support from Prince Henry but was thrown into difficulties by his death. In 1617 he was appointed Secretary to the Merchant Adventurers at Middelburg. 343

John **Taylor** (1580–1653) was a 'sculler' or waterman on the Thames. He engaged in a series of sponsored journeys of which he published versified accounts. A staunch royalist, he engaged in several skirmishes with George Wither (q.v.). In his last years he fell foul of Parliament's growing control over royalist writings. See Wallace Notestein, *Four Worthies*, 1956. 197, 289, 364

Chidiock **Tichborne** (1558?–86) came from an old Catholic family. In 1586 he became involved in a plot to assassinate Queen Elizabeth. He was disembowelled while still alive. His speech on the scaffold and his poem of farewell became widely known. 311

Anna **Trapnel** (*c.* 1622–?) was the daughter of a shipwright. Both her parents were dead by the time she was twenty; selling most of her goods to support the parliamentarian army, she went to live with various women friends. In 1654 she was seized by a series of very public trances in which she prophesied in verse. *The cry of a stone* and three other texts appeared in 1654, followed by a huge untitled collection of verse prophecies in 1658 and *Voice for the king of saints and nations* in 1658. See Nigel Smith, *Perfection Proclaimed: Language and Literature in English Radical Religion 1640–1660*, Oxford 1989. 304

George **Turbervile** (*c.* 1544–*c.* 1597) was educated at New College, Oxford, and the Inns of Court. In 1568 he went on a diplomatic mission to Russia. Besides his *Epitaphes, epigrams, songs and sonets*, 1567, he published translations from Ovid and Mantuan and from Italian novelists. 59

W. **Turner** (fl. 1612). Nothing is known about this ballad-writer. 196

Henry **Vaughan** (1621–95) was probably educated, like his brother Thomas, at Jesus College, Oxford; he embarked on legal studies in London, but on the outbreak of the Civil War he returned to his native Wales; eventually he practised medicine. His interest in the mystical Hermetic ideas circulating in the 1640s and 1650s is manifested in the two volumes of *Silex scintillans*, 1650 and 1655. He published one further volume of poems, *Thalia rediviva*, 1678. See ed. L. C. Martin, *The Works of Henry Vaughan*, 2nd edn, Oxford 1957; F. E. Hutchinson, *Henry Vaughan: A Life and Interpretation*, Oxford 1947. 212, 299–302, 328, 374

Edward de **Vere** (1550–1604), seventeenth Earl of Oxford, had a turbulent career at court. His public quarrel with Philip Sidney (q.v.) in 1579 aligned him with the opponents of Sidney's strongly Protestant faction. Although his extravagant and erratic way of life earned him many enemies, he was a generous patron of the arts as well as writing a number of courtly lyrics. Theories that he wrote Shakespeare's plays emerged only in the twentieth century. See B. M. Ward, *The Seventeenth Earl of Oxford*, 1928. 226

Edmund **Waller** (1606–87) was educated at Eton and King's College, Cambridge. He served in Parliament during the 1620s. During the 1630s he courted Dorothy Sidney, the granddaughter of Robert Sidney, Earl of Leicester (q.v.), as 'Sacharissa'. His allegiances in the 1640s were divided: returning to Parliament, he made some celebrated speeches calling for reform, but in 1643 became involved in a royalist plot and was banished. He returned to England in the 1650s, writing a panegyric of Cromwell. After the Restoration he again returned to Parliament, speaking for religious toleration. See Warren L. Chernaik, *The Poetry of Limitation: A Study of Edmund Waller*, New Haven and London 1968. 159–61, 240, 290

Isabella **Whitney** (fl. 1567–73) was a member of the family of Whitney which came from Coole Pilate in Cheshire. As well as the volume which contains the poem printed above, Isabella Whitney also published a collection of poems called *A sweet nosgay*, [1573]. Her brother was the emblem-writer Geoffrey Whitney (1548?–1601). 60

Robert **Wild** (1609–79) was educated at St John's College, Cambridge, where he gained a reputation as a wit. He was ordained a minister in 1647. Though he welcomed General Monck's inauguration of the Restoration in his most famous poem, *Iter boreale*, 1660, his Presbyterian allegiances led to his ejection from his ministry in 1662.. 295

George **Wither** (1588–1667) was educated at Magdalen College, Oxford, but his studies were curtailed, apparently for financial reasons. He spent some time in Ireland before studying law in London, being admitted to Lincoln's Inn in 1615. He wrote some popular lyrics but also gained a reputation as a prophet. In a series of long versified prophecies, from *Abuses stript and whipt*, 1613, through to the 1660s, he attacked religious and political authoritarianism and called for electoral reforms, being several times imprisoned for his outspokenness. He fought for Parliament in the Civil War and was one of the few poets to celebrate the execution of Charles I in verse. See Charles S. Hensley, *The Later Career of George Wither*, The Hague and Paris 1969. 202, 369

Sir Henry **Wotton** (1568–1639) was educated at Winchester and at New College and Queen's College, Oxford. During extensive Continental travels, he supplied intelligence for the Earl of Essex. Under James I he served for a time as ambassador to Venice; in 1624 he became Provost of Eton. He wrote poems, essays and a treatise on architecture; he died without completing a projected life of his friend John Donne (q.v.). 36, 321

Lady Mary **Wroth** (1586?–1651?) was brought up in the highly literary atmosphere of the Sidney dynasty, her father being Sir Robert Sidney (q.v.). Her arranged marriage to Sir Robert Wroth was unhappy: she was in love with William Herbert, third Earl of Pembroke, by whom she had two children after her husband's death. Her romance the *Urania* appeared in 1621 and caused scandal for alleged topical allusions; a long second part remained unpublished. Wroth also wrote the dramatic entertainment *Love's victorie*. 143–7

Sir Thomas **Wyatt** (*c.* 1503–42) was educated at St John's College, Cambridge. His service as a diplomat brought him in contact with contemporary writing on the Continent. In 1528 he published *The quyete of mynde*, a translation from Plutarch. He was intermittently under suspicion of disloyalty and sexual misconduct; he separated from his wife, Elizabeth Brooke, a few years after their marriage. In 1536 he was arrested and banished to the country for a time, probably because of his relations with Anne Boleyn, whom Henry VIII had decided to marry. After a second trial in 1541 he was apparently ordered to abandon further infidelities on pain of death. See Kenneth Muir, *Life and Letters of Sir Thomas Wyatt*, Liverpool 1963. 5–7, 53–6, 223

Appendix 5: Index of Authors

References are to poem numbers

Anonymous (*by title or first line; see also under* Ballads; Dowland, John; 'Eliza'; Ravenscroft, Thomas)
A Lament for our Lady's Shrine at Walsingham, 250
Epitaph on the Duke of Buckingham, 39
Feltons Epitaph, 38
Jack of the North, 177
Of Sir Frauncis Walsingham Sir Phillipp Sydney, and Sir Christopher Hatton, Lord Chancelor, 15
On Francis Drake, 195
The Diggers' Song, 211
The Mode of France, 238
Upon Arch-bishop Laud, Prisoner in the Tower. 1641, 294
Vox populi vox Dei, 176
Westron wynde when wylle thow blow, 52
Yet if his Majestie our Sovareigne lord, 287
Askew, Anne, 248

Ballads (*see also under* Birch, William; Corbett, Richard; Heywood, John; Parker, Martin; Turner, W.; Wild, Robert)
A new Courtly Sonet, of the Lady Greensleeves, 62
John Arm-strongs last good night, 9
The Jolly Pinder of Wakefield, 178
A Song bewailinge the tyme of Christmas, 187
The wanton Wife of Bath, 127
Barclay, Alexander, 174
Barnes, Barnabe, 97
Barnfield, Richard, 102–3
Birch, William, 12
Boyd, Mark Alexander, 78
Brome, Alexander, 51, 242
Browne, William, 37, 198, 317, 358
Buchanan, George, 175

Campion, Thomas, 129–31, 237
Çarew, Thomas, 154–6, 320, 365–6
Cavendish, Margaret, Duchess of Newcastle, 219–21, 371–2
Chapman, George, 124, 344, 356
Churchyard, Thomas, 347
Clarkson, Laurence, 298
Cleveland, John, 41, 163
Collins, An, 305
Constable, Henry, 254
Corbett, Richard, 200
Cowley, Abraham, 210, 373
Crashaw, Richard, 209, 291–3
Crowley, Robert, 10

Daniel, Samuel, 90–2, 194, 231, 353
Davenant, Sir William, 201, 303, 370
Davies, Sir John, 93–4, 184
de Vere, Edward, Earl of Oxford, *see* Vere, Edward de, Earl of Oxford
Dekker, Thomas, 230
Deloney, Thomas, 126, 229
Denham, Sir John, 42
Devereux, Robert, Earl of Essex, 30
Donne, John, 28–9, 96, 132–7, 188, 228, 256–61, 313, 350
[Dowland, John], 128
Dowriche, Anne, 17

Drayton, Michael, 138–40, 191–3, 239, 360–2
Drummond, William, 267–8

'Eliza', 327
Elizabeth I, Queen, 13, 20
Essex, Robert Devereux, Earl of, *see* Devereux, Robert, Earl of Essex

Fairfax, Edward, 342
Fanshawe, Sir Richard, 40
Fletcher, Giles, 265
Fletcher, Phineas, 269

Gascoigne, George, 61, 224–5
Godolphin, Sidney, 288
Golding, Arthur, 334
Googe, Barnabe, 179
Gorges, Sir Arthur, 35
Greene, Robert, 79
Greville, Fulke, Lord Brooke, 26, 73–7, 262–4
Grimald, Nicholas, 310
Guilpin, Everard, 186

Hall, Joseph, 185
Harington, Sir John, 24–5, 255, 341, 349
Harrington, James, 172
Herbert, Edward, Lord Herbert of Cherbury, 199
Herbert, George, 276–86, 319
Herbert, Mary, Countess of Pembroke, *see* Sidney, Mary, Countess of Pembroke
Herrick, Robert, 44, 148–53, 205–8, 322–4, 367–8
Heywood, John, 11, 251
Howard, Henry, Earl of Surrey, 8, 57, 308–9, 332
Hume, Alexander, 183

Jonson, Ben, 34, 141–2, 190, 232–3, 314–15, 354–5

King, Henry, 318

Lanyer, Æmilia, 189, 266
Lindsay, Sir David, 4
Llwyd, Morgan, 297
Lodge, Thomas, 227
Lovelace, Richard, 164–8, 213, 241

Marlowe, Christopher, 98–9, 339–40
Marston, John, 125, 352
Marvell, Andrew, 45, 50, 169–71, 214–18, 306
Milton, John, 48–9, 203–4, 243, 270, 296, 325–6, 345, 363
Montgomerie, Alexander, 23
More, Sir Thomas, 2–3
Mure, Sir William, 46

Nashe, Thomas, 95
Newcastle, Margaret Cavendish, Duchess of, *see* Cavendish, Margaret, Duchess of Newcastle

Ó Heóghusa, Eochaidh, 33
Oxford, Edward de Vere, Earl of, *see* Vere, Edward de, Earl of Oxford

Parker, Martin, 43, 157–8
Peele, George, 27
Pembroke, Mary Sidney (Herbert), Countess of, *see* Sidney, Mary, Countess of Pembroke
Philips, Katherine, 47, 173, 222, 244–6, 329–30
Phylip, Siôn, 180
Puttenham, George, 16, 252

Quarles, Francis, 271–5

Ralegh, Sir Walter, 18–19, 21–2, 89, 316, 357
[Ravenscroft, Thomas], 234–6

Scott, Alexander, 58
Shakespeare, William, 100–1, 104–19, 312, 351
Shepherd, Luke, 249
Shirley, James, 331
Sidney, Mary, Countess of Pembroke, 31, 336–8
Sidney, Sir Philip, 14, 63–72, 181
Sidney, Robert, Earl of Leicester, 120–3
Skelton, John, 1, 247, 307, 346
Southwell, Robert, 253
Speght, Rachel, 359
Spenser, Edmund, 32, 80–8, 182, 335, 348
Stanyhurst, Richard, 333
Suckling, Sir John, 162
Surrey, Henry Howard, Earl of, *see* Howard, Henry, Earl of Surrey
Sylvester, Josuah, 343

Taylor, John, 197, 289, 364
Tichborne, Chidiock, 311
Trapnel, Anna, 304
Turbervile, George, 59
Turner, W., 196

Vaughan, Henry, 212, 299–302, 328, 374
Vere, Edward de, Earl of Oxford, 226

Waller, Edmund, 159–61, 240, 290
Whitney, Isabella, 60
Wild, Robert, 295
Wither, George, 202, 369
Wotton, Sir Henry, 36, 321
Wroth, Lady Mary, 143–7
Wyatt, Sir Thomas, 5–7, 53–6, 223

Index of First Lines

References are to the numbers of poems. Punctuation at the end of lines has usually been omitted, and words in upper case have had all but their first letter lowered. Since the spelling in this index is unmodernized, users are reminded that 'y' was often used for 'i'. The first lines of editorial translations have not been indexed. Both sonnets at the beginning and end of Thomas Nashe's 'The choise of valentines' (no. 95) have been included, but not the thirteen sonnets following the first one in Lady Mary Wroth's 'A crowne of Sonetts' (no. 145).

A Paradice on earth is found 362
A sweet disorder in the dresse 148
A womans face with natures owne hand painted 105
Absence, the noble truce 76
Accept thou Shrine of my Dead Saint 318
Ah Mater, quo te deplorem fonte? Dolores 319
Ah silly pugge wert thou so sore afraid 20
Alas how barbarous are we 222
Alas my love, ye do me wrong 62
Alas why say yow I ame ritch? when I 120
An unreasonable ryche manne 10
And, for our tongue, that still is so empayr'd 356
And now to the Abbyss I pass 218
And thus as we wer talking to and fro 4
And yett not lowng agoo 176
Art thou poore yet hast thou golden Slumbers 230
As close as you your weding kept 60
As Gold is better that's in fire tride 197
As I in hoarie Winters night stoode shivering in the snow 253
As virtuous men passe mildly away 137
As when it hapneth that some lovely Towne 268
As when the cheerfull Sunne, elamping wide 265
As when the glorious Magazine of Light 47
As you came from the holy land 89
At last shee cals to mind where hangs a peece 101

Batter my heart, three person'd God; for, you 259
Because you have thrown of your Prelate Lord 296

Behold, the King of glory now is come 298
Behold this needle; when the *Arctick* stone 273
Behold what hap *Pigmalion* had to frame 90
Brave Infant of *Saguntum*, cleare 315
Busie old foole, unruly Sunne 133
But be contented when that fell arest 112
By this noble pourtrayt 16

Can we not force from widdowed Poetry 365
Change thy minde since she doth change 30
Christmas is my name, Farr have I gone, have I gone, have I gone 187
Clora come view my Soul, and tell 170
Come a *brimmer* (my bullies) drink whole ones or nothing 242
Come live with mee, and be my love 98
Come, Madam, come, all rest my powers defie 96
Come, my *Lucasia*, since we see 244
Come over the born bessy 12
Come wee Shepheards who have seene 291
Comming to kisse her lyps, (such grace I found) 84
Cosmus hath more discoursing in his head 184
Cromwell, our cheif of men, who through a cloud 48
Cupid, in *Myra's* faire bewitching eyes 74

Dazel'd thus, with height of place 36
Dean-bourn, farewell; I never look to see 205
Desire, though thou my old companion art 68
Devouring time blunt thou the Lyons pawes 104
Dew sate on *Julia's* haire 152
Disswasion hearing her assigne my helpe 359
Downe in the depth of mine iniquity 263

Eftsoones they heard a most melodious sound 80
Eternal God! maker of all 374
Even as the sunne with purple-colourd face 100
Even now that Care which on thy Crowne attends 31
Even suche is tyme that takes in trust 316

Faith (wench) I cannot court thy sprightly eyes 94
Farewell Rewards and *Faeries* 200
Farewell sweet Boy, complaine not of my truth 77
Farewell (sweet *Cooke-ham*) where I first obtain'd 189
Farewell, thou child of my right hand, and joy 314
Farewell thou fertyll soyle 179

Father of lights! what Sunnie seed 301
Fine knacks for ladies, cheape choise brave and new 128
Followe thy faire sunne unhappy shaddowe 129
Fond man *Musophilus*, that thus dost spend 353
For all the gallantry of him 293
For Godsake hold your tongue, and let me love 134
For round about, the wals yclothed were 82
For shame, thou everlasting Woer 163
For sport my *Julia* threw a Lace 150
Forbear bold Youth, all's Heaven here 173
Forsaken woods, trees with sharpe storms opprest 122
Fra banc to banc fra wod to wod I rin 78
Fresh spring the herald of loves mighty king 86
Fúar liom an adhaighsi dh'Aodh 33
Fy Satyre fie, shall each mechanick slave 352

Get up, get up for shame, the Blooming Morne 206
Give *Mee* the *Free*, and *Noble Stile* 371
Give way, give way ye Gates, and win 208
Go lovely Rose 160
Go, the rich *Chariot* instantly prepare 373
Gods boundles bownties gods promise ever abyding 337
Gods *Houses*, almost like *Troyes Ilion* 289
Goe soule the bodies guest 22
Good brother *Philip*, I have borne you long 70

Had *Dorothea* liv'd when mortals made 240
Had *Lucan* hid the truth to please the time 357
Had we but World enough, and Time 169
Hail native Language, that by sinews weak 363
Happy those early dayes! when I 299
Happyer those times were, when the Flaxen clew 358
Having been tenant long to a rich Lord 277
He first deceas'd: She for a little tri'd 321
He who at first a womans mind 172
Heere uninterr'd suspendes (though not to save 38
Hence loathed Melancholy 204
Here a pretty Baby lies 324
Here lies Wise and Valiant Dust 41
Here take my Picture, though I bid farewell 132
Hey hoe what shall I say 234
Hous-keping's dead, *Saturio*: wot'st thou where 185

How fresh, O Lord, how sweet and clean 283
How vainly men themselves amaze 217

I am two fooles, I know 350
I did not live until this time 246
I, in your frutefull woomb conceyved, born was 310
I joy to see how in your drawen work 87
I now thinke, Love is rather deafe, then blind 142
I pray thee leave, love me no more 140
I saw Eternity the other night 300
I saw him dead; I saw his Body fall 272
I scarce beleeve my love to be so pure 135
I struck the board, and cry'd, No more 282
I will enjoy thee now my *Celia*, come 156
I wish a greater knowledge, then t'attaine 275
I with whose colors *Myra* drest her head 73
If by mischance the people in the street 202
In a grove most rich of shade 71
In a melancholly studdy 295
In *Bath* a wanton wife did dwell 127
In the wrackes of walsingam 250
In this strang labourinth how shall I turne 145
In *wakefield* there lives a jolly Pinder 178
Is not thilke the mery moneth of May 182
Is there never a man in all *Scotland* 9
'Is this, saith one, the Nation that we read 50
It may be good like it who list 55
It was the merie moneth of Februarie 95

Just like unto a *Nest* of *Boxes* round 219

Kinde pitty chokes my spleene; brave scorn forbids 256
Know *Celia*, (since thou art so proud) 155

Late in the Forest I did Cupid see 146
Late 'twas in *June*, the Fleece when fully growne 191
Lately on yonder swelling bush 161
Lawrence of vertuous Father vertuous Son 243
Let mans Soule be a Spheare, and then, in this 257
Let me confesse that we two must be twaine 108
Let me powre forth 136
Let me sleep this night away 323
Let others sing of Knights and Palladines 92

Let others to the Printing Presse run fast 368
Let the bird of lowdest lay 312
Like to *Diana* in her Summer weede 79
Long have I lov'd this bonny Lasse 126
Lord when the wise men came from Farr 288
Lord, who createdst man in wealth and store 278
Love bade me welcome: yet my soul drew back 285
Loving in truth, and faine in verse my love to show 65
Lucy, you brightnesse of our spheare, who are 232
Luxurious Man, to bring his Vice in use 216
Lyke as a huntsman after weary chace 85
Lyke as the armed knyght 248

Maides to bed, and cover coale 236
Marke how this polisht Easterne sheet 366
Me thinks I heare some Cavillers object 364
Methought I saw my late espoused Saint 326
My dearely loved friend how oft have we 361
My God, the poore expressions of my Love 276
My Love is of a birth as rare 171
My lute awake perfourme the last 56
My Maisters all attend you 196
My prime of youth is but a froste of cares 311
My voice to thee it self extreamly strayning 338
My worthy Lord, I pray you wonder not 225
Myn owne John poyntz sins ye delight to know 223

New light gives new directions, Fortunes new 124
No more bee greev'd at that which thou hast done 107
Norfolk sprang thee, Lambeth holds thee dead 308
Not at first sight, nor with a dribbed shot 66
Not marble, nor the guilded monuments 109
Nothing could make mee sooner to confesse 313
Now for that slawnders sake 177
Now ore the sea from her old Love comes she 339
Now that the winter's gone, the earth hath lost 154
Now the bright morning Star, Dayes harbinger 203
Now warre is all the world about 40
Now winter nights enlarge 237

O he is a rest that requires 304
O Heavens! O Earth! heer I must pause a space 46
O kisse, which doest those ruddie gemmes impart 69

O mightye Muse 252
O Perfite light, quhilk schaid away 183
O! should all Potentates whose higher birth 37
O Whither will you lead the Fair 201
O, why should Nature niggardly restraine 360
Oh thou that swing'st upon the waving haire 241
On *Hellespont* guiltie of True-loves blood 99
One of King *Henries* Favorites beganne 255
Our Canterburye's great Cathedrall Bell 294
Our Mother *Eve*, who tasted of the Tree 266
Our storme is past, and that storms tyrannous rage 28
Out upon it, I have lov'd 162
Over this the foresayd lay 247

Pardon sweete flower of matchless Poetrie 95
Penelope for her *Ulisses* sake 83
Pigmalion, whose hie love-hating minde 125
Pla ce bo 307
Praisd be Dianas faire and harmles light 18
Praise, is devotion fit for mighty Mindes 303
Pray why should any man complain 51
Prayer the Churches banquet, Angels age 279
Proud *Paulus* late my secrecies revealing 349

Quæris uter melius, Rex ne imperet an ne Senatus 3
Queene *Vertues* court, which some call *Stellas* face 67
Quid bonus est princeps? Canis est custos gregis inde 2
Quid tu? quæ nova machina 209

Religion stands on tip-toe in our land 286
Remembers thou in Æsope of a taill 23
Rime, the rack of finest wits 354
Rose-cheekt *Lawra* come 130

Salvete sacris deliciis sacræ 175
See! with what constant Motion 165
See'st thou that Cloud as silver cleare 151
Shall *Reason* rule where *Reason* hath no right 59
She brought her to her joyous Paradize 81
Show me deare Christ, thy spouse, so bright and cleare 261
Sighing, and sadly sitting by my Love 103
Since I am comming to that Holy roome 258
Since she whome I lovd, hath payd her last debt 260

Since ther's no helpe, Come let us kisse and part 139
Sing we now merily 235
Sir *Drake* whom well the world's end knew 195
Sir *Frauncis* and *Sir Phillip* have noe Tombe 15
Sir, more then kisses, letters mingle Soules 228
Sitting alone (as one forsook) 149
So him at first *De Nance* commanded was to kill 17
Soe well I love thee, as without thee I 239
Some act of *Love's* bound to reherse 141
Some doe, perhaps, both wrong my love, and care 147
Sometimes I wish that I his pillow were 102
Such maner time there was (what time I n'ot) 14
Sufficeth it to yow my joyes interred 21
Sure there are Poets which did never dream 42
Sweet love renew thy force, be it not said 110
Sweete Saynt: Thow better canst declare to me 254
Syon lyes waste, and thy *Jerusalem* 264

Tagus fare well that westward with thy strems 6
Take heed mine eyes, how you your lookes doe cast 144
Tell me not (Sweet) I am unkinde 164
Than, if this noble kyng 346
Thassyryans king in peas with fowle desyre 8
hat for seven *Lusters* I did never come 322
That humor now, declines for age drawes on 347
That Prince, who may doe nothing but what's just 44
That shipwrackt vessel which th'Apostle bore 290
The Booke of *Common Pray'r* excels the rest 274
The common speech is, spend and God will send 224
The cunning Painter, that with curious care 343
The dowbt off future foes exiles my present joye 13
The drearie trumpet blew a dreadfull blast 342
The egles byrde hath spred his wings 11
Th'expence of Spirit in a waste of shame 116
The forward Youth that would appear 45
The glories of our blood and state 331
The harbingers are come. See, see their mark 284
The Hearts thus intermixed speak 245
The Lady *Mary Villers* lyes 320
The last and greatest Herauld of Heavens King 267
The little Hearts, where light-wing'd Passion raignes 26
The *Manicheans* did no Idols make 262
The minde through thee divines on endlesse things 227

The Muses friend (gray-eyde *Aurora*) yet 198
The Nightingale as soone as Aprill bringeth 63
The *nurse-life* Wheat within his greene huske growing 75
The piller pearisht is whearto I Lent 7
The Rose both white and Rede 1
The sacred Muse that firste made love devine 93
The soote season, that bud and blome furth bringes 57
The *Sun* hath run his course through all the Signes 369
The Sunn is set, and masked night 123
The thriftles thred which pampred beauty spinnes 61
The Town believes thee lost, and didst thou see 212
The *Waves* like *Ridges* of *Plow'd-land* lies high 221
The Winter being over 305
The winter snowes, all covered is the grounde 174
The *worst Fate Bookes* have, when they are once read 372
Theare be great Prince, such as will tell you howe 194
Thee whilst thee dawning Aurora fro the Ocean hastned 333
Then, as if he would have sold 29
Then do I thinke in deed, that better it is to be private 181
Then from the seas, the dawning gan arise 332
There is a Garden in her face 131
There, when they thought they saw in well sought Books 370
They are all gone into the world of light 328
They fle from me that sometyme did me seke 53
They that have powre to hurt, and will doe none 113
Thirsis a youth of the inspired train 159
This Damsell was not famous for the place 334
This is the Month, and this the happy morn 270
This little Grave embraces 39
This said, the restles generall through the darke 340
Tho when they came to the sea coast, they found 32
Thou art not, Penshurst, built to envious show 190
Thou knowst I lov'd thee well 157
Though virtue be the same when low she stands 231
Through the wall, uprore stood up on end 344
Thus all that day, they spent in divers talke 341
Thus hath my penne presum'd to please my friend 95
Thus now I leave my love in fortunes handes 19
Tis better to be vile then vile esteemed 114
Tis strang 220
Tis the yeares midnight, and it is the dayes 188
To luve unluvit it is ane pane 58
To night, grave sir, both my poore house, and I 233

To nothing fitter can I Thee compare 138
Treason doth never prosper, what's the reason 25
'Twas not for some calm blessing to receive 167
Twice forty months of Wedlock I did stay 330
Two loves I have of comfort and dispaire 119
Tyrant, whie swel'st thou thus 336
Tyr'd with all these for restfull death I cry 111

Underneth this Marble Hearse 317
Unto this place when as the Elfin Knight 348

Vane, young in yeares, but in sage counsell old 49
Vast Ocean of light, whose rayes surround 269

W. resteth here, that quick could never rest 309
Weare I a Kinge I coulde commande content 226
Well then; I now do plainly see 210
Westron wynde when wylle thow blow 52
What *Booker* doth prognosticate 43
What heav'n-intreated Heart is This 292
What is the *World*? A great *Exchange* of ware 271
What more variety of pleasures can 186
What on Earth deserves our trust 329
What slender Youth bedew'd with liquid odours 345
What spirit can lift you up, to that immortall praise 192
What? summer now? divisions ring 297
What's in the braine that Inck may character 351
When doome of Peeres and Judges fore-appointed 24
When every one to pleasing pastime hies 143
When first my lines of heav'nly joyes made mention 281
When for the Thorns with which I long, too long 306
When from the world, I shall be tane 327
When *Hercules* did use to spin 229
When in disgrace with Fortune and mens eyes 106
When Love with unconfined wings 166
When my devotions could not pierce 280
When my love sweares that she is made of truth 118
When was there contract better driven by *Fate* 34
When winter snowes upon thy sable haires 91
Where do'st thou carelesse lie 355
Where others love, and praise my Verses; still 367
Where the remote *Bermudas* ride 214
Whilst my heart bleeding writes that deadlie wound 35

Whither away good neighbour 158
Who ever hath her wish, thou hast thy *Will* 117
Who hath not knowne or herd 249
Who is it that this darke night 72
Who lists to see, what ever nature, arte 335
Who lyst his welth and eas Retayne 5
Who so list to hount I knowe where is an hynde 54
Why do I draw this coole releeving ayer 97
Will you heare the Mode of france 238
Wilt thou use turners craft still? ye by my trouth 251
Wise Emblem of our Politick World 213
With paste of Almonds, *Syb* her hands doth scoure 153
With what deep murmurs through times silent stealth 302
Write write yow Croniclers of Tyme and Fame 27

Ye have been fresh and green 207
Ye learned sisters which have oftentimes 88
Ye living Lamps, by whose dear light 215
Yee Gote-heard Gods, that love the grassie mountaines 64
Yet if his Majestie our Sovareigne lord 287
Yet once more, O ye Laurels, and once more 325
Yet there belongs a Sweetnesse, softnesse too 168
Yf my deare love were but the childe of state 115
You brave Heroique Minds 193
You noble diggers all stand up now 211
You well compacted Groves, whose light and shade 199
Yow that take pleasure in yowr cruelty 121
Yr wylan deg ar lan dŵr 180

Index of Titles

References are to the numbers of poems. Poems with titles beginning 'A', 'An' and 'The' are listed under their second words.

Alas poore Scholler, whither wilt thou goe 295
Amoretti *Sonnet 23* 83
Amoretti *Sonnet 64* 84
Amoretti *Sonnet 67* 85
Amoretti *Sonnet 70* 86
Amoretti *Sonnet 71* 87
Anglorum Feriae 27
Another Song exciting to spirituall Mirth 305
Answer to another perswading a Lady to Marriage, An 173
Antiplatonick, The 163
Arcadia, The Countesse of Pembrokes 14, 64, 181
Ariosto's Orlando Furioso Book 34 341
Astrophil and Stella 1 65
Astrophil and Stella 2 66
Astrophil and Stella 9 67
Astrophil and Stella 72 68
Astrophil and Stella 81 69
Astrophil and Stella 83 70
Astrophil and Stella Eight song 71
Astrophil and Stella Eleventh song 72
At a Vacation Exercise 363
At Pens-hurst 240

Balade whych Anne Askewe made and sange whan she was in Newgate, The 248
Ballad on the Marriage of Philip and Mary, A 11
Belmans Song, A 236
Bermudas 214
Book, The 374
Britain's Remembrancer Canto 4 202
Britannia's Pastorals Book 2 37, 198, 358
Budd, The 161
Bulla 209
Burning Babe, The 253

Cælica Sonnet 22 73
Cælica Sonnet 27 74
Cælica Sonnet 39 75
Cælica Sonnet 44 76
Cælica Sonnet 78 26
Cælica Sonnet 84 77
Cælica Sonnet 89 262
Cælica Sonnet 99 263
Cælica Sonnet 109 264
Calendæ Maiæ 175
Calme, The 28
Canonization, The 134
Certain Sonnets: 4 63
Certayne Egloges 5 174
Choise of valentines, The 95
Christs Victorie, and Triumph in Heaven, and Earth, over, and after death 265
Church Militant, The 286
Claspe, The 371
Cock-crowing 301
Collar, The 282
Collyn Clout 247
Common Fate of Books, The 372
Comparison betwixt a *Whore* and a *Booke*, A 364
Complaynt of the Comoun weill of Scotland, The 4
Content and Resolute 268
Coopers Hill 42
Corinna's going a Maying 206
Coronet, The 306
Countess of Anglesey lead Captive by the Rebels, at the Disforresting of *Pewsam*, The 201
Countesse of Mountgomeries Urania 7, The 147
Countesse of Pembrokes Arcadia, The 14, 64, 181
Crowne of Sonetts dedicated to Love, A 145
Cry of a Stone, The 304
Cry of Blood, and of a Broken Covenant, The 46
Cupid's Wrongs Vindicated 157
Cynthia Sonnet 8 102
Cynthia Sonnet 11 103

De Principe Bono Et Malo 2
Definition of Love, The 171
Delia Sonnet 13 90

Delia Sonnet 39 91
Delia Sonnet 52 92
Delight in Disorder 148
Deniall 280
Description of Cooke-ham, The 189
Description of Elizium, The 362
Dialogue betwixt *Man*, and *Nature*, A 220
Diggers' Song, The 211
Divine Fancies On Christ and our selves 275
Divine Fancies On the Booke of Common Prayer 274
Divine Fancies On the contingencie of Actions 272
Divine Fancies On the Needle of a Sun-diall 273
Dorons description of *Samela* 79
Dreame, The 359

Easter wings 278
Elegie upon the death of the Deane of Pauls, Dr. John Donne, An 365
Epigrammes In Cosmum 17 184
Epistle. To Prince Henrie 194
Epitaph. On her Son *H.P.* at St. *Syth*'s Church where her body also lies Interred 329
Epitaph on the Duke of Buckingham 39
Epitaph on the Earl of *Strafford* 41
Epitaph on the Lady *Mary Villers* 320
Epithalamion 88
Epygrams Of turnyng. 67 251
Exequy To his matchlesse never to be forgotten Freind, An 318

Faerie Queene Book 2, The 80
Faerie Queene Book 3, The 81, 82
Faerie Queene Book 5, The 32
Faerie Queene Book 6, The 348
Faeryes Farewell, A Proper New Ballad Intituled, The: Or God-A-Mercy Will 200
Fancy, A 366
Feltons Epitaph 38
Fifth Ode of *Horace*. Lib. *I*, The 345
First Anniversary of the Government under O.C., The 50
Fit of Rime against Rime, A 354
Flaming Heart, The 293
Flower, The 283
For the *Baptiste* 267
Forerunners, The 284

Fraus Mundi 271
French Historie, The 17
Friendship in Embleme, or the Seal. To my dearest *Lucasia* 245
Friendship's Mystery, To My Dearest *Lucasia* 244
Funerall song, upon the deceas of Annes his moother, A 310

Gallery, The 170
Garden, The 217
Gascoignes wodmanship 225
Gondibert Book 2 303, 370
Goodfriday, *1613.* Riding Westward 257
Goyng towardes Spayne 179
Grasse-hopper, The. To my Noble Friend, Mr. *Charles Cotton.* Ode 241
Gratiana dauncing and singing 165
Greensleeves, A new Courtly Sonet, of the Lady 62
Groome of the Chambers religion in King *Henry* the eights time, A 255
Gullinge Sonnets 6 93

Her Bed 151
Her Majestie resembled to the crowned piller 16
Her Muffe 167
Here followeth the unfashionable fashion, or the too too homely Worshipping of God 289
Hero and Leander 99
Hero and Leander Sestiad 3 124
His Picture 132
Holy Sonnets 10 259
Homer's Iliad Book 12 344
Homer's Iliad, To the Reader 356
Horace. Lib. *I*, The Fifth Ode of 345
Horatian Ode upon *Cromwel's* Return from *Ireland*, An 45
Hymne of the Nativity, sung by the Shepheards, A 291
Hymne to God my God, in my sicknesse 258

I.W. To her unconstant Lover 60
Idea 10 138
Idea 25 360
Idea 61 139
In Cosmum 17 184
In Lectores prorsus indignos 352
In Spayn 6
Inconstancy 172

Ingratefull beauty threatned 155
Inviting A Friend To Supper 233

Jack of the North 177
John Arm-strongs last good night 9
Jolly Pinder of Wakefield, The 178
Jordan 281

King and no King, A 44

L'Allegro 204
Lament for our Lady's Shrine at, Walsingham, A 250
Lawde and Prayse Made for Our Sovereigne Lord the Kyng, A 1
Lie, The 22
Love 285
Loves growth 135
Lucan's Pharsalia Book 1 340
Lucrece 101
Lycidas 325

Memoriae Matris Sacrum 319
Metamorphosis of Pigmalions Image, The 125
Mode of France, The 238
Mower against Gardens, The 216
Mower to the Glo-Worms, The 215
Muse, The 373
Muses Elizium The Description of Elizium, The 362
Musicall Consort, A 347
Musophilus 353
My Picture left in *Scotland* 142

New Courtly Sonet, of the Lady Greensleeves, A 62
Nocturnall upon S. *Lucies* day, Being the shortest day, A 188

Ocean to Scinthia, The 21th: and last booke of the 21
Ode, An. To himselfe 355
Ode Upon occasion of His Majesties Proclamation in the yeare 1630, An 40
Of honest Theft. To my good friend Master *Samuel Daniel* 349
Of many *Worlds* in this *World* 219
Of Sir Frauncis Walsingham Sir Phillipp Sydney, and Sir Christopher Hatton, Lord Chancelor 15
Of the day Estivall 183

Of the Progres *of the Soule* 313
Of Treason 25
Of turnyng. 67 251
Of unsaciable purchasers 10
On Christ and our selves 275
On Francis Drake 195
On Maguire's Winter Campaign 33
On My First Sonne 314
On *Sanazar's* being honoured with six hundred Duckets by the *Clarissimi* of *Venice*, for composing an *Elegiack Hexastick* of The City. A Satyre 168
On Sir *G.B.* his defeat 51
On the Booke of Common Prayer 274
On the contingencie of Actions 272
On the Countesse *Dowager* of *Pembrooke* 317
On the morning of Christs Nativity 270
On the Needle of a Sun-diall 273
On the new forcers of Conscience under the Long Parliament 296
On the 3. of *September*, 1651 47
On the Union 34
21th: and last booke of the Ocean to Scinthia, The 21
Orinda upon little *Hector Philips* 330
Orlando Furioso Book 34, Ariosto's 341
Ovid's Metamorphoses Book 6 334
Ovids Elegies Book 1 Elegia. 13. *Ad Auroram ne properet* 339

Pamphilia to Amphilanthus 23 143
Pamphilia to Amphilanthus 34 144
Pamphilia to Amphilanthus A crowne of Sonetts dedicated to Love 145
Pamphilia to Amphilanthus 2 146
Partheniad 11 252
Parthenophil and Parthenophe Sonnet 27 97
Passionate Sheepheard to his love, The 98
Pastorals The Ninth Eglogue 191
Pentelogia Fraus Mundi 271
Perseverance 276
Phoenix and Turtle, The 312
Phyllyp Sparowe 307
Pinder of Wakefield, The Jolly 178
Poly-Olbion Song 6 192
Posting to Printing 368
Prayer 279

Prisoners Written when *O.C.* attempted to be King, The 242
Proper New Ballad Intituled The Faeryes Farewell: Or God-A-Mercy Will, A 200
Psalm 52 336
Psalm 89 Misericordias 337
Psalm 142 338

Quid gloriaris? Psalm 52 336
Quis Optimus Reipublicae Status 3

Rapture, A 156
Redemption 277
Replycacion, A 346
Retreate, The 299
Ruines of Rome: by Bellay 5 335

Saluste du Bartas' Devine Weekes 343
Salve Deus Rex Judæorum 266
Satire [John Donne] 4 29
Satyre [John Donne] 3 256
Scillaes Metamorphosis 227
Scourge of Villanie *In Lectores prorsus indignos*, The 352
Sculler Epigram 22, The 197
Second Anniversarie Of the Progres *of the Soule*, The 313
Shepheardes Calender Maye, The 182
Silken Snake, The 150
Similizing the *Sea* to *Meadowes*, and *Pastures*, the *Marriners* to *Shepheards*, the *Mast* to a *May-pole*, *Fishes* to *Beasts* 221
Single Eye All Light, no Darkness, A 298
Skialetheia Satire 5 186
Snayl, The 213
Sonet [Mark Alexander Boyd] 78
Sonet written in prayse of the brown beautie, A 61
Song [Edmund Waller] 160
Song On *May* morning 203
Song. To Lucasta, Going to the Warres 164
Songe [Robert Sidney, Earl of Leicester] 17 123
Songe betwene the Quenes majestie and Englande, A 12
Songe bewailinge the tyme of Christmas, So much decayed in Englande, A 187
Sonnet [Edward Herbert, Lord Herbert of Cherbury] 199
Sonnet [Robert Sidney, Earl of Leicester] 21 120
Sonnet [Robert Sidney, Earl of Leicester] 25 121

Sonnet [Robert Sidney, Earl of Leicester] 31 122
Sonnets [William Shakespeare] 19 104
Sonnets [William Shakespeare] 20 105
Sonnets [William Shakespeare] 29 106
Sonnets [William Shakespeare] 35 107
Sonnets [William Shakespeare] 36 108
Sonnets [William Shakespeare] 55 109
Sonnets [William Shakespeare] 56 110
Sonnets [William Shakespeare] 66 111
Sonnets [William Shakespeare] 74 112
Sonnets [William Shakespeare] 94 113
Sonnets [William Shakespeare] 108 351
Sonnets [William Shakespeare] 121 114
Sonnets [William Shakespeare] 124 115
Sonnets [William Shakespeare] 129 116
Sonnets [William Shakespeare] 135 117
Sonnets [William Shakespeare] 138 118
Sonnets [William Shakespeare] 144 119
Spring, The 154
Story of *Phoebus* and *Daphne* appli'd, The 159
Summer, The 297
Sunne Rising, The 133

Tasso's Godfrey of Bulloigne Book 4 342
These verses weare made By Michaell Drayton Esquier Poett Lawreatt the night before hee dyed 239
To Althea, From Prison 166
To *Dean-bourn*, a rude River in *Devon*, by which sometimes he lived 205
To Edward Lawrence 243
To His Coy Love, A Canzonet 140
To his Coy Mistress 169
To his Love that sent him a Ring wherein was gravde, *Let Reason rule* 59
To his Mistress going to bed 96
To his retired friend, an Invitation to *Brecknock* 212
To Lucasta, Going to the Warres, Song 164
To Lucy, Countesse of Bedford, with Mr. Donnes Satyres 232
To Meddowes 207
To my Excellent *Lucasia*, on our Friendship 246
To my Husband 327
To my most dearely-loved friend Henery Reynolds Esquire, of *Poets and Poesie* 361

To Penshurst 190
To Queen Elizabeth 31
To Sir Henry Vane the younger 49
To Sir *Henry Wotton* 228
To St Mary Magdalen 254
To the Detracter 367
To the immortall memorie, and friendship of that noble paire, Sir Lucius Cary, and Sir H. Morison 315
To the Lady Lucie, Countesse of Bedford 231
To the Lord Generall Cromwell May 1652 48
To The Noblest and best of Ladyes, the Countesse of Denbigh 292
To the reverend shade of his religious Father 322
To the Translator 357
To The Virginian Voyage 193
Tragicall Epigram, A 24
Triple Foole, The 350
Turners dish of Lentten stuffe, or a Galymaufery 196

Upcheringe of the Messe, The 249
Upon a child 324
Upon Appleton House, to my Lord *Fairfax* 218
Upon Arch-bishop Laud, Prisoner in the Tower. 1641 294
Upon defacing of *White-hall* 43
Upon himselfe being buried 323
Upon his Majesties repairing of Pauls 290
Upon *Julia's* haire fill'd with Dew 152
Upon *Sibilla* 153
Upon the death of Sir *Albert Morton's* Wife 321
Upon the graving of her Name upon a Tree in *Barnelmes* Walks 222
Upon the sudden Restraint of the *Earle* of *Somerset*, then falling from favor 36
Upon the theme: *Magnum vectigal parcimonia* 224
Urania 7, The Countesse of Mountgomeries 147

Valediction forbidding mourning, A 137
Valediction of weeping, A 136
Venus and Adonis 100
Virgidemiarum Book 5 185
Virgil's Aeneid Book 4 332, 333
Vision, The 149
Voce mea ad Dominum Psalm 142 338
Vox Pacifica 369
Vox populi vox Dei 176

Walsingham, A Lament for our Lady's Shrine at 250
Wanton Wife of Bath, The 127
Wassaile, The 208
Water-fall, The 302
Weavers Song, The 229
Well met Neighbour 158
Why I Write Not Of Love 141
Wish, The 210
World, The 300
Written upon the death of the most Noble Prince *Henrie* 35
Written when *O.C.* attempted to be King 242

Yr Wylan 180

READ MORE IN PENGUIN

READ MORE IN PENGUIN

A CHOICE OF CLASSICS

Charles Dickens	**American Notes for General Circulation**
	Barnaby Rudge
	Bleak House
	The Christmas Books (in two volumes)
	David Copperfield
	Dombey and Son
	Great Expectations
	Hard Times
	Little Dorrit
	Martin Chuzzlewit
	The Mystery of Edwin Drood
	Nicholas Nickleby
	The Old Curiosity Shop
	Oliver Twist
	Our Mutual Friend
	The Pickwick Papers
	Pictures from Italy
	Selected Journalism 1850–1870
	Selected Short Fiction
	Sketches by Boz
	A Tale of Two Cities
George Eliot	**Adam Bede**
	Daniel Deronda
	Felix Holt
	Middlemarch
	The Mill on the Floss
	Romola
	Scenes of Clerical Life
	Silas Marner
Fanny Fern	**Ruth Hall**
Elizabeth Gaskell	**Cranford/Cousin Phillis**
	The Life of Charlotte Brontë
	Mary Barton
	North and South
	Ruth
	Sylvia's Lovers
	Wives and Daughters

READ MORE IN PENGUIN

A CHOICE OF CLASSICS

READ MORE IN PENGUIN

A CHOICE OF CLASSICS

Walter Scott	**The Antiquary**
	Heart of Mid-Lothian
	Ivanhoe
	Kenilworth
	The Tale of Old Mortality
	Rob Roy
	Waverley
Robert Louis Stevenson	**Kidnapped**
	Dr Jekyll and Mr Hyde and Other Stories
	In the South Seas
	The Master of Ballantrae
	Selected Poems
	Weir of Hermiston
William Makepeace Thackeray	**The History of Henry Esmond**
	The History of Pendennis
	The Newcomes
	Vanity Fair
Anthony Trollope	**Barchester Towers**
	Can You Forgive Her?
	Doctor Thorne
	The Eustace Diamonds
	Framley Parsonage
	He Knew He Was Right
	The Last Chronicle of Barset
	Phineas Finn
	The Prime Minister
	The Small House at Allington
	The Warden
	The Way We Live Now
Oscar Wilde	**Complete Short Fiction**
Mary Wollstonecraft	**A Vindication of the Rights of Woman**
	Mary and Maria (includes Mary Shelley's **Matilda**)
Dorothy and William Wordsworth	**Home at Grasmere**